A GUIDE TO

JOHN HENRY NEWMAN

A GUIDE TO

JOHN HENRY NEWMAN

His
LIFE
and
THOUGHT

EDITED BY

JUAN R. VÉLEZ

The Catholic University of America Press
Washington, D.C.

The portrait on the cover is a reproduction
with permission from the artist, Mary Fotheringham.

The paper used in this publication meets the minimum requirements
of American National Standards for Information Science—
Permanence of Paper for Printed Library Materials, ANSI Z39.48–1984.

∞

Cataloging-in-Publication Data available from the Library of Congress

ISBN 978-0-8132-3585-1
eISBN 978-0-8132-3586-8

CONTENTS

CONTENTS

II. John Henry Newman's Doctrine

ACKNOWLEDGMENTS

This volume is the result of the generous contribution of many scholars. I wish to thank each one for their collaboration, and especially Barbara H. Wyman, Michael Dauphinais, Michael Pakaluk, Paul Shrimpton, Fr. Keith Beaumont, Fr. Uwe Michael Lang, Jeff L. Morrow, Scott Goins, Dave P. Delio, and Christopher J. Lane for their advice in my work as editor. I also wish to express gratitude to my friend Pat Sharp, to Mary Fotheringham, the portrait artist of the cover of this book, the reviewers of the manuscript, the staff at Catholic University of America Press, the marketing editor Brian Roach, the copy editors Allyson Drucker and Robert Harig, the indexer Matthew White, and Victoria and Jean Nelson for assisting me in its preparation for publication. I am especially grateful to John Martino, executive acquisitions editor at Catholic University of America Press. This work might have been completed sooner but not as well without his generosity and professional expertise.

A word of thanks is also due to *Scripta Theologica, Nova et Vetera, New Blackfriars,* and *Gracewing Publishers* for allowing the use of parts of some articles and material from a book chapter.

I am confident that the contributors would join me in dedicating this work to our respective family members, friends, and students whose friendship we treasure.

While we were preparing this book for publication, Rev. John T. Ford, CSC, passed from this life. He was a leading scholar of the life and work of John Henry Newman, founding editor of the *Newman Studies Journal* (2004), and editor of the same for its first ten years. He graciously accepted to contribute to this volume. We are all indebted to his friendship, generosity, and scholarship. Requiescat in pace.

Juan R. Vélez

February 21, 2022

ABBREVIATIONS

Unless otherwise specified below, the works of Newman cited in this volume are those of the uniform edition that was begun in 1868 and reprinted by Longmans, Green and Co., London (1909–1910). These texts are available at www.newman-reader.org. When reference is made to an edition other than the online editions or the ones noted below, it will be indicated in a footnote.

Add.	*Addresses to Cardinal Newman with His Replies*
Apo.	*Apologia Pro Vita Sua (1865)*
Ari.	*The Arians of the Fourth Century*
Ath. i, ii	*Select Treatises of St. Athanasius in Controversy with the Arians*
AW	*Autobiographical Writings, edited by Henry Tristram. London: Sheed and Ward, 1957*
BOA	*Birmingham Oratory Archives (Manuscript)*
Cal.	*Callista, A Sketch of the Third Century*
Campaign I	*My Campaign in Ireland, Part I, edited by William P. Neville (printed for private circulation 1896). Edited with an introduction, Paul Shrimpton. Leominster, England: Gracewing, 2021*
Cons.	*On Consulting the Faithful in Matters of Doctrine (Rambler, 1859). Edited with an Introduction by John Coulson. New York: Sheed & Ward, 1961*
Critic	*British Critic, Quarterly Theological Review and Ecclesiastical Record*
DA	*Discussions and Arguments on Various Subjects*
Dev.	*An Essay on the Development of Christian Doctrine*

Diff. i, ii	*Certain Difficulties Felt by Anglicans in Catholic Teaching*
EH i, ii	*Essays Critical and Historical*
FP	*Faith and Prejudice and Other Unpublished Sermons, edited by Fathers of the Birmingham Oratory. New York: Sheed and Ward, 1956*
GA	*An Essay in Aid of a Grammar of Assent*
HS i, ii, iii	*Historical Sketches*
Idea	*The Idea of a University, Defined and Illustrated*
IS i, ii	*On the Inspiration of Scripture*
Jfc.	*Lectures on the Doctrine of Justification*
LD i–xxxii	*The Letters and Diaries of John Henry Newman, edited by Charles Stephen Dessain and others, vols. 1–6. Oxford: Oxford University Press, 1978–1984; vols. 11–22. London: Nelson, 1961–1972; vols. 23–32. Oxford: Clarendon Press, 1973–2008.*
LG	*Loss and Gain*
MD	*Mediations and Devotions of the Late Cardinal Newman*
Mir.	*Two Essays on Biblical and on Ecclesiastical Miracles*
Mix.	*Discourses to Mixed Congregations*
Norfolk	*A Letter to His Grace the Duke of Norfolk* (in *Diff. ii*)
NO	*Newman the Oratorian: His Unpublished Oratory Papers, edited by Placid Murray. Leominster: Gracewing, 1980*
OS	*Sermons Preached on Various Occasions*
PN i, ii	*The Philosophical Notebook, edited by Edward Sillem, 2 vols. New York: Humanities Press, 1969*
Prepos.	*Lectures on the Present Position of Catholics in England*
PS i–viii	*Parochial and Plain Sermons*
SD	*Sermons Bearing on the Subject of the Day*
Serm. i–v	*John Henry Newman: Sermons 1824–1843, edited by Placid Murray, Vincent F. Blehl, and Francis J. McGrath. Oxford: Clarendon Press, 1991–2012*

ABBREVIATIONS

SN	*Sermon Notes of John Henry Newman, edited by Fathers of the Birmingham Oratory. London: Longmans, 1913*
TP i	*The Theological Papers of John Henry Newman on Faith and Certainty, edited by Hugo M. de Achaval and J. Derek Holmes. Oxford: Clarendon Press, 1976*
TP ii	*The Theological Papers of John Henry Newman on Biblical Inspiration and Infallibility, edited by J. Derek Holmes. Oxford: Clarendon Press, 1979*
Tract	*Tracts for the Times. Those identified as Newman's by Vincent F. Blehl and available at www.newmanreader.org*
TT	*Tracts Theological and Ecclesiastical*
US	*Fifteen Sermons Preached Before the University of Oxford Between A.D. 1826 and 1843*
VM i–ii	*The Via Media*
VO	*Verses on Various Occasions*

INTRODUCTION

Fr. Juan R. Vélez

John Henry Newman (1801–1890), the English writer, former Anglican clergyman, and Catholic convert who became a cardinal, was declared a saint by Pope Francis on October 13, 2019. St. John Henry Newman's life and work have been, and will continue to be, studied extensively, teaching and inspiring readers and theologians, as well as helping the lives of ordinary Christians and the body of believers that is the Church.[1]

The purpose of this collection of essays is to advance scholarship on Newman in keeping with his well-deserved place of honor. The outright avowal of Newman's place of honor, though formally declared by the Church, might seem incongruous with an academic work. Is it not distance from a subject studied and a critical appraisal of his or her work that defines scholarly objectivity? It is true that an excessive attachment to a subject carries the risk of creating an idealized version of the person, glossing over inconsistencies or failings. But the converse applies as well: intense dislike of a subject impedes a fair appraisal of a person's work. Many scholars have judged such a prejudice to be evident in the case of a recent, highly influential biography of John Henry Newman.[2] Our goal in this work is to strike a balance, disagreeing at times with

---

1   One of the latest studies, published while this volume was being prepared, is *St. John Henry Newman, Preserving and Promulgating His Legacy*, ed. Robert C. Christie (Newcastle upon Tyne: Cambridge Scholars Publishing), 2019.

2   See Frank M. Turner, *John Henry Newman: The Challenge to Evangelical Religion* (New Haven: Yale University Press, 2001), 1–11. With reference to Turner, Peter Nockles writes: "Others have set up a modern quarrel with Newman as '*J'accuse*' (in one case on the basis of 'I know the man is a liar and I am determined to prove him so') from a historical set of assumptions, while at the same time appropriating him as a 'cultural apostate' who demanded a pluralism within the English Church for himself and his followers to do

Newman, indicating omissions or completing ideas he put forth without diminishing his contributions or, worse, denigrating him. We aim to provide an overall picture consonant both with scholarly rigor, sympathy for Newman's viewpoint, and the conviction that he still has much to teach us today.

SCOPE OF THE VOLUME AND AUTHORS

This work has been arranged into two parts. The first section, which explains much of Newman's thinking and his work, contains essays about his life and person, such as the influence of the classics on him and his engagement with the Church Fathers. The second focuses on the teaching contained in his sermons and his lectures, his verses and books, even though naturally some chapters from the first part could have been placed also in this second part. The volume is not intended to cover all the possible aspects of Newman's life and teaching—his novels, for instance, are not fully examined—but the chapters offer a wide view of the breadth and depth of his thought. Although some chapters are of particular interest to Newman scholars, the essays will also appeal to general readers who know about Newman and wish to learn more about his work.

Our volume opens with chapters on Newman's understanding of the Oxford Movement, his lifelong conversion, and his call to celibacy. These are followed by chapters on his use of imagination ("realizing the image of Christ as the principle for religious action"), and interpretation of history. This book examines the familiar but nevertheless important contributions of Newman to theology and education. In the area of theology, the chapters deal with his teaching on faith and reason, development of doctrine, the theological doctrines underlying his sermons, the study of conscience, soteriology, Mariology, ecclesiology, the laity, and the relationship between theology, morality, and spirituality. In addition, this work offers a presentation of aspects of Newman much less studied, such as his approach to philosophy, Sacred Scripture, the Church Fathers, and poetry, as well as his understanding of liturgy and his broad grasp of the classics. It includes chapters on his friendships, teaching on Christian holiness, and the foundation of the Oratory in England, and it closes with a study of his disputed use of the term liberalism.

The contributors to this volume—laywomen, laymen, and clergymen—provide perspectives from their fields of specialty, and from their research and publications. Most of them are academics with teaching experience. They work in the United States, Britain, France, Spain, Australia, and Macao. At least eight of the contributors were Christian Protestant converts to Roman Catholicism and therefore have personal knowledge of these denominations. As editor, I bring to this work my experience in independent research, teaching seminars in theology, and pastoral work in the United States.

---

as they liked." Peter B. Nockles, "The Oxford Movement" in *The Oxford Handbook of John Henry Newman*, ed. F. D. Aquino and B. J. King (Oxford: Oxford University Press, 2018), 24.

METHODOLOGY AND LIMITS
OF THE HISTORICAL METHOD

The methodology of the contributions varies depending on the author's discipline or sub-discipline, whether it be philosophy, theology, history, liturgy, education, or literature. These sciences make use of the historical method to a certain extent. During the nineteenth and twentieth centuries the historical-critical method has been privileged, especially in the analysis of ancient and Biblical texts, but also of texts from the not-so-distant past. There are benefits and dangers to this type of criticism. Over the last few decades some scholars have emphasized the need for the historical-critical method in research on Newman. These scholars have correctly spoken of the need for a contextual history, going beyond the lenses of Newman's letters, diaries, and memoranda to understand his milieu and writing. As others before them, they have underlined the value of looking at sources and influences upon an author's works, and the changes in his beliefs over time.

There can be, however, various biases in historical methods examining the past, as scholars engaged in Biblical studies have made clear. One of these is giving foremost importance to the context of an author's life and writings with less attention to the content of his teaching and his truth claims, which often require philosophical and theological appraisal. Naturally in a scholarly work it can be appropriate to ask one type of question (how do we understand this author in his context?), without also asking another question (is this author right?). However, when the scholar then also assumes his or her own unexamined answers to these truth claims—especially those at odds with the claims of the subject in question—what results is not genuine historical inquiry but the appearance of objectivity masking a pre-existing bias built upon a hermeneutic of suspicion.[3]

A hermeneutic of suspicion has frequently been applied to Newman but not to his contemporaries, leading some to consider that Newman's personal recollections are false until proven true. The following questions can illustrate our point: What are we to think of Newman's *Apologia*, written by him precisely to counter claims of duplicity and untruthfulness? Is it a book full of errors, exaggerations, self-aggrandizement, and selective memories? It is certainly a personal narrative, written in hindsight and with a particular polemic purpose, but this does not therefore invalidate Newman's account. Even though some of his contemporaries disagreed with arguments in the *Apologia*, it would be strange to think that the great majority of English readers of the mid-nineteenth century were duped by Newman on facts to which they themselves had access.

---

3 Brad S. Gregory points out the error of a hermeneutic of suspicion that applies modern or postmodern sensibilities to judge people's actions and motivations. See Brad S. Gregory, *Salvation at Stake, Christian Martyrdom in Early Modern Europe* (Cambridge: Harvard University Press, 1999), 14–15.

Reading the *Apologia,* any educated person can discover an account on the whole consistent with Newman's intellectual journey and corpus. Furthermore, it is not surprising that it is a major and primary source of study for Newman's thinking and doctrinal development. To claim otherwise would be analogous to diminishing the importance the *Confessions* has for the study of St. Augustine simply because he had spent years reflecting upon the events described and the composition of the work.

A related objection raised by some academics is to call into question or cast doubt about what Newman said about himself. Newman certainly had human failings, for instance, being indecisive; he also made mistakes in his reasoning, and his religious opinions and beliefs changed in successive periods of his life. In this context it is appropriate to give his oft-quoted (and sometimes misused) phrase "here below to live is to change, and to be perfect is to have changed often."[4] There is maturation in his thinking on various subjects, for example, in ecclesiology, development of doctrine, and Mariology; his formulation of these subjects is at first partial and incomplete, and subject to improvement. Such changes indicate serious reflection on his part. Moreover, while undeniably brilliant, Newman was not immune to the vicissitudes of human memory, nor does his particular purpose in writing the *Apologia* have no impact on how he presents certain facts and developments. As such, investigation into other sources of historical data—including Newman's own early writings—does help to nuance or qualify this one source, as well as fill in gaps and make sense of puzzling passages. Nevertheless, a premise for a just appraisal of Newman and his work is trust in the basic reliability of his personal integrity and records as testified by living eyewitnesses and the consistency of his thought across his vast correspondence and his many other writings.

A predominantly historical analysis of certain subjects, especially the Scriptures and theology, also has another important limitation. It is unable to reach the interior of the author as a person, in order to convey aspects of religious truth which go beyond facts. This approach requires other methods for the study of its subject. Newman invites men and women to a deeper understanding of religious truths and the moral life, which can be studied academically but not reduced to the historical-critical method or literary analysis, nor measured simply by the comparison of varying editions of an author's work or by tracing the intellectual genealogy of his ideas.

Another frequent objection made in contemporary historiography against Newman's reading of the Church Fathers and history, or of the account of his own life in the *Apologia,* is that 'he is reading back into the Fathers or into his own earlier life, problems and situations of a later period.' It is normal, however, for a reader of history to seek parallels with his own age, and keys for understanding the past. He may be mistaken in the analogies and conclusions that he

---

4 *Dev.,* 40.

reaches, and his judgments can be compared to other accounts of the history, ancient or personal, that his arguments encompass, but he should not be faulted for attempting to reach truths through looking at the past. Indeed, is not all history, as Collingwood says, a kind of re-enactment of the past in the present?[5] Conversely, scholars should take care that they are not reading back into Newman's day the cultural preoccupations of their own age, much less offering psychological explanations for Newman's changes when he himself offers ample intellectual reasons for them.

As we look to the future scholarship on Newman, we can aspire to integrate historical research on his contemporaries and his unpublished texts with the theological, philosophical, and literary analysis of his thought. More study of the influence he received from Anglican and Catholic sources will provide a better appreciation for his work. It is also to be desired that his contribution to other areas of study, such as biblical exegesis, liturgy, and poetry, will be borne out. In this volume the contributors have attempted to further this effort, and hopefully we have succeeded in larger measure.

CONCLUSION

Since Newman's death one hundred and thirty years ago, thinkers have wished to enlist Newman into their camp. To the question "Was Newman a liberal or conservative theologian?" Ian Ker has responded, asserting that Newman was neither; instead he was a "radical conservative or conservative reformer."[6] The contributors to this collection of essays wish to present, through the lenses of their respective disciplines, the rich and varied teaching drawn from Newman's life and work, and to offer some new insights to this body of doctrine. We have attempted this in a positive manner, respectful of differences of opinion, but fully convinced of Newman's integrity, spiritual greatness, and orthodoxy.

Lastly, the contributors to this volume naturally express their own thoughts and account of Newman and Newman scholarship, independent from the editor and the ideas expressed in this introduction, but they share the desire to contribute to an objective and well-rounded understanding of Newman, open to further study of his historical, theological, and philosophical context and development. We hope the readers of this volume will benefit from our research and work.

Juan R. Vélez

February 21, 2022

---

5 See Robin G. Collingwood, *The Idea of History*, ed. T. M. Knox (Oxford: Clarendon Press, 1946), 282–302. I am indebted to Matthew C. Briel for pointing out to me this idea of Collingwood characteristic of Newman.

6 Ian Ker, *Newman on Vatican II* (Oxford: Oxford University Press, 2014), 39.

I. JOHN HENRY NEWMAN

CHAPTER 1

NEWMAN'S IDEA
OF THE OXFORD MOVEMENT

David P. Delio and Matthew C. Briel

I n *The Oxford Movement, Twelve Years: 1833–1845,* Richard W. Church, former Tractarian and friend of John Henry Newman, remarked that so much had been written on or about the movement that any addition would seem superfluous.[1] Almost 135 years later, the thousands of pages of personal reflections and scholarly development on the Oxford Movement— its characters, context, and implications—is overwhelming. The perspectives are almost too many to count. And yet according to a leading scholar of the movement, Peter Nockles, there are certain persons, events, and facts that have achieved consensus while others have been discarded.[2] John Henry Newman's central impact on the movement is among those accepted.

Yet understanding Newman's role in the movement, how he viewed his place, and how others have interpreted his actions is still an ongoing work.

---

*   Portions of this chapter derive from David P. Delio, *"An Aristocracy of Exalted Spirits": The Idea of the Church in Newman's Tamworth Reading Room* (Leominster: Gracewing, 2016), used with permission.

1   Richard W. Church, *The Oxford Movement, Twelve Years, 1833–1845* (London: Macmillan and Co., 1891), vii–viii.

2   Peter Nockles, "The Oxford Movement" in *The Oxford Handbook of John Henry Newman*, ed. Frederick D. Aquino and Benjamin J. King (Oxford: Oxford University Press, 2018), 7.

Nockles has pointed to several distinct lines of interpretation of the Oxford Movement that have coalesced over the centuries: an awakening destined for Rome, a restoration of the Anglican Church, a revival, schismatic yet failed endeavor, or an ongoing ecclesial reality. Each variously situates Newman's place in the movement. There is perhaps another approach that accounts for Newman's architectonic influence and his eventual rejection of the Anglican Church for Rome, while also depicting the movement's impetus, unfurling, and continuity: approaching the Oxford Movement through Newman's concepts of ideas and developments. Specifically, this chapter asks whether the Oxford Movement is a distinct aspect of the Idea of Christianity. In raising this question, this chapter engages history while departing from an historicist account and rather uses Newman's concepts as a heuristic to interpret the contexts of the movement, Newman's involvement, and his eventual departure.[3]

Viewed from a certain angle, portions of Newman's first chapter in the *Essay on the Development of Christian Doctrine*, appear as a philosophical account of ideas and developments infused with a personal retrospective on his involvement in the Oxford Movement. Here, Newman comments that if "an idea is very complex, it is allowable, for the sake of convenience, to consider its distinct aspects as if separate ideas."[4] The very Idea of Christianity, he goes on to note, is real because it has a supernatural identity, but is complex as it moves between persons and nations in time.[5] Often, he continues, scholars or ecclesial leaders (orthodox and heretical) artificially reduce Christianity down to a "leading idea" that distorts its reality. This inquiry will approach the Oxford Movement not as a "leading idea." Rather, it will ask whether the movement is a "distinct aspect" of the Christian Idea, one which presents "as if a separate idea."

---

3   We choose Newman's approach over certain contemporary approaches, such as Kenneth L. Parker's historical hermeneutic. See Kenneth L. Parker, "Re-visioning the Past and Re-sourcing the Future: The Unresolved Historiographical Struggle in Roman Catholic Scholarship and Authoritative Teaching," in *The Church on its Past*, ed. Peter D. Clarke and Charlotte Methuen, Studies in Church History 49 (Woodbridge, Suffolk: Ecclesiastical History Society and Boydell, 2013), 389–416. In his analysis of Christian theology he discerns four historiographical metanarratives, three of which he maintains are in Newman. Each of the four metanarratives he outlines identifies some of the truth (including the successionism that he first proposes and then rejects), but these aspects of Parker's metanarratives are already found in Newman's *Essay on the Development of Doctrine*. Parker's presentation of the metanarrative of development inadequately discerns corruptions (false developments). His reading and appropriation of Newman's notion of development and his artificial division of an organic approach to the past (development) into four metanarratives has important consequences. It not only breaks up Newman's unified approach to the past but also allows Parker the opportunity to add and subtract elements to the three metanarratives he accepts in order to argue that the best understanding of the truth is to be found in the ever-advancing present.

4   *Dev.*, 35.

5   *Dev.*, 36.

Considered in this way, the Oxford Movement as an "idea," "may be said to have life, that is, to live in the mind which is its recipient . . . not merely received passively in this or that form into many minds, but it becomes an active principle within them, leading them to an ever-new contemplation of itself, to an application of it in various directions, and a propagation of it on every side."[6] To regard the Oxford Movement as a living "idea," an "active principle" in many minds, especially in Newman's recollections in his *Apologia Pro Vita Sua*, this chapter will look at aspects of its origins, development, and ultimately its demise in his life.[7]

Initially drawing upon ancient ecclesial resources and contemporary Anglican traditions, the Oxford Movement did not fully realize itself as true aspect of the Christian Idea, at least in Newman's mind and many others. He gradually recognized this in the years subsequent to his construction of the *Via Media* in 1837. As he reflected in the *Essay on Development*, "development then of an idea is not like an investigation worked out on paper."[8] Over the next eight years, the Oxford Movement, outlined in the *Via Media*, devolved into what Newman called a "corruption" of a living idea. This corruption was not one that collapsed at once, but decayed over time.[9] Perhaps, to pluck a contemporary analogy from atomic theory, Newman, especially in the *Apologia*, regarded the Oxford Movement as having an initial burst of energy yet disintegrating in its "half-life" even after he left it.

The problem of Newman's understanding of the Oxford Movement leads to a question that must be answered, even if cursorily. Just how reliable a guide to the Oxford Movement is Newman's 1864 retrospective *Apologia Pro Vita Sua*? For it is here that Newman hopes that the movement, especially in the form of the *Via Media*, was a living "idea" yet paradoxically describes its disintegration.[10] Some recent scholars have claimed that Newman has been given too prominent a role in historical reconstructions of the Oxford Movement.[11] One way that current historians have diminished Newman's agency is by "contextualization," a method that claims to bring more voices to the table but in fact is frequently

---

6   *Dev.*, 36.

7   In ch. 2 of this volume, Juan Alonso explores what might be considered the personal counterpart to the development of this "living idea," that is, Newman's gradual conversions (editor's note).

8   *Dev.*, 38. Perhaps Newman was referring to his comment in *Via Media* 1, "the *Via Media* . . . viewed as an integral system, has never had existence except on paper." See *V.M.* I, 16.

9   *Dev.*, 204–5.

10   E.g., Newman noted, "The *Via Media* was an impossible idea; it was what I had called 'standing on one leg.'" *Apo.*, 149.

11   Although the literature is extensive, currently none is more prominent, and yet unconvincing, than Frank M. Turner, *John Henry Newman: The Challenge to Evangelical Religion* (New Haven: Yale University Press, 2002), 7–10.

employed as a sleight of hand.[12] Often his contemporaries are brought in to contradict Newman's claims, but contextualist historians employ an imbalance in their suspicion of sources: Newman's claims (and motives) are much more often doubted than other sources, usually without strong arguments for these preferences.

Thus certain contemporary scholars challenge Newman's recounting of the Oxford Movement in the *Apologia* because of his personal motives and the distance of years. Yet there exist many concurrent accounts that validate much of Newman's narrative,[13] while also allowing for his grafting of memories and sources into a fresh account. This chapter seeks to restore Newman's agency,[14] while also acknowledging the contextual studies surrounding the movement. The *Apologia* remains one of the most important sources for any historical understanding of the movement and is central to our approach because it outlines the animating "idea" of the Oxford Movement. As with all historical enquiry, this chapter attempts to provide a real insight into the past in fidelity to all of the sources. We draw particularly upon the *Apologia*, however, because it adumbrates the "idea" of the movement while chronicling Newman's egress.

In what follows, this chapter explores the "idea" of the Oxford Movement through the prism of development in Newman's thought and its relationship to the fullness of the Christian Idea. Therefore, the chapter will situate the context of its origins, its development, including Newman's concerns over contradictory principles within the "idea," and his conviction that the movement ultimately did not participate in the true Idea of Christianity.

---

12   As John Milbank, reflecting on Charles Péguy, has noted, "the historical point of view suppresses the inexplicability (beyond a certain point) of every historical event by fantasizing an exhaustive circumstantial or causal account . . . which idolatrously seems to mimic the mind of God." "The Gift of Ruling: Secularization and Political Authority," *New Blackfriars* 85, no. 996 (March 2004): 226.

13   See for example, Newman to William and Catherine Froude, 2–3 April 1844, *LD* x, 183–85. These letters offered a first glimpse into Newman's mind about the Oxford Movement, and twenty years later, they provided structure to his *Apologia Pro Vita Sua*. Newman had rehearsed these same themes some months earlier to then Archdeacon Henry Manning (*LD* ix, 584–85). What was important in the Froude and Manning exchanges and eventually in his *Apologia* was that Newman's ideal theological position (*Via Media*) fell apart and so he proceeded to act cautiously, rather than controversially, in his capacity as an Anglican minister. By contrast, Frank Turner offered a wayward psychological account of the Froude letters mixed with his erroneous thesis regarding Evanglicalism that missed their significance for both the Oxford Movement and the *Apologia* (*Challenge*, 507–10).

14   Newman acknowledged that the *Apologia* is in no sense an objective history. For example, Newman wrote to W. J. Copeland that his narrative of the Oxford Movement would be disappointing to those involved in so far as "it is not a history of the movement but of me—it is an egotistical matter from beginning to end." *LD* xxi, 97.

ORIGINS OF THE MOVEMENT

As Newman himself remarked, and later histories have shown, the Oxford Movement emerged out of Anglican religious traditions, political events of Oxford in the late 1820s and early 1830s, the spread of political liberalism, the Reform Act of 1832, shifts in ecclesial alignments, Oxonian friendships, rereading of the Fathers of the Church, and Newman's voyage to the Mediterranean.

In January 1864, as the controversy between Newman and Charles Kingsley was starting to take shape that resulted in the writing of the *Apologia Pro Vita Sua*, Newman wrote to Sophia Ryder, reflecting on his founding of the Oratory at Birmingham fifteen years prior. Waxing nostalgic, he added, "Fifteen years may be called a fourth of a man's life. What a time! Why it was only 15 years, from 1830, when the first steps were laid towards the Oxford movement, to 1845, when, for me, it ended. And then to think what has one been doing all this time?"[15] This recollection, written months before he began composing his *Apologia* does not contradict his claim that the movement *began* in 1833. Newman's memory served him that around 1830 the "first steps were laid" in terms of persons and principles that would form the movement.[16] Three years later, he believed the "start of the religious movement" began with Keble's Assize Sermon and the high-spirited meetings that followed.[17] It was then that the Oxford Movement came into itself as an "idea," through members and principles.

Among these "first steps" of the Oxford Movement were powerful currents in British society and in Newman's own life that gave it sustenance. Newman had imbibed the Idea of Christianity as a boy, but it was refracted through what he later recounted as the "bible religion" of Christianity in England.[18] At fifteen years old he became convinced of certain evangelical teachings through his teacher, Walter Mayers, seeing in them a greater fidelity to the truths of the Bible than he had seen in the tepid Anglicanism in which he had been born.

In 1816 he experienced a living encounter with God and became convinced that the Church has definite doctrines to preserve the truth of the Gospel. Newman came under the influence of Evangelicalism, and as he recounted in 1835 to Sir James Stephen, "When I was a youth of 19 and 20, I held their opinions myself, as far as I had any."[19] Newman never fully defined what he meant by his evangelical opinions. Later histories have found "Evangelicalism" of the early nineteenth century notoriously difficult to define. Grayson Carter for example

---

15 *LD* xxi, 19.

16 Peter Nockles dates the Oxford Movement to 1829, which is close to the time Newman observed, "For it was the campaign against Peel that first brought together the future Tractarian constellation on the basis of political discontent underpinned by moral principle." Peter Nockles, "'Church and King': Tractarian Politics Reappraised" in *From Oxford to the People*, ed. Paul Vaiss (Leominster: Fowler Wright Books, 1996), 96–97.

17 *Apo.*, 35.

18 *GA*, 56–67.

19 *LD* v, 31.

has noted that this movement eschewed some of the austerities of Calvinist Puritanism, and rather adapted to the times. The Evangelicalism that Newman experienced was unique in stressing "individual conversion, reason, and empiricism," and acted "as an unruly stepchild of the Enlightenment."[20] Although it accented habits of mind informed by the Gospel, Evangelicalism also emphasized doctrine, a revival of liturgy, and an "appeal to the heart."[21] By the mid-1820s, under the influence of several persuasive mentors, Newman held that the visible Church and doctrinal tradition were more true to the Idea of Christianity than what he found in certain evangelical teachings as a young man. Over a period of years, Newman was able to reconcile true principles and precepts in evangelical traditions and reject those that did not adhere to the High Church tradition, and perhaps did not redound in the deeper Idea of Christianity he experienced in his conversion. Nevertheless, evangelical elements remained as almost permanent features in Newman's life and actions, as well as many other future Tractarians who came from an evangelical background.[22] These young men, inspired by evangelical zeal for reform, were able to transfer their energies into a new movement that promised a revival of antiquity to meet the challenges of their moment.[23]

An interest in the Church Fathers was omnipresent in the High Church tradition preceding the Oxford Movement. Sir Henry Savile of Eton, for instance, published the first and very well done eight folio volume Greek edition of John Chrysostom (1610–1613). Richard Sharp has shown that in the eighteenth century there were continued efforts at scholarly retrievals of the Fathers and attempts to bring certain practices to bear upon the Church of England.[24] In continuity with these Hanoverian retrievals, and closer to the Oxford Movement, the High Church of the late eighteenth and early nineteenth centuries developed elements of antiquity while forming a distinctive theo-political tradition. This tradition was embodied in Martin Routh, president of Magdalen College, and editor of the influential five-volume *Reliquiae Sacrae*.[25] The High Church appropriation of the Fathers eventually provided the grist for the future Tractarians' mill. Because Newman was not born into the High Church tradition, he learned to gradually adopt aspects of it, especially a reading of the Fathers, from Froude and others at Oxford.[26] Newman made use of evangelical (especially Milner) and

---

20 Grayson Carter, "The Evangelical Background," in *The Oxford Handbook of the Oxford Movement* (Oxford: Oxford University Press, 2017), 40.

21 Carter, "The Evangelical Background," 48.

22 Carter, "The Evangelical Background," 46–49.

23 Peter Nockles, "The Oxford Movement and the Legacy of Anglican Evangelicalism: Religious Reform in the Early 19th Century Church of England" in *The Churches*, ed. Joris Van Eijnatten & Paula Yates (Leuven: Leuven University Press, 2010), 54–55.

24 Richard Sharp, "The Communion of the Primitive Church? High Churchmen in England, c. 1710–1760," in *The Oxford Handbook of the Oxford Movement*, 26–27.

25 Nigel Aston, "High Church Presence and Persistence in the Reign of King George III, c. 1760–1811," in *The Oxford Handbook of the Oxford Movement*, 54–55; 62–63.

26 Pierre Gauthier, "Richard Hurrell Froude's Influence on Newman and the Oxford

High Church patristic scholarship, with unprecedented intensity, as well as early German *Wissenschaft*, in his early reading of the editions of the Fathers (with their Latin introductions) produced in Germany and acquired by Pusey.[27]

These convictions grew and were further refined in his experiences at Oxford. In 1829, Newman became highly engaged in the Oxford elections for MP, as he and some compatriots resisted Sir Robert Peel's bid to keep his seat, for they felt that his support for repealing the Catholic Emancipation was a betrayal. This was Newman's first and brief entry into political activism. At the time he recounted to his mother, "We have achieved a glorious Victory. It is the first public event I have been concerned in, and I thank God from my heart both for my cause and its success. We have proved the independence of the Church and of Oxford."[28] For several years, Newman had been under the influence of Oxford Noetics such as Richard Whately and later traditionalists Hurrell Froude and John Keble regarding the Church's independence, and this event presented the power of the Church (and the University) in crystalline form. However, despite Newman's trenchant observations about the pyrrhic political victory at Oxford and his growing awareness that something called "liberalism" was ascendant, he did not intimate, nor did his compatriots seem to augur, a movement afoot.

Newman may have begun to sense changes were nigh, however, when he preached "Witnesses of the Resurrection" in April 1831. The sermon, a combination of sound exegesis and personal reflection, noted how God chose a small band of disciples to carry out his will in forming the Church for the World:

> It is plain every great change is effected by the few, not by the many; by the resolute, undaunted, zealous few. Nothing is *done* except by those who are specially trained for action. . . . One or two men, of small outward pretensions, but with their hearts in their work, these do great things. These are prepared, not by sudden excitement, or by vague general belief in the truth of their cause, but by deeply impressed, often repeated instruction.[29]

Newman reprised this same argument in his *Apologia* thirty-three years later and applied it directly to the formation of the Oxford Movement.[30] Increasingly, these "few" who were called Tractarians were concerned about ecclesiastical reform on the basis of principles drawn from the Apostolic Church and continued to

---

Movement," in *From Oxford to the People*, ed. Paul Vaiss (Leominster: Fowler Wright Books, 1996), 259–65.

27 Sheridan Gilley, "Keble, Froude, Newman, and Pusey," in *The Oxford Handbook of John Henry Newman*, 101.

28 *LD* ii, 125–26.

29 *PS* i, no. 22; 287–88.

30 *Apo.*, 39.

be increasingly uneasy about the relationship that had developed between the Church and State.[31]

In 1832, the Whigs sponsored the Reform Act, which, by granting broader political rights to the middle classes and consolidating "rotten boroughs," overturned the political landscape. Although the Act was widely heralded—and feared by many Tories—it only brought about modest changes. What was more important was what the Act signified and initiated: an age of social reform. The previous decade had been characterized by a return to fiscal stability, governmental reform, and a successful thwarting of radicalism. In contrast, the Reform Act brought with it calls for the transformation of many aspects of society.[32]

In December 1832, six months after the Reform Act passed, Newman began a Mediterranean voyage with his colleague, Hurrell Froude and Froude's father. Prior to sailing, Newman seemed to anticipate more "first steps" toward a movement, remarking to his mother that the journey was to be "a preparation and strengthening time for future toil."[33] Newman, Froude, and others had also planned a poetry series designed to resist what seemed like sweeping social changes. They hoped that upon their return, their status as Oxford men and clergy would allow them to "bring out certain truths and facts, moral, ecclesiastical, and religious, simply and forcibly" to the wider populace. As Juan Vélez has noted, "These poems first appeared in the British Magazine in a section entitled *Lyra Apostolica*—a title suggested by Newman that evokes one of the main themes of the Oxford Movement: a return to the apostolical origins of tradition and authority in the Church."[34]

Not only was this Newman's first journey outside England, but it was providential—he was able to speak at length with his intellectual companion about current and future problems in their Church, drink in real imagery of classical lands and heroes as well as Catholic and Orthodox cultures. Newman also suffered gravely from illness and the depths of loneliness, much like the classical heroes and biblical saints he admired. As Mary Katherine Tillman observed, Newman descended into Hades, emerging, not to inherit an earthly heaven of home and hearth, but to go on a new mission for the Gospel.[35] One of his evangelically inspired compositions, "A Word in Season," penned during his first days at sea and in Gibraltar, anticipated a coming "season" in which he was to "speak,"

---

31 Proponents of the Oxford Movement were also called "Tractarians" after the *Tracts for the Times* (1833–1841), which were written by different authors about the theology and aims of the movement. Newman wrote 29 of the ninety *Tracts*.

32 Eric J. Evans, *The Shaping of Modern Britain: Identity, Industry and Empire, 1780–1914* (Harlow: Pearson Educational, 2011), 214–19.

33 LD iii, 123.

34 Juan R. Vélez, "Newman's Mediterranean 'Verses': Poetry at the Service of Doctrinal Teaching and Religious Renewal," *Newman Studies Journal* 3, no. 2 (Fall 2006): 82.

35 See Mary Katherine Tillman, "'Realizing' the Classical Authors: Newman's Epic Journey in the Mediterranean," *Newman Studies Journal* 3, no. 2 (Fall 2006): 60–77.

Thy holy Paul, with soul of flame,
Rose on Mars' hill, a soldier lone:
Shall I thus speak th' Atoning Name,
Though with a heart of stone?
"Not so," He said: "hush thee, and seek,
With thoughts in prayer and watchful eyes,
My seasons sent for thee to speak,
And use them as they rise.[36]

On returning from his travels in the Mediterranean, Newman recognized the beginning of a protest at Oxford—different in kind from Catholic Emancipation. John Keble preached his staid Assize Sermon over parliament's suppression of Irish Bishoprics. He articulated the anxieties of Oxonians that gone were the days of an interdependent Church and State. Although removing these bishoprics was negligible and overdue, Keble believed that the state usurped the rights of the Church by taking action that resided in the authority of the bishops. Soon after, as David DeLaura has remarked, "The Oxford Movement began, practically speaking, in a series of meetings between July 25 and 29 at Rose's rectory at Hadleigh, Suffolk. Palmer, Froude, Perceval, and Rose agreed to unite in defending the doctrine of the Apostolic Succession and the Prayer Book."[37]

DEVELOPMENT OF THE MOVEMENT

Newman recounted in his *Essay on Development* that development was a process of long or short duration "by which the aspects of an idea are brought into consistency and form . . . being the germination and maturation of some truth or apparent truth on a large mental field."[38] Principles and personalities, especially Newman's kinetic energy pent up from his journey, electrified a cadre of Oxford dons, students, and sympathizers. They began to develop what appeared to be a "living idea." The Oxford Movement now unfurled into "the warfare of ideas under their various aspects striving for the mastery, each of them enterprising, engrossing, imperious, more or less incompatible with the rest, and rallying followers or rousing foes, according as it acts upon the faith, the prejudices, or the interest of parties or classes."[39]

As Newman took on a more prominent role and compatriots and disciples followed (while others fell away), the movement began to be articulated and clarified. It is here that the Oxford Movement departed from past precedents

---

36   *Verses on Various Occasions* (London: Longman's, Green and Co., 1903), 87.
37   *Apologia Pro Vita Sua*, ed. David J. DeLaura (New York: W. W. Norton and Co., 1968), 42n1.
38   *Dev.*, 38.
39   *Dev.*, 38.

and took on its own personality. Indeed, members of the Movement began to enlist yet distinguish themselves from the Evangelicals and High Churchmen. They increasingly believed that an Erastian state could no longer be a trusted ally for the Church.[40] The movement's response was not reactionary; rather it conformed to the age by advocating reform—something akin to an Evangelical revival, seeking to restore the Church to herself, but in ancient and Anglican vestiges. Yet it was this energy and a combination of other forces that made this "idea" inherently unstable, and ultimately unsustainable for Newman.

However, at the time he and others thought that the movement was a participation in the restoration of the "Holy Church . . . a solemn religious fact, so to call it,—as a picture, a revelation of the next world, as itself the Christian Dispensation."[41] The bond of renewal was not to last long however, as both High Churchmen such as Hugh James Rose and William Palmer[42] and eventually evangelical allies[43] saw not an "idea" of renewal, but a faction unable to unite or renew the Church. Behind this, for better and for worse, Newman began "revealing himself as the master strategist" of the movement.[44] The ecclesiastical reforms which Newman and his allies proposed consisted in a return to the Church Fathers, promulgation of the *Tracts for the Times*, and the construction of the *Via Media*.

The Tractarians innovated from the earlier High Church tradition, bringing forth the Fathers to fight the contemporary battle against anti-dogmatic Liberalism.[45] This began with Froude and Keble, who helped Newman give focused attention to the Fathers. Once the Oxford Movement began, the Tractarians, and especially Newman, reconceived the early Church as a living idea and hoped to inspire bishops along the lines of Ambrose and Athanasius, while implementing changes in the liturgy, vestments, and ecclesial architecture. The principle means to accomplishing this was through the *Tracts for the Times*, which were Newman's signal achievement for the movement and were solely his undertaking.[46] Newman wrote almost a third of all published tracts, and most had a proposed audience, for example, the clergy or the laity, yet were very popular, exhortative, and meant to ferment discussion and change in ecclesial practices. The *Tracts* at first were short bursts of argument and encouragement. As the

---

40 A term associated with Thomas Erastus (1524–1583), a Swiss Protestant theologian, in which the Church is subject to the State. M. L. Fell, *New Catholic Encyclopedia*, s.v. "Erastianism," 2nd edition (Detroit: Gale, 2003), vol. 5, 317–18. Newman wrote extensively on Erastianism in his *Certain Difficulties Felt by Anglicans in Catholic Teaching*, vol. 1.

41 *PS* ii, no. 6: 66.

42 Nockles, "Oxford Movement," 12.

43 Carter, "The Evangelical Background," 48–49.

44 Ian Ker, *John Henry Newman: A Biography* (Oxford: Clarendon Press, 1988), 81.

45 See David Delio, "Liberalism: Personal and Social Aspects in Newman's Thought" in this volume.

46 Nockles, "The Oxford Movement," 11.

movement grew, they did too in length and complexity, especially as Pusey joined the fray. Time and again, they drew from the well-springs of the Church Fathers to provide a model and exemplar for Church renewal.

Newman came to his conclusions by reading the Fathers in a particular way. He and most of the other Tractarians were neither antiquarians (interested in the past for its own sake), nor dogmaticians (looking for dogma without historical context) but more akin to ecclesiastical historians, who searched the past for answers to contemporary questions.[47] More important than the specific doctrines discerned in the early Church which became principles of the Oxford Movement was a retrieval of the Rule of Faith, a *ressourcement* that was not merely academic but something to be lived.[48] This is especially apparent in Athanasius, to whom Newman devoted four years near the end of his Anglican life. The Rule of Faith, for Athanasius and Newman, is the authoritative tradition of the Church that is the guarantor of the correct interpretation of scripture.[49] Like Eusebius's ecclesiastical mind, the Rule of Faith is something that the believer participates in. It removes the necessity of a pure private judgment. As Newman's appreciation for the Rule of Faith (which was living, adapting, and incorporating new terminology) grew he saw it was integral to the Church. If the Church lost the living

---

47 This approach to early tradition has recently been criticized. Benjamin J. King, for instance, has repeatedly considered Newman's approach to the Fathers as not up to "scholarly standards" because of its "lack of historical consciousness." See Benjamin J. King, "The Church Fathers," in *The Oxford Handbook of John Henry Newman*, 113–14. See also Benjamin J. King, *Newman and the Alexandrian Fathers: Shaping Doctrine in Nineteenth-Century England.* (Oxford: Oxford University Press, 2009), 216–17. King levels several charges against Newman's approach to history. King's greatest concern can be summed up as Newman writes to change the present (King, *Newman and the Alexandrian Fathers*, 14, 16, 25). Benjamin King, like Charles Kingsley in 1864, attacks Newman's transparency, ignoring what he knew to be historical anachronisms "in order to please the new pope Leo" ("The Church Fathers," 131). What is striking in King's three texts that address Newman's reading of the past is that King simply criticizes it as not up to "scholarly standards" as if distinguishing it from the practices of academic history of the twenty-first century, rather than trying to understand Newman's work on its own terms, was itself an exercise of historical consciousness. Instead of reading Newman's work as simply bad, or even dishonest, history, it seems more worthwhile to understand Newman as engaged in an endeavor that does not have an antiquarian interest that stops at understanding the *dicta* of Christians in their historical context, but rather understands those pre-modern Christians as they understood themselves: witnesses to the Gospel, or what one might call the Apostolic Deposit or what Newman called the Idea of Christianity. (See *HS* i, 385–86 and *Ari.*, 52). Newman, then, is accountable to critical history, but his scope is not limited to it, and in this way one recent commentator has failed to understand him. This is crucial for understanding the Tractarian *ressourcement*.

48 King, *Alexandrian Fathers*, 37.

49 John Henry Newman, ed., *Select Treatises of S. Athanasius, Archbishop of Alexandria, in Controversy with the Arians* (London: J. J. Parker, 1844), 440 (28.7). See also, 482 (3.58, section 5): "Had Christ's enemies thus dwelt on these thoughts, and recognized the ecclesiastical scope [σκοπός] as an anchor for the faith . . ."

Rule of Faith, not only would she be in a state of decay, but she would cease to exist. Newman was divided on the question of whether or not the Rule of Faith continued to develop in his own day as early as his *Arians* (1833) and therefore was inconsistent through the publication of the *Via Media*.

For Newman, along with some of the Tractarians, antiquity was the standard by which to judge the later Church. Others in the Oxford Movement, especially John Keble, thought that antiquity was the model for the Anglican Church and that the latter ought to be reformed in the light of the early Church, but their fundamental act of faith was in the Church of England, rightly understood. For Newman "his fundamental act of faith was in the Apostolic Church and the Church of the Fathers."[50] This can be seen in his presentation of his earlier opinions in a letter to Samuel Wilks of November 8, 1845. Newman's principles included "taking *Antiquity*, not the *existing Church*, as the oracle of truth; and holding that the *Apostolical Succession* is a sufficient guarantee of Sacramental Grace, without *union with the Christian Church throughout the world*."[51] The Roman Catholic Church, accordingly, did not need to be taken seriously because the purity of ancient doctrine was the criterion for identifying the Church. Having added to the doctrine of the early Church, the Roman Catholic Church forfeited doctrinal purity.[52]

DISINTEGRATION

In his *Essay on Development* Newman makes a distinction between authentic developments and corruptions, insofar as an idea develops by remaining true to its type, principles and organization while incorporating new aspects in time.[53] Inversely, a corruption that does not occur quickly, is a decay or disintegration. Its demise is slow and although "there is no violent or vigorous action" that ends an idea quickly, it nevertheless cannot sustain its own life: "And thus we see opinions, usages, and systems, which are of venerable and imposing aspect, but which have no soundness within them, and keep together from a habit of consistence, or from dependence on political institutions."[54]

Newman began to see the disintegration of the Oxford Movement with the construction of a novel ecclesiology which occupied his attention throughout the 1830s. He had designed a paper church, although he hoped it would become real. Eventually the *Via Media* was introduced, which presented Anglicanism as the "middle course" between Protestant Christianity and Roman Catholicism.

---

50 Christopher Dawson, *The Spirit of the Oxford Movement* (Washington, DC: The Catholic University of America Press, 2022), 106.

51 *LD* xi, 27–28.

52 Pierre Gauthier, "Richard Hurrell Froude's Influence on Newman and the Oxford Movement," 262.

53 *Dev.,* 171.

54 *Dev.,* 204–5.

The *Via Media* began to reveal latent contradictions in the application of the Rule of Faith, ones that neither antiquity nor scripture alone could answer.

Thus, the disintegration of the movement as an "idea" began in Newman's mind almost in mid-stream. It took him years to see the once radiating appearance of an idea slowly fade away. He was pushed to reconsider this understanding of the Church by deeper readings in the Fathers, exchanges with Abbé Jager, prominent evangelicals, his brother Francis, Pusey's immense learning, and especially by the influence of Hurrell Froude. Froude himself carried forward the principles of the early Church to their logical development in the Middle Ages and nearly to communion with the Roman Catholic Church.[55] Froude died in 1836 but his influence on Newman continued, both in the form of remembered conversations and in the four volumes of his controversial *Remains* which Newman edited after his death.[56]

The Oxford Movement held that antiquity was the model for Newman's church. But that principle started to rupture for Newman with the publication of his "Home Thoughts from Abroad," written in March 1836.[57] Here Newman presents two conceptions of Catholicism.[58] Froude's shadow looms in this text because he favored a developing understanding of Catholicism over a frozen, even sclerotic view of the early Church as the standard for the contemporary Church.[59] While a fissure can be seen in 1836 in Newman's attachment to the Oxford Movement's principle that the early Church displays the true form of the Church, Newman held as late as 1837 that antiquity was the rule and that a living teaching authority (ordinary magisterium in nineteenth century Catholic parlance) that claimed to develop the doctrine of the early Church betrayed it.

> In like manner in their teaching and acting, they [Roman Catholics] begin as if in the name of all the Fathers at once, but will be found in the sequel to prove, instruct, and enjoin simply in their own name. . . . The infallibility of the existing Church is then found to be its first principle. Whatever principles they profess in theory, resembling, or coincident with our own, yet . . . when they have to prove this or that article of

---

55 For instances of Froude bringing Newman beyond the limits of the Oxford Movement towards Rome, see *LD* iv, 18, 24, 32, 37, 38–39, 46, 47, 48–49, 50, 51, 83, 112, 190, 254, 271; v, 12, 17, 68, 100, 128, 155, 156, 163; x 188.

56 For example, Newman wrote J. W. Bowden on January 17, 1840, that *The Record* had written something "that was most *bitter* (that's the only word) against Keble, and me [Newman], and the new volumes of Froude. They are past *anger*; they say we are far worse than the unspiritual High Church of the last century, as sinning more against light—*i.e.* there was no 'Record' then." *LD* vii, 216.

57 Henry Parry Liddon, *Life of Edward Bouverie Pusey*, vol. 2 (London: Longmans, 1894), 503.

58 Dawson, *The Spirit of the Oxford Movement*, 115.

59 See Froude's letter of January 9, 1834, to Keble in Dawson, 110. See also William Palmer 1843 and Nockles, "Histories and Anti-Histories," 607.

their creed, they supersede the appeal to Scripture and Antiquity by putting forward the infallibility of the Church, thus solving the whole question, by a summary and final interpretation both of Antiquity and of Scripture.[60]

Here Newman proposes a rejection of the living Rule of Faith. The Rule of Faith had been ossified and the task of the Oxford Movement was to re-instate it.[61] This contradictory trajectory would begin to end in the *Via Media*.

In the wake of "Home Thoughts" and the *Via Media*, Newman's activities in the movement increased even as the inherent contradictions in the movement gradually fragmented its core idea. Newman became the editor of *The British Critic* in January 1838.[62] Under his direction, the quarterly produced Tractarian-themed articles.[63] During Newman's tenure as editor, philosophical, theological, and social questions received frequent and prominent attention. Newman not only was aware of these questions, but he actively *cultivated* them, especially among up-and-coming Tractarians.[64] Between 1839 and 1841, Newman faced critical questions about his role in the Oxford Movement. Suspicions that he was drifting from his native communion towards the Roman Catholic Church appeared in various letters and journals.[65] Such criticism weighed heavily upon him.[66]

Newman continued to edit and write theological tracts that attempted to reassure the adherents of the Oxford Movement, while simultaneously provoking the wrath of his critics.[67] Newman relished this role as a "controversialist" mediating

---

60 *VM* i, 47–48.

61 The Tractarians were not consistent in this, however, as can be seen in their advocation of medieval vestments and ecclesial architecture rather than, say, the early Church's basilica form.

62 Ker, *Biography*, 158–59; 173. See Esther Rhoads Houghton, "'The British Critic' and the Oxford Movement," *Studies in Bibliography* 16 (1963): 119–23.

63 For a recent and complete account of Newman as editor of the *British Critic*, see Simon Skinner, *Tractarians and the 'Condition of England': The Social and Political Thought of the Oxford Movement* (Oxford: Clarendon Press, 2004), 31; 36–58. Unfortunately, Skinner's revisionist work used unnecessarily caustic language; e.g., Newman was described as "Machiavellian" in his "abduction" of the *British Critic* (*Tractarians*, 14; 36); in spite of such defects, he has provided a usable description of Newman's editorship of the *British Critic*.

64 Anne Mozley commented on Newman's editorship "One incidental use of the review was to furnish a field—a sort of practice-ground—for the younger members of the party." *The Letters of Rev. J. B. Mozley, DD*, ed. Anne Mozley (London: Rivingtons, 1885), 71.

65 W. F. Mandel, "Newman and His Audiences: 1825–1845," *Journal of Religious History* 24, no. 2 (June 2000): 143–58.

66 See David Delio, "A Multitude of Subtle Influences: Faith, Reason, and Conversion in Newman's Thirteenth Oxford University Sermon," *Newman Studies Journal* 5, no. 1 (Spring 2008): 77–86.

67 For example, Newman wrote to Mr. J.W. Bowden "by the by have you observed between the goals and aspirations of the Oxford Movement and those who would question his loyalty to the Anglican tradition. Indeed, Newman had reached his apogee of influence within the movement.[68]

However, Newman's exalted, "controversial *status*" was short lived. In the summer of 1839, Newman retreated for the "Long Vacation" to study patristic authors as well as the history of the Monophysite controversy of the fifth century. He was particularly "absorbed in the doctrinal issue" raised by this crisis in the early Church, and this was linked to his ongoing interest in the *Via Media*.[69] Towards the close of his vacation, Newman became alarmed by surge of doubt about "the tenableness of Anglicanism."[70]

Two separate occasions marked the gradual abeyance of his Anglican identity:[71] Newman's discovery of the Anglican Church not as a *Via Media* but alienated from the true Church in heresy and the Catholic Fr. Nicholas Wiseman's article about the power and universality of the Church.[72] Even with the reassurance of his "old convictions," Newman experienced moments of uncertainty over the next few months, for example, finding himself in prayer for unity with Rome and publishing a provocative exposition in January of 1840, "On the Catholicity of the English Church."[73] Yet, his correspondence and other writings during this tumultuous period revealed that he was still seeking to maintain some form of Anglican identity that would distance himself from what he thought were the excesses of the Roman Catholic Church.[74]

During the winter of 1840–1841, Newman focused on a commentary that treated the *Thirty-Nine Articles* of the Church of England according to Catholic principles: *Tracts for the Times, No. 90: Remarks on certain Passages of the Thirty-nine Articles*. Newman hoped that *Tract* 90, an interpretative analysis capable of generating scholarly debate,[75] would allay those who had started clamoring for defection to Rome and would bolster the Tractarian position on the catholicity of

---

that most grotesque of pieces of news in the *Christian Observer* of this month about me? One step alone is wanted—to say that I am the Pope *ipsissimus* in disguise." *LD* vii, 5.

68 *Apo.*, 92–94.

69 *Apo.*, 113–14.

70 *Apo.*, 114.

71 See David Delio, "Calculated to Undermine Things Established: Newman's Fourteenth Oxford University Sermon," *Newman Studies Journal* 5, no. 2 (Fall 2008): 69–83.

72 *Apo.*, 115–17.

73 *Apo.*, 124, 129.

74 Ker, *Biography*, 193.

75 Newman (*Apo.*, 88) did not anticipate that *Tract* 90 would create the "sudden storm of indignation" that it did; however, he did anticipate that his interpretations might provoke controversy: e.g., in the conclusion of *Tract* 90 he defended his Catholic interpretation: "the Articles are evidently framed on the principle of leaving open large questions, on which the controversy hinges" (*VM* ii, 345). After 1839, Newman had wanted to remain peaceful concerning "subjects of the day"; *Tract* 90 and the *Catholicus* letters to *The Times* were the two exceptions.

the English Church.[76] Newman's reading of the *Thirty-Nine Articles* revealed his desire for ecclesial communion between churches, for he believed both communities shared an underlying, fundamental faith. However, this gambit proved disastrous for him, as he was essentially censured, forced to discontinue the *Tracts for the Times* and to retreat from controversy and even his ministry at St. Mary's. *Tract 90* was also significant in that it fully exposed to Newman and the wider public that the hairline fractures anticipated in "Home Thoughts" and the *Via Media* between Rome and England were in fact acute and irreconcilable differences. In so many ways, the inability to unite the living magisterial tradition of Rome with the *Thirty-Nine Articles* and other Anglican traditions signaled the ongoing collapse, in Newman's mind, of the "idea" of the movement.

Following *Tract 90*, and the tumult it produced, Newman increasingly became critical of this changeless conception of the early Church, for the application of the ethos and Rule of Faith of that earlier period to the present required the use of a pure private judgment, and the rejection of private judgment in matters of religion was one of the principles of the Oxford Movement.[77] In some ways Newman's increasing realizations had precedent and paralleled his earlier movement away from evangelical traditions into the Anglican High Church. Now in his forties, he found that a church without a developing Rule of Faith (or living teaching authority) was not living the same life as the early Church. Newman realized that even ecclesial tradition, lifted from antiquity without the guidance of a living teaching authority, was homeless and dependent on private judgment.

The Fathers were the germ of the "idea" of the Oxford Movement, especially appropriated by Newman, Keble, and Froude. Their influential way of looking at the Fathers came through disputes in the *Tracts*, sermons, and letters. It was the warfare of minds and ideas that ultimately led to development and thereby forced Newman to see the contradictions inherent in the "idea" of the Oxford Movement and its insufficiency in relation to the Idea of Christianity.

Faced with these contradictions, Newman could not, as some Tractarians seem to have done, live with what they considered an antinomy. He knew he had to choose either the living Rule of Faith or the timeless authority of the Church as she existed in antiquity as truer to the Idea of Christianity. Newman rejected one principle (the early Church as the timeless, unalterable model for all succeeding ages) of the Oxford Movement to preserve another (the rejection of a pure private judgment in matters of religion). In militating against private judgment Newman began to see the need for a living magisterium. Therein he distanced himself from the decaying "idea" of the Oxford Movement (disintegrating because it contained contradictory principles) and towards the living Idea of Roman Catholic Church.

---

76 *VM* i, 269.
77 *Apo.,* 113.

CONCLUSION

Newman's conclusion to Sophia Ryder of the momentous interval in his life between 1830–1845 is illuminating. He noted quite definitively that 1845 represented the end of the movement for him, yet not the movement itself. Indeed, it lived on, but no longer showed growth and force as it did in the heady days of 1833–39.[78]

The further this "idea" of the Oxford Movement expanded through tests and attacks, the *Tracts for the Times* and other periodicals, as well as through sermons and internal arguments, the less vigorous it became. Newman and others came to see some of these principles, now in their mature form, to be contradictory and stultifying. Some of his friends and disciples recognized this early on and after a series of external events, as well as internal movements of grace, Newman grew in the knowledge that the movement could not become a true aspect of the Christian Idea. The movement that he in so many ways brought to life, died for him, even if it has continued on as embers glowing grey, sparking and popping, never to rekindle. By 1845 Newman was persuaded by grace and reason to see the Roman Catholic Church as the true Idea of Christianity.

Others involved in the movement, such as Pusey and Keble, seemed content either not to develop the various aspects of the Oxford Movement or to rest with the paradox of principles without resolving them, and therefore keep the disintegrating "idea" alive. Tractarians like Mark Pattison or James Froude also saw the contradictions of movement's principles but went in an opposite direction, either leaving the Church entirely or becoming ensconced in the growing leviathan of the liberal political order.

The Oxford Movement was something like a "revival," but it neither achieved a telos in the Church of Rome nor reformed the Church of England. Rather the movement forced many of its ardent adherents to come to grips with the paradoxes and contradictions inherent to its "idea" and accept, unconsciously, its disintegrating half-life while remaining in the Anglican communion in some form, to opt for another Christian denomination, to reject it for an agnostic or atheistic life in the liberal order, or, finally, to choose a living idea, the Roman Catholic Church, as Newman did.

---

78 "To see that what was once a small, focused band of clergymen with clear intents, although contradictory principles, is now a memory diffused in many directions, slowly drifting amid its many contradictions. Perhaps the 'personal ordinariates' established in 2009 by the Catholic Church would have been a fulfillment that Newman and others after 1841 would have welcomed." See Colin Podmore, "The Oxford Movement Today—'The Things that Remain,'" in *The Oxford Handbook of the Oxford Movement*, 622; 626–30.

Suggested Reading

Brown, Stewart J., Peter Nockles, James Pereiro, eds. *Oxford Handbook of the Oxford Movement*. Oxford: Oxford University Press, 2017.

Dawson, Christopher. *The Spirit of the Oxford Movement*. New York: Sheed and Ward, 1933.

Delio, David P. *"An Aristocracy of Exalted Spirits:" The Idea of the Church in Newman's Tamworth Reading Room*. Leominster: Gracewing, 2016.

———. "A Multitude of Subtle Influences: Faith, Reason, and Conversion in Newman's Thirteenth Oxford University Sermon." *Newman Studies Journal* 5, no. 1 (Spring 2008): 77–86.

———. "Calculated to Undermine Things Established: Newman's Fourteenth Oxford University Sermon." *Newman Studies Journal* 5, no. 2 (Fall 2008): 69–83.

Ker, Ian. *John Henry Newman, A Biography*. Oxford: Clarendon Press, 1988.

Nockles, Peter. *The Oxford Movement in Context: Anglican High Churchmanship, 1760–1857*. Cambridge: Cambridge University Press, 1997.

Vaiss, Paul. *From Oxford to the People*. Leominster: Fowler Wright Books, 1996.

CHAPTER 2

JOHN HENRY NEWMAN'S LIFELONG JOURNEY OF CONVERSION

Fr. Juan Alonso

One of the most well-known aspects of John Henry Newman is that he is "a convert." His entry into the Catholic Church on October 9, 1845, is considered a major event in the modern history of the Church.[1] For many, Newman occupies the highest place among the converts to Catholicism coming from churches arising with the Reformation. Furthermore, he is one of the most influential converts in the history of the Church, alongside St. Augustine.

His reception into the Catholic Church signified a radical change in the direction of fundamental aspects of his life. Nevertheless, if we look at his entire existential itinerary, we see that this event was nothing more than the endpoint of a series of "conversions" that Newman had experienced up until then: a long and suffering process in search for the truth and fidelity to his inner voice. As Joseph Ratzinger pointed out in 1990, "throughout his entire life, Newman was a person converting, a person being transformed, and thus he always remained

---

* This a revised version of an article that appeared in *Scripta Theologica* 51, no. 3 (2019): 649–77.

1 See Ian Ker, "Introduction," in *Newman and Conversion*, ed. Ian Ker (Edinburgh: T&T Clark, 1997), 1.

and became ever more himself."[2] An attentive consideration of these "conversions" will help us get to know better the history of the great convert, but also the soul and thought of a great teacher who teaches both with his thought and with his life.[3] Additionally, the figure of Newman stands out for the influence he had on numerous people journeying the path toward faith.[4] But before we begin that route, we must address a preliminary question.

SOURCES FOR RESEARCH ON THE CONVERSION OF JOHN HENRY NEWMAN

Apologia Pro Vita Sua (1864) is the richest and most vivid source where the reader can satisfy his desire to learn Newman's intellectual trajectory, since in it the author narrates the relevant milestones in his own conversion. The text was born in response to slanderous accusations cast against him by Charles Kingsley, an Anglican clergyman. Over the course of a month, filled with strenuous stretches of some fifteen or more hours of work, Newman put forth with enormous effort and documentation to prove with clarity his spiritual development and to explain his religious choices; the result being the "history of his religious opinions," as the subtitle reads. The book was greatly welcomed in the English world, among Catholics and Protestants alike.[5] Recently, the now departed historian Frank Turner posed a revisionist approach to Newman's figure,[6] specifically calling into question the value of his testimony in the *Apologia*, and accusing him of offering in a retrospective and deceitful manner, not just a religious motivation for his journey to Rome, but also a falsified intellectual and theological construct.[7] Turner's widely debated attempt to provide an alternative account is, however, a reductionist and warped vision of Newman's conversion.[8]

---

2   Joseph Ratzinger, "Presentation on the Occasion for the First Centenary of the Death of Card. John Henry Newman," Rome, April 28, 1990.

3   "The characteristic of the great Doctor of the Church, it seems to me, is that he teaches not only through his thought and speech but also by his life, because within him, thought and life are interpenetrated and defined." Joseph Ratzinger, "Presentation for the First Centenary of the Death of Card. Newman."

4   Peter Willi, "Newman as a Convert and Counsellor of Converts" (October 9, 2008), available from http://www.newmanfriendsinternational.org/en/newman-as-a-convert-and-counsellor-of-converts/ (accessed July 20, 2020).

5   See J. Morales and V. Garcia Ruiz, "La retórica de la verdad," Introduction to J. H. Newman, *Apologia Pro Vita Sua. Historia de mis ideas religiosas* (Madrid: Ediciones Encuentro, 1996), 17–20.

6   Frank M. Turner, *John Henry Newman: The Challenge to Evangelical Religion* (New Haven and London: Yale University Press, 2002).

7   In a provoking manner Turner affirms that in his path toward the Catholic Church Newman was not guided by principles, nor oriented by his conscience, nor followed a determined theological direction: "In reality, contingency after contingency determined the emergence of Newman's religious character and thought." Turner, *John Henry Newman*, 110.

8   Nockles criticizes the fact that throughout his book Turner "erases with increasingly

In addition to the *Apologia*, several other interesting Newman texts serve as sources for this study. In his *Essay on the Development of Christian Doctrine*, published in 1845, the same year as his entrance in the Catholic Church, the English convert reveals his vision of the type of personal development that guides a person toward individual conversion. The *Essay in Aid of a Grammar of Assent* (1870)—that comes to be an attempt at the epistemology of knowledge— deals with the nature of religious assent that is implied in the journey toward faith or conversion.[9] We must also mention the rich collection of letters and diaries composing thirty-two volumes, as well as other hidden references in his numerous sermons.

His two novels, *Loss and Gain* (1848) and *Callista* (1855), also serve as a valuable place to delve into the Newmanian vision of Christian conversion since they pertain as much to the genre of conversion stories as to the genre of auto-biography. *Loss and Gain* could be considered the first draft of the *Apologia*.[10] The novel arose as a response to a short anonymous account in which Oxford converts to Catholicism were accused of fraud and disloyalty.[11] Newman hoped to show that those converts were not blind followers to some foreign creed, but were authentic Englishmen, lovers of their traditions but bearers of an incorrupt-ible religious and moral choice. Following the steps of the young protagonist, Charles Reding, in his years as a student at Oxford, Newman demonstrates that the conversion is a gradual process of interior growth, in which man—spurred by God and guided by a well-disposed conscience—comes to recognize the real Christianity that responds to one's internal restlessness and to one's search for truth. The expressive title, *Loss and Gain*, evokes the internal state of a potential

---

alarming ease what should be clear limits between conjecture, claims, and theorizing, on the one hand, and fact, evidence, and proof on the other." Peter Nockles, review of *John Henry Newman: The Challenge to Evangelical Religion* by Frank M. Turner, in *Albion: A Quarterly Journal Concerned with British Studies* 35, no. 4 (2003): 670. Although Turner deserves recognition for insisting on the importance of historical contextualization for the study of Newman, his eagerness for revisionism and de-mythification of the figure of Newman turn his considerations into a sterile reductionism. Peter Nockles has affirmed that "Turner's Newman is too much of a one-dimensional caricature of a complex person." "The Current State of Newman Scholarship," *British Catholic History* 35, no. 1 (2020): 125). In sum, "The judgment that the *Apologia* does not give us a comprehensive or fair account of Newman's life up until 1845 is, in itself, a banality." Lawrence S. Cunningham, review of Frank M. Turner, *John Henry Newman: The Challenge to Evangelical Religion*, in *Horizons: The Journal of the College Theology Society* 30, no. 1 (2003): 146.

9   This book had a great influence on Bernard Lonergan's thinking about the justification of belief. See Richard Liddy, "John Henry Newman's Influence on Bernard Lonergan," in *St. John Henry Newman, Preserving and Promulgating His Legacy*, ed. Robert C. Christie (Newcastle upon Tyne: Cambridge Scholars Publishing, 2019).

10   See J. Morales and V. Garcia Ruiz, "La retórica de la verdad," 25.

11   Elizabeth Harris, *From Oxford to Rome: And How It Fared with Some Who Lately Made the Journey*, 1847. The author was a convert to Catholicism who later returned to Anglicanism.

convert facing the dilemma of risking his station in life for fidelity to a divine call that is perceived with certainty.[12]

Callista is set in north Africa at the end of the third century. The context is the life of the first Christian communities in a pagan world, during a time in which persecution under Emperor Decius threatens and at the same time strengthens Christianity. The novel narrates the conversion experience of a young pagan, Callista, but also the experiences of other characters close to her, like Juba, an ancient catechumen, or Agelio, a Christian who has allowed his faith to grow cold. Newman offers a view of conversion as a complex process in which, in addition to an intellectual component, there is a more decisive and vital element: an encounter with Jesus. The novel sharply reflects central aspects of Newman's thought, like the role of the conscience in a conversion and the existential dimension of faith.

In Newman's biographical trajectory we can distinguish four fundamental experiences of conversion; their analysis allows us to go deeper into the meaning of the qualifier—"convert"—that is applied to him, as well as the significance and transcendence that he himself attributes to conversion.[13]

1. "A GREAT CHANGE OF THOUGHT TOOK PLACE IN ME." AUTUMN, 1816

As a starting point in his spiritual history Newman recalls in his *Apologia* the spontaneous religiosity of his childhood years before his religious convictions had even begun to take shape.[14] A boy of keen intellect, extraordinarily perceptive and reserved but at the same time emotional, he possessed a lively imagination that led him to recreate an invisible world inhabited by spirits with magical powers. He recognized that these thoughts and feelings as a child had great influence on his future religious convictions.

Growing up in a family in which the religious atmosphere of Anglicanism of the time prevailed, he had acquired a taste for Bible readings, and he possessed "a perfect knowledge of [his] Catechism."[15] He was a voracious reader. At age 14 his reading of some of the Enlightenment authors who were hostile toward Christianity—citing Voltaire and Thomas Paine—awoke in him a certain skepticism.

---

12 See Victor Garcia Ruiz, "Para leer al principio o al final," Introduction to *Perder y ganar*, 19–20. John Henry Newman, *Perder y ganar*, translation, introduction, and notes by Víctor García Ruiz, Madrid, Ediciones Encuentro, 2017.

13 Regarding the notion of conversion, see Juan Alonso and J. Jose Alviar, eds., *Conversión cristiana y evangelización*, XXXI Simposio Internacional de Teología (Pamplona: Eunsa, 2011); Juan Alonso, *La conversión cristiana. Estudios y perspectivas* (Pamplona: Eunsa, 2011).

14 *Apo.*,1–2.

15 *Apo.*, 1.

His spiritual state was such that he sought "to be virtuous, but not religious," and he did not "see the *meaning* of loving God."[16]

In his final year at the Ealing School in London, the young Newman met the reverend Walter Mayers, a 25-year-old Anglican clergyman with a Calvinist evangelical leaning, whose pedagogy and example fully permeated the future cardinal. In his *Apologia*, Newman comments that Mayers was an "excellent man, . . . the human means of this beginning of divine faith in me."[17] Mayers placed in his hands some books of Calvinist orientation that helped foster his piety, dispelling doubts and clarifying his religious vision. The spiritual autobiography of the evangelical author Thomas Scott (1747–1821), titled *The Force of Truth* (1779), emblazoned a piercing sense of dogma on Newman.[18] The reading of *History of The Church of Christ* (1794–1809) by Joseph Milner (1744–1797) led him to discover texts by the Church Fathers, like St. Augustine and St. Ambrose, igniting in his youthful heart a passion for the Fathers that would last his entire life. But at this time he also fell under the influence of some doctrines that later he would have to renounce, like the idea expounded by the Calvinist William Romaine that conversion was the infallible sign of predestination, or the book by Thomas Newton about the prophecies[19] that attempted to prove through Scripture that the pope was the Antichrist.

What he denoted as his "first conversion" took place in 1816 in this intellectual and religious context marked by Evangelicalism, though not in all its extremes.[20] It was not a sudden and emotional experience in a conventional evangelical style.[21] It is better defined as a change that took place from the first days of August until a few days before Christmas. During that summer he stayed at the Ealing School due to the collapse of his father's bank. There he suffered his first encounter with illness that, according to words he wrote some time later, "made [him] a Christian—with experiences before and after, awful, and known only to God."[22] He sums up his experience in few words: "When I was fifteen, (in the autumn of 1816) a great change of thought took place in me. I fell under the influences of a definite Creed, and received into my intellect impressions of dogma, which, through God's mercy, have never been effaced or obscured."[23]

---

16 *AW*, 169.

17 *Apo.*, 4–5.

18 *Apo.*, 5.

19 William Romaine, *Dissertations on the Prophecies*, 1758.

20 See Keith Beaumont, *Dieu intérieur: La théologie spirituelle de John Henry Newman* (Paris: Éditions Ad Solem, 2014), 92–97.

21 In a written memory, many years later (1876) he recalls that: "he had not been converted in that special way which it laid down as imperative, but so plainly against rule, as to make it very doubtful in the eyes of normal Evangelicals whether he had really been converted at all." *AW*, 79.

22 *AW*, 268.

23 *Apo.*, 4. See Letter to Anne Mozley (1885), in *LD* xxxi, 31.

Newman always considered this occasion as the beginning of his consciousness of Christianity, and he asserted graphically that he was more certain of his inward conversion than he was of the fact that he had hands and feet.[24] What kind of experience was this? What are its main characteristics? We can distinguish the following:

a) *An invisible world.* Newman's "first conversion" does not seem to be about a mystical event, nor is it a type of intuitive understanding of God, but rather an ordinary grace of notable intensity that bestowed upon the young evangelical a solid conviction about the existence of an invisible world, absolutely real, to which the Christian mysteries belong, as well as a sharp sensibility in order to perceive it in all its significance.[25]

This theme of the "invisible world" permeates through all of Newman's works. One of his Anglican sermons from 1837 ("The Invisible World") describes it as such: Through this visible world "there is another world, quite as far-spreading, quite as close to us, and more wonderful; another world all around us, though we see it not, and more wonderful than the world we see, for this reason if for no other, that we do not see it. All around us are numberless objects, coming and going, watching, working, or waiting, which we see not: this is that other world, which the eyes reach not unto, but faith only."[26]

The existence of this invisible world is at the base of the theology of faith that Newman develops. In his sermon given in 1830 ("Faith and Obedience") Newman ponders the nature of believing: "What is meant by faith? It is to feel in good earnest that we are creatures of God; it is a practical perception of the unseen world; it is to understand that this world is not enough for our happiness, to look beyond it on towards God, to realize His presence, to wait upon Him, to endeavour to learn and to do His will, and to seek our good from Him."[27] The existence of an invisible world which escapes our senses constitutes a necessary preamble to our faith.

This discovery of the invisible world during his "juvenile conversion" connects to the distinction that Newman will make later between *notional* knowledge and *real* knowledge. The first—he will say in the *The Grammar of Assent*— is the result of reasoning and abstraction; the second is the fruit of a communication with the real world, which also includes the invisible. It is in the confines of real assent that knowledge of the concrete and the practical are inscribed as is the case with faith and religious knowledge.[28]

---

24 *Apo.,* 4.

25 See José Morales, "Experiencia religiosa. La contribución de J. H. Newman," *Scripta Theologica* 27 (1995): 84.

26 *PS* iv, no. 13: 201.

27 *PS* iii, no. 6: 79.

28 For more on how the concepts of apprehension and *true* assent confer a personalist character to Newman's thought, see John F. Crosby, "Imagination and Intellect," in *The Personalism of John Henry Newman* (Washington, D.C.: The Catholic University of America Press, 2014), 33–65.

In summary, the invisible world is acting above us, although we are not conscious of it. Not only is it authentically real, but it also sustains and makes possible all created reality. Converting and believing means precisely choosing that invisible reality.

b) *The presence of Another.* In keeping with the above, for Newman one's "first conversion" is an awareness of the presence of God and an effective encounter with Him. He was able to rest—he commented later—in the thought of two and only two beings, absolute and luminously self-evident: "myself and my Creator."[29] In this point he follows the pattern for all Christian conversion, as is evident in the great converts, such as St. Paul ("I do not live, since it is Christ who lives in me," Gal 2:20), or St. Augustine ("you were more inward to me than my most inward part," "*interior intimo meo*"),[30] or to mention a closer figure, the spiritual conversion of St. Teresa of Avila in 1554 at age 39: a conversion rooted in her encounter with the image of *Ecce Homo* and the reading of St. Augustine's *Confessions*.[31]

This "luminous self-evidence" of God's absolute reality and His relationship to the believer is described in one of the first annotations of his personal diary as the core characteristic for conversion: "The reality of conversion, as cutting at the root of doubt, providing a chain between God and the Soul, that is with every link complete; I know I am right. How do you know it? I know I know. How? I know I know I know &c &c."[32] Thus, for Newman—as he expresses in one of his sermons—the Christian is "the one who has a ruling sense of God's presence within him."[33]

At one point in his first novel, *Loss and Gain*, Newman recreates the spiritual disposition of Charles Reding, the young Oxford student: "Charles's characteristic, perhaps about anything else, was an habitual sense of the Divine Presence; a sense which, of course, did not insure uninterrupted conformity of thought and deed to itself, but still there it was—the pillar of the cloud before him and guiding him."[34] In the other novel, *Callista*, the protagonist also recognizes that "voice" that is carrying her to God: "No, it is the echo of a person speaking to me. Nothing shall persuade me that it does not ultimately proceed from a person external to me. It carries with it its proof of its divine origin."[35]

Following his "first conversion," God occupies the center of life for Newman, and this event gives rise to a recurring theme in his sermons and his own spirituality: the importance of inner *solitude*, which is not closing oneself from others or egocentric individualism, but rather becoming conscious of the personal individuality in

---

29 *Apo.*, 4.
30 Augustine of Hippo, *Confessions*, Bk. V, 2, 2.
31 Teresa of Avila, *The Life of Teresa of Jesus*, ch. 9.
32 *AW*, 150.
33 "Sincerity and Hypocrisy," *PS* v, no. 16: 225.
34 *LG*, 230–31.
35 *Cal.*, 314.

relation to God, to others and to the world.[36] It is possible to assert that a large part of the insistence in Newmanian thought on the personal and individual character and the relationship between God and man is the result of the influence of the simple yet vigorous evangelicalism that Newman received in his youth.[37]

c) *One call, one mission.* One consequence of his spiritual experience in 1816 is the rise in him of a "deep imagination" that imposed itself upon him: "that it would be the will of God that I should lead a single life."[38] This inkling remained in him almost uninterrupted until 1829 and was strengthened from that year forward. He had a clear conviction that his divine vocation called for "such a sacrifice as celibacy involved," just as was required by the missionary work among pagans, which deeply attracted him for some years.[39]

In *Loss and Gain* we see a conversation between Charles and his tutor and confidant, Carlton, who holds that celibacy does not belong in the Anglican religious system. Charles responds: "It's no new notion taken up . . . ; you will smile, but I had it when a boy at school, and I have ever since fancied that I should never marry. Not that the feeling has never intermitted, but it is the habit of my mind. My general thoughts run in that one way, that I shall never marry."[40] In Newman's time celibacy was a practically inconceivable choice among the

---

36 See, for example, "The Immortality of the Soul," *PS* i, no. 2; "The Individuality of the Soul," *PS* iv, no. 6.

37 Gareth Atkins has reclaimed a major role of the influence of evangelism in John Henry Newman's conversion, a role that, in his opinion, had been distorted by researchers and that Newman himself wanted to conceal. According to him, there is a need for a major study on the spiritual climate that sustained Newman's worldview between 1816–1826, since it has frequently been overlooked (see Gareth Atkins, "Evangelicals," in *The Oxford Handbook of John Henry Newman*, ed. Frederick D. Aquino and Benjamin J. King (Oxford: Oxford University Press, 2018), 173.

Publisher's note: Such a study seems to be the goal of Geertjan Zuijdwegt in a forthcoming book *An Evangelical Adrift: The Making of John Henry Newman's Theology*, due to be released by the Catholic University of America Press in 2022.

Although it certainly seems necessary to make such a more attentive study of evangelism's influence on Newman's intellectual and spiritual itinerary, it is clear that Newman, in addition to rejecting what he perceived to be defects and limitations of evangelism, recognized just as well the influence of many positive aspects. In any event, there is no evidence of the alleged radical "anti-evangelism" of which Turner accuses Newman, and less still of his willingness to falsify in the *Apologia* his genuine feelings towards it. See criticism from Ian Ker, "John Henry Newman and his Distorters," in *Saint John Henry Newman: Preserving and Promulgating His Legacy*, ed. Robert Christie (Cambridge: Cambridge Scholars Publishing, 2020). Ultimately, as Avery Dulles maintains, Newman's conversion to Rome is better understood, not as a condemnation but rather an affirmation and finalization of his evangelical past. See Avery Dulles, "Newman, Conversion and Ecumenism," *Theological Studies* 51 (1990): 723.

38 *Apo.*, 7.

39 *Apo.*, 7.

40 *LG*, 192.

Anglican clergy. It was only much later, with the rise of the Oxford Movement led by Newman, that it became a religious ideal, a manifestation of generosity, a devotion and purity of the saints, though little was talked about it directly.[41]

d) *Discovery of dogma*. One final consequence of notable relevance from his first conversion is the importance of Christian dogma, which our author mentions explicitly in the cited text: "I fell under the influences of a definite Creed, and received into my intellect impressions of dogma, which, through God's mercy, have never been effaced or obscured."[42] This is the intellectual or doctrinal dimension of that first experience of conversion.

In the *Apologia* he refers to the "principle of dogma" as one of the "three great principles" of the Oxford Movement[43] and he declares: "I have the satisfaction of feeling that I have nothing to retract, and nothing to repent of. The main principle of the movement is as dear to me now, as it ever was. I have changed in many things: in this I have not. From the age of fifteen, dogma has been the fundamental principle of my religion: I know no other religion; I cannot enter into the idea of any other sort of religion; religion, as a mere sentiment, is to me a dream and a mockery. As well can there be filial love without the fact of a father, as devotion without the fact of a Supreme Being. What I held in 1816, I held in 1833, and I hold in 1864. Please God, I shall hold it to the end."[44]

This first conversion coincides with the end of Newman's schoolboy years. At age 16 he was prepared to begin his studies at Trinity of Oxford, where he arrived in June of 1817.

2. "I WAS DRIFTING IN THE DIRECTION OF THE LIBERALISM OF THE DAY. I WAS RUDELY AWAKENED FROM MY DREAM AT THE END OF 1827 BY TWO GREAT BLOWS." END OF 1827

Newman's second conversion must be situated at the end of 1827 and beginning of 1828. Since his arrival at Oxford he had developed a brilliant career, and he had enjoyed great prestige. First he had been named fellow of Oriel College and later an official tutor. He had been ordained an Anglican deacon and afterwards Anglican priest, and he had entered into a prestigious intellectual and academic environment. These had not been easy years. Three painful incidents helped him mature as a person: 1) an academic failure in the summer of 1820 from which he learned—as he indicates in a letter at the time to Reverend Mayers—that "honor

---

41   See Richard W. Church, *The Oxford Movement; Twelve Years, 1833–1845*, 1970, 117. Available from: http://www.gutenberg.org/ebooks/12092 (Accessed July 27, 2020).

42   *Apo.*, 4.

43   *Apo.*, 48–52.

44   *Apo.*, 49.

and fame are not desirable" and that "God is leading me through life in the way best adapted for His glory and my own salvation"[45]; 2) another bankruptcy for his father's business; and 3) the death of his father in September of 1824 following a sudden illness.

But two other sorrowful events shook Newman's life: "I was rudely awakened from my dream at the end of 1827 by two great blows—illness and bereavement."[46] The first is a physical and nervous collapse that he suffered while acting as examiner in November 1827.[47] His mind went blank, and he had to abandon his post on an examination tribunal. The other event was the unexpected death of his youngest sister, Mary, on January 5, 1828, at age 18. Of his three sisters, she was the one with whom John Henry had enjoyed the closest bond.[48]

This double commotion, to use his own words, woke him rudely from a dream. Over time he was able to see that these crises were preparing him for the beginning of a new phase in his life. In the *Apologia* he summarizes his interior situation at that time: "The truth is, I was beginning to prefer intellectual excellence to moral; I was drifting in the direction of the liberalism of the day."[49]

The liberalism to which he refers paid scarce attention to doctrinal orthodoxy and treated Evangelicals with certain disdain. Liberalism was interested in the role of the Church within the moral order of society, but its jealous defense of tolerance for religious matters was accompanied by the idea that "all opinions are the same" and, therefore, by skepticism regarding objective truth in religious matter. Today we would call this liberalism a theological, philosophical, or religious "relativism."

This second conversion was in part spiritual—in fact he considered the death of his sister as "the heaviest affliction with which the good hand of God has ever visited [him]"[50]—but above all it was a conversion of an intellectual order. In a diary entry, dated July of 1826, he summarized his intellectual itinerary of the previous two years: "In that time I have greatly changed my views in many points."[51] Indeed, during his years as fellow at Oriel he had been in contact with his cloistered colleagues, many of whom tended toward liberal rationalism,[52] and sometimes were called the "noetics." It was commented ironically that the professors' lounge at Oriel "stank of logic."[53] He had begun a special familiarity with one of them, Richard Whately, who opened intellectual and academic horizons

---

45   Letter to Rev W. Mayers (January 1821), *LD* i, 99.
46   *Apo.*, 14.
47   See Entry for February 21, 1828, in *AW*, 211–13.
48   *AW*, 211.
49   *Apo.*, 14.
50   *AW*, 213.
51   Entry for July 26, 1826, in *AW*, 172.
52   Thomas Arnold, Richard Whatley, and José Blanco White.
53   Meriol Trevor, *Newman's Journey* (Huntington, Ind.: Our Sunday Visitor, 1985), 27.

for him, and who invited him to collaborate on various projects, although this friendship did not last long. He had also met other colleagues of a more doctrinal and spiritual religious orientation than that of the liberals, like John Keble, who quickly abandoned the academic life, and Edward Pusey, an intelligent and devout man. These two, together with Newman and others (Hurrell Froude, Hugh Rose, William Palmer and Arthur Perceval) would later start the Oxford Movement.

At 27 years of age, Newman was aware of the liberal traits that had entered into his mindset. His second conversion made him aware of the inherent danger of skepticism. From then on, he would fight against it for the rest of his life, as he expressed many years later in 1879, in his moving address upon being named cardinal.[54]

3. "I HAVE NOT SINNED AGAINST LIGHT."
A TASK TO ACHIEVE. SUMMER OF 1833

His quarrels with Edward Hawkins, the new Provost at Oriel since 1828, over the tutorial system led him to resign from his official post as tutor and to focus on preparing his sermons for the parish church of St. Mary, and on the study of the Fathers and the early councils. In the summer of 1832, he completed the draft of his first work: *The Arians of the Fourth Century*. Drained from the previous month's exertion and the lack of much-needed rest, he departed with his friend Hurrell Froude and Hurrell's father, for a trip through the Mediterranean that lasted until the summer of the following year and that had very significant consequences.

During his stay in Sicily he became gravely ill, and for ten days he was on the brink of death, to the point that his servant, who now acted as his nurse, asked him for his final instructions. He did so, but told him—without fully understanding the significance of his own words: "I shall not die . . . I shall not die, for I have not sinned against light, I have not sinned against light."[55] Once recovered and about to embark upon his return to London, the servant noticed that his master was despondent and weeping and asked him the cause of his affliction.

---

54 See *Biglietto Speech*, available from http://www.newmanreader.org/works/addresses/file2.html (Accessed July 27, 2020)]. According to Turner, Newman had deliberately rewritten the history of his conversion to disguise the fact that the true enemy of the Oxford Movement was not liberalism but Evangelicalism: this way Newman would have tried to placate his fellow Roman Catholics, many of whom suspected he was a liberal. But Turner's speculations are not supported by facts. As John T. Ford has commented, the problem with Turner's interpretation is, on the one hand, his tendency to superimpose motives conjecturally on Newman's actions, with the use of citations that do not actually support these interpretations, and on the other hand, his inclination to offer psychological explanations for Newman's actions, thus frequently obscuring and complicating the questions at hand. See John T. Ford, review of *John Henry Newman: The Challenge to Evangelical Religion* by Frank M. Turner, in *The Catholic Historical Review* 89 (October 2003): 788–91.

55 *Apo.*, 34–35.

Newman only responded: "I have a work to do in England."[56] That work would be none other than the start of the Oxford Movement, or Tractarian Movement, of which he would be the main inspiration and organizer.[57]

In this third conversion experience we can distinguish two dimensions. The first is essentially spiritual: the feeling of the closeness of death and the perception of a mission with which God entrusted him, which seem to have helped him to abandon himself in God and trust in his Providence. An indication of this is the autobiographical poem he wrote during his return trip to England that later would become the well-known hymn "Lead, Kindly Light."[58] This poem itself was a prayer:

> LEAD, Kindly Light, amid the encircling gloom
> Lead Thou me on!
> The night is dark, and I am far from home—
> Lead Thou me on!
> Keep Thou my feet; I do not ask to see
> The distant scene—one step enough for me.

The second dimension of this experience is ecclesiological. Newman understood that his mission going forward consisted in renewing the Church of England from within. For that reason, after his return from the Mediterranean, he began to devise a specifically Anglican ecclesiology, as a *Via Media* between the Protestantism of the Reformers from the sixteenth century and Roman Catholicism.[59] This was not about an intellectual whim or a speculative exercise. At the bottom of the *Via Media* lay the desire to reactivate a national church in decline, a decline as much in the doctrinal sphere as in the sacramental and spiritual spheres. And that required relying on another fundamental principle of the Oxford Movement: the sacramental principle, inseparably united to the dogmatic principle. Newman remembered in 1864: "I was confident in the truth of a certain definite religious teaching, based upon this foundation of dogma; viz. that there was a visible Church, with sacraments and rites which are the channels of invisible grace. I thought that this was the doctrine of Scripture, of the early Church, and of the Anglican Church. Here again, I have not changed in opinion; I am as certain now on this point as I was in 1833, and have never ceased to be certain."[60]

However, over time Newman became aware of the fragility of such an undertaking as the *Via Media*. Indeed, in the summer of 1839 he wrote "for the first

---

56 *Apo.*, 35.

57 Newman always considered Keble's Sermon, "National Apostasy" (July 14, 1833) as the beginning of the Oxford Movement. See *Apo.*, 35.

58 "The Pillar of the Cloud" ["Lead, Kindly Light"], *VO*, 156.

59 For more on Newman's ecclesiology, see John T. Ford, "La eclesiología en John Henry Newman," *Scripta Theologica* 51, no. 3 (2019): 741–73.

60 *Apo.*, 49.

time a doubt came upon me of the tenableness of Anglicanism."[61] The history of the first Councils showed him that the *Via Media* was an erroneous path.[62] This shock was followed quickly by another: in 1839 he was struck by a phrase from St. Augustine that he encountered in an article on Catholic theology by Nicholas Wiseman, future cardinal and first Archbishop of Westminster (1850): "*securus iudicat orbis terrarum*" (the entire world [the Catholic sphere] judges right). It was about the basic principle of all the first Councils: everyone should support what the majority of the Church accepts as truth. Preferring one's own opinion over the consent of the majority is the beginnings of a pathway toward error and heresy, "*Securus iudicat orbis terrarum*." By those great words of the ancient Father, interpreting and summing up the long and varied course of ecclesiastical history, the theory of the Via Media was absolutely pulverized."[63] Following the first blow Newman reassured himself, thinking that things still needed to be investigated and hoping to receive later on a new illumination.[64]

What did he do in this situation? It is worth quoting at length a text by our author that gives testimony of his right intention and passion for the truth:

> I determined to be guided, not by my imagination, but by my reason. . . . Had it not been for this severe resolve, I should have been a Catholic sooner than I was. . . . Then I said to myself, Time alone can solve that question. It was my business to go on as usual, to obey those convictions to which I had so long surrendered myself, which still had possession of me, and on which my new thoughts had no direct bearing. That new conception of things should only so far influence me, as it had a logical claim to do so. If it came from above, it would come again;—so I trusted,—and with more definite outlines and greater cogency and consistency of proof.[65]

Newman's attitude—not just prudent but, above all, faithful to his conscience and committed to the truth—is reflected in the commentary of Charles Reding (the protagonist in *Loss and Gain*) about the crossroads in which he is caught during his search for the true Church of Christ: "But . . . surely God wills us to be guided by reason; I don't mean that reason is everything, but it is at least something. Surely we ought not to act without it, against it."[66] The beginning of Newman's conduct is also shared by his alter ego in *Loss*

---

61   *Apo.*, 114.

62   *Apo.*, 114.

63   *Apo.*, 117.

64   Newman wrote: "The thought for the moment had been, The Church of Rome will be found right after all'; and then it had vanished. My old convictions remained as before." *Apo.*, 118.

65   *Apo.*, 119–20.

66   *LG*, 110.

and Gain: "our strength in this world is, to be the subjects of reason, and our liberty, to be captives of the truth."[67]

Our purpose here is not to examine the details of Newman's intellectual trajectory from 1839 until his reception into the Catholic Church on October 9, 1845. Here it suffices to enumerate some events that weakened his faith in the Anglican Church even more: his historical research on the Arian heresy of the fourth century, that persuaded him that Rome already was the rightful defender of orthodoxy; the publication of *Tract* 90, in February 1841, where he attempt-stut to demonstrate that the doctrine of the ancient Church can be found—using a Catholic, not Protestant interpretation—in the official Anglican texts, especially in the *Thirty-Nine Articles*; the creation in 1841, on the part of the British and Prussian governments, of a common bishopric in Jerusalem, whose bishop would alternate between an Anglican and a Lutheran-Calvinist; and his research into the development of the Christian doctrine, that confirmed his belief that the Roman Catholic Church of the nineteenth century was the authentic "development" from the primitive Church.[68]

These were years of doubts and anxieties that affected his demeanor and his relationship with the Anglican Church; years of tireless effort in order to lay foundations for an Anglican ecclesiology, despite the blows he was receiving. In the *Apologia* he expressed his feelings: "From the end of 1841, I was on my deathbed, as regards my membership with the Anglican Church."[69]

On April 19, 1842, he retired to Littlemore, a small village situated three kilometers from Oxford and incorporated in St. Mary's parish, where earlier he had remodeled some barns into a house. There he shared with some disciples and friends that had followed him an almost "monastic" lifestyle based on study, prayer, and penance. In 1843 he resigned as pastor of St. Mary. His final sermon was September 25, and the following Monday in Littlemore he gave a heartfelt farewell address.[70] This period in Littlemore was a time of hope and discernment.[71] He did not wish to take steps without first making sure that he was not under the effects of a delusion.[72] When the moment arrived, at 44 years of age, Newman, an "already dying Anglican" took a final and definitive step: communion with Rome.[73]

---

67   *LG*, 18.

68   Newman decided to make a kind of test: to complete his *Essay on the Development of Christian Doctrine*, and to make the decision to convert if at the end he confirmed what he sensed about the Roman Catholic Church.

69   *Apo.*, 147.

70   "The Parting of Friends," *SD*, no. 26: 409.

71   In ch. 16 of this volume, Frédéric Libaud explores the element of time, and the need for patience in the process of religious conversion (editor's note).

72   Avoiding sudden conversions was the advice he would give in the future to his friends and acquaintances: "the Church must be prepared for converts, as well as converts prepared for the Church." *AW*, 258.

73   See Ian Ker, *La espiritualidad personal a la luz de J. H. Newman: Sanar la herida de la humanidad* (Madrid: Encuentro, 2006), 8.

4. "IT WAS LIKE COMING INTO PORT AFTER A ROUGH SEA." OCTOBER 9, 1845

The final events and details of John Henry Newman's life leading up to his reception into the Roman Catholic Church were quite moving. Two of his disciples, residents of Littlemore, had been received into the Church of Rome a few days before: John Dalgairns and Ambrose St John. It was only then that Newman suddenly entered into action. He renounced his position at Oriel College, leaving aside where he was in the composition *Essay on the Development of Christian Doctrine*,[74] and preparing himself interiorly for the arrival of the expected moment. The Passionist priest Dominic Barberi, who had once visited Littlemore, and whom Dalgairns had asked to stop by again, was passing through Oxford on his way back to the continent. Dalgairns recorded that, as he was going to receive the carriage that was bringing Barbieri, Newman told him, in a low and serene tone: "When you see your friend, will you tell him that I wish him to receive me into the Church of Christ." He did so. He told Father Barbieri once he stepped off the coach, completely soaked, after hours of riding on the box cover of a carriage, under dreadful weather. Barbieri responded: "God be praised," and—as the reporter tells it—"neither of us spoke again till we reached Littlemore."[75] They arrived late, at 11 p.m. on the night of October 8, while it continued to pour.

And now it is Father Barbieri who recounts: "I took up my position by the fire to dry myself. The door opened—and what a spectacle it was for me to see at my feet John Henry Newman begging me to hear his confession and admit him into the bosom of the Catholic Church! And there by the fire he began his general confession with extraordinary humility and devotion."[76] The conversation ended the following day, October 9. Logically, it is not possible to know its contents, but perhaps one can find a glimmer of it in the letter that Newman wrote a year later to Mrs. Bowden, the widow of his friend, who asked him advice about some setbacks. He told her: "The moment before acting may be, as can easily be imagined, peculiarly dreary—the mind may be confused—no reason for acting may be forthcoming to our mind—and the awful greatness of the step itself, and without any distinct apprehension of its consequences, may weigh on us. Some persons like to be to themselves in such a crisis—others find comfort in the presence of others—I could do nothing but shut myself up in my room and lie down on my bed."[77] On October 9, 1845, Newman and two of his young followers recited their confession of faith with fervor and piety. The following morning Barbieri celebrated Mass in the small chapel in Littlemore, using the table on which Newman had been writing his *Essay on the Development of Christian Doctrine*.

---

74 *Apo.*, 234.
75 Quoted in Trevor, *Newman's Journey*, 108.
76 Trevor, *Newman's Journey*, 108–9.
77 Quoted in Trevor, *Newman's Journey*, 109.

Entering the Catholic Church was, for Newman, like "departing for the high seas."[78] It was not easy to leave behind people and places that had formed so much of his life. In the *Apologia* he writes, with a laconism that reveals suffering and nostalgia: "I left Oxford for good on Monday, February 23, 1846. . . . I have never seen Oxford since, excepting its spires, as they are seen from the railway."[79] He had a similar sentiment upon leaving Littlemore, as he reflected in a letter at the time.[80] A man of acute sensibility and a deep sense of gratitude, he could not bid farewell to those places in any other way.[81]

His entrance into the Catholic Church certainly meant a deep undoing of his personal, academic, and institutional plans; he lost a large number of his friends and acquaintances, he was rejected by his own family, he was forced to abandon his university activities and his beloved St. Mary's parish; in short, he went from being one of the most well-known men in the Anglican Church to being an unfamiliar figure in a church that, although universal, did not have much room for the Anglo-Saxon world at that time. However, on the intellectual and spiritual level, Newman's conversion was more a continuity rather than a rupture. "I was not conscious to myself, on my conversion, of any change, intellectual or moral, wrought in my mind. I was not conscious of firmer faith in the fundamental truths of Revelation, or of more self-command; I had no more fervour; but it was like coming into port after a rough sea; and my happiness on that score remains to this day without interruption."[82] It was a slow but steady process that carried him from the intense awareness of God as a youth until his conviction of the truth of the Roman Catholic Church.[83]

CONCLUSION

A passion for truth gave John Henry Newman the strength during his life to search for the authentic face of God and of the Church. None of the phases of his personal itinerary were superfluous: the simple but vigorous evangelism of his early youth; his years spent fascinated by the liberalism of the time coupled with the events that awoke him from that dream; the lights received during his trip through the Mediterranean; the two decades' worth of effort to reconstruct the apostolic tradition in order to legitimize the Anglican Church, as a *Via Media* between the Church of Rome and Protestantism; and, after his reception into the Catholic Church, his decision to serve the Church in the difficult circumstances that he met along his path. His successive conversions were not the result of a

---

78 Letter to Ambrose St John, in *LD* XI, 95.

79 *Apo.*, 236–37.

80 Letter to W. J. Copeland, in *LD* XI, 132–33.

81 A moving scene from *Loss and Gain* appears to recall that farewell. See *LG*, 374–75.

82 *Apo.*, 238.

83 Newman's feelings upon embracing the Catholic faith can be understood in the description of Charles Reding as a recent convert. See *LG*, 430–31.

muddled, unstable, or resentful personality,[84] rather each personal experience guided his path, oriented his mission, and shaped his extraordinary figure.

Even though the historical and theological context of his life is quite different from our own, his personal journey allows us to outline some important characteristics of the Christian conversion: God—not ourselves—is the protagonist in conversion; each conversion is unique and unrepeatable; its driving force is the personal conscience, which like a "stern monitor" leads us to obey the "divine voice speaking within us"; its dynamism is not to be found in the purely rational logic but rather in the convergence of all the dimensions of the person, engaging the head and the heart, emotions and imagination; a true conversion is not instantaneous, since "Great acts take time"[85]; an authentic conversion does not destroy one's personality, but instead leads it to fullness; and some personal dispositions are an indispensable requisite for faith, since believing means being willing to take a risk: "faith is a venture before a man is Catholic; it is a gift after it."[86]

At one point in his *Essay on the Development of Christian Doctrine*, Newman wrote down a basic principle of the human condition and, therefore, applicable as well for the Christian life: "In a higher world it is otherwise, but here below to live is to change, and to be perfect is to have changed often."[87] Of course not all change or development is for the better; but it is indisputable that perfection and holiness are always the fruit of a passion for truth and fidelity to conscience, in other words, a life lived according to the dynamic of permanent conversion.

John Henry Newman's spiritual journey demonstrates that conversion is the path of a lifetime.

Suggested Reading

Alonso, Juan. *La conversión cristiana. Estudios y perspectivas*. Pamplona: Eunsa, 2011.

Conn, Walter E. *Conscience and conversion in Newman. A Developmental Study of Self in John Henry Newman*. Milwaukee: Marquette University Press, 2010.

Dulles, Avery. "Newman, Conversion and Ecumenism." *Theological Studies* 51, no. 4 (1990): 717–31.

Honoré, Jean. *The Spiritual Journey of Newman*. New York: Alba House, 1992.

Ker, Ian. *Newman and Conversion*. Edinburgh: T&T Clark Ltd., 1997.

---

84   Jean Honoré, *The Spiritual Journey of Newman* (New York: Alba House, 1992), 225–31.

85   *Apo.*, 169.

86   *LG*, 385.

87   *Dev.*, 40.

CHAPTER 3

TO REALIZE AN EVERYDAY HOLINESS: NEWMAN, IMAGINATION, AND THE VIRTUE OF RELIGION

Deacon Stephen Morgan

Unlike so many academic philosophers and theologians, Newman's work was not primarily abstract or speculative, nor yet undertaken as part of some systematic academic project, but was essentially and immediately pastoral, as his correspondence, journals and notes provide ample proof. It is not, however, this extrinsic evidence nor even the wide range of issues upon which he wrote that give the clue to the enterprise with which he understood himself to be engaged but the very manner in which he wrote. Should one be entirely ignorant of the biographical circumstances of their creation, it is possible to detect even in Newman's more developed works (e.g., the *Lectures on Justification*, the *Essay on Development* or the *Grammar of Assent*) hints of the urgent controversial necessities that lay behind their production in their literary style and choice of vocabulary. His choice of illustrative examples, turns

---

*   The phrase "to realize an everyday holiness" in the title of this chapter comes via Bernard Dive, *John Henry Newman and the Imagination* (London: T & T Clark, 2019), 11.

of phrase, and narrative composition all seem chosen to appeal to more than the intellectual aspect of the mental faculties. His informing, impelling, and over-riding concern appears always to have been the same: the communication of the saving truth of Jesus Christ and the conditions necessary for the appropriation of the same by his readers and, in the case of his preaching, his hearers such that their lives were transformed by that truth. It is as if he had ever before his eyes the canonical maxim *salus animarum suprema lex*.[1]

Although always desirous of expressing himself regarding that truth in a manner that was intellectually coherent and faithful to ecclesial tradition, Newman was, ultimately, more concerned with the question of the reality of true religion and the claims it makes upon his audience than with its formal theoretical expression, although he by no means disdained philosophical and theological precision. He sought ever to make the idea of Christianity "real" in the minds and lives of those to whom he addressed himself and so can be seen to have addressed their imaginations as much as their intellect. A lack of clarity about his writing regarding the imagination abounds: authors have confused his notion of the imagination with his concept of the illative sense,[2] seen it as primarily aesthetic,[3] or ignore it altogether.[4] It is, however, a recurrent theme in both his writing as a subject explicitly addressed and in his manner of expression, and it deserves to be taken seriously. Terrence Merrigan's writing on the subject stands unequalled for its comprehensive and convincing treatment,[5] and 2018 brought Bernard Dive's *John Henry Newman and the Imagination*, an eminently readable book to be recommended to any who wants to explore the theme more fully. The ambition of this chapter is more modest: to present

---

1   This expression has a long pedigree. It first appears, in the form *salus populi suprema lex* in Marcus Tullius Cicero, *De Legibus—Liber Tertius*, accessed June 1, 2021, https://www.thelatinlibrary.com/cicero/leg3.shtml#3, pt iii, sub viii., and became a staple of both civil and canonical interpretation, especially in those systems drawing their form from Roman Law. It is found in the current law of the Catholic Church in, for example, the 1983 Code of Canon Law in the form, *"prae oculis habita salute animarum, quae in Ecclesia suprema semper lex esse debet,"* *Codex Iuris Canonici* (Rome: Typica Vaticanis Polyglotis, 1983), can.1752.

2   Stephen Prickett, *Romanticism and Religion: The Tradition of Coleridge and Wordsworth in the Victorian Church* (Cambridge: Cambridge University Press, 1976), 194–95.

3   Robert C. Christie, "Eleven Major Elements of Newman's Legacy Critical for Our Time" in *John Henry Newman: Preserving and Promulgating His Legacy*, ed. Robert C Christie (Newcastle: Cambridge Scholars Publishing, 2019), 13–18.

4   The curious choice—given the breadth of scope of the work and the themes otherwise explored—made by Frederick D. Aquino and Benjamin J. King, eds., *The Oxford Handbook of John Henry Newman*, First edition (Oxford: Oxford University Press, 2018).

5   The author of this chapter makes no apology for citing Merrigan often and fundamentally adopting his perspective.

Newman's thought on the imagination in outline and tie it closely to the necessity of the virtue of religion.

In a sense, for Newman, the imaginative sphere, *ethos*,[6] the practice or virtue of religion and the "impressions of dogma"[7] are inseparable and interdependent. As such, they rely upon an apprehension in the imagination of the idea of Christianity, of "God's saving revelation, His self-disclosure in history:"[8] that is of the image of Christ not as conjured-up figure but as concrete reality present in the mind, "to realize things unseen and unknown,"[9] such that they make a claim upon our beliefs and actions, and, "representing as they do the concrete, have the power of the concrete upon the affections and passions."[10] Accordingly, the following pages seek to use Newman's understanding of the imagination to explain the role of the virtue of religion in bringing about the real assent to the saving idea of Christianity, believed, practiced, and integrated, by which we are "made like unto the Son of God" (Heb 7:3).

This chapter proposes that the manner in which the communication of the idea of Christianity and its appropriation by the individual are closely, one might even say inextricably related in Newman's thought, and that the way he considers them to find expression is in the religious imagination of the individual, informed and sustained by the landscape of the practice of true religion. It is contended that the question of what the imagination is, how it functions, and its purpose are, for Newman, less a question of epistemology than of the cultivation of an existential holiness. This will first require a brief examination of the historical evidence for early development of the idea of the imagination in Newman's thought, before, in the second section, offering a sketch of the fully worked out form of the concept, as it appears in *The Grammar of Assent*. In the third and final section of this chapter, the circumstances under which Newman believes the religious imagination functions in a manner best predisposed to religious truth will be examined: the imagination formed, conditioned, and cultivated through what might reasonably be called the virtue of religion.

---

6   See James Pereiro, *'Ethos' and the Oxford Movement: At the Heart of Tractarianism* (Oxford: Oxford University Press, 2008); See also Owen Chadwick, *The Mind of the Oxford Movement* (London: Adam and Charles Black, 1957); Peter Nockles, *The Oxford Movement in Context: Anglican High Churchmanship, 1760–1857* (Cambridge: Cambridge University Press, 1994).

7   *Apo.*, 107.

8   Nicholas Lash, "Faith and History: Some Reflections on Newman's 'Essay of the Development of Christian Doctrine,'" *Irish Theological Quarterly* 38, no. 3 (1971): 232.

9   *Serm.* ii, 18.

10   *GA*, 89.

FROM "CHILDISH IMAGINATIONS"[11]
TO "A LIVING HOLD ON TRUTHS."[12]

The Evangelicalism which made its claim upon Newman's soul in the autumn of 1816 was a religion that begged a place at the table of religious belief for the imaginative faculty. The narrative of that conversion Newman gives in the *Apologia*, makes explicit the role of that faculty—albeit here tied to the idea of "childish imaginations"—in creating a religious landscape as real as it is imagined, remembered but, above all, real, ". . . confirming me in my mistrust of the reality of material phenomena, and making me rest in the thought of two and two only absolute and luminously self-evident beings, myself and my Creator."[13]

This idea of the imagined as the truly real is a theme to which Newman returned again and again but which creates some difficulty because of the specific way in which Newman deploys his vocabulary. The contemporary pragmatic fields for both "real" and "imagination" are such that Newman's use of them requires some preliminary explanation.

Under the influence both of empiricism and scientific materialism, not to mention the cyberworld, contemporary use of the term "real" often juxtaposes the word with "virtual" or "imaginary," understood as its anonyms: not only as "unreal" but as "non-real": real is, thus, often confined to the purely physical. This is not how Newman understood the term. He and here, as Terrence Merrigan observes, his classically educated intended audience and readership,[14] was conscious of the word's derivation from the Latin word *res* meaning thing and so, when using it, he "means something like 'thingish.'"[15]

Newman's meaning of the word "imagination" also differs considerably from its use in current language. Although not normally thought to be a reliable source for the scholar, as evidence of the contemporary popular understanding of terms, the internet site Wikipedia has some value. It explains the word "imagination" as a cognitive process by which the human mind forms "experiences in one's mind, which can be re-creations of past experiences such as vivid memories with imagined changes, or they can be completely invented and possibly fantastic scenes."[16] Here the term is used to mean a mental process of engagement with memory of sense data in a non-rational manner to create the non-real or

---

11   *Apo.*, 4.
12   *GA*, 117.
13   *Apo.*, 4.
14   Terrence Merrigan, "The Image of the Word: Faith and Imagination in John Henry Newman and John Hick," in *Newman and the Word*, ed. Terrence Merrigan and Ian Turnbull Ker (Leuven: Peeters Press, 2000), 8.
15   Henry Price, *Belief; the Gifford Lectures Delivered at the University of Aberdeen in 1960* (London: Allen and Unwin, 1960), 317., cited in Merrigan, "The Image of the Word," 8.
16   "Imagination," in *Wikipedia*, January 5, 2021, https://en.wikipedia.org/w/index.php?title=Imagination&oldid=998413546.

counterfactual, and thereby posits the product of the imagination as precisely the imaginary or fantastical. Newman's use of the word however was as a faculty or power "which allows us to bring home to ourselves the objects of experience,"[17] as "concrete, full of life,"[18] with, as he was later to write, "the power of the concrete upon the affections"[19] to effect change.

Newman's later practice of attempting always to imagine, that is, "to believe as if I saw,"[20] the hand of the Divine as real, active, and requiring response in the mundane circumstances of life, echoes the practice of his schoolmaster, the Reverend Walter Mayers, to whom Newman accredited "the human means of this beginning of divine faith in [himself]."[21] Falling from his horse and nearly ending up in what would have been a watery grave in the River Severn at Gloucester in the autumn of 1814, Mayers had written a memorandum that reveals precisely the same mental and spiritual disposition: "Lord give me grace to discern thy hand . . . [e]nable me to glorify thee for my preservation, by devoting myself more exclusively to the work of Your ministry."[22] Newman offered a strikingly similar explanation, grounded in the imagination, when writing to Mayers to give an account of his poor performance in his Final Honours Schools, "God is leading me through life in the way best adapted for His glory and my own salvation."[23]

From his earliest sermons it is possible to detect a strong sense of the place of the imagination in Newman's understanding of the life of faith. Although not yet using the later more technically and philosophically developed vocabulary, as early as his eleventh sermon, in August 1824 he adopted the language of seeing "by the eye of faith" what cannot otherwise be seen and of the concrete consequences of that realization. He described a process of imagination as religious reflection which, in the subject, has the effect that "day by day fresh scenes open upon his view . . . he realizes . . . sees more of the spaciousness and depth of those divine appointments . . . feels overpowered . . . his heart is full, and he has fervent longings after the blessed time when his knowledge will be perfected and he shall see God as He is."[24] The following year, in his first Good Friday sermon, Newman

---

17   Terrence Merrigan, "Newman and Faith in the Trinity," in *Newman and Faith*, ed. Ian Turnbull Ker and Terrence Merrigan, Louvain Theological and Pastoral Monographs 31 (Louvain: Peeters Press, 2004), 97.

18   Zeno, *John Henry Newman: Our Way to Certitude: An Introduction to Newman's Psychological Discovery, the Illative Sense, and His Grammar of Assent* (Leiden: Brill, 1957), 123.

19   *GA*, 89.

20   *GA*, 102.

21   John Henry Newman, *Apologia Pro Vita Sua*, ed. Martin Svaglic (Oxford: Clarendon Press, 1974), 17.

22   Walter Mayers, *Sermons by the Late Reverend Walter Mayers to Which Is Annexed a Brief Memoir of His Life* (London: James Nisbet, 1831), iii.

23   *LD* i, 99.

24   Sermon no. 14, "Illumination," August 22, 1824, *Serm.* v, 65.

concluded the first part of the sermon by saying, "I have said quite enough to make any one, who can bring the subject before his mind's eye, very sorrowful and very thankful."[25] A commonplace enough aspiration for any preacher, one might say, but in the context of Newman's trajectory and to adopt the vocabulary of the *Essay on Development*, it is evidence of an early example of recurrent intimations in anticipation of what later became the fully developed idea of the imagination as "the intellectual act that grasps the real and the concrete . . . as something with a claim on us."[26] The 1829 sermon "Introductory.—character of Abraham,"[27] provides further early anticipation of the technical language of imagination he was later to deploy, when, as Joseph F. Keefe notes, Newman "encouraged his listeners to 'realize things unseen and unknown.'"[28]

The homiletic evidence for Newman's concern for and development of his understanding of the workings and purpose of the imagination continues to accumulate in the following decades. Two significant sermons of the 1830s, both reproduced in *Parochial and Plain Sermons*, further developed Newman's thought as they considered the act of realization of the religious imagination.[29] Keefe argues convincingly that the act "is a type of self-appropriation by which a fact or an object (real in itself) is assimilated (made personally real to the subject)."[30] He goes on to show that in these sermons another aspect of the later developed concept is also present in embryo in these sermons: "Regarding the mystery of Christ, Newman understood the role of imagination as a reception of the impression of the image of Christ on the mind through an act of faith. In this respect, realization is the assimilation and self-appropriation of that image. Christ is the central 'object of faith.'"[31]

The final *University Sermons*, especially the thirteenth and fifteenth, reveal Newman grappling with another aspect of his developing concept of imagination: the idea as the object of realization in relationship to or as mediating

---

25 Sermon no. 74, "Review of Christ's sufferings and death," April 1, 1825, *Serm.* v, 214. He was to preach this sermon, with minor amendments, no less than eight times between 1825 and 1843.

26 Terrence Merrigan, *Clear Heads and Holy Hearts: The Religious and Theological Ideal of John Henry Newman*, Louvain Theological and Pastoral Monographs 7 (Louvain: Peeters, 1991), 60.

27 Sermon no. 202, "Introductory.—character of Abraham," July 12, 1829, *Serm.* ii, 18.

28 Joseph F. Keefe, "'The Intellectual Difficulty of Imagining and Realizing Emmanuel': Newman's Concept of Realizing Christ in 'Parochial and Plain Sermons,'" *Newman Studies Journal* 12, no. 1 (Spring 2015): 32–33. Keefe is, himself, quoting Newman in sermon no. 202, although he incorrectly asserts that it was "one of the first sermons (Newman) ever preached" and dates it to 1824. See Keefe, "Intellectual Difficulty," 32.

29 Sermon no. 380, "The Humiliation of the Eternal Son," March 8, 1835, in *PS* iii, no. 12: 156–72., and Sermon no. 534, "Difficulty of Realizing Sacred Privileges," March 31, 1839, in *PS* iv, no. 8: 94–104.

30 Keefe, "Intellectual Difficulty," 32.

31 Keefe, "Intellectual Difficulty," 34.

the object of faith in the mind not just of the individual but of the Church. Of course, what we see treated by Newman with the brevity demanded in a sermon (even in its rather extended nineteenth century Anglican form), he dealt with more expansively in the *Essay on Development*, where the understanding of the idea of Christianity as an individual and ecclesial mental correlate to the facts of revelation is more fully explored. This ecclesial dimension is of crucial importance. At this point in Newman's life, the question of where the Church was to be found, where her authoritative voice was to be heard had become an almost all-encompassing preoccupation for Newman, and so, it is inevitable that in seeking to identify the idea, "Newman turns to the living tradition of the Church to forge his image of Jesus."[32]

It is a passage from that final University Sermon, "The Theory of Developments in Religious Doctrine" that expresses most succinctly where Newman had reached in his consideration of the concept of the imagination on the eve of his reception into the Catholic Church. When he claims that in the sermon "one finds an understanding of the imagination that is as rich, and certainly as profound as the view which is operative in the *Grammar*,"[33] Merrigan is surely correct, as the following passage from it, worth quoting *in extenso*, demonstrates:

> Religious men, according to their measure, have an idea or vision of the Blessed Trinity in Unity, of the Son Incarnate and of His Presence, not as a number of qualities, attributes, and actions, not as the subject of a number of propositions, but as one, and individual, and independent of words, as an impression conveyed through the senses. Particular propositions, then, which are used to express portions of the great idea vouchsafed to us, can never really be confused with the idea itself which all such propositions taken together can but reach, and cannot exceed. As definitions are not intended to go beyond their subject, but to be adequate to it, so the dogmatic statements of the Divine Nature used in our confessions, however multiplied, cannot say more than is implied in the original idea, considered in its completeness, without the risk of heresy. Creeds and dogmas live in the one idea which they are designed to express, and which alone is substantive; and are necessary only because the human mind cannot reflect upon that idea, except piecemeal, cannot use it in its oneness and entireness, nor without resolving it into a series of aspects and relations. And in matter of fact these expressions are never equivalent to it; we are able, indeed, to define the creations of our own minds, for they are what we make them and nothing else; but it were as easy to create what is real as to define it;

---

32 Merrigan, "The Image of the Word," 37.
33 Merrigan, *Clear Heads and Holy Hearts*, 51.

and thus the Catholic dogmas are, after all, but symbols of a Divine fact, which, far from being compassed by those very propositions, would not be exhausted, nor fathomed, by a thousand.[34]

In addition to the conceptual, however, Newman had long been engaged with the question of the practical, so far as the imagination was concerned. In his remark and associated note about his increasing noeticism in the *Apologia*, it is possible to detect a sense that, whilst Newman felt that in the late 1820s his intellectual star was in the ascendant, the intellectualization of his religion lacked an important dimension and one that made it unsatisfactory.[35] There was, as Isaac Williams noted, another way: one which "set *ethos* above intellect."[36] In 1827, John Keble had produced *The Christian Year*, a volume of devotional poetry concerned to evoke rather than explain (or explain away) the mysteries of the Christian faith as they were presented in the liturgical cycle of the Church of England.[37] The book was immediately successful and its popularity endured throughout the nineteenth century. The modest advertisement with which it begins hints at a desire to add the landscape of evoked memories to that of orthodox doctrine—"a sound rule of faith"—with the intention of enabling the reader to bring "his thoughts and feelings into more entire unison."[38] The effect of it on Newman was profound. He records it as having reinforced and recast in him the idea of the "the Sacramental system; that is, the doctrine that material phenomena are both the types and the instruments of real things unseen,"[39] that he had learned from Joseph Butler. It also introduced him to "the living power of faith and love ... directed towards an Object; in the vision of that Object they live; it is that Object, received in faith and love, which renders it reasonable to take probability as sufficient for internal conviction."[40] Although the terminology is different, it is impossible to overlook the similarity of this passage with the language he used later in the *Grammar*.

The possibilities of the creation of an imaginative landscape in the mind as a necessary and fruitful counterpart to the intellectual were not lost on Newman. During his writing of *The Arians of the Fourth Century*, and particularly in his exchange of correspondence with Archdeacon Lyall concerning the drafts, Newman had become seized of the need to make the Church of antiquity live again: to "prepare the *imaginations* of men for a changed state of things."[41] To do

---

34 *US* no. 15, 331–32.

35 *Apo.*, 14; 285–97.

36 Isaac Williams, *The Autobiography of Isaac Williams*, ed. George Prevost (London: Longmans, Green and Co, 1892), 46.

37 John Keble, *The Christian Year* (London: C. and J. Rivington, 1827).

38 Keble, *The Christian Year*, Advertisement.

39 *Apo.*, 18.

40 *Apo.*, 17.

41 *LD* iv, 24. See also Nockles, *The Oxford Movement in Context*, 113.

this would require precisely the cultivation of impressions not merely upon the intellect but upon the imagination. Shortly before departing on the Mediterranean voyage that was to provide so many imaginative impressions, both positive and negative, and give rise to perhaps the most imaginatively evocative poem of the first half of his life, "The Pillar of the Cloud,"[42] Newman wrote to Hugh James Rose proposing to address this issue. "Our object is, to bring out certain truths and moral, ecclesiastical, and religious, simply and forcibly, with greater and clearness than in the Christian Year. I will not go on to say, with greater poetry . . . It might be called Lyra Apostolica."[43] Newman was to write forty-six of the one hundred and seventy-nine poems to appear from June 1833 onwards in Rose's *British Magazine*.[44] Whilst the controversial pamphleteering of the *Tracts for the Times* was to give a name to the movement, the poems or "ballads"[45] of the *Lyra Apostolica* and *Records of the Church*,[46] a series of translations of patristic material, arguably did as much to provide the imaginative substrate necessary to create its *ethos* and "to familiarize the imagination of the reader to an *Apostolical state* of the Church."[47]

IMAGINATION IN *THE GRAMMAR OF ASSENT*

The publication of *An Essay in Aid of a Grammar of Assent* in 1870, marked the completion of Newman's long held objective of offering a fully worked out account of the philosophical principles upon which he believed his contemporaries could navigate what he had once called "the ocean of interminable scepticism [*sic*],"[48] and come to religious, and specifically Christian belief as a principle of action. Although Newman had long conceived of the idea of "working on towards a philosophical polemic, suited to these times,"[49] and writing "a work embodying all the principles I have implied in my books,"[50] it was the correspondence with William Froude in December 1859 and carried

---

42   Better known now as the hymn "Lead, Kindly Light", it was written at sea as Newman returned to England in the summer of 1833. See *LD* iii, 322 n1. Newman wrote a great deal of poetry during this Mediterranean voyage. Fr. Juan R. Vélez has considered the value and significance of them in "Newman's Mediterranean 'Verses': Poetry at the Service of Doctrinal Teaching and Religious Renewal," *Newman Studies Journal* 3, no. 2 (Fall 2006): 78–88. See Barbara Wyman's chapter, n. 15 of this volume, for a study of Newman's poetry, which serves as a window into the unseen world (editor's note).

43   *LD* iii, 120.

44   Others were variously written by John Bowden, Hurrell Froude, Robert Wilberforce, Isaac Williams, and John Keble himself.

45   *LD* iv, 109.

46   "Records of the Church Nos. I-XVIII," November 11, 1833, in *Tract* 1.

47   *LD* iv, 109.

48   *Ari.*, 76.

49   *LD* xiv, 206.

50   *LD* xiv, 381.

on through the first quarter of 1860, that provided the proximate impetus for what was to become *Grammar of Assent*. In that correspondence Froude had expressed the view,

> That on no subject whatever,—distinctly not in the region of the ordinary facts with which our daily experience is conversant—distinctly not in the domain of history or politics, and yet again a fortiori, not in that of Theology, is my mind, (or as far as I can tell the mind of any human being,) capable of arriving at an absolutely certain conclusion. That though of course some conclusions are far more certain than others, there is an element of uncertainty to all.[51]

He went on to deny that probability is a sufficient cause for action due to the tendency "to overate the degree of probability" when "the mind is strongly drawn and inclined" to act in accordance with it—what might today be called "confirmation bias." That inclination is, he wrote, "a temptation to be resisted, not an intimation to be relied on."[52] Newman believed this position—which might stand as a paradigmatic example of religious skepticism (which alone justifies having quoted it at such length)—was a fallacy but confessed "I don't think it easy to show it to be so."[53] It was not. The eventual product of these reflections—together with those he had worked up in the late-1840s regarding "concurring and converging probabilities"[54] for the certainty of faith and thus as a principle of action, and, as has been shown, his long concern with the nature and purpose of religious imagination—only appeared with the publication of the *Grammar of Assent*.

Terrence Merrigan suggests that the purpose of the *Grammar* "might be described as the attempt to justify the existence and the operation of [the image of Christ] among Christians" by means of "an analysis of the process of human perception."[55] The dynamic sense he imparts to the work corresponds closely to what might be called the over-arching pastoral and soteriological preoccupations that ring out from Newman's letters and sermons. Accounts of the *Grammar* which present it as being primarily epistemological, psychological or even aesthetic certainly capture aspects of the whole, but it can only be properly understood as dealing with those aspects in order to establish the conditions for realizing the image of Christ in the minds of human beings as the principle of religious action, both in terms of belief and conduct.

The *Grammar of Assent* is divided into two sections: the first, called by Newman "Assent and Apprehension," deals with the question of how it is possible to believe what is not understood (and, in so doing, it also develops Newman's

---

51 *LD* xix, 270.
52 *LD* xix, 270.
53 *LD* xix, 272.
54 *Apo.*, 30–31.
55 Merrigan, "The Image of the Word," 6.

argument from conscience for the existence of God;[56] the second section deals with belief and arriving at certitude—precisely the question in the correspondence with William Froude. Both parts required Newman to engage with the question of human cognition as both rational and non-rational, as intellectual and imaginative, as (to use, in reversed order, the language of the thirteenth University Sermon) explicit and implicit. It is in the latter that he located the primary impetus to religious faith, thus the question of the imagination—what it is, what it is for, how it operates and the necessary conditions for its proper operation—becomes a persistent and recurring theme in the book, running like a musical fugue throughout the entire composition. This fugal character of imagination in the *Grammar* requires, appropriately enough, an approach to reading it that reflects Newman's account of the proper functioning of the synthetic aspect of the intellect itself in *The Idea of a University*: that of arriving at a "a connected view or grasp of things."[57] Consideration of the detailed distinctions Newman drew in the *Grammar* between the types of assent, specifically between "notional assent," of which the subject is the theological intellect, and "real assent," with which the religious imagination is primarily concerned, must, for reasons of space here, be left for another occasion.

At root, the concept of the imagination expressed in the *Grammar* is that of the mental faculty or power (Newman uses the words virtually indistinguishably) which impresses upon the mind of the individual subject the reality of an object through the apprehension, both synthetic and evocative, of images of that same object. This process enables the subject to relate and respond to the object as real. By means of the imaginative process, "the 'objects' of (religious) consciousness, in all their paradoxical complexity, are so vividly 'realized' (and so existentially 'charged') that they are able to command the subject's enduring commitment."[58] These images are not, of course, the object itself as concrete, but, in Newman's words "representing as they do the concrete, have the power of the concrete upon the affections and passions, and by means of these indirectly become operative."[59] In the specifically religious context, that is in the question of the real assent and response to the truth claims of faith, Newman understood the imagination as being the means by which believers have real access to the object of their faith, not merely to a notional assent to the *fides quae creditur*. It

---

56 Geertjan Zuijdwegt and Terrence Merrigan, "Conscience," in *The Oxford Handbook of John Henry Newman*, ed. Frederick D. Aquino and Benjamin J. King, First edition (Oxford: Oxford University Press, 2018), 444. In this otherwise excellent essay on the operations of conscience, and given the extent to which one of the co-authors has written on the imagination in Newman, the omission of the role of the imagination in "realizing" images that otherwise remain only "an object of faith or belief" (445), is difficult to explain.

57 *Idea*, xvii.

58 Merrigan, "The Image of the Word," 39.

59 *GA*, 89.

functions by means of both evocative or realizing imagination, "focused on the fact grasped,"[60] and by synthetic or, to use Merrigan's expression, "prehending imagination," "by means of which imagination's object is grasped, or, as it were, set before the mind's eye."[61]

At this point, it may be helpful to consider Newman's use of the term "image," since it is a word that has the capacity both to clarify and obscure Newman's meaning. The obvious allusions of the word can mislead the reader into believing that Newman intends it to convey the purely visual—to repeat the point made earlier, "to believe as if I saw."[62] His use of the word is, however, much wider in scope. Indeed, early in the *Grammar*, when considering the question of apprehension and memory—upon the proper operation of both he understood imagination to depend—he explicitly stated so in terms that are themselves a powerful example of both the evocative and synthetic aspects of the way in which the imagination apprehends ideas:

> I have hitherto been adducing instances from (for the most part) objects of sight; but the memory preserves the impress, though not so vivid, of the experiences which come to us through our other senses also. The memory of a beautiful air, or the scent of a particular flower, as far as any remembrance remains of it, is the continued presence in our minds of a likeness of it, which its actual presence has left there. I can bring before me the music of the *Adeste Fideles*, as if I were actually hearing it; and the scent of a clematis as if I were in my garden; and the flavour of a peach as if it were in season; and the thought I have of all these is as of something individual and from without,—as much as the things themselves, the tune, the scent, and the flavour, are from without,—though, compared with the things themselves, these images (as they may be called) are faint and intermitting.
>
> Nor need such an image be in any sense an abstraction; though I may have eaten a hundred peaches in times past, the impression, which remains on my memory of the flavour, may be of any of them, of the ten, twenty, thirty units, as the case may be, not a general notion, distinct from every one of them, and formed from all of them by a fabrication of my mind.[63]

---

60 Merrigan, *Clear Heads and Holy Hearts*, 51. Merrigan notes here that what the *Essay on Development* has to say about imagination is primarily concerned with prehending imagination, the *Grammar* with realizing imagination.

61 Merrigan, 52. Merrigan adopts the term "prehending imagination" to express the synthetic power of the imagination to bring together the whole idea presented by the image to the mind and in so doing setting it "before the mind's eye." Merrigan, "The Image of the Word," 14.

62 *GA*, 102. See n. 22 above.

63 *GA*, 24–25.

In the case of the Christian, Newman understood the image apprehended by the religious imagination is simply the idea of Christ or, as noted above "God's saving revelation, His self-disclosure in history."[64] As has been shown, this apprehension is a realization of a "thing," "a personal grasp of the reality of a particular object or truth, a grasp so profound that it can move the believer to action."[65] The object to be made real to the mind of the subject by the evocative capacity of the imagination is itself subject, the person of Jesus Christ. In "realizing Emmanuel" then, the concrete that has the power of the concrete on the subject is no less than God with us. It is precisely this Christocentricity that, Lash observes, causes Newman constantly "to express the transcendence of the 'idea' by hypostasizing, or personalizing it" and gives the "idea" its power.[66]

Where Newman drew his intellectual inspiration for this conception of the imagination from is a matter of some debate. Empiricist influences from Locke and Hume can be detected in some of his vocabulary and Jan Walgrave sees parallels with German Romanticism.[67] Newman himself gave credit to Joseph Butler's principle of analogy and Edward Sillem to the unlikely figure of the obscure Adam Tucker—it appears, on the sole grounds of a similarity in the functioning of prehending imagination.[68] John Coulson claimed forcefully that "Newman's original conception of imagination was purely Coleridgean" because of its "inventive (or 'esemplastic') power"[69] and, insofar as Newman's perspective also requires the "displacing of the primacy of the merely literary in favour of the pictorial, the devotional, the lyrical, hymnic and liturgical"[70] that is surely so, but it is most assuredly not Coleridge's "fancy." Whilst this capacity of the mind for Coleridge was an "assembling" or "aggregating power," and so analogous to Newman's prehending imagination, it was also "a mode of memory emancipated from the order of time and space," devoid of the philosophical realism underpinning Newman's thought.[71] Ian Ker, in his introduction to the Clarendon Press edition of the *Grammar*, takes further issue with Coulson's attribution on the

---

64 Lash, "Faith and History," 232.

65 Denis Robinson, "Preaching," in *The Cambridge Companion to John Henry Newman*, ed. Ian Ker and Terrence Merrigan, Cambridge Companions to Religion (Cambridge: Cambridge University Press, 2009), 248.

66 Nicholas Lash, *Change in Focus: A Study in Doctrinal Change and Continuity* (London: Sheed and Ward, 1973), 92.

67 Jan Hendrick Walgrave, *Newman the Theologian: The Nature of Belief and Doctrine as Exemplified in His Life and Works*, trans. A.V. Littledale (London: Geoffrey Chapman, 1960), 110.

68 *PN* i, 122

69 John Coulson, *Religion and Imagination: "In Aid of a Grammar of Assent"* (Oxford: Clarendon Press, 1981), 60.

70 John Milbank, "What Is Living and What Is Dead in Newman's Grammar of Assent," in *Newman and Truth*, ed. Terrence Merrigan and Ian Ker, Louvain Theological and Pastoral Monographs 39 (Louvain: Peeters Press, 2008), 35.

71 Merrigan, "The Image of the Word," 37.

grounds that the it makes too facile and direct a connection which overlooks the primacy of memory, the bringing to mind of something remembered, in the operation of the imagination.[72] It seems most likely that Newman's position, at least as set out in the *Grammar*, which, he came to after a lifetime's consideration, reflected his own compelling synthesis drawing on many, if not all of these sources.

FORMING A PROPERLY FUNCTIONING IMAGINATION: "TILLING AND MANURING THE LAND:"[73]

Newman was not naïve. His anthropology and understanding of cognitive processes meant that his thinking about the operation of the imagination was not divorced from an awareness of the effects of appetites, biases, predispositions, and habits on its operation. Whilst he could conceive of a more or less purely intellectual consideration of the theological intellect, he was aware that the religious imagination was something that required formation, conditioning, and cultivation. As early as that 1824 sermon from which the title of this section is taken, he was expressing what he called there "the necessity of a preparation of heart for receiving Christian doctrine."[74] Despite the different vocabulary, the sentiment remains the same: the heart—understood as the seat of the intellect, imagination, and affections—needs to be made ready to receive the truth of Christ, in order that it may be realized and become the principle of action. At this point it is clear that Newman saw this "preparation" as taking place primarily in the devout reading of Sacred Scripture and in mental prayer but, in time, he would come to share Keble's opinion in the "Advertisement" to *The Christian Year*, that the practice and formularies of the Church's liturgy were both the source material and place in which it took place. As Newman was to put it in his sermon "The Visible Church, an Encouragement to Faith," preached in September 1834, "He who comes to Church to worship God, be he high or low, enters into that heavenly world of Saints of which I have been speaking. For in the Services of worship we elicit and realize the invisible."[75] By the time he was a Catholic, Newman could observe to Henry Wilberforce: "I have been exceedingly struck with the abiding φαντασία of religion which Catholics have. The articles of faith are external facts taken for granted—worship is an offering really made to a real Presence etc etc."[76] The relationship between this worship

---

72   John Henry Newman, *An Essay in Aid of a Grammar of Assent*, ed. Ian Ker (Oxford: Oxford University Press, 1985), 23.

73   Sermon no. 18, "Parable of the Sower," September 5, 1824, *Serm.* v, 89.

74   *Serm.* v, 89.

75   *PS* iii, no. 17: 250.

76   *LD* xi, 191–92. As Stanley Jaki observed, "By φαντασία Newman meant 'the power by which an object is made apparent to the mind.'" Stanley L. Jaki, *Newman to Converts: An Existential Ecclesiology* (Pinckney, Mich.: Real View Books, 2001), 60.

made to a real Presence and the religious imagination, is made even clearer in the seventh of Newman's lectures of 1850, later published as *Certain Difficulties Felt by Anglicans in Catholic Teaching*, when he wrote:

> Thus the usages and ordinances of the Church do not exist for their own sake; they do not stand of themselves; they are not sufficient for themselves; they do not fight against the State their own battle; they are not appointed as ultimate ends; but they are dependent on an inward substance; they protect a mystery; they defend a dogma; they represent an idea; they preach good tidings; they are the channels of grace. They are the outward shape of an inward reality or fact, which no Catholic doubts, which is assumed as a first principle, which is not an inference of reason, but the object of a spiritual sense.[77]

In *Idea of a University*, Newman had looked at the question of the contrasting formative power of the religion of culture and revealed religion, primarily in their moral aspect.[78] Nevertheless, his concern here was with the reality of beliefs as the principle of action and, therefore, with the formation of that faculty by which they were realized: "it is not a matter of what one and the other make a man believe but what they make him *do* as a result of his beliefs."[79] In this discourse Newman witheringly (and not lacking a note of sarcasm) points up the inadequacy of the religion of culture in preparing the mind for the task of producing a believing and acting Christian. Robert Gassert called this "the hollow sepulchre of a religion of civilization, which is made beautiful *to look upon*—and nothing more."[80] What was needed was the practice of true religion to form properly the mind—intellect and imagination— so that the object of belief, the idea of Christianity, Christ who has come in the flesh, realized and assimilated, becomes the operative principle of belief and action. As Newman put it, the purpose of religious practice " is to realize [the Divine Word]; to make the facts which [the Gospels] relate stand out before our minds as objects, such as may be appropriated by a faith as living as the imagination which apprehends them."[81] Newman was here speaking explicitly of mediation on the facts of Divine revelation, but, by extension, it is reasonable to assume he would have included devotion and—given the liturgy—in other words, the virtue of religion. Peter Kwasniewski has recently demonstrated

---

77   *Diff.* i, 216.

78   Discourse VIII, "Knowledge viewed in relation to Religion," *Idea*, 179–211.

79   Philip Boyce, "Christian Perfection in the Writings of John Henry Newman," *Ephemerides Carmeliticae* 24, no. 2 (1973): 250.

80   Robert G. Gassert, *The Christian Character according to Cardinal Newman: A Study of His Ideal of Catholic Higher Education* (Rome: 1958), 41.

81   *GA*, 79.

"allusions to liturgical rites are ubiquitous in Newman's writings . . . when he is preaching on the reverent worship Christians owe to God" because he "is rooted in a deeply personal conviction of the infinite holiness of God, to which the only appropriate response is a profound reverence towards God in Himself and in all His works, natural and supernatural."[82]

CONCLUSION

This chapter has looked at the place of the imagination in Newman's thought and, with that examination given an insight not only to the development of the idea but also of the man. By surveying the evidence for the presence of the language he was later to use in the *Grammar of Assent* from its earliest intimations in letters and sermons preached as a young Anglican and on through his life as minister, convert and priest, this chapter has considered the centrality of the imagination to Newman's thinking across half a century and more. The fully-formed notion of the imagination, laid out in the *Grammar of Assent*, has been examined and shown to consist in a deeply sophisticated and subtle understanding of the human mind, the human person in relation to that image of Christ as foundational to salvation what may be referred to (today, under the influence of Husserl, Stein, and Wojtyła) as the irreducibility of the human subject before the saving reality of the Incarnation.[83] Finally, by acknowledging the need to form and cultivate the imagination by means of the virtue of religion, it has been shown that Newman's thought here is no mere theorizing but related to his awareness of the urgency of the salvation of souls.

In a famously long life, the question of the nature and role of the imagination was ever present in Newman's considerations. Limitations of space have prevented any substantial consideration of the use to which Newman put literature, both verse and prose, in the service of creating and forming a landscape for the imaginative apprehension, for the realization of the saving image of Christ. The omission of a consideration of Newman's novel is much regretted,[84] as is the supremely synthetic and evocative power of *The Dream of Gerontius*— to say nothing of Edward Elgar's peerless musical setting of it, which adds superabundantly to its imaginative force. Nevertheless, it has been shown that in his sermons, letters, discourses, essays and, supremely, in the *Grammar of Assent*, the imagination plays a central role in the realization "of an everyday

---

82 John Henry Newman, *John Henry Newman on Worship, Reverence, and Ritual: A Selection of Texts*, ed. Peter A Kwasniewski (Os Justi Press, 2019), vii.

83 These aspects are considered at length in John F. Crosby, *The Personalism of John Henry Newman* (Washington, D.C: The Catholic University of America Press, 2014).

84 In ch. 2 of this volume, Juan Alonso draws attention to Newman's novels both as a locus for autobiographical notes as well as a reflection on the nature of conversion (editor's note).

holiness,"[85] not as a mental faculty independent of external influences but as one tilled and manured by the virtue of religion. Through worship, devotion, study, and suffrages, through "offering services and ceremonial rites to [the] Divine"[86] to adopt the language of Aquinas, the imagination is properly conditioned to receive not merely the "impressions of dogma"[87] but the reality of Christ.

The vivid power and synthetic originality of Newman's idea of the imagination casts a glimpse on an understanding of the human person and its apprehension of, engagement with and transformation by the reality of Christ, experienced and remembered as experienced, that caused Edward Sillem, with perhaps only just a touch of hyperbole, to call Newman, "a Christian Socrates."[88]

Newman himself must be given the last word:

> When men begin all their works with the thought of God, acting for His sake, and to fulfil His will, when they ask His blessing on themselves and their life, pray to Him for the objects they desire, and see Him in the event, whether it be according to their prayers or not, they will find everything that happens tend to confirm them in the truths about Him which live in their imagination, varied and unearthly as those truths may be. Then they are brought into His presence as that of a Living Person, and are able to hold converse with Him, and that with a directness and simplicity, with a confidence and intimacy, *mutatis mutandis*, which we use towards an earthly superior; so that it is doubtful whether we realize the company of our fellow-men with greater keenness than these favoured minds are able to contemplate and adore the Unseen, Incomprehensible Creator.[89]

Suggested Reading

Boyce, Philip. "Christian Perfection in the Writings of John Henry Newman." *Ephemerides Carmeliticae* 24, no. 2 (1973): 215–90.

Coulson, John. *Religion and Imagination: "In Aid of a Grammar of Assent."* Oxford: Clarendon Press, 1981.

Crosby, John. *The Personalism of John Henry Newman.* Washington, D.C.: The Catholic University of America Press, 2014.

Dive, Bernard. *John Henry Newman and the Imagination.* London: T & T Clark, 2019.

Keefe, Joseph F. "'The Intellectual Difficulty of Imagining and Realizing Emmanuel': Newman's Concept of Realizing Christ in 'Parochial and Plain Sermons.'" *Newman Studies Journal* 12, no. 1 (Spring 2015): 30–42.

Ker, Ian. *John Henry Newman: A Biography.* Oxford: Oxford University Press, 2010.

---

85 Dive, *Newman and the Imagination*, 11.
86 Thomas Aquinas, *Summa Theologiae*, IIa-IIae, q. 81, a. 1.
87 *Apo.*, 4.
88 *PN* i, 250.
89 *GA*, 117–18.

Merrigan, Terrence. *Clear Heads and Holy Hearts: The Religious and Theological Ideal of John Henry Newman*. Louvain Theological and Pastoral Monographs 7. Louvain: Peeters Press, 1991.

_____. "Newman and Faith in the Trinity." In *Newman and Faith*, edited by Ian Turnbull Ker and Terrence Merrigan, 93–116. Louvain Theological and Pastoral Monographs 31. Louvain: Peeters Press; W.B. Eerdmans, 2004.

_____. "The Image of the Word: Faith and Imagination in John Henry Newman and John Hick." In *Newman and the Word*, edited by Terrence Merrigan and Ian Ker. Leuven: Peeters Press, 2000.

Newman, John Henry. *John Henry Newman on Worship, Reverence, and Ritual: A Selection of Texts*. Edited by Peter A Kwasniewski. Os Justi Press, 2019.

Nockles, Peter. *The Oxford Movement in Context: Anglican High Churchmanship 1760–1857*. Cambridge: Cambridge University Press, 1994.

Vélez, Juan R. "Newman's Mediterranean 'Verses': Poetry at the Service of Doctrinal Teaching and Religious Renewal." *Newman Studies Journal* 3, no. 2 (Fall 2006). 78–88.

Walgrave, Jan Hendrick. *Newman the Theologian: The Nature of Belief and Doctrine as Exemplified in His Life and Works*. Translated by A.V. Littledale. London: Geoffrey Chapman, 1960.

Williams, Isaac. *The Autobiography of Isaac Williams*. Edited by George Prevost. London: Longmans, Green and Co, 1892.

Zeno the Capuchin. *John Henry Newman: Our Way to Certitude: An Introduction to Newman's Psychological Discovery, the Illative Sense, and His Grammar of Assent*. Leiden: Brill, 1957.

CHAPTER 4

NEWMAN'S CALLING
TO CELIBACY

Fr. Carter Griffin

Three years after his conversion to Catholicism, John Henry Newman wrote a philosophical novel entitled *Loss and Gain* that recounts the intellectual conversion of a young Oxford student to the Catholic faith. The protagonist of the story, Charles Reding, is often seen as an autobiographical figure because of his obvious parallels to Newman's own conversion story. At one point Reding has a revealing conversation about celibacy with his Anglican friend Carlton. The notion of remaining celibate, Reding tells Carlton, occurred to him "when a boy at school, and I have ever since fancied that I should never marry. Not that the feeling has never intermitted, but it is the habit of my mind. My general thoughts run in that one way, that I shall never marry."[1]

The conversation later continues with Reding praising celibacy as a "make-up for sin," and Carlton reproaching him for an apparent contradiction. "You began by saying that celibacy was a perfection of nature, now you make it a penance; first it is good and glorious, next it is a medicine and punishment." To which Reding responds, "Perhaps our highest perfection here is penance" and then confesses, "but I don't know; I don't profess to have clear ideas upon the subject. I have talked more than I like. Let us at length give over."[2]

Like Reding, Newman never relished conversations about celibacy, least of all his own reasons for choosing it. He wrote little on the topic, and that almost

---

1   *LG*, 192.
2   *LG*, 200–1.

entirely in personal correspondence. Only once does he address it at length, and that is after his conversion, to fellow Catholics who find themselves defending celibacy against criticism from Protestants. The short dialogue between Reding and Carlton reflects Newman's own reserve and his lack of "clear ideas" on the subject in his youth, but also his quiet, consistent confidence in a personal call to forego marriage. With that confidence, and his eventual conversion to Catholicism, Newman's ideas about celibacy gained clarity and strength through the years.

CELIBACY IN THE CHURCH OF ENGLAND

Newman's ambivalent ideas about celibacy are echoed in the *Thirty-Nine Articles*, the doctrinal foundation of the Church of England. Article thirty-two states that "Bishops, Priests, and Deacons, are not commanded by God's Law, either to vow the estate of single life, or to abstain from marriage: therefore it is lawful also for them, as for all other Christian men, to marry at their own discretion, as they shall judge the same to serve better to godliness."[3] Many Anglican thinkers, influenced by strong Reformation tendencies, interpreted this article as a repudiation of clerical celibacy altogether.[4] Others, such as Jeremy Taylor, attempted an uphill apologetic in defense of celibacy despite widespread reservations in the Anglican Church.[5] Without question, however, in the time of Newman the assumption was that most Anglican clergymen would—and indeed should—marry. Newman himself, in his Anglican years, acknowledged that clergy not only had a right to marry, but that in general they ought to do so.[6]

At the same time, it was not unheard-of for clergymen to remain single. There was an ancient tradition at Oxford and Cambridge for clerical "dons" to refrain from marriage in order to dedicate themselves to the care and teaching of undergraduates.[7] Given his interest in academia, Newman's choice to remain single was therefore not too unusual. (He nonetheless found amusing a declaration by one Oxford Provost that St. Paul's endorsement of celibacy in First Corinthians was "fulfilled in College Tutors."[8]) Newman lived to see the tradition of celibacy fade at both Oxford and Cambridge, thereby dismantling one of "the

---

3 Edward Welchman, *The Thirty-Nine Articles of the Church of England* (London: Gilbert and Rivington, 1842), 74.

4 B. W. Young, "The Anglican Origins of Newman's Celibacy," *Church History* 65, no. 1 (1996): 15–18.

5 Young, "The Anglican Origins of Newman's Celibacy," 18–19.

6 See John Henry Newman, *John Henry Newman: A Portrait in Letters*, ed. Roderick Strange (Oxford: Oxford University Press, 2015), 49.

7 Juan R. Vélez, *Holiness in a Secular Age: The Witness of Cardinal Newman* (New York: Scepter, 2017), 101.

8 *LD* v, 221.

most influential bastions of institutionalized clerical celibacy."[9] In his youth, though, celibacy remained a viable and respected option for at least a handful of Anglican clergymen.

NEWMAN'S CHOICE FOR CELIBACY

Newman made his choice for celibacy at an early age. It would be a mistake, however, to think that Newman's celibacy was some kind of reaction against elements of his own upbringing. Quite the contrary—he had received a positive example of marriage from his parents. Apart from some serious financial setbacks, his "family and those of his close friends were a sound reference point in his universe. . . . Respect and affection, support and obedience were a natural part of family life."[10] Nevertheless, in the autumn of 1816, Newman writes in the *Apologia*, a "deep imagination . . . took possession of me,—there can be no mistake about the fact; viz. that it would be the will of God that I should lead a single life."[11] It was as a fifteen-year-old boy that Newman first became convinced that he should forego marriage, and "with the break of a month now and a month then" his conviction held for thirteen years—and after that, "without any break at all."[12]

Newman acknowledged that this "deep imagination" was somewhat obscure. It was "more or less connected in my mind with the notion, that my calling in life would require such a sacrifice as celibacy involved; as, for instance, missionary work among the heathen, to which I had a great drawing for some years. It also strengthened my feeling of separation from the visible world."[13] After his father's death in 1824, Newman wrote in his diary, "When I die, shall I be followed to the grave by my children? My Mother said the other day, she hoped to live to see me married; but I think I shall either die within college walls, or as a missionary in a foreign land. No matter where, so that I die in Christ."[14]

Despite this personal conviction of a celibate vocation, however, Newman made clear his objection to the more universal approach towards clerical celibacy in the Catholic Church. In an 1833 letter to Rev. Samuel Rickards, he inveighs against the "crafty, relentless and inflexible" policy of the Roman Church which "still sacrifices the good of its members to the splendour and strength of the Republic (what can be a greater instance of this than the custom of the forced

9   Young, "The Anglican Origins of Newman's Celibacy," 26.

10   Vélez, *Holiness in a Secular Age*, 99. See also Meriol Trevor, *Newman: The Pillar of the Cloud, A Biography of John Henry Cardinal Newman* (New York: Doubleday & Company, 1962), 93.

11   *Apo.*, 110–11.

12   *Apo.*, 111.

13   *Apo.*, 111.

14   John Henry Newman, *Letters and Correspondence of John Henry Newman*, vol. 1, ed. Anne Mozley (London: Longmans, Green, and Co., 1903), 79–80.

celibacy of the clergy?)."[15] Later, in more measured tones, he comments on clerical celibacy as "grounded not on God's law, but on the Church's rule, or on a vow.... Our Church leaves the discretion with the clergy; and most persons will allow that, under our circumstances, she acts wisely in doing so."[16]

Even in his Anglican years, though, he always saw celibacy itself as an objective good and came to view it as a tradition dating back to the apostles. His Anglican friend Hurrell Froude opened his eyes to the excellence of celibacy and to the Blessed Virgin Mary as its most perfect expression.[17] Newman writes in the *Apologia* that "in my weary days at Palermo, I was not ungrateful for the comfort which I had received in frequenting the churches; nor did I ever forget it. Then, again, her zealous maintenance of the doctrine and the rule of celibacy which I recognized as Apostolic, and her faithful agreement with Antiquity in so many other points which were dear to me."[18]

CELIBACY AFTER CONVERSION

Newman's very personal motives for celibacy as an Anglican took on a more defined shape as a Catholic. Certainly there is continuity in his choice for celibacy throughout his life. One of his biographers, Zeno the Capuchin, remarks that Newman's decision for celibacy as a teenager was

> comparable with the call heard by a Catholic boy, to lead a life of total dedication to God by becoming a priest. Young though he was, he realized that this would entail the sacrifice of his deep need for affection, but youthful enthusiasm—in the true meaning of the word—helped him to follow God's will. How genuine this call was will appear from the faithfulness with which he followed it till the end of his life.[19]

Newman's estimation of celibacy grew over the years and became more confident and general in application after his conversion. His only systematic treatment of celibacy occurs in a lecture on the *Present Position of Catholics in England*. Here Newman responds to the (surprisingly modern-sounding) Protestant claim that clerical celibacy causes sexual repression and moral corruption among the clergy. He replies to this objection first indirectly, then directly. Indirectly, he points to the rigorous selection and formation of priests that he had observed in the Catholic Church, and the natural and supernatural

---

15 Newman, *Letters and Correspondence of John Henry Newman*, vol. 1, 342.

16 *VM* ii, 327–28.

17 See Vélez, *Holiness in a Secular Age*, 101.

18 *Apo.*, 54.

19 Zeno the Capuchin, *John Henry Newman: His Inner Life* (San Francisco: Ignatius Press, 1987), 25.

means that are fostered in them to observe the discipline of celibacy. Once a man is called to the priesthood, Newman writes, "unless he be wonderfully wanting to himself, the power of divine grace abundantly poured upon him, without which all human means are useless, but which can do, and constantly does, miracles, as the experience, not of priest merely, but of every one who has been converted from a life of sin, will abundantly testify."[20]

He then directly responds to the objection. He writes that Protestants mistakenly assume that married clergy are less prone to temptations or scandals. While insisting upon the virtue of the married clergymen of his acquaintance, he nevertheless argues that

> a Protestant rector or a dissenting preacher is not necessarily kept from the sins I am speaking of, because he happens to be married: and when he offends, whether in a grave way or less seriously, still in all cases he has by matrimony but exchanged a bad sin for a worse, and has become an adulterer instead of being a seducer. Matrimony only does this for him, that his purity is at once less protected and less suspected. . . . the terrible instances of human frailty of which one reads and hears in the Protestant clergy, are quite enough to show that the married state is no sort of testimonial for moral correctness, no safeguard whether against scandalous offences, or (much less) against minor forms of the same general sin. Purity is not a virtue which comes merely as a matter of course to the married any more than to the single.[21]

Turning to the celibate priest, he then says:

> But if matrimony does not prevent cases of immorality among Protestant ministers, it is not celibacy which causes them among Catholic priests. It is not what the Catholic Church imposes, but what human nature prompts, which leads any portion of her ecclesiastics into sin. Human nature will break out, like some wild and raging element, under any system; it bursts out under the Protestant system; it bursts out under the Catholic; passion will carry away the married clergyman as well as the unmarried priest.[22]

For a man who wrote little about celibacy in his life, this defensive broadside of the practice reveals how much more confidence, as a Catholic, he had in widespread clerical celibacy. It was no longer merely a fruit of his "deep imagination" but an apostolic practice eminently suitable to priestly ministry as a whole.

---

20 *Prepos.,* 133.
21 *Prepos.,* 134–35.
22 *Prepos.,* 136.

IN SERVICE TO THE CHURCH

Over the years, Newman's reasons for embracing celibacy broadened as well. He writes in the *Apologia* that his conscious choice for celibacy in 1816 was primarily associated with his "calling in life" that "would require such a sacrifice as celibacy involved; as, for instance, missionary work among the heathen."[23] Six years later, he had written in his dairy that he might die "within college walls, or as a missionary in a foreign land. No matter where, so that I die in Christ."[24] The initial impetus for Newman's celibacy, then, was a desire to serve the Church without the "tug of a home life."[25] He writes that celibacy "is a high state of life, to which the multitude of men cannot aspire. I do not say that they who adopt it are necessarily better than others, though the noblest 'ethos' is situated in that state."[26] Clerical celibacy, in the mind of the young Newman, was primarily ordered to service.

Over time, Newman began to envision a dedicated core of celibate Anglican clergymen who could devote their entire lives to the Church in the critical times it was passing through. "The Church wants *expeditos milites*—not a whole camp of women at its heels."[27] There "should be among the clergy enough unmarried," he wrote to Henry Wilberforce in 1832, "to give a character of strength to the whole."[28] Indeed he even wistfully looked at the Catholic Dominicans in Oxford, feeling "more strongly than ever the necessity of there being men in the Church, like the R Catholic friars, free from all obstacles to their devoting themselves to its defence."[29] The committed clergymen Newman had in mind would live in community, imitating "the *mode* in which the Monastic orders rose, in order to see whether one could not in all simplicity and godly sincerity found such a society, if times get bad."[30] Such communities would serve the poor, evangelize the cities, and prepare men intellectually to defend Church doctrine in the face of liberalizing tendencies. These thoughts were first embodied in the Oxford Movement and eventually came to fruition in the Birmingham Oratory after his conversion to Catholicism.

SEPARATION FROM THE WORLD

The other reason given by Newman for his initial attachment to celibacy was his "feeling of separation from the visible world."[31] This motive is not in contrast to his desire for missionary labors or other work that demands total dedication,

---

23 *Apo.*, 111.
24 Newman, *Letters and Correspondence of John Henry Newman*, vol. 1, 79–80.
25 Juan R. Vélez, *Passion for Truth: The Life of John Henry Newman* (Charlotte, N.C.: TAN Books, 2012), 64.
26 Strange, *John Henry Newman: A Portrait in Letters*, 49.
27 *LD* iii, 43.
28 *LD* iii, 23.
29 *LD* ii, 133.
30 *LD* iii, 107.
31 *Apo.*, 111.

but rather presupposes and builds upon it. A passage in the first draft of the *Apologia*, which Newman chose to leave unpublished, shows the relationship in his mind between these two motives. The anticipation that he would live a single life, Newman wrote,

> has held its ground almost continuously ever since, and it has been closely connected with that feeling of dissociation from scenes about me, of which I have already spoken. . . . This imagination, which I will speak of once for all, and then dismiss, was not founded on the Catholic belief of the moral superiority of the single life over the married, which I did not hold till many years afterwards, when I was taught it by Hurrell Froude. It arose from my feeling of separation from the visible world, and it was connected with a notion that my mission in life would require such a sacrifice as it involved. When I was first on the Oriel foundation it was associated in my mind with Missionary employment, or with duties at Oxford.[32]

The "separation from the visible world" was therefore not that of a man retreating from responsibility. He saw it as inseparably linked to the very responsibilities that God was calling him to. There was "a real early awareness of what we would call the supernatural," Joseph Tolhurst writes, that exercised in Newman "a fascination and an invitation to detach oneself from the hold of the world so as to enter more fully into the things which God has prepared for those who love him."[33] Nor was it that of a man fleeing the duties of domestic life out of fear or sloth. He was keenly aware of the sacrifice that celibacy involved. He lamented, very naturally, losing the kind of attentive love that only a wife can truly provide.

> This is the sort of interest which a wife takes and none but she—it is a woman's interest—and that interest, so be it, shall never be taken in me. Never, so be it, will I be other than God has found me. All my habits for years, my tendencies, are towards celibacy. I could not take that interest in this world which marriage requires. I am too disgusted with this world—And, above all, call it what one will, I have a repugnance to a clergyman's marrying. I do not say it is not lawful—I cannot deny the right—but, whether a prejudice or not, it shocks me. And therefore I willingly give up the possession of that sympathy, which I feel is not, cannot be, granted to me. Yet, not the less do I feel the need of it.[34]

---

32 Louis Bouyer, *Cardinal Newman: His Life and Spirituality* (San Francisco: Ignatius Press, 2011), 31.

33 Joseph Tolhurst, "The Interchange of Love: John Henry Newman's Teaching on Celibacy," *Irish Theological Quarterly* 59, no. 1 (1993): 218.

34 *AW*, 137–38.

Commenting on this passage, one biographer writes, "To be interested in the small worries, in a man's health, in his moods, in his material needs and well-being and to give him her sympathy . . . this is one of the most important offices of Eve the 'helpmate', and Newman was painfully aware of this unfulfilled need of his nature."[35] It is an example of Newman's emotional honesty that tended to startle his contemporaries, who often "did not admit to feelings contrary to the ideals they professed, did not recognize them except possibly as temptations."[36]

Celibacy, then, was no easy decision for Newman. He was a man capable of giving and receiving a great deal of love and his "separation from the world" did not come without a struggle. It pained him when friends, whom he had hoped would constitute part of the brotherly cadre of celibate clergymen in the Oxford Movement, left to get married. He knew that their decision to marry, while completely within their rights, meant a natural and necessary distancing from him. Hearing of his intention to marry, for example, Newman writes to Henry Wilberforce that their friendship must necessarily change, whatever the latter might say. "It is a little hard for a friend to separate himself from familiarity with me (which he has a perfect right, and perhaps lies under a duty to do,) and then to say, 'Love me as closely, give me your familiar heart as you did, though I have parted with mine.' Be quite sure that I shall be free to love you, far more than you will me."[37]

UNDIVIDED LOVE

As he approached his conversion to Catholicism, Newman's reasons for celibacy continued to mature. The initial motive of wholehearted service to the Church did not change but rather assumed new depths. Celibacy became less about separation from the world than about cleaving more ardently to Christ. Newman's choice for celibacy, precisely because of its sacrifice, became a path towards more radical love for God. Muriel Spark, the English novelist and convert, captured this tension when she described the *Apologia* as the "saddest love story in the world."[38]

Twenty years after his youthful choice for celibacy, Newman wrote to his sisters that the feeling of "dejection" that overtook him at times was "not unwelcome—I am speaking of dejection from solitude; I never feel so near heaven as then." After all, he writes, "this life is very short, and it is a better thing to be pursuing what seems God's call, than to be looking after one's own comfort."[39] Biographer Ian Ker writes that by this time Newman had already understood that the gift of celibacy "was not so much that it provides freedom from the ties of marriage and

---

35 Hilda Graef, *God and Myself: The Spirituality of John Henry Newman* (London: Peter Davies, 1967), 72.

36 Trevor, *Newman: The Pillar of the Cloud*, 95.

37 Strange, *John Henry Newman: A Portrait in Letters*, 76.

38 John Henry Newman, *Realizations: Newman's Selection of His Parochial and Plain Sermons*, ed. Vincent Ferrer Blehl (Collegeville, Minn.: Liturgical Press, 2009), vii.

39 Newman, *Letters and Correspondence of John Henry Newman*, vol. 2, 175–76.

family for a fuller commitment to the work of a religious profession, but rather that the very pain of the lack of intimate human love is meant to impel the celibate to find affective fulfillment in the exclusive love of God."[40]

Echoing the dialogue between Reding and Carlton in *Loss and Gain*, by 1840 Newman was writing to Faber that celibacy could be "a penance for past sin" but, by this point, "I consider it also a more holy state."[41] Going still further, Newman said at the religious profession of Mary Anne Bowden in 1854 that the "Virginity of the Gospel" was more than a mere separation from the world. It is not a

> state of independence or isolation, or dreary pride, or barren indolence or crushed affections; man is made for sympathy, for the interchange of love, for self-denial for the sake of another dearer to him than himself. The Virginity of the Christian soul is a marriage with Christ. . . . And this it is to be married to Jesus. It is to have Him ourselves wholly, henceforth, and for ever—it is to be united to Him by an indissoluble tie—it is to be His, while He is ours.[42]

The most poignant expression of Newman's mature view of celibacy as a longing for divine love occurs in a poetical dialogue between allegories of the "Married" and the "Single" that he wrote in 1834. Marriage, instituted at the dawn of creation, boasts that she is a place of companionship and love, the progenitor of all, a source of trust and human affection.

> *Take love away, and life would be defaced,*
> *A ghastly vision on a howling waste,*
> *Stern, heartless, reft of the sweet spells which swage*
> *The throes of passion, and which gladden age.*

Marriage concludes that

> *A life which scorns the gifts by heaven assign'd,*
> *Nor knows the sympathy of human kind.*

Then Virginity has her turn:

> *Dim is her downcast eye, and pale her cheek;*
> *Untrimm'd her gear; no sandals on her feet;*
> *A sparest form for austere tenant meet.*

---

40   Ian Ker, *John Henry Newman: A Biography* (Oxford: Clarendon Press, 1988), 132–33.

41   *LD* vii, 422.

42   *NO*, 277.

And after being prompted to overcome her shy reluctance, the "Single" life replies:

> *Ah, who has hither drawn my backward feet,*
> *Changing for worldly strife my lone retreat?*
> *Where, in the silent chant of holy deeds,*
> *I praise my God, and tend the sick soul's needs;*
> *By toils of day, and vigils of the night,*
> *By gushing tears, and blessed lustral rite.*
> *I have no sway amid the crowd, no art*
> *In speech, no place in council or in mart.*
> *Nor human law, nor judges throned on high,*
> *Smile on my face, and to my words reply.*
> *Let others seek earth's honours; be it mine*
> *One law to cherish, and to track one line,*
> *Straight on towards heaven to press with single bent,*
> *To know and love my God, and then to die content.*[43]

Truly Newman had come to an appreciation of celibacy that far outpaced his early motives for it. It had become, for him, a path to union with God. It had become a way to "know and love my God, and then to die content."

CONTROVERSY

Newman was no stranger to doctrinal and even legal controversy in his own day, but his choice for celibacy provoked virtually no murmuring or gossip during his lifetime. Remaining single was an intelligible—if uncommon—choice for Anglican clergymen in his day. His intention to forge a group of committed, celibate clergymen to serve the Church of England raised no eyebrows, even when the strident doctrines of the Oxford Movement did. It was not until long after his death that a new source of controversy emerged. Nearly forty years after Newman's death, Geoffrey Faber wrote a withering account of Newman and his Oxford friends using the latest Freudian theories which were then at their apex of influence. Faber speculated that Hurrell Froude struggled with homosexual desires,[44] and that there were homosexual undertones to the community of celibate men surrounding Newman. Faber construed the emotional attachment between Newman and other Tractarians to be an indication of homosexuality.[45]

---

43 *VO*, 202–7.

44 See Geoffrey Faber, *The Oxford Apostles: A Character Study of the Oxford Movement* (London: Faber and Faber, 1933), 218–22.

45 See Faber, *The Oxford Apostles,* 227.

More recently, Yale historian Frank Turner has argued that Newman's sexuality was "at best indecisive and the question not firmly resolvable"[46] but that he was certainly preoccupied with the affections of his younger celibate friends. Newman, according to Turner, restrained his young protégés at Littlemore from converting to Catholicism out of fear that he would cease "to be the center of their attention and affection."[47] Turner admitted that there is "no evidence of open homosexual orientation"[48] but the magisterial tone of Turner's work has left a lasting impression.[49] Furthermore, heads wagged when Newman was exhumed, and it became widely known that he chose to be buried in the same grave as his friend Father Ambrose St John. It was assumed by many that Newman's funeral instructions reflected suppressed (or perhaps not suppressed) same-sex attractions. Some homosexual activists, sensing opportunity, even declared publicly that Newman should not be separated from Fr. Ambrose out of respect for their shared feelings.[50]

It should first be noted that sharing graves was not uncommon in Victorian England, and certainly did not imply romantic affection or sexual overtones. In a book written in 1907, an early biographer of Newman betrays not a hint of embarrassment when he describes the burial. "At Rednal, he was laid to rest by loving hands. His grave he shares with Ambrose St. John," the biographer writes simply, "who died in 1875, and in whose memory Newman planted the now spreading bed of St. John's wort down one side of the small enclosure. They loved each other in life; in death they are not divided."[51] We can be certain that if such a burial was at all shocking in 1907, it would never have been stated so unguardedly in that reverential biography. It took a more cynical age like ours to read anything further into Newman's funeral arrangements.

Why, then, did Newman choose to be buried with Ambrose St John? Biographer Ian Ker offers several suggestions. First, Newman blamed himself for St John's death, having essentially (and of course unintentionally) worked him beyond his capacities in translating a German theologian's work on papal infallibility.[52] Second, Newman may have feared that Church authorities would wish to erect a tomb for the deceased cardinal that would take him away from the resting

---

46 Frank M. Turner, *John Henry Newman: The Challenge to Evangelical Religion* (New Haven: Yale University Press, 2011), 425.

47 Turner, *John Henry Newman*, 595.

48 Turner, *John Henry Newman*, 434.

49 See Simon Skinner, "History versus Hagiography: The Reception of Turner's Newman," *Journal of Ecclesiastical History* 61, no. 4 (2010): 764–81. Also Eamon Duffy, "The Reception of Turner's Newman: A Reply to Simon Skinner," *Journal of Ecclesiastical History* 63, no. 3 (2012): 534–48. Also Simon Skinner, "A Response to Eamon Duffy," *Journal of Ecclesiastical History* 63, no. 3 (2012): 549–67.

50 Ian Ker, "John Henry Newman and the Sacrifice of Celibacy," *L'Osservatore Romano*, Sept 3, 2008.

51 Wilfrid Meynell, *Cardinal Newman* (London: Burns and Oats, 1907), 122–23.

52 Ker, "John Henry Newman and the Sacrifice of Celibacy."

spots of his beloved fellow Oratorians. By being buried in the same grave as Fr. Ambrose, he might avert that possibility. Third, St John had been buried between Joseph Gordon and Edward Caswall, the three of whom he called the "life and centre of the Oratory," and being buried among them would be a last opportunity to show his gratitude and respect.[53] Most importantly, however, Newman had a great affection for Ambrose—they were the spiritual equivalent of brothers. For thirty years St John "had been his most faithful and loyal supporter, from the days of his virtual exile at Littlemore through all his trials and tribulations as a Catholic."[54] In fact, as Ker has pointed out, Newman's request to be buried with Fr. Ambrose cuts in the other direction.

> After all, Newman would scarcely have left such an instruction had he even dreamed that it could ever be interpreted as having any significance beyond the significance which he attached to it—nor would the Oratory or the Church authorities have ever permitted such a joint burial if they had the slightest suspicion about what must have seemed to them a totally innocent, not to say praiseworthy gesture. Newman had plenty of critics, not to say enemies, in his time; yet not one of them, not one newspaper, not one casual observer even dreamed of reading a significance into an act of loving friendship, and indeed of humility, such as was left to the twentieth century to read into it.[55]

Beyond the question of his burial, though, there is much evidence to debunk the hypersexualized claims of our day. Most obviously, as has already been pointed out, Newman understood celibacy to be a painful sacrifice. Since the notion of same-sex "marriage" had not emerged in his day, this manifestly meant sacrificing marriage to a woman. In addition, Ker points out a clear piece of evidence from Newman's youth that sheds light on his affections. Shortly after his choice for celibacy at the age of fifteen, Newman recalled his misgivings about returning home from boarding school for the holidays—mentioning in particular the temptations associated with dances and parties. That is, he was worried about being in situations where he would encounter girls. Ker writes, had "the pious Evangelical Newman been [homosexually] inclined in the slightest way—and adolescent boys in all-male boarding school environments are often sexually confused—we would have found him praying fervently for the school holidays and the accompanying release from an all-male society."[56]

---

53 Ian Ker, *John Henry Newman: A Biography* (Oxford: Oxford University Press, 2019), 748.

54 Ker, *John Henry Newman*, 747.

55 Ker, *John Henry Newman*, 750.

56 Ker, *John Henry Newman*, 749.

FRIENDSHIP

Biographer Meriol Trevor observes that "nobody who actually knew Newman, however hostile to his views, ever classed him as effeminate. It was a charge only made by those, personally unacquainted with him, who misunderstood his views on celibacy."[57] It was, rather, Newman's capacity for deep friendships that fuels much of the speculation about Newman's sexuality and his choice of celibacy. Certainly he had female friends—apart from his mother and sisters, for instance, Newman had a lifelong friendship with Maria Giberne, who eventually became a Catholic and a nun of the Visitation of Mary Order.[58] Most of his deep friendships were with men, though, and they were characterized by warmth, sincerity, loyalty, intellectual curiosity, and spiritual kinship.[59] Newman had an exceptional gift for friendship.[60] He saw in human affections the most favorable ground for growing in divine love. Newman "never forgets that man is a social being, that he does not live in a vacuum, and that only by cultivating natural love and friendship will he learn to love also supernaturally."[61] Christ himself, Newman believed, showed us the importance of affection for those who are immediately about us.[62] Friendships, to Newman, were a "special token of God's mercy."[63]

Newman's power of friendship did not diminish but actually expanded over the course of his life. Despite a reserved temperament, his heart continued to expand to include new relationships. Trevor argues that this remarkable and unusual achievement in Newman's latter years was the reward of persevering through the tempests of inner struggle and outward trial.

> This enlargement of heart, which cannot happen to anyone if he remains merely passive to experience, Newman won by the way he passed through the successive crises of his personal development. Often the power to love was threatened with constriction and even extinction: in his youth from within, by the dangers of intellectualism and self-will; after he had passed his physical prime by reiterated blows from without, ordeals by rejection. He not only survived these crises,

---

57   Trevor, *Newman: The Pillar of the Cloud*, 89–90.
58   In ch. 6 of this volume, Barbara H. Wyman describes Newman's friendship with Maria R. Giberne and Francis Wootten (editor's note).
59   See Joyce Sugg, *Ever Yours Affly: John Henry Newman and His Female Circle* (Leominster: Gracewing, 1996), and Vélez, *Holiness in a Secular Age*, 29–37.
60   In ch. 5 of this volume, Víctor García-Ruiz gives an account of many interesting details of Newman's male friends (editor's note).
61   Graef, *God and Myself: The Spirituality of John Henry Newman*, 71.
62   Zeno, *John Henry Newman*, 257.
63   Zeno, *John Henry Newman*, 257–58.

some very severe, but each time came out more alive and with greater power of sympathy. The signs of the struggle marked his features, but so, increasingly, did the resulting gentleness.[64]

In an age that has largely reduced human intimacy to sexual activity, it is perhaps inevitable that Newman's close friendships with men, including Fr. Ambrose St John, should be mistaken for homosexual, or at least subconsciously homosexual, proclivities. The evidence, however, simply is not there. Given his status and reputation in nineteenth century England, it is simply inconceivable that Newman was flouting religious and social conventions so brazenly. He is accused of fostering homosexual associations simply because of the depth of friendship that prevailed at Oxford and the Oratory. This controversy, in short, has said more about our times and the sorry state of male friendship today than it ever has about John Henry Newman.

CHURCH TEACHING AFTER NEWMAN

Prior to the twentieth century, references to celibacy in official documents of the Catholic Church are surprisingly spare. They typically deal with the canonical, and occasionally ascetical, implications of clerical continence. In the century after Newman's death, however, celibacy was increasingly addressed as a subject in itself, something worth considering and valuing in its own right. It is interesting to note that the themes Newman associated with celibacy—service to the Church, detachment from the world, and union with Christ—show up in these documents again and again.[65] One notable example is the document on the priesthood of the Second Vatican Council, *Presbyterorum Ordinis*. Through celibacy, the Council fathers taught,

> priests are consecrated to Christ by a new and exceptional reason. They adhere to him more easily with an undivided heart, they dedicate themselves more freely in him and through him to the service of God and men, and they more expeditiously minister to his Kingdom and the work of heavenly regeneration, and thus they are apt to accept, in a broad sense, paternity in Christ.[66]

---

64 Trevor, *Newman: The Pillar of the Cloud*, 95.

65 It is beyond the scope of this chapter to examine the theology of celibacy that has been developing in recent years. Interested readers may wish to consult Gary Selin, *Priestly Celibacy: Theological Foundations* (Washington, D.C.: The Catholic University of America Press, 2016) or the author's dissertation on priestly celibacy and spiritual fatherhood: Carter Griffin, *Supernatural Fatherhood through Priestly Celibacy: Fulfillment in Masculinity* (Rome: Pontifical University of the Holy Cross, 2011).

66 Vatican Council II, *Presbyterorum Ordinis* (December 7, 1965), 16.

Pope St. John Paul II again emphasized these general themes in his Post-Synodal Apostolic Exhortation *Pastores Dabo Vobis* on the formation of priests. The Church, he wrote, "as the spouse of Jesus Christ, wishes to be loved by the priest in the total and exclusive manner in which Jesus Christ her head and spouse loved her. Priestly celibacy, then, is the gift of self in and with Christ to his Church and expresses the priest's service to the Church in and with the Lord."[67]

The two most extensive magisterial treatments of celibacy, however, are the encyclicals *Sacra Virginitas* by Pope Pius XII and *Sacerdotalis Caelibatus* by Pope St. Paul VI. In *Sacra Virginitas* the pope, like Newman, identifies service as one of the primary motivations for celibacy. "We feel the deepest joy," he writes, "at the thought of the innumerable army of virgins and apostles who, from the first centuries of the Church up to our own day, have given up marriage to devote themselves more easily and fully to the salvation of their neighbor for the love of Christ, and have thus been enabled to undertake and carry through admirable works of religion and charity."[68] Pope Paul VI continues the thought in *Sacerdotalis Caelibatus*, casting celibacy in the key of love. When someone responds to a priestly call, he wrote,

> grace increases the longings of love. And love, when it is genuine, is all-embracing, stable and lasting, an irresistible spur to all forms of heroism. And so the free choice of sacred celibacy has always been considered by the Church "as a symbol of, and stimulus to, charity": it signifies a love without reservations; it stimulates to a charity which is open to all.[69]

Later in the document he continues, "by a daily dying to himself and by giving up the legitimate love of a family of his own for the love of Christ and of His kingdom, the priest will find the glory of an exceedingly rich and fruitful life in Christ, because like Him and in Him, he loves and dedicates himself to all the children of God."[70]

However limited his writings on celibacy, Newman's was a prophetic voice of the century to come. His commitment to the practice, and his slow unpacking of its merits, was echoed in the Church's own prayerful reflection regarding this "brilliant jewel" of her priestly life.[71] While Newman himself did not live long enough to see the rapid development of teaching on this topic, it is certain that he would have warmly embraced it.

---

67 John Paul II, Post-Synodal Apostolic Exhortation *Pastores Dabo Vobis* (March 15, 1992), 29.

68 Pius XII, Encyclical Letter *Sacra Virginitas* (March 25, 1954), 26.

69 Paul VI, Encyclical Letter *Sacerdotalis Caelibatus* (June 24, 1967), 24.

70 Paul VI, *Sacerdotalis Caelibatus*, 30.

71 Paul VI, *Sacerdotalis Caelibatus*, 1.

CONCLUSION

In the fictional dialogue between Reding and Carlton written a few years after his conversion, Newman encapsulates his own youthful ambivalence about celibacy. Certainly he clearly felt the call to celibacy very early in life and never veered far from his early intuitions. At the same time, he was reluctant to draw more general conclusions about celibacy from his personal experience alone. It was not until later that he embraced the Catholic approach to universal clerical celibacy.

Compared to his more illustrious theological contributions, Newman wrote (and thought) far less about celibacy. Nevertheless, he makes some important contributions to the topic.

First, Newman's voluntary choice for celibacy when the Church of England did not require it of its clergy—in fact largely discouraged it—is illuminating. For Newman, celibacy was a conscious and personal choice, one made in the light of prayer and with the intention to serve the Lord and the Church more fully. Young Catholic men who are discerning a vocation to the priesthood can sometimes fail to see celibacy as a distinct charism but rather as a mere requirement for ordination. Newman's choice reminds us of the intrinsic value of celibacy and the need to embrace it freely, personally, and unreservedly while one discerns the call to Holy Orders.

Second, we can learn from Newman's approach to celibacy, particularly in his later years, that celibacy is best understood as an act of love. The blessing of celibacy is not to be found only—or even primarily—in expanding one's availability for ministry. Lived well, celibacy expands the heart. It is an invitation to join in a deeper relationship with God. Like all celibates Newman experienced the "desolation" that sometimes accompanies this life. It is love that turns such feelings into an opportunity to be drawn into a greater intimacy with God. Celibacy is not about loving less, but loving more—and the expansive heart of well-lived celibacy finds room for many souls, as the celebrated history of saintly "eunuchs for the sake of the Kingdom" (Mt 19:12) makes clear.

Third, precisely because celibacy is about "loving more," Newman shows us that in most circumstances it will be supported through deep and abiding friendships. Certainly Newman would insist first of all upon the supernatural means—prayer, sacraments, and asceticism. But of the natural means, Newman would assuredly count friendship among the first. In his mind, friendship is a "special token of God's mercy" and the natural training ground for supernatural love. It is true that Newman had a singular capacity for friendships, but he also labored to sustain them. His is an important lesson today, particularly when many priests feel increasingly isolated from one another. Newman is a reminder that the hard work of sustaining friendships, especially priestly friendships, is more imperative than ever if a priest is to joyfully adhere to his own choice for celibacy.

Suggested Reading

Ker, Ian. "John Henry Newman and the Sacrifice of Celibacy." *L'Osservatore Romano*. Sept 3, 2008.

Newman, John Henry. *John Henry Newman: Autobiographical Writings*. Edited by Henry Tristram. New York: Sheed and Ward, 1957.

Newman, John Henry. "True Testimony Insufficient for the Protestant View." In *Lectures on the Present Position of Catholics in England*, 133–42. London: Longmans, Green, and Co., 1908.

Newman, John Henry. *Loss and Gain: The Story of a Convert*. London: Longmans, Green, and Co, 1906.

Tolhurst, Joseph. "The Interchange of Love: John Henry Newman's Teaching on Celibacy." *Irish Theological Quarterly* 59, no. 1 (1993): 218–25.

Trevor, Meriol. "1829: The Idea of Virginity." In *Newman: The Pillar of the Cloud, A Biography of John Henry Cardinal Newman*, 88–96. New York: Doubleday & Company, 1962.

Vélez, Juan R. "On Friendship" and "Celibacy in Marriage." In *Holiness in a Secular Age: The Witness of Cardinal Newman*, chs. 2 and 9. New York: Scepter, 2017.

Young, B.W. "The Anglican Origins of Newman's Celibacy." *Church History* 65, no. 1 (1996): 15–27.

Zeno the Capuchin. *John Henry Newman: His Inner Life*. San Francisco: Ignatius Press, 1987.

CHAPTER 5

NEWMAN, THE UNFAILING FRIEND— AND AN OLD BLUE CLOAK

Víctor García Ruiz

John Henry Newman, a distinguished man of letters, was a person with many close lifelong friends. This article, which is partly descriptive and partly narrative, is primarily a study of characteristics common to Newman and his friends.[1] It begins with a consideration of his affective life and early decision to remain celibate that was intrinsically tied to his ideal of a complete dedication to God, and a detachment from earthly goods, which enabled him to have such rich friendships. Newman admired the apostle Paul as a hero—a Romantic one, perhaps—and clearly understood that when the apostle writes that "thrice was I beaten with rods, once was I stoned, thrice I suffered shipwreck, a night and a day I have been in the deep; in journeyings often, in perils of waters, in perils of robbers, in perils by mine own countrymen, in perils by the heathen, in perils in the city, in perils in the wilderness, in perils in the sea, in perils among false brethren" (2 Cor 11:25–26), it went largely unstated that such perils entailed a determinedly single life. It was this life as well as the

---

* This a revised version of an article that appeared in *Scripta Theologica* 52, no. 2 (2020): 351–81.

1 In technical terms this is called prosopography which is "a study that identifies and relates a group of persons or characters within a particular historical or literary context." *Merriam-Webster.com Dictionary*, s.v. "prosopography," accessed June 13, 2021, https://www.merriam-webster.com/dictionary/prosopography.

heroic lives of those early Christians and Fathers of the Church which filled Newman with amazement and love as a youth.[2] Although he never openly criticized it, Newman could not reconcile himself with the idea that the natural successors of such apostles, the Anglican clergy, would lead a life so regular, so established, so grounded in benefices, so sweetened by the angel in the house, a spouse in the flesh. In "the autumn of 1816, [a deep imagination] took possession of me,—there can be no mistake about the fact; viz. that it would be the will of God that I should lead a single life."[3] Nevertheless this "will of God" did not imply for Newman quenching his capacity to love others—which is precisely what the present article wishes to show. The death of friends such as Hurrell Froude and later Ambrose St John left Newman "truly widowed,"[4] to compare with the loss of a married man as "the greatest affliction I have had in my life."[5] In 1840, while finishing a long-delayed account of his Sicilian odyssey ("My Illness in Sicily"), Newman had two thoughts. The first—Henry Wilberforce as the only living person who would "be pleased with such details" about his trip—indicates a key reason for Newman's celibacy: that marriage and a full self-dedication to God would seem, to him, incompatible:

> This is the sort of interest that a wife takes and none but she—it is a woman's interest—and that interest, so be it, shall never be taken in me.... All my habits . . . are towards celibacy. I could not take that interest in this world that marriage requires. I am too disgusted with this world.... I willingly give up the possession of that sympathy, which I feel is not, cannot be, granted to me. Yet, not the less do I feel the need of it.[6]

The second thought was of "an old blue cloke [sic] of mine which I had since 1823" and which he did not give away to his servant Gennaro because "I had an affection for it":

> It had nursed me all through my illness; had even been put on my bed, put on me when I rose to have my bed made etc. I had nearly lost it at Corfu—it was stolen by a soldier but recovered. I have it still. I have

---

2   See *Apo.*, 7.
3   *Apo.*, 7.
4   Feb. 21, 1836; *LD* v, 241.
5   *LD* xxvii, 313. Newman's pointed allusion to marriage served to indicate the depth of a chaste affection between friends of the same sex, which today is so often misconstrued as a sexual relationship. In ch. 4 of this volume, Carter Griffin discusses and dismisses the spurious claims to Newman's "confused sexuality" and the homosexual overtones of his friendships (editor's note).
6   *AW*, 137–38. For an account of Newman's chaste friendship with women see Edward Short, *Newman and His Contemporaries* (New York: T & T Clark, 2011), 177–212; Juan R. Vélez, *Holiness in a Secular Age: The Witness of Cardinal Newman* (New York: Scepter Publishers, 2017), 29–37.

brought it up here to Littlemore, and on some cold nights I have had it on my bed. I have so few things to sympathize with me, that I take to clokes.[7]

This passing reference to solitude symbolized by attachment to a material object may point to a deeper truth later expressed when, before leaving Oxford for good, he was alone for some days at Littlemore. He then wrote: "numquam minus solus quam cum Deo solus."[8] Newman liked to read, muse, and study, but he was anything but a hermit. His motto as a cardinal (*Cor ad cor loquitur*) sums up Newman's peculiar gift for inspiring affection: face to face, from the pulpit or from unforgettable passages in his writings, Newman *hits* the heart. Even today this still happens; recently a young academic came across a copy of *Apologia* in a secondhand bookshop. He recounted, "I read the book from start to finish—not because I wanted to learn from Newman, but because I wanted to hate him." Unexpectedly the young academic was totally overwhelmed by Newman's story and literary powers: "Decades later, I still keep it close at hand and reread favorite passages."[9] In the thick of the last century, in a deeply post-war metaphor, the novelist Muriel Spark came to the same conclusion: "Newman has *a voice* . . . radioactive from the page."[10]

John Henry Newman knew himself to be a solitary young man in need of timely advice which he later recounted: "[at the beginning of my life at Oriel college] I was very much alone, and I used often to take my daily walk by myself. I recollect once meeting Dr Copleston, then Provost, with one of the Fellows. He turned round, and with the kind courteousness which sat so well on him, made me a bow and said, 'Nunquam minus solus, quam cum solus.'"[11]

Newman was then a young *fellow* surrounded by eminent academics—only a few were such, though; others were affecting donnish mannerisms in a college that featured as the intellectual aristocracy of pre-Victorian England. And some of them may have thought they made a poor choice in his election. But Newman would thrive in climates warmed by friendly conversation. He might have been the happiest man on earth living a life among a few friends, a small group of colleagues, and later within the circle of his disciples and parishioners in his beloved Oxford, a scholarly and uneventful life.

---

7   *AW*, 138.

8   These words were an adaptation of the Latin expression *"numquam minus solus quam cum solus."*

9   Carl R. Trueman, "Newman for Protestants: How Newman Drove Me to Geneva," *First Things*, October 2015.https://www.firstthings.com/article/2015/10/newman-for-protestants

10   Muriel Spark, "Foreword," *Realizations: Newman's Selection of his Parochial and Plain Sermons*, ed. Vincent Ferrer Blehl (London: Darton, Longman & Todd, 1964), v-ix.

11   *Apo.*, 15–16.

Things turned out very differently, and Newman's influence in nineteenth century England, though unintended, was vast. It's my intention in this paper to focus on a number of the male friends of this man so markedly inclined toward solitude and at the same time deeply affectionate. Newman himself was well aware of this paradox and accepted, as God's will, the loss of dear ones. After the death of his mother in May 1836, Newman wrote two letters to his sisters with one common topic: his loneliness and the emptiness of their house at Iffley. In the one to Harriet he remembers his anxieties in the years 1822–1826 when he had no friend "near me—no one to whom I opened my mind" and how "since that time I have learned to throw myself on myself."[12] But to Jemima he opens himself freely, and loneliness is seen in a different and deeper light: "I have said all this . . . that you might not think me lonely. . . . God intends me to be lonely. He has so framed my mind that I am in a great measure beyond the sympathies of other people and thrown upon Himself," the main point being that "God, I trust, will support me in following whither He leads.[13]"

Nevertheless, along the years he paid homage many times to his friends, a telling testimony to a tender heart, can be divided into two periods. The first covers his Anglican years and can be read in the *Apologia*: "it was not I who sought friends, but friends who sought me. Never man had kinder or more indulgent friends than I have had." And echoing Job he adds: "They have come, they have gone; they came to my great joy, they went to my great grief. He who gave took away."[14] The second, from his Catholic years, consists of a eulogy of his brothers—only six—at the Oratory in Birmingham. The memorable text begins as panegyric and continues as a prayer, and it is better left as an appropriate ending to this article.[15]

THE TASTE OF FRIENDSHIP: FIRST TWO FRIENDS

Tuberculosis took away the most intimate friends of Newman's youth: John Bowden and Richard Hurrell Froude. Although Bowden (1798–1844) was three years his elder—but born, like Newman, on February 21—both entered the "very gentlemanlike" Trinity College at the same time. Newman was at that time a Calvinist, so it did not take very long for him to realize that in an unreformed Oxford "a gentlemanlike college" meant that the idle noblemen and gentleman commoners spent their time drinking, gambling, and engaging in profligate

---

12   *LD* v, 311–12.

13   *LD* v, 313.

14   To Robert Wilberforce Newman confessed that losing his friends was the hardest for him during the two years prior to his conversion, "and it affected my health most seriously." *LD* xvi, 242.

15   A window into Newman's affective landscape on becoming a Catholic—next to a wasteland—can be found in a letter of January 1846 to Maria Giberne, who was suffering a similar fate. See *LD* xi, 102.

behavior. An understandably annoyed Newman recorded in his diary how he was taken in by a party of drinking students who managed to persuade him to bring along his violin and play for them: "the first thing that surprised me on entering the room was to see a long table: the next to hear a smothered laugh on my conductor's announcing: 'Mr Newman and his fiddle.'"[16] In his naïveté, he would shelter his shyness and his desire for academic success in Bowden's friendship, a man he had met for the first time very soon after arriving in Oxford, immediately finding him congenial. The two wrote jointly and published a poem on a very anti-papist topic, *St. Bartholomew's Eve* (1818). From the start Bowden contributed enthusiastically to the Tractarian Movement: six hymns for the *Lyra Apostolica*, five of the *Tracts for the Times* and various articles for the *British Critic*. After wintering in 1839 in Malta—the island Newman had visited with Hurrell, another friend who, a few years before, was stricken with tuberculosis—Bowden's health declined, and he died four years later. These were, precisely, years of interior agony for Newman who, always the faithful friend, would travel regularly to London to visit Bowden during his illness. He never hinted to Bowden his deep-seated misgivings that, after all, Anglicanism was not a Church, and never had been but a schism. After Bowden was gone, his widow and some of his children followed Newman into the Roman Catholic Church; the two sons became Oratorians, and one of the daughters, a nun, was able to attend Newman's funeral. In Bowden's house Newman was referred to as "the great man," and he once wrote to Keble (Sept. 14, 1844) that in Oxford Bowden and himself would spend all day long in each other's rooms, the other students would mix them up, and—what's most startling and even comical—is that when Bowden married he would make that same mistake and call his wife "Newman" and Newman "Elizabeth."[17] The day after Bowden's death, Newman bitterly sobbed and wept over his friend's coffin at the thought "that he left me still dark as to what the way of truth was, and what I ought to do in order to please God and fulfil His will." He also wrote: "when one sees so blessed an end, and that, the termination of so blameless a life, of one who really fed on our ordinances and got strength from them, and sees the same continued in a whole family, the little children finding quite a solace of their pain in the Daily Prayer, it is impossible not to feel more at ease in our Church, as at least a sort of Zoar, a place of refuge and temporary rest, because of the steepness of the way."[18]

Newman and Richard Hurrell Froude (1803–1836) became best friends at Oriel College. But their first real meeting was not until 1821, when Newman was elected fellow and Hurrell entered the college as an undergraduate, since up at Oxford "you choose your friend, not so much by your tastes, as by your

---

16   *AW*, 156.
17   *LD* x, 337.
18   *Apo.*, 227.

staircase."[19] The close friendship began slowly in 1826 when Hurrell himself was elected fellow. Certainly Hurrell rubbed people the wrong way. He was rash and had extreme High Church views conveyed through a sharp and brilliant tongue. He was a radical and made Newman a radical. At the same time he was disarming and possessed an intense and intriguing interior world, as would later emerge in his *Remains*. Newman found in him a twin soul, and his loss was utterly tragic. As tutors, Newman and Hurrell led a bold reform in the teaching methods at Oriel. Both wanted a less detached and more pastoral, face to face dealing with students. But their move gained them disfavor from Provost Hawkins and cost them their tutorial posts. Such reform was abolished—almost stillborn—and no more students were assigned to any of the reformers or their friend, Robert Wilberforce.[20]

The end of their tutorship coincided with a crisis in Hurrell's lingering lung disease, which led in the winter of 1833 to a four-month trip together with Newman across the Mediterranean. Hurrell's lungs did not improve at all but his friendship with Newman did benefit immensely. As a consequence the Oxford Movement fermented and burst into life: "You shall know the difference, now that I am back again"[21] Newman would write in the *Apologia* borrowing words from Homer's Achilles, to express the feeling of both friends at the time of the "sacrilegious" *Irish Bill* of that same 1833. Poor Hurrell could contribute very little to the Movement while alive, just a handful of *Tracts* (Nos. 9, 59, 63, perhaps 8, and a draft of No. 75 finished by Newman). But he did contribute, in a posthumous and resounding way, when Newman and John Keble—his tutor at Oriel—decided to publish his private papers. The *Remains of the late Rev. Richard Hurrell Froude* fell like a heavy thundershower upon Anglicanism and divided the Tractarians forever. There was widespread rage, scorn, and breakups with the reckless editors for not only airing the Romanizing *ethos* and devotional observances of the deceased—celibacy, devotion to the Blessed Virgin, belief in the Real Presence, use of the Roman Breviary, corporal mortifications, asceticism, and self-examination—but especially for revealing Hurrell's irreverent opinions about the Protestant Reformers, whom he detested and accused of poisoning Christianity with the spirit of rationalism. Hurrell was an outright agitator and would prompt Newman to become one himself. Nevertheless his main contribution to the Movement, in his own words, was this: "Do you know the story of the murderer who had done one good thing in his life? Well, if I was ever asked what good deed I have ever done, I should say I had brought—and—to understand each

---

19   *LG*, 3.

20   See A. Dwight Culler, *The Imperial Intellect: A Study of Cardinal Newman's Educational Ideal* (New Haven: Yale University Press, 1955), 75–76, and Paul Shrimpton, "More Poet than Policeman: Newman and Education 'in a large sense of the word,'" *Scripta Theologica* 51, no. 3 (2019): 775–800.

21   *Apo.*, 34.

other."[22] Historian Christopher Dawson was certainly right when, in 1933, he pointed at Hurrell as the most clear-sighted member of the Oxford Movement, by then in its first centenary.[23]

THE OXFORD MOVEMENT:
KEBLE, PUSEY, AND NEWMAN

The Oxford Movement had a triumvirate at its forefront. To commemorate this there are physical reminders: in Oxford there has been a Keble College since 1870 and a Pusey House since 1884. On the road to Littlemore, beyond Rose Hill and just before the Ring Road, a side road bears the sign Newman Road, and leads to Cardinal Close. As far as I know, this is the one memorial Oxford has dedicated to Newman, which is only to be expected. John Keble and Edward Pusey, especially the latter, made Anglo-Catholicism possible; whereas the *Establishment* has always viewed Newman's standing with ambivalence, at least until his beatification in 2010: they thought him admirable but still a renegade; brilliant, but after all, a traitor. It does not seem Newman had a special appetite for recognition. It is beyond doubt that a Tractarian Movement without Newman would never have achieved the huge impact it made on Victorian England. Nevertheless, with both humility and grace he saluted an occasional sermon by John Keble, "National Apostasy," in this fashion: "I have ever considered and kept the day, as the start of the religious movement of 1833."[24]

Edward Pusey's influence is made obvious by the fact that the Tractarians were sometimes called Puseyites. At the end of that same 1833 Newman tried to gain Pusey, a former colleague at Oriel and now a Regius Professor, to write a tract for the series. Pusey accepted on condition that he would sign it—the *Tracts* were anonymous—to avoid any implication that he was one of those agitating.[25] Surprisingly, not only was Pusey thought to be one "of those people" but, what is more, their leader as well, and the whole group was named after him. Keble and Pusey responded with magnanimity on that fateful day in October 1845 when Newman sent them message that "I am expecting Father Dominic the Passionist, . . . I trust he will receive me, Bowles and Stanton into what I believe to be the

---

22 Richard Hurrell Froude, *Remains of the late Reverend Richard Hurrell Froude, MA Fellow of Oriel College, Oxford*, vol. 1, ed. J. H. Newman and J. Keble (London: Rivington, 1838–1839), 438. In the *Apologia* Newman supplied the missing names: Keble and Newman (see *Apo.* [Combined edition], 120).

23 See Christopher Dawson, *The Spirit of the Oxford Movement* (London: Sheed & Ward, 1933), 10–11, 23–24, 84, 100.

24 *Apo.*, 35.

25 See George Prevost, ed., *The Autobiography of Isaac Williams: As Throwing Further Light on the History of the Oxford Movement* (London: Longmans, Green & Co., 1892), 70–72.

one and only fold of the Redeemer."[26] In the Summer 1863, on his return from one of his few travels abroad, Newman found a letter from Keble on his desk, the first in seventeen years. His reply is a tribute to their friendship and a full display of tact.

> Never have I doubted for one moment your affection for me—never have I been hurt at your silence. I interpreted it easily—it was not the silence of men, nor the forgetfulness of men, who can recollect about me and talk about me enough, when there is something to be said to my disparagement. You are always with me a thought of reverence and love—and there is nothing I love better than you, and Isaac, and Copeland and many others I could name, except Him whom I ought to love best of all and supremely. May He Himself, who is the over abundant compensation for all losses, give me His own Presence—and then I shall want nothing and desiderate nothing—but none but He, can make up for the losses of those old familiar faces which haunt me continually.[27]

Only once would the three meet again. It was in September 1865, in Hursley, in Keble's rural parish (near Southampton, Hampshire). Newman's diary reads, laconically: "Tuesday 12 September went to Keble's, where Pusey—dined with them—then to Ryde to the Bowdens."[28] Newman produced a bittersweet account of the meeting in a letter to Ambrose St John, his last great friend, written in the house of his first great friend, the late Bowden, in which he speaks about two other great friendships recovered after 20 years of silence. A truly marvelous concentration of coincidences![29]

John Keble (1792–1866) was the closest to a spiritual guide Newman had in his Anglican years, almost until the very eve of his reception into the Catholic Church. Most of the time this guidance was by letter since the two never reached face-to-face intimacy, given the short periods of time Keble spent in Oxford and also because Keble was almost ten years his elder. Newman admired him deeply because, after a legendary "double first" when he was just eighteen, Keble had resigned all the privileges of an Oxford don that so many—including young Newman—coveted, and instead "buried himself" in rural parishes as a pastor of souls. Still a fellow of Oriel, Keble had an influence in Oxford through his disciples whom he would gather in study parties before the exams: people like Robert Wilberforce, Isaac Williams, and Hurrell Froude, who in due course would become intimate with Newman and integral to the Movement.

Keble could have been elected Provost of Oriel College but, ironically, Newman managed to get the other candidate elected. And this new Provost,

---

26 *LD* xi, 9.
27 *LD* xx, 503.
28 *LD* xxii, 51.
29 See *LD* xxii, 52–53.

Edward Hawking, turned out to become one of Newman's lifelong antagonists. Newman relished finding God, hidden in nature and present in Anglican liturgy through Keble's verses in *The Christian Year* (1827). Keble was one of the last of a nearly extinguished race in England: the Non-Jurors, a group of clerics who refused to swear allegiance to the new King William of Orange in 1688 because of their previous allegiance to the former, and still-living Catholic king, the Stuart James II. These clerics espoused the theology of the Caroline Divines: a high regard for the sacraments and the liturgy, belief in the apostolic succession of bishops, and the divine origin and catholicity of the Church. Keble handed Hurrell Froude all these traditional doctrines, while Newman, still a Calvinist with liberal leanings and friends, was an untrustworthy Common Room colleague. But in due course Hurrell made his new friend acquainted with those doctrines and Newman absorbed them deeply and spread them across England and beyond. It could be argued that the Oxford Movement was a vigorous revival of those "Church principles" that cost Archbishop Laud and King Charles I their heads. Keble wrote nine of the *Tracts for the Times*, and he reportedly said that if the Church of England perished, it could still be found in his parish.[30]

Edward Pusey (1800–1882), a member of an aristocratic family, an erudite and somber man, in part due to the illness of various close family members, was shy and reserved. With time, he and Newman developed a close tie and friendship. It was Pusey who, in tears, officiated in the Eucharistic service at which Newman preached his last sermon "The Parting of Friends" and acted for the last time as a minister of the Anglican Church. On that September 25, 1843, in the little church of Littlemore, before one hundred and fifty attendants Newman bade farewell to his parishioners. The future barrister, Edward Bellasis, then only a distant admirer, tried to describe to his wife the sorrow and solemnity of the event.[31]

DISCIPLES

The first of Newman's student disciples was Isaac Williams (1802–1865), the poet of the Movement, a steady Tractarian, who was equipped with an invincible antipathy towards the Church of Rome. During his Mediterranean journey Newman wrote to him abundantly because Williams was then his curate at St. Mary's and would also later be his curate, and his main support, at Littlemore. Williams remained deeply attached to Newman in spite of the "catastrophe" of October 1845. Williams belonged to the circle of Keble, authored a controversial *Tract* (No. 80) and has to be given credit for his co-editing ten volumes of *Plain Sermons by Contributors to the Tracts for the Times* (1839–1848) with a view to

---

30 Owen Chadwick, *The Spirit of the Oxford Movement: Tractarian Essays* (Cambridge: Cambridge University Press, 1995), 62.

31 Edward Bellasis, *Memorials of Mr Serjeant Bellasis, 1800–1873*, 3rd ed. (London: Burns Oates and Washbourne) 1923, 63–65.

calm the hysteria brought about by the publication of Froude's *Remains* through a more palatable Tractarianism. But it was of little avail. When, soon after, the Professorship of Poetry at Oxford was to be appointed, and though Williams was the most obvious candidate, he was forced to give up his candidacy due to his Tractarian affiliations. Williams lived his last twenty years discretely and in poor health. Newman knew that Williams had always been an affectionate friend and visited him in Stinchcombe shortly before his death. In 1857, Newman lengthened and reworded the dedication to Williams of *The Church of the Fathers* (1840).

William Copeland (1804–1885) seems to be of a type with Isaac Williams: he was a High Church clergyman, a fellow of Trinity college, and the co-editor with Williams of the above-mentioned *Plain Sermons*. He also was Newman's curate in Littlemore during the last years. Even more reserved than Isaac, and almost invisible, he felt so frustrated that the Catholic Church didn't allow any reunion with Anglicans that he made a point that none of Newman's letters to him should ever end up in Catholic hands after his death. But he sincerely loved Newman and was one of the very few who saw him off the evening of February 23, 1846, when Newman left Oxford for good.

The diffident Copeland proved crucial for Newman fifteen years later in June 1862 when the two estranged friends literally bumped into each other in the streets of London. Copeland was soon to visit Newman in Birmingham and stayed at the Oratory. Word got around of this visit and friends and disciples on the other side of the fence started to write and then to show up in the house of the lost, but never forgotten, Newman. These newly recovered friends would come to the rescue soon after, in 1864, when Newman was thrown into the controversy with Charles Kingsley, which gave rise to *Apologia Pro Vita Sua*.

Henry Arthur Woodgate (1801–1874), once a fellow of St John's College, Oxford, was an obscure cleric—there is no entry for him in the *Oxford Dictionary of National Biography*—and the incumbent of a rural church near Birmingham, the city where Newman spent the best part of his forty-five years as a Catholic. They had befriended each other at least by the end of 1828; Woodgate was with the Newmans in Brighton when young Mary died suddenly in January 1829. Woodgate dedicated his Bampton Lectures of 1839 to Newman who was godfather to his elder daughter. Newman hinted at him in *Apologia* as one of "the two persons who knew me best at that time . . . still alive, beneficed clergymen, no longer my friends."[32] Woodgate immediately wrote to let Newman know that he didn't complain about such words, but he had always kept him in the highest regard and affection. From then on, Woodgate visited the Oratory and Rednal, the recreation estate owned by the Oratorians a few miles off Edgbaston (Birmingham). Newman managed to be near Woodgate shortly before his death, as he had done with Mark Pattison, who had once been a Tractarian.

---

32 *Apo.*, 16.

Samuel Rickards (1796–1865) was "the other" one who knew Newman best at that time. A close friend of the family and an Oriel man both as a student and then as a fellow, they had met briefly in college. Over the first half of 1833 they corresponded frequently since Rickards was deeply involved in the Movement at the time when the constitutional reforms kept Anglican clergymen extremely concerned. But soon there emerged disagreements between them and they parted ways for ever. Nevertheless, one of Newman's nephews—a son of Jemima's—was given Rickards as his middle name.

ORIEL:
CONVERTS AND NON-CONVERTS BUT FRIENDS

Newman had close ties with the Wilberforce family, whose head was William (1759–1833), the "emancipator," or politician, who brought about the end of slave traffic within the British Empire. From among his children, Robert Wilberforce (1802–1857) was a colleague at Oriel and a close friend. Henry was probably his dearest disciple. Both Robert and Henry went to Oriel, became Tractarians, and followed Newman into the Catholic Church. The former was a brilliant student and sided with Newman and Froude in the controversy over the new tutorial system; it seems that it was actually he who first had the idea which, typically, Newman took up and brought to the final consequences. After their dismissal as tutors, Robert left Oxford and married, and the daily intercourse came to an end just as Robert became the main theological mind of post-Newman Tractarianism. Up to 1854 after a long religious crisis, Robert went to Paris and was quietly received into the Catholic Church.

Newman's relation with the younger Henry Wilberforce (1807–1873) was entirely like that of a father and son; it had much to do with the Newmanian ideal of the celibate apostle he wanted for himself and others. Newman had a soft spot for Henry after four Long Vacations "reading" for exams in rented cottages in the countryside along with a few other students. Henry was a brilliant and enthusiastic Tractarian, but he had a volatile character. After toying with a career as a lawyer, he ended up taking up orders. When the disciple-son thought of getting married, he feared the master-father would feel disappointed in him and found the worst way out: he asked Newman's sister Harriet to tell her brother that he was going to get married. But Harriet never told her brother. When he finally got the news, Newman drafted a letter to Henry, which he never sent. The letter opened: "My poor dear foolish Henry, Dear, for auld lang syne—foolish, for being suspicious of me—poor, because I suppose you have been pained at your own suspicions."[33] The intimacy between beloved master and beloved disciple was mended and never lost again. This explains why, years later, amid the austerities of Littlemore, Henry often came to Newman's mind.

---

33 *LD* iv, 169.

In 1840 Newman was, at last, finishing off an extremely private account of his illness in Sicily, tracing God's hand and Providence during those weeks in the island and the experience of his near death. In the last paragraphs, Henry is mentioned and linked with Newman's desire for self-dedication to God and celibacy as a protest against worldliness:

> The thought keeps pressing on me, while I write this, what am I writing for? For myself, I may look at it once or twice in my whole life, and what sympathy is there in *my* looking at it? Whom have I, whom can I have, who would take interest in it? I was going to say, I only have found one who even took that sort of affectionate interest in me as to be pleased with such details—and that is Henry Wilberforce, and what shall I ever see of him?[34]

Henry became a Catholic in 1850, soon after his wife. Having resigned a rich benefice of one thousand pounds a year, Henry was forced to work for a living as a writer and a journalist for the next twenty years. He bought the *Weekly Register* and made this weekly Catholic paper an organ of more balanced views than those coming from the ultramontane *Tablet* and other periodicals. In April 1873 Newman wrote to his sister Jemima about the days he spent in the house of a worn-out, dying Henry. Newman travelled there at the end of the month to preach at Henry's funeral. His children collected and published Henry's writings as *The Church and the Empires;* the opening was a biographical note by Newman.

At a similar level of intimacy and expectations on the part of a master was Frederic Rogers (1811–1889), Newman's last pupil at Oriel. The conversion of Newman, nevertheless, proved a severe setback in the friendship with this man who would become a top-ranking civil servant for colonial affairs in the British Empire. Rogers was said to have made his way from Eton into Oriel College as the result of a request from Newman to one of the masters there to send him the best pupils. Rogers entered Oriel in 1828, got the only "double first" of 1832, and was elected fellow of the college next year. Newman, unable to vote for him in the elections because he was away on his Mediterranean trip, was slightly regretful about his absence and worried in case things went the wrong way. Always diligent, he wrote to the Provost from Gibraltar to fill him in on confidential and relevant details concerning Rogers's family financial affairs.[35] Newman got the news about Rogers's election in Palermo by the chance reading of a newspaper that he could not help kissing in excitement. Newman had been Rogers's tutor, supervised his reading, and let him stay in his own rooms at Oriel at no charge so that he did not have to go home to prepare for the elections. Rogers was, as were some of Newman's other close disciples, a frequent visitor at Iffley, where

---

34 *AW*, 137.
35 See *LD* iii, 140.

Newman's mother and sisters lived. Having Newman as *paterfamilias* to provide his two sisters with husbands, he had envisaged that "something" on the way of an engagement might occur between sisters and disciples.

At some stage Newman realized that the periods of intimacy with several friends—*contubernium* he called them—spanned precisely seven years. That had been the case with Froude between 1827 and 1834, and it was later to apply to Rogers from 1833 to 1840.[36] The melancholy remark came as a result of Rogers being one of the very few to whom Newman had disclosed his serious misgivings about the Church of England. In 1843 Rogers decided to separate from his teacher: "I do not like to meet you again without having said, once for all, what I hope you will not think me hollow or false. I cannot disguise from myself how very improbable, perhaps impossible a recurrence of our former terms is."[37] It was reassuring that loyal Rogers spoke highly of Newman as a friend during the controversy over *Tract* 90. When both met again in Birmingham in 1863, Rogers "burst into tears, and would not let go my hands; then his first words were 'How altered you are.'" Immediately, they resumed their contact and again became "like two clocks keeping time."[38] Up to 1845 Rogers continued as a fellow of the college but his home base was divided between Oriel and London where he met the lawyer James Hope, with whom he spent a winter in Rome, and group of laymen and Tractarians, who like Hope, were part of the circle of the future Prime Minister William Gladstone. While at Oxford, Rogers had made an intimate friendship with Richard W. Church, future dean of St. Paul's, and travelled one summer with him around the North of France. The reason for tracing these details is to indicate the fluid network of Tractarian circles and friendships, which though numerous were closely interconnected. After leaving Oxford, Rogers's public career in London quickly rose, and although already a baronet through family, he became the first civil servant to be knighted as Baron Blachford. He spent his last twenty years in his large estate, near Dartington, the place where another one for whom Newman had great affection, Hurrell Froude, had died many years before.[39]

Richard W. Church (1815–1890) or *Dean* Church of St. Paul's, London, signaled as a key moment in his life a precise afternoon in February 1836 when he listened to Newman preaching one of his memorable parochial sermons, "The Ventures of Faith." That Sunday Church felt a direct call to a more religious life.[40] Although coming from an Evangelical college, Wadham, Church won an Oriel fellowship against Mark Pattison. In Oriel he became intimate with Newman and

---

36 See Henry Tristram, *Newman and His Friends* (London: John Lane, 1933), 122.

37 *LD* ix, 301, note 5.

38 *LD* xx, 513.

39 For the "friendship violin" which Rogers and Church gave Newman in 1865, see *LD* xxi, 503; and *LD* xxix, 213–14 for the Brougham Carriage present on being made a cardinal.

40 Tristram, *Newman and His Friends*, 183.

Rogers in the momentous years between 1841 and 1845. Church did translation work for the *Library of the Fathers* and, being a proctor, had the courage to veto the formal censure by the University of Newman's *Tract* 90 against the heads of Houses and the vice-chancellor, who had incited it. The following year, Church visited the Radcliffe Observatory where Newman was spending his last night in Oxford to see him off. Many years later, then a cardinal and eighty-five years old, Newman spent three days with the Churches in their London house next to St. Paul's. This was one of his last trips away from Birmingham. All three of Church's daughters were immensely fond of Newman, and one of them received from him the so-called "friendship violin" when Newman was no longer able to play it. He had probably got too attached to the violin as he was attached to that old blue cloak many years before. According to one of the girls in that household Newman "was a name apart."[41] And Church himself in an obituary for the *Guardian* would make it abundantly clear "how unique he was." His classic book *The Oxford Movement: Twelve Years, 1833–1845* exudes reverence—perhaps too much—for his friend.

THREE LAWYERS

We can easily single out a compact group of three lawyers, all three committed Tractarians, all three converts to Catholicism, all three a firm support for Newman at different moments of his life: Hope-Scott, Bellasis, and Badeley. Moreover, as laymen, the three most likely strengthened the insights about the role of the laity within the Church that Newman brought with him from the Anglican tradition and through his own familiarity with the early Church.[42]

James Robert Hope-Scott (1812–1873), the son of the founder and first governor of the Royal Military College, Sandhurst, was a parliamentary barrister who specialized in legislation for railways, which was at that time the great social revolution. His overwhelming brilliance and professional competence gained him a fortune that he gave away largely to charities, the building of churches and schools, and the Catholic cause. In Scotland alone he spent 40,000 pounds on such endeavors in the last years of his life. His career included Eton College (1828), Christ Church (1829), and a fellowship at college (1833), where he also served as bursar. His life as a barrister and his great friendship with Newman began more or less at the same time, in 1838.

Hope's way into the Catholic Church resembles that of Newman: the long crisis of a Tractarian culminating in the Jesuit church on Farm Street, London. The conferences Newman gave in 1850 about the Anglican prejudices against the Catholic Church (*Certain Difficulties Felt by Anglicans in Catholic Teaching*)

---

41   Tristram, *Newman and His Friends*, 193.
42   See ch. 26 in this volume, "Newman's Farsighted Understanding of the Laity's Role in the Church," by Juan R. Vélez.

made a real impression on him and helped him to take the final step. He was a man of deep piety and exemplary conduct, universally sought after as an adviser. "Ask Hope" became a common saying in the Birmingham Oratory before making decisions. When sounded out about the Catholic University of Ireland, he characteristically replied "First, get Newman."[43] An unhappy concurrence of circumstances came together to produce many tribulations and exhaustion: being an Englishman in Ireland, a convert from Anglicanism, starting a university in a hungry and gentryless Ireland; and all this on the heels of the unjust Achilli trial, a libel case in which Newman was found guilty and nearly sent to prison. Hope staunchly supported Newman and offered him Abbotsford, his country house south of Edinburgh, as a place to rest. Newman spent six weeks there at his bishop's command, recovering from chronic exhaustion. Abbotsford had previously belonged to Sir Walter Scott and Hope had inherited the estate through his first wife, a granddaughter of the novelist. This is the reason why he changed his name to Hope-Scott.

Hope was a principal adviser and fundraiser for both the Oratory School and the failed Oratory Mission in Oxford. The life of this man, charming and nevertheless reserved, included a heavy quota of suffering. His first wife, who had become a Catholic, died at the birth of their second child, who also died. His other child died also shortly after, while still only one-year old. Three years later Hope married a daughter of the 15th Duke of Norfolk, who also died days after giving birth to a son. This second blow happened in 1870, and poor Hope never recovered. He gave up his legal practice, and his health declined. His daughter would remember the deep-seated melancholy of her father and her own terror to find him crying after the death of his wife.[44] Hope died only three years later in his London house (7 Hyde Park Place): "In the afternoon, dear papa . . . said out loud his favourite prayer, *Fiat, laudetur, atque in aeternum superexaltetur, justissima, altissima, et amabilissima voluntas Dei in omnibus. Amen.*"[45] From 1903 Hyde Park Place became the site of Tyburn Convent, a community of Benedictine nuns. Two beautiful plaques found there keep alive the memory of the two great friends.

On April 29, 1873, Newman preached at the funeral of Henry Wilberforce at Stroud, Gloucestershire. Upon his return to Birmingham Newman found on his desk a telegram with the news of Hope's death. A few days later, Newman would travel on one of those trains his friend had contributed to expand to preach a poignant sermon whose title wonderfully summarizes Hope's entire life: "In the world but not of the world."[46] In that same church on Farm Street, both Hope and his friend Archbishop Manning, there attending the funeral, had been received

---

43 *LD* xxi, 549.

44 Maisie Ward, *Unfinished Business* (London: Sheed and Ward, 1964), 15.

45 Robert Ornsby, *Memoirs of James Robert Hope-Scott of Abbotsford*, vol. 2 (London: John Murray, 1884), 246.

46 *OS*, no. 14: 263–80.

into the Catholic Church in the same ceremony years earlier. The portrait of this remarkably handsome man features prominently among those Newman hung on a wall in his study and bedroom in Birmingham.

Edward Bellasis (1800–1873), did not discover Newman and Tractarianism in Oxford, but through a Tractarian circle in London—whose existence owes a lot to Samuel F. Wood, another too-soon-departed close friend of Newman.[47] At the church of All Saints on Margaret Street, where Bellasis worshiped on a daily basis, a number of young lawyers would congregate during the 1830s, precisely the years of the first constitutional reforms in England, strongly drawn by the idea of a Church of England reformed in a Catholic fashion.

Bellasis's bond with Newman was increasing and determined; initially, through reading *Tracts* and sermons. Deeply impressed, Bellasis chose to return to London from the Isle of Wight via Oxford—which is not, precisely, on the way—in order to hear Newman preach in person. Next year, 1839, equipped with a letter of introduction, Bellasis set foot in Oriel College to meet the vicar of St. Mary's. As mentioned earlier he was present and narrated in a moving manner Newman's farewell as an Anglican cleric in Littlemore in 1843. Bellasis was sick of the Protestant prejudices against the Church of Rome, and also deeply edified by the simplicity with which the old landed Catholics would say their prayers in their country house chapel before going hunting in their red coats and riding boots; or by the devotion with which the lady of the same country house would prepare the altar linen for Mass and genuflect before the Blessed Sacrament.[48] From his entry into the Catholic Church, along with his wife and children in 1850, and up to his death, Bellasis was a constant support and an unfailing stay for Newman.

Many ties and a few common endeavors linked Bellasis and his close friend James Hope-Scott. Bellasis was an outstanding man of the law as *Serjeant at Law*—one of the three main London magistrates. He rushed to help Newman in the Achilli trial and, thinking of his many sons and the sons of other fellow converts, insisted that Newman should start a Catholic boarding school as similar as possible to the *public schools* where they themselves had been educated. The outcome was the Oratory School in Birmingham. It was customary that if going to or coming from the Parliament buildings he coincided in the cab with Hope-Scott each would pull out their rosaries from their pockets and pray it on their way back home. If the ride was in the company of a priest or headed for a Catholic building, Bellasis would generously tip the driver in order to blow away his almost certain anti-Catholic prejudices. Although not particularly rich, he owned a house in Hyères, in the south of France, where he would spend the winter, next to Villa Madonna, the estate of Hope-Scott. Both died

---

47   James Pereiro, *'Ethos' and the Oxford Movement: At the Heart of Tractarianism* (Oxford: Oxford University Press, 2008), 14–25.

48   See Bellasis, *Memorials of Mr Serjeant Bellasis*, 117.

within four months of each other. In between the date of their deaths another of Newman's intimates, Henry Wilberforce, died in 1873; it was a truly *deadly* year for Newman.

Bellasis's great goodness would catch people's eyes and hearts. He used to say that the "greatest of pleasures is giving pleasure. The next best thing to cultivate is a pain in giving pain. Two feelings to be suppressed: the pleasure in giving pain, and the pain in giving pleasure."[49] This offers a nice variation to Newman's theme regarding a gentleman: "one who never inflicts pain."[50] He loved a joke in the *Punch*: "If you have nothing to say, say it and sit down!" With such a disarming character—Bellasis was said to "find a good side to a bad shilling"—deserved that Newman, when dedicating the *Grammar of Assent* to him, described their long friendship as "sunny."[51] The Bellasis family remained always close to Newman. Out of Bellasis's thirteen children, two became Oratorians at Birmingham and three became nuns.

Edward Badeley (1803–1868) played a decisive role in two moments of Newman's life: the Achilli trial and the *Apologia*. Giovanni Achilli (1803–1860) was a womanizer and former Dominican from the Papal States who declared himself a Protestant and, invited by the Evangelical Alliance, was welcomed by the Foreign Office and then travelled across the country leading massive anti-Catholic rallies; this was part of the "No Popery!" campaign of 1850, which accompanied the restoration of the Catholic hierarchy and the wave of conversions of prominent Anglicans following the Gorham case. In one of his conferences in *The Present Position of Catholics in England,* Newman directly spoke of several misdemeanors by Achilli, who sued Newman for libel. Badeley and other legal advisers were unable to prevent Newman—more than anything a victim of the collective hysteria—of being found guilty of libel by a prejudiced jury and by an anti-Catholic judge. The magistrate accepted as a proof what clearly was a false testimony by Achilli, and did not allow Newman to read his allegation, and furthermore rejected proofs and witnesses on the part of the accused. Newman blamed the scandal and trial for the death of his sister Harriet.

Apologia Pro Vita Sua, arguably Newman's greatest book, was the occasion of a brilliant comeback from obscurity and oblivion into general esteem by the public opinion of Victorian society. The *Apologia*'s origin lies in the insolent calumny by Charles Kingsley, a then-popular clergyman and novelist who accused Newman, and the whole Catholic clergy, of a systematic disregard for truth. In response to Newman's protest, Kingsley offered apologies that Newman and especially Badeley found wanting and unacceptable. Written in a few frantic weeks, between April and June 1864, Newman published, in installments, an overwhelming narrative of his conversion in which he at last gave the history

49 Bellasis, *Memorials of Mr Serjeant Bellasis*, 127.
50 *Idea*, 208.
51 Dedication, *GA*.

of his religious opinions, explaining in full daylight how and why he became a Roman Catholic. When, physically and emotionally exhausted after many days of up to twenty solid hours writing and thereby reawakening the past, the last of the issues was published, few readers in England remembered the "reckless" Anglican clergyman. But without the sturdy advise from Badeley, it is unlikely that the *Apologia* would have ever come to be.

Badeley's conversion had a similar course to those of his friends, Hope and Bellasis. An Oxford man, Badeley was called to the Bar in 1841 and became an expert in navigating the maze of ecclesiastical legislation. He took a prominent part in the Gorham case (1850), a legal case after which many Tractarians could no longer bear with the Church of England and went over to Rome. Badeley was one of those Tractarians, as was also the case with the future Archbishop and Cardinal, Edward Manning, as well as Bellasis and Hope-Scott. Newman was always deeply grateful to Badeley, although his friendship to Newman did not compare to that which Newman had with the two other convert lawyers. When Hope found out that Badeley was ill in London, where he lived as a bachelor in rooms at the Inner Temple, he travelled all the way from Hyères and visited him daily and remained at his bedside until Badeley's death.

FRIENDSHIPS, OLD AND NEW

Newman's Catholic years as an Oratorian explain the tribute he paid to his brothers (and spiritual sons) members of the Birmingham Oratory, of whom there were only six:

> I have closed this history of myself with St. Philip's name upon St. Philip's feast-day; and, having done so, to whom can I more suitably offer it, as a memorial of affection and gratitude, than to St. Philip's sons, my dearest brothers of this House, the Priests of the Birmingham Oratory, Ambrose St John, Henry Austin Mills, Henry Bittleston, Edward Caswall, William Paine Neville, and Henry Ignatius Dudley Ryder? who have been so faithful to me; who have been so sensitive of my needs; who have been so indulgent to my failings; who have carried me through so many trials; who have grudged no sacrifice, if I asked for it; who have been so cheerful under discouragements of my causing; who have done so many good works, and let me have the credit of them; with whom I have lived so long, with whom I hope to die.[52]

Having said this, Newman dedicates a special paragraph to Ambrose St John, the last of these micro-biographies. St John (1815–1875), a Christ Church man who had probably listened to Newman's parochial sermons at St. Mary's,

---

52 *Apo.,* 283.

was Henry Wilberforce's curate (1841–1843) until his growing religious doubts and misgivings prompted him to go to Littlemore with a view of living for a time a semi-monastic life with Newman. But after that he never parted from Newman. The latter would see a particular providence in that his beloved disciple Henry Wilberforce sent him another beloved disciple in the person of St John, who became a Catholic a few days before Newman—without waiting for Newman to be received in the Catholic Church. St John went to Rome with Newman, was ordained together with him, and lived with him together as an Oratorian in Birmingham, as his right hand in the priestly work there, in the failed translation project of the Bible, and in governing the Oratory. Ambrose, a competent linguist in both modern and classical languages, who was very keen on Oriental languages such as Hebrew and Syriac, had been a student of Pusey. He mastered French, Italian, German and Spanish—Newman could only read French and bits of Italian—and had his own literary projects separate from Newman's. In January 1862, St John left all those things he so relished doing when Newman asked him to take over the Oratory School, then a sinking boat. His staunch loyalty and devotion to Newman deserved a hundred times this wonderful tribute that so keenly caught George Eliot's sensitive eye[53]:

> And to you especially, dear Ambrose St John; whom God gave me, when He took every one else away; who are the link between my old life and my new; who have now for twenty-one years been so devoted to me, so patient, so zealous, so tender; who have let me lean so hard upon you; who have watched me so narrowly; who have never thought of yourself, if I was in question.[54]

There was more to add, though, to this memorable ending to the *Apologia*. Asthmatic and worn out, Ambrose had recently left the Oratory School when, in order to help Newman in the commotion after the dogmatic declaration of infallibility, he overworked himself translating a book by patristic scholar Joseph Fessler (1813–1872), *Die Wahre und die falsche Unfehlbarkeit der Päpste [The True and the False Infallibility of the Popes]*. Newman, who could not read German, badly needed to know the views of Fessler, the Secretary of the Vatican Council at which the doctrine was declared, before finishing his *Letter to the Duke of Norfolk* in reply to William Gladstone's accusations (*The Vatican decrees in their bearing on civil allegiance: a political expostulation* (1874–1875) that English Catholics could not be loyal to both an infallible pope and to the Queen. Given the political and religious circumstances—there were a good deal of ultramontane Catholics in England at that time—Newman could not afford the slightest mistake or misunderstanding.

---

53   Tristram, *Newman and His Friends*, 221.
54   *Apo.*, 283.

St John managed to finish the translation and publish it in time,[55] but he became sick and a few months later lost the use of his reason and died unexpectedly. Newman, who regularly visited the place where Ambrose was trying to recover, was not present at his death. In a letter to a female correspondent, Newman wrote that the last time both were together, Ambrose "threw his arms about my neck and said he loved no one as he loved me."[56] Writing to Rogers, nevertheless, Newman hid his emotions and even said "in joke 'He will give me a stiff neck,'"[57] referring to the close hug that Ambrose had given him. Newman had not understood this affectionate gesture at the time, and this would fill him with distress. He would reproach himself because he had failed to express to Ambrose "how much I felt *his* love."[58] As a way of making up for it, Newman specified in strong terms,[59] that he was to be buried in the same tomb as St John, and so it was done.

"As far as this world was concerned I was his first and last."[60] Nevertheless, St John was not a mere appendix to "the great man." They were quite different in character, qualities, and preferences. Newman relished and loved music, was an accomplished violinist, composed and arranged hymns, but he could not stand such things as tobacco. Ambrose would smoke good cigars with gusto, had no ear at all for music, but did paint with some skill. Newman was a born teacher and educator in a family devoid of real pedigree. Ambrose, who was from aristocratic descent and enjoyed private means, devoted himself to teaching, not by choice but out of devotion for Newman. The ever grateful friend closes his *Apologia*:

> And in you [Ambrose St John] I gather up and bear in memory those familiar affectionate companions and counsellors, who in Oxford were given to me, one after another, to be my daily solace and relief; and all those others, of great name and high example, who were my thorough

---

55 Joseph Fessler and Ambrose St John, *The True and the False Infallibility of the Popes: A Controversial Reply to Dr. Schulte* (London: Burns and Oates, 1875).

56 *LD* xxvii, 304.

57 *LD* xxvii, 306.

58 *LD* xxvii, 311. A very similar feeling seems to have occurred with the loss of Froude in 1836: "He afterwards, Henry Wilberforce told me [Tom Mozley], lamented with tears (not a common thing for him) that he could not see Froude just to tell him how much he felt that he had owed to him in the clearing and strengthening of his views." Mozley, *Letters*, vol. 2, 154.

59 Alan Bray has said all that is fitting to say about loyalty, sworn brotherships, and shared tombs from Achilles and Patroclus's to Newman and St John's: Alan Bray, *The Friend* (Chicago: University of Chicago Press, 2003), 289–306. Admiral Nelson, one-armed, one-eyed and a moribund, famously said "Kiss me, Hardy" to Captain Thomas Hardy, his second in command aboard HMS Victory. Oliver Warner, *A Portrait of Lord Nelson* (London: The Reprint Society, 1958), 310.

60 *LD* xxvii, 305.

friends, and showed me true attachment in times long past; and also those many younger men, whether I knew them or not, who have never been disloyal to me by word or deed; and of all these, thus various in their relations to me, those more especially who have since joined the Catholic Church.[61]

CONCLUSION

John Henry Newman had many friends, some intimate ones who died early on (Bowden and Hurrell), others lifelong ones who remained Anglican (Keble, Pusey and Rogers), and yet others who became Roman Catholic and shared deeply in his life's work (Ambrose St John, Henry William Wilberforce, James R. Hope-Scott, Edward Bellasis and Edward Badeley), and many others, including the spouses and sisters of some of his friends. His friendships constitute a sort of a treatise comparable to any of his theological masterpieces.

Newman followed a vocational call to celibacy in which he lived a special and intimate friendship with God, but this calling did not remove him from others; rather it enabled him to serve them generously with a big heart and to develop wonderful friendships. He treasured his many friendships as God's gifts. These relationships were sincere, affectionate, and lifelong. They were, indeed, a foretaste of heaven on earth. Human friendship opened his eyes both to a personal friendship with Jesus Christ, and to a blessed communion with the many relations and departed friends in purgatory[62] whom he could still love and help from here below; friends whom he expected to meet again on the Resurrection, on the Last Day.

Suggested Reading

Bellasis, Edward. *Memorials of Mr Serjeant Bellasis, 1800–1873*. 3rd ed. London: Burns Oates and Washbourne, 1923.

Chadwick, Owen. "The Limitations of Keble." In *The Spirit of the Oxford Movement: Tractarian Essays,* 54–62. Cambridge: University Press, 1995.

Froude, Richard Hurrell. *Remains of the Late Reverend Richard Hurrell Froude, MA Fellow of Oriel College, Oxford*. 4 vols. Edited by J. H. Newman and J. Keble. London: Rivington, 1838–1839.

Mozley, Anne, ed. *Letters and Correspondence of John Henry Newman During His Life in the English Church*. 2 vols. London, New York and Bombay: Longmans, Green, and Co., 1903.

---

61 *Apo.,* 283–84.

62 James Tolhurst, "A Blessed and Ever Enduring Fellowship: The Development of John Henry Newman's Thoughts on Life and Beyond," *Recusant History* 22, no. 3 (1995): 424–57.

Ornsby, Robert. *Memoirs of James Robert Hope-Scott of Abbotsford*. 2 vols. London: John Murray, 1884.

Shrimpton, Paul. "More Poet than Policeman: Newman and Education 'in a large sense of the word,'" *Scripta Theologica* 51, no. 3 (2019): 775–800.

Tristram, Henry. *Newman and His Friends*. London: John Lane, 1933.

Ward, Maisie. *Unfinished Business*. London: Sheed and Ward, 1964.

CHAPTER 6

COMPLETING THE ALBUM: ST. JOHN HENRY NEWMAN AND HIS FEMALE CIRCLE OF FRIENDS

Barbara H. Wyman

Photography transformed forever how people, places, and events are viewed and remembered. Even the most realistic artist's rendering of things cannot elicit the response as does, say, a snapshot from a friend standing on top of the Great Wall of China, his familiar height dwarfed by the Wall stretching into the horizon, impossible to comprehend, except we see it. Yet for all the realness photography brings us, there are disadvantages, especially with early photography. Most of us have that one portrait of ancestors, dressed in their Sunday best, sitting stiffly in an unknown studio, surrounded by their children, all somber, all unsmiling. There was an awkward posing, the subjects aware of the occasion's importance. Even if our mind knows that they were probably jolly and happy, we do not see it. We see serious and somber faces.

So it is with St. John Henry Newman. Existing photographs of him are the expected: a studious priest, in his library or with a volume in his hand. He always seems serious. Perhaps worse are the unflattering ones of the old, shrunken Newman, almost buried in his cardinal's regalia. It is hard not to imagine these pictures when we think of Newman. Nevertheless, there are a couple of him with a slight smile, and one with him tugging on his ear, a small but unexpected detail. Let us imagine which photographs would allow Newman to spring to life. What would complete an album of the whole Newman? There would have to be a walking Newman. He walked daily; he loved to walk and talk with others. There would be a Newman on horseback and a Newman playing the violin. There would be a Newman making faces at his sisters across the table. And most certainly, there would be a laughing Newman, perhaps slapping his knee, thinking of Trollope.[1] Additionally, a group of essential photographs for this album would be Newman with his female friends.[2] He had an incredible capacity for friendship with both women and men. A knowledge of these friendships is indispensable for understanding the whole Newman.

Newman's ease with women should come as no surprise, as he grew up in a close family with three precocious and intelligent sisters, along with a very capable mother with whom he had a close relationship. Newman had an intuitive sensitivity for what is now known as "the feminine genius."[3] Through his interactions with many women who made up his "Female Circle," we can witness how much he appreciated the feminine genius, and not only guided the vocations of his female friends but depended on their friendship as well. His letters to many of these women are discretely affectionate, showing a refined warmth of feeling for them.[4] There could be several photographs of Newman with these women friends, but two women in particular would be pictured throughout the whole of our imaginary album for both the duration and depth of their friendships. These two would be Maria Rosina Giberne and Frances Wootten.

MARIA ROSINA GIBERNE

Photographs of Newman with Maria Rosina Giberne (1802–1885) would be plentiful because it is she whose friendship with Newman was the most constant and devoted for the longest period of time, and it is she to whom Newman gave the most consistent encouragement in the various periods of their friendship, culminating with her vocation to the religious life when, at last, she became a nun.

---

1 Newman read and enjoyed Trollope greatly. Through their common friend Lord Emly, Trollope learned that Newman was amused by his novels. See Letter by Anthony Trollope to Newman and his reply (October 27–28, 1882) in *LD* xxix, 155.

2 These include Maria Holmes, a governess; Elizabeth Bowden, wife of Newman's friend William Bowden; Emily Bowles; Catherine Froude and her daughter Elizabeth; authors, Geraldine Penrose Fitzgerald, Lady Chatterton, and Lady Georgiana Fullerton; Lady Lothian, the Duchess of Norfolk; and Mrs. William Robinson Clark. See Edward Short, *Newman and His Contemporaries* (London: T & T Clark, 2011), 176–212. Joyce Sugg includes other friends and divides these into groups: the converts, the writers, the nuns, and nunnish ladies. See *Ever Yours Affly: John Henry Newman and His Female Circle* (Leominster: Gracewing, 1996).

3 John Paul II, Apostolic Letter *Mulieris Dignitatem: On the Dignity and Vocation of Women on the Occasion of the Marian Year* (August 15, 1988). The phrase "feminine genius," usually attributed to St. John Paul II, was originally outlined in exhortations of Pope Pius XII in 1957. Four aspects of this genius highlighted in *Mulieris*, key to the feminine contribution to aid humanity are: receptivity, sensitivity, generosity, and maternity. John Henry Newman showed through his interaction with his female friends that he appreciated these qualities.

4 See Sugg, *Ever Yours*, 25–27. This author has done excellent work of compiling Newman's most interesting and important correspondence with his female friends.

Maria Rosina Giberne was the sister-in-law of Walter Mayers. It was at the Mayers' where she met Frank Newman, who would introduce her later to his sisters. She was described by Tom Mozley, the husband of Newman's sister Harriett, as: "Tall, strong of build, majestic, with aquiline nose, well-formed mouth, dark penetrating eyes, and a luxuriance of glossy black hair; she would command attention anywhere."[5] Maria was evidently lovely and full of pluck. She had many talents; she played the harp, she drew and painted, and she wrote. She also spoke several languages. Her vivacious nature lasted throughout her life, even when she was an aged nun. She surely turned the head of Newman's brother Frank, who proposed to her at least twice. But she declined his offer each time. She was engaged to an Army officer named Robert Murcott, who went to India, where he died; however, he left her his money. Maria Rosina kept his picture with her until she entered the religious life, when she gave it up in a moment of scrupulosity.[6]

Maria was initially friends of the Newman sisters through Frank. She was there on the fateful night when the youngest sister Mary, aged 19, died suddenly, an event which marked John Henry for the entirety of his life.[7] It was with Mary that Newman had felt a very close bond of his three sisters. The shared experience of this tragic event especially drew him close to Maria Rosina, for she alone of his later friends knew Mary and could reminisce about her with him.[8] It is thanks to Maria's talent at drawing that we have Mary's portrait, one drawn with Harriet and one drawn postmortem as she lay on her death bed, the latter painting especially treasured by Newman.[9]

Maria was of Huguenot background, like John Henry's mother, and her family was inclined towards the evangelical branch of Anglicanism. Eventually she, like Newman, would also become a Tractarian and eventually a Roman Catholic.[10] Maria and Newman saw each other on her visits to Newman's family and began a lifelong correspondence, initially regarding the Oxford Movement but later concerning all sorts of topics.[11] She approached all of life, it seems, with fervor. As a Tractarian she slept on the floor, arising to say Matins at 3:00 a.m. In response to Newman's request that she author some popular material in support

---

5   See Giberne Sieveking, *Memoir and Letters of Frances W. Newman* (London: Kegan Paul, Trench, Trubner & Co, 1909). http://www.fullbooks.com/Memoir-and-Letters-of-Frances-W-Newman1.html. Ch 2.

6   See Maisie Ward, *Young Mr. Newman* (New York: Sheed and Ward, 1948), 171.

7   Newman described her death to his friend Robert I. Wilberforce. See *LD* ii, 49.

8   See Sugg, *Ever Yours*, 30–32; 286–87.

9   See Ward, *Young Mr. Newman*, 150.

10   Joyce Sugg mainly uses Maisie Ward and Meriol Trevor for biographical sources. See Maisie Ward, *Young Mr. Newman*, and Meriol Trevor's two-volume biography: *Newman, The Pillar of the Cloud* and *Newman, Light in the Winter* (Garden City, New York: Doubleday and Company, 1962).

11   See Rosario Athie, "'My Dear Miss Giberne' Newman's Correspondence with a Friend: 1826–1840," *Newman Studies Journal* 2, no. 1 (2005): 63. Roderick Strange's *John Henry Newman: A Portrait in Letters*, (Oxford: Oxford University Press, 2015), is a good companion to Joyce Sugg's book. This volume contains complete letters with an excellent introduction.

of the Oxford Movement, she tried her hand at writing a children's book, titled *Little Mary*. Newman not only proofread it and gave her feedback, but he saw to it that it was published. In a letter he told her that her story was "really quite beautiful"[12] and thanked her for a drawing of Christ Church which she had sent him. Newman asked her for help in disseminating the *Tracts for the Times*.[13] In 1845, two months after Newman became Catholic, so too did Maria Rosina.

For some years she lived in Rome, maintaining an artist's studio. She was there when Newman and Ambrose St John spent the year at Propaganda Fide College, studying Catholicism. Some believe she moved to Rome to be close to Newman. It is at this time that she painted Ambrose and John Henry at their books under a picture of the Blessed Virgin Mary. This painting was obtained by Newman to put outside the door of his room at the Oratory, where it remains today.[14]

It is within the context of the Achilli debacle that we can observe firsthand how much Newman appreciated the feminine genius of sensitivity, and in particular Maria Rosina's generosity, for he entrusted to her an incredibly important task. After Newman's lecture against the rogue and defrocked priest Giovanni Achilli, he was sued for libel by the anti-Catholic establishment in England. Achilli had been brought to England specifically to lecture on the evils of Catholicism. The English libel laws were so contorted that Newman could be charged with the most severe penalty. He desperately needed witnesses who could testify against the debauchery of Achilli. He asked Maria, at fifty years of age, to set off to Italy to fetch witnesses. She was fluent in French and Italian, and, showing her pluck, set off alone with a crucifix and New Testament.[15] Newman needed a woman with a feminine touch who could win the trust of the witnesses, the unfortunate women who had been abused by Achilli, to convince them to come back to England with Maria.[16] She was successful in convincing one witness, Elena, who (along with her husband, Vincenzo) was willing to make the arduous trek with her to England. All of her sensitivity was needed in dealing with the boorish Vincenzo.[17] Every step of the way she was afraid he would want to turn back, depriving Newman of an important witness in Elena.

The tales of this journey are humorous and endearing. We learn in one letter that she was having a hard time keeping Vincenzo entertained on the long trip, and Newman, revealing his sharp wit, wrote:

> We think you don't let Gippina's (Elena's) husband have cigars enough—
> let him have an unlimited supply. Let him have anything else he takes
> to—perhaps he would get tired if he rode in legno [the carriage] every

---

12   *LD* vi, 20.
13   See *LD* v, 137, 281.
14   See Sugg, *Ever Yours*, 82.
15   See Sugg, *Ever Yours*, 85–92.
16   *LD* xiv, 450, 457.
17   *LD* xv, 14, 29, 77.

day—but is there nothing else? Is there no equestrial exhibition? No harmless play? No giant or dwarf? No panorama, cosmorama, diorama, dissolving views, steam incubation of chickens, or menagerie which he would like to see? Surely beasts are just the thing for him. . . .[18]

Maria was successful in getting them to England, and Elena turned out to be credible and powerful. Nonetheless, Newman was found guilty by the anti-Catholic court. Yet out of her loyalty, generosity, and ingenuity, for five months Maria looked after this couple, even painting their portrait.

Newman was able to return Maria's kindness by encouraging her at an important spiritual turning point for her. Almost out of the blue, he had received a letter from Maria from Rome reporting that she had had a vision of the Blessed Virgin Mary,[19] who told her that she was called to be a nun. Maria, in her usual fervor, single-mindedly made the rounds of several different orders, which, because of her age, would not accept her. In this difficult time, Newman supported and encouraged her, generously writing letters of recommendation for her. His guidance even took the form of a mild correction. When she wrote a negative and uncharitable assessment of one Mother Superior, Newman wrote Maria that obedience needed to include charity.[20] When she was becoming despondent that she would never find a place, he suggested that she could, instead, live by a church, attend Mass frequently as possible, and live a life of prayer and painting, passing the time as best she could. He never discouraged her. However, her long pilgrimage finally paid off, and in late 1863 she found a home in the Visitation convent at Autun in France. Little did both dear friends know that they would never see each other again, though their robust correspondence would continue.[21]

From the time she entered the convent until her death in 1885, Newman's letters to Maria (now Sister Mary Pia), give us a window into their close friendship. The letters range from a sharing of his difficulties in meditating to answering her questions about biblical interpretation and the meaning of grammatical terms. They speak of everyday difficulties of growing older. Maria was still drawing and sketching and writing, and Newman encouraged this.[22]

One particularly touching letter to Maria Rosina, after the death of Ambrose St John, shows both Newman's capacity for friendship and his ability to express affection. Sister Maria Pia, who also loved Fr. Ambrose, was one of the first to hear

---

18 *LD* xv, 25.

19 Sugg, *Ever Yours*, 216–17 and Trevor, *Light in Winter*, 213.

20 Sugg, *Ever Yours*, 214–16.

21 During the last years of Maria's life, Newman continued to write to her. See *Letters and Diaries* in 1876 (xxviii, 94), 1881 (xxix, 371), 1882 (xxx, 109), 1883 (xxx, 255) and 1885 (xxx, 397). In the last one he wrote to her: "My oldest living friends are, besides you, Rogers and T. Mozley—is it not so?"

22 Trevor, *Light in Winter*, 573 and Sugg, *Ever Yours*, 220–21. In 1870, Newman wrote Charlotte Wood, that in the past eighteen months, Maria had brought her convent £80 from her paintings. *LD* xxv, 217.

of his death. Newman wrote her a long letter commiserating with her on their shared loneliness with the death of so many dear and close friends. He wrote:

> What a faithful friend he has been to me for thirty-two years! Yet there are others as faithful. What a wonderful mercy it is to me that God has given me so many faithful friends! He has never left me without support at trying (and other times), and I have never thanked you, as I ought to have done. This sometimes oppresses me, as if I was very ungrateful. You truly say that you have seen my beginning, middle and end. Since his death, I have been reproaching myself for not expressing to him how much I felt his love—and I write this lest I should feel the same about you, should it be God's will that I should outlive you. . . . [the Achilli matter] is only one specimen of the devotion, which by word and deed and prayer, you have been continually showing towards me most unworthy. . . .[23]

Newman also shared his ups and downs of being named Cardinal. On his way home from the ceremonies in Rome, he very much wanted to visit his beloved friend, knowing that age was upon them both. Unfortunately, John Henry contracted pneumonia and was too weak for the visit. Not long after, Maria died suddenly at age 83, which did not bring him grief; rather, he rejoiced that she would soon be in heaven. The sisters from the convent wrote to her old friend, now Cardinal Newman, that they had all loved Sister Mary Pia because she was vivacious and full of life.[24]

MRS. FRANCES WOOTTEN

The next photograph that would have to be in this album would depict another woman whom Newman knew for a very long time, Mrs. Frances Wootten. It is with Mrs. Wootten that Newman's appreciation of the feminine genius is perhaps the most impressive. In his attitude towards Mrs. Frances Wootten, Newman shows that he is aware of just how capable women can be in positions of authority. Newman saw in her maternal ways great generosity, sensitivity, and organizational skills.[25] At Oxford she had been the wife of a Tractarian physician, John Wootten, who had treated many leaders of the movement. After her husband's death, Mrs. Wootten became a Catholic and moved to Birmingham. Here Catholic converts, with prodding by Newman, considered starting a school for boys. After his frustrating experience at the founding a university in Dublin, he realized that a good school was needed to prepare boys for university life, a sort of Catholic Eton. The concept of this boys' school was both logical

---

23 *LD* xxvii, 311.
24 Sugg, *Ever Yours*, 220–21, and Trevor, *Light in Winter*, 629.
25 See Ian Ker, *John Henry Newman: A Biography* (Oxford: Oxford University Press, 1988), 189–90, 210, 504–7, and 734.

and sound, showing evidence of Newman's understanding of the importance of caring for the whole person. There was to be a headmaster in charge of the academic side, but Newman's prescience served him again, for he realized that young boys need more than rules and rigor. They also need love and affection. Newman realized that the human and religious side of the boys' development needed to be in hands of a sympathetic woman, known as a Dame, who would be appointed as the "Guardian of the Children." He knew from the beginning exactly who would fill the bill: Mrs. Frances Wootten. She was not only maternal and kind, but she was also intelligent and capable. And she was no shrinking violet. He had a high opinion of her, stating that she was "more like a saint than most people."[26] She likewise won the approval of the boys' parents, because in her generosity, she took the time to write them regularly. The mothers felt comfortable with asking her to do specific things for their young sons. Mrs. Wootten's feminine genius, her understanding of the needs of boys and mothers, helped make the school successful.[27] However, as was the custom at that time, caning was used for discipline in the classroom. It is here that Mrs. Wootten's sensitivity became extremely important. She realized that harsh corporal punishment could break the spirit of young boys. She became a courageous intercessor with Fr. Darnell, the headmaster, who was often too harsh. Despite the disagreements with Darnell, she was happy in the school, even donating some of her own funds as well as deeding her property to the Oratory in return for an annuity.[28]

The Oratory School was ahead of the time under Newman's presidency, allowing for a partnership between the headmaster and the Dame, giving equal stature to a woman in a leadership role. An example of Newman's confidence in Mrs. Wootten's leadership abilities came early. The headmaster, the Oratorian priest, Fr. Nicholas Darnell, disliked the sharing of authority and wanted Mrs. Wootten gone. Several altercations occurred where Mrs. Wootten's kind approach to a sick boy, for example, caused her to defy Fr. Darnell's demands.[29] In other areas as well, including the harsh caning, Mrs. Wootten would preempt Fr. Darnell. He did not like her authority and demanded her removal. Newman brought the problem to the parents, who unanimously stood behind Newman and Mrs. Wootten. Newman tried to keep Fr. Darnell at the school and told the Oratorians that Darnell and Mrs. Wootten were the two pillars of his undertaking,[30] but he reminded Darnell that school would not be what it was without his name (Newman's). Regrettably Fr. Darnell resigned and later left the Oratory. For Newman it was the greatest blow that the Oratory had suffered.[31]

---

26 *LD* xix, 188. For Newman, she was also a strong maternal figure. See Shrimpton, *A Catholic Eton? Newman's Oratory School* (Leominster: Gracewing, 2005), 91

27 Sugg, *Ever Yours*, 251–53 and Shrimpton, *A Catholic Eton?*, 87.

28 Shrimpton, *A Catholic Eton?*, 87.

29 Shrimpton, *A Catholic Eton?*, 104, 120 and Sugg, *Ever Yours*, 255.

30 *LD* xx, 86.

31 *LD* xx, 96, and Shrimpton, *A Catholic Eton?*, 127–31.

Newman believed that the success of the school was due to Mrs. Wootten's great care for the persons of the boys, both soul and body, and the parents would have agreed. The school had started with nine boys and in Newman's lifetime grew to eighty boys. A small school allowed maximum pastoral care, which was a central part of the Dame's charge. For its first seventeen years, Frances Wootten was the life of the school. She is a perfect example of a lay woman who flourished because of Newman's support and encouragement.[32] In turn, society and the Church benefitted. At her death, her doctor, who was not Catholic, said he had never met anyone like her—her one aim was to serve God, and she had no fear of death.[33] The Oratorians honored her so much that she was buried in their cemetery, the only woman who received such an honor.[34]

CELIBACY

The account of Newman's friendship with Maria Rosina Giberne, Mrs. Frances Wootten, and others[35] indicates Newman's appreciation for women and his affection for them. These friendships point to his natural inclination for the female sex and the goodness of marriage and the home. At age fifteen he consciously decided to embrace celibacy, which he felt was more conducive to a religious calling. His diary entries in the mid-1820s indicate a desire to serve God with a total dedication, particularly since at the time he wished to become a missionary.[36] Newman's thoughts would not have seemed as strange in his period as in

---

32 After Darnell sought Mrs. Wootten's dismissal, Newman wrote a friend, "Every woman's heart would have cried shame on me, if I had been the coward to banish, or permit to be banished a lady and benefactress, at a minute's warning, (whatever may be her alleged faults,) at the dictation of a lot of men." Letter to Mrs. Peter Bretherton, January 11, 1862, *LD* xx, 119.

33 Trevor, *Light in Winter*, 536.

34 Sugg, *Ever Yours*, 271.

35 Besides Maria Giberne and Frances Wootten, there were other women with whom Newman shared a longstanding friendship. One of these was Emily Bowles, to whom he also wrote a brief, loving letter after St. John's death: "Don't be surprised that I have written to some others before you—this is because I love you so much and trust you so well, that I have wanted to send you a longer letter than I could now. . . ." Letter to Emily Bowles, June 3, 1875, *LD*, xxvii, 309.

36 In the *Apologia* he recalls, "I am obliged to mention, though I do it with great reluctance, another deep imagination, which at this time, the autumn of 1816, took possession of me,—there can be no mistake about the fact; viz. that it would be the will of God that I should lead a single life . . . that my calling in life would require such a sacrifice as celibacy involved; as for instance, missionary work among the heathen, to which I had a great drawing for some years" (*Apo.*, 7). Similarly, he wrote, "I am conscious of horrible pride . . . but still I think the Missionary Office the highest privilege from God I can possess, though I speak blindly, it will not be wrong to pray to God to make me a Missionary" (*AW*, 75–76). Also "My Mother said the other day she hoped to live to see me married, but I think I shall either die within College walls, or as a missionary in foreign lands. . . ." 88.

our own. Married tutors were not allowed at Oxford, since the foundation of the university which was initially for the training of unmarried men, mostly for the priesthood. W. B. Young describes the seventeenth and eighteenth century debate in England between those in favor and against obligatory priestly celibacy. He notes, "The nature of specifically clerical celibacy, however, and its influence on the young Newman, have tended to be overlooked in favor of a general psychosexual understanding of his own unwillingness to marry."[37]

In correspondence with Pusey, Newman expresses the importance he envisioned for virginity and a celibate clergy.[38] It is in light of this ideal of service to God that Newman was initially disappointed with his younger friend Henry Wilberforce's decision to marry and hurt by Henry's failure to inform him directly of this choice. Beyond this, however, Newman, held that the virginity of a Christian soul is marriage with Christ. This idea is found in a draft of an unpublished 1854 sermon for the ceremony in which Marianne Bowden, the daughter of his late friend, was clothed as a bride of Christ in the Visitation Order.[39] For a man who is a priest the symbolism of a bride could be applied to the Church; his bride is the Church.[40]

Some have assumed that Newman's desire to remain celibate and his deep friendships with men suggest that he was attracted sexually to men.[41] Yet we find in the Letters and Diaries no mention of sexual desire for other men or of sexual improprieties with either gender. It is impossible to know Newman's sexual feelings, but his interest in celibacy for the sake of holiness and his tendency to be self-revelatory in his Letters and Diaries would suggest that we take his decision to be celibate at face value.

Deep emotional attachments to both women and men based on religious and human ideals are hardly an indication of sexual desires for them. Newman seems to have had a healthy balance in his friendships, which is evident in his Letters, in which he seems to have allowed himself freer rein than in everyday speech. He had deep friendships with both genders, and he tried to express his

---

37 B. W. Young, "Anglican Origins of Newman's Celibacy," *Church History* 65, no. 1 (March 1996): 15–27.

38 See *LD* vi, 283. For a theological explanation of Newman's view of marriage and celibacy, see Daniel Cere, "Newman's 'Lesson of the Marriage Ring': Celibacy and Marriage in the Thought of John Henry Newman," *Louvain Studies* 22 (1997): 59–84.

39 See Trevor, *The Pillar of the Cloud*, 90.

40 See Trevor, *The Pillar of the Cloud*, 91.

41 In 1933, Geoffrey Faber, in an apologia for homosexuality, suggests that Hurrell Froude had homosexual desires because Froude confessed to unspecified carnal desires. See *The Oxford Apostles: A Character Study of the Oxford Movement* (London: Faber and Faber, 1933), 218–22. From this, Faber gratuitously suggests the there was an undertone of sexuality to Newman and his celibate friends. See more recently J. M. I. Klaver, "The Apologia," in the *Oxford Handbook of John Henry Newman*, ed. Frederick D. Aquino and Benjamin J. King (Oxford: University Press, 2018), 471–72.

love for both men and women in an appropriate and honest manner.[42] In the case of women, his letters indicate special fondness for Maria Giberne, Frances Wootten, Elizabeth Bowden, and Emily Bowles.[43]

CONCLUSION

St. John Henry Newman was a genuine and devoted friend to many persons. He had many female friends with whom there would be photographs in the ideal album; he corresponded with and guided spiritually these women throughout his life. Knowing how much he appreciated and was loved by these women brings a depth of gratitude for his gift of celibacy, since a married Newman could not have had such close feminine ties. Newman showed a great capacity to understand and interact with women on many different levels. He encouraged each of his female friends in their own vocations: as wives, as mothers, as writers, as educators, and as nuns. Any number of them could be used as examples of his understanding of the feminine genius, but Maria Rosina Giberne and Frances Wootten are two of his closest friends who allow us deep insight into his appreciation and affection for women. Newman's friendship with these women exemplified "the beauty of holiness,"[44] showing the fruits of love and compassion, kindness and empathy: a heart which speaks to hearts. Newman's rich friendships full of warmth and charity, both with men and women, were chaste because they were based on supernatural love and pointed to that higher Love which the world cannot understand.

Suggested Reading

Athie, Rosario. "'My Dear Miss Giberne' Newman's Correspondence with a Friend: 1926–1840." *Newman Studies Journal* 2, no 1 (2005): 58–78.

Short, Edward. *Newman and His Contemporaries*. London: Bloomsbury Publishing, T & T Clark, 2011.

Strange, Roderick. *John Henry Newman, A Portrait in Letters*. Oxford: Oxford University Press, 2015.

Sugg, Joyce. *Ever Yours Affly: John Henry Newman and His Female Circle*. Leominster: Gracewing, 1996.

Trevor, Meriol. *Newman: The Pillar of the Cloud* and *Light in Winter: A Biography of John Henry Cardinal Newman*. 2 vols. New York: Doubleday and Company, 1962.

42　See Strange, *Newman a Portrait*, 20–21.

43　One such example is a letter to Emily Bowles, sister of the Oratorian Frederick Bowles, in which he wrote: "You are one of my faithful friends and I am always grateful to you. I have said Mass for you by name, as one of them, four times this year" (*LD* xx, 439, Letter to Emily Bowles, May 13, 1863). Another example is that of a letter to the widow of his good friend, John Bowden. He wrote to her: "I have just felt like you—wishing to write, and having nothing to say. We must remember each other at holy times and seasons the more." In this letter as in others to her, he signed "Ever Yours affecty in Xt." *LD* xvi, 534. Letter to Mrs. J. W. Bowden, August 31, 1855.

44　*PS* vii, no. 10: 134.

CHAPTER 7

NEWMAN:
BIBLICAL SCHOLAR

Jeffrey L. Morrow

John Henry Newman has long been revered as a towering theological voice within the Catholic Church, a voice which has only been magnified now that he has been raised to the altars as a canonized saint.[1] More than a decade ago, a collection of excerpts of Newman's works on Scripture was published; this is a topic that always lay at the core of Newman's thought.[2] Yet, unfortunately, to date, comparatively very little has been written on Newman's use of Scripture.[3] This present chapter will provide a cursory

---

1   Helpful biographies of St. John Henry Newman abound: Ian Ker, *John Henry Newman: A Biography* (Oxford: Oxford University Press, 2019 [1988]); Juan R. Vélez, *Passion for Truth: The Life of John Henry Newman* (Charlotte, N.C.: TAN Books, 2012); and Louis Bouyer, *Newman. Sa vie. Sa spiritualité* (Paris: Éditions du Cerf, 2012 [1952]). An English translation of Bouyer's volume is available as *Newman: His Life and Spirituality* (San Francisco: Ignatius Press, 2011). All citations in this chapter will be to the French edition, and, unless otherwise mentioned, all English translations (including those of Bouyer) are my own.

2   William Park, ed., *Newman on the Bible: Theory and Commentary: An Anthology* (New York: Scepter, 2006).

3   To date, the most thorough treatment of this topic remains W. F. Jaak Seynaeve, *Cardinal Newman's Doctrine on Holy Scripture according to His Published Works and Previously Unedited Manuscripts* (Louvain: Publications universitaires Louvain, 1953), which is dated and needs to be revisited. See also his much briefer study, "Newman's Biblical Hermeneutics," *Louvain Studies* 15, no. 2–3 (1990): 282–300; and the study that focuses more on the role of the Bible and tradition in Newman's understanding of doctrinal

overview of Newman's thoughts on Scripture. After a brief look at the place of Scripture in Newman's life and preaching, I will discuss the importance of the Church Fathers for Newman's biblical interpretation.[4] Then I will discuss Newman's apologetical use of Scripture in his Anglican period. I will conclude this chapter with an examination of Newman's thoughts on Scripture, its inspiration, and the place of modern biblical scholarship, from after his conversion to Catholicism.

SCRIPTURE'S PLACE
IN NEWMAN'S LIFE AND PREACHING

Newman was an assiduous reader of Sacred Scripture; he once confessed that he had committed much of the King James Version of the Bible to memory as a youth, and he knew the Latin Vulgate well.[5] After his entrance into the Catholic Church, Newman was selected to produce an English translation of the Bible, although it never materialized.[6] Keith Beaumont explains: "The thought of Newman draws on three principal sources: his intimate knowledge of the Bible; his diligent time spent with the works of the Fathers of the Church; and his own spiritual experience."[7] Such was his attention to the Sacred Page that W.F. Mandle opines, "if the Bible were to disappear, a remarkable amount of it could be reconstructed from Newman's Anglican sermons."[8] Louis Bouyer likewise remarks that "Newman's knowledge of the Bible is extraordinary, even in a country that flatters itself of having no other religion than the religion of the holy book. . . . It is the divine Word that is, and always remains his immediate source

---

development, Jean Stern, *Bible et tradition chez Newman: Aux origines de la théorie du développement* (Paris: Aubier, 1967). For Bible reading practices among Catholics in the nineteenth century of Newman's era, see Justin Taylor, SM, "Reading the Bible in the Time of the Curé of Ars," *Angelicum* 88, no. 4 (2011): 1103–13.

4 In ch. 23 of this volume, Nicholas Gregoris offers a good example of Newman's biblical exegesis of Marian doctrines, based on the Church Fathers (editor's note).

5 *AW*, 194–95.

6 Ker, *John Henry Newman*, 466–68; and Alan H. Chadwallader, "Star-cross'd Lovers: John Henry Newman and the Revision of the Bible," *Australian eJournal of Theology* 19, no. 3 (2012): 234 and 236–40. Newman was actually approached for three separate English translations of the Bible. See Chadwallader, "Star-cross'd Lovers," 229–43.

7 Keith Beaumont, *Dieu intérieur, la théologie spirituelle de John Henry Newman* (Paris: Éditions Ad Solem, 2014), 36–37.

8 W.F. Mandel, "Newman and his Audiences: 1825–1845," *Journal of Religious History* 24, no. 2 (June 2000): 152. On Newman's love of Scripture, see also, Philip Griffin, "Newman's Thought on Church and Scripture," *Irish Theological Quarterly* 56, no. 4 (1990): 287; and "Revelation and Sacred Scripture in the Writings of John Henry Newman," *Excerpta e Dissertationibus in Sacra Theologia: Cuadernos Doctorales de la Facultad de Teología de la Universidad de Navarra* 9, no. 5 (1985): 273–74. For his biblical interpretive work as an Anglican see, Jeffrey W. Barbeau, "Newman and the Interpretation of Inspired Scripture," *Theological Studies* 63, no. 1 (2002): 60–67.

[for everything]."[9] It should not surprise us, then, that Newman's preaching, both as an Anglican and as a Catholic, was suffused with quotations from and allusions to Sacred Scripture.[10]

Beaumont explains, "In the era of his Anglican preaching, he followed the custom, then in force, of writing an entire sermon and reading it. Becoming a Catholic, he adapted to the manner of Catholic preachers who spoke more freely, without an entire written text; but he always had his Bible in his hand, ready to open and to cite it at a desired moment."[11] Throughout his life as a preacher, what John Cavadini writes of the *Catechism of the Catholic Church*, is true of Newman, that he uses Scripture often as his very own words; to express himself.[12] Or, as Jean-Louis Guérin-Boutaud puts it, regarding Newman's preaching, "Scripture is woven into Newman's own wording."[13] One excellent and rich source for examining Newman's use of Scripture in his preaching is his *Parochial and Plain Sermons* from while he was still an Anglican.[14]

THE OLD AND NEW TESTAMENTS: NEWMAN'S READING OF SCRIPTURE WITH THE CHURCH FATHERS

In light of Newman's well-known work on the development of Christian doctrine, especially in his *The Arians of the Fourth Century* and his *An Essay on the Development of Christian Doctrine*, which he discovered as the result of his painstaking patristics research, it should come as no surprise that Newman's reading of Scripture was influenced by the Church Fathers.[15] Even as an Anglican, as can be seen,

---

9   Bouyer, *Newman*, 229. See also Seynaeve, "Newman's Biblical," 282–83.

10   See Jean-Louis Guérin-Boutaud, "L'ombre de la main providentielle de Dieu dans les *Sermons paroissiaux* de John Henry Newman," *Transversalités* 128 (2013): 93–105; and Seynaeve, "Newman's Biblical," 282.

11   Beaumont, *Dieu intérieur*, 38.

12   John C. Cavadini, "The Use of Scripture in the Catechism of the Catholic Church," *Letter & Spirit* 2 (2006): 43–54, esp. 52–54.

13   Jean-Louis Guérin-Boutaud, "John Henry and the Beloved: Newman Reading the Fourth Gospel," *Newman Studies Journal* 12, no. 1 (2015): 14. Jaak Seynaeve remarks that "like St. Augustine and the medieval authors, Newman, in his sermons, employs a mosaic of biblical texts, such that one can hardly tell the difference between the language of the Bible and his own." Seynaeve, "Newman's Biblical," 282.

14   See Paul V. Harrison, "A Scripture Index to Newman's *Parochial and Plain Sermons*," *Newman Studies Journal* 3, no. 2 (2006): 119–23, for a useful and complete index of all the Scripture citations in Newman's *Parochial and Plain Sermons*.

15   See Guérin-Boutaud, "John Henry," 16; Beaumont, *Dieu intérieur*, 167–70 and 343–47; Uwe Michael Lang, "Newman and the Fathers of the Church," *New Blackfriars* 92 (2011): 144–56; Inos Biffi, "I Profili storici di John Henry Newman," in *Una ragionevole fede: Logos e dialogo in John Henry Newman: Atti del convegno internazionale, Università cattolica del Sacro Cuore, Milano, 26–27 marzo 2009*, ed. Evandro Botto and Hermann Geissler (Milan:

e.g., from his *Lectures on Justification*, Newman was already heavily influenced by the Church Fathers.[16] Barbeau notices this and writes, "the section on Scripture [in *Lectures on Justification*] reveals Newman's reliance on a patristic conception of *words* and *things*, an implicit argument against the rise of historical criticism, and the primacy of the rule of antiquity."[17] In assessing this implicit critique of historical criticism, Barbeau points to Newman's cautions against simply reading passages of Scripture within their immediate contexts, where he praises patristic approaches above such modern methods.[18] We will return to the complicated issue of Newman's relationship with historical biblical criticism below. Suffice it to say that, for Newman, "without the Fathers, one is left stranded, reading words without a guide to their meaning."[19]

John Britt points out that, when it came to selecting passages of Scripture for his works, Newman "used Scripture as a whole, with the reading of the Fathers as his guide and the liturgy as his inspiration."[20] Beaumont has pointed out how important the Old Testament was in Newman's work, even in his Anglican sermons, and how he employed the patristic category of typology in so much of his exegesis of the Old Testament.[21] Early in his career, he wrote that the Scriptures "themselves have certainly an allegorical structure, and seem to countenance and invite an allegorical interpretation."[22]

Vita & Pensiero, 2009), 155–81; Benjamin John King, *Newman and the Alexandrian Fathers: Shaping Doctrine in Nineteenth-Century England* (Oxford: Oxford University Press, 2009), 24, 34, 38, and 40; Brian E. Daley, "The Church Fathers," in *The Cambridge Companion to John Henry Newman*, ed. Ian Ker and Terrence Merrigan (Cambridge: Cambridge University Press, 2009), 29–46; Seynaeve, "Newman's Biblical," 293; John F. Britt, "Newman's Use of Sacred Scripture in Texts on the Incarnation and Mary (Excerpts)," *Marian Library Studies* 24 (1995): 214–15; Seynaeve, *Cardinal Newman's Doctrine*, 307–30; and Bouyer, *Newman*, 230, where Bouyer explains that for Newman, "the value of the Fathers in understanding the Scriptures is not in the details of their exegesis, but is in the fact that they have a living familiarity with the realities of which the Bible speaks."

16   See Lang, "Newman and the Fathers," 144–46; Barbeau, "Newman and the Interpretation," 62; and Britt, "Newman's Use," 214–15. The fifth lecture of Newman's *Jfc.*, 104–29, entitled, "Misuse of the Term Just or Righteous," has a whole section devoted to biblical exegesis, where his indebtedness to the Fathers becomes evident.

17   Barbeau, "Newman and the Interpretation," 62.

18   See Barbeau, "Newman and the Interpretation," 63–64.

19   Barbeau, "Newman and the Interpretation," 64.

20   Britt, "Newman's Use," 215.

21   See Beaumont, *Dieu intérieur*, 167. On the importance of typological readings of the Old Testament for Newman see also Mikhail Stetckevich, "The Old Testament and Judaism in the Last Anglican Sermons of John Henry Newman," *Hebrew Studies* 57 (2016): 218–20; Guérin-Boutaud, "John Henry," 16; Muller, "Newman's Poetics," 15–16 and 19–23; Seynaeve, "Newman's Biblical," 291–94; Britt, "Newman's Use," 262; and Seynaeve, *Cardinal Newman's Doctrine*, 257–305. Britt, "Newman's Use," 197–264, provides numerous examples of Newman's use of typology as it applies to the figure of the Blessed Virgin Mary. Newman's early understanding of allegory was much broader than typology. See Muller, "Newman's Poetics," 20–23; and Seynaeve, "Newman's Biblical," 291n39.

22   *Ari.*, 57.

In his *Essay on the Development of Christian Doctrine*, after surveying patristic exegetical practices, Newman goes so far as to suggest, "It may be almost laid down as an historical fact, that the mystical interpretation and orthodoxy will stand or fall together."[23]

In his sermons, Newman not only emphasized the importance of the Old Testament in the context of salvation history (using typology) as preparing for the coming of Christ, but also as exemplary for moral lessons applicable to his hearers, as tropological or moral exegesis.[24] In his published doctoral dissertation, Jaak Seynaeve observes that "for Newman, not only the words of Christ but the books of the Old Testament also possess a religious meaning for all times. . . . For him, the Old Testament is a permanent instruction and commands our imitation, though not always our literal imitation."[25] Before becoming Catholic, the "Old Testament figures and images . . . [were] above all an anchor of sorts, with which he desperately struggle[d] to secure himself in the Church of England while already setting his sights toward Roman Catholicism."[26]

When it came to the New Testament, Newman seemed especially drawn to the writings of St. John and St. Paul.[27] If we take the example of his *Parochial and Plain Sermons*, we find numerous references to the Old Testament and twice as many from the New Testament. He mostly quotes from the Gospels and of these primarily from Matthew and John, as well as the letters of Paul and John.[28] In the New Testament, Newman found, as had St. Augustine before him, the full flowering of the Old Testament where the pages of salvation history recorded therein found their fulfilment in the life of Christ.

NEWMAN'S UNDERSTANDING OF
REVELATION AND HIS APOLOGETICS

One of the most important works Newman wrote which addressed the nature of Revelation was his famous *Tract 85*, from within the larger work, *Tracts for the Times*.[29] *Tract 85* was entitled, "Lectures on the Scripture Proof of the Doctrines of the Church," and, even though he was still Anglican when he wrote this, it was

---

23 *Dev.*, 344.

24 See Stetckevich, "Old Testament," 212–14; and Seynaeve, *Cardinal Newman's Doctrine*, 218–20.

25 Seynaeve, *Cardinal Newman's Doctrine*, 218–19.

26 Stetckevich, "Old Testament," 216.

27 See Beaumont, *Dieu intérieur*, 167.

28 See *Parochial and Plain Sermons* (San Francisco: Ignatius Press, 1997), 1723–46. Here the index of biblical references occupies 23 pages in small print (9 pages for the Old Testament and 5 pages for the New Testament). The Gospel of St. Matthew and St. John each have 2 pages. The references to St. Paul's writings include over 5 pages.

29 The *Tracts* 83 and 85, written by Newman, were republished in *Discussions and Arguments*. *Tract 85* is found in *DA*, 109–253.

focused on refuting the Protestant principle of *sola Scriptura*.[30] It contains, in Ian Ker's opinion, "some of his most brilliant Biblical criticism."[31] This tract grew out of Newman's frustration with Protestants unable to come to grips with the importance of the authority of the early Church in the thinking of Tractarians, or the "Oxford Movement."[32]

Newman's response in *Tract 85* was, to show the impossibility of adhering to the Bible without also revering patristic tradition.[33] Newman's logic connected the canonization of the Scriptures with the other doctrines promulgated by the same Church Fathers.[34] In Newman's own words: "but, if you do consider the fourth and fifth centuries enlightened enough to decide on the Canon, then I want to know why you call them not enlightened in point of doctrine."[35] Newman calls this "a happy inconsistency."[36] To quote again from Newman, "if the doctrines cannot be proved true, neither can the Bible; they stand or fall together."[37]

Newman comes to the logical conclusion that the tradition bequeathed by the Church Fathers is essential to understanding Scripture properly. Part of this is because of the Bible's mysterious nature, and part of this is in connection with the determination of the biblical canon which occurred in the fourth century. For Newman, "the Scriptures are full of mysteries."[38] He more often phrases it

---

30 See *DA*, 110–13, 125, and 201–15. For more on *Tract 85*, see Ker, *John Henry Newman*, 160–62; Keith Beaumont, "Newman's Reflections on Biblical Inspiration," *Newman Studies Journal* 11, no. 1 (2014): 8–9; Frank M. Turner, *John Henry Newman: The Challenge to Evangelical Religion* (New Haven: Yale University Press, 2002), 275–83; and Norbert Schiffers, "Schrift und Tradition bei John Henry Newman," in *Schrift und Tradition*, ed. Deutsche Arbeitsgemeinschaft für Mariologie (Essen: Hans Driewer, 1962), 250–66, esp. 251–52. In surveying Newman's works on Scripture, Philip Griffin claims, "Newman sets before us what must surely be one of the most comprehensive critiques of the Protestant *sola Scriptura* principle ever made." See "Revelation," 310.

31 Ker, *John Henry Newman*, 162. On the same page he elaborates that this is "particularly in respect of the literary form of Scripture."

32 See Turner, *John Henry Newman*, 275. On Newman and the Tractarians, or the "Oxford Movement," see Ker, *John Henry Newman*, 54–157; Peter Nockles, "The Oxford Movement," in *The Oxford Handbook of John Henry Newman*, ed. Frederick D. Aquino and Benjamin J. King (Oxford: Oxford University Press, 2018), 7–27; George Herring, *The Oxford Movement in Practice: The Tractarian Parochial World from the 1830s to the 1870s* (Oxford: Oxford University Press, 2016); Peter Nockles, *The Oxford Movement in Context: Anglican High Churchmanship, 1760-1857* (Cambridge: Cambridge University Press, 1994); Bouyer, *Newman*, 181–202, 223–43, and 265–88; and Christopher Dawson, *The Spirit of the Oxford Movement* (London: Sheed & Ward, 1945; reprint Washington, D.C.: The Catholic University of America Press, 2022).

33 See Ker, *John Henry Newman*, 160; Griffin, "Revelation," 277–78; and Schiffers, "Schrift und Tradition," 251–52.

34 *DA*, e.g., 201–17, 236–37, 240–41, and 252; Ker, *John Henry Newman*, 160; Griffin, "Revelation," 277–78; and Schiffers, "Schrift und Tradition," 251–52.

35 *DA*, 241.

36 *DA*, 201.

37 *DA*, 252.

38 Barbeau, "Newman and the Interpretation," 66. Newman comments on this as

as truths "obscurely conveyed in Scripture."[39] This underscores the necessity, for Newman, of using the Church Fathers as a guide to proper biblical interpretation.[40] It also underscored the fact that Newman understood the literal sense to have serious limits, hence the need for the spiritual sense.[41]

Newman's view here is perfectly at home with early Jewish and Christian assumptions about Scripture. James Kugel explains these early assumptions shared among Jews and Christians:

> [1] They assumed that the Bible was a fundamentally cryptic text: that is, when it said A, often it might really mean B. . . . [2] Interpreters also assumed that the Bible was a book of lessons directed to readers in their own day. It might seem to talk about the past, but it is not fundamentally history. It is instruction, telling us what to do. . . . Ancient interpreters assumed this not only about narratives like the Abraham story but about every part of the Bible. . . . [3] Interpreters also assumed that the Bible contained no contradictions or mistakes. It is perfectly harmonious, despite its being an anthology. . . . In short, the Bible, they felt, is an utterly consistent, seamless, perfect book. . . . [4] Lastly, they believed that the entire Bible is essentially a divinely given text, a book in which God speaks directly or through His prophets.[42]

Newman goes beyond the Fathers, however, in trying to show his readers the challenges of reading Scripture. This is where most scholars put their emphasis: Newman underscores the human qualities of the Bible in order to highlight how essential doctrine and tradition are for interpreting Scripture.[43] Sometimes in *Tract* 85 Newman writes as if he were pointing out problems with Scripture, e.g. its obscurity, apparent contradictions, etc.[44] One aspect Newman brings to the

---

the Bible being full of obscurities or that it teaches in a hidden way, e.g., *DA*, 122–23, 142, 148, 152, 156, and 170. See also Juan R. Vélez, "Newman's Influence on Vatican II's Constitution *Dei Verbum,*" *Scripta Theologica* 51, no. 3 (2019): 715; Griffin, "Revelation," 303–6; Seynaeve, *Cardinal Newman's Doctrine*, 216; and "La doctrine du Cardinal Newman sur l'inspiration d'après les articles de 1884," *Ephemerides Theologicae Lovanienses* 18 (1950): 364. Griffin cautions that, for Newman, "The almost universal lack of clarity in Scripture is . . . by no means an argument against the divinity of its doctrines; on the contrary it seems to be the characteristic hallmark of their divine Author, who will undoubtedly have had 'some wise and unknown reasons' for not stating them clearly." Griffin, "Revelation," 305.

39 *DA*, 156.

40 See Barbeau, "Newman and the Interpretation," 66; and Britt, "Newman's Use," 214–15.

41 See C. Michael Shea, *Newman's Early Roman Catholic Legacy 1845–1854* (Oxford: Oxford University Press, 2017), 6; Seynaeve, "Newman's Biblical," 291–94; and Britt, "Newman's Use," 253.

42 James L. Kugel, *How to Read the Bible: A Guide to Scripture, Then and Now* (New York: Free Press, 2007), 14–16.

43 See, e.g., *DA*, 111–13, 122–23, 125, 127, 140–42, 146, 168, 170, and 216–35.

44 See, e.g., *DA*, 146, 168, 170, and esp. 216–35.

fore in *Tract* 85 is the importance of the Bible canon in interpretation.[45] As he mentions in *Tract* 85, the Bible's very canon was grounded in Catholic doctrine developed in the early Church.[46]

Scholars sometimes view all of this discussion on the difficulties involved in biblical interpretation as Newman raising questions stemming from nineteenth century historical biblical criticism, in order to use it as a foil. The sorts of difficulties he brings up, however, are more akin to problems raised in the seventeenth century. Newman's intended audience accepts Scripture as true and from God, but they doubt the value of tradition and patristic witness and exegesis. Newman is pointing out their inconsistency more so than he is pointing to Scripture's incoherence. Thus, he writes:

> though the Bible is inspired, and therefore, in one sense, written by God, yet very large portions of it, if not far the greater part of it, are written in as free and unconstrained a manner, and (apparently) with as little apparent consciousness of a supernatural dictation or restraint, on the part of His earthly instruments, as if He had no share in the work.[47]

And later he mentions, "distinct portions of Scripture itself are apparently inconsistent with one another, yet are not really so."[48]

CATHOLIC PERIOD:
ON THE INSPIRATION OF SCRIPTURE AND
A CATHOLIC HERMENEUTIC

Newman saw "in Catholicism the continuation of the Church of the New Testament and of the Fathers."[49] In his Catholic period, one of the most direct works Newman published dealing with the Bible were two short essays on inspiration from 1884.[50] His views here were not entirely different from what he held as an Anglican.[51] The notion of biblical inspiration was important in Newman's

---

45   See Guérin-Boutaud, "John Henry," 26–28; and Britt, "Newman's Use," 262.

46   Ker, *John Henry Newman*, 162; and Griffin, "Revelation," 277–78.

47   *DA*, 146. After reviewing the different accounts of Judas's death, Newman concedes, "I do not mean to say, of course, that these accounts are irreconcilable even by us; but they certainly differ from each other" (168).

48   *DA*, 170.

49   Bouyer, *Newman*, 362.

50   On Newman's essay, "On the Inspiration of Scripture," see, e.g., Vélez, "Newman's Influence," 718–20; and Beaumont, "Newman's Reflections," 14–15.

51   See especially Muller, "Newman's Poetics," 5–24, who focuses on Newman's *Arians of the Fourth Century*, to demonstrate the role of poetry and the imagination in Newman's early views on biblical inspiration as an Anglican. He notes, however, "It is significant for understanding his view of inspiration because he described divine

thought even though he did not publish much on the topic.[52] Beaumont writes that since the doctrine of inspiration had not been the focus on serious Christian reflection before the modern period, "Newman, in addressing the question of biblical inspiration, is working in relatively uncharted territory."[53] This is an important point to keep in mind when reading Newman.

Newman reads the various books of the Bible in light of the other books of the Bible, what we have come to call a canonical reading, canonical interpretation, or canonical criticism.[54] He likewise reads Scripture Christologically, with Christ as the key unlocking the Bible, as the Fathers had before him.[55] The Catholic tradition and the creeds forged in the controversies of the early Church prove essential to Newman for proper biblical exegesis.[56]

The notion of the development of doctrine played a significant part in his thinking on Scripture as well as on patristic exegesis. It is important to note, however, that "the *Essay on Development* was not an argument for Roman Catholicism directed toward the Enlightenment ideal of an unbiased observer without rational commitments. Rather, it was for those who began to discern the universal Church in some way but still harbored intellectual difficulties in accepting those teachings that were not plainly revealed in scripture."[57] As a Catholic, the Rule of Faith, in the context of the development of doctrine, as well as in the Church's living tradition in the Magisterium, became essential components in Newman's biblical interpretation.[58] Such Catholic tradition was a *sine*

---

inspiration as a gift of illumination and instruction to the imagination. One should not regard Newman's association of inspiration with the imagination as accidental or inconsequential given the context of British Romanticism in general and the Tractarian reception of Romanticism in particular. Indeed, a poetic ethos guided much of the thought and practice of the Oxford Movement. Good poetry came from the imagination as a way of expressing moral and religious sentiments. It was contrary to rationalism and scientific or discursive reasoning. There was more to 'poetry' than written communications using rhyme and meter. Rather, anything that could evoke moral and religious sentiments or associations could serve as poetry. Finally, true poetry never sought originality or excessive use of language" (15).

52 Vélez, "Newman's Influence," 717–25; Beaumont, "Newman's Reflections," 4–17, esp. 5; Seynaeve, "Newman's Biblical," 283; *Cardinal Newman's Doctrine*, esp. 49–194; and "La doctrine," 356–82. Keith Beaumont observes that "this question [of inspiration] forms a thread that runs through all of Newman's work and seems to have been in his mind for a period of sixty years." Beaumont, "Newman's Reflections," 5.

53 Beaumont, "Newman's Reflections," 5.

54 Guérin-Boutaud, "John Henry," 26–28; and Britt, "Newman's Use," 262.

55 Guérin-Boutaud, "John Henry," 26–28.

56 *DA*, 111–13 and 125; Ker, *John Henry Newman*, 142–43; Griffin, "Revelation," 297; and Schiffers, "Schrift und Tradition," 254–57.

57 Shea, *Newman's Early Roman Catholic*, 65.

58 *IS* i, 188 and 190–92; Vélez, "Newman's Influence," 716; Britt, "Newman's Use," 260–61; Griffin, "Newman's Thought," 291–93; "Revelation," 277; and Seynaeve, "La doctrine," 364.

qua non of authentic Christian exegesis.[59] This was in sharp contrast to nineteenth century historical biblical critics for whom Christian dogmas obscured Scripture's true meaning. As Juan R. Vélez puts it, for Newman, "dogmas are windows that peer into the mysteries of faith; they always allow for deeper understanding."[60]

J. Derek Holmes argues that "Newman was strongly influenced by his appreciation of the results of scientific or historical criticism in understanding biblical inspiration."[61] Newman's relationship to modern historical biblical criticism, however, is a complicated one and one which I think needs further exploration. On one extreme, scholars have linked Newman's views on inspiration with the later Alfred Loisy, as well as with Newman's contemporary François Lenormant.[62] Part of this linking is due, no doubt, to Loisy's own embracing of Newman as an inspiration to his own work and thus Newman was associated with the Roman Catholic Modernist movement early on in some circles.[63] Newman's very careful tentative questions about *obiter dicta*, the possibility of certain portions (phrases or lines) of Scripture as we now have the texts as not pertaining to faith or morals, but rather as human elements of Scripture, have often been read in this context, leading some to see Pope Leo XIII's 1893 *Providentissimus Deus* as a condemnation of Newman's ideas.[64] Holmes and others argue that Newman was receptive to modern trends in historical criticism that would have been approved by Loisy and others, later in his life.[65]

There are indications in Newman's works that he was aware of what was happening in historical criticism in the nineteenth century.[66] He shows familiarity

---

59 *DA*, 122–23, 127, and 140–42; Vélez, "Newman's Influence," 716; Griffin, "Newman's Thought," 291–93; "Revelation," 271–73 and 282; Schiffers, "Schrift und Tradition," 250–66; Seynaeve, *Cardinal Newman's Doctrine*, 38–44; and "La doctrine," 364.

60 Juan R. Vélez, "Newman and Last Things," *Downside Review* 119 (2001): 51.

61 J. Derek Holmes, "Newman's Attitude towards Historical Criticism and Biblical Inspiration," *Downside Review* 89, no. 294 (1971): 22.

62 See H. J. T. Johnson, "Leo XIII, Cardinal Newman and the Inerrancy of Scripture," *Downside Review* 69, no. 218 (1951): 412.

63 On the relationship between Newman's thought and Loisy's, see, e.g., Jeffrey L. Morrow, *Alfred Loisy and Modern Biblical Studies* (Washington, D.C.: The Catholic University of America Press, 2019), 130–57.

64 See Seynaeve, *Cardinal Newman's Doctrine*, 153 and 171–73; and "La doctrine," 358 and 374. Griffin comments: "While wholeheartedly admitting the doctrine of the Vatican Council that the sacred books themselves were inspired, he proposed the *obiter dicta*, as a possibility. That theory proved later unacceptable, as being out of keeping with the Catholic doctrine of plenary inspiration and inerrancy . . . in all his teachings, including this rather infamous *cause celèbre* (which he forwarded as a mere personal opinion: a somewhat loosely conceived hypothesis), Newman takes for granted their submission to the 'correction of the Church'" ("Newman's Thought," 300). See *IS* i, 197–99; and *IS* ii, 50–57.

65 Seynaeve, "Newman's Biblical," 291 and 297; and Holmes, "Newman's Attitude," 22–37.

66 For the broad history of these developments stretching from the end of the

with at least some of the works of Renan, Ewald, and others.[67] He has knowledge of the idea that the Pentateuch originated with other sources and that Daniel in Hebrew, Aramaic, and Greek portions may come from different authors.[68] He mentions that Isaiah may have had different authors.[69] Newman was quite comfortable engaging in intellectual discussions and arguments that emerged from historical critical study of the biblical texts.[70] Early on, however, as modern biblical criticism gained traction in England, Newman was critical of the rationalistic tendencies he detected.[71] Newman linked the roots of this rationalism with the Protestant Reformation.[72] And yet, despite his predilection for allegorical exegesis, Newman did appreciate the literal sense as well.[73]

In writing on this topic, Beaumont explains that "Before the first Vatican Council in 1870, in fact, he does not seem to have considered that developments in biblical scholarship created particular theological problems. But as a 'pastor' concerned about the faithful in his charge, he was fully conscious of the confusion created in many minds by these developments."[74] Beaumont further observes, "Newman called for freedom in historical and scientific research, declaring that it was his aim to show that there was no dispute between the results of this research and the truths of Revelation."[75] Beaumont even sees Newman as in some way anticipating the helpful insights of the sort of form

---

medieval period through the end of the nineteenth century, see, e.g., Scott W. Hahn and Benjamin Wiker, *Politicizing the Bible: The Roots of Historical Criticism and the Secularization of Scripture 1300–1700* (New York: Herder & Herder, 2013); and Scott W. Hahn and Jeffrey L. Morrow, *Modern Biblical Criticism as a Tool of Statecraft (1700–1900)* (Steubenville: Emmaus Academic, 2020).

67   *IS* i, 185 and 190; Beaumont, "Newman's Reflections," 4–17.

68   *IS* i, 195.

69   *IS* i, 196.

70   Beaumont, "Newman's Reflections," 7–8.

71   See, e.g., Bedeau, "Newman," 127–42; Griffin, "Newman's Thought," 288; and Seynaeve, *Cardinal Newman's Doctrine*, 376–83. Regarding "rationalism," Turner's comments are helpful: "in 1836 the meaning of *rationalism* within Tractarian and high-church circles was quite complicated. A few years earlier, during their debate on rationalism in Germany, both [Hugh James] Rose and [Edward Bouverie] Pusey had acknowledged the difficulty of precise definition. Commentators on their dispute in the *Edinburgh Review* alluded to 'the system called Rationalism in Germany,' by which they meant a critical use of reason, a naturalistic interpretation of natural phenomena, an empirical account of human experience, a critical examination of biblical history, and a rejection of 'whatever is supernatural in the Judaical and Christian revelations.'" *John Henry Newman*, 236.

72   Ker, *John Henry Newman*, 121–23 and 258. There is a way in which Newman understood the Arians of the early Church as similar to the rationalists of the nineteenth century. See, e.g., Ker who notes that for Newman, "In disputing the orthodox creed, the Arians, too, were guilty of misapplying reason to the mysteries of revelation." *John Henry Newman*, 48.

73   Seynaeve, "Newman's Biblical," 295.

74   Beaumont, "Newman's Reflections," 11.

75   Beaumont, "Newman's Reflections," 12. See also Vélez, "Newman's Influence," 725.

criticism the Second Vatican Council's *Dei Verbum* would later imply with its reference to literary forms.[76] Vélez thinks it is indeed likely that Newman's thought influenced *Dei Verbum*.[77]

After the First Vatican Council, Newman understood *Dei Filius* to have described biblical inspiration in such a way that it was in conflict with some of modern biblical criticism.[78] This was the context for Newman's writing on biblical inspiration in the wake of Vatican I, to help Catholic biblical scholars have due concern for the guidance of the Magisterium.[79]

Newman was aware of and concerned with the growing skeptical and rationalist biblical criticism that was developing.[80] He was aware of development within the biblical text, which is how Loisy would later use Newman in defense of his form of historical criticism. For Newman, however, and in contrast to Loisy and others, this was a prophetic development, following the unfolding of salvation history as the Old Testament progressively moved towards its fulfillment in the New Testament, and not the sort of development behind the texts that are envisioned in the historical critical method.[81]

Nicholas Lash writes, "Newman takes it for granted that the process of doctrinal elaboration in the church as a whole is the fruit of its meditation on scripture . . . the guarantee of the faithfulness of this process is the guiding presence of the Spirit. . . ."[82] As Mikhail Stetckevich notes, "the idea of development of Christian doctrine as formulated by Newman stems from the concept of the New Testament as continuation of the Old Testament. . . ."[83] In Newman's own words from his *Essay on the Development of Christian Doctrine*, "the whole Bible, not its prophetical portions only, is written on the principle of development. As the Revelation proceeds, it is ever new, yet ever old."[84]

---

76   Beaumont, "Newman's Reflections," 16.

77   Vélez, "Newman's Influence," 712. Vélez includes a helpful chart comparing key teachings of *Dei Filius*, Newman, and *Dei Verbum* (726–28) and explains what might be a more direct form of influences (729–38).

78   Vélez, "Newman's Influence," 718; and Beaumont, "Newman's Reflections," 13. For the history of the Catholic Magisterium's teachings (and its development) on the notion of biblical inspiration, see especially Pablo T. Gadenz, "Magisterial Teaching on the Inspiration and Truth of Scripture: Precedents and Prospects," *Letter & Spirit* 6 (2010): 67–91.

79   *IS* i, 187; and Beaumont, "Newman's Reflections," 13. Beaumont thinks that the work of Ernest Renan is what roused Newman to write on inspiration more than a decade after the Council (14).

80   Ker, *John Henry Newman*, 193.

81   Ker, *John Henry Newman*, 305–6; and Stetckevich, "Old Testament," 220–21. Gerard McCarren notes a slightly different point when he observes that for Newman, "Scripture itself contains doctrinal developments and in fact warrants further development by the use of reason in theological reflection. Doctrinal development enshrines this progressive understanding. ("Development of Doctrine," in *Cambridge Companion*, 120).

82   Nicholas Lash, *Newman on Development: The Search for an Explanation in History* (Shepherdstown: Patmos Press, 1975), 90.

83   Stetckevich, "Old Testament," 221.

84   *Dev.*, 65. See his further comments in this vein, "Thus with respect to the

At some level, historical criticism focused on the literal sense, and yet, for Newman, the literal sense, even as traditionally understood and as he himself appreciatively used it, was limited and insufficient of itself to explain all of Scripture.[85] Newman understands Scripture as very much like a sacrament.[86] Thus, the full panoply of traditional patristic exegesis was necessary in order to plumb Scripture's depths. Ultimately, what distanced Newman from modernist exegetes was not simply their different appropriations of historical criticism, which Newman too was able to value, but rather in their different approaches to the authority of the Magisterium, and the nature of biblical inspiration.

Newman began heavily researching inspiration and biblical interpretation in 1861.[87] He eventually wrote drafts on this topic, focusing on inspiration, in 1861 and 1863, but they were never completed in final form, nor published.[88] From his letters and notes it seems he had a more nuanced approach to inspiration, focusing on the inspiration of the authors more than the texts, following Trent.[89] Holmes overstates the case for Newman adhering to a view of restricted inspiration, e.g., eliminating historical matters, when he argues that Newman held only the focus of infallibility to be "religious truth" in the Bible. This problematically makes it seem that Newman could have exempted historical matters from inspiration, which he did not do.[90] Newman, rather, held to a much closer view to that espoused by *Dei Verbum*, which we might speak of as the "mystery of dual authorship."[91] The human aspects underscore the humility of the divine condescension in Scripture, including its difficulties.[92]

---

evangelical view of the rite of sacrifice, first the rite is enjoined by Moses; next Samuel says, 'to obey is better than sacrifice;' then Hosea, 'I will have mercy and not sacrifice;' Isaiah, 'Incense is an abomination unto me;' then Malachi, describing the times of the Gospel, speaks of the 'pure offering' of wheatflour; and our Lord completes the development, when He speaks of worshipping 'in spirit and in truth'" (65–66).

85 Britt, "Newman's Use," 253.

86 *IS* i; Seynaeve, "Newman's Biblical," 295; *Cardinal Newman's Doctrine*, 214 and 231–35; and "La doctrine," 365.

87 See Ker, *John Henry Newman*, 734.

88 Ker, *John Henry Newman*, 735; Vélez, "Newman's Influence," 717; Beaumont, "Newman's Reflections," 11. On these papers, see also Seynaeve, *Cardinal Newman's Doctrine*, 54–73, 97–151, 174–77, and 182–90.

89 Ker, *John Henry Newman*, 735–36.

90 Holmes, "Newman's Attitude," 27–28. Much of Holmes's discussion is focused on the drafts from 1861–1863. Holmes explains, "These notes, however, must be used very cautiously as the results of a man thinking with pen in his hand. Much of the material is in the form of drafts or notes corrected several times so that parts of it are no longer legible . . . he was feeling his way towards a solution, seeing how far the question was open, and in an attempt to examine various possibilities, occasionally adopting 'contradictory' positions" (23).

91 I am borrowing this phrase of "mystery of dual authorship" to explain *Dei Verbum*'s teaching from Brant Pitre, "The Mystery of God's Word: Inspiration, Inerrancy, and the Interpretation of Scripture," *Letter & Spirit* 6 (2010): 47–66.

92 See, e.g., Scott W. Hahn, "For the Sake of Our Salvation: The Truth and Humility

It is helpful to consider Newman's own words, as when he writes, "As God rules the will, yet the will is free,—as He rules the course of the world, yet men conduct it,—so He has inspired the Bible, yet men have written it."[93] Newman explains further:

> Whatever else is true of it, this is true, that we may speak of the history or the mode of its composition, as truly as of that of other books; we may speak of its writers having an object in view, being influenced by circumstances, being anxious, taking pains, purposely omitting or introducing matters, leaving things incomplete, or supplying what others had so left. Though the Bible be inspired, it has all such characteristics as might attach to a book uninspired,—the characteristics of dialect and style, the distinct effects of times and places, youth and age, or moral and intellectual character; and I insist on this, lest what I am going to say, I seem to forget (what I do not forget), that in spite of its human form, it has in it the Spirit and the Mind of God.[94]

Finally, Newman later comments, "they have a human side, which manifests itself in language, style, tone of thought, character, intellectual peculiarities. . . ."[95]

Newman clearly articulates that the whole of Scripture is inspired, including the historical narratives, beyond merely select statements on faith and morals, since, in Newman's understanding the narratives themselves pertain to faith.[96] In his defense after he was publicly challenged on this point, he responds, "Are historical statements of fact included? It makes me smile to think that any one could fancy me so absurd as to exclude them. . . ."[97] On the one hand, one could see how early on he might be misinterpreted to limit inspiration to statements of faith and morality, but Newman is careful to clarify that it is also in matters of fact that Scripture is inspired:

> the sacred narrative carried on through so many ages, what is it but the very matter for our faith and rule of our obedience? What but the narrative itself is the supernatural teaching, in order to which inspiration is given? What is the whole history, traced out in Scripture from Genesis to Esdras and thence on to the end of the Acts of the Apostles, but a manifestation of Divine Providence. . . ?[98]

---

of God's Word," *Letter & Spirit* 6 (2010): 21–45; and John R. Betz, "Glory(ing) in the Humility of the Word: The Kenotic Form of Revelation in J.G. Hamann," *Letter & Spirit* 6 (2010): 141–79.

   93 *DA*, 146.
   94 *DA*, 146.
   95 *IS* ii, 41.
   96 *IS* ii, 41.
   97 *IS* ii, 47.
   98 *IS* i, 189.

When Newman speaks of "limits" on inspiration, he does not mean what is often attributed to him, namely a limit on what is inspired, rather he means more that Scripture is not a science textbook, etc., and points out logical limits in things like textual transmission.[99]

It is helpful, again, to turn to Newman's own words on the matter. Consider when he writes:

> Its pages breathe of providence and grace, of our Lord, and of His work and teaching, from beginning to end. . . . In this point of view it has God for its author, even though the finger of God traced no words but the Decalogue. Such is the claim of Bible history in its substantial fulness to be accepted *de fide* as true. In this point of view, Scripture is inspired, not only in faith and morals, but in all its parts which bear on faith, including matters of fact.[100]

In contrast to his earlier unpublished notes which were written prior to the First Vatican Council, after the Council, Newman makes clear how he understands the Bible's divine inspiration in light both of Trent and Vatican I, with both the sacred authors and the text they wrote as inspired: "Are the books or are the writers inspired? I answer, Both . . . The books are inspired, because the writers were inspired to write them. They are not inspired books, unless they came from inspired men."[101]

Lawrence Feingold—following the teachings of Vatican I, as well as Popes Leo XIII and Benedict XV, and Vatican II—clearly explains the Thomistic view on the uniqueness of biblical inspiration, which, although never articulated as clearly by Newman, is nonetheless consistent with what Newman writes:

> It is God's Word because He inspired its composition in such a way that the human author, using his faculties under the influence of divine grace, *wrote what God wished him to write, only that and nothing more.* . . . Inspiration implies three distinct effects in the human author: illuminating the mind, efficaciously moving the will, and assisting in the execution of the work. . . . It is not enough, however, for God to enlighten the intellect of the sacred writer. He must also move the author's will to desire to write that which divine illumination has enabled him to conceive. . . . Since God is the principal author, He must have not only inspired the ideas of the sacred authors, but also guided their mode of expression, since this is clearly the responsibility of an author. . . . God's inspiration of the sacred writer consisted in an influence of efficacious grace that *illuminated* his intellect and reasoning (including historical research),

---

99 *IS* ii, 41 and 57–61.
100 *IS* i, 190.
101 *IS* i,192.

moved his will, and *guided* all his faculties involved in the composition of his work, especially his imagination, memory, and literary judgment . . . the human authors of Scripture were intelligent and free in the use of all their capacities, like any other author. The fact of being inspired did not in any way diminish their use of their human faculties and human choice. It simply guided, aided, and elevated those truly human faculties. . . . The human authors had to employ ordinary human means in their work, such as historical research and literary composition, like any other true author.[102]

CONCLUSION

As a Catholic, for instance, in his 1864 *Letter to Pusey*, Newman evidenced "an exegesis which took into account everything previously developed, along with an awareness of the following aspects of doctrine: the biblical, the patristic, the ecclesiological, the liturgical, and the ecumenical."[103] To Catholic exegetes, Newman implored them never to forget that what they are "handling is the Word of God, which . . . cannot be put on the level of other books . . . but has the nature of a Sacrament, which is outward and inward, and a channel of supernatural grace."[104]

In all he wrote, Newman had a very keen and logical sense of whatever topic he treated and as a Catholic he had a robust sense of fidelity to the Magisterium. Yet, his theology was not a rigid abstraction. He was aware of the personal implications of theology. Vélez puts it thus, "In Newman's thought there is a good and necessary tension between mystery and dogma: between personal assent and dogmatic formulations. Newman's approach to theology manifests two important categories of Christianity . . . a historical and a personal character."[105] This is not to say that Newman was subjective: truth was the anchor, but that truth was known by a subject.[106] Furthermore, as expressed by Beaumont, for Newman, truth was found through "the *union* between this unwavering fidelity to the Church and the exercise of critical intelligence."[107] For this reason, St. John

---

102 Lawrence Feingold, *Faith Comes from What Is Heard: An Introduction to Fundamental Theology* (Steubenville: Emmaus Academic, 2016), 283, 285, 288–91, and 293.

103 Britt, "Newman's Use," 261.

104 *IS* i, 192.

105 Vélez, "Newman's Influence," 714.

106 Ratzinger's comments are helpful here: "Newman was much more taken by the necessity to obey recognized truth than his own preferences, that is to say, even against his own sensitivity and bonds of friendship and ties due to similar backgrounds. It seems to me characteristic of Newman that he emphasized truth's priority over goodness in the order of virtues. Or, to put it in a way that is more understandable for us, he emphasized truth's priority over consensus, over the accommodation of groups," Joseph Ratzinger/Benedict XVI, *Faith and Politics* (San Francisco: Ignatius Press, 2018), 118.

107 Beaumont, "Newman's Reflections," 16.

Paul II mentioned Newman by name as an exemplar of unifying faith and reason in his papal encyclical on that topic, *Fides et Ratio*.[108] We can learn much from Newman today on this union of faith and reason. Greater attention to Newman's use of Scripture promises to serve as a helpful guide to Catholic exegetes and theologians concerned for fidelity to God's Word.[109]

Suggested Reading

Barbeau, Jeffrey W. "Newman and the Interpretation of Inspired Scripture." *Theological Studies* 63, no. 1 (2002): 53–67.

Beaumont, Keith. "Newman's Reflections on Biblical Inspiration." *Newman Studies Journal* 11, no. 1 (2014): 4–17.

Britt, John F. "Newman's Use of Sacred Scripture in Texts on the Incarnation and Mary (Excerpts)." *Marian Library Studies* 24 (1995): 197–264.

Griffin, Philip. "Newman's Thought on Church and Scripture." *Irish Theological Quarterly* 56, no. 4 (1990): 287–306.

_____. "Revelation and Sacred Scripture in the Writings of John Henry Newman." *Excerpta e Dissertationibus in Sacra Theologia: Cuadernos Doctorales de la Facultad de Teología de la Universidad de Navarra* 9, no. 5 (1985): 255–311.

Muller, Matthew. "Newman's Poetics and the Inspiration of the Bible in *Arians of the Fourth Century*." *Newman Studies Journal* 14, no. 2 (2017): 5–24.

Seynaeve, W. F. Jaak. *Cardinal Newman's Doctrine on Holy Scripture According to His Published Works and Previously Unedited Manuscripts*. Louvain: Publications universitaires Louvain, 1953.

_____. "La doctrine du Cardinal Newman sur l'inspiration d'après les articles de 1884." *Ephemerides Theologicae Lovanienses* 18 (1950): 356–82.

_____. "Newman's Biblical Hermeneutics." *Louvain Studies* 15, no. 2–3 (1990): 282–300.

Vélez, Juan R. "Newman's Influence on Vatican II's Constitution *Dei Verbum*." *Scripta Theologica* 51, no. 3 (2019): 711–40.

---

108 Pope John Paul II, *Fides et Ratio* (September 14, 1998), 74, online at: www.vatican.va.

109 I owe a word of thanks to Fr. Pablo Gadenz and Elizabeth Huddleston for providing me with additional references, and to Fr. Keith Beaumont for showing me an early draft of his chapter in this volume, as well as to Maria Morrow and Biff Rocha for reading through a draft of this chapter.

CHAPTER 8

NEWMAN AND
THE FATHERS OF THE CHURCH

Fr. Uwe Michael Lang

In his *Letter to Pusey on Occasion of His Eirenicon* of 1866, John Henry Newman gave his well-known testimony:

Of course I maintain the value and authority of the "Schola," as one of the *loci theologici*; nevertheless I sympathize with Petavius in preferring to the "contentious and subtle theology" of the middle age, that "more elegant and fruitful teaching which is moulded after the image of erudite Antiquity." The Fathers made me a Catholic, and I am not going to kick down the ladder by which I ascended into the Church.[1]

Newman adds that even the process of development of doctrine, "does not supersede the Fathers, but explains and completes them." In the context of the *Letter to Pusey*, he refers in particular to Catholic teaching on the Blessed Virgin Mary and notes: "with the Fathers I am content. . . . Here, let me say, as on other points,

---

*   This chapter is a revised and extended version of my article "Newman and the Fathers of the Church," *New Blackfriars* 92 (2011): 144–56. The Dominican Society. Published by Blackwell Publishing Ltd. 2011, 9600 Garsington Road, Oxford OX4 2DQ, UK, and 350 Main Street, Malden, MA 02148, USA. Reproduced with permission of Wiley-Blackwell through PLSclear.

1   John Henry Newman, *A Letter Addressed to the Rev. E. B. Pusey, D.D., on Occasion of his Eirenicon of 1864*, in *Diff.* ii, 24.

the Fathers are enough for me. I do not wish to say more than they suggest to me, and will not say less."[2] Newman then develops his central argument: Catholic devotion to the Blessed Virgin may have developed over time, but the Church's teaching on her is firmly grounded in the Church Fathers' conception of Mary as the Second Eve, which Newman identifies already in St. Irenaeus of Lyon (c. 130–202 AD).[3]

In this chapter I intend to retrace Newman's reading of the Church Fathers and examine what precisely attracted him in the writings of the early Christian bishops and theologians. In doing so, I follow a well-trodden path that has been explored in many different ways by Newman scholars, but I am confident that, in the light of recent contributions, a clearer picture will emerge of Newman's contribution to the revival of patristic studies, in the English-speaking world and beyond.[4]

EARLY YEARS UNTIL THE PUBLICATION
OF *ARIANS OF THE FOURTH CENTURY*

According to his own evidence, Newman's first encounter with the Fathers of the Church was at the age of fifteen, when he read Joseph Milner's *Church History*. He writes in retrospect that he "was nothing short of enamoured of the long extracts from St. Augustine, St. Ambrose, and the other Fathers which I found there. I read them as being the religion of the primitive Christians."[5]

---

2 *Diff.* ii, 24–25.

3 Nicholas Gregoris examines Newman's reliance on the Fathers for the doctrine of Mary as the New Eve. See ch. 23 of this volume (editor's note).

4 See George D. Dragas, "John Henry Newman's Rediscovery of the Catholicity of the Greek Fathers," *One in Christ* 17, no. 1 (1981): 46–68; Jaroslav Pelikan, "Newman and the Fathers: The Vindication of Tradition," *Studia Patristica* 18, no. 4 (1990): 379–90, and G. Tokarsik, "John Henry Newman and the Church Fathers," *Eastern Churches Journal* 7 (Autumn 2000): 101–16; Brian E. Daley, "Newman and the Alexandrian Tradition: 'The Veil of the Letter' and the Person of Christ," in *Newman and Truth*, ed. Ian Ker and Terrence Merrigan, Louvain Theological & Pastoral Monographs 39 (Louvain: Peeters, 2008), 147–88; Brian E. Daley, "The Church Fathers," in *The Cambridge Companion to John Henry Newman*, ed. Ian Ker and Terrence Merrigan (Cambridge: University Press, 2009), 29–46; Benjamin J. King, *Newman and the Alexandrian Fathers: Shaping Doctrine in Nineteenth-Century England* (Oxford: Oxford University Press, 2009); Benjamin J. King, "The Church Fathers," in *The Oxford Handbook of John Henry Newman*, ed. Frederick D. Aquino and Benjamin J. King (Oxford: Oxford University Press, 2018), 113–34. See also the contributions in *Etudes Newmaniennes* 21 (2005)—*Actes du colloque des 20 et 21 novembre 2004: Newman et les Pères de l'Église*. In the volume *Una ragionevole fede: Logos e dialogo in John Henry Newman*, ed. Evandro Botto and Hermann Geissler (Milan: Vita & Pensiero, 2009), see the papers of Kathleen Dietz, "John Henry Newman and the Fathers of the Church: The Birth of an Ecclesiology," 211–20, and Inos Biffi, "*I Profili storici* di John Henry Newman," 155–81.

5 *Apo.*, 7; cited from the 1865 edition, which was reprinted as: *Apologia Pro Vita*

The Fathers did not feature much in Newman's intellectual formation nor in his theological studies before 1828; however, he professes to have developed a preference for ante-Nicene Trinitarian theology, so much so that Richard Whately (1787–1863) of Oriel College told him he had been "Arianizing" in an Easter sermon preached in the College Chapel in 1827, which contained some comments on the Son's being subordinate to the Father.[6] Around the same time Newman, expressed his view that the Athanasian Creed compared unfavourably to the Nicene Creed, because it was "unnecessarily scientific" in some of its expressions. Newman seemed to have preferred the more expressive theological language of the earlier Fathers to the doctrinal formulae of the great Councils. From the vantage point of the *Apologia*, he charged himself with a "certain disdain for Antiquity" in that period of his life.[7]

It was the encounter with High Churchmen at Oxford that led to Newman's scholarly engagement with the theologians of Christian antiquity. In the Long Vacation of 1828, he set out to read the Fathers systematically, beginning with St. Ignatius of Antioch and St. Justin Martyr. In his lectures given at the London Oratory in 1850,[8] Newman recalls that back then he had read only Fathers of the ante-Nicene period and claims that he "had read them simply on Protestant ideas, analysed and catalogued them on Protestant principles of division, and hunted for Protestant doctrines and usages in them."[9] The Birmingham Oratory Archives contain Newman's *Theological Commonplace Book* from that time, in which he wrote notes under such headings as justification by faith alone, personal conversion, and so on.[10] In retrospect, Newman does not make much of this reading, with one exception:

> I knew not what to look for in them; I sought what was not there, I missed what was there; I laboured through the night and caught nothing. But I should make one important exception: I rose from their perusal with a vivid perception of the divine institution, the prerogatives, and the gifts of the Episcopate.[11]

Sua, Being a History of His Religious Opinions, new impression (London: Longmans, Green, and Co., 1908).

6 *Apo.*, 14. Whately was regarded as a liberal theologian, but nonetheless had considerable influence on Newman's thinking; see Sheridan Gilley, "Life and Writings," in *The Cambridge Companion to John Henry Newman*, 1–28, at 3.

7 *Apo.*, 15.

8 They were published in the same year under the title *Lectures on Certain Difficulties Felt by Anglicans in Submitting to the Catholic Church*, and are, according to Gilley, "Life and Writings," 16, "Newman's most anti-Anglican publication." Later they were published in the first volume of *Diff.*

9 *Diff.* i, 371.

10 See Dietz, "John Henry Newman and the Fathers of the Church," 212n3.

11 *Diff.* i, 371–72.

This comment shows one of the key motives for Newman's attraction to the Fathers: their ecclesiology. Newman was profoundly impressed by the early Christian writers as witnesses to the Church's understanding of herself and of her offices, and this was to remain a theological interest in Newman's life, both in his Anglican and in his Catholic period.

In March 1831, the High Churchman Hugh James Rose (1795–1838) asked Newman to write a "History of the Principal Councils," which was to be part of a new series of publications intended to raise the Church of England's awareness of its own doctrinal and liturgical tradition.[12] Newman embarked on this project, but soon found that the complex theological issues involved made it necessary to limit the temporal scope of the investigation to period around the Council of Nicaea.

Newman was working within an existing tradition of scholarship, which he received and transformed. He stood on the shoulders of the Anglican divines who had studied the early Fathers with a view to defending their claims against the Roman Catholic Church and with a view to maintaining traditional Christian doctrine against the growing sectarian movements in the Church of England. In 1850, Newman looked back on those years, noting that he read the Fathers "with Bull's Defensio, as their key, as far as his subject extended."[13] The *Defence of the Nicene Creed* by George Bull, Anglican Bishop of St. David's (1634–1710), published in 1685, attempted to demonstrate that the ante-Nicene Fathers' Trinitarian theology was essentially that of the Nicene Creed. Newman also acquired some familiarity with French patristic scholarship, which flourished in the age before the Revolution, for instance, Pierre Daniel Huet's *Origeniana* of 1668.[14]

The fruit of these labours was Newman's first book and major contribution to theology: *The Arians of the Fourth Century*, in which he presents the historically most improbable thesis that the doctrine of Arius, who was an Alexandrian presbyter, was in fact influenced by Antiochene theology. Newman dedicates about a third of the book to what he identifies as two profoundly different schools of exegesis and theology: on the one hand, there was the school of Antioch and surrounding Syria, which developed a rationalist and historicising reading of the Bible and consequently gave birth to the Arian doctrine of Jesus Christ as a created mediator between the transcendent God and the world. On the other hand, there was the school of Alexandria, which privileged the spiritual sense of the Scriptures and consequently developed a theological vision that was, according to Newman, "based on the mystical or sacramental principle, and spoke of the various Economies or Dispensations of the Eternal."[15]

---

12   *Apo.*, 26.
13   *Diff.* i, 372.
14   See King, *Newman and the Alexandrian Fathers*, 41.
15   *Apo.*, 26–27.

Newman saw these ideas already exemplified in the works of Clement and Origen, and he believed that they naturally led to the theology of Athanasius, the great defender of the Trinitarian profession of faith. What attracted Newman to Alexandrian theology was its sacramental reading not just of Scripture, but of the whole of reality. He writes about this encounter:

> I understood these passages to mean that the exterior world, physical and historical, was but the manifestation to our senses of realities greater than itself. Nature was a parable: Scripture was an allegory: pagan literature, philosophy, and mythology, properly understood, were but a preparation for the Gospel.[16]

Newman was also fascinated by the spiritual life and vigour of the Alexandrian Church; in his eyes it compared very favourably with the state of his own Church of England, which he saw threatened by the strong tide of liberalism.

The Arians of the Fourth Century shows that Newman's study of the Fathers was inextricably linked to the arguments and controversies he faced in his own ecclesial context. Thus several commentators have observed that Newman's "Antioch" and "Alexandria" are ideal types rather than historical realities.[17] The Antiochenes Diodore of Tarsus, Theodore of Mopsuestia, John Chrysostom and Theodoret of Cyrus are often seen—and were certainly seen by Newman—as constituting a "school of exegesis," but their approach as biblical commentators is by no means as uniform as that term would suggest, even if they share common patterns of interpretation, which are quite distinct from those of their Alexandrian contemporaries.[18] The Antiochenes gave priority to the "historical" and "literal" interpretation of the Old Testament and were reluctant to read it from the perspective of the New. However, they were not completely opposed to allegory, as is sometimes claimed, and by the time of Theodoret and Cyril there is a clear cross-fertilisation between Antioch and Alexandria (where, incidentally, the "historical" reading of the Old Testament was considered to be the foundation of its Christological and ecclesiological interpretations). Nonetheless, with the exception of Chrysostom, there is something prosaic in the Antiochenes' understanding of the spiritual life, which has been characterised by Louis Bouyer as "asceticism without mysticism."[19]

---

16   *Apo.*, 27.

17   See Rowan Williams, "Introduction," in John Henry Newman, *The Arians of the Fourth Century*, Birmingham Oratory Millennium Edition 4 (Leominster: Gracewing, 2001), xix–xlvii.

18   See Robert C. Hill, *Reading the Old Testament in Antioch*, Bible in Ancient Christianity, vol. 5 (Leiden: Brill, 2005).

19   Louis Bouyer, *The Spirituality of the New Testament and the Fathers*, trans. Mary P. Ryan (London: Burns & Oates, 1963), 436.

In short, *The Arians of the Fourth Century* is the work of a neophyte in patristic studies. In the years to come, Newman had much opportunity to deepen his knowledge of the early Christian centuries. What never left him, however, was his fondness for the Alexandrian tradition, which profoundly resonated with his own intellectual and spiritual convictions.

THE OXFORD MOVEMENT

John Keble's "Assize Sermon" of July 14, 1833, denouncing what he identified as the nation's detachment from the practice of the Christian faith, marked the beginning of the religious movement later known as the Oxford Movement. Its founders were alarmed by the Whig government's Irish Church Temporalities Act and saw in it the rising tide of theological liberalism and rationalism in society. From September 1833, the work of the movement centred on the publication of the *Tracts for the Times*, which were originally short pamphlets, but later adopted a more learned character. The scholarly aspect of the *Tracts* was strengthened especially when Edward Bouverie Pusey (1800–1882), Professor of Hebrew at Oxford, joined the group. Unlike Newman and most of his Oxford contemporaries, Pusey read German, had spent some time in Germany, and had direct familiarity with the rationalist theology emerging from Protestant Universities such as Tübingen.

Newman soon came to realise that the polemic against religious liberalism needed to be founded on sound theology and that the study of the Fathers was an essential element in it. The claim of the Oxford Movement was that the Church of England was one of the "branches" of the undivided Church of the first centuries, along with the Roman and the Orthodox Churches, without suffering from the same "corruptions" as they did.[20] The two pillars of the Oxford Movement were the Fathers of the Church and the Anglican divines of the seventeenth century. In the early years of the Oxford Movement, Newman wrote a number of essays of a biographical character that were published first in the *British Magazine* and were later reprinted in the volume *The Church of the Fathers* in 1840. In 1834, he began to work on an edition of the extant works of Bishop Dionysius of Alexandria, a disciple of Origen who in the third century exchanged a number of letters on Trinitarian theology with his contemporary Bishop Dionysius of Rome. This correspondence played an important role in

---

20 Newman formulated the Oxford Movement's programme as follows: "I had a supreme confidence in our cause; we were upholding that primitive Christianity which was delivered for all time by the early teachers of the Church, and which was registered and attested in the Anglican formularies and by the Anglican divines. That ancient religion had well-nigh faded away out of the land, through the political changes of the last 150 years, and it must be restored. It would be in fact a second Reformation:—a better reformation, for it would be a return not to the sixteenth century, but to the seventeenth." *Apo.*, 43.

the Arian crisis of the fourth century. Newman never completed this work, but through this research became more familiar with the technical, philological aspect of patristic studies. In 1836, Newman and Pusey had the idea of making patristic theology available in English translation in a new series entitled *Library of the Fathers*. Newman's most significant contribution to the series was the volume *Select Treatises of St. Athanasius*, which appeared after several years' work in two parts, in 1842 and 1844.

Newman's studies of early Christianity also shaped his preaching and his theological writing in general. This is evident from his *Lectures on the Doctrine of Justification* of 1838, where he proposes to overcome one of the key disputes of the Reformation period by introducing the idea of man's deification, which he knew from his studies of the Alexandrian Fathers. Andrew Louth comments on this important theological contribution:

> Newman gives expression to this central conviction of the Oxford Movement, the conviction that as we respond to God in Christ, God Himself is present to us, in our hearts, drawing us to Himself: a conviction which expresses . . . the heart of the patristic doctrine of deification.[21]

In the *Apologia*, Newman wrote with hindsight that his study of the Fathers was a voyage into unchartered territory and that its outcome was uncertain. He was aware that the energetic recovery of the early Fathers questioned some of the Protestant principles of the Church of England in his day. In his lengthy *Preface* to the first volume of the *Library of the Fathers*, which contained the works of St. Cyril of Jerusalem and was published in 1838, Newman compared the task of the editors to that of architects,

> who lie under the disadvantage, from which Painters and Sculptors are exempt, of having their work exposed to public criticism through every stage of its execution, and being expected to provide symmetry and congruity in its parts independent of the whole.[22]

In the face of suspicions that the Oxford Movement would eventually lead to Roman Catholicism, Newman urged his readers not to jump to conclusions and asked above all for patience; in case of perplexity, they should submit their judgments to that of the Church of England as final arbiter.

---

21   Andrew Louth, "Manhood into God: The Oxford Movement, the Fathers and the Deification of Man," in *Essays Catholic and Radical: A Jubilee Group Symposium for the 150th Anniversary of the Beginning of the Oxford Movement 1833–1983*, ed. Kenneth Leech and Rowan Williams (London: Bowerdean Press, 1983), 70–80, at 74–75.

22   John Henry Newman, "Preface," *The Catechetical Lectures of S. Cyril, Archbishop of Jerusalem,* translated, with notes and indices, 4th ed. (Oxford/London: James Parker & Co./Rivingtons, 1872), xii.

This *Preface* also shows what I consider another key motive for Newman's attraction to the Fathers, that is, the question of Scriptural hermeneutics.

> Nothing can be more certain than that Scripture contains all necessary doctrine; yet nothing, it is presumed, can be more certain either, than that, practically speaking, it needs an interpreter; nothing more certain than that our Church and her Divines assign the witness of the early ages of Christianity concerning Apostolic doctrine, as that interpreter.[23]

Newman was very aware of the question of biblical exegesis, a question that was as relevant in his age as it is today. In the Fathers, Newman saw authentic interpreters of Scripture, and they taught him to read the Bible in and with the Church. There is an important passage in his *Lectures on Justification*, written around the same time as the *Preface*, which helps to illustrate this point. In the fifth lecture, entitled "Misuse of the Term Just or Righteous," Newman discusses the biblical sense of "being made righteous," which was at the heart of the Reformation controversy. Being aware of the variety and uncertainty of Scriptural interpretations, he wants to find "the one real sense" of the term, for which a philological methodology is not sufficient. Newman claims:

> Our duty is to be intent on things, not on names and terms; to associate words with their objects, instead of measuring them by their definitions; . . . in short, when we speak of justification or faith, to *have* a meaning and grasp an idea, though at different times it may be variously developed, or variously presented, as the profile or full face in a picture.[24]

For Newman, the Fathers are exemplary as interpreters of Scripture, because they "acquaint us with the things Scripture speaks of."[25] This passage is remarkable because it anticipates what scholars, such as Basil Studer and Robert Louis Wilken, have said more recently about patristic exegesis: the Fathers move from *res* to *verba*, that is, they start from an established (theological, moral, spiritual) reality, which is centred on the mystery of Christ, and explore how the words illustrate or express this truth.[26] This method has its obvious limitations, as any reader of a Church Father's biblical commentaries will find. However, the growing study of patristic exegesis in recent years has made more people realise

---

23 Newman, *The Catechetical Lectures of S. Cyril*, xii.
24 *Jfc.*, 121.
25 *Jfc.*, 121.
26 See Robert Louis Wilken, "Interpreting Job Allegorically: The *Moralia* of Gregory the Great," *Pro Ecclesia* 10, no. 2 (2001): 213–26 and "Allegory and the Interpretation of the Old Testament in the 21st Century," *Letter and Spirit* 1 (2005): 11–21; Basil Studer, *Schola christiana: Die Theologie zwischen Nizäa (325) und Chalcedon (451)* (Paderborn: Ferdinand Schöningh, 1998).

that it represents a legitimate approach to Holy Scripture. In fact, where patristic exegesis is at its best, it provides an example of the criteria given for biblical interpretation in the Second Vatican Council's Dogmatic Constitution on Divine Revelation.[27]

In the 1830s, Newman adopted the theory of the *Via Media*, according to which the Church of England, one of the branches of the undivided primitive Church, had preserved the doctrines of the patristic Church best and thus represented the *Via Media* or "middle way" between the doctrinal errors and apostasy of Protestantism and the corruptions and abuses of the Church of Rome (at least on the popular level). The *Lectures on the Prophetical Office of the Church* of 1837 are his fullest expression of this theory, which hinged on the dogmatic principle, the sacramental system and anti-Romanism. In the second edition of the *Lectures* of 1838, Newman chose to speak of "Anglo-Catholicism" instead of "Anglicanism."[28] However, in studying the history of the Church in the fourth century with its great controversies, Newman made a great discovery: even in the early Church doctrinal problems were not resolved solely on the basis of the principle of antiquity.

THE CRISIS OF THE *VIA MEDIA*

The controversial reception of the Oxford Movement in the Church of England at large, as well as a series of events at Oxford itself, made the theory of the Anglican *Via Media* appear fragile. An event in the summer of 1839 threw Newman into intellectual turmoil and started a process of reflection that would eventually bring him to the Roman Catholic Church.

The background to this intellectual crisis was formed by Newman's continued study of the Fathers. His initial research on Dionysius of Alexandria, though never published, led him further into the Christological controversies of the fourth and fifth centuries.[29] In the summers of 1834 and 1835 he carried this research further, and in the fateful "Long Vacation" of 1839, Newman read extensively on the years leading up to the Council of Chalcedon in 451. In these Christological debates, Newman saw St. Leo the Great, Bishop of Rome, as the supreme witness to the confession of the apostolic faith against the Monophysites, whose extreme representative, Eutyches, claimed that the human nature of Christ was completely absorbed in His divine nature:

---

27   Vatican Council II, Dogmatic Constitution on Divine Revelation *Dei Verbum* (November 18, 1965), 12: "But, since Holy Scripture must be read and interpreted in the sacred spirit in which it was written, no less serious attention must be given to the content and unity of the whole of Scripture if the meaning of the sacred texts is to be correctly worked out. The living tradition of the whole Church must be taken into account along with the harmony which exists between elements of the faith."

28   See Gilley, "Life and Writings," 8.

29   See King, *Newman and the Alexandrian Fathers*, 127–80.

My stronghold was Antiquity; now here, in the middle of the fifth
century, I found, as it seemed to me, Christendom of the sixteenth and
the nineteenth centuries reflected. I saw my face in that mirror, and I
was a Monophysite. The Church of the *Via Media* was in the position of
the Oriental communion, Rome was where she now is; and the Protestants were the Eutychians.[30]

In *Certain Difficulties Felt by Anglicans*, a text that is about fifteen years
closer to the events than the *Apologia*, Newman described his "reasonings and
feelings" of that summer with powerful rhetoric:

It was difficult to make out how the Eutychians or Monophysites were
heretics, unless Protestants and Anglicans were heretics also; difficult to
find arguments against the Tridentine Fathers, which did not tell against
the Fathers of Chalcedon; difficult to condemn the Popes of the sixteenth
century, without condemning the Popes of the fifth. The drama of religion, and the combat of truth and error, were ever one and the same.
The principles and proceedings of the Church now, were those of the
Church then; the principles and proceedings of heretics then, were those
of Protestants now. I found it so,—almost fearfully; there was an awful
similitude, more awful, because so silent and unimpassioned, between
the dead records of the past and the feverish chronicle of the present.
The shadow of the fifth century was on the sixteenth. . . . What was the
use of continuing the controversy, or defending my position, if, after all, I
was forging arguments for Arius or Eutyches, and turning devil's advocate
against the much-enduring Athanasius and the majestic Leo?[31]

The point of comparison between the Monophysites of the fifth century and
the Anglicans of the nineteenth century was not the contents of their teachings,
but the principle according to which controversial points were resolved. Thus, what
was at issue was theological methodology and ecclesial authority. Newman realised
that the truths of the Catholic faith were not found on the "*Via Media*," and their
point of reference was not just "antiquity," as the Oxford Movement was claiming.[32]

In that same summer of 1839, Newman's friend Robert Williams[33] showed
him a lengthy article in the *Dublin Review* by Nicholas Wiseman, then still
Rector of the English College in Rome, on the "Anglican claim." Wiseman
compared the Church of England with the schismatic Donatists of North Africa
in the time of St. Augustine of Hippo. At first, Newman was not at all convinced

---

30 *Apo.*, 114.

31 *Diff.* i, 387–88; see also *Apo.*, 115–16.

32 Nicholas Wiseman, "The Anglican Claim of Apostolic Succession," *Dublin Review*
7 (1839): 139–80.

33 See *LD* ii, 256.

of Wiseman's argument, but Williams pointed Newman to a phrase of Augustine's that Wiseman quoted to illustrate his main point: "*Securus judicat orbis terrarum.*" This phrase was taken from Augustine's lengthy reply to a letter of Parmenianus, the Donatist Bishop of Carthage.[34] Augustine's argument against the Donatists, who claimed to be the true church, indeed the church of the pure and holy, was catholicity: the whole world judges securely that those are not good who separate themselves from the whole world, in whatever part of the world. This is said against the backdrop of Augustine's ecclesiology of the Church as a *corpus permixtum*: it contains wheat and tares, good and bad fish, which will be separated only at the end of times. The supreme principle therefore is catholicity. Wiseman applied this argument to the contemporary situation of Anglicans, and his words resonated with Newman not primarily because of the Donatist struggle but because of the Christological controversies he was studying during this summer of 1839.[35]

Newman was able to lay aside the disturbing questions that this summer of study had raised for him. However, as he expressed it, with a vivid biblical image: "I had seen the shadow of a hand upon the wall." He could no longer forget Augustine's phrase "*Securus judicat orbis terrarum,*" that is, in his own paraphrase: "The universal Church, in her judgments, is sure of the Truth." Newman pursued his patristic studies and continued to work on the translation of Athanasius. However, the thoughts of the summer of 1839 returned to haunt him. In 1841, he writes, he "received three blows which broke me." First, he saw the same theological principle underpinning the Christological debates of the fifth century, to be at work in the Arian controversies of the fourth century and, in fact, "in a far bolder shape." Newman admits that he "had not observed it in 1832." His reading of the history of Arianism was now thus: "the pure Arians were the Protestants, the semi-Arians were the Anglicans, and . . . Rome now was what it was then. The truth lay, not with the *Via Media*, but with what was called "the extreme party.""[36]

Two further events accelerated Newman's move towards Rome: the general condemnation of his *Tract* 90 on the interpretation of the *Thirty-Nine Articles* by the Anglican Bishops and the question of the Jerusalem Bishopric, which was set up jointly by the Church of England and the United Protestant Church of Prussia. In this period, the focus of Newman's patristic studies changed, as noted by King: "Newman abandoned his aim of making the ancient Church live once more in England. Instead, he sought an authority who would guarantee that developments in doctrine were legitimate, and in his reading of Athanasius he found such a guarantor."[37]

---

34   "Quapropter securus iudicat orbis terrarum bonos non esse qui se diuidunt ab orbe terrarum, in quacunque parte terrarum Augustine of Hippo, *Contra epistulam Parmeniani*, III,4,24: CSEL 51,131.

35   See *Apo.*, 117.

36   See *Apo.*, 119.

37   King, *Newman and the Alexandrian Fathers*, 19.

TOWARDS ROME

The importance of Newman's studies of the Christological controversy of the fourth and fifth centuries for his theological development cannot, in my view, be overestimated.[38] This is all the more remarkable, because Newman's own theological reasoning was closer to the Alexandrian tradition, which is centred on the Divine Word, the Second Person of the Trinity, and on his union with a human nature that he made his own as the instrument of salvation. Even the more "monophysite" expressions of Cyril of Alexandria would have appealed more to Newman than the more "symmetrical" Christology of Pope Leo's *Tome*, affirming the undiminished reality of divinity and humanity in Christ. There is a debate in patristic scholarship as to what extent Chalcedon was actually shaped by Leo's *Tome*, and some historians argue that the Christology of Cyril was considered the supreme authority and that Leo was seen to agree with it.[39] In Newman's reading, however, it was Leo's *Tome* that settled the controversy. For him it was above all a question of teaching authority, and for this he was ready to relinquish his own theological preferences.[40]

Newman's ever-more extensive reading on the doctrinal controversies in the patristic period made him realize that the principle of "antiquity" alone, because it cannot account for the development of Christian doctrine that took place already in the Apostolic age and continued through the Middle Ages until the present day, being authenticated by the Magisterium of the Catholic Church. In other words, Newman discovered the principle of the development of doctrine, which is one of his major contributions to modern Catholic theology. It is interesting to note that he approached the position of the French Jesuit Dionysius Petavius, who in his *De theologicis dogmatibus* (1644–1650) argued that there was indeed a development in the theological understanding of the Trinity that led to the Creed of Nicaea and conceded that many ante-Nicene Fathers held positions that were not so different from that of Arius. In fact, Petavius admitted that, judged by the formulae of later orthodoxy, the language of theologians in the first three centuries would be found lacking. It was against Petavius that Bull wanted to show the agreement of ante-Nicene Trinitarian theology with the Nicene Creed.[41]

---

38 See *Apo.*, 149 and his letter to Archdeacon Manning, Oct. 25, 1843. "This thought came to me last summer four years . . . I mentioned it to two friends in the autumn . . . It arose in the first instance from the Monophysite and Donatist controversies, the former of which I was engaged with in the course of theological study to which I had given myself." The letter is quoted in *Apo.*, 221.

39 See, above all, Richard Price and Michael Gaddis, *The Acts of the Council of Chalcedon, translated with an introduction and notes*, Translated texts for historians, vol. 45, 2nd rev. ed. (Liverpool: Liverpool University Press, 2007).

40 See Daley, "Newman and the Alexandrian Tradition," 179–81.

41 See Daley, "The Church Fathers," 32–33 and 35. Daley sees this new position expressed in the last of Newman's Oxford University Sermons of February 2, 1843: "The Theory of Developments in Religious Doctrine."

THE FATHERS IN THE
ESSAY ON THE DEVELOPMENT OF CHRISTIAN DOCTRINE

Newman's critique of the Anglican divines and their patristic hermeneutics is contained in the introduction to his *Essay on the Development of Christian Doctrine*. In his account, the foundation for the Anglican position that distinguishes between "a pure Christianity in East and West" in antiquity and a "corrupt" one in its present Roman form is the famous principle of Vincent of Lérins: Catholic doctrine is distinguished from heresy by having been held at all times, in all places, and by all believers (*quod semper, quod ubique, quod ab omnibus*).[42] Vincent formulated this principle in his *Commonitorium* (or "aide-memoire") of 434, in opposition to Augustine's "new" theology of grace.

Newman had already felt the difficulties of this when, still fully confident of the *Via Media* theory, he delivered in his *Lectures on the Prophetical Office of the Church* of 1837.[43] As a student of the early Church, Newman was keenly aware of the problems in applying Vincent's criteria to even the most fundamental articles of the Christian faith. On the Trinity, he professes not to see "in what sense it can be said that there is a *consensus* of primitive divines in its favour, which will not avail also for certain doctrines of the Roman Church which will presently come into mention."[44] For example, it is questionable where any ante-Nicene theologian clearly affirms the numerical unity or the coequality of the three divine persons in the way this would be required by post-Nicene orthodoxy, apart perhaps from Tertullian (c. 160–220) in his important treatise *Adversus Praxean*, which he wrote during his Montanist period. Moreover, the divinity of the Holy Spirit was not distinctly articulated in theology before the momentous contributions of the Cappadocian Fathers in the later part of the fourth century.

Newman does not mean to say that there was no such thing as pre-Nicene orthodoxy; on the contrary, he sees the early Fathers as important witnesses for the Apostolic faith. His point is rather that the principle *quod semper, quod ubique, quod ab omnibus* requires what he calls a "fair" interpretation, as opposed to "that *unfair* interpretation of Vincentius, which is necessary in order to make him available against the Church of Rome."[45] In other words, it is not possible to draw a clear line between a "pure" antiquity that would fulfil the Vincentian criteria, and a later period of corruption.

Newman's sober judgment of Vincent's principle is this: "The solution it offers is as difficult as the original problem." This leads him to consider a second hypothesis, which he presented already in his *Arians of the Fourth Century*, that of the *disciplina arcani*: "It is maintained that doctrines which are associated with the later ages of the Church were really in the Church from the first,

---

42 *Dev.*, 10.
43 *VM* i, 55–56.
44 *Dev.*, 13.
45 *Dev.*, 19.

but not publicly taught, and that for various reasons."[46] The concept of a *disciplina arcani* has come under criticism in recent patristic scholarship, because it suggests that Christians were obliged to keep strict silence especially about the baptismal and Eucharistic liturgy in a way parallel to the pagan mystery cults, where the sacred rites were only known to the initiates. The Church's sacraments were certainly never "*arcana*" in that sense; at the same time, however, early Christians observed some reticence in speaking about their ritual and worship to outsiders.[47] The case of St. Ambrose of Milan (c. 340–397) is instructive: In his *De mysteriis*, which bears the characteristics of catechetical homilies but is a literary work intended for publication, he explains the meaning of the sacraments of baptism and the Eucharist, but he does not cite any of the liturgical texts on which he draws extensively in his *De sacramentis*, a text that is based on unrevised notes taken directly from his mystagogical preaching in Milan. In these instructions for the newly baptised, the bishop quotes large parts of the formula of renunciation and the formula of Baptism and substantial parts of the Eucharistic Prayer. He also speaks about Christian prayer and gives a commentary on the Our Father, which is omitted in *De mysteriis*.[48]

Thus it would be reasonable to conclude with Newman that "the fact of this concealment can hardly be denied."[49] However, Newman goes on to concede that this theory of *disciplina arcani*, while going "some way to account for that apparent variation and growth of doctrine . . . is no key to the whole difficulty."[50] In other words, appeal to the *disciplina arcani* to account for the gaps between ante-Nicene and post-Nicene orthodoxy is largely wishful thinking. At this point Newman introduces his theory of the development of Christian doctrine, which he defines as

the increase and expansion of the Christian Creed and Ritual, and the variations which have attended the process in the case of individual writers and Churches, are the necessary attendants on any philosophy or polity which takes possession of the intellect and heart, and has had any wide or extended dominion; that, from the nature of the human

---

46 *Dev.*, 27.

47 See Douglas Powell, "Arkandisziplin," *Theologische Realenzyklopädie* 4 (1979), 1–8; Jorg Christian Salzmann, *Lehren und Ermahnen: Zur Geschichte des christlichen Wortgottesdienstes in den ersten drei Jahrhunderten*, Wissenschaftliche Untersuchungen zum Neuen Testament II/59 (Tübingen: Mohr Siebeck, 1994), 396–99 and 427–29 (on Tertullian); Edward J. Yarnold, *The Awe-Inspiring Rites of Initiation: The Origins of the R.C.I.A.* (Edinburgh: T & T Clark, 1994), 55–56, and *Cyril of Jerusalem*, The Early Church Fathers (London: Routledge, 2000), 49–50.

48 See Josef Schmitz, *Gottesdienst im altchristlichen Mailand: Eine liturgiewissenschaftliche Untersuchung über Initiation und Meßfeier während des Jahres zur Zeit des Bischofs Ambrosius († 397)*, Theophaneia 25 (Köln: Hanstein, 1975).

49 *Dev.*, 27.

50 *Dev.*, 29.

mind, time is necessary for the full comprehension and perfection of great ideas; and that the highest and most wonderful truths, though communicated to the world once for all by inspired teachers, could not be comprehended all at once by the recipients, but, as being received and transmitted by minds not inspired and media which were human, have required only the longer time and deeper thought for their full elucidation. This may be called the *Theory of Development of Doctrine*.[51]

Newman illustrates his theory with a striking image:

It is indeed sometimes said that the stream is clearest near the spring. Whatever use may fairly be made of this image, it does not apply to the history of a philosophy or belief, which on the contrary is more equable, and purer, and stronger, when its bed has become deep, and broad, and full.[52]

The concept was not an entirely new one; as we have seen, Petavius in the seventeenth century identified a development in Trinitarian theology in the centuries before Nicaea. Newman also acknowledged that the principle of development had been presented by two very different Catholic authors before him, the French writer Joseph De Maistre (1753–1821) and the Tübingen theologian Johann Adam Möhler (1796–1838).[53] It required the historical consciousness of the nineteenth century to make the principle of development of doctrine a central element of Catholic teaching. As Sheridan Gilley has observed, this principle has become so commonplace "that it is difficult to imagine a world in which Catholic theologians defended dogma by insisting that it was simply unchanging."[54]

In the *Essay*, Newman does not fully explore his theory of development; this "would be the work of a life," which cannot be undertaken by "one who, in the

---

51 *Dev.*, 29–30.

52 *Dev.*, 30. In June 1846, Newman wrote to Henry Wilberforce: "The fact I believe to be this—the early Fathers made incorrect intellectual developments of portions or aspects of that whole Catholic doctrine which they held, and so far were inconsistent with themselves. . . . I really do not think you can deny, that the Fathers, not merely did not contemplate true propositions, (afterwards established), but actually contemplated false." *LD* xi, 183.

53 Owen Chadwick, *From Bossuet to Newman*, 2nd ed. (Cambridge: Cambridge University Press, 1987), 111, contends that, despite this reference, Möhler exerted no influence on Newman (who did not know German). Dietz, "John Henry Newman and the Fathers of the Church," 215, n. 9, suggests a parallel between Möhler and Newman, in that both saw the Fathers as "testimonies" to the apostolic faith, even where they failed to articulate with the precision of language characteristic of later orthodoxy.

54 Gilley, "Life and Writings," 12.

middle of his days, is beginning life again."[55] Instead Newman presents "notes" that help to authenticate genuine development and distinguish it from distortions and corruptions. In fact, the principle of development ensures for Newman that the "idea of Christianity" remains the same.

NEWMAN AS A PATRISTICS SCHOLAR

Despite the many different claims on his time and attention, Newman continued his patristic scholarship until the last years of his life. The writings of his Catholic period include technical, scholarly pieces, such as the study "On St. Cyril's Formula of the μία φύσις τοῦ θεοῦ λόγος σεσαρκωμένη,"[56] as well as lively and sympathetic articles of a more biographical character, such as "The Last Years of St. Chrysostom."[57]

Newman's seminal contributions to the study of the Church Fathers, especially those of the Greek tradition, have been widely acknowledged by Anglican, Catholic, and Orthodox scholars.[58] At the same time, given the intimate connection of Newman's studies of the Fathers with his own intellectual and spiritual journey, there has been some controversy about their value as historiography. In the early twentieth century, W. R. Inge judged Newman's patristic writings "autobiographical" and saw in him "historical falsity" mixed with "philosophical truth."[59] More recently, Rowan Williams has found fault with Newman's *Arians of the Fourth Century* from a historian's point of view: "Newman's own perspectives and proposals are often flawed by a colossally over-schematic treatment and a carelessness in detail."[60] On the other hand, Benjamin King, who in his monograph on *Newman and the Alexandrian Fathers* provides a critical reading of how Roman Catholic theology conditioned Newman's later interpretation of the Fathers, grants that Newman was "a more serious historical scholar than Inge allowed."[61] King shows how Newman's patristic studies developed in various stages of his life and notes the impact they had on subsequent Anglophone scholarship. However, I am not convinced by King's claim that by the 1870s Newman "was reading the Greek Fathers through the lens of scholasticism,"[62] let alone the kind of "Neo-Thomism" that was promoted by Pope Leo XIII's encyclical *Aeterni Patris* of 1879. It is somewhat ironic to make Newman into a scholastic, since as a Catholic he was criticized by members of the Roman school of theology for precisely *not* being scholastic enough. I would rather suggest that the

---

55 *Dev.*, 31.
56 First published in *Atlantis*, July 1858 and later reprinted in *TT*, 329–82.
57 First published in *Rambler*, 1859–60 and later reprinted in *HS* ii, 217–302.
58 See the testimonies gathered by King, "The Church Fathers," 113.
59 See King, *Newman and the Alexandrian Fathers*, 224.
60 Williams, "Introduction," xxxvi.
61 King, *Newman and the Alexandrian Fathers*, 224.
62 King, *Newman and the Alexandrian Fathers*, 19.

anachronisms in Newman's later, revised translation of Athanasius can be explained more easily by an ill-suited attempt to make fourth century theology conform to the language of orthodoxy that emerged from the doctrinal struggles between Nicaea and Chalcedon.

Newman found in the Fathers a theological method that was congenial to his own, precisely because it was not scholastic. The limitations of his patristic writings from a historian's point of view lie in the fact that he read the Fathers as contemporaries, as participants in the theological conversations and controversies of his own day. Henri Brémond noted that Newman treated the Fathers with great intimacy and conversed with them as with friends. This is evident particularly in Newman's biographical sketches, which are written with great warmth and sympathy.[63] Newman could not take the role of an impartial, detached historian; he was always too closely involved in the subject matter he was treating. In this sense, he was very similar to the Fathers themselves, whose theological method he once characterised with the following words:

> Instead of writing formal doctrinal treatises, they write controversy; and their controversy, again, is correspondence. They mix up their own persons, natural and supernatural, with the didactic or polemical works which engaged them. Their authoritative declarations are written, not on stone tablets, but on what Scripture calls "the fleshly tables of the heart."[64]

Thus, the relationship between Newman and the Fathers provides a vivid illustration of his cardinalitial motto, taken from St. Francis de Sales and inspired by St. Augustine, *Cor ad cor loquitur*—"Heart speaks to heart."

Suggested Reading

Biffi, Inos. "*I Profili storici* di John Henry Newman." *Una ragionevole fede: Logos e dialogo in John Henry Newman*, ed. Evandro Botto and Hermann Geissler, 155–81. Milan: Vita & Pensiero, 2009.

Chadwick, Owen. *From Bossuet to Newman*, 2nd ed. Cambridge: Cambridge University Press, 1987.

Daley, Brian E. "Newman and the Alexandrian Tradition: 'The Veil of the Letter' and the Person of Christ." In *Newman and Truth*, ed. Ian Ker and Terrence Merrigan, 147–88. Louvain Theological & Pastoral Monographs 39. Louvain: Peeters, 2008.

Daley, Brian E. "The Church Fathers." In *The Cambridge Companion to John Henry Newman*, ed. Ian Ker and Terrence Merrigan, 29–46. Cambridge: University Press, 2009.

---

63   See Biffi, "*I Profili storici* di John Henry Newman," 155, 163–65, with reference to Henri Brémond, *Newman: Essai de biographie psychologique* (Paris: Bloud et Gay, 1906).
64   *HS* ii, 223.

Dietz, Kathleen. "John Henry Newman and the Fathers of the Church: The Birth of an Ecclesiology." In *Una ragionevole fede: Logos e dialogo in John Henry Newman*, edited by Evandro Botto and Hermann Geissler, 211–20. Milan: Vita & Pensiero, 2009.

Dragas, George D. "John Henry Newman's Rediscovery of the Catholicity of the Greek Fathers." *One in Christ* 17, no. 1 (1981): 46–68.

Various. *Actes du colloque des 20 et 21 novembre 2004: Newman et les Pères de l'Église. Etudes Newmaniennes* 21 (2005).

King, Benjamin J. "The Church Fathers." In *The Oxford Handbook of John Henry Newman*, edited by Frederick D. Aquino and Benjamin J. King, 113–34. Oxford: Oxford University Press, 2018.

King, Benjamin J. *Newman and the Alexandrian Fathers: Shaping Doctrine in Nineteenth-Century England*. Oxford: Oxford University Press, 2009.

Louth, Andrew. "Manhood into God: The Oxford Movement, the Fathers and the Deification of Man." In *Essays Catholic and Radical: A Jubilee Group Symposium for the 150th Anniversary of the Beginning of the Oxford Movement 1833–1983*, edited by Kenneth Leech and Rowan Williams, 70–80. London: Bowerdean Press, 1983.

Pelikan, Jaroslav. "Newman and the Fathers: The Vindication of Tradition." *Studia Patristica* 18, no. 4 (1990): 379–90.

Tokarsik, G. "John Henry Newman and the Church Fathers." *Eastern Churches Journal* 7 (2000): 101–16.

Williams, Rowan. "Introduction" to *The Arians of the Fourth Century*, Birmingham Oratory Millennium Edition 4, xix–xlvii. Leominster: Gracewing, 2001.

CHAPTER 9

NEWMAN:
A STUDENT AND TUTOR
OF CLASSICS

Scott Goins

From childhood until the end of his life, the study of the Classics was an important constant for John Henry Newman. Newman was not only engaged in teaching the Classics on the university level, especially during his early career, but ancient authors provided him with much of his model for education. In particular, Aristotle and, to a lesser extent, Cicero were foundational in offering him inspiration for his concept of education.[1] The Classics, notably Cicero, also provided Newman his model for composition, contributing to his reputation as one of the greatest prose writers of the time. Moreover, like C. S. Lewis and many others, Newman saw classical writings as propaedeutic for Christianity. Although he was certain of the superior revelation to be found in Scripture and the teachings of the Church, he also considered

---

1   On Aristotle, see Angelo Bottone, *The Philosophical Habit of Mind: Rhetoric and Person in John Henry Newman's Dublin Writings* (Bucharest: Zeta Books, 2010); Paul Shrimpton, *The 'Making of Men': The Idea and Reality of Newman's University in Oxford and Dublin* (Leominster: Gracewing, 2014). See also Joshua P. Hochschild, "The Re-Imagined Aristotelianism of John Henry Newman," *Modern Age* 45, no. 4 (2003): 333–42, especially at 335, and Mary Katherine Tillman, *John Henry Newman: Man of Letters* (Milwaukee, Wisc.: 2015), 261–81. On Cicero, see Angelo Bottone, "The Influence of Cicero on Newman's Idea of a Liberal Education," *Yearbook of the Irish Philosophical Society* (2009): 1–14.

classical wisdom as inspired. He believed that the Classics offered much of the best of human wisdom, along with elements of the divine, and he considered the subject foundational to the formation of the young human mind.

NEWMAN THE STUDENT

Like most well educated persons of his era, Newman became acquainted with the standard authors of ancient Greece and Rome at a young age. By the age of nine, he was reading some Virgil and Ovid in Latin, and he had begun learning Greek with a text of *Aesop's Fables* (Eton 1807).[2] A year later he had tried his hand at writing Latin verse, and about a year after that, at the age of eleven, he began to read Homer in Greek.[3] While at Ealing, Newman delighted in performing in the annual Latin plays, a tradition he would continue at the Oratory School. From 1813–1816 he performed in Terence's *Phormio, Eunuch, Adelphoe*, and *Andria*.[4] In 1817, at the age of sixteen, Newman enrolled at Trinity College, Oxford, where he took his new role very seriously. In preparing for college, he covered a large amount of ancient literature, including Sophocles, Horace, Cicero, and Juvenal.[5] Similarly, in the fall term, he had taken on the whole of Xenophon's *Anabasis* (when he would have been allowed to do only one book), and two "tracts of Tacitus."[6] During this period and throughout most of his life, he was also dedicated to learning the skillful writing of Latin prose, and, to a lesser extent, Latin poetry. Newman even records pledging with his close friend John William Bowden that they would speak to each other only in Latin.[7] These talents impressed his instructors. At Ealing his Headmaster, George Nicholas, said of him that "nobody had run through the school from the bottom to the top as rapidly as John Newman."[8] In 1813, at age eleven, Newman's talents were enough to make his teacher, Mr. Mullins, deem him worthy of the gift of a Greek New Testament.[9] Similarly, five years later at Trinity, his tutor gave him a lexicon of Ionic Greek to enhance his studies of Herodotus.[10] Newman wrote his mother that Mr. Kinsey, who judged the Latin declamations at Trinity, said that his declamation "did [him]

---

2   *LD* i, 6 and n. 3.

3   *LD* i, 11.

4   See Maisie Ward, *Young Mr. Newman* (New York: Sheed and Ward, 1948), 7, and Henry Tristram, "The Classics," in *A Tribute to Newman: Essays on Aspects of His Life and Thought*, ed. Michael Tierney (Dublin: Browne and Nolan, 1945), 252.

5   See A. Dwight Culler, *The Imperial Intellect: A Study of Newman's Educational Ideal* (New Haven, Conn.: Yale University Press, 1955), 5. See similarly Culler's list of Newman's reading on a summer vacation: a book of the *Aeneid*, Tacitus's *Germania*, seven chapters of Genesis from the Septuagint, Herodotus, and seven plays of Sophocles (7).

6   *LD* i, 45.

7   See Ward, *Young Mr. Newman*, 41.

8   *AW*, 29.

9   *LD* i, 13.

10   *LD* i, 49.

much credit."[11] Despite his accomplishments, Newman's early academic career was not a series of unbroken successes. At Trinity he records feeling behind his cohort in Latin and Greek, although this could simply be attributable to a lack of self-confidence often found in serious students.[12] More significantly his attempt at testing for Honors at Trinity was a disaster, probably because of studying too much, having insufficient guidance, and perhaps also suffering from fears that he was moving outside God's will in his desire to excel. Despite his good efforts, Newman had a breakdown and performed poorly.[13]

NEWMAN'S PROFESSIONAL LIFE AS A CLASSICIST

If we look at Newman's failure we might be tempted to agree with some who have questioned his credentials as a classicist. Edward Copleston, Provost at Oriel, and later Bishop of Llandaff, claimed that Newman was "not even a good classical scholar," and the polyglot Irish Cardinal Francis Moran observed that he was "a bad Latinist."[14] Mark Pattison, who entered Oriel just as Newman was ceasing to tutor there, likewise criticized Newman and the other Oriel tutors in his *Memoirs* on the grounds that "their knowledge of the classics was extremely limited."[15] Yet these claims can hardly be taken seriously at face value. It is evident that there were times when Newman, both as a student and as a teacher, read huge amounts of material in the original languages, and although he stuck mostly to the standard authors, he seems to have been thoroughly familiar with them.[16] Newman naturally gravitated to works that were recommended by his tutor or later that would be useful to his students. As his career progressed and his attention moved towards doctrine and the Church Fathers, he still remained interested

---

11   *LD* i, 45.

12   *LD* i, 48.

13   See Culler, *Imperial Intellect*, 17–22; Ward, *Young Mr. Newman*, 51–52; Ian Ker, *John Henry Newman: A Biography* (Oxford: Oxford University Press, 1988), 12–14; and *AW*, 51–52.

14   For Copleston's remark, see Ward, *Young Mr. Newman*, 70, and *AW*, 64. In the full quote from a letter to Edward Hawkins, dated May 2, 1843, he adds "yet in mind and powers of composition, and in taste and knowledge, he was decidedly superior to some competitors, who were a class above him in the Schools." For Moran's comment, see Tristram, "Classics," 260, who disagrees with Moran's assessment.

15   Mark Pattison, *Memoirs* (London: Macmillan, 1985), 92, cited in Tristram, "Classics," 265. Tristram suggests that Pattison refers to breadth of reading rather than depth of reading.

16   Culler, *Imperial Intellect*, 276–78, has a useful list of the classical texts in Newman's library. One has only to read "University Life. Athens," in *Rise and Progress of the Universities* to see how thoroughly Newman's mind was steeped in the knowledge of antiquity (*HS* iii, 33–46). With regard to classical rhetoric, Walter Jost, *Rhetorical Thought in John Henry Newman* (Columbia, S.C.: University of South Carolina Press, 1989), 9, claims that Newman's "Scattered remarks . . . reveal an easy familiarity with the rhetorical tradition from the time of Gorgias to the Second Sophistic."

in the Classics. Although Newman did publish in the Classics, as we shall see, he did not see research as his primary goal. Instead, like most of his colleagues, Newman rejected the German idea of a highly specialized, research-oriented professoriate.[17] It is therefore unfair to judge him by the German model of the 1800s or by the standards of the modern research university.[18] It would be better to compare Newman to a good teacher at a university dedicated to the liberal arts, especially as those teachers saw their role a generation or two ago, rarely intent on extensive publication.

An examination of Newman's publications in the Classics certainly suggests that he was a generalist rather than a specialist. For Newman, publications were largely based on opportunity rather than on an attempt to establish himself as an expert in one or two areas, as a career-oriented classicist of today would do. Newman's first foray into publishing actually began as a fellow at Oriel when he wrote an essay that Whately would later adapt for his textbook, *The Elements of Logic*.[19] Whately warmly praised Newman for his help in writing the book, although Newman demurred to him in a letter claiming that his contribution was not significant.[20] Whately also secured Newman's most important classical publication, an article on Cicero for the *Encyclopaedia Metropolitana*.[21] The editor of the *Encyclopaedia* had been disappointed by a previous submission from another author, so Whately suggested Newman, then aged only twenty-three, as the author of its replacement. In a mere two months he completed the lengthy article, which amounted almost to a monograph. This accomplishment is especially amazing when we consider the vast oeuvre of Cicero, ranging from letters to orations to philosophical discourses. The article is comprehensive and sensitive, with an astute treatment of Cicero's philosophy. It was praised by Mary Rosner as "the most qualified and complex response" to Cicero's oratory currently available.[22] Being a skilled rhetorician, Newman was

---

17   See Alasdair Macintyre, "The Very Idea of a University: Aristotle, Newman, and Us," *British Journal of Educational Studies* 57, no. 4 (2009): 348, and *Idea*, 168. Although Newman saw instruction of the mind and character as a tutor's main role, he was a strong proponent of professorial publication. See Mary Katherine Tillman, ed., *Rise and Progress of Universities and Benedictine Essays* (Leominster: Gracewing, 2001), lxx–lxxiv, and Tillman, *Letters*, 304–5. On the secular basis of the German research model, see Reinhard Hütter, *John Henry Newman on Truth and Its Counterfeits: A Guide for Our Times* (Washington, D.C. : The Catholic University of America Press, 2020), 168–69.

18   In ch. 10 of this volume, Christopher Lane critiques the "noble dream" of objectivity (editor's note).

19   See Culler, *Imperial Intellect*, 39–43, and *AW*, 18–19.

20   See *LD* i, 306–7.

21   Reprinted in *HS* i, 245–300. *LD* i, 176 and n. 2, includes a letter in which the article is highly praised in a letter from the editor. See also Bottone, "Influence of Cicero," 1–2.

22   Mary Rosner, "Reflections on Cicero in Nineteenth Century England and America," *Rhetorica* 4, no. 2 (1986): 169. See also Bottone, "Influence of Cicero," 1–2.

able to see the virtues as well as the flaws of the great orator.[23] Newman went on to write articles on Apollonius of Tyana, a first century Neopythagorean philosopher, and an "Essay on Miracles" for the *Encyclopaedia* in the following year.[24] During this period he collaborated with the Rev. J. E. Tyler on *Indices Attici or a Guide to the Quantity of the Greek Penultima, Chiefly with Reference to Attic Writers* (Oxford and London 1824), an obviously specialized book the authors began writing as a substitute for a text they felt was no longer afford-able for students.[25] Four years later Newman wrote a more general study of Aristotle's *Poetics* for the *London Review*.[26] Newman would later write several works relating to Classics and education designed for a popular, mostly Irish, audience when he was assigned the task of creating the Catholic University in Dublin.[27] In these articles Newman displays a thorough acquaintance with clas-sical authors, culture, and customs.

Like many classical scholars, Newman's interest and talent in the Classics contributed to his involvement with patristics. He began reading the Church Fathers in 1828, intending to carry out a systematic study in his search for reli-gious truth. By 1833 he had written the *Arians of the Fourth Century*, in which he shows a proclivity for the Alexandrian School.[28] His next step, which he would work on intermittently for over a decade, was a translation of two volumes of Athanasius (1842 and 1844). Newman's study of Athanasius, Clement of Alexan-dria, and Origen contributed to his adopting an eastern view of *theosis* (deifica-tion) seen in his work on *Lectures on the Doctrine of Justification*.[29] Further study of the Fathers eventually caused him to see the Anglican Church as acting simi-larly to the heretical groups that had broken with the Roman Catholic Church during the past.[30] Newman truly loved and admired the Fathers, and he would

---

23 See, for example, *HS* i, 291–93, where he notes the positive and negative aspects of Cicero's *Orations*.

24 See *LD* i, 209, n. 1.

25 See *LD* i, 181, n. 1.

26 Originally published as "Greek Tragedy—poetry," *London Review* 1 (1828): 153–71; reprinted in *EH* i, 1–26.

27 See, for example, "Site of a University," "University Life. Athens," and "Discipline and Influence" *HS* iii. 18–32, 33–46, and 60–76. For a full list, see Vincent Ferrer Blehl, *John Henry Newman: A Bibliographical Catalogue of His Writings* (Charlottesville, Va.: University Press of Virginia, 1978), 87–92.

28 See Brian E. Daley, "The Church Fathers," in *The Cambridge Companion to John Henry Newman*, ed. Ian Ker and Terrence Merrigan (Cambridge: Cambridge University Press, 2009), 29–43; Uwe Michael Lang, "Newman and the Fathers of the Church," *New Blackfriars* 92, no. 1038 (2011): 146–47 (revised and expanded in this volume); Benjamin J. King, *Newman and the Alexandrian Fathers: Shaping Doctrine in Nineteenth-Century England* (Oxford: Clarendon, 2009); and Benjamin J. King, "The Church Fathers," in *The Oxford Handbook of John Henry Newman*, ed. Frederick D. Aquino and Benjamin J. King (Oxford: Oxford University Press, 2018), 113–34.

29 King, "The Church Fathers," 124–26.

30 See Lang, "Newman and the Fathers," 150–51. See also *Apo.*, 114.

study them, especially Athanasius, until the end of his life.[31] Newman has usually been considered an excellent student of the Fathers, although recent scholars have noted that he is not as objective as he might be, and that he tends to read the Fathers through the lens of his own time.[32] While there is some justification for these criticisms, we must realize that Newman's primary intent was to seek an understanding of the faith by returning to the Fathers. He was not content to read them with complete detachment but instead passionately sought to learn Christian truths from them. Newman's love for the Fathers and their era is also revealed in *Callista*, a novel about a third century convert in North Africa that illustrates his knowledge of late antiquity as well as his versatility in writing.[33]

THE CLASSICS AND NEWMAN'S STYLE

Another area of accomplishment related to the Classics is Newman's talent as a prose stylist. Newman is well known and often anthologized as one of his period's greatest prose writers. Newman influenced the style of Arnold and Pater and garnered high praise from James Joyce.[34] One prevailing characteristic of his writing that can be linked to his classical training is his amplification of ideas by examining them from many angles and employing extensive and applicable exemplification. As Wall aptly notes, Newman's "gyrations are those of a falcon before it has isolated and swooped on its prey. And this roundabout analytic way to truth was, he knew, the opposite of the poet's intuitive grasp at the heart of things. It was the orator's way, Cicero's way."[35] In support of his claim, Wall goes on to quote from Newman's essay on Aristotle's *Poetics*:

> the talent of the orator consists in making much of a single idea. . . . This is the great art of Cicero himself, who, whether engaged in statement, argument, or raillery, never ceases till he has exhausted his subject; going round about it, and placing it in every different light, yet without repetition to weary the reader.[36]

---

31 Lang lists a few other patristic works. See Lang, "Newman and the Fathers," 155. For a complete listing, see Blehl, *Bibliographical Guide*, 1978. Newman also wrote poems on the Fathers, such as "The Greek Fathers" and "St. Gregory Nazianzen" VV, 102 and 151.

32 See King, "The Church Fathers," 113–34. Stephen Prickett, "Literary Legacy," in *Oxford Handbook*, 583, claims that there was "probably none better in his generation." See also Lang, "Newman and the Fathers," 156.

33 For an appreciation of *Callista* see, e.g., Margaret C. Frank, "The Literary Stylist," in *Oxford Handbook*, 484–86, and Prickett, "Literary Legacy," 590–94.

34 See David DeLaura, *Hebrew and Hellene in Victorian England* (Austin, Tex.: University of Texas Press, 1969), and Frank, "The Literary Stylist," 477. See also James Joyce's letter to Harriet Shaw Weaver in James Joyce, *Selected Letters of James Joyce*, ed. Richard Ellmann (London: Faber & Faber, 1975), 375.

35 Thomas Wall, "The Writer and Preacher," in *Tribute to Newman*, 354. See similarly Tillman, *Letters*, 51 and 54.

36 Wall, "The Writer and Preacher," 354; see *EH* i, 17. Compare Newman on Cicero:

Wall is right on both counts: Newman is effective in his use of examples, and Newman did indeed call Cicero "the only master of style I have ever had."[37] But unlike Cicero, Newman sought always to give precedence to substance over style. Newman recalled, "I think I have never written for writing sake; but my one and single desire has been to do what is so difficult—viz. to express clearly and exactly my meaning; this has been the principle motive of all my corrections and re-writings."[38] It is this devotion to the matter discussed and Newman's own candor that caused Alastair Fowler to praise the honesty of Newman's prose. He notes that Newman's writing, with its "conversational informality" and its "personal coloration communicates an unostentatious, pleasant good nature."[39] This openness is especially evident in the *Apologia*, which Ker found as having an "(almost) disconcertingly calm, limpid tone of the author's conversational, indeed confidential, voice."[40] Newman could indeed employ Ciceronian style while revealing his inner self more openly than the Roman orator.

Although one will find Ciceronian sentences in Newman's novels, *Loss and Gain* (1848) and *Callista, A Tale of the Third Century* (1855), the style of these works seems to be formed at least equally from Newman's view of the poetic, seen in a broad sense.[41] In his article "Poetry, with Reference to Aristotle's *Poetics*," Newman notes that while Cicero analyzes the subject intellectually from all logical angles, the poet should create a different effect, one relying on beauty and the imagination.[42] Poetry is seen as "originality energizing in the world of beauty; the originality of grace, purity, refinement, and good feeling."[43] Although Newman takes his start from Aristotle, poetically he recasts his favorite philosopher through a Platonic lens. Newman saw Aristotle as too prescriptive and mechanical, and he argues instead that "the poetical mind is one full of the eternal forms of beauty and perfection; these are its material of thought."[44] Therefore instead of giving priority to plot, as Aristotle advised, Newman argued

---

"Here he goes (as it were) round and round his object; surveys it in every light; examines it in all its parts." *HS* i, 293.

37 *LD* xxiv, 242. See also Frank, "Literary Stylist," 483, on Newman's use of the "extended list." Although Newman credits Cicero as his guide, it should be noted that Newman was fond of Gibbon's style (*LD* i, 67) and was also a dedicated student of Aristotle's *Rhetoric*. See Bottone, *Philosophical Habit*, 60, on Aristotle.

38 *LD* xxiv, 242.

39 Alastair Fowler, *A History of English Literature* (Cambridge, Mass: Harvard University Press, 1987), 242.

40 Ker, *John Henry Newman*, 549.

41 For Newman's broad understanding of poetry, see his article on the *Poetics* (*EH* i, 1–27) and "The Mission of St. Benedict," *HS* ii, 365–430. In the latter work he sees the Benedictines as rooted in the sphere of the poetic. "Poetry," he says, "does not address the reason, but the imagination and affections; it leads to admiration, enthusiasm, devotion, love." *HS* ii, 387.

42 *EH* i, 17.

43 *EH* i, 21.

44 *EH* i, 10.

that art is displayed more in "the characters, sentiments, and diction."[45] This view is definitely seen in Newman's novels, and as Friedman notes, it reflects elements of Romanticism and Victorianism.[46] Charles Reding in *Loss and Gain* and Callista and Agellius in *Callista* are carefully drawn characters whose aspirations, desires, and fears the readers can experience. We also see in Newman's novels the Victorian idea that literature should be morally uplifting. The poet should reflect beauty in his interior life, since "in proportion to the standard of a writer's moral character, will his compositions vary in poetical excellence."[47] In his view of literature as idealizing and lifting up the soul of the reader, Newman takes the very non-Aristotelian view that it "is scarcely possible for a poet satisfactorily to connect innocence with ultimate unhappiness."[48] Here perhaps is why both of Newman's novels stress the ultimate happiness of their protagonists. Reding, after much persecution, joyfully embraces Catholicism, and Callista accepts martyrdom to gain Christ.

NEWMAN THE TEACHER

For a final consideration of Newman's credentials as a classicist, we should look at the accomplishments of his students. Dedicated teachers find great satisfaction in the accomplishment of students, since their achievements confirm the quality of teaching. Evidence of Newman's proficiency as a tutor can be seen in the success of Henry Wilberforce, who in 1830 won first-class honors in Classics and second-class honors in Mathematics.[49] In 1831 Samuel Francis Wood and Robert Francis Wilson, two of Newman's students, also obtained firsts in Classics.[50] A year later Francis Roger won a double first. Although Newman ceased to be a tutor at Oriel after 1832, he remained a zealous teacher all of his life. At Littlemore, while engaged in translating Athanasius and in the Tractarian movement, he tutored a village boy in elementary Classics and instructed William Henry Welch, the nephew of Ambrose St John, in Euclid and in Greek in 1843.[51] At the Catholic University in Dublin, while organizing the university and raising funds, he continued to devote many hours to instructing pupils.[52]

---

45 *EH* i, 2.

46 Norman Friedman, "Newman, Aristotle, and the New Criticism," *PMLA* 81, no. 3 (1966): 261–71, especially at 264. Newman's favorite novelist was Sir Walter Scott, whose characterization in the Waverley novels is praised at *EH* i, 18. For Newman's place within the genre of historical fiction, see Prickett, *Literary Legacy*, 590–92.

47 *EH* i, 21.

48 *EH* i, 16.

49 See Juan R. Vélez, *Passion for Truth: The Life of John Henry Newman* (Charlotte, N.C.: TAN Books, 2012), 89. See also Newman's letter to Wilberforce, *LD* ii, 305. For a look at Newman's teaching style, see his letter to Wilberforce, *LD* ii, 189–90.

50 See Vélez, *Passion for Truth*, 128, and *LD* ii, 333.

51 See Vélez, *Passion for Truth*, 372 and 487.

52 See Shrimpton, *Making of Men*, 195.

Newman always considered the Classics to be fundamental in education, as is evident from the university's exams, its curriculum, and his *Idea of a University*.[53] Newman's attention to hands-on instruction can be seen from Charles de la Pasture's comment that he learned more about Latin composition in a few sessions from Newman than in the courses taught by Ornsby and Stewart.[54] When he returned to Birmingham, Newman once again turned his attention towards education, founding a school with a connection to the Oratory. There he continued his devotion to teaching through the Classics. Only weeks before his death, the students at the Oratory school presented a version of Terence's *Andria* that Newman had revised for them.[55]

The dedication to teaching seen throughout Newman's life surely suggests a love of the subject matter that is also evident in Newman's many references to the Classics in his Diaries, Letters, and other works. The descriptions of his Mediterranean tour, when he reread Homer's *Odyssey*, Thucydides, and Virgil, manifest a lifelong affection for antiquity. He delighted in finding cites described in ancient epic and history. He was particularly fond of Sicily, which filled him "with inexpressible rapture."[56] This trip was also a rich time in Newman's poetic career. The overtly classical poems include "The Isles of the Sirens," "Corcyra," and "Messina."[57] But Newman's love for his subject matter does not entirely account for his dedication to teaching the Classics. Newman saw the role of the teacher, especially the individual tutor, in terms of the intellectual and spiritual formation of those he taught. After considering both parish and missionary work, Newman eventually discerned that he was honoring God's purpose best by helping form the mental and spiritual character of his students. According to Culler, "Newman had come to believe that his ordination vow, though he had as deep a sense of its solemnity as anyone, could be, might be fulfilled through the office of college tutor, if that office were interpreted in its primitive religious sense."[58] This appreciation for the role of the tutor caused him and his companions to seek to reform the tutorial system at Oriel, restoring its original purpose as expressed in the Laudian Code of 1636, in which the tutor was to be a personal guide

---

53   See Shrimpton, *Making of Men*, 222n62. For Newman's establishment of prizes and scholarships in the Classics, see 198. On the Classics in the *Idea*, see 120–24 and 192–98.

54   See Shrimpton, *Making of Men*, 195, and Charles de la Pasture, "Letter to the Editor," *The Tablet* 114 (September 11, 1909): 416. Also showing the importance Newman gave to Latin composition is his article published on that topic in the *Catholic University Gazette*, which is included in *Idea*, 366–71, as "Elementary Studies: Old Mr. Black's Confession of his Search after a Latin Style."

55   On the school at the Oratory, see Paul Shrimpton, *A Catholic Eton: Newman's Oratory School* (Leominster: Gracewing, 2005).

56   *LD* iii, 213. On the trip as a realization of Newman's experience with the Classics, see Tillman, *Letters*, 12 and 23–43.

57   *VO*, 83, 109, and 129.

58   Culler, *Imperial Intellect*, 51.

rather than simply an academic resource.[59] In the opinion of Newman and his fellows, Robert Wilberforce and Hurrell Froude, the role of the tutor included offering uplifting guidance and setting an example of religious practice. Teaching the Classics was to be the main vehicle for providing a personal and enriching education. The Classics offered depth, variety, and a cultural distance whereby virtue could be taught, somewhat indirectly and in the light of a long-standing tradition. As Newman noted, "The way to a young man's heart lies through his studies, certainly in the case of the more clever and diligent. . . . Obscurities of thought, difficulties in philosophy, perplexities of faith are confidentially brought out, sifted, and solved; a pagan poet or theorist may thus become the occasion of Christian advancement."[60]

THE CLASSICS AND THE UNIVERSITY

Although the faith was a constant assumption between tutor and student, religion was never to be the primary focus; the Classics were to be the academic backbone. One reason for this choice was the period in which Newman lived, when knowledge of the Classics was still expected of any educated person. Despite the arguments of Locke, the *Edinburgh Review*, and others for adopting a utilitarian approach to education,[61] Classics remained the major subject for preparatory schools and universities in England. Exams were based primarily on construing the meaning of the ancient authors and on one's ability to compose in Latin.[62] Yet Newman did not stress the Classics simply because it was in accord with contemporary practice. Indeed, Newman saw value in all fields, as is evident from his establishing a medical school at the Catholic University. Nevertheless, he always felt that the Classics provided the ideal basis for the training of the mind in what he called the philosophical habit. Throughout the *Idea of a University* we see that the purpose of an education is foremost to teach individuals to probe questions and to examine themselves. As Shrimpton notes, to Newman, "education is a higher word [than instruction]; it implies an action upon our mental nature, and the formulation of character; it is something individual and permanent."[63] If we look at "Elementary Studies" in the *Idea of a University*, where Newman compares different students taking oral exams, we can see the

---

59 See Shrimpton, *Making of Men*, 15, 20n49, and 48n35. See also Ward, *Young Mr. Newman*, 196. On Newman's career and aspirations as a tutor, see Culler, *Imperial Intellect*, 51–79; Shrimpton, *Making of Men*, 16–32; and Tillman, *Letters*, 219–32.

60 *Campaign I*, 119 (original text by Newman cited by Tillman, *Rise and Progress*, lxvii).

61 See Shrimpton, *Making of Men*, 73–75; Bottone, *Philosophical Habit*, 102–22; and Jane Rupert, "Newman on Pedagogical Studies," *Newman Studies Journal* 17, no. 1 (2020): 111–15.

62 See Martin J. Svaglic, "Newman and the Oriel Fellowship," *PMLA* 70, no. 5 (1955): 1014–32.

63 Shrimpton, *Making of Men*, 79.

Socratic nature of his method applied even to a school text like the *Anabasis*.[64] On deeper topics Newman was especially fond of using Aristotle's *Nichomachean Ethics*, a well-annotated copy of which still exists at the Oratory.[65] Newman's fondness for the *Nichomachean Ethics*, as well as for Cicero's *de Officiis*, illustrates his desire to focus on questions fundamental to the fulfillment of the human person. What is it that makes a human being good and accordingly gives him happiness, *eudaimonia*? The *Nichomachean Ethics* linked personal happiness to the development of the mind and to the exercise of virtue. Only the virtuous man possesses true happiness. Similarly, the *de Officiis*, which Cicero wrote to his son, dealt with the virtues and the inner life.

Newman's deep appreciation for Aristotle and Cicero has been stressed and closely studied during the last decade. Shrimpton claims justifiably that "Newman was a natural Aristotelian,"[66] and he reminds us that Newman, along with Whately and Wilberforce (his colleagues at Oriel College) relied on the *Nicomachean Ethics* for teaching ethics. But the Aristotelianism of Oriel went much deeper than subject matter. Oriel's core of teachers was led by the eminent Aristotelian Edward Copleston, and they embraced an Aristotelian understanding of education. This group, which became known as the Noetics, stressed "a rigorous catechetical style of teaching"[67] that can be seen in Newman's in "Elementary Studies," mentioned above. In this amusing dialogue, we see two exams, one taken by a weak, undisciplined student and one by a well-prepared, logically minded pupil. In both exams the teacher tries to elicit thoughtful answers rather than rote learning. This philosophical approach characterizes Newman's view of education for its own purpose. Both practically in Newman's work with the Catholic University and theoretically in the *Idea of a University* we can see that Newman's understanding of education follows "Aristotle's argument that everything has its own perfection, whether intellectual, aesthetic, moral, or pastoral."[68] Education is not primarily a practical goal to achieve a particular utilitarian end, but an effort at developing the mind to engage in the philosophical habit. Education could be practical, but practicality was not its purpose, strictly speaking. Education "brings the mind to form";[69] that is its essential purpose. As Newman argued, "There is a physical beauty and a moral [beauty]; . . . and in like manner there is a beauty, there is a perfection, of the intellect."[70] The goal of education is to produce the ability to think and to make connections between

---

64 For an analysis of Newman's pedagogy, see Rupert, "Pedagogical Practice," 103–11.

65 See Shrimpton, *Making of Men*, 18–19.

66 Shrimpton, *Making of Men*, xxvii; see also 21. See similarly, Tillman, *Letters*, 263.

67 Shrimpton, *Making of Men*, 12.

68 Shrimpton, *Making of Men*, 73.

69 Shrimpton, *Making of Men*, 78.

70 *Idea*, 122.

subjects. As Hütter summarizes: "a philosophical habit of mind is the acquired mental *habitus* that facilitates inquiry into the principles, the inner coherence, and the interconnectedness of all the sciences."[71]

Like Shrimpton, Angelo Bottone has also argued that Aristotle was the essential influence for Newman's view of education, especially as it is depicted in the *Idea* and in *Rise and Progress of the Universities*. Bottone observes that "most of his ideas on the intellectual dimension of the human being come from a creative interpretation of Aristotle."[72] Indeed, Newman surely bases his theories on Aristotle's famous maxim that "All men by their nature yearn to know."[73] Knowing fulfills the most human aspect of a person, his mind, and thus contributes to his having happiness, *eudaimonia*. As Newman wrote, "Not to know the relative disposition of things is the state of slaves or children; to have mapped out the Universe is the boast, or at least the ambition of philosophy."[74] Here we see why Newman so objected to the utilitarian approach advocated by Locke and the *Edinburgh Review*. Bottone notes that Locke's constant point of reference is to the adult in society. According to Locke, children should be taught what their parents see as gentlemanly conduct and what will help them be successful as adults—the individual child as a person is not an important issue. As Bottone observes, "For Locke, in every case the ultimate end of education is an adult, whether it be the father or a child in his future years, while for Newman the core of education was the student and his mind."[75]

The flourishing of the mind explains much of Newman's attitude regarding the structure of the university. Since Newman stressed so strongly the relational aspect between tutor and pupil, and between fellow pupils, he insisted upon the college model, with the bulk of teaching done by tutors rather than lecturing professors, as an ideal. The tutor inspired his pupils with his "personal presence," the truth to be firmly planted "by propounding it and repeating it, by questioning and requestioning, by correcting and explaining. . . ."[76] Using Aristotle's concept of a moral actor, Newman contends that a university can exist without the college model, but it cannot flourish.[77] It cannot, so to speak, have *eudaimonia*. Rather, since "intellectual and moral virtues can be developed only inside a community,"[78] the university does not fulfill its calling if it is simply a place where content is ladled out.

---

71 Hütter, *John Henry Newman*, 178. See similarly, Tillman, *Letters*, 236.

72 Bottone, *Philosophical Habit*, 63.

73 Aristotle, *Metaphysics* 1.1 (my translation).

74 *Idea*, 113. See Bottone, *Philosophical Habit*, 65.

75 Bottone, *Philosophical Habit*, 118. See also p. 110. Rupert, "Newman," 112, notes that Newman, unlike the utilitarians, supported teaching literature, partially because it fed the imagination of young persons.

76 *HS* iii, 14.

77 Bottone, *Philosophical Habit*, 69–70.

78 Bottone, *Philosophical Habit*, 71.

Bottone also argues that, after Aristotle, Cicero was the leading inspiration for Newman's vision of education.[79] Newman considered Cicero a prime example of the intellectually flourishing man. Though realizing Cicero's limitations, he frequently praised him, as seen in an article for the *Catholic University Gazette*.[80] He uses one of Cicero's *Epistulae ad familiares* for an example in his mock exam in "Elementary Studies" in the *Idea of a University*, and knowledge of Cicero's *de Officiis* was expected for the entrance exam at the Catholic University. Although Newman admits that Cicero sometimes displayed hypocrisy and shallowness, he considered the Roman orator an example of and a spokesman for the philosophical habit of mind. Cicero represents "a specimen of the liberal educated man" and is "employed to demonstrate the excellence of intellectual activity, but also the limits of the man educated outside of the Christian faith."[81]

In the Fifth Discourse of *Idea*, "Knowledge Its Own End," Newman uses Cicero for his main argument, that knowledge should be sought for its own purposes rather than for extrinsic goals. As Newman quotes from the beginning of *de Officiis*, "This pertains most of all to human nature . . . for we are all drawn to the pursuit of knowledge, in which to excel we consider excellent, whereas to mistake, to err, to be ignorant is both an evil and a disgrace."[82] It is noteworthy that this letter was written to Cicero's son, Marcus, who was studying philosophy in Greece, a subject that obviously would be considered to have little direct practicality in worldly terms.[83] Newman contrasts this Ciceronian attitude with that of Cato, who stressed the importance of practicality in education, as Locke would later do.[84] Newman notes that liberal arts, as opposed to the servile arts, have their own sufficiency:

> that alone is liberal knowledge, which stands on its own pretensions, which is independent of sequel, expects no complement, refuses to be *informed* (as it is called) by any end, or absorbed into any art, in order duly to present itself to our contemplation. The most ordinary pursuits have this specific character, if they are self-sufficient and complete; the highest lose it, when they minister to something beyond them.[85]

He further cites Aristotle in calling things that bear fruit useful, and "those *liberal, which tend to enjoyment . . . where nothing accrues of consequence beyond*

---

79 See Bottone, "Influence of Cicero," 1–3.

80 John Henry Newman, "Athens, Considered as a Type of a University," *Catholic University Gazette* 5 (June 29, 1854), 34, found in HS iii, 35.

81 Bottone, *Philosophical Habit*, 93. On Cicero's limitations, see *HS* i, 263 and Bottone, 91–93.

82 *Idea*, 104.

83 On the purpose of the *de Officiis*, see e.g., Bottone, "Influence of Cicero," 7–8.

84 *Idea*, 106.

85 *Idea*, 108.

the using.[86] Liberal education "is simply the cultivation of the intellect;" it is to be tended like a garden, so that it will be beautiful.[87] We should no more question the beautification of the mind than we would object to the beautification of a garden, even though that garden had no functional purpose.

Cicero was himself like a garden, a man who showed excellence of the mind. It has been argued that the model for Newman's famous passage regarding the gentleman in Discourse 8 may be partially based on Cicero.[88] As eloquent and inspiring as the passage is, however, as Tillman and others have noted, it carries a definite note of irony.[89] The ideal of a man should not be to resemble "an easy chair or a good fire."[90] The man of the description is a model from only a secular viewpoint; he displays no overt religiosity or heroic virtue. Newman believed that education could go only so far in promoting moral goodness. As Newman noted in Discourse 5, education in and of itself does not intrinsically cause a person to lead a moral or certainly a religious life. Morality is not the true end of education; its true end is only that of improving the mind. He contends, "I insist upon it, that it is a real mistake to burden it [Knowledge] with virtue or religion as with the mechanical arts."[91] Newman is consistent in his application of the idea that the improvement of the mind is its own reward. Learning hones the mind, but it does not guarantee religiosity.

CLASSICS AS A PROPAIDEIA TO CHRISTIANITY

Given Newman's religious fervor and his awareness of the limitations of the ancient pagan world, one might wonder why he did not provide religion as the foundational subject matter for the university. One of Newman's difficulties in establishing the Catholic University in Dublin was precisely that he refused to create a university that was based on the model of a seminary. Moreover, he did not use a churchman for his educational inspiration, but rather Aristotle and to a lesser extent Cicero. One reason Newman employs figures from the ancient world in offering his theory of education is that they force him to use reason rather than rely on faith or religion as a trump card. In a time of burgeoning atheism and secularity even in religious thinking, Newman was aware that his arguments would have a better chance of being accepted by more persons if they

---

86 *Idea*, 109; cf. Aristotle, *Rhetoric*, 1.5.

87 *Idea*, 121.

88 *Idea*, 208–11. On the relevance of Cicero, see Bottone, "Influence of Cicero," 10–11. Bottone does not suggest that Cicero is per se the model, but that the model is partially based on a general ideal of a Roman statesman and orator. Bottone, 11n51, cites Charles Frederick Harrold, *John Henry Newman: An Expository and Critical Study of His Mind, Thought and Art* (New York: Longmans, Green, 1945), 92.

89 M. Katherine Tillman, *Philosophy of Education in Oxford Handbook*, 426.

90 *Idea*, 209.

91 *Idea*, 120.

were based on the ancients. In his writings on education one might compare him with Boethius, who, though a Christian, chose to present his *Consolation of Philosophy* in almost purely philosophical terms without reliance on Scripture and Church teachings.[92] Second, as Bottone observes, the use of Aristotle and Cicero offered an approach that could be accepted by any religious faction.[93] There was no appeal to any specific Christian approach or sect.

But Newman's use of Aristotle, Cicero, and other ancient authors in the development of his theory of education more importantly points to his view of the propaedeutic nature of the Classics. Newman believed that studying these ancient authors prepared one to understand Christianity better and be more receptive to it. Especially using Aristotle, who "told us the meaning of our words and ideas before we were born," the Classics could form the mind so as to be open to the truth.[94] Though Newman was adamant that education did not produce religious faith, he did suggest that the comprehensive, relational approach to knowledge that he termed the philosophical habit was conducive to theism and even to an understanding of the world from a divine perspective. As Tillman observes, "Worldly wisdom or philosophy, then, in its most full and positive sense, as the fruit of an enlightened mind, contains within itself an orientation and a directedness, an intentionality, towards divine wisdom."[95] Newman notes that the reasons why educated persons are not always oriented towards faith is because of pride or because of a failure to grasp the larger view of knowledge, that is, a failure to acquire the philosophical habit.[96] Persons who focus too sharply on their own subject do not acquire even worldly wisdom; hence we see again a need for the liberal inclusiveness of the Classics. These studies help a person map the world and see things in their relationship to each other, as Newman suggests when he cites Virgil in the *Idea of a University*: "Felix qui potuit rerum cognoscere causas."[97] But more importantly, Newman truly believed that the ancients had been gifted in a special way with their own, obviously limited, revelation. Hugo Rahner has drawn attention to Newman's critique of Milman's *History of Christianity*, in which the claim is made that Christianity cannot be true since it shares so many commonalities

---

92   See Scott Goins and Barbara H. Wyman, trans. *Boethius: The Consolation of Philosophy* (San Francisco: Ignatius Press, 2012), xv, and, more fully, Henry Chadwick, *Boethius: The Consolations of Music, Logic, Theology, and Philosophy* (Oxford: Oxford University Press, 1981), 247–53.

93   See Bottone, *Philosophical Habit*, 73.

94   *Idea*, 109–10.

95   Tillman, "Philosophy of Education," 422.

96   *Idea*, 137–38. See also Tillman, *Letters*, 125 and 244.

97   "Happy the man who is able to understand the causes for things." *Idea*, 138. See Virgil, *Georgics* 2.490. See also *Idea*, 137–39, for Newman's description of the perfection of the intellect. Here he attributes the perfection of the intellect to philosophy, which of course to Newman suggested Aristotle above all others.

with paganism.[98] Newman turns the tables, however, contending that the truth of Christianity can be partially seen in its continuation (and correction) of pagan truth. Newman writes:

> we prefer to say, and we think that Scripture bears us out in saying, that from the beginning the Moral Goodness of the world has scattered the seeds of truth far and wide over its extent; that these have variously taken root, and grown up in the wilderness, wild plants indeed but living.[99]

In the *Apologia* Newman writes of being attracted to the Alexandrian School with its love of allegory and openness to pre-Christian thought. He asserts that "pagan literature, philosophy, and mythology, properly understood were but a preparation for the gospel. The Greek poets and sages were in a certain sense prophets; for 'thoughts beyond their thoughts to these high bards were given.'"[100] This understanding of ancient wisdom as a divine gift was characteristic of St. Paul, as Newman argues in his book on the Arians.[101] Newman also notes in this book the tendency of the Alexandrian School to begin catechesis with Natural Theology and Natural Law before moving to divine matters.[102] Some elements of Ancient thought thus become part of the divine economy of salvation.

CONCLUSIONS

The wisdom of the ancients, then, was in Newman's eyes a great gift to mankind, given by a God who, in the words of St. Paul to the Romans, purposefully revealed himself "at sundry times and in divers manners."[103] Here we find the logic, order, and grasp of human understanding of Aristotle "the great Master [who] does but analyze the thoughts, feelings, views, and opinions of human kind. He has told us the meaning of our own ideas, before we were born."[104] Here we also encounter the great orator and humanist, Cicero, an eloquent advocate for the liberal arts, despite the inconsistencies of his conduct. There too we meet with Homer, Thucydides, Horace, and Virgil, whom Newman loved and delighted in quoting.

Although Newman is not remembered primarily as a classicist, to a great extent the Classics shaped his way of thinking and helped to make him memorable.

---

98 Hugo Rahner, *Greek Myths and Christian Mysteries*, trans. Brian Battershow (London: Burns & Oates, 1963), 95–96.

99 *EH* ii, 231–34.

100 *Apo.*, 27; Newman quotes from the poem *The Christian Year*, by John Keble.

101 *Ari.*, 73.

102 Vélez, *Passion for Truth*, 133, and Tillman, *Letters*, 97 and 290.

103 Hebrews 1:1, KJV.

104 *Idea*, 109–10.

His classically formed view of the world helped create much of the vision of the *Idea of a University*, *Rise and Progress*, and his other writings on education. He saw the Classics as a superior way to train the mind and as a propaideia to Christianity. The Classics also contributed to another one of his claims to fame, his great Victorian style, because of which he is so often anthologized in textbooks of English literature. For all of his academic life, Newman labored and excelled in style and rhetoric. And while he had other influences, his prose was formed primarily by the study of Cicero and Aristotle's *Rhetoric*.

The Classics had a tremendous impact on Newman's thinking and writing. In his life they were a perfect illustration of his claim that the good is always useful, even if it is not to be sought for its utility.[105] A field that he had enjoyed, even played with as a child making verses, helped to ensure his reputation as a skilled writer and an eloquent advocate of a liberal education.

Suggested Reading

Bottone, Angelo. *The Philosophical Habit of Mind: Rhetoric and Person in John Henry Newman's Dublin Writings*. Bucharest: Zeta Books, 2010.

Culler, A. Dwight. *The Imperial Intellect: A Study of Newman's Educational Ideal*. New Haven, Conn.: Yale University Press, 1955.

Shrimpton, Paul. *The 'Making of Men': The Idea and Reality of Newman's University in Oxford and Dublin*. Leominster: Gracewing, 2011.

Tristram, Henry. "The Classics." In *A Tribute to Newman: Essays on His Life and Thought*, edited by Michael Tierney, 246–78. Dublin: Browne and Nolan, 1945.

---

105 See *Idea*, 164.

CHAPTER 10

NEWMAN AND
A HISTORIAN'S CRAFT

Christopher J. Lane

I n writing about Newman, I am tempted to echo my subject's claim, from one of his *Historical Sketches*, of doing "nothing more than to group old facts in his own way," and to feel his fear of giving the reader mere "superficial generalizations."[1] One such generalization, oft-repeated, includes the fact that Newman was not a historian in the professional sense of the term and did not consider himself to be one. Yet some contrasting oft-repeated generalizations—offered by some of the same commentators as the first—are arguably more important. Newman did indeed engage in historical work, and, moreover, historical arguments permeated his intellectual and religious life.[2] On that score,

---

*   The author dedicates this chapter to the memory of friend and colleague Brendan J. McGuire, whose analysis of Newman's approach to history helped shape the author's thinking and who passed from this life on Newman's feast day, October 9, 2020. A recording of McGuire, speaking on Newman as an early Church historian, can be found here: Brendan J. McGuire, "Newman's Historical Epistemology," St. John Henry Newman Lecture Series, Christendom College, October 30, 2019, video of lecture, https://media. christendom.edu/2019/10/newmans-historical-epistemology/.

1   *HS* i, xi.

2   E.g., Kenneth L. Parker, "Historiography," in *The Oxford Handbook of John Henry Newman*, ed. Frederick D. Aquino and Benjamin J. King (Oxford: Oxford University Press, 2018), 557. Parker also notes that Newman expressed a preference to be called a "controversialist," rather than a historian or even a theologian. For a brief discussion of the contrary claim that Newman did indeed call himself a historian, see Stephen D. Lawson,

one scholar has proclaimed that a key aspect of Newman's life was his "adventure in history," and his conversion particularly was rooted in the study of the past, especially the history of the early Church.[3] Not everything about Newman as a historian can be counted as either "superficial generalizations" or "old facts," however, since his historical thought continues to give rise to lively debates. Scholars have given wildly divergent assessments as to the quality of his historical arguments and as to his astuteness as a reader of patristic texts, for instance. Rooted thus both in old facts and in lively debates, this essay will seek to show something of Newman's historical "adventure." In so doing, we might see not only the role of historical arguments in his own life but also how his work is of continuing relevance as a model for engaging the past with nuance and integrity. This model, I suggest, might have something in it even for those of us who, unlike him, willingly take on the professional moniker of "historian."

THE HISTORICAL BOOKENDS
OF NEWMAN'S TRACTARIANISM:
ARIANS AND THE *ESSAY*

The first and last books of Newman's Anglican career—*The Arians of the Fourth Century* (1833) and *An Essay on the Development of Christian Doctrine* (1845), respectively—are keys to understanding how his historical engagement issued in his embrace of Rome. Neither work was written from the ostensibly detached position of one seeking to understand the past for its own sake. In both cases, he engaged with the past in order to speak to present religious questions. The two works are nevertheless very different—and not only in terms of genre. They respectively exemplify different stages in the evolution of his philosophy and theology of history.

Arians was Newman's first book and also the only one of his full-length books that can be called "a history" without qualification.[4] This, despite the fact that he later called this tome of over 400 pages "a historical sketch."[5] According to Newman, the book came forth from an ongoing study of the Church Fathers, begun around 1828, and a request in 1830 that he write a history of the early Church councils. He let his project run away from him, and it morphed into a large book on a much narrower span of Church history than was originally intended.[6] Writing about the Arian crisis stemmed from his already-formed conviction "that Antiquity was the true exponent of Christianity and the basis

---

"'To Be Deep in History': The Role of History in the Conversions of John Henry Newman and Erik Peterson," *Newman Studies Journal* 16, no. 2 (2019): 11n19.

    3   Josef L. Altholz, "Newman and History," *Victorian Studies* 7, no. 3 (1964): 287.

    4   Of course, some of the connected sets of essays that make up his *Historical Sketches* have often been reprinted as standalone volumes.

    5   *Ari.*, vi.

    6   *Apo.*, 35.

of the Church of England."[7] In his view at the time, the early Church was in unbroken succession with his own Established Church, and its conflicts mirrored those of his own day.[8] If the Church of England faced doctrinal conflicts, so had the early Church. If the heterodox were ascendant in England, so had they been in the fourth century Church.

But could one find an orthodox continuity in the face of historical evidence that suggested massive change between the ante-Nicene and the post-Nicene period, as well as massive division during the latter? Newman's case for a coherent early Church orthodoxy—one that remained valid even when on the political (and ecclesiastical) outs—was an intricate one, involving claims of an imbalance between faith and reason in religious thought, distinctions between the respective theologies of Antioch and Alexandria, and arguments about the early Church's deployment of the principle of "economy" and of the *disciplina arcani*. The "economical method," based in the Pauline dictum to "become all things to all men" and exemplified by the apostle's sermon at Athens, entailed accommodating one's language to "the feelings and prejudices of the hearer, in leading him to the reception of a novel or unacceptable doctrine."[9] In order to avoid "abuse of the Economy in the hands of unscrupulous reasoners," however, churchmen were "ever to maintain substantial truth" when leading a hearer "by degrees."[10] The related and more specific concept of the *disciplina arcani* entailed withholding, for a variety of reasons, the fullness of doctrine from those not yet fully initiated into the Church: "The elementary information given to the heathen or catechumen was in no sense undone by the subsequent secret teaching, which was in fact but the filling up of a bare but correct outline."[11] Newman persuasively argued from scriptural and patristic examples that both of these practices were not uncommon in the early Church, and he especially finds evidence for their deployment in Alexandria.

These practices then helped him to explain some of the apparent doctrinal changes among early Church texts, especially the contrast between ante-Nicene and post-Nicene approaches to Trinitarian and Christological dogmas. In the earliest times, he argued, the fullness of doctrine had been handed down, without alteration, among the bishops and revealed to fully-initiated Christians, but only some of it was published to the world. As heresies arose, the public expression of doctrine through creeds and definitions effectively eliminated the *disciplina arcani* and substantially altered the use of economy. Error had necessitated a clear and open response. In using the *disciplina arcani* to argue for a coherent early Church orthodoxy, Newman appears to have been influenced by the works of Roman apologists, such as seventeenth century French Jesuit Denis

---

7 *Apo.*, 35–36.
8 Parker, "Historiography," 559–61.
9 *Ari.*, 71–72.
10 *Ari.*, 72.
11 *Ari.*, 53.

Pétau.[12] Recourse to these theories about unwritten tradition had led William Rowe Lyall, one of Newman's original editors, to critique the manuscript for its departure from the Protestant orthodoxy of the Established Church.[13] Nevertheless, in Newman's view at the time, economy and the *disciplina arcani* were integral to maintaining claims that doctrine had been passed down unchanged, when other readers of the early Fathers might hold that seismic doctrinal shifts had occurred.

Continued study and reflection, however, cast increasing doubt on this approach to continuity and eventually opened Newman to the idea of doctrinal development. He could not securely maintain the principle that his own Anglican Church held simply the ancient faith that, in the words of the so-called Vincentian Canon of St. Vincent of Lérins, was believed "everywhere, always, and by all." It took several years of consideration, however, before Newman could reconcile the idea of development with an acceptable account of doctrinal continuity.[14] His *Essay on the Development of Christian Doctrine* was, of course, the result of his working out a theory that explained to his satisfaction the appearance of doctrinal change in Church history—much more to his satisfaction than a static continuity that depended excessively on the *disciplina arcani*.

The *Essay* was not itself a history but a theological argument founded in part on underlying historical arguments. Newman opens the work by asking to what extent the history of Christianity can teach us about what true Christianity may be. After considering theories that imply a radical discontinuity between the religion of Christ and the historical churches that have claimed to instantiate it, he asserts as a reasonable assumption the claim that "the Christianity of the second, fourth, seventh, twelfth, sixteenth, and intermediate centuries is in its substance the very religion which Christ and His Apostles taught in the first, whatever may be the modifications for good or for evil which lapse of years, or the vicissitudes of human affairs, have impressed upon it."[15] But then, more subtle difficulties faced anyone who sought in history a guide to right doctrine. Doctrine was "so variously represented, and so inconsistently maintained" by Christians of various ages that the only viable solution seemed to be *sola scriptura*.[16] Such, Newman notes, had been classically stated by seventeenth century Protestant controversialist William Chillingworth: "There have been Popes against Popes: Councells against Councells:

12   Parker, "Historiography," 560.

13   *LD* iii, 105; Ian Ker, *John Henry Newman: A Biography* (Oxford: Oxford University Press, 2019), 48; Parker, "Historiography," 560. Decades later, Newman would refer back to his nuanced discussion in *Arians* of economy and the *disciplina arcani* to defend himself against Charles Kingsley's claim that approval of those practices entailed approval of deceit; *Apo.*, 439–43.

14   Lawson, "'To Be Deep in History,'" 14–15.

15   *Dev.*, 5. References are to the 1878 edition. Newman significantly reorganized the book from its 1845 original, but he left virtually unaltered the substance of his original argument.

16   *Dev.*, 6.

Councells confirmed by Popes, against Councells confirmed by Popes: Lastly the Church of some Ages against the Church of other Ages."[17] In other words, the changes evident in the visible Church over the centuries had been corruptions. The 1845 *Essay* is in part an answer to such objections and a means to reconcile seemingly conflicting historical evidence about Christian truth, using more subtle conceptual tools than Newman had possessed when writing *Arians* in 1833.

With these more subtle tools, Newman argued against other nuanced accounts of historical Christianity, especially the views of many of his Tractarian-aligned contemporaries—including views he once held himself. One of the biggest casualties of Newman's theory of development was the Vincentian Canon, or at least its use in defense of the continuity between the early Church and the Church of England. The Canon as used by "the English school of divines" for several centuries, was meant to be "a short and easy method for bringing the various informations of ecclesiastical history" into harmony and to know what teachings to treat as mere private theological opinion or even as corruption.[18] Newman objected that the Canon, though valuable, could never be interpreted in a way which consistently protected the doctrines of the Established Church while simultaneously undermining Roman Catholicism and Continental Protestantism.[19] With only the Vincentian Canon, one could not defend infant baptism, for instance. One could not argue that it was practiced "always, everywhere, and by all" in the early Church, certainly not until around the turn of the fifth century. This question could easily appear to be a matter of "the Church of some Ages against the Church of other Ages" and of some Fathers against others. Hence, no Anglican divine could defend his Church's doctrine against that of the Baptists, on the basis of the Canon.[20] It was insufficient as an interpretive key to the history of Christianity.

How then, could one use historical evidence in service of true Christianity? Newman's answer is basically two-fold. On the one hand, authentic developments were such that they could be, and often had been, eventually approved by legitimate ecclesiastical authority. And, on the other hand, authentic development was marked by seven "tests" or "notes." The core of Newman's claim runs thus: "From the first age of Christianity, its teaching looked towards those ecclesiastical dogmas, afterwards recognized and defined, with (as time went on) more or less determinate advance in the direction of them; till at length that advance became so pronounced, as to justify their definition and to bring it about, and to place them in the position of rightful interpretations and keys of the remains and the records in history of the teaching which had so terminated."[21] That is, the

---

17   William Chillingworth, *The Religion of Protestants a Safe Way to Salvation* (Oxford: Leonard Lichfield, 1638), 131; *Dev.*, 6.

18   *Dev.*, 10–11.

19   *Dev.*, 11–12.

20   *Dev.*, 127–29.

21   *Dev.*, 122.

fully-developed dogmas were the legitimate flowering of doctrines and practices contained in seed form from the beginning, and the dogmas themselves help us to make sense of the incomplete historical evidence. Most of Newman's book is spent illustrating this claim with historical examples, organized around the "notes" that distinguish genuine development from corruption. These notes he summarizes thus: "There is no corruption [of an idea] if it retains one and the same type, the same principles, the same organization; if its beginnings anticipate its subsequent phases, and its later phenomena protect and subserve its earlier; if it has a power of assimilation and revival, and a vigorous action from first to last."[22] To the Newman of 1845, affirmation of authentic Catholic doctrine need not fear historical silences and ambiguities. Moments of doctrinal definitions had not been merely publications of hitherto secret doctrines, and one need not find any doctrine to have been taught "always, everywhere, and by all"—at least, not in narrowly-defined senses of the terms—before accepting its truth. Development of doctrine happened in time, and intra-church conflict was often part of the process of gaining clarity, of coming to the full flowering of the apostolic doctrinal seed.

The significance of Newman's concept of development has been considerable.[23] Lord Acton—historian, politician, liberal Catholic, and sometime critic of Newman—praised Newman as having "helped to make History essential to men who reasoned" and declared that the *Essay on the Development of Christian Doctrine* "did more than any other book of his time to make his countrymen think historically, and watch the process as well as the result."[24] And contrary to occasional scholarly claims that the book received a cold reception among Catholic hierarchs, Newman's theory has been shown to have played an important role in Vatican doctrinal deliberations during the latter half of the nineteenth century, including the declaration of papal infallibility at Vatican I.[25] This is not to mention the fact that Newman has been called "the Father of Vatican II," for his influence on the theological *ressourcement* that preceded and guided the Council.[26] Lord Acton was not far off at least in this respect: Newman thoroughly integrated rigorous historical thinking into Catholic theological inquiry, and many of his insights on doctrinal development have become second nature among theologians.

And so, in these two works, we have two of the most important episodes in Newman's "adventure in history." *Arians* was an expression of his return to the Church Fathers as a basis for Christian orthodoxy, something he took in part

---

22 *Dev.*, 171.

23 See ch. 20 of this volume by Tracey Rowland for further discussion on development (editor's note).

24 Cambridge University Library, Add. 4987, quoted in Josef L. Altholz, "Newman and History," *Victorian Studies* 7, no. 3 (1964): 286, 288.

25 Parker, "Historiography," 568–70.

26 Ian Ker, *Newman on Vatican II* (Oxford: Oxford University Press, 2014), 1.

from reading at the time the seventeenth century Anglican bishop and theologian George Bull.[27] To return to the Fathers was to plant his theological claims in history. The *Essay* expressed a more nuanced approach to the Christian past, coming from one who had, in the intervening years, struggled with the theological problems raised by historical evidence. Church history, and the history of doctrine in particular, yielded no easy answers. Only the careful thinking enabled by the concept of development, thought Newman, could make a space for continuity amid the confusion of apparent doctrinal contradictions over time. It ultimately enabled him to find in Rome not the fruit of corruption but the fruit of authentic development.

NEWMAN AND THE "NOBLE DREAM" OF OBJECTIVITY

Given his larger goals with respect to doctrine, was Newman still a "good historian"? Did a lack of detachment—e.g., he mentions his "partiality" toward the Alexandrian Church when writing *Arians*—vitiate his reasoning?[28] Did his theological concerns too strongly determine his historical conclusions? Scholars have widely varied in their judgments as to whether, in the last analysis, Newman made good historical arguments. There is general agreement that he lacked the interest and the resources—including German language skills—needed to take up the new historical methods coming out of German universities starting in the middle decades of the nineteenth century.[29] Assuming we do not judge his work as if he were trained by the great German historian Leopold von Ranke, how indeed shall we judge it?

As a historian of the early Church, Newman has received mixed reviews. The Catholic historian Ignaz von Döllinger, steeped as he was in new German methods, believed Newman was an eminent authority on the Fathers whose arguments about Arianism would remain valuable.[30] Among the more negative assessments of Newman's historical work in *Arians* comes from Rowan Williams, who bases that assessment partly on evidence that Newman himself later looked down on the book. James J. Crile, however, argues that Williams has misread Newman's diffidence and thus missed the book's enduring value.[31] Much depends on whether one generally finds Newman to be an astute reader of the Fathers. It has been noted—sometimes but not always critically—that Newman maintained no "critical distance from his heroes" in the early Church, whom he instead "read as contemporaries, as participants in the theological conversations and controversies of his own

---

27 *Apo.*, 35–36.

28 *Apo.*, 36.

29 Altholz, "Newman and History," 287.

30 Altholz, "Newman and History," 286; Stephen Kelly, "John Henry Newman and the Writing of History," *Newman Studies Journal* 8, no. 2 (2011): 29.

31 James J. Crile, "John Henry Newman's *The Arians of the Fourth Century*: An Embarrassment?" *Newman Studies Journal* 10, no. 2 (2013): 46–58.

day."[32] Never would he wish to be a mere historian of the Fathers, explicating their doctrine without interest in its present-day theological import. It remains debated the degree to which, out of zeal or partiality, he attributed to certain Fathers concepts foreign to them.[33] Regardless of valid critiques one could make of some of Newman's particular arguments and conclusions, would his lack of detachment ultimately necessitate weak historical argumentation?

Among nineteenth century intellectuals, Newman was far from alone in eschewing the objectivity that has sometimes been proclaimed the gold standard of professional historical scholarship. In the 1980s, Peter Novick famously chronicled the story of the "noble dream" of objectivity, at least among professional historians in the United States, suggesting that such an ideal had been subject to rancorous debate throughout much of the previous century.[34] He noted that the German historians who supposedly pioneered scientific objectivity were often motivated by rampant nationalism. And the great Leopold von Ranke, hailed in late nineteenth century America as the father of a purely empirical history, was in fact "a thoroughgoing philosophical idealist" who "promoted an historiography grounded on the fundamental principle that the course of history revealed God's work."[35] While Newman and Ranke differed in method and in philosophical disposition, they shared the convictions that the historical discipline needed stronger theoretical underpinnings than mere empiricism and that the historian ought *not* be detached from the past he studied.

Many professional historians in more recent times have sought to integrate their deeply held convictions with a mitigated form of objectivity in method. For example, scholars of progressive leanings have openly professed political motivations for their interests and approaches, sometimes also offering self-critiques in their continued search for balance.[36] In a less partisan way, Brad Gregory explains that he wrote *The Unintended Reformation* both to give more nuanced historical argument about the rise and character of modernity and to engage with present-day practical problems, including political and cultural polarization, unexamined relativism about truth claims, and the rampant consumerism that contributes to intractable global environmental problems.[37] From another

---

32 Benjamin J. King, "The Church Fathers," in *The Oxford Handbook of John Henry Newman*, ed. Frederick D. Aquino and Benjamin J. King (Oxford: Oxford University Press, 2018), 113; Uwe Michael Lang, "Newman and the Fathers of the Church," *New Blackfriars* 92, no. 1038 (2011): 156 (a revised version of this article is ch. 8 in this volume).

33 See Lang, "Newman and the Fathers," 155–56; and King, "Church Fathers," 131.

34 Peter Novick, *That Noble Dream: The "Objectivity Question" and the American Historical Profession* (Cambridge: Cambridge University Press, 1988), 16–17.

35 Novick, *That Noble Dream*, 27.

36 E.g., see the desire to maintain a "politically committed intellectual project" after the fall of the Soviet Union in Florencia E. Mallon, "The Promise and Dilemma of Subaltern Studies: Perspectives from Latin American History," *American Historical Review* 99, no. 5 (1994): 1515.

37 Brad S. Gregory, *The Unintended Reformation: How a Religious Revolution*

perspective, Christian academic historians in recent decades have kept up a robust conversation about how faith might be involved their work without undermining their professional scholarly integrity.[38] And so, if the emperor objectivity is not totally unclothed, his robes are more than a bit tattered.

At their best, efforts at critical distance remain worthwhile if not absolutized, and the example of Newman illustrates this. Although he wrote his historical arguments in relation to doctrinal ones, he allowed the evidence to guide him to the most uncomfortable places. Looking at the early Church gradually led him away from an Anglican *Via Media*, away from his early Tractarian convictions, away from branch theory, and into the arms of the Church of Rome, which he had often denounced before as having corrupted much of its inheritance of faith and practice from antiquity. Famously, he recalled that one of the biggest blows to his former beliefs came through an effort in 1839 to study and master the history of the Monophysites: "It was during this course of reading that for the first time a doubt came upon me of the tenableness of Anglicanism. . . . I was seriously alarmed. . . . My stronghold was Antiquity; now here, in the middle of the fifth century, I found, as it seemed to me, Christendom of the sixteenth and the nineteenth centuries reflected. I saw my face in that mirror, and I was a Monophysite."[39] He notes that he did not enter upon this study with the intention of exploring present-day controversies about Rome's claims; rather, the analogy struck him unexpectedly. This new favor to Rome was no motivated reasoning, for it was precisely contrary to his motivations at the time, and it would be some years before he fully accepted the implications of the shock. In the end, he let his religious convictions follow his historical research.

THE LIMITS OF THE HISTORICAL DISCIPLINE

Despite being thus doctrinally moved by historical evidence, Newman was careful not to absolutize the historical discipline. He had been indeed—as Acton had so boldly declared—a key figure in the nineteenth century for elevating the place of

---

Secularized Society (Cambridge, Mass.: The Belknap Press of Harvard University Press, 2012), 14–20.

38 Discussion of these issues has often been found in the pages of *Fides et historia*, the journal of the Conference on Faith and History. Particularly influential in inspiring further conversation was George M. Marsden, *The Outrageous Idea of Christian Scholarship* (Oxford: Oxford University Press, 1997). Two important compendia of recent thinking are John Fea, Jay Green, and Eric Miller, eds., *Confessing History: Explorations in Christian Faith and the Historian's Vocation* (Notre Dame, Ind.: University of Notre Dame Press, 2010); and Jay D. Green, *Christian Historiography: Five Rival Versions* (Waco, Tex.: Baylor University Press, 2015). Two recent proposals for ways forward are Christopher Shannon and Christopher O. Blum, *The Past as Pilgrimage: Narrative, Tradition, and the Renewal of Catholic History* (Front Royal, Va.: Christendom Press, 2014); and Mark Sandle and William Van Arragon, *Re-Forming History* (Eugene, Ore.: Cascade Books, 2020).

39 *Apo.*, 108.

history among the disciplines. History, Newman suggested, was essential not only for researchers in almost every academic discipline but also for those whose baili-wick was more practical. Yet, contrary to some of his contemporaries, Newman held that historical arguments could not trump all other kinds of reasoning. The honest historian would recognize the limits of his evidence and maintain humility about his degree of certainty. History could not teach all things.

The argument of the *Essay* assumed that historical evidence alone could not answer all questions about true Christianity. The theory of development, however, facilitated the use of historical evidence as part of the bigger picture. To Chill-ingworth and others who argued that *sola scriptura* was the only solution to the seeming contradictions and lacunae in historical evidence, Newman granted that "history is not a creed or a catechism; it gives lessons rather than rules."[40] In his original 1845 edition, he included stronger verbiage arguing that historical evidence was "sufficient to condemn Protestantism, though not sufficient to imprint upon our minds the living image of Christianity." He went on: "It does not bring out clearly upon the canvass the details which were familiar to the ten thousand minds of whose combined movements and fortunes it treats. Such is it from its very nature; nor can the defect ever fully be remedied." And so, historical evidence needed theo-retical help, "principles" that would be "keys to its various notices, enabling us to arrange and reconcile them."[41] These principles he provided in the *Essay*.

Later in the *Essay*, Newman offered a brief epistemology of history opposed to the empiricist aspirations of many nineteenth century historians, and thus he illumined a path to making compelling historical arguments without a hubristic search for mathematical certainty. Newman mildly praised Francis Bacon's scien-tific empiricist mode of reasoning and insistence on avoiding presuppositions but then insisted that such an approach could not apply to historical evidence: "Physical facts . . . are submitted to the senses, and the senses may be satisfactorily tested, corrected, and verified. . . . But it is otherwise with history, the facts of which are not present. . . . We must do our best with what is given us, and look about for aid from any quarter; and in such circumstances the opinions of others, the traditions of ages, the prescriptions of authority, antecedent auguries, analogies, parallel cases, these and the like, not indeed taken at random, but, like the evidence from the senses, sifted and scrutinized, obviously become of great importance."[42] He went on to quote favorably Barthold George Niebuhr (1776–1831), the great Danish-German historian of ancient Rome, as a corrective to pure empiricism, especially when dealing with scant evidence on obscure matters: "Instances are not arguments, but in history are scarcely of less force."[43] Moreover, Newman pointed

---

40 *Dev.*, 7.

41 *Dev.* (1845), 7.

42 *Dev.*, 111. See also his discussion in *The Idea of a University* of different disciplines being rooted in different sources of evidence: *Idea*, 37–38.

43 B. G. Niebuhr, *The History of Rome*, trans. Julius Charles Hare and Connop Thirl-wall (Cambridge: John Taylor, 1828), vol. 1, 345, quoted in *Dev.*, 113.

out that much of our reasoning, even on "our dearest interests," proceeds "not on proof but on a simple probability" and that "presumption verified by instances, is our ordinary instrument of proof, and, if the antecedent probability is great, it almost supersedes instances."[44] These epistemological principles—in accord with his more expansive theory in *An Essay in Aid of a Grammar of Assent*—have two effects on the historical scholar. First, the historian must abandon pretensions to unassailable empirical argumentation. Secondly, he or she can reasonably make arguments rooted in probability or a convergence of evidence. Most historians today—even those who wish to cling to scraps of a mitigated version of nineteenth century empiricism and impartiality—would have difficulty finding objections to the core of Newman's methodological principles. Like it or not, we historians must stake our claims without mathematical or empirical certitude.

From this reality stems the fact that historical arguments are often more subject to uncertainty and to debate than are purely empirical demonstrations in, say, the natural sciences. (And even the latter are often far from irreformable.) A seemingly settled historical question can be upended by new evidence, new questions about old evidence, or new theoretical foundations. A piece of historical argumentation that seems initially plausible may be found to be built on sand when looked at in another light. In a passage of *The Idea of a University*, he demonstrated this with respect to "silences," arguing against eighteenth and nineteenth century thinkers who rejected religious claims that had not been otherwise verified by historical evidence. Mere "silences" in secular sources—Edward Gibbon's skepticism, for example, regarding the darkness that covered the land at the Passion—had been treated as evidence that a thing had not been: "Well might he argue against the existence of Christianity itself in the first century, because Seneca, Pliny, Plutarch, the Jewish Mishna, and other authorities are silent about it."[45] Rather than maintaining humility about its uncertainties, history had arrogated to itself the right to answer questions that were beyond its ken and had done so in service of an anti-religious polemic. Newman concludes: "The evidence of History, I say, is invaluable in its place; but, if it assumes to be the sole means of gaining Religious Truth, it goes beyond its place. We are putting it to a larger office than it can undertake, if we countenance the usurpation."[46] No one could doubt that Newman elevated the place of historical evidence—especially in its essential role in doctrinal arguments—but it was not the master discipline trumping all others that some wished it to be.

Along these lines, one of Newman's recurrent claims in *Idea of a University* was that all the disciplines, including history, needed the others; there was no universal trump. One of his clearest definitions of the "philosophical habit of mind"—which he saw as one of the chief goals of university education—was "the

---

44   *Dev.*, 113–14, 115.

45   *Idea*, 90.

46   *Idea*, 90.

comprehension of the bearings of one science on another, and the use of each to each, and the location and limitation and adjustment and due appreciation of them all."[47] If even theology needed to recognize its limits and to accept the insights of every other discipline from philosophy to geology, then neither could history stand alone.[48] Newman believed an intellectual balance could issue from the university's social character: "An assemblage of learned men, zealous for their own sciences, and rivals of each other, are brought, by familiar intercourse and for the sake of peace, to adjust together the claims and relations of their respective subjects of investigation."[49] The historian thus rightly would insist on the bearings of his science on all the others, but he never would claim to be the master above all his fellows.

THE PROMISE OF THE HISTORICAL DISCIPLINE

Within its due limits, history remained in Newman's eyes essential to the life of the educated man. Put another way, history undermined the fuzzy thinking that pervaded the writing and conversation of his day—and that, some would argue, pervades the flood of words of our own day, as well. In the preface to *Idea of a University*, Newman lamented the fact that so many men did "not know what they are talking about" and had "no difficulty in contradicting themselves in successive sentences, without being conscious of it." Other "intellectual infirmities" included a monomaniacal recourse to "most unfortunate crochets . . . or hobbies," an inability to "see the point," an obstinacy and prejudice that made change of opinion impossible regardless of evidence, and an intemperate manner of defending positions that consistently drove hearers from those positions.[50] Even should he lack these more obvious intellectual vices, a polished, seemingly well-educated man might fall into what Newman calls "spurious philosophism" or "viewiness," the tendency to express "'views' on all subjects of philosophy, on all matters of the day," regardless of one's qualifications to do so.[51] The study of history was an antidote to these ills, as an essential part of the liberal education that aimed "at raising the intellectual tone of society, at cultivating the public mind, at purifying the national taste, at supplying true principles to popular enthusiasm and fixed aims to popular aspiration, at giving enlargement and sobriety to the ideas of the age, at facilitating the exercise of political power, and refining the intercourse of private life."[52]

Newman's account of historical education can roughly be expressed under the two related concepts of historical thinking and historical literacy, the former

---

47 *Idea*, 57.
48 *Idea*, 57–58.
49 *Idea*, 95; see also *Idea*, 369.
50 *Idea*, 11.
51 *Idea*, 12, 13.
52 *Idea*, 154.

of which was the more important in itself. As much as Newman valued erudition and the acquirement of knowledge, mere accumulation of large masses of facts formed people "who have too much on their hands to indulge themselves in thinking or investigation, who devour premise and conclusion together with indiscriminate greediness, who hold whole sciences on faith."[53] History could instead be approached with an eye toward cultivating the mind, at giving order and structure to one's thinking. History can "enlarge and enlighten the mind" insofar as "it gives a power of judging of passing events, and of all events, and a conscious superiority over them."[54] But to have such effects, it was to be studied with careful attention to chronology and geography as principles of "science, method, order, principle, and system; of rule and exception, of richness and harmony"; for otherwise history would be "little better than a storybook."[55] Truly to understand, "to get up . . . any one chapter of history" was "a lesson in memory and discrimination."[56] In other words, Newman was not interested in providing mere knowledge of the past, but in forming minds that could discern continuities, discontinuities, and, ultimately, the causes of events and changes within human affairs as they played out in time and space. Rather than merely memorizing stories and factoids, the student of history would practice giving a coherent analysis of contingent matters, even from imperfect evidence.[57]

For all his critique of *mere* accumulation of knowledge, Newman nevertheless strongly advocated the inculcation of historical literacy—not only in the university student but also in the Christian faithful—often for overtly practical purposes. While still an Anglican, he lamented ignorance of Church history as "perhaps the greatest of wants" in the religious literature being published in his day.[58] This want he linked with a general historical ignorance that greatly vitiated ecclesiastical and political public discourse: "Men enter into life, and take what they find there, and put their own interpretation upon it, if their imaginations are not pre-occupied with the one true historical comment. This is why there is such difficulty in rousing the public mind to understand the importance of certain measures, proposed or resisted: to the public they are facts without meaning."[59] Without historical context, we are at sea in the present: "The history of the past ends in the present; and the present is our scene of trial;

---

53 *Idea*, 132.

54 *Idea*, 119.

55 *Idea*, 12–13.

56 *Idea*, 403.

57 Contrary to this ideal would be Newman's caricature Mr. Brown, the dabbling candidate for university admission who "knows *something* about a great many things" but cannot "see exactly the *point* of things." Telling, in Newman's view, is the pride Brown's father expresses about his son's "good memory," "great talent for history," and *speed* in reading a multitude of works (*Idea*, 287–89).

58 *EH* ii, 249. He anticipates here some of his later ideas about development of doctrine.

59 *EH* ii, 251.

and to behave ourselves towards its various phenomena duly and religiously, we must understand them; and to understand them, we must have recourse to those past events which led to them. Thus the present is a text, and the past its interpretation."[60] Many of Newman's historical essays, found especially in the collections *Historical Sketches* and *Essays Critical and Historical*, precisely aim to dispel such ignorance in a wider reading audience, on issues ranging from the Church Fathers to the Benedictines to medieval universities to the role of the Ottoman Turks in Europe.

After his conversion, Newman saw wider dissemination of historical knowledge as integral to the defense of Catholicism. The year before publishing *Idea of a University*, Newman had spoken of this apologetic purpose, in one of his *Lectures on the Present Position of Catholics in England*: "I want a laity, not arrogant, not rash in speech, not disputatious, but men who know . . . their creed so well, that they can give an account of it, *who know so much of history that they can defend it*."[61] As for the graduate of the Catholic university, he was to be "on par" with Oxbridge men in knowing things like "the great primitive divisions of Christianity, its polity, its luminaries, its acts, and its fortunes; its great eras, and its course down to this day."[62] Just as with other matters pertaining to Church life and his own religion, the educated Catholic must be not only as well-informed in history as his Protestant contemporaries, so as to converse with them creditably and amiably, but still more well informed, so as always to have "a few direct words stating the fact" that will dispel misinformation and prejudice.[63]

A final word on Newman's approach to history can be seen through his efforts to build Christian culture by making known the lives of the saints. As has been noted already, the Fathers were close to his heart from very early in his career, and he wrote in the 1830s a series of biographical essays known as *The Church of the Fathers* that were included with some modification in his *Historical Sketches*. These essays he later described as "polemical, . . . being directed against certain Protestant ideas and opinions," and so it fits with many of his other historical projects, such as *Arians* and the *Essay on Development*. But a further comment is noteworthy, for he defends his willingness to portray the saints in their full humanity: "Their lingering imperfections surely make us love them more, without leading us to reverence them less, and act as a relief to the discouragement and despondency which may come over those, who, in the midst of much error and sin, are striving to imitate them."[64] More controversial was a short-lived series called *The Lives of the English Saints*, edited by Newman during his last years as an Anglican.[65] Newman's alleged indifference

---

60 *EH* ii, 250.
61 *Prepos.*, 390 (emphasis added).
62 *Idea*, 305.
63 *Idea*, 307–8.
64 *HS* ii, xiii.
65 See Elizabeth Macfarlane, "John Henry Newman's *Lives of the English Saints*," in

to historical truth in the *Lives* ended up being prominent in Charles Kingsley's accusations and Newman's response in the *Apologia*.[66] Indeed, Newman himself approved of the idea that the work of the hagiographer was distinct from that of the historian.[67] These arguments aside, the *Lives* was a series meant to form Englishmen via knowledge of their own history. His descriptions of the project's goals varied—whether it might be "devotion" or "polemical"—but he above all wished "to kindle love for the national Church *and yet* to inculcate a Catholic tone," to instill in his countrymen "an interest in the English soil and the English Church."[68] Insofar as the work was polemical, he was still hoping to prevent defections to Rome by more strongly identifying the Established Church with the medieval Church in England.[69] But insofar as it was devotional, the project was really meant to "kindle love," to help Englishmen embrace their own saints. In this way, historical literacy would be a means to reform in the individual heart and in the wider Church.

CONCLUSION

Newman allowed historical evidence to provoke some of his most important life decisions, and he never lost faith in the study of the past, either as a form of learning for its own sake or as a necessity in the practical life of Church and society. He did not fear history because he did not fear the legitimate claims of reason in the Christian's intellectual life: "If we invite reason to take its place in our schools, we must let reason have fair and full play. If we reason, we must submit to the conditions of reason. We cannot use it by halves; we must use it as proceeding from Him. . . . To be ever interrupting its processes, and diverting its attention by objections brought from a higher knowledge . . . argues surely some distrust either in the powers of Reason on the one hand, or the certainty of Revealed Truth on the other. . . . Let us eschew secular history, and science, and philosophy for good and all, if we are not allowed to be sure that Revelation is so true that the altercations and perplexities of human opinion cannot really or eventually injure its authority."[70] History, in all its limitations and in all its promise, was essential to Newman's life and his vision.

Making and Remaking Saints in Nineteenth-Century Britain, ed. Gareth Atkins (Manchester: Manchester University Press, 2016), 245–61. This article highlights recent research showing Newman was more heavily involved in the project than has sometimes been asserted. See also J. Derek Holmes, "Newman's Reputation and *The Lives of the English Saints*," *The Catholic Historical Review* 51, no. 4 (1966): 528–38.

66 *Apo.*, 423–29.

67 *Apo.*, 425.

68 *LD* ix, 299; *LD* viii, 155; *LD* ix, 349; see Macfarlane, "John Henry Newman's *Lives of the English Saints*," 247.

69 Macfarlane, "Newman's *Lives of the English Saints*," 247.

70 *Idea*, 382–83.

In the last analysis, nineteenth century thinkers like St. John Henry Newman did not follow every rule of scholarly engagement that we have subsequently laid down, and that is an important reason we should attend to them. It is true that "great historians are obsolete historians, who have stimulated others into superseding their work," and our intellectual forbears' arguments and methods are certainly worthy of critique.[71] New evidence is discovered, new methods are developed, and new questions are asked. Nevertheless, we might not reject all that bygone greats have bequeathed us, as Noah Shusterman has argued in speaking of his engagement with nineteenth century historians of the French Revolution: "The classic accounts still have much to teach us, and receive far less attention than they merit."[72] Present-day scholars of early Christianity are free to make judgments about this or that aspect of Newman's arguments about the patristic era. Even if we would reject many of Newman's conclusions—and it is doubtful that we should—we might still learn from Newman the proper place of history vis-à-vis other disciplines. History professors might better learn from Newman how and why to help their students "get up" some "chapter of history," in a way that instills a sense of "science, method, order, principle, and system." Academic historians might imitate Newman by writing essays that promote historical literacy among a wider audience. And they might do so, like Newman, in service of deeply held convictions about the common good or about religious truth. A historian of Christian convictions might even entertain the notion of hagiographical writing that conforms with the best historical evidence.[73] Newman, in short, models for us ways to harmonize faith and reason in our study of the human past. But even the religious skeptic can ponder Newman's claim that the historical discipline—for all its pretensions to objectivity and detachment over the past century and more—is eminently practical and necessary, since "the history of the past ends in the present; and the present is our scene of trial."

Suggested Reading

Altholz, Josef L. "Newman and History." *Victorian Studies* 7, no. 3 (1964): 285–94.

Blum, Christopher O. "The Historian and His Tools in the Workshop of Wisdom." *Logos* 13, no. 4 (2010): 15–34.

Bokenkotter, Thomas S. *Cardinal Newman as an Historian.* Leuven: Editions Nawelaerts, 1959.

Green, Jay D. *Christian Historiography: Five Rival Versions.* Waco, Tex.: Baylor University Press, 2015.

Holmes, J. Derek. "Newman's Reputation and *The Lives of the English Saints.*" *The Catholic Historical Review* 51, no. 4 (1966): 528–38.

---

71   Altholz, "Newman and History," 287.

72   Noah Shusterman, *The French Revolution: Faith, Desire, Politics,* 2nd ed. (Abingdon, UK: Routledge, 2021), 5.

73   Christopher O. Blum "The Historian and His Tools in the Workshop of Wisdom," *Logos* 13 (2010): 29.

Holmes, J. Derek. "Cardinal Newman on the Philosophy of History." *Tijdschrift Voor Filosofie* 32 (1970): 521–35.

Kelly, Stephen. "John Henry Newman and the Writing of History." *Newman Studies Journal* 8, no. 2 (2011): 29–41.

Lawson, Stephen D. "'To Be Deep in History': The Role of History in the Conversions of John Henry Newman and Erik Peterson." *Newman Studies Journal* 16, no. 2 (2019): 5–33.

Macfarlane, Elizabeth. "John Henry Newman's *Lives of the English Saints*." In *Making and Remaking Saints in Nineteenth-Century Britain*, edited by Gareth Atkins, 245–61. Manchester: Manchester University Press, 2016.

Parker, Kenneth L. "Historiography." In *The Oxford Handbook of John Henry Newman*, edited by Frederick D. Aquino and Benjamin J. King, 557–77. Oxford: Oxford University Press, 2018.

Russell, David L. "John Henry Newman." In *Historians of the Christian Tradition: Their Methodology and Influence on Western Thought*, 191–207. Nashville, Tenn.: Broadman & Holman, 1995.

Sandle, Mark, and William Van Arragon. *Re-Forming History*. Eugene, Ore.: Cascade Books, 2020.

Shannon, Christopher, and Christopher O. Blum. *The Past as Pilgrimage: Narrative, Tradition, and the Renewal of Catholic History*. Front Royal, Va.: Christendom Press, 2014.

Short, Edward. *Newman and History*. Leominster, U.K.: Gracewing, 2017.

CHAPTER 11

NEWMAN'S FOUNDATION OF THE ORATORY IN ENGLAND

Fr. Daniel Seward

When, on the 8th of October 1845, John Henry Newman (1801–1890) entered the "one fold" of the Redeemer, he had the question of what to do and where to go next, not only for himself but also for his friends. Since Oxford was in the Midland District under the Vicar Apostolic Nicholas Wiseman, Newman and the other converts ended up at Old Oscott. Wiseman had previously been Rector of the English College in Rome and had met Newman there in 1833. Now as his bishop he suggested the Oratory of St. Philip Neri as a possible home for Newman. With this thought in mind, Newman and Ambrose St John headed to Rome in 1846. On his way, praying to know God's will, St. John Henry wrote, "I shall do just what they tell us in Rome."[1]

This chapter will discuss why Newman eventually took Wiseman's suggestions and chose the Oratory of St. Philip Neri and not any other institute in the Church for himself and his close friends. We will also consider which features of the Oratory were particularly consonant with Newman's outlook and temperament, especially the idea of "home," and how he came to be a stimulus to further growth in Philippine life in the twentieth century and beyond.

Newman himself would regard all this as the action of Providence working through him. "It continually happens in the history of the Church, that the immediate and direct notion which has stimulated holy men to begin their labour, is but a part of that work, or is not that work, which the event proves

---

1   *LD* xi, 227.

to have been their mission. They have their own object before their mind, and Providence had led them on by means of it to accomplish His own."[2]

Such has been the history of John Henry Newman's own call to found the Oratory in England, and the subsequent development and growth of the houses which have sprung from that inspiration.

WHAT IS THE ORATORY?

St. Philip Neri (1515–1595) began the Oratory in sixteenth century Rome simply as a way of providing the *Exercises* of the Oratory, which he led first in his room and later in an oratory above the church of *San Girolamo della Carità*. At a certain point, Philip's followers pressed him to give them a Rule, and the new Congregation was given formal approval in 1575, together with a church, *Santa Maria in Vallicella*. This church Philip had demolished, and a larger, new church built in its place, which is still known as the *Chiesa Nuova*—"the New Church."

Oratorians are not religious, in the sense that they do not take religious vows. They are secular priests living under a Rule. Hence a priest of the Oratory is always free to leave it without incurring sin. This gives a certain fragility to each individual Oratory, dependent as it is upon the daily perseverance of its members, and Newman cites the saying of an old Father: "The true sons of St. Philip are known at their burial."[3] St. Philip had no ambition to extend his institute beyond the city of Rome: "Rome was his India; he dedicated himself to Rome; to ask him to take interest in other places, was nothing short of asking him to intermit his exertions in behalf of Rome."[4]

Philip insisted that different houses should have no role in governing each other. The growth of the Oratory through Italy and elsewhere came through individual communities being founded, copying the customs of the *Chiesa Nuova*, with their mutual relations being simply of charity.

AN ANSWER TO PRAYER

There was still a great uncertainly in Newman's mind in January 1847. With faint praise, he says,

> Well then, we have said to ourselves, let us see what the Oratorians are like. We do not hear much about them—they are said to be good *Confessors*—Theiner is a very *learned* man—here certainly are some lineaments of the primitive Oratorians retained—but here our information ends.[5]

---

2   *NO*, 185.
3   *NO*, 336.
4   *NO*, 165.
5   *LD* xii, 16.

At this time, the attraction of Dominican learning and teaching was still strong. Also, the possibilities for Oratorian life in Birmingham seemed meager. Both Newman and St John felt that London would be a much better center of operation, if they could migrate there, but they felt an obligation to the place where God had placed them, from the circumstance of having found themselves in the Midland District. Certainly the Oratorian Rule would need substantial alteration to be put into practice in England.

On the 17th of January 1847, the vigil of the feast of the Chair of Peter, John Henry went to St. Peter's and began a novena for light as to his vocation, which was completed on the 25th of January, the feast of the Conversion of St. Paul. On the first day of the novena, Newman wrote to Wiseman, "It is curious and very pleasant that, after all the thought we can give to the matter, we come round to your Lordship's original idea, and feel that we cannot do better than be Oratorians."

On Newman's 46th birthday, the 21st of February 1847, he wrote to Cardinal Franconia with a request that he ask Pope Pius IX for approbation of the idea of founding the Oratory in England.

PERSONAL INFLUENCE

In an age of industrialization and mass-production—a phenomenon often reflected in the Church by the elimination of local custom and the centralization of authority—St. John Henry chose to attach himself to an institution that was deliberately small and local. Whereas St. Philip's friend, St. Ignatius Loyola, founded a highly successful body with a military-style discipline borrowed from the experiences of his early life as a soldier, Philip's Oratory embodied a complementary but opposite spirit. Newman admired the Jesuits and for a short time considered the Society of Jesus as a possible home for himself and his friends. There is no disapproval in the contrast he draws between the Philippine and Ignatian ways, but Newman saw the Oratorian as the "Athenian" in contrast to the Jesuit "Spartan":

> He [the Oratorian] fights by himself—he guides himself by "carità"— which means by tact, self-knowledge, knowledge of others. This requires a specific training—more, it requires training *with* those with whom he is to live. Again, if you come to us with the grave, unmoved bearing of a Jesuit, you might be as good a Christian as a disciple of St. Philip—but you would not be a Philippian, whose spirit is to conceal seriousness under great cheerfulness, simplicity, modesty, and humour.[6]

6　*LD*, xii, 113.

The Jesuit could be characterized by his "staid and upright figure, his down-cast or uplifted eyes, his abstracted countenance and his high biretta" whereas the Oratorian, "sits in an easy chair, in a lounging posture, one hand stretched on a table, with bright sparkling eyes and a merry countenance."[7]

Newman identifies here a key feature of Oratorianism: it cannot be mass-produced because it depends not on any theory but on living with a particular set of people. Whereas religious orders usually keep the noviciate separate from the main body, sometimes even in a separate house, for the Oratorian the test of his vocation is not an abstract keeping of the Rule but being able to live in one house with one set of people for the remainder of his life.[8] The clothing ceremony Newman devised, still used at the Birmingham Oratory and its foundations, asks the prospective novice a remarkable question: "Will you love us with a brotherly affection, without particular friendship or party combination, being gentle with the impetuous, winning the froward, and bearing the perverse?"[9]

It is in the voluntary love of community life that sanctity is to be reached. *Vita communis mortificatio maxima*, runs a favourite Oratorian maxim.[10]

When visiting the Oratory at Naples, St. John Henry observed the democratic spirit of the house: "The giovani are pleasant, brightfaced, modest looking youths, silent perhaps because they are young and backward in giving their opinion, but they have nothing of the external gravity, composed attitude, and reserve of a Jesuit novice."[11]

There is a reason for this: the Oratorian must be an equal member of a body, able to depend upon his own resources as well as to be supported by a community. While St. Philip gave the Oratory a Rule, the Rule is not the key to understanding Philippine life. Newman realized that community life would not remain in its perfection by mere observance of the Rule. The well-conduct of the house depended not on blind obedience but on each member individually as a first spring of action.

These facets of Oratorian life give a vital continuity to Newman's spiritual and intellectual life. The man who was convinced of the Apostolic Succession during a walk around Christ Church meadow, who wrote on the day of his ordination to the Anglican diaconate that he had the responsibility of souls on him until death, upon being made a cardinal in 1879, remarked,

> When I was public tutor of my College at Oxford, I maintained even
> fiercely that my employment was distinctly pastoral. I considered that,
> by the statutes of the University, a tutor's profession was of a religious

---

7   *NO*, 207.

8   See ch. 5 of this volume by Víctor García Ruiz for Newman's description of his fellow Oratorians, especially Ambrose St John (editor's note).

9   *Sanctus Philippus Birminghamiensis*, (Birmingham Oratory: 1856), 10.

10   *NO*, 345.

11   *NO*, 208.

nature. I never would allow that, in teaching the classics, I was absolved from carrying on, by means of them, in the minds of my pupils an ethical training. I considered a College tutor to have the care of souls. . . . To this principle I have been faithful throughout my life.[12]

For the tutor in Oxford as for the priest in Birmingham the care of souls by *personal influence* was the golden thread that ran through Newman's life, and it was thus that he found a perfect fit with St. Philip's Oratory.[13] Philip Neri was one of the most important figures of the Counter-Reformation, even though he remained quietly in Rome for six decades. It was the quiet influence of the confessional and personal contact that earned him the title of the third Apostle of Rome. Hence, "It would seem that influence, whether secret or open, is the mainspring of the Oratory."[14]

Newman points out that personal anecdotes about St. Philip in Rome abound, whereas there are few of St. Ignatius's long stay. The Oratorian bishop of Geneva, St. Francis de Sales, originated the saying that heart shall speak unto heart, though Newman could not remember where he had originally read the phrase when adapting these words as his cardinal's motto. This choice—*Cor ad Cor loquitur*—shows why John Henry Newman brought the Rule of St. Philip to England.

In 1853 Newman spent his holiday at Abbotsford cutting up (literally with a pair of scissors) the *Life of St. Philip* into daily segments to be read in the refectory: "and it is a thought in which they may find an occasion for boasting and for thankfulness, that hardly a Saint can be named, whose recorded history admits of being separated into so many small wholes, for the year's course, as that of their own St. Philip."[15] Whereas in Benedictine monasteries the Rule of St. Benedict is read at meals, in the Oratory it is the *Life of St. Philip*. Benedict left a Rule that transformed Europe, Philip re-converted Rome by the winning force of his personality.

THE ORATORY AS A REDISCOVERY OF ANTIQUITY

Cesare Baronius, (1538–1607), one of the first Oratorians and the author of the *Annals of the Christian Church*, when speaking of the re-unions of the primitive Christians, according to the form described in the Epistles to the Corinthians, declared that the Divine disposition had renewed this ancient and profitable

---

12   *Sayings of Cardinal Newman*, 35.
13   In ch. 12 of this volume, Paul Shrimpton expounds on the "pastoral care" which Newman considered the mission of an educator (editor's note).
14   *NO*, 215.
15   Dedication, *The Life of Saint Philip Neri Apostle of Rome by Father Pietro Giacomo Bacci of the Roman Oratory Arranged for the Days of the Year by Blessed John Henry Newman*, (Birmingham Oratory, 2015), 1.

custom. Similarly, in his litany of St. Philip, Newman used the title, "Man of Primitive Times." Philip's ten years praying in the catacombs gave him an affinity for antiquity, and he sometimes compared himself with the desert Fathers. For Newman, who found his way into the Church by reading the Church Fathers, the Oratory, "is a return to the very first form of Christianity, as it existed in the lifetime of the Apostles."[16]

Another advantage of the Oratory was its similarity to Oxford colleges as they were then constituted. Such echoes are more than coincidental. Jerome Bertram has shown in his book *Vita Communis* that the college or minster was once the common model for "secular" or pastoral clergy, and that the Oxford collegiate system owes its existence to it.[17] When St. Philip lived at *San Girolamo*, he was part of a collegiate house whose members worked and prayed together.[18] St. Philip's Oratory was not a radical new venture in the sixteenth century, but an adaptation of what had come before. It is by no means the only possible structure for the common life of secular clergy, and perhaps it challenges other bodies, such as colleges of canons, to live according to their original purpose. St. Philip's intuitive continuation of the collegiate structure in his time, and Newman's rediscovery of it three hundred years later, might serve as a prompt to reform clerical life far beyond the confines of the Oratory itself.

Sometimes the lack of vows in the Oratory is spoken of as an historical accident, but for Newman it was an essential feature. Writing to Dalgairns on the last day of 1846, he said:

> They have a good library, and handsome sets of rooms apparently. It is like a College with hardly any rule. They keep their own property and furnish their own rooms. It is what Dr Wiseman actually wishes, and really I should not wonder, if at last I felt strongly inclined to it, for I must own I feel the notion of giving up property try my faith very much.[19]

St. Philip himself had insisted that if any group of fathers at the *Vallicella* should ever propose the idea of taking vows, they should be dismissed from the Congregation and the remaining fathers to be considered the whole of the Oratory, even if the latter should be the minority. Here again, we see Philip's particular genius, reflecting his origins in the Florentine Republic. The Oratory is a democracy where the majority should not be able to dominate a minority. Change occurs only when all agree: "The great advantage of the Oratory is, that it leaves scope for persons of very different tastes and qualifications."[20]

---

16 *NO*, 203.

17 See Jerome Bertram, *Vita Communis* (Leominster: Gracewing, 2009).

18 However, unlike the Oratorians, the community at San Girolamo did not eat in common.

19 *LD* xi, 305.

20 *LD* xii, 60.

A SIGN OF CONTRADICTION

Much of the thrust of the religious revival of the nineteenth century, in both the Anglican and Catholic communions, was an interest in the cultural and artistic forms of the Middle Ages. Pugin pioneered the rediscovery of Gothic architecture, along with the techniques of encaustic tiles, stained glass, and a more ancient cut of vestment. In France, Dom Prosper Guéranger recreated the monastic world that had already disappeared long before 1789 and restored the use of Gregorian chant to a preeminent position in Church music. We might have expected Newman, as one of the foremost churchmen of the age, to be in the vanguard of the Gothic revival, but things turned out very differently, and unexpectedly. Both the Birmingham and London Oratories employed (and employ) baroque architecture, Roman vestments, and polyphonic music. Guy Nicholls writes of Newman's concern that the altar should be visible and approachable as "clearly antithetical" to the ideas of Pugin.[21] Sadly, when Dom Guéranger visited the Birmingham Oratory in 1860, Newman was unresponsive, "answering only in monosyllables and declining to give extended answers to the abbot's overtures."[22]

Despite his unfashionable dislike of Gothic, Newman was also cautious in his response to the increased emphasis on the person of the Roman Pontiff and the position of the Curia; and yet he attached himself to that most Roman of institutions: the Oratory of St. Philip Neri, himself the third Apostle of Rome. It might seem as though Newman and the English Oratorians were deliberately perverse, swimming against the stream on just about every hot matter of the day: full of Romanità, and yet not ultramontane; bringing to England an institution that was to become peculiarly English, and yet eschewing rood "skreens" and pointed arches.

Many nineteenth (and twentieth) century converts to Catholicism expressed their fervor in their new religion by becoming extreme ultramontanists. W. G. Ward wanted to read a papal bull at every breakfast with his *Times*. All this reflected the spirit of the age: industrialization brought about a new uniformity. Whereas previous generations had set their clocks by the sun, "Railway Time" put whole countries onto standard, legal hours. Smaller, regional identities were swept away by the new, "national" states. Victorian city planners demolished decayed, mediaeval streets in favour of wide, brash avenues. Ancient, quirky, irregular churches were knocked down, to be replaced with soulless off-the-shelf models, so many of which now stand draughty and disused. Once Newman had left Oxford, he left the field open for the great "reformer," Benjamin Jowett, who began the process of dismantling the Anglican establishment to create a "modern" secular university.

---

21 Guy Nicholls, *Unearthly Beauty, The Aesthetic of St. John Henry Newman* (Leominster: Gracewing, 2019), 263.
22 Mary David Totah, *The Spirit of Solesmes* (Tunbridge Wells: Burns & Oates, 1997), 31.

What Newman found in the Oratory was the contradiction of all this. St. Philip Neri is the antithesis of strategy, risk assessments, and central planning. He used to say, when people described him as the founder of the Oratory, that Our Lady was the true foundress. This is more than the conventional humility of saints. Philip came to Rome with no particular objective other than to do God's will. He lived as a layman until his fortieth year. Only when his confessor, Persiano Rosa, told him that he should be ordained did Philip become a priest. Those who gathered around him he collected not by design, but by the sheer force of his personality, illuminated as it was by the Holy Spirit. It was these accidental disciples who formed the nucleus of the Oratory, and so reluctant was Philip to be regarded as its author, that when the pope gave the new Congregation the church of *Santa Maria in Vallicella*, Philip remained at *San Girolamo* for a further eight years, until ordered to move by papal authority.

There are parallels to be seen in the life of Newman. He would naturally have gravitated to London, but stayed in Birmingham, where he considered that God had put him. Other people seem to have realized that the Oratory was a natural fit while he was still dithering and hesitating about what next to do. The Oratory's combination of pastoral care and the possibility of intellectual work seems almost to have been designed with Newman in mind.

Newman knew that he would offend by the choices he made. Once the decision had been made to found the Oratory in England, he wrote to Bishop Wiseman, "I am afraid I shall shock Pugin."[23] Similarly, Newman wrote in wry tones about M. Olivier, who attempted to teach plainchant at Maryvale, and of Henry Formby, who was put off joining the English Oratorian novitiate in Rome, since as Newman put it, "I know him still to be mad on the subject of Gregorians."[24] By contrast, he saw that a less purist approach, that which he found in the Oratorian tradition, might be more adaptable to English needs:

> We were at an Oratorio last Sunday, not a real one of St. Philip's, but after his pattern. The boys and youths sang with great spirit and animation choruses and the like—and they had a collection of texts all set to music, some grave, some gay—I cannot conceive this being done with Gregorians—I am not sanguine about interesting boys in Gregorians.[25]

Already in Milan, before ever visiting the *Chiesa Nuova*, St. John Henry was thinking along lines of external secularism with a gentle bond of asceticism, which is what he conceived the Oratory to be.

It was not a superficial love of the exotic that drew Newman to the baroque. Whereas the young Anglican travelling abroad for the first time in 1833 was

---

23 *LD* xii, 52.

24 *LD* xii, 65.

25 *LD* xi, 260.

affected by the romance of Italy, the more mature convert found Rome rather trying. The mud, the deadening protocol, the jejune studies—all of these wearied him. "O how dreary *Santa Croce* and Fr Rossi!"[26] It has to be admitted that the middle-aged Newman had become, on the whole, the sort of Englishman who is uneasy beyond Dover. In November 1846, he wrote to Richard Stanton to describe the hotel where he was staying in Rome:

> It is a palace of filth. . . . We thought it bad enough in France . . . bad enough at Milan . . . but here the carpet is a nest of fleas and they have milk pans for slop pails. This is but a type of the whole. We dare not unpack our clothes lest fleas and dirt should infect the whole. And to complete it we are obliged to dress in the queerest fashion.[27]

Things did not much improve once they had gone to live at the *Propaganda Fide* College:

> I never saw any city with the tenth part the quantity of dung in the streets as Rome—When the rain comes this is formed into a thickish fluid—Last Sunday it rained hard—and when we came in, our mantellas at bottom had a *very deep* fringe of the nastiest stuff I ever saw and all wet.[28]

The homesickness of the English exiles is shown by their habit of describing the journey from *Santa Croce* into the city of Rome as "walking into Oxford,"[29] as if they were still at Littlemore, but there was plenty of the atmosphere of the Eternal City that was to become incarnate in Edgbaston.

Complaints about food and living conditions by no means exhaust Newman's attitude to Rome. Writing to Henry Wilberforce a few weeks later he said: "I was happy at Oriel, happier at Littlemore, as happy or happier still at Maryvale—and happiest here."[30]

THE VITAL IMPORTANCE OF HOME

The status of the son of St. Philip as a secular, living in community, came to be seen by Newman as allowing community in the fullest sense of the word, since it is a continually chosen community. Hence the importance of the idea of *home*. The Father of the Oratory usually joins one community and stays there for the remainder of his life. The love shown by the people of Birmingham for

---

26 *AW*, 256.
27 *LD* xi, 267.
28 *LD* xi, 285.
29 *LD* xii, 100.
30 *LD* xi, 294.

Cardinal Newman as his hearse passed through the streets on its way to Rednal came from their knowledge that this man had fixed his dwelling among them, that he had become one of them. He had achieved what he set out to do, that is, to form the Oratory as a *native* body of priests. When visiting the Oratory in Naples, Newman had noticed the good relationship between the fathers and the local merchants—surely as good a barometer of inculturation as any! In Turin, he observed that many of the local clergy went to confession to the fathers—a feature of English Oratories today. In the idea of home, Newman found another happy congruity between St. Philip's ideas and his own sense of English identity.

Newman's willingness to embrace places and situations that were naturally repugnant to him is one of the marks of his sanctity. Already as an Anglican he had shown concern for the welfare of his poor and ordinary parishioners at Littlemore that was far from typical of Oxford dons at the time. Newman's first concern in coming into the Catholic Church was to keep together with his friends. He was not responsible for himself only. Nicholas Wiseman, the Vicar Apostolic of the Midland District, offered him Old Oscott as a home, which he accepted despite finding it "dismally ugly."[31] At that point, the new converts were influenced by Fr. Dominic Barberi's wish that they should form a congregation, giving missions and helping the local clergy—in short, not unlike the Passionists. The happenstance of being received within the Midland District remained a firm imperative in Newman's mind that they should remain in Birmingham, even though "Brummagem is no centre."[32]

Nevertheless, he was to call "Brummagem" home for the rest of his life. Some people live in a place as strangers, without particular attachment. Such was not the way of St. John Henry. He had a strong, and peculiarly English, sense of home. Although to many, Littlemore's low stable block can have had little to recommend it, it had become a place of affection for Mr. Newman, no less than the dressed stones of Trinity or Oriel. On taking leave of his room at "The College," Newman sentimentally kissed the furniture. Later he wrote to Ambrose St John, "I can't help writing to dear Littlemore now that I am a pilgrim at a distance from it. I suppose it is good penance going from home."[33]

To Dominic Barberi he wrote, "You may fancy what pain the thought gives me of leaving Littlemore."[34] For someone who attached such importance to place, to home, Newman's departure from Littlemore was an agony. He wrote to Ambrose St John in January 1846: "*Obliviscere populum tuum et domum patris tui* has been in my ears for the last twelve hours. I realize that we are leaving Littlemore and it is like going on the open sea."[35]

---

31   *LD* xi, 29.
32   *LD* xi, 30.
33   *LD* xi, 45.
34   *LD* xi, 77.
35   *LD* xi, 95.

It was on the 6th of January 1846 that Newman first referred to the "dismally ugly" Old Oscott as "Mary Vale." Four days later he wrote in a memorandum in York, "We did not know our vocation yet,"[36] but those who believe in Providence will note that the church given to St. Philip Neri in 1575 is *Santa Maria in Vallicella*—Saint Mary in the little Valley. Later in January Newman would write of "Sancta Maria in Valle"[37] and in March of "St. Mary in the Vale."[38]

Professor Roger Scruton writes that,

> Ideas of race, tribe and religion, which have played a dangerous part in continental politics, have also shaped English identity. But they were qualified and moderated by the concept of home. England was first and foremost a *place*—though a place consecrated by custom . . . Home is not just a place, it is also what goes on there. A place *becomes* a home, by virtue of the habits that domesticate it.[39]

In February 1848, Newman wrote,

> The Congregation is to be the *home* of the Oratorian. The Italians, I believe, have no word for home—nor is it an idea which readily enters into the mind of a foreigner, at least not so readily as into the mind of an Englishman. It is remarkable then that the Oratorian Fathers should have gone out of their way to express the idea by the metaphorical word *nido* or nest, which is used by them almost technically.[40]

It is precisely in the perseverance in the "humdrum and twaddling"[41] life of routine, which Blessed Sebastian Valfrè of the Turin Oratory called the "slow fever" of the Oratorian's life, that the Philippine vocation consists. Hence the three ideal, wooden places for the father of the Oratory to die: the chair for giving sermons in the Little Oratory, the confessional, or the predella of the altar. Newman, always sensitive to his environment, attached great importance to the physical setting of the Oratory. The present, magnificent church of the Birmingham Oratory was built after the cardinal's death—a temporary building was used in his lifetime—but the Oratory house, which the community occupied from 1852, is a tangible testament to the realization of his idea:

> This large House is in some sense a *subject* of the Oratory, and has to go through its noviciate, before it can be said really to belong to us. And again, since the Congregation has to grow *into* the House as into its outward covering or shell, almost a corresponding process must

---

36 *LD* xi, 89.
37 *LD* xi, 99.
38 *LD* xi, 143.
39 Roger Scruton, *England: An Elegy* (London: Bloomsbury, 2006), 7.
40 *NO*, 192.
41 *LD* xxvi, 48.

be undergone by ourselves, before we can be considered to be established on the spot of ground, to which our dear and Holy Father has conducted us.[42]

While the Oratory is not a community of vowed religious, still less is it a boarding house, and hence the physical spaces of the house take on a sacred aspect. The refectory, says St. John Henry, is a sort of domestic chapel and is provided with a ceremonial. While the same might be said of a monastic refectory, it takes on a greater importance for the Oratorian, because,

> Only at rare intervals does our Rule bring us together in Church; we do not keep choir, we seldom have high mass, vespers or other functions; our own masses one by one, our attendance in the Confessional, our instructions, our whole work, is necessarily personal and isolated, or nearly so; but twice a day, besides the stated Oratory meeting, does our Holy Father bring us together, to take part, each in his own place, in that great Sacrament of nature, which is recognized by the Patriarchal Dispensation, by the Mosaic Law, and by the Gospel.[43]

THE PAPAL BRIEF

Pope Pius IX's 1847 brief for the English Oratory directed the new foundation's ministry towards the "*coetus doctoris, honestioris, et splendidoriosis ordinis*"[44] to be found in England, often loosely translated as the "upper classes." Keith Beaumont notes that this stipulation was not one that Newman had asked for, describing it as a mission to "the wealthy and educated classes."[45] Clearly, the scope of the pastoral work of the Birmingham and London Oratories was to include the poorest in nineteenth century England: fleas were common in the confessionals of both houses. However, Newman was also keenly aware that the papal brief gave him an obligation to influence the higher echelons of society, so as to affect the whole of it. Four months before the foundation brief, Newman said,

> The more I understand it, the more the Oratory seems the proper thing for England at this moment—the object of St. Philip was to educate a higher class of priests for parish work—most of his followers were highly educated men, corresponding precisely to the fellows of our English Universities.[46]

---

42 *NO*, 287.
43 *NO*, 289.
44 *NO*, 427.
45 Keith Beaumont, "The Oratory," in *The Oxford Handbook of John Henry Newman*, ed. Frederick D. Aquino and Benjamin J. King (Oxford: Oxford University Press, 2018), 40.
46 *LD* xii, 101.

Newman himself recognized that times had altered since the sixteenth century, so that new classes of society had come into existence. Whereas in St. Philip's time there was no medium between the highest and the lowest, in the nineteenth century the "upper class" in England could be said to consist not only of those of "birth" but of all those who have "liberal education and refinement of mind." Therefore, it would be more accurate to say that Pius IX intended that Newman and his confreres should seek out and convert the middle classes. In 1856, Newman stated, "much as I desire to encourage plans of conversion among the Protestant poor of Smethwick, I think distinctly we have prior duties to the Protestant rich of Edgbaston."[47]

Raleigh Addington notes that Newman accepted contemporary social distinctions, while counselling his brethren against a superior attitude to others, "but he believed that those who had been given advantages of birth or education should use them for the common good."[48] In one of his first Chapter Addresses in 1848, Newman said, "it does not follow, because refinement is worthless without saintliness, that it is needless and useless without it. It may set off and recommend an interior holiness."[49] His interpretation of the value of worldly finesse can be compared then with St. Paul's attempt to "become all things to all men, that I might by all means save some" (1 Cor 9:22).

Newman saw the papal mandate to the *ordo honestior* as a recognition that effective missionaries must in temporal matters resemble those to whom they are sent. There is an important feature of Newman's Oratorian mission to be gleaned from the papal brief: it is that the Oratory in England, being composed at first mainly of graduates from the two ancient universities, was a demonstration that Catholics could hold their own in intellectual and cultural life, and thus help to form men and women who could transform a society that would become increasingly hostile to all religious belief. Newman's foundation of the Oratory School, his work with the Catholic University in Ireland, and his lengthy correspondence are all part of this work of influencing and guiding. This is also why the brief speaks of going to the larger cities of the country: Oratorian houses are nearly always in cities, because only there can be found sufficient population to form and influence.

Newman understood the need to be on a level with those whom a priest serves pastorally as a reason for cultivating art, learning, and science. Cesare Baronius, the author of the *Annals of the Christian Church*, is certainly preeminent among learned Oratorians, but there are others too. Newman writes of Fr. Justiniani of the Roman Oratory, who "rummaged libraries, and turned over the pages of books, without any immediate aim before him, or prospect of utility."[50]

---

47 *NO*, 307.
48 Raleigh Addington, *The Idea of the Oratory* (London: Burns & Oates, 1966), 123.
49 *NO*, 189.
50 *NO*, 324.

LOVE TO BE UNKNOWN

We have seen that Newman's discovery of his Oratorian vocation enabled him to be a "light to others," and to create a body which would perpetuate this call. Like St. Philip Neri, John Henry Newman was hidden from the world's gaze for much of his life. In this he fulfilled the Philippine maxim, *amare nesciri:* Love to be unknown. The Oratory, he said, "dislikes whatever savours of pomp, pretence, or violence. It has a hidden life, neither is its voice heard in the streets."[51] The program for holiness that Father Newman set before his brethren in Birmingham is disarmingly simple: "He is perfect who does the duties of the day perfectly."

While we can say that Newman's adaptation of the Rule to English circumstances enabled new growth, this growth was typically Newmanian in that it was a development that preserved type, not a wholesale change. Having discovered St. Philip and his Congregation, Newman had an instinctive understanding of how to bring this to nineteenth century England. A demonstration of the vital, organic power of this transplantation into the land of "heretics and Saxons"[52] is in the subsequent history of the English Oratories. The Birmingham and London houses, despite inevitable challenges and vicissitudes of fortune, have remained substantially true to the spirit of their founder, and from the centenary of Newman's death onwards, new shoots have grown: in Oxford (1993), Manchester (2019) and York (2019) there are new Congregations, and also now houses-in-formation in Cardiff and Bournemouth. Further afield, Oratories such as Pittsburgh, Toronto, and Vienna all owe their inspiration to John Henry Newman.

When in the 1930's autocratic government was in vogue, there was an attempt to turn the Oratory into a centralized body with a Superior General. Fr. Denis Sheil, the final novice to have been clothed by Cardinal Newman in 1890, drew up a "Solemn Protest" in 1936 on behalf of both English Congregations against proposals to diminish the autonomy of individual houses. The Confederation of the Oratory was still formed, but the loss of independence was considerably reduced by Fr. Sheil's intervention. He saved the Oratory from destruction by the homogenizing spirit of the age, and he was described as *un uomo tremendo*, "a tremendous man" by Fr. Larraona, the first Apostolic Visitor. Raleigh Addington writes, "Fr Sheil was certainly right in one respect—there *is* something alien to the Socratic, humanist spirit of St. Philip's Oratory in regimentation, codifying or forcing a living organism into definite categories whether Aristotelian or legal. Such was not St. Philip's way."[53]

The preservation of this way of St. Philip into the twenty-first century came through the tenacity of Newman's spiritual heirs.

---

51 *NO*, 216.

52 *LD* xii, 22.

53 Addington, *The Idea of the Oratory*, 195.

NEWMAN'S INFLUENCE ON THE GROWTH
OF ST. PHILIP'S ORATORY

Speculation about "what-ifs" is one of those fascinating but inconclusive hobbies of historians. What if the coachman had been directed to turn right towards Cambridge in 1817 instead of left towards Oxford? It seems likely that the intelligence and gifts of John Henry Newman might have been channeled in an entirely different direction. There would have been no Oxford Movement, no Second Spring, and no cardinal living on the Hagley Road in Birmingham. Similarly, we might ask what the result would have been had Newman decided upon another vocation within the Catholic Church after his conversion, instead of becoming the founder of the Oratory in England.

With the benefit of hindsight, St. John Henry's discovery of the Oratory and his transplanting it to England appear inevitable, yet this is to see Providence acting with the large view of history. To the new convert in 1845, nothing about his future seemed certain, except that he would be a Catholic. Newman thought about the Dominicans, the Sulplicians, the Vincentians, the Passionists, and the Jesuits, and had he attached himself to any of these bodies, his own development (and theirs) would have been different, and the Oratory might be still unknown in the English-speaking world.

Until the twentieth century and the establishment of the Confederation of the Oratory, it is surprisingly difficult to be certain and exact about how many Congregations of the Oratory there were, or how many members they had. While the prominent houses of Rome and Naples, still in the last flower of their glory when Newman went to Rome in 1846, were large establishments with dozens of priests, an examination of smaller houses elsewhere, for example in the *Marche* of Italy, suggests that they must always have had few members. In 1878 Newman said,

> I have never wished, I have never liked, a large Oratory. Twelve working Priests has been the limit of my ambition. One cannot love many at one time; one cannot have many friends. An Oratory is a family and a home; a domestic circle, as the words imply, is bounded and rounded.[54]

Today, twelve priests would be considered a very large Oratory—especially twelve working priests.

A century before the foundation of the English Oratory, there were one-hundred-and-forty-six congregations, of which ninety-six were in the Italian peninsula.[55] Only fourteen of all these houses exist today. Dozens of

---

54 *NO*, 387.
55 *Catalogo delle città dove esiste la Congregazione dell'Oratorio*, Roma, Archivio della Procura Generale, 1749.

long-established foundations were swept away in the wake of revolutionary events of the nineteenth century, especially in Italy. Of the nineteen Oratories now in Italy, most occupy only a fraction of their former house, the bulk having been confiscated. The Oratory remains a footnote in ecclesiastical history. Yet the picture of Philippine life is far from unhealthy, given that there are (in 2020) eighty-seven established Congregations of the Oratory in the world.[56] Fifty-eight of these have been founded (or re-founded) since Newman began the Birmingham Oratory on the 2nd of February 1848, and of these, thirty-six have been founded since the opening of the Second Vatican Council. In the words of Keith Beaumont:

> By the middle of the nineteenth it [the Oratory] was languishing, if not semi-moribund, with the exception of a few communities in the north of Italy. However, the foundation by Newman of the Oratory in England would eventually lead to a widespread renewal of the institution which continues to this day. And Newman's conception of the Oratory remains an important point of reference.[57]

CONCLUSION: NEWMAN, THE ORATORIAN

If it was uncertain in 1845 what John Henry Newman would become within the Catholic Church, when we look back, every other thing he did must be seen through the prism of his vocation as an Oratorian. During his stay in Rome Newman discovered first a person, St. Philip Neri, and from him a way of life. In bringing the love of St. Philip and his Rule to England, Newman reignited the Oratorian charism and launched an institute that seemed to have been designed with the English specifically in mind, especially in their love of home and of stability. Newman's hymn to St. Philip, *On Northern Coasts*, expresses this:

> *And when he died, he did but go*
> *In other lands to dwell,*
> *A traveller now, who in his life*
> *Ne'er left that one dear cell.*
>
> *He travelled, and he travelled on,*
> *He crossed the swelling sea,*
> *He sought our island's very heart,*
> *And here at length is he.*[58]

---

56 www.oratoriosanfilippo.org/congregazioni
57 Beaumont, "The Oratory," 46.
58 *Birmingham Oratory Hymn Book*, 1857.

John Henry Newman discovered the Oratory by the promptings of others, especially Nicholas Wiseman. It was peculiarly suited to his temperament and outlook by virtue of its organic development and humane structure. The rediscovery of St. Philip Neri's charism by Newman has brought it to new prominence and life. Still, like Philip himself, John Henry had no plan to do anything. His foundation of the Oratory in England was above all an act of obedience to the voice of the Holy Spirit as he understood it, mediated through the Church. When considering the possibility of "some body such as the Oratorians" in 1846, he said simply, "I shall do just what they tell me to do in Rome."[59]

Suggested Reading

Addington, Raleigh. *The Idea of the Oratory*. London: Burns & Oates, 1966.
Bertram, Jerome. *Vita Communis*. Leominster: Gracewing, 2009.
Nicholls, Guy. *Unearthly Beauty, The Aesthetic of St. John Henry Newman*. Leominster: Gracewing, 2019.

---

59 *LD* xi, 227.

CHAPTER 12

NEWMAN THE EDUCATOR, "FROM FIRST TO LAST"

Paul Shrimpton

Newman once remarked, "Now from first to last, education, in this large sense of the word, has been my line."[1] This observation identifies one of the recurring strands of his life, and it also says something about what he meant by "education." The qualification "in this large sense of the word" indicates that Newman had a very broad conception of "education" and that he resisted the tendency to reduce its meaning and narrow its scope. Then, as now, there was a common mistake of viewing education as the imparting of knowledge rather than the training of the mind, the acquisition of habits, and character formation. Nor did Newman consider education as something confined to its more formal moments or institutional settings: for him, education takes place not just in the formal settings of classrooms, laboratories, and libraries, but in semi-formal activities such as sport, music-making, journalism, drama, and debating, and even in the informal moments of relaxation and amusement, such as meals and parties.

According to conventional wisdom a successful educator is someone who excels either at teaching or at inspiring or organising others to teach: someone who possesses a special talent for dealing with children, adolescents, students, or adults in a particular setting, which might be either informal or institutional. What is unusual about Newman as an educator is that over a seventy-five-year

---

1   Journal entry, January 21, 1863, *AW*, 259.

period he dealt with every age group, instructing them both individually—in person and by letter—and collectively—in tutorial classes, lecture halls, the schoolroom, and the pulpit. The range of his contributions to the organisation of teaching and learning is equally impressive. He reorganised a parish school; played a leading part in the nineteenth century revival of Oxford University; was the founding rector (i.e., president) of a Catholic university in Ireland; and founded the first Catholic public school in England. But it is for his written legacy that Newman is best known as an educator, principally for his educational classic *The Idea of a University* (1873), which a leading historian of education describes as "unquestionably the single most important treatise in the English language on the nature and meaning of higher education."[2]

It is not a simple task to summarise such a busy and productive life and to do justice to such a range of accomplishments; nor is it easy to illustrate how intellectual genius and down-to-earth practicality combined in one and the same person. By focusing on his literary output and overlooking the man of action, the reader of Newman can easily acquire a distorted impression of him as an educator. Many have been hypnotised by the brilliance of his prose and the force of his rhetoric, only to conclude that, however wonderful, the *Idea* is ultimately an unworkable ideal.[3] The mistake comes from ignoring the broader picture: that Newman was using the Dublin lectures (that form the first half of the *Idea*) for a specific purpose: to rally support for a new university in a complex political situation. Other writings from Newman's time in Dublin—articles, letters, memoranda, university documents—fill out the themes developed in the *Idea* and provide a counterbalance to it; and actual practice at the Catholic University illustrates how his erudite discourses could be translated into action, even in very difficult circumstances. Any reader of Newman's educational writings would do well to remember that he was immersed in the practice of education all his life, and that his thinking derived from constant exposure to learning environments as well as from reflection on how best to shape education to match man's deepest needs.

SCHOOLBOY AND UNDERGRADUATE

Newman's lifelong stress on the role of personal influence in education can be traced back to his formative days at Ealing School, where he was befriended by the headmaster and deeply influenced by the sermons, conversations, and reading advice of the senior Classics master. Ealing School, a large, successful private boarding school, was quite unlike the great public schools of England: it had first-class facilities, a homely atmosphere, a broad curriculum, specialist

---

2   Sheldon Rothblatt, "An Oxonian 'Idea' of a University: J. H. Newman and 'well-being,'" *The History of the University of Oxford*, vol. 6, ed. M. G. Brock & M. C. Curthoys (Oxford: Clarendon Press, 1997), 287.

3   For a good example of this, see Roy Jenkins, "Newman and the Idea of a University," in *Newman: A Man for our Time*, ed. D. Brown (London: SPCK, 1990), 155.

teachers, and small classes. Newman excelled in his studies and participated enthusiastically in school life, acting in Latin plays, taking part in debates, playing the violin, and editing several school magazines. Going up to Trinity College Oxford at the age of 16, after what he called his "seven years of plenty," was a chastening experience, for he learnt little from his tutors and suffered from a lack of guidance.[4] Almost despite Trinity and its undergraduate rowdiness, Newman continued to pursue a wide range of interests. He took up the works of Gibbon and Locke, entered himself for university prizes, studied manuals and tried experiments in chemistry, and attended lectures in the emerging science of geology. He joined a music club at St John's College, playing first violin in quartets by Hayden and Mozart, and co-founded the Trinity College Book Society. With a close friend he composed a verse romance called *St. Bartholomew's Eve*—two hundred and fifty copies were printed and sold—and started a periodical called *The Undergraduate*, which was the second ever student-run magazine at Oxford. He also took on his first (voluntary) educational assignment: the tutoring—by post—of his three sisters and two brothers.

FELLOW AND TUTOR AT ORIEL

After winning one of the coveted fellowships at Oriel College in 1822, Newman received Anglican orders and was appointed curate of the nearby working-class parish of St Clement's, where he threw himself into parish work, visiting all his parishioners and raising funds for the building of a new church. In 1826 he was appointed a college tutor and, after weighing up his options and praying for light, decided to pursue his "care of souls" in education rather that in parish or missionary work. He gave up the curacy of St Clement's, justifying his decision on the grounds that the tutorship was a *spiritual* office, and one way of fulfilling his Anglican ordination vows. The point was that the sixteenth century Laudian statutes were still on the books, and these gave the tutor moral and religious as well as academic oversight over his tutees; though the system had fallen into neglect, Newman sought to revive it. He soon became worried by the "considerable profligacy" of the undergraduates, most of whom were from well-connected families, and by the lack of "direct religious instruction" for them.[5] In doing battle with those privileged young men, whom he considered to be the ruin of the place, Newman and the other three Oriel tutors implemented various reforms: expelling students who they considered beyond reform; tightening up the admissions system; introducing written work into termly college exams; reviving the Chapel sermon at Eucharist; and making changes to the lecture system to favour serious students.[6]

---

4   For some of the classic authors and works studied by Newman at Ealing and Trinity, see ch. 9 of this volume by Scott Goins (editor's note).
5   Newman's diary, May 7, 1826, *LD* i, 286.
6   K. C. Turpin, "The Ascendancy of Oriel," *History of the University of Oxford*,

The background to these changes is important. By the 1820s Oxford was in the process of rousing itself after over a century of academic torpor, and Oriel was at the forefront of reform. The problem was that, for the majority of Oxford students, there were few incentives to work, and so much of their time was spent socialising and in outdoor pursuits. The main academic incursion into their leisure time was the daily requirement to attend "college lectures" for two or three hours; during these a college tutor would oversee a group of up to fifteen students translating Latin and Greek texts, to which he might add a commentary of a grammatical, historical, or philosophical nature. It was an unwieldy system, as the tutors were expected to tackle too many subjects, and the pace was reduced by the presence of many backward and idle students. As a consequence, there had emerged a parallel semi-official system in which the serious students engaged private coaches for individual tuition. Along with two other Oriel tutors, Newman offered the more deserving pupils as much time and attention as the best private coaches, thus eliminating the need and expense of the duplication; in doing so the Oriel tutors provided "the germ of the modern tutorial system" at Oxford.[7]

The Oriel tutors, however, were unlike modern-day tutors in that their aim was as much moral and religious as intellectual; they shared Newman's view that secular education should, if conducted properly, be "a pastoral cure." Arguing from the Laudian statutes, Newman held that "a Tutor was not a mere academical Policeman, or Constable, but a moral and religious guardian of the youths committed to him."[8] In a sermon to the Oriel undergraduates, he spoke of his responsibility for their welfare: "Account of us as thinking much and deeply of your eternal interests, as watching over your souls as those who must give account."[9] These ideas were not unusual for the time, as families of the lesser gentry, clergy, and professional classes were eager to find educational settings which were conducive to moral growth: indeed, one of the reasons for parents employing private tutors in Oxford was so that they could oversee their charges and act *in loco parentis*. This pastoral responsibility was an additional function of the private tutor that Newman had integrated into his role as college tutor, and which rendered it still more effective. By finding extra time for the more worthy undergraduates, Newman "cultivated relations, not only of intimacy, but of friendship, and almost of equality, . . . seeking their society in outdoor exercise, on evenings, and in Vacation."[10] The interest he showed was contagious, one tutee describing him as "an elder and affectionate brother."[11] However, the Provost of

---

vol. 6: 188–89. The University introduced written exams in 1830, two years after Oriel introduced them.

   7   M. G. Brock, "The Oxford of Peel and Gladstone, 1800–1833," *History of the University of Oxford*, vol. 6, 61.

   8   Memoir, June 13, 1874, *AW*, 91.

   9   Sermon preached on April 15, 1827, *Serm.* i, 341.

   10   Memoir, June 13, 1874, *AW*, 90.

   11   Thomas Mozley, *Reminiscences: Chiefly of Oriel College and the Oxford Move-*

Oriel became uneasy with what he saw as the "proselytising" influence of his Tractarian tutors, and feared that the college might lose its connections with wealthy families, and after a dispute over the tutors' role—strictly disciplinary in the Provost's view, fully pastoral in theirs—he simply refused to assign them any more students from the summer of 1830 onwards.

Though Oriel's academic reputation slumped after the tutors were replaced, Newman's influence on the university's tutorial system did not end. The explanation for this forms part of the story of the Oxford Movement, which spread in grassroots fashion to the undergraduates and younger graduates of the University through the more personalised form of tuition initiated by Newman and continued by his immediate successors and followers. While the spread of Tractarian ideals and principles was fostered by what Newman called "the force of personal influence and congeniality of thought,"[12] the educational value of the new tutor-pupil relationship was prized even by those who were unsympathetic to the Tractarian cause; over the two decades after Newman's dismissal a growing number of tutors came to regard their office as a pastoral one. Valued as an intellectual training, individual tutorial instruction eventually became the norm at Oxford—and to this day this ideal sets it (and Cambridge) apart from the rest of the educational world.

In 1832, the great "year of reform," after a long period of Tory rule, the incoming Whig administration presented the reforming Liberals with the opportunity to challenge vested interests. In educational matters it was becoming fashionable to speak of the improvement of society as a goal to be achieved, not by nurturing virtue and training the will, but by nourishing the intellect with knowledge. In 1834 a bill was introduced in Parliament to remove the religious "tests" (the requirement to swear to the *Thirty-Nine Articles*) at Oxford and Cambridge, triggering a pamphlet war that lasted for two years. The first pamphlet was written by Newman, and it argued that religion was so much part of the very fabric of an Oxford education—with its daily routine of morning and evening chapel—that to admit Dissenters (i.e., Protestants who were not part of the Church of England) would destroy the whole. After this Newman left to others the task of penning the pamphlets, and he joined Edward Pusey and William Sewell on the committee that ran the campaign, using the structures that had recently been put in place for distributing the *Tracts for the Times*.

Largely thanks to the united front it put up, Oxford was able to see off calls for reform inspired by Whig influence outside the University, but shortly after the bill's defeat in Parliament (in the summer of 1835), bitter controversy erupted within the university over proposals to replace subscription to the *Thirty-Nine Articles* with a Declaration of Conformity. The battle over the reform of the

---

ment vol. 1 (London: Longmans, Green, and Co., 1882), 181. Mozley became Newman's brother-in-law by marrying his sister Harriet.

12 *Apo.*, 40.

religious tests raged for a decade, pitting liberal reformers against the rising Tractarian party, each side arguing for a set of beliefs which concerned the whole spirit and method of education. This is not the place to chart the involvement of Newman and the Tractarians in the complicated and protracted dispute, but it is worth emphasising that—though the Tractarians were determined to infuse a religious spirit into education—they were deeply intellectual and in no sense minded to turn the University into a simple seminary.[13] Far from undervaluing academic values, they enriched and strengthened Oxford's collegiate life. This applied above all to Newman, and it helps to explain why he was widely regarded during these years as "the greatest force both morally and intellectually in the University."[14]

NEWMAN'S DUBLIN DISCOURSES

Newman resigned his Oriel fellowship in October 1845 and a few days later was received into the Catholic Church. He was sent to Rome to prepare for ordination and returned as an Oratorian priest with a commission to establish the first Oratory of St. Philip Neri in England, at Birmingham. In 1851 he was invited by the Irish hierarchy to become the founding rector of a Catholic university in Ireland. To prepare his Irish co-religionists for the new university, Newman composed ten lectures on education, five of which were delivered and all of which published in 1852. Newman's fame in education is almost entirely due to the discourses—the first half of the *Idea of a University*—and they are endlessly cited, especially by those who take a "high" view of a university education and see Newman as the most inspiring advocate of a liberal education. Many see in the *Idea* an attractive alternative to the shapeless, uninspiring outlook of so many contemporary universities, which increasingly function as performance-oriented, heavily bureaucratic organisations committed to a narrowly economic conception of "human excellence." Just as Newman battled against destructive trends within education in his own day, so others fight in our own times against the lack of direction and loss of vision of the modern university. In attempting to recover a sense of purpose, several of these modern critiques use the *Idea* as a key point of reference,[15] and some use Newman as the pivotal figure in their analysis.[16]

---

13   For an account of these battles, see Peter Nockles, "Lost Causes and . . . Impossible Loyalties: The Oxford Movement and the University," *History of the University of Oxford* vol. 6: 195–267.

14   W. C. Lake, *Memorials of William Charles Lake, Dean of Durham* (London: E. Arnold, 1901), 41.

15   Examples include: Duke Maskell and Ian Robinson, *The New Idea of a University* (London: Black Springs Press Ltd, 2001); Gordon Graham, *Universities: The Recovery of an Idea* (Thorverton: Imprint Academic, 2002); Stefan Collini, *What Are Universities For?* (London: Penguin Books, 2012); Mike Higton, *A Theology of Higher Education* (Oxford: Oxford University Press, 2012); as well as Alasdair MacIntyre, *God, Philosophy, Universities* (Lanham, Md.: Rowman & Littlefield, 2009).

16   Newman is the pivotal figure in Jaroslav Pelikan, *The Idea of the University:*

In the discourses Newman argues knowledge can be pursued either with a view to the cultivation of the intellect, or for more immediate practical purposes. The cultivation of the intellect, Newman explains, is a good in itself and constitutes the primary aim of a university. Thus, while all subjects tend to the cultivation of the intellect, some are particularly suited to fostering this aim, and a university should concentrate on those subjects above all. While it is the case that universities prepare directly for the professions through disciplines such as medicine and law, they also do so indirectly; indeed, teaching people how to think is the best preparation for such an aim.

For Newman, "All that exists, as contemplated by the human mind, forms one large system or complex fact, and this of course resolves itself into an indefinite number of particular facts, which, as being portions of a whole, have countless relations of every kind, one towards another." The effect of a proper university education is an enlargement of the mind:

> the action of a formative power, reducing to order and meaning the matter of our acquirements; it is a making the objects of our knowledge subjectively our own, or, to use a familiar word, it is a digestion of what we receive, into the substance of our previous state of thought.[17]

This organic, living knowledge—not just of things themselves, but of their mutual relations—enables the intellect to gain,

> a connected view of old and new, past and present, far and near, and which has an insight into the influence of all these one on another; without which there is no whole, and no centre. It possesses the knowledge, not only of things, but also of their mutual and true relations; knowledge, not merely considered as acquirement, but as philosophy.[18]

Acquiring this overview or "philosophical habit of mind" is one of the chief goals of a university education.[19] In this way, a lawyer, physician, geologist, or economist studying at university,

> will just know where he and his science stand, he has come to it, as it were, from a height, he has taken a survey of all knowledge, he is kept

A Re-examination (New Haven: Yale University Press, 1992) and in Sheldon Rothblatt, *The Modern University and its Discontents: the Fate of Newman's Legacies in Britain and America* (New York: Cambridge University Press, 1997).

17   *Idea*, 45 & 134.

18   *Idea*, 134.

19   *Idea*, 51. This elusive concept is explored at length in Angelo Bottone, *The Philosophical Habit of Mind: Rhetoric and Person in John Henry Newman's Dublin writings* (Bucharest: Zeta Books, 2010).

from extravagance by the very rivalry of other studies, he has gained from them a special illumination and largeness of mind and freedom and self-possession, and he treats his own in consequence with a philosophy and a resource, which belongs not to the study itself, but to his liberal education.[20]

In arguing that the end of a university is intellectual culture,[21] Newman is defending the university against those who would burden it with some other end, such as practical utility or even religious training and morality. Following Aristotle's argument that everything has its own perfection, whether it be intellectual, aesthetic, moral or practical, Newman holds that,

> To open the mind, to correct it, to refine it, to enable it to know, and to digest, master, rule, and use its knowledge, to give it power over its own faculties, application, flexibility, method, critical exactness, sagacity, resource, address, eloquent expression, is an object as intelligible ... as the cultivation of virtue, while, at the same time, it is absolutely distinct from it.[22]

In saying this, he is simply proposing what a liberal education is in itself: not what it is worth, nor what use the Church makes of it. It is an important distinction to draw, because Newman was faced with two dominant outlooks, each of which showed a marked tendency to use the university as a vehicle for something other than its primary end, and thus tended to distort the education that was imparted. Besides their obsession with "useful knowledge," the intellectual descendants of John Locke held that education alone was enough to make the public moral, and that religious teaching was redundant; ecclesiastics, on the other hand, had a tendency to be interested in education only insofar as it ministered to religion and matters ecclesiastical. Newman addresses both tendencies by defending what he maintains is the proper business of a university:

> Its direct business is not to steel the soul against temptation or to console it in affliction, any more than to set the loom in motion, or to

---

20   *Idea*, 166–67.

21   Note that Newman's idea of intellectual culture is not at all the same as Matthew Arnold's. When Newman speaks of "intellectual culture" he means "the culture of the intellect," that by which the intellect is "generally exercised in order to its perfect state" (*Idea*, 165). By contrast Arnold sees it as "a pursuit of our total perfection by means of getting to know ... the best which has been thought and said in the world." Matthew Arnold, *Culture and Anarchy: An Essay in Political and Social Criticism* (London: Sam, Elder & Co., 1869), xviii. For Newman, therefore, a liberal education is about learning how to think, whereas for Arnold it is something similar to a "great books" programme.

22   *Idea*, 122–23.

direct the steam carriage; be it ever so much the means or the condition of both material and moral advancement, still, taken by and in itself, it as little mends our hearts as it improves our temporal circumstances.[23]

NEWMAN'S PASTORAL IDEA OF THE UNIVERSITY

Though the *Idea* is usually quoted for its purple passages on a liberal education, it does contain a few glimpses of Newman's wider, pastoral vision. A champion of education outside the lecture hall and library, Newman recognises that wherever students are gathered, "they are sure to learn one from another, even if there be no one to teach them; the conversation of all is a series of lectures to each, and they gain for themselves new ideas and views, fresh matter of thought, and distinct principles for judging and acting, day by day." Convinced that half the education a student received was derived from the self-perpetuating tradition of the place of learning, Newman attributes great importance in an educational institution to the *genius loci*, or "spirit of the place"; it constitutes "a sort of self-education" which "haunts the home where it has been born, and which imbues and forms, more or less, and one by one, every individual who is successively brought under its shadow." This "ethical atmosphere" amounts to "a real teaching"—and its impact, naturally, was all the greater in a residential university.[24]

These glimpses of Newman's pastoral vision occur rarely in the *Idea*, because the discourses were not composed as an exhaustive exposition of a theme, though they have often been treated as such; they are about the *essence* of a university, not about its fully functioning existence or well-being. They contain a great deal about the intellectual formation of the student, but relatively little about character formation and residential student life. To discover Newman's larger view we need to look at the idea of the university illustrated in history—the twenty "university sketches" that Newman wrote for the *Catholic University Gazette* in 1854[25]—and at what Newman carried out in practice at the Catholic University, which opened its doors in November 1854. The university sketches trace the organic growth and development of the "university" over time, and illustrate the role played by the "college" and the "tutor" in his educational ideal. In them Newman looks at the traditional division of labour at the two ancient universities—however distorted it was in practice—which concerned both methods of teaching (lecturing at the university, tutoring at the college) and the purpose of

---

23 *Idea*, 120.

24 *Idea*, 146–47.

25 The sketches form the first and major part of *HS*, 3:1–251. Though they are far less well-known than the Dublin lectures, Newman scholars have argued that they are vital for a full understanding of Newman's educational views. For an analysis of the sketches, see Katherine Tillman's preface to *The Rise and Progress of the Universities and Benedictine Essays* (Leominster/Notre Dame: Gracewing, 2001).

education (the pursuit of knowledge at the university, the formation of character at the college). By giving this distinction a new twist, Newman makes his own original contribution. Having identified the communication of knowledge as the "essence" of a university, Newman argues that the purpose of the college (or its equivalent) is to bring about its harmonious functioning: its role is to complement that of the university, and to stretch the "strict idea" of a university—what is essential to its "being"—into "well-being" and fullness of life.[26]

Newman's historical sketches illustrate the perennial dangers and hardships that students are exposed to when living away from home, and the need for a second home; they show how a collegiate house or hall of residence can provide the necessary paternal oversight, discipline and order. No doubt influenced by memories of Oxford, Newman speaks of the collegiate residence in rousing images of security and sanctuary as "the shrine of our best affections, the bosom of our fondest recollections, a spell upon our after life, a stay for the world-weary mind and soul."[27] When setting up the Catholic University in Dublin, he gave careful thought to the question of student accommodation, and for those living away from home he oversaw the provision of lodging-houses. Each residence was to have its own private chapel and chaplain, one or two lecturers, resident tutors, and up to twenty students, presided over by a dean. Their number and size would "make the large body of students *manageable*," and their variety was intended to "introduce a spirit of emulation."[28] Since the Catholic University was only partly residential, Newman grappled with the problem of how to extend collegiate living to those living at home or with relatives. He tried various schemes for attaching "externs" to the lodging houses, such as stipulating their presence there for the working hours of the day, so that they might benefit from some aspects of collegiate living rather than simply attending lectures.

Newman also wanted the "externs" to benefit from collegiate teaching, as he regarded the tutors—not the lecturers—as the engine of the university. The tutors were to be two or three years older than their pupils, "half companions, half advisers . . . thrown together with them in their amusements and recreations . . . gaining their confidence from their almost parity of age."[29] As well as conferring academic benefits, tutors would be able to exert "those personal influences, which are of the highest importance in the formation and tone of character."[30] To an Oxford friend, Newman explained that the tutor's work was,

> more of influence than of instruction. But at the same time influence
> is gained *through* the reputation of scholarship etc, and the very duty

---

26 Rothblatt, "An Oxonian 'Idea' of a University," 293.
27 *HS* iii, 215.
28 Newman to Paul Cullen, August 14, 1852, *LD* xv, 146.
29 Report for the Year 1854–55, *Campaign I*, 145–46.
30 Report read to the Thurles Committee, November 12, 1851, *Campaign I*, 192.

which comes on a Tutor is to do that which the pupil cannot do for himself, e.g. to explain difficulties in the works read in lecture, and to give aid in the higher classics, or to cram for examinations.[31]

No stranger to the student scene, Newman saw the need for tutors to anticipate in many of their tutees "little love of study and no habit of application, and, even in the case of the diligent, backwardness," and to make adjustments accordingly. The reason he laid such emphasis on the idea of a college tutor was because he saw in it,

> that union of intellectual and moral influence, the separation of which is the evil of the age. Men are accustomed to go to the Church for religious training, but to the world for the cultivation both of their hard reason and their susceptible imagination. A Catholic University will but half remedy this evil, if it aims only at professorial, not at private teaching. Where is the private teaching, there will be the real influence.[32]

In proposing guidelines for dealing with students "in that most dangerous and least docile time of life, when they are no longer boys, but not yet men," Newman laid down the guiding principle that "the young for the most part cannot be driven, but, on the other hand, are open to persuasion and to the influence of kindness and personal attachment." University residence he saw as "a period of training" linking boyhood and adulthood, designed "to introduce and to launch the young man into the world." This was an enormously important office, because "nothing is more perilous to the soul than the sudden transition from restraint to liberty." Consequently, it was both duty and privilege for the authorities to lead the young men,

> to the arms of a kind mother, an Alma Mater, who inspires affection while she whispers truth; who enlists imagination, taste, and ambition on the side of duty; who seeks to impress hearts with noble and heavenly maxims at the age when they are most susceptible, and to win and subdue them when they are most impetuous and self-willed.[33]

This being the case, Newman thought university discipline should be characterised by "a certain tenderness, or even indulgence on the one hand, and an anxious, vigilant, importunate attention on the other."[34]

These words are not the polished phrases of a distant administrator, but of a rector who had to deal with disciplinary matters personally when he found

---

31 Newman to T. W. Allies, November 6, 1857, *LD* xviii,164.
32 "Scheme of Rules and Regulations," April 1856, *Campaign I*, 228 & 231.
33 "Scheme of Rules and Regulations," 226–27.
34 "Scheme of Rules and Regulations," 227.

himself without a vice-rector. Besides, it should be emphasised that virtually every aspect of life at the Catholic University came into being through Newman's hands. Apart from overseeing academic affairs, the appointment of staff, the financial administration, the launching of new faculties and schools, devising statutes, writing rules and regulations, editing the weekly *Catholic University Gazette*, delivering lectures each term and preaching sermons, Newman gave priority to the pastoral needs of the students and his dealings with the academic staff. Despite all the managerial burdens he shouldered, Newman led the way by establishing the rector's house (called St Mary's) as one of the first three collegiate houses. While he could easily have distanced himself from the residences and the problems they threw up, instead Newman wished to deal with individuals rather than retreat into academic and administrative isolation. He personally oversaw the servants, the kitchen staff and all the domestic finances at St Mary's, and in addition undertook the duties of dean, chaplain and tutor, alongside those of university rector—and all this while continuing to act as Provost of the Birmingham Oratory. The vigilance he exerted over his charges—which can be seen in his correspondence—reflected his conviction that the University under-took a grave responsibility of oversight for those who entered its doors; it acted as a surrogate parent to the students, "an Alma Mater, knowing her children one by one, not a foundry, or a mint, or a treadmill."[35]

It was no simple task for Newman to translate his vision into a living insti-tution, for he faced a series of nearly insurmountable difficulties: an absence of a university tradition among Irish Catholics, and little appreciation of the purpose of a liberal education; a complete lack of experience in dealing with students *qua* students; serious financial constraints in the years following the Great Famine (1845–49); a population which was dispirited and had little confidence in new ventures; deep divisions between the clergy and the educated laity, manifested in clerical high-handedness and lay anticlericalism; a British government which refused to recognise the new foundation, let alone provide financial aid or a charter; and a generous dose of anti-English feeling within Ireland. Despites all these difficulties and limitations, Newman's plans and deeds are instructive because they present a clear picture of how he adapted his principles to the Irish situation of the mid-1850s.

FOUNDING AND OVERSEEING THE ORATORY SCHOOL

Just as he was making preparations to withdraw from the University, Newman became involved with a different, though equally significant, educational foun-dation. The Oratory School, Edgbaston opened in May 1859 and over three decades—a third of Newman's long life—it was nurtured and formed by him. The school was a remarkable foundation in a number of ways, both within

---

35 *Idea*, 144–45.

the Catholic system and on the national stage. The impulse for the foundation came from converts from the Oxford Movement who were unimpressed with the boarding education available to Catholics: they disliked the arrangements at the Catholic colleges (such as Oscott and Ushaw) where those intended for the priesthood were mixed with lay boys in what were effectively minor seminaries. They also disliked their "un-English" customs: the close supervision of pupils, the impossibility of providing female care for young boys, and the reliance on novices and seminarians as teachers. What they wanted for their sons was an English public school—a Catholic one, but a real one. In the spring of 1858 a group of converts led by the parliamentary barrister Edward Bellasis petitioned Newman to create a Catholic public school, promising financial backing and pupils. The Birmingham Oratory sanctioned the plan, and a year later the new school opened its doors to seven boys, aged between eight and twelve, all sons of converts. By the mid-1860s it had grown into a boarding school for seventy boys aged up to eighteen.

Several of the converts called the new foundation "a Catholic Eton." The phrase would have made little sense to mid-nineteenth century Victorians, since the Catholic colleges of the time were strictly run, like seminaries, while the public schools were characterised by the wide liberty given to the boys and by the delegation of power through the prefect system. The gulf between the two systems—Catholic college and the Anglican public school—is illustrated by the comment of the convert W. G. Ward twenty years *after* the foundation of the Oratory School, when he declared that "the evils of a public school are insepa-rable from its very essence"; and he added dismissively that "A 'Catholic Eton' is (to our mind) a contradiction in terms."[36] The fact that Newman was attempting the impossible partly explains why every bishop but Newman's own opposed the school, and why a campaign of gossip against the school persisted for over a decade.

Besides creating the first Catholic public school, Newman was also a pioneer within the Catholic system in forming the first *lay* boarding school in England. The Catholic colleges were run either by the secular clergy or by the religious orders, and the education given was generally suited to those aspiring to the priesthood or religious life. Most of Newman's convert friends had been educated at the public schools, and what they wanted was a purely *lay* school; they were concerned that the high moral standards at the colleges—which they recognised as important—were "apparently purchased at the expense of many valuable qualities of manliness, energy and readiness to face the world."[37] Their desire for a greater stress on the natural or human virtues met with Newman's full approval, and the statement in his draft manifesto that the Oratory School

---

36 W. G. Ward, "Catholic Colleges and Protestant Schools," *Dublin Review* 31 (October 1878): 313 and 315.
37 John Simeon to Newman, April 30, 1857, *BOA*.

was intended "for youths whose duties are to lie in the world"[38] incorporated this concern and signalled an important shift in emphasis. This stress on "facing the world" can also be seen in the advice Newman gave to boys who thought they might have a priestly vocation, for he invariably urged them to be patient and avoid narrowing their options too early; his attitude shows that he regarded preparation for "the world" on same footing as preparation for the priesthood, as one calling for serious and appropriate training. Whether leaving for further study or for the world of work, the boys were prepared for life and trained to hold their own in a Protestant society. The number of leavers going into the priesthood—twenty-three in Newman's own time—vindicated, besides, his belief that a curriculum consisting mainly of secular studies would not deter those truly called to Holy Orders.

The fact that the school was the result of parental initiative responded to Newman's conviction that a school's main task is not to replace but to assist parents in their duty to care for and educate their children. This idea was not explicitly stated in school documents, but it showed itself in practice, shaping the Oratory School's attitude to the boys and their parents. When Edward Bellasis told Newman that the school had been a great success for his sons, Newman replied that it could only take a "due portion of credit . . . seeing the patterns and guidance they have at home"[39]—in other words, a school had to build on the education received in the family.

To make his idea of partnership with parents come about, Newman sent them reports about their sons twice a year—an uncommon practice at the time. Besides writing reports, he personally undertook the task of dealing with parental demands, a task which kept him busy in term and out. His highly-educated convert friends badgered him about the curriculum, teaching methods, textbooks—even the boys' pronunciation of Latin. When parents visited the Oratory or passed through Birmingham, and particularly when they came to drop off or collect their sons at the beginning and end of term, Newman used the opportunity to speak to them at length. This degree of parental contact was unknown elsewhere, either at the public schools or at the Catholic colleges.

In order to make the school a second home for the younger boys, Newman placed a "dame" in charge of them outside school hours; for this role, he chose Mrs. Frances Wootten, a widowed friend of his who lived near the Oratory. The dame arrangement was largely borrowed from Eton, where dames ran some of the boarding houses and were responsible for the comfort and well-being of the boys in them; in Newman's more elevated vision, her role included overseeing the acquisition of good habits and virtues. Unfortunately, the first Oratorian headmaster had his own ideas of what a Catholic public school should be, and as a result he and the entire teaching staff resigned in December 1861 after a

---

38 Draft school manifesto, n.d. [November 1858], *BOA*.
39 Newman to Edward Bellasis, September 4, 1865, *LD* xxii, 42.

disagreement with Newman about the role of the dame. Newman's closest friends rallied round him, and together they rescued the situation. Ambrose St John, Newman's right-hand man at the Oratory, also played a crucial role by stepping in as headmaster, and over the next ten years he and Newman re-formed the school between them.

One effect of the staff mutiny was that Newman's involvement with the school was much closer thereafter. He was now able to mould the school along lines which reflected his lifelong insistence on the pastoral role of the educator. The tone he managed to set can be seen in a variety of ways. When writing his school reports, he pulled together observations and opinions from the whole staff to provide a balanced overview; the insights they contain show that he had a real gift for judging individuals and a keen understanding of what boys were like. A theme Newman repeatedly emphasised to parents was the need for patience with their sons. He calmed their eagerness for quick gains, insisting that the phases of growing up be respected and that irritating but passing habits be over-looked: boys could not be forced like plants. Another expression of his pastoral concern was the introduction of "characters" after the end-of-term exams. At these individual interviews the headmaster would read out an account of the boy's progress and behaviour, then Newman would give a few words of encour-agement or approval—or, if necessary, a telling-off. (A similar arrangement had existed at the Catholic University, where once a year students were summoned one by one to appear before the rector and listen to a report of behaviour and progress read by their dean, tutor and lecturers.[40]) Newman attached great importance to hearing the termly "characters," refusing to depute the task to others. Nor was he satisfied with a mere acquaintance with the boys; he aimed to know them well and even to make their personal friendship—and this in spite of the age-gap, for he was fifty-eight when the school began. A clue to his ability to relate to boys comes from Oscar Browning, educational reformer at Eton and King's College Cambridge. Browning stayed overnight at the Oratory in 1866 and was struck by "Newman's marvellous copiousness of language and abundant fluency, also with his use of harmless worldly slang, that he might not appear priggish or monkish."[41]

Unlike the students in Dublin, who held Newman in great awe, the young-sters at the Oratory School generally regarded him with affection. One pupil described "Jack" or "old Jack"—as Newman was rather irreverently known—as a gentle, understanding and approachable figure for whom nothing was too trivial: thus when the editorial of the *Weekly Wasp* (a school magazine run entirely by boys) criticised the lack of school facilities, Newman saw to it that their

---

40 Newman copied and adapted this custom from Oriel. These brief, end-of-term interviews, which are known as "collections," still take place in Oxford colleges today and are usually chaired by the head of college.

41 Oscar Browning, *Memories of Sixty Years at Eton, Cambridge and Elsewhere* (London: John Lane, 1910), 269.

grievances were met. In chapel the younger boys found him softly spoken and given to long quotations from Scripture, but they were held spellbound by his readings from the Bible, and at times his silvery voice and beautiful intonation moved them to tears.

From the outset Newman insisted that relations between staff and boys should be characterised by trust, and that they should dispense with the surveillance system used at the Catholic colleges. So, when the boys were granted an hour a week during school time to write letters home, Newman preferred to trust that the boys did so, rather than check up, even though he knew that some would abuse the privilege. The Oratory School incorporated a full public-school prefect system: senior boys were appointed as prefects not only to play a part in the smooth running of the school, but also to set the younger boys an example, and the boys themselves elected the school captain.[42] Reliance on older boys as prefects was part and parcel of Newman's overall strategy of achieving a new balance in that precarious transition from boyhood to manhood, by placing a premium on trust.

As one might expect, Newman attempted to impart a truly liberal education. The school, he felt, ought to make good scholars out of the boys—he declared to one parent, "it is not simply our aim, but our passion to do so."[43] From the advice he gave, it is clear he considered there was no substitute for hard graft. Yet he was *equally* insistent—particularly with parents—that boys needed downtime; his normal reaction to parents who asked for extra tuition for their sons was to remind them of the boys' natural reluctance to forfeit free time outside lessons. He also ensured that sporting enthusiasms were respected: for example, he would rearrange the afternoon timetable in summer, to allow for longer cricket matches. Organised games coexisted with a large variety of other outdoor pursuits; and extra-curricular activities such as music, journalism, debating and acting thrived. Newman himself oversaw the production of the annual Latin play, and he sometimes joined boys in their music recitals, playing second violin.

Newman's arrangements for religious training and instruction are interesting, bearing in mind that the Oratory School was a lay school. Before breakfast the boys said their prayers and attended Mass; at the end of morning lessons they prayed the Angelus; after tea there was optional Rosary; and at night there were joint prayers followed by a reading from a spiritual classic. In Holy Week

---

42 Newman adapted the prefect system introduced by Thomas Arnold at Rugby School which played a key part in reforming the English public-school system. During the middle decades of the nineteenth century it gradually became accepted that character training was enhanced by a delegation of authority to the boys themselves and that, besides instilling virtues, self-government had two practical advantages: it made the headmaster's job easier, and it prevented rebellion by uniting some of the most influential boys with the masters. Though theologically at odds with Arnold's liberalism, Newman clearly appreciated his use of surrogate authority and employed it himself.

43 Newman to John Simeon, August 22, 1864, *LD* xxi, 205.

all the boys made a three-day retreat. The school had two spiritual directors, whose main duty was to hear the boys' Confessions, as well as being available for boys to chat to. The boys learnt their catechism thoroughly and tested each other in pairs every week, in the presence of Newman or the headmaster; and there were instructions and sermons for the whole school. Newman himself gave the catechetical lectures to the older boys, and he carefully marked and annotated the essays they were required to write afterwards. And, in order to stimulate boys' piety, he involved them in devotions throughout the liturgical year.

CONCLUDING THOUGHTS

One feature which is common to all Newman's ventures is that in christianising education he was careful not to distort it. Rather than over-stress the Christian dimension, he respected the inner autonomy of education; he understood the connaturality of education and religion, while recognising that "Knowledge is one thing, virtue is another."[44] His harmonious synthesis of the secular and religious in education—"to fit men for this world while it trained them for another"[45]—explains why Christians and non-Christians alike admire him. Nevertheless, Newman recognised the ultimate supremacy of holiness over intellectual attainment. This is evident from his words of consolation to the mother of a boy, who died just five years after leaving the Oratory School: "what was your mission . . . except to bring him to heaven? That was your very work,—not to gain him a long life and a happy one, but to educate him for his God."[46]

Whether at school or university, Newman's influence derived from dealing with the young separately or in small groups, rather than from addressing them *en masse*. Indeed, his mind instinctively recoiled from an identical treatment of individuals, for he felt that "An academical system without the personal influence of teachers upon pupils, is an arctic winter."[47] While his educational activity shows his insights and reforms to have been both wide-ranging and ahead of his time, his contribution to education cannot be measured simply in terms of new arrangements, but by a variety of indirect means. His sensitivity to both the aspirations and the foibles of adolescents and young men enabled him to make demands of them in a way that they would respond to. Newman's original contribution to the ever-present dilemma of an authentic Christian presence in the world is reflected in the down-to-earth training for the challenges and duties of life that he provided in Dublin, in Birmingham and elsewhere. The principles that guided him in his educational tasks owe much to his understanding of the condition of lay Christians, and their need for an education suited to

---

44 *Idea*, 120.
45 *HS* iii, 152.
46 Newman to Mrs F. R. Ward, September 22, 1866, *LD* xxii, 292.
47 *HS* iii, 74.

their condition. If Newman's university and school appear strangely familiar to modern eyes, it is because his insights into the truth about the human condition enabled him to anticipate a future age. And yet, when we see in contemporary education the effects of educational policies pursued in the name of "efficiency" and "good management," and the intellectual poverty resulting from production-line learning, we would do well to heed Newman's shrewd observation that while the world is "content with setting right the surface of things," the Church aims "at regenerating the very depths of the heart."[48]

Suggested Reading

Arthur, James A., and Guy Nicholls. *John Henry Newman.* Continuum Library of Education Thought 8. Edited by R. Bailey. London: Continuum, 2007.

Culler, A. Dwight. *The Imperial Intellect: A Study of Newman's Educational Ideal.* New Haven: Yale University Press, 1955.

Shrimpton, Paul. *A Catholic Eton? Newman's Oratory School.* Leominster: Gracewing, 2005.

_____. *The 'Making of Men': The Idea and Reality of Newman's University in Oxford and Dublin.* Leominster: Gracewing, 2014.

---

48 *Idea*, 203.

CHAPTER 13

APPROACHES TO READING NEWMAN AS A PHILOSOPHER

Michael Pakaluk

John Henry Newman was and is acknowledged to have been a great churchman, an extraordinary preacher and stylist, a theologian, a spiritual and devotional writer, an educator, controversialist, essayist, historian, classicist, and poet. But should he also be accounted a *philosopher*? If so, then why would the name "philosopher," as we can agree, not commonly be put on such a list? Why is he rarely if ever taught in philosophy courses, even in institutions which aim to pass on the entire Catholic intellectual tradition? The question is not, absurdly, whether he was a philosopher mainly, or above all, or underlying everything, but whether his life and writings are properly philosophical in important respects, and whether he made, in his own way, contributions to philosophy (perhaps undiscovered), just as he has, for instance, to English poetry.

To make a start on these questions, I consider three instances taken from his life which together establish, I think, an antecedent probability that he should be accounted by us as a philosopher. These are: his candidacy for White's Professor of Moral Philosophy in the University of Oxford, his collaboration with Richard Whately on the latter's textbook on logic, and his unfinished manuscript which had the working title for him, "Discursive Enquiries on Metaphysical Subjects," sometimes called his "Philosophical Notebook." My investigation is intended to give credence, so to speak, to the project of reading Newman as a philosopher. If my claims about these instances are correct, then a foundation is established for sound work in uncovering and more directly exploring Newman's distinctively philosophical contribution. I do not think that these initially historical consid-erations can be side-stepped. Unless we undertake them, we are constrained simply *to use philosophy* (e.g. pragmatism, personalism) *to interpret Newman*, which is something other than reading Newman as an original philosopher. We need to establish, as it were, a matter of fact—about Newman's powers, interests, purposes, and aims—and not merely propose a way of seeing his works, as valu-able as that may be.

CANDIDATE FOR WHITE'S PROFESSOR
OF MORAL PHILOSOPHY

Today the White's Professorship of Moral Philosophy is highly prestigious: noteworthy holders of the chair have included T. H. Green (1878–1881), W. D. Ross (1923–1927), and Bernard Williams (1990–1995). But when Newman was a fellow of Oriel College, it had just been revived: founded originally in 1621 through a gift of Thomas White, canon of Christ Church, from the late 1670s onward, with a single strange exception, the professorship was unoccupied and apparently forgotten.[1] In 1829 it was re-founded, and William Mills of Magdalen College was elected its first holder in the new period.

When the White's chair was originally founded, "moral philosophy" meant what was covered by Aristotle's *Nicomachean Ethics*.[2] Presumably the earlier holders of the chair would have been familiar with that work and taught it in Greek. But they were also clerics who for the practical instruction of their youthful charges mainly expounded Scripture.[3] So, implicit from the founda-tion of the chair at its beginning were the questions of whether and to what extent could instruction in moral philosophy be separated from Christian faith and practice. During the century of desuetude of the chair, the "British Moral-ists" began to expound moral philosophy on broadly empiricist principles; also, German philosophy had begun to acquire a new prestige. Therefore, when the chair was revived in Newman's time, the additional question became important of whether the *Nicomachean Ethics*, and related classical works, such as Plato's *Dialogues* and Cicero's *De Officiis*, were to remain foundational texts in the

---

1   Edward Thwaytes, a scholar of Anglo-Saxon, held the chair 1708–1711. Renn Hampden in his inaugural lecture as the second White's Professor after the chair's revival speculates that "The Proctors, as having charge of the moral discipline of the University, were . . . regarded in that interval as representing the Moral Philosophy Professor." Renn Hampden, *A Course of Lectures Introductory to the Study of Moral Philosophy*, 2nd ed, revised (London: T. Fellowes, 1856), 16.

2   "Young men, whom Aristotle thought Vnfit to heere Morrall Philosophie," William Shakespeare, *Troilus & Cressida*, II.ii.166 (1609), as cited in the *Oxford English Dictionary*.

3   See for example the *Three Decades of Sermons, Lately Preached to the University of Oxford* by Henry Wilkinson, White's Professor 1649–1653 (London: Printed by H. H. A. and W. H. Lichfield for Thomas Robinson, 1660).

academic treatment of personal practical philosophy, or instead the contributions of recent and contemporary philosophers, especially English and Scottish, but also German, were to be given equal or greater status.

Both of these controversies—whether moral philosophy was independent of Christianity, and whether the exposition of ancient texts should enjoy a certain primacy—would naturally figure in the battle that was ongoing in Oxford in the 1820s and 1830s, between the leaders of the incipient Tractarian movement, and those rather who favored "liberalism," that is, Socinianism (i.e. Unitarianism) in theology, disestablishmentarianism in ecclesiology, and a more impersonal model of university instruction. Thus it should not be completely surprising that Newman would have been promoted as a candidate for the White's chair, as we discover in his letter to J. W. Bowden in 1834: "There is a chance of my being elected Professor of Moral Philosophy. I have no especial wish for it. It would oblige me to take up a line of reading somewhat out of my present course; yet it might be the means of giving me influence with the undergraduates, and there is no situation which combines respectability with lightness of responsibility and labour so happily as the office of a professor."[4] That Renn Hampden, Newman's nemesis in the controversy in Oriel over the role of tutors, and notorious Bampton lecturer, was elected instead, was a large victory for the liberalizing party, as seen in the fact that Hampden thereby became positioned to be appointed Regius Professor of Divinity two years later.[5]

What form would lectures in moral philosophy have taken from Newman as White's Professor? From the lectures of Mills and Hampden, we can form plausible conjectures, which at the same time show us where to look in Newman to begin reading him as a moral philosopher. The year before his election, Mills had published a short and learned treatise arguing that in Plato and Aristotle one could find fairly robust teachings on a personal God, the immortality of the soul, and a particular providence.[6] In his inaugural lecture as White's Professor,[7] he argues in an Aristotelian manner, starting as it were with *endoxa* presented by eminent moralists—the doctrine of "eternal fitness or relations of things"

---

4   Oriel: January 3, 1834 in *Letters and Correspondence of John Henry Newman*, vol. 2, 14–15. The tenure of the White's Professorship was limited by the terms of its foundation to five years. Thus Newman was entertaining a relatively short-term commitment.

5   The electors are listed in the dedication of Hampden's book, *A Course of Lectures Introductory to the Study of Moral Philosophy*. The Provost of Oriel, Edward Hawkins, was not among them but enjoyed considerable influence through his shared service on the old Hebdomadal Board.

6   William Mills, BD, *The Belief of the Jewish People and of the Most Eminent Gentile Philosophers, Most Especially of Plato and Aristotle, on A Future State, Including an Examination of the Leading Principles Contained in Bishop Warburton's Divine Legation of Moses* (Oxford: Oxford University Press, 1828). William Warburton, *The Divine Legation of Moses* (London: A. Millar, 1765).

7   William Mills, BD, *Lecture on the Theory of Moral Obligation* (Oxford: Samuel Collingwood, 1830).

in Wollaston and Clarke; the theory of "immutable distinctions which the understanding of itself perceives" in Plato and Cudworth; the moral internal sense of Hutchinson; Butler's recourse to "the law and benevolent tendencies of our nature;" and Paley's doctrine of the "expediency of [virtuous] action to promote the general happiness of mankind[8]—to arrive at a harmonizing definition of morality, "considered as an internal quality in ourselves," as "an obedience to the law and constitution of man's nature, assigned him by the Deity, in conformity to his own essential and unchangeable attributes, the effect of which is the general happiness of his creatures."[9] He ascribes this view to Aristotle himself, who "believed in the existence of natural and unchangeable principles of right."[10]

Somewhat astonishingly he dismisses the philosophy of Kant's *Critik der practischen Vernunft*, so prestigious to us today, as merely a repackaging of Cudworth.[11] His remarks on conscience are noteworthy. He criticizes Butler for imprecision in the matter, and for his suggestions that conscience is the origin of moral obligation: rather, Mills says, the moral law is discerned by reason, whereas the role of conscience is to inflict punishment internally when we act against the moral law, and to assure and praise when we act well.[12]

On the question of the priority of the ancients, Mills approvingly cites Berkeley, "no mean judge on such subjects," who "warmly recommended [Plato and Aristotle] in preference to more recent and shallow speculations."[13] "In our study of the ancient writers indeed it is by no means necessary to disregard the modern," Mills comments, "But if we are compelled to choose between them, and to decide which ought to have the preference as text-books in a system of education, those who are best acquainted with their respective merits will have

---

8   Mills, *Theory of Moral Obligation*, 16.

9   Mills, *Theory of Moral Obligation*, 30.

10   "We might ask, what is his theory of equity, but a return, when written laws have accidentally deviated from them, to those eternal principles of justice, from which legal ordinances, in the first instance, derived all their origin and authority", he writes, citing *Nic Eth* V.10, and *Rhetoric* I, 14 and 16, Mills, *Theory of Moral Obligation*, 33–34, notes 10 and 11.

11   It is not too much to assert, he says, "that what is most valuable in the hypothesis of the German metaphysician may be traced to the discussions of the English philosopher." Mills, *Theory of Moral Obligation*, 37.

12   "If at any time [Butler] is erroneous, it is when he speaks somewhat inaccurately of conscience, as if the province of this heavenly monitor were to inspire and prescribe moral duties, instead of pronouncing its decisions when they have been infringed or observed." Mills, *Theory of Moral Obligation*, 38; see also 27–29.

13   Mills, *Theory of Moral Obligation*, 31–32. He quotes Berkeley's *Siris*: "It might very well be thought serious trifling to tell my readers, that the greatest men had ever an high esteem for Plato . . . whose philosophy has been the admiration of the ages . . . in these free-thinking times, many an empty head is shook at Aristotle and Plato, as well as at the holy scriptures." George Berkeley, *Siris: A Chain of Philosophical Reflexions* (London: W. Innys and C. Hitch, 1747), 159–60.

no hesitation in assigning the first rank to the ancients."[14] As to its relation to Christian revelation, moral philosophy has the task of applying more accurately the general precepts of the gospel, and of confirming the wisdom of Christian teaching. But "if it be entitled to the name of philosophy . . . it must search after principles; it must ascend to the source of duty and obligation; it must examine the nature of man, and analyse his mental faculties; and must lay the foundation of morals in the phenomena of mind."[15]

If silence implies consent, we might interpret the absence of commentary by Newman's circle on Mills's lectures as a sign of their general support. The case was different with Hampden. Upon the appearance in print of Hampden's lectures as White's professor, Newman's friend H. J. Rose wrote to Newman, presumably aware that Newman had been a candidate,

> *Quousque tandem?* How long are such books as Hampden's come forward from professors and Heads of Houses? How long are they to come forth unreproved? Hampden's lectures are such an aggravation of the offence of his former book, are in themselves so mischievous, and so anti-Christian, that it does seem to me something very like a public calamity that they should be allowed to pass with no rebuke more weighty than an anonymous review.[16]

Newman forwarded this letter in agreement to Pusey along with his own note that the publication of Hampden's lectures was "a deplorable evil; a breach, it seems to me, of Vincentius' great rule that—as a witness for posterity—error should be protested against on its first appearing."[17] It becomes clear that Hampden's appointment as White's Professor was viewed as official support for him to develop Lecture VI from his Bampton Lectures, which was precisely on "Moral Philosophy."

> The close connexion of Theological and Moral Truth, has been of serious injury to both departments of human knowledge . . . Theology and Ethics are entirely distinct in their nature," Hampden began that lecture. What most contributed to the confusion, he continues, was

---

14   Mills, *Theory of Moral Obligation*, 7.

15   Mills, *Theory of Moral Obligation*, 12.

16   See Harry Parry Liddon, "The Hampden Controversy," in *Life of Edward Bouverie Pusey*, (London: Longmans, 1894), vol. 1, 365. The "former book" would be Hampden's Bampton Lectures of 1832, on *The Scholastic Philosophy Considered in its Relation to Christian Theology* (Oxford: Printed by Samuel Collingwood for the author: Sold by J.H. Parker, 1833), which was interpreted by its critics as an attempt to explain away nearly all of Christian doctrine as a "scholastic" accretion upon a putative primitive Christianity of Scripture.

17   Liddon, *Life of Edward Bouverie Pusey*, vol. 1, 365. But see the apparently distinct letter of Newman to Froude dated January 3, 1836, in *Letters and Correspondence of Newman to 1845*, ed. Anne Mozley (London: Longmans, Green, & Co.), vol. 2, 133.

"the spiritual power, which the Latin Church had been acquiring. . . . The laity were brought into captivity to the imperious sense of their spiritual leaders.

As a result, "the right of private judgment, in *morality*, was as effectually excluded by the spiritual power of the Church, as it was in articles of faith."[18]

Hampden's final White's lecture is valuable for our purposes in proposing a reading list in moral philosophy and therefore as giving us roughly a good sense of what texts Newman presumably thought he would have to take into account, if he had been elected White's Professor: Xenophon, Plato, Aristotle, and Cicero, as expected, but also Adam Smith, *Theory of the Moral Sentiments*; Paley's *Moral and Political Philosophy*; and Dugald Stewart's *Philosophy of the Active Powers*. Butler reassuringly receives the greatest recommendation, as "most of all deserving of the attention of the moral student, and which will assist him in understanding the Ethics of Aristotle,"—the *Analogy* of course but especially the Preface to the Rolls Sermons.[19] If we include the other authorities cited by Mills, Hampden's list depicts what the discipline of "moral philosophy" amounted to at the time.

But presumably what alarmed Rose was Hampden's dismissive view of the practice of teaching moral philosophy by tutors through a close reading of Aristotle's *Ethics*: "our highest classical honours have been not unfrequently attained by persons who, in fact, were ignorant of the very nature of Moral Philosophy," Hampden complains, "who had read through the Ethics of Aristotle, and made themselves masters of his text, without really knowing the connexion of that work with Moral Philosophy, much less its bearing on the questions discussed in modern speculation on the subject."[20] Also, Hampden's insistence of "the independence of moral obligation, theoretically, on any religious sanction," and that "pure morals neither necessarily follow in fact a pure faith, nor are exclusively the result of it. All that can be truly affirmed is, that where the good fruits of upright conduct are wanting, there the real adoption of a true faith by the individual must be wanting."[21]

Newman of course was not inactive while Hampden was lecturing: he commanded the pulpit of St. Mary's.[22] Indeed, various sermons from volumes

---

18   Hampden, *The Scholastic Philosophy*, 264, 275–76, and 277. Quotations are from the Third Edition (London: Simpkin, Marshall, and Co, 1848). When Newman in his *Biglietto Speech* of 1879 described himself as having struggled with "liberalism" for a full fifty years, that is, going back to 1829, it is not implausible to take him to have had Hampden's lectures primarily in mind. See http://www.newmanreader.org/works/addresses/file2.html

19   Hampden, *The Scholastic Philosophy*, 268–71. Joseph Butler, *Fifteen Sermons preached at the Rolls Chapel* (London: Robert Horsfield, 1765).

20   Butler, *Fifteen Sermons*, x.

21   Butler, *Fifteen Sermons*, 20–21.

22   "Upon becoming Provost, Hawkins had had to leave to Newman what proved,

2 and 3 of *Parochial and Plain Sermons*, from the years in which he would have been White's Professor, if he had been elected, may be studied as developments of Mills's views, or criticism of Hampden's, and therefore as material for a contribution to moral philosophy as it was understood at the time. But to read the *Sermons* in this way, we need to know what we are looking for. The task, to be done well and thoroughly, would require a book.

Let us consider here just one instance, selected at random, Newman's Sermon 23 in volume ii, "Tolerance of Religious Error," on the Feast of St. Barnabas the Apostle (presumably June 11, 1834). Newman begins by insisting that grace typically converts us only progressively: "The especial graces poured out on the Apostles . . . had no tendency to destroy their respective peculiarities of temper and character . . . or to preclude failings and errors." Already this statement clears away some felt difficulties about the relation between faith and morals. Next, Newman in effect shows how the Gospel provides a viewpoint for a critique of conventional morality: "in every age [the world] chooses some one or other peculiarity of the Gospel as the badge of its particular fashion for the time being, and sets up as objects of admiration those who eminently possess it." But it is not very difficult to possess only one virtue, disproportionately: the real challenge of the moral life, Newman says, is to combine virtues which cannot easily stand together. For example, in his day, he proposes, kindness is praised in isolation from "firmness, manliness, and godly severity." In the manner of Aristotle, Newman then unfolds various characteristic expression of this kind of unbalance, such as "We allow men to speak against the Church, its ordinances, or its teaching, without remonstrating with them"—exactly what Rose had lamented about the authorities and Hampden.[23]

In the second part of the sermon, Newman discusses three different schools or philosophies, first, the followers of Paley, "men who are advocates of Expedience," who out of kindness deny the reality of retributive justice. Second, there are the sentimentalists, who "believe themselves to be converted from sin to righteousness by the mere manifestation of that love to their souls, drawing them on to Him." Third and finally, there are "others of a mystical turn of mind"—he seems to have in mind abstracted scholars who resemble Cudworth—"with untutored imaginations and subtle intellects, who follow the theories of the old Gentile philosophy." All three schools, Newman maintains, although differing from one another, are united in "overlooking that the Christian's God is represented in Scripture not only as a God of Love, but also as 'a consuming fire.'" He then

---

in his hands, the far more important and influential position of vicar of St. Mary's, including the parochial occupancy of the pulpit from which the University sermons were delivered. . . . [Newman's] sermons became the staple of many a college conversation; admired by all." *The Times of London*, August 12, 1890, p. 8.

23 In ch. 9 of this volume, Scott Goins indicates other areas of Aristotle's influence on Newman, namely rhetoric, poetry and theory of education (editor's note).

makes a point which would have been clearly recognized by his listeners as in the manner of Butler's *Analogy*: "Rejecting the testimony of Scripture, no wonder they also reject that of conscience, which assuredly forebodes ill to the sinner." They say that conscience is not the voice of God at all, or that it is "mere benevolence," or that it is "a kind of passion for the beautiful and sublime."

By the end, the sermon has become an argument against Hampden's moral philosophy and raises the questions: Would the fact that grace works progressively explain the phenomena Hampden uses to deny any connection between moral philosophy and religion? Is each system of modern moral philosophy actually founded upon a simplification of the moral life, related to some favored virtue of an age, which gets cultivated in disproportion, and which makes the theory seem more compelling than it rationally is? Does the Gospel prove itself uncannily indispensable, because construed wisely it provides a viewpoint for judging even the culture in which one is immersed? (Could this be shown case by case?) Does the account of conscience which results from this kind of self-criticism ring true?

This sermon is just one example, of course. One might proceed, next, by taking discussions from later works and similarly construing them as answers to disputes within "moral philosophy," as they were presented to Newman in the late 1820s and early 1830s. How different, then, to read Newman on conscience in this way in the *Grammar of Assent*—not as an implicit proof of the existence of God, but as text which gives a phenomenology of "what reason says" in Aristotle's ethics,[24] which points to the integration of moral philosophy with religious piety. How different to examine his ideal of a gentleman, or "the religion of philosophy," in *Idea of a University*, as an argument that when conscience is not interpreted as a voice from without, but rather mere self-reproach, then would a person's virtues of necessity become distorted and risk becoming vices: as Newman remarks there, "if we will make light of what is deepest within us, nothing is left but to pay homage to what is more upon the surface. To seem becomes to be; what looks fair will be good, what causes offence will be evil; virtue will be what pleases, vice what pains."[25]

It becomes clear that within this question of whether Newman is a moral philosopher are philosophical questions about the nature of that discipline itself. Newman might be a moral philosopher in the way that discipline should have been or might reasonably have been construed, although not in how it has been construed and developed. The question is not unimportant for the historiography of philosophy. For example, a common view which springs from Alasdair MacIntyre's *After Virtue* is that the tradition of the virtues was lost after the Middle Ages and out of sight for centuries, leaving us only "fragments of a conceptual scheme

---

24 *Nic Eth* 1115b2, 1117a8, 1138b20.

25 *Idea*, 201. The entire discourse on "Knowledge Viewed in Relation to Religion" should be consulted in this regard. *Idea*, 179–211.

. . . simulacra of morality."[26] But in reality, as we see, the "virtue theory" of Plato, Aristotle, and Cicero was alive and well in Oxford in the 1830s, and the dispute over the direction of the White's Professorship was in part a dispute as to whether it would remain dominant.[27] Thus, to read Newman as a moral philosopher despite his not being elected White's Professor is, in part, to consider how this tradition was passed on now, in a sense, outside the usual channels of the academy, as the academy began to divest itself of that tradition.[28]

At the same time, from the controversy over the White's Professorship we see why Newman is not generally thought of as a moral philosopher or even potentially a moral philosopher. The works which established the topics and questions for that discipline, at that time, are not studied or even much known today—take Joseph Butler and Dugald Stewart as instances. Dugald Stewart, so highly esteemed in that generation with his many treatises, honorary degrees, and academic distinctions, would not quickly come to anyone's mind as a moral philosopher today, nor even Thomas Reid, his teacher: how surprising is it, then, that Newman is not thought of in that way?[29] Note of course that we are not saying that someone neglected as a moral philosopher is nonetheless a great or important moral philosopher, only that he is at least a moral philosopher.

COLLABORATION WITH RICHARD WHATELY
ON *ELEMENTS OF LOGIC*

Whately's *Logic* was enormously successful and became the standard university text in logic in the Anglophone world for most of the nineteenth century.[30] Published in 1836, within ten years it had gone through six editions in London

---

26 Alasdair MacIntyre, *After Virtue: A Study in Moral Theory*, 3rd ed. (Notre Dame: University of Notre Dame Press, 2007), 2.

27 Hampden in his first White's Lecture even takes it for granted that his listeners will know that the *Secunda Secundae* of the "Sum of Theology" of Thomas Aquinas contains "an exposition, admirable indeed in itself for its exactness and copiousness, of the ethical system of Aristotle," Hampden, *Course of Lectures*, 14.

28 See ch. 14 of this volume for a discussion by John F. Crosby on Newman's understanding of the unity of the intellectual and moral virtues (editor's note).

29 The third and final volume of Stewart's acclaimed *Elements of the Philosophy of the Human Mind* was published in 1827 (London: A. Strahan, and T. Cadell). His *Outlines of Moral Philosophy* (Edinburgh: W. Creech, and T. Caddell, London, 1793), was a highly influential textbook for decades. It is indeed possible that the prestige of Stewart's work in Edinburgh was the occasion for the revival of the White's Professorship in Oxford. Heads of Oxford colleges might reasonably have believed they could quickly surpass in sophistication a textbook which, to corroborate a claim about virtue in Aristotle's *Ethics*, cites as its authority Lord Monbaddo's *Ancient Metaphysics*: see Stewart, *Outlines*, 288. Compare James Burnett, Lord Monboddo, *Ancient Metaphysics*, vol. 3 (London: T. Cadell, 1784).

30 Or more precisely, *Elements of Logic: Comprising the Substance of the Article in the Encyclopaedia Metropolitana, with Additions, &c* (London: B. Fellowes, 1826). It first appeared in the *Encyclopaedia* in 1823.

and also separate printings in New York, Philadelphia, and Boston. Newman's assistance in the preparation of the book was substantive enough that Whately wrote in the Preface: "I have to acknowledge assistance received from several friends who have at various times suggested remarks and alterations. But I cannot avoid particularizing the Rev. J. Newman, Fellow of Oriel College, who actually composed a considerable portion of the work as it now stands, from manuscripts not designed for publication, and who is the original author of several pages."[31] Note the language of "composed a considerable portion" and "original author of several pages."[32] Newman apparently took Whately's notes and went a long way in turning them into the finished book.

More than a work in Aristotelian syllogistic, Whately's treatise covered topics in what we should call "philosophical logic" and philosophy of logic, discussing the nature, scope, and utility of logic. Many important British logicians of the Victorian era were influenced by it, but an American reaction is noteworthy. Whately's book was a textbook at Harvard in 1851–1852, when Charles Sanders Peirce as a boy first came upon it in his older brother's rooms.[33] Peirce frequently cited the encounter as his intellectual conversion to philosophy of logic:

> It must have been in the year 1851, when I should have been 12 years old, that I remember picking up Whately's Logic in my elder brother's room, and asking him what logic was. I see myself, after he had told me, stretched on his carpet and poring over the book, and I must have passed most of my time so during that week, since subsequent severe tests showed that I had then mastered Whateley's [sic] work with the exception of two or three sections of pedantic nonsense. From that day to this logic has been my passion; although my training was chiefly in mathematics, physics, and chemistry.[34]

---

31 Whately, *Logic*, xiv–xv.

32 "Newman copied [Whately's logical "dialogues"] in 1822, dated his copy, and then constructed a 'rough draft' of an article which he returned to Whately 'as a sort of basis for his work.'" Newman to William John Fitzpatrick, March 7, 1864 (*LD* xxi, 72), as cited in Ray E. McKerrow, "'Method of Composition': Whately's Earliest 'Rhetoric,'" *Philosophy and Rhetoric* 11, no. 1 (Winter 1978): 43–58 at 44.

33 For evidence that philosophical trends at Harvard in the early 1800s were dominated by Scottish Commonsense philosophy, as was Oxford, see Edgeley Woodman Todd, "Philosophical Ideas at Harvard College, 1817–1837," *The New England Quarterly* 16, no. 1 (Mar. 1943), 63–90, which finds no basis whatsoever in the Harvard curriculum at the time for the Transcendentalism which was soon to break out through Emerson and Thoreau.

34 Peirce MS 905: 12, 1907 et seq., as quoted in Charles Seibert, "Charles Peirce's Reading of Richard Whately's Elements of Logic," *History & Philosophy of Logic*, 26, no. 1 (Feb. 2005): 1–32 at 7.

Clearly, a text which could have so inspired an admittedly precocious Peirce must be accounted philosophical.[35] Thus, to identify Newman's thought in relation to Whately's text is to identify Newman as working specifically as a philosopher.

Now, while Whately was composing his article in the *Encyclopaedia Metropolitana*, Newman was composing his own article, on miracles, which was later published separately as the first of his *Two Essays on Biblical and Ecclesiastical Miracles*. Near the start of that first essay, in a section entitled, "On the Antecedent Credibility of a Miracle, Considered as a Divine Interposition," Newman addresses Hume's famous argument. Hume had argued that it is always more plausible that the report of a miracle is false than that the reported miracle is true, or, more elaborately: a miracle should be defined as a violation of a law of nature; but as the evidence for a law of a nature is uniformly in favor, the antecedent probability of any such violation is zero; moreover, as we are fallible and flawed, when someone reports something, the antecedent probability that that person is deceived or deceiving is always greater than zero; thus, in any report of a miracle, the probability that the reporter is deceived or deceiving is always greater than the probability that the miracle occurred; but it is rational to believe the more likely of two alternatives; thus, it is never rational to believe that a reported miracle occurred.[36] Note that the argument lends itself well to analysis in terms of "antecedent probability," which as we shall see is an important idea in Newman.

Of this argument in particular, Newman remarks near the start of his Essay,

> This latter objection has been so ably met by various writers, that . . . it need not be considered here. It derives its force from the assumption, that a Miracle is strictly a causeless phenomenon, a self-originating violation of nature; and is solved by referring the event to divine agency, a principle which (it cannot be denied) has originated works indicative of power at least as great as any Miracle requires. An adequate cause being thus found for the production of a Miracle, the objection vanishes, as far as the mere question of power is concerned; and it remains to be considered whether the anomalous fact be of such a character as to admit of being referred to the Supreme Being. For if it cannot with propriety be referred to Him, it remains as improbable as if no such agent were known to exist.[37]

---

35 And indeed Pierce grappled most of his life with certain distinctive theses in Whately's book, especially Whately's rejection of psychologism and his understanding of hypothetical judgment. See Seibert, "Charles Peirce's Reading of Richard Whately's Elements of Logic," 7.

36 "No testimony is sufficient to establish a miracle, unless the testimony be of such a kind, that its falsehood would be more miraculous, than the fact, which it endeavours to establish," David Hume, *Philosophical Essays Concerning Human Understanding* (London: Andrew Millar, 1748), Section X, "Of Miracles," 115–16.

37 *Mir.*, 15.

Note that even this summary of the refutation of Hume gets to deep grounds: not satisfied with simply a logical or dialectical reply, Newman diagnoses what he regards as the crucial, hidden assumption. In any case, this objection being taken as sufficiently addressed, Newman promptly turns his attention to the problem which interests him more, namely: given the analogy between nature and revelation which Butler had so well described, it is antecedently likely that a miraculous and supernatural act of God would have similar characteristics to the ordinary, natural acts of God: therefore, we may reasonably ask, what are these characteristics, and how can they be used to mark out reports of miracles which have a claim to be believed? That is, Newman regards the "logical" refutation of Hume as serviceable mainly for clearing the way for an investigation of the grounds on which someone might assign antecedent probability to miracles. If they are not antecedently impossible, as Hume in effect argued, then what contributes to their antecedent likelihood?

Now Whately's *Logic* repeatedly addresses Hume's argument, with great acuity. Surely in the phrase "so ably met by various writers," Newman understands Whately, then, among others.[38] But in his Essay, Newman had just referred, on the previous page, to Whately's *Rhetoric*, as the source for his own invocation of the notion of "antecedent probability." Why, then, wouldn't Newman have referred to Whately's *Logic* too in that connection, as exhibiting some of the "able" refutations of Hume, which he was indeed presupposing?— Presumably because, in view of his own contributions to that text, he did not wish to appear to recommend himself.

Whately's *Logic* in fact deals with Hume's objection in five distinct passages, and Newman seems to enter implicitly into at least three of these. The first passage is a discussion of how to expose an argument as a fallacy.[39] One method is to "bring forward a similar one whose conclusion is obviously absurd."[40] In a note, Whately refers the reader to his pamphlet, "Historic Doubts Relative to Napoleon Buonaparte," which had exposed Hume's fallacy, by cleverly making use of Hume's principles to argue that no reasonable person should affirm the existence of Napoleon.[41]

In a second passage, he dismisses Hume's argument as a violation of the *Dictum de omni*. To see this, consider the fallacy, "Food is necessary to life; corn

---

38 Another other figure regarded then as prominent in this connection was George Campbell, who is cited by Newman on pages 5 and 50. See his *Dissertation of Miracles*, 3rd ed. (London: T. Cadell, Jr. and W. Davies, 1797). But Newman cites no one else in this regard, either in the *Two Essays on Biblical and on Ecclesiastical Miracles* or anywhere else in his corpus.

39 Note that to expose a fallacy is not yet to explain why it is a fallacy.

40 Whately, *Logic*, 33.

41 Richard Whately, *Historic Doubts Relative to Napoleon Buonaparte* (London: J. Hatchard, 1819). Whately's pamphlet was reprinted many times by Christian publishers in Britain and the United States. Note that Napoleon had died in the very year the pamphlet was published.

is food; therefore, corn is necessary to life." In this fallacy, the term "necessary to life" is affirmed of food, but not universally. But Hume clearly commits the same fallacy: "It may be stated thus," Whately comments, "Testimony is a kind of evidence more likely to be false, than a miracle to be true . . . the evidence on which the Christian miracles are believed, is testimony; therefore the evidence on which the Christian miracles are believed is more likely to be false than a miracle to be true." In the first premise, Whately observes, what is referred to must be only "some testimony," not "all testimony," since otherwise one assumes what one wants to prove. Thus, "this apparent argument has exactly the same fault" as the foolish fallacy about corn and food.[42]

He returns to Hume a third time in discussing *ignoratio elenchi* or the fallacy of "irrelevant conclusion." A common form of the fallacy is when a parallelism is drawn between two cases, in view of a similarity, whereas "perhaps they differ in the very point which is essential to the argument." Whately gives the following example: "From the circumstance that some men of humble station, who have been well educated, are apt to think themselves above low drudgery, it is argued, that universal education of the lower orders would beget general idleness." The argument is based on a parallelism between two cases, and yet "there is a circumstance that is absolutely essential, in which they differ; for when education is universal, it must cease to be a distinction: which is probably the very circumstance that renders men too proud for their work."

Then, in the following paragraph, as if making an additional point, he claims that Hume commits the same mistake: "Again, parallels have been drawn by Hume, (in his Essay on Miracles) . . . between the miracles recorded in the New Testament, and those in the Legends of pretended Saints; which last were received just as counterfeit coin is, from its *resemblance* to the genuine."[43] It is an interesting claim, and yet it does not, so far, show Hume to have committed the fallacy. One needs to say something further about "a circumstance that is absolutely essential, in which they differ." But this is exactly the burden of Newman's Essay. So Newman has entered into the discussion implicitly, because that paragraph in the *Logic* makes little sense except supplemented by that essay.

In a fourth passage, the *Logic* returns to Hume's objection, in an Appendix on ambiguous terms. Under the heading, "Experience," it is pointed out astutely that there are two different meanings of the word: "we sometimes understand [by it] our own personal Experience; sometimes general Experience." Then comes a succinct diagnosis of Hume's error:

> Hume has availed himself of this (practical) ambiguity, in his Essay on Miracles; in which he observes that we have Experience of the frequent falsity of Testimony, but that the occurrence of a Miracle is contrary

---

42 Whately, *Logic*, 45–46.
43 Whately, *Logic*, 229–30.

to our Experience, and is consequently what no testimony ought to be allowed to establish. Now had he explained *whose* Experience he meant, the argument would have come to nothing: if he means, the Experience of man kind universally, *i.e.* that a Miracle *has never* come under the Experience of *any one*, this is palpably begging the question: if he means the Experience of each individual who has never himself witnessed a Miracle, this would establish a rule (*viz.* that we are to believe nothing of which we have not ourselves experienced the like) which it would argue insanity to act upon.

The lines that next follow give what ends up being in Newman's *Grammar of Assent* a stock example of a certainty, the certainty that each man has that he is to die: if we take "experience" to mean personal experience, a man would be irrational to believe that he is going to die, as his experience in that sense is uniformly against it.[44]

So far so good: one would think the refutation of Hume's objection is done. But the discussion goes on, and it takes a new tack in a fifth and final passage, this time relying implicitly on the Aristotelian idea that generalizations which are true only for the most part cannot settle how a particular case is to be dealt with: it is always the health of "this particular man" not health in general which is a physician's concern:[45]

> In any other individual question, as to the admissibility of evidence, it would be reckoned absurd to consider merely the average chances for the truth of Testimony in the abstract, without inquiring what the Testimony is, in the particular instance before us. . . . Experience tells us that "a destructive hurricane is not a common occurrence;" certain persons tell us that "a destructive hurricane occurred in the West Indies, at such a time;" there is (as Dr. Campbell has pointed out) no opposition between these two assertions.[46]

This seems a Newmanian note, and, indeed, Newman will echo the point many years later, in a passage in the *Grammar of Assent*:

> Unbelievers use the antecedent argument from the order of nature against our belief in miracles. Here, if they only mean that the fact of that system of laws, by which physical nature is governed, makes it antecedently improbable that an exception should occur in it, there is no objection to the argument; but if, as is not uncommon, they mean

---

44 *GA*, 299–300.
45 See Aristotle, *Nicomachean Ethics*, I.6.1097a11–14.
46 Whately, *Logic*, 334.

that the fact of an established order is absolutely fatal to the very notion of an exception, they are using a presumption as if it were a proof. They are saying,—What has happened 999 times one way cannot possibly happen on the 1000th time another way, because what has happened 999 times one way is likely to happen in the same way on the 1000th. But unlikely things do happen sometimes. If, however, they mean that the existing order of nature constitutes a physical necessity, and that a law is an unalterable fact, this is to assume the very point in debate, and is much more than asserting its antecedent probability.[47]

But consider carefully the passage above from the *Logic*. Its upshot, strictly, is only that there is nothing irrational in belief in a miracle. Yet those sentences as I have quoted them contain an ellipsis, and in that gap there occurs this sentence, which reverts to a very different point (which is why I omitted it at first): "As if, e.g. any one had maintained that no testimony could establish Columbus's account of the discovery of America, because it is more common for travellers to lie, than for new Continents to be discovered," and then a footnote points the way, once more, to Whately's *Historic Doubts Relative to Napoleon*.

Observe the use of the word, "establish," and attend carefully to what is going on here. It is one thing to say that the uniformity of nature is consistent with testimony to a miracle; it is another altogether to say that testimony to miracles can "establish" them, as much as it can establish the existence of Napoleon. This stronger assertion was, of course, the conviction of the school of "Christian evidence," to which Whately subscribed. But it was not the conviction of Newman, who was at that time turning in dissent away from Whatley and toward his own view of faith as a real, miraculous power distinct from reason, but which functions like reason in leading its bearer from some truths to other new truths.[48] So here we see implicitly another influence of Newman, an attempt to moderate or reign in, in an Aristotelian spirit, the stronger and more rationalist stance that Whately wished to take.

It is perhaps through Newman's hand that this three-page treatment of Hume in the Appendix concludes with an unusual afterthought, "But this celebrated Essay [on Miracles], though it has often perhaps contributed to the amusement of an anti-christian sophist at the expense of those unable to expose its fallacy, never probably made one convert"[49]—a turn of phrase very close to Newman's famous assertion in one of his *University Sermons* (see below) that

---

47 *GA*, 382–83. Note that the passage never mentions Hume, and that sixty years after Whately, Newman is still grappling with Hume.

48 See Geertjan Zuijdwegt, "Richard Whately's Influence on John Henry Newman's Oxford University Sermons on Faith and Reason," *Newman Studies Journal* 10, no. 1 (2013): 82–95.

49 Whately, *Logic*, 335.

Hume was right, that the faith of Christians in miracles is itself a miracle, regardless of what "reason" says in a narrow sense.

I have dwelt on the treatment of miracles in Whately's logic for two reasons. First, in order to prove, as is my goal, the "fact" of Newman's powers and purposes as a philosopher, I want to show the quality of his training under Whately, assuredly a logician and philosopher, which, it is reasonable to suppose, we can see expressed especially in the passages on miracles in the *Logic*, since Newman who helped Whately compose that book was, at that very time, writing his own, complementary treatise on miracles.

But, second, it turns out that the proper handling of Hume on miracles was regarded by Newman and others as a kind of seedbed of original theological reflection; therefore, it is important to see just how, and how carefully, Newman thought about Hume (which in the first instance is of course a philosophical matter). Newman himself speculates that the masterwork which is Butler's *Analogy* was simply an elaborate response to Hume on Miracles.[50] James Froude, in his brief memoir of the Tractarian Movement, interprets Newman's decisive step away from Protestantism as bound up with his handling of Hume:

> I was something more than surprised, therefore, when I heard Newman say that Hume's argument against the credibility of miracles was logically sound. The laws of nature, so far as could be observed, were uniform, and in any given instance it was more likely, as a mere matter of evidence, that men should deceive or be deceived, than that those laws should have been deviated from. Of course he did not leave the matter in this position. Hume goes on to say that he is speaking of evidence as addressed to the reason; the Christian religion addresses itself to faith, and the credibility of it is therefore unaffected by his objection. What Hume said in irony Newman accepted in earnest.[51]

A careful reading the *Grammar of Assent* would reveal that a preoccupation with Hume runs right through it.

---

50 "I have sometimes thought that Hume's question at the end (I think) of his Essay on Miracles . . . was the stimulus which led to Butler's writing the Analogy." John Henry Newman, "The Text," in *The Philosophical Notebook of John Henry Newman*, ed. Edward Sillem (Louvain: Nauwelaerts Publishing House, 1970), vol. 2: 107–9. Hume's Essay was published more than ten years after the *Analogy*. But apparently Newman was aware that Hume had shown the Essay to Butler in a draft version of the *Treatise*. Hume removed the Essay from the *Treatise* before it was published, later joking that he had "castrated" it, so as not to displease Butler. See *The Letters of David Hume*, edited by J. Y. T. Greig, 2 vols, (Oxford: Clarendon Press, 1932), 6.2.

51 James Anthony Froude, "The Oxford Counter-Reformation," *Short Studies on Great Subjects*, vol. 4 (London: Longmans, Green, and Co., 1899), 287–88. He is referring to Newman's Oxford University sermon, "The Usurpations of Reason." Of course he misstates Newman's view, which is not that Hume's argument is "logically sound."

Newman in his *Apologia* says of Whately that "He, emphatically, opened my mind, and taught me to think and to use my reason."[52] Therefore, we should not leave this question of Newman's training under Whately without at least mentioning the vast subject of how Newman takes from Whately the notion of "antecedent probability." One sees this concept and methodological principle at work in nearly all of Newman's writings: for example, one must get straight the antecedent probability of a miracle as having such-and-such characteristics, he thinks (as we have seen), before examining directly the evidence for any miracle; or one must first see that developments in Christianity are antecedently probable before looking at the evidence for development.[53] His whole treatment of the problem of faith and reason involves dividing their work, with faith bearing upon the antecedent probabilities with which we approach experience, and reason examining the available evidence, perhaps slight, in light of these antecedent probabilities.

One can see that, complementary to this principle, is the idea which he also takes from Whately, that because our experience is as it were fecund, then different people experience the same thing in different ways, depending upon the antecedent probabilities they bring to bear on it. In editions of the *Logic* after 1831, Whately explained this principle, which he also called "abstraction," by reference to a passage from his Third Lecture on *Political Economy*:

> If you will be at the pains carefully to analyze the simplest descriptions you hear of any transaction or state of things, you will find, that the process which almost invariably takes place is, in logical language, this; that each individual has in his mind certain *major-premises* or principles, relative to the subject in question; that observation of what actually presents itself to the senses, supplies *minor-premises*; and that the statement given (and which is reported as a thing experienced) consists in fact of the *conclusions* drawn from the combinations of those premises. . . . And this explains the fact, that we find so much discrepancy in the results of what are called Experience and Common-sense, as contra-distinguished from theory.[54]

Antecedent probabilities are therefore, Newman will later say, the characteristic work of a living mind:

> After the aspects in which a question is to be viewed, and the principles on which it is to be considered, come the arguments by which it is decided;

---

52 *Apo.*, 11.

53 Part I, Section 2, of *Development of Doctrine* is entitled, "The Antecedent Argument in behalf of Developments in Christian Doctrine."

54 Richard Whately, *Introductory Lectures on Political Economy* (Oxford: London, B. Fellowes, 1831), 76–77.

among these are antecedent reasons, which are especially in point here, because they are in great measure made by ourselves and belong to our personal character, and to them I shall confine myself.[55]

The notion of "antecedent probability," only a methodological principle for Whately, becomes then a substantive principle for Newman. But Newman had taken it from Whately's *Rhetoric*, or, rather, from an early precis of the main ideas of the *Rhetoric*, which, again, Newman as an assistant to Whately helped compose.[56] And that is why Newman joked "I thought of dedicating my first book to him, in words to the effect that he had not only taught me to think, but to think for myself."[57] What Whately had set down as a principle of persuasion, Newman applied as a principle of the limitation of explicit reasoning in practice.

NEWMAN'S "DISCURSIVE ENQUIRIES ON METAPHYSICAL SUBJECTS"

I have been following Newman's own preferred method in this chapter, by examining three instances which establish an antecedent probability, and leaving for another time a direct consideration of the "body of evidence." If Newman is right, then getting these antecedent probabilities right is by far the most important thing. The first two were taken from the beginning of Newman's life as a scholar, while the last, as if to establish a continued path throughout his life, is taken from 1859–1888, years in which he sketched ideas in a philosophical notebook for a planned book which would have the title noted above.

It is well known that Newman as it were complained that his life was taken up with controversy and that he hardly had leisure to expound a subject just for its own sake.[58] A White's Professorship would have given him such leisure.

---

55   *GA*, 381. Butler's analogy is cited as a great example of this.

56   Newman assisted in the composition of Whately's *Rhetoric* as much as the *Logic*, and from 1822 was using an early outline and precis of that book in instruction at Oriel. See McKerrow, "Whately's Earliest 'Rhetoric,'" which gives that precis in full, (49–56). That text says that arguments for a thesis should be divided into an "A" class and a "B" class. In a footnote added to later editions of the *Rhetoric*, Whately explained that the symbols are a mnemonic: "Some students . . . have found it useful to adopt, in drawing up an outline or analysis of any composition, certain arbitrary symbols, to denote, respectively, each class of arguments and of propositions: viz., A, . . . to denote 'a priori' or 'antecedent probability,' . . . and B, for . . . 'the body of evidence.'" *Elements of Rhetoric*, From the Last Enlarged and Revised Edition (Nashville, Tenn.: Southern Methodist Publishing House, 1861), 58.

57   *Apo.*, 11.

58   John Henry Newman, *Sayings of Cardinal Newman*, ed. Anonymous (London: Burns & Oates, Ltd.), 1890, 32–33.

Yet old age and the relative retirement of the Oratory in Birmingham did as well, and, when he had time at last (excepting the necessity of putting his affairs in order) to write on whatever he wished, he chose to investigate "metaphysical subjects," and, relatedly, to examine the phenomenology of conscience and the conditions of certainty in the *Grammar*. If Aristotle is correct that what we choose when we have leisure, we esteem most of all,[59] then Newman's preference for "metaphysics" above all else was revealed only near the end of his life.

However, what did he mean by "metaphysics" in his intended book? It is not what Aristotle meant, the study of being *qua* being, which would include too the study of theology, if it turned out that the primary beings were gods—though Newman in one place suggests that that is how he would have used the term in Oxford in the 1830s.[60] Rather, by the middle of the nineteenth century Dugald Stewart's definition had become controlling. For Stewart, "metaphysics" meant "not the Ontology and Pneumatology of the schools, but the inductive Philosophy of the Human Mind."[61]—however, such philosophy as pursued speculatively, not with a view to practice, which is why Newman could write, "My turn of mind has never led me towards metaphysics; rather it has been logical, ethical, practical."[62]

That this is the controlling definition at the time is shown by how the first Waynefleet Professor of Metaphysics in Oxford, 1859–1867, Henry Longueville Mansel, explicitly defines the term: he quotes Stewart from the *Dissertation* and

---

59   Aristotle, *Nicomachean Ethics*, IX.12, and X.6–8.

60   "As regards the term "reason"—Certainly in 1831 and the following years the terminology which [Dr. Fairbairn] takes for granted was little known in Oxford, nor indeed any terminology but Aristotle's," see John Henry Newman, *Stray Essays on Controversial Points variously illustrated*, by Cardinal Newman, 1890, privately printed, https://archive.org/details/a618244801newmuoft. Newman in a note refers to a work which appeared then, which might have provided a broader viewpoint, but which apparently was little studied, namely, Wilhelm Gottlieb Tennemann, *A Manual of a History of Philosophy*, trans. Arthur Johnson (Oxford: D.A. Talboys, 1832). Although Tennemann does say that for Aristotle "metaphysics" is "Primary philosophy, treating of the nature of Being" (at 128). However, his general outlook is that the term means rather the investigation of any subject to the greatest degree of abstraction, there being a sequence from *physics*, to *mathematics*, to *metaphysics* (at 124).

61   Dugald Stewart, *Dissertation: Exhibiting the Progress of Metaphysical, Ethical, and Political Philosophy*, in Sir William Hamilton, *Collected Works of Dugald Stewart*, vol. 1 (Edinburgh: Hamilton, Adams, & Co., 1854), 22.

62   Newman, *Stray Essays*, 94. Logic is purely formal and linguistic, he thinks, following Whately, thus it is excepted. His remark was a confession of ignorance, that he did not have time to study in effect Stewart and his school well: "Some of my University sermons will be very hard, but I have now for twelve years been working out a theory, and whether it is true or not it has this recommendation, that it is consistent; and this is the only encouragement I have to publish, considering its unpopularity and my own ignorance of metaphysical writers." Newman to Mrs. J. Mozley, Littlemore (January 23, 1843), *LD* ix, 214.

then glosses it as: "all those inquiries which have for their object to trace the various branches of human knowledge to their first principles in the constitution of our nature."[63]

At the same time the view was becoming dominant, which was later popularized in a famous article in the *Encyclopedia Britannica* by Thomas Case, that the Aristotelian term had always been misunderstood, as *ta meta ta physica*, "the things after the physics," was simply a placeholder for the order of volumes in the edition of Aristotle's works by Andronicus of Rhodes, not a substantive name of the subject matter itself.[64] "Metaphysics" in its Aristotelian and Scholastic sense always having been based on a misconception, then, the term was free to be applied in the new way preferred by the Scottish school.

We saw that Mills dismissed Kant as Cambridge Platonism repackaged. But by the mid-nineteenth century, with the ascendancy of Hegelianism on the Continent, it was not so easy for Oxford professors to dismiss or ignore German philosophy. Thus Mansel and others were obliged to developed arguments as to why Reid and Aristotle are to be preferred, even in areas which might be thought to be strong suits for the Germans. One sees Newman grappling with the question too. He takes seriously a translation of a book by Heinrich Moritz Chalybäus, *The Historical Development of Speculative Philosophy*,[65] which argues that German philosophy carries forward the great traditions in philosophy. But he clearly is casting around for some reason to ignore the Germans altogether, and he thinks he has found them: "The question is, not what is difficult, but what is true. Here we get at the real fundamental proposition assumed—viz that the human mind is the measure of all things. Perhaps the German writers have discussed all this—I do not think I am bound to read them in spite of what Chalybaus [sic] says, for notoriously they have come to no conclusion."[66] One might add that German philosophy starting with Kant is a reaction to Hume, but Newman, reasonably enough, implicitly takes himself to have engaged with and responded to Hume in his own way.

It would be pointless to attempt to give an exegesis of the "Discursive Enquiries" here, as they never were so organized as to serve as an outline for a book, and to supply this additional work "for" Newman posthumously would involve a subtle project in reconstruction, which would require its own book.[67]

---

63 Henry Longueville Mansel, *Metaphysics* (Edinburgh: Adam and Charles Black, 1860), 2–3.

64 Mansel, *Metaphysics*, 2–3.

65 Heinrich Moritz Chalybäus, *The Historical Development of Speculative Philosophy*, trans. Alfred Edersheim (Edinburgh: T. & T. Clark, and London: Hamilton, Adams, & Co., 1854).

66 *PN* ii, 90.

67 It is as if: suppose one had only Beethoven's sketch books for the Opus 109 sonata in E, could one reconstruct the sonata? It is difficult enough to interpret the sketch books, given the sonata. See the subtleties in Nicholas Marston, *Beethoven's Piano Sonata in E, Op. 109*, (Oxford: Clarendon Press, 1995).

Some extraordinary ideas presented in it are: that the knowledge of all sciences is implicit in the power of abstraction which each person has;[68] that the mind through reflection on its own operation can arrive at ideas of totality and parts, rule and subjection, power, time, and causation;[69] that we cannot be said to have faith or trust in faculties which are such that in the activity of those faculties I see that I exist;[70] that when we regard a concept as "beyond reason" we are dealing with a form of words implying a contradiction, which is interpreted as not being a contradiction, because each claim is assigned to a different respect, and yet what those respects are, or fully are, we are ignorant of.[71] He considers certain puzzles too, such as how is it appropriate to interpret the system of revelation in light of the system of nature (as Butler presumed), if God could create an infinitude of worlds each strikingly dissimilar to every other;[72] or how could we know whether what look to be relationships in experience are not governed by an underlying hidden law, not by real action of one thing upon the other, just as phenomena governed by an algebraic equation might appear to be acting in relationship to one another, independent of that equation.[73]

But in conclusion I will draw attention to a deep conviction evident in the "Enquiries," which is a guiding insight for his entire life. The conviction is that what is really true is unseen. In the *Apologia*, Newman tells how he had such a conviction even as a child:

> I used to wish the Arabian Tales were true: my imagination ran on unknown influences, on magical powers, and talismans . . . I thought life might be a dream, or I an Angel, and all this world a deception, my fellow-angels by a playful device concealing themselves from me, and deceiving me with the semblance of a material world." Again: "Reading in the Spring of 1816 a sentence from [Dr. Watts's] Remnants of Time, entitled 'the Saints unknown to the world,' to the effect, that 'there is nothing in their figure or countenance to distinguish them,' &c. &c., I supposed he spoke of Angels who lived in the world, as it were disguised.[74]

In an unpublished essay, "Letter on Matter and Spirit," he argues thoroughly and with ingenuity that everything we sense, through an instinct which we have no power over, leads us to infer the existence of what we do not sense, and which carries the burden of our belief and reasoning about the world. We speak of "material objects," and yet we sense only

---

68 *PN* ii, 11.
69 *PN* ii, 23–25.
70 *PN* ii, 83.
71 *PN* ii, 101–6.
72 *PN* ii, 107–10.
73 *PN* ii, 111–20.
74 *Apo.*, 2.

external phenomena betokening the unknown, not revealing it. The word *rose*, in its properties, does not belong to the senses; whether the thing itself can even be called a rose we do not know. It may be an Angel; it may be the soul of a child; it may be as I have hinted . . . one of the innumerable immediate acts of the Ever-present Creator Himself . . . what we call matter . . . is simply and nothing else but a divine action, mediately, or immediately.[75]

He returns to the theme in his notebook, in an entry entitled, "The Unseen World," dated September 10, 1876: each of us has "as clear a proof of the unseen world and its constituent parts as the seen."[76] Our experience both conveys knowledge and brings home to us our ignorance:

Here at once is an unseen world. The action of the mind of each individual is at once a reality, yet to the others but ourselves a hidden reality. Each man thinks, hopes, fears, loves, likes, dislikes, has pleasure & pain, plans & performs, yet in himself, not to others. In the aggregate of this acting & suffering we have the fact of an unseen, unknown world. How infinitesimal is the knowledge I have of it in its detail and fulness! An unseen God then, Angels, devils, &c &c, are not strange ideas, they are but a carrying out of a conception, which experience has brought home to us together with a knowledge of the visible world.[77]

His Proof of Theism in the notebook needs to be understood in light of this assumption. Sensations are not inert, but actions or passions, which already point to something that complements them, but which is unseen. We might have thought Newman favored a proof of theism which was practical or moralistic: say, we search for a God who is the source of revelation, and effectively believe, in a kind of faith, that such a God exists, because that would help us clarify our conscience, and any refinement of conscience leads us to look earnestly for light. However, this is not the character of his argument. Rather, his view is that the sensation we feel of a "voice" of conscience is a kind of passivity, which is an aspect of something active, which we sense as commanding, in the manner of a person, and which, although unseen, we no more believe to exist on faith, than we believe that we exist on faith, when we reason.[78]

---

75 *NP* ii, 208. I omit the signs used by the editor to indicate insertions and changes in the Newman's draft of the letter.

76 *NP* ii, 189.

77 *NP* ii, 189.

78 *NP* ii, 31–78.

CONCLUSION

This essay establishes that the project of reading Newman as a philosopher rests on solid foundations, based upon an accurate construal of his life as and of the history of philosophy: it is not a matter of interpreting Newman's thought with respect to general similarities, or vague associations, which it shares with various philosophies.[79]

The history of philosophy needs to be understood both genetically and not in separation from questions of institutions and perceived authority. *Genetically*: the history of philosophy has developed in certain ways that make it difficult to place Newman within the discipline in the way it is understood today. We can take this as a *fait accompli* only if we take philosophy to be an inherently progressive discipline like a technology or physical science, which it is not. *Not in separation from institutions and authority*: Newman lost every contest over the direction of an institution in which he was engaged. The Tractarian movement failed to change the direction of the Church of England; his reform of the office of tutor at Oriel College, to find a place for "personal influence," also failed; his attempts to secure the authority of Oxford for his conception of the reasonable openness of moral philosophy, in a Christian culture, to considerations of revelation and grace, in the extended Hampden Controversy, failed as well; his founding of the Irish university of course failed. We can take this state of affairs as a *fait accompli* only if we can convince ourselves that the culture and character imparted by the modern university system are fine.

Newman has been made an exile as a philosopher from history and institutions. The study of Newman as a philosopher, then, properly undertaken, aims to end this condition of exile: not by keeping the subsequent history of philosophy as something fixed, and asking whether and how Newman could fit into it—as, in truth, he hardly has a home here—but rather by returning to Newman's works in their context, and considering how philosophy might take a different direction starting from there, and what sorts of institutions would nurture that concept of philosophy and provide for its best expression and support—as it might be suspected that we, truly, could find an intellectual home there.

---

79 This other approach was first undertaken by Wilfrid Ward in his Lowell lecture, "Newman's Philosophy" in *The Genius of Cardinal Newman*, ed. Wilfrid Ward (Josephine Mary Hope-Scott), *Last Lectures by Wilfrid Ward* (London: Longmans, Green, and Co., 1918), 72–101. By taking Newman's fundamental philosophical insight to be expressed in a chance comment by Newman in a letter of 1840 to "Miss H.," viz. "The human mind in its present state is unequal to its own powers of apprehension" (*Letters and Correspondence of John Henry Newman*, ed. Anne Mozley, vol. ii [London: Longmans, Green, & Co., 1903], 278), Ward discovers very general similarities between Newman and the American pragmatists, and Newman and German Idealism. And yet Newman goes on to say, in the next line of that letter, "Absolute certainty, then, cannot be attained here"—which is so far from expressing his considered view that it contradicts a main holding of the *Grammar*!

Suggested Reading

Butler, Joseph. *The Analogy of Religion, Natural and Revealed*. London: James, John and Paul Knapton, 1736.

Campbell, George. *A Dissertation of Miracles*. 3rd. ed. London: T. Cadell, Jr. and W. Davies, 1797.

Corona, Marial. *John Henry Newman and the Pragmatist Tradition*. Washington, D.C.: The Catholic University of America Press, forthcoming.

Crosby, John F. *The Personalism of John Henry Newman*. Washington, D.C.: The Catholic University of America Press, 2016.

Nubiola, Jaime. "La relación de Charles S. Peirce con John H. Newman." *Acta Philosophica*, II, 23 (2014): 340–43.

Ward, Wilfrid. *The Genius of Cardinal Newman, Last Lectures by Wilfrid Ward*, edited by Wilfrid Ward (Josephine Mary Hope-Scott). London: Longmans, Green, and Co., 1918.

CHAPTER 14

NEWMAN'S VISION OF INTELLECTUAL VIRTUE IN ITS RELATION TO MORAL AND RELIGIOUS VIRTUE

John F. Crosby

"**N**ow from first to last, education, in this large sense of the word, has been my line."[1] Thus wrote Newman in his personal diary in 1863. He was not only, first to last, an educator, but he reflected on education and wrote about it, and these writings form an important part of his legacy.

The world is taking a new interest in Newman's legacy now that he has become a canonized saint. This is an auspicious moment for all who are committed to liberal education to go back to Newman's writings on the subject. One thinks above all of his magisterial work, *The Idea of a University*, which grew out of his labors to establish a Catholic university in Dublin in the early 1850's. This work is *the* classic defense of liberal education; it has no peer, in my opinion. I want to call attention to an idea in Newman's book that is easily overlooked, and that, once noticed, is provocative and challenging for us.

Newman states the idea in this beautifully crafted sentence: "Quarry the granite rock with razors, or moor the vessel with a thread of silk; then may you hope with such keen and delicate instruments as human knowledge and human

---

1   *AW*, 259.

reason to contend against those giants, the passion and the pride of man."[2] If we think of the cultivation of "human knowledge and human reason" as the work of liberal education, and if we think of moral virtue as bringing order into "the passion and the pride of man," then Newman seems to be saying that liberal education does not directly promote moral virtue or moral character. This is indeed what he teaches. In fact, he goes so far as to say that liberal education is no more about forming moral character than it is about developing professional skill. It is not controversial to say that liberal education is not a matter of cultivating professional skill; well, for Newman it is just as little controversial to say liberal education does not have the task, or the ability, to contend against those giants, "the passion and the pride of man," and to form good moral character in those who receive a liberal education.

As I say, this claim of Newman is sure to provoke objections from many of us. Whenever my colleagues defend liberal education against its detractors, they almost always praise its power of moral formation. A merely professional education is said to be deficient precisely because it neglects moral character; we need liberal education just because moral character has to be front and center in the work of education. Let us, then, allow ourselves to be challenged by Newman; let us examine his reasons for drawing this sharp distinction between moral and intellectual virtue. Let us see if liberal education is perhaps best defended by abstaining from certain excessive claims on its behalf, and by focusing with greater precision on what it really accomplishes in the liberally educated person, and what it cannot accomplish.

SETTING ASIDE A MISUNDERSTANDING

Let us begin by warding off a misunderstanding. Newman does not mean that a university, least of all a Catholic university, has no interest in the moral development of its students, as if it were exclusively interested in the cultivation of intellectual virtue. In a sermon preached at his fledgling university in Dublin and entitled, "Intellect, the Instrument of Religious Training," he said:

> The human mind, as you know, my brethren, may be regarded from two principal points of view, as intellectual and as moral. The perfection of the intellect is called ability and talent; the perfection of our moral nature is virtue. And it is our great misfortune here, and our trial, that, as things are found in the world, the two are separated, and independent of each other; that, where power of intellect is, there need not be virtue; and that where right, goodness, and moral greatness are, there need not be talent. It was not so in the beginning. . . .[3]

---

2   *Idea*, 121.
3   *OS*, no. 1: 5–6.

Newman proceeds to consider the original integrity of human nature, that is, the original unity of moral and intellectual virtue, and the shattering of this unity as a result of the fall of man. He says that our task at this point in salvation history is to strive to recover the lost integrity. In the setting of a university, and especially of a Catholic university, this means that we have the task of recovering the unity of moral and intellectual excellence—not indeed blending the latter into the former, but restoring the unity that obtains between them as distinct excellences. Towards the end of the same sermon he says, "Here, then, I conceive, is the object of the Holy See and the Catholic Church in setting up Universities; it is to reunite things which were in the beginning joined together by God, and put asunder by man." And he explains his point in these often-quoted words:

> I want to destroy that diversity of centres, which puts everything into confusion by creating a contrariety of influences. I wish the same spots and the same individuals to be at once oracles of philosophy and shrines of devotion. It will not satisfy me, what satisfies so many, to have two independent systems, intellectual and religious, going at once side by side, by a sort of division of labor, and only accidentally brought together.[4]

But the same Newman who wants to restore a lost unity of moral and intellectual excellence also wants to preserve the distinction between moral and intellectual, and he wants to say that the liberal education imparted by a university aims at intellectual virtue; it does not equally aim at moral virtue. Liberal education alone does not give you what you need to "contend against those giants the passion and the pride of man." Insofar as the university supports its students in this moral struggle, it draws on other resources than liberal education.

THE INTELLECTUAL VIRTUES THAT ARE
CULTIVATED BY LIBERAL EDUCATION,
AS SHOWN THROUGH THEIR CONSPICUOUS ABSENCE

We will understand Newman better if we look more closely at the intellectual virtue wrought by liberal education. This is the best way to come to see why he teaches that intellectual virtue is irreducible to moral.

In the *Idea of a University* Newman throws intellectual virtue into relief by way of two contrasts: the contrast between intellectual virtue and the conspicuous absence of it, and the contrast between intellectual virtue and a certain deformation of it. Let us consider the first contrast in the following section, and the second contrast in the section after that.

---

4 *OS*, no. 1: 13.

The first goes like this. Newman considers a man born blind who wakes up from the surgery that has restored his power of seeing. This person does not immediately see the world that we see, but rather has only chaotic sensations of light and color. He does not at first see where one thing ends and another begins, nor can he tell what is close up and what is far away. Only gradually does he learn to apprehend distinct things and to situate them in space, so that "what was an unintelligible wilderness becomes a landscape or a scene."[5] This is just the way it is, Newman says, with our mental life before we have received a liberal education:

> when we hear opinions put forth on any new subject, we have no prin-
> ciple to guide us in balancing them; we do not know what to make
> of them; we turn them to and fro, and over, and back again, as if to
> pronounce upon them, if we could, but with no means of pronouncing.
> It is the same when we attempt to speak upon them: we make some
> random venture, or we take up the opinion of some one else, which
> strikes our fancy.[6]

The helplessness of such a mind makes manifest the absence, the painful absence of any intellectual virtue. It is liberal education that empowers us to bring order into the world of opinions and judgments, to begin to discriminate in the world of the mind like the person who awakens to sight begins to discriminate in the world of sight.

Newman gives us some other remarkable pictures of the mind as it functions prior to receiving a liberal education. He says of a clever schoolboy:

> For some years his intellect is little more than an instrument for taking
> in facts, or a receptacle for storing them; he welcomes them as fast as
> they come to him; he lives on what is without; . . . he has a lively suscep-
> tibility of impressions; he imbibes information of every kind; and little
> does he make his own in a true sense of the word, living rather upon
> his neighbours all around him. He has opinions, religious, political, and
> literary, and for a boy, is very positive in them and sure about them; but
> he gets them from his schoolfellows, or his masters or his parents. . . .[7]

So when you hear this schoolboy speak, what you hear is mainly his teachers and parents speaking through him, since he has as yet very little mind of his own; as Newman says, he is at this point in his life "mainly a creature of foreign influ-ences." He is ready for, and urgently in need of, a liberal education.

---

5   *Idea*, 495.
6   *Idea*, 497.
7   *Idea*, 127–28.

We are reminded here of Newman's personalism. Newman is concerned, not just with the truth of the schoolboy's opinions, but with the boy's personal ownership of them. As long as the boy just transmits what he has heard from others, not realizing that he does not really understand what he transmits, he is not really alive as a distinct person; the boundary between self and other is only faintly drawn. If liberal education does nothing else for him, it teaches him to recognize the opinions that he really owns, and not to confuse these with opinions which he has heard but not yet made his own. Of course, Newman says that it is all-important to have true opinions; but true opinions devoid of real personal ownership of them are of no benefit to the person holding the opinions, nor does it give any evidence of the presence of real education in that person.

Here is another picture from Newman's gallery of pictures of the mind devoid of real intellectual virtue. I realize that I am quoting him more extensively than is usual; but his characterizations are so perfectly drawn, that I cannot resist quoting him, and using his words rather than my own.

> Seafaring men, for example, range from one end of the earth to the other; but the multiplicity of external objects, which they have encountered, forms no symmetrical and consistent picture upon their imagination; they see the tapestry of human life, as it were on the wrong side, and it tells no story. They sleep, and they rise up, and they find themselves, now in Europe, now in Asia; they see visions of great cities and wild regions; they are in the marts of commerce, or amid the islands of the South; they gaze on Pompey's Pillar, or on the Andes; and nothing which meets them carries them forward or backward, to any idea beyond itself. Nothing has a drift or relation; nothing has a history or a promise. Every thing stands by itself, and comes and goes in its turn, like the shifting scenes of a show, which leave the spectator where he was.[8]

Newman proceeds to show the absence of any intellectual discrimination in these seafaring men by imagining an encounter with them:

> Perhaps you are near such a man on a particular occasion, and expect him to be shocked or perplexed at something which occurs; but one thing is much the same to him as another, or, if he is perplexed, it is as not knowing what to say, whether it is right to admire, or to ridicule, or to disapprove, while conscious that some expression of opinion is expected from him; for in fact he has no standard of judgment at all, and no landmarks to guide him to a conclusion.[9]

---

8   *Idea*, 136.
9   *Idea*, 136.

Newman wants to say that these people are deficient precisely in respect of intellectual virtue. He wants to say that it is liberal education that imparts to the mind the power of judging that is so painfully absent in them.

But what exactly is the activity of the mind whereby it begins to focus and to discriminate and to have a "mind of its own"? Newman intimates his answer when he says, as we just heard, that for the seafaring men "nothing has a drift or relation; nothing has a history or a promise. Every thing stands by itself." Behind these statements lies an idea that is fundamental to Newman's epistemology: he thinks that the finite human mind, facing the immensity of reality, can in any given act only take in a very limited aspect of the whole of reality. He thinks that we have to compensate constantly for the finitude of our impressions by knitting them together and apprehending the larger whole that they make up. This is why Newman says that the "imperial intellect" of the liberally educated person "never views any part of the extended subject-matter of Knowledge without recollecting that it is but a part. . . . It makes every thing in some sort lead to every thing else; it would communicate the image of the whole to every separate portion."[10] This is a striking expression for the actual work of intellectual virtue: to communicate the image of the whole of knowledge to each part of it. You see how Newman brings intellectual virtue to evidence by contrasting it with a habit of mind that remains stuck in its present impression, as if the impression stood alone without history or promise, and it did not belong to any greater whole.

Let us now revisit our question about intellectual virtue in relation to moral virtue. The conspicuous lack of intellectual virtue is not a moral failing. The schoolboy described by Newman is not morally deficient, nor are the seafaring men morally deficient. They lack intellectual virtue, not moral virtue. If the schoolboy receives a liberal education, and learns to order his thoughts, and to discern a scene or a landscape where he had previously only seen a wilderness, then he advances indeed in intellectual virtue but not necessarily equally in moral virtue. He may be helpless in contending against those giants, the passion and the pride of man, even while he is learning, as Newman puts it, "to leaven the dense mass of facts with the elastic force of reason."[11] Thus we can say: just as the deficiency of intellectual virtue is not necessarily a moral failing, so the presence of intellectual virtue does not guarantee moral excellence.

One might object that intellectual virtue is inseparable from moral virtue; that surely no one has intellectual virtue who is not truthful, diligent, persevering, etc., all of which are moral qualities. Newman does not deny this. But as we will see below, he has a "high" notion of moral virtue as a result of the religious dimension that he discerns in it. Morally good qualities that are

10 *Idea*, 137.
11 *Idea*, 138.

possible without this religious dimension do not really count for Newman as moral virtue in the full and proper sense.

One might think that Newman is bound to depreciate intellectual virtue once he has distinguished it from moral virtue. But he does nothing of the kind; he brings out by his contrasts the beauty of intellectual virtue, and in fact he makes a great point of teaching, as every reader of Newman knows, that intellectual virtue is worth having for its own sake. One might think that a pastor and evangelist, such as Newman was, would either reduce intellectual virtue to moral, or else reduce it to a mere instrumental means for attaining moral virtue. But he does neither; he is a true Christian humanist who esteems intellectual virtue for its own sake. He acknowledges that liberal education is not necessary for salvation, but he still esteems it for its own sake.

THE AUTHENTIC INTELLECTUAL VIRTUES AS CONTRASTED WITH A CERTAIN DEFORMATION OF THEM

I said that there was another contrast that Newman uses for thinking about intellectual virtue; it is the contrast between intellectual virtue and a certain deformation of it. He has in mind the deformation that comes from exalting one part of knowledge into the whole of it. He deplores those who:

> conceive that they profess just *the* truth which makes all things easy. They have their one idea or their favourite notion, which occurs to them on every occasion. They have their one or two topics, which they are continually obtruding, with a sort of pedantry. . . . Perhaps they have discovered, as they think, the leading idea, or . . . sum and substance of the Gospel; and they insist upon this or that isolated tenet . . . to the disparagement of the rest of the revealed scheme.[12]

In his letters Newman gives a most interesting specimen of this fault of wrenching a part out of its place within the whole. He knew the English architect Pugin, who was the driving force behind the revival of Gothic church architecture in the nineteenth century. Newman expresses great admiration for his talents, but at the same time calls Pugin "a bigot."[13] Newman meant that Pugin made Gothic architecture into *the* norm for church architecture and held every other style in contempt. Pugin even said that St. Peter's Basilica in Rome, which is not a Gothic church, was pagan. He thought that only Gothic architecture was compatible with Catholic orthodoxy, and that all other church styles had heretical tendencies. He did not know how to combine his admiration for the Gothic with respect for other styles of church

---

12 *US*, no. 14: 306.
13 So wrote Newman of Pugin in a letter of June 15, 1848 (*LD* xiii, 220).

building. This is for Newman at least analogous to that deformation of intellectual virtue that he deprecates.[14]

If we were to look for an example today of this deformation of intellectual virtue, we might mention the neuroscientists who want to explain human consciousness and human action exclusively in terms of brain function, as if there were no mind that is irreducible to the brain. For many neuroscientists, the idea of appealing to our conscious experience of moral agency is dismissed as naïve; they say that conscious experience is something merely subjective, and that we have to go behind it and examine the brain with its synapses and dendrites if we are going to find the real ground of mental activity. Newman's point is not exactly that neuroscientific materialism is a gross metaphysical error, though he would certainly say that too. But in the setting of the *Idea of a University* he wants above all to say that these neuroscientists are deficient in intellectual virtue, for they take one aspect of the human mind, namely the brain, and try to explain everything else, even moral agency, in terms of it.

You see why I speak here of a deformation of the mind rather than a simple lack of the formation that it ought to have. These neuroscientists, or artists like Pugin, are not unable to bring order and reason into their thinking; their minds do not represent a bundle of undigested information, like the schoolboys, nor do they just passively endure sensations, like the seamen do. They have indeed standards for organizing their thought, but the standards are too narrow, so that they end up doing violence to those parts of reality that do not correspond to their standards.

But their narrowness is not exactly a moral failing. Pugin is not exactly morally bad for overrating his beloved Gothic. It may be somewhat different with the neuroscientists; they may have a hostility to the very idea of a spiritual principle in man, and that would certainly be morally objectionable. But insofar as they too are overrating the thing that they happen to know best, they show a malformed intellect more than they show a wayward or malicious will.

Again we see that Newman is not disparaging intellectual virtue as a result of conceiving of it as something other than, and in a way less than, moral virtue. For if a person knows how to impart the image of the whole of knowledge to every separate portion of the whole, how to give every portion its due, how to let the different realms of knowledge explain each other, and how to avoid privileging one at the expense of the others, then that person has achieved something eminently worth having for its own sake, even if it is not exactly a growth in moral virtue. In fact, Newman is so far from disparaging intellectual virtue that we can say that, in his view, intellectual virtue contributes something for the full flourishing of the person that is not contributed by moral virtue alone, just as bodily health contributes something to the full flourishing of the person that is not contributed by moral virtue alone.

---

14 For a full account of Newman's relation to Pugin, see Guy Nicholls, *Unearthly Beauty, The Aesthetic of St. John Henry Newman* (Leominster: Gracewing, 2019), 245–59.

AN OBJECTION

It is now time to consider an objection to Newman's way of distinguishing intellectual and moral virtue. It is an objection that can in fact be formulated in Newman's own words. In the course of speaking about the "influence exerted by intellectual culture upon our moral nature" he mentions "veracity, probity, equity, fairness, gentleness, benevolence, and amiableness." He continues,

> a character more noble to look at, more beautiful, more winning, in the various relations of life . . . is hardly conceivable . . . [than the character of the liberally educated person] If you would obtain a picture for contemplation which may seem to fulfil the ideal, which the Apostle has delineated under the name of charity, in its sweetness and harmony, its generosity, its courtesy to others, and its depreciation of self, you could not have recourse to a better furnished studio than to that of Philosophy.[15]

Philosophy with a capital P is Newman's name not for one discipline among others, resident in one academic department among others, but rather for that vision of the whole that is formed by liberal education. In this sense Philosophy encompasses all disciplines and all academic departments. The objection, then, is that Newman himself seems to acknowledge a profound and positive moral influence of such Philosophy on the liberally educated person. Did he perhaps misspeak when he said, as we heard above, that you can no more get moral virtue out of intellectual virtue, than you can tie up a ship in the harbor with a thread of silk?

In response Newman performs an impressive "discernment of spirits." It must be remembered that for Newman the truth about the moral life is nowhere so clearly revealed to us as in the experience of conscience. By conscience he means our sense of being subject to moral imperatives, and of living our moral life "under judgment." As a result, conscience for Newman has not only a deep moral but also a religious meaning, which is why Newman speaks of conscience as the "creative principle of religion."[16] In the promptings of conscience we discern the divine Other under whose judgment we choose and act. Now Newman thinks that the intellectual life as cultivated in liberal education does have a certain tendency to obscure the truth about conscience. He says,

> Conscience . . . inflicts upon us fear as well as shame; when the mind is simply angry with itself and nothing more, surely the true import of the voice of nature, and the depth of its intimations have been forgotten, and a false philosophy has misinterpreted emotions which ought to lead to God. Fear implies the transgression of a law, and a law implies a lawgiver and judge; but the tendency of intellectual culture is to swallow up the

---

15   *Idea*, 189–90.
16   *GA*, 110.

fear in the self-reproach, and self-reproach is directed and limited to our mere sense of what is fitting and becoming. Fear carries us out of ourselves, whereas shame may act upon us only within the round of our own thoughts. Such, I say, is . . . the ordinary sin of the Intellect; conscience tends to become what is called a moral sense; the command of duty is a sort of taste; sin is not an offence against God, but against human nature.[17]

We can draw out Newman's thought by saying that conscience tends to become *aestheticized* in the sensibilities of a liberally educated person. In such a person, he says, "a sense of propriety, order, consistency, and completeness gives birth to a rebellious stirring against miracle and mystery, against the severe and the terrible."[18] The unadulterated sense of conscience is for Newman full of the severe and the terrible; this is in fact the reason why it functions as the "creative principle of religion."[19] Conscience is blunted when our aesthetic sensibilities are too fastidious to endure impressions of the severe and the terrible. Newman finds a striking expression of this aestheticism in a famous line from Edmund Burke. In his *Reflections on the Revolution in France*, Burke offers a kind of valedictory to the spirit of chivalry, saying: "It is gone, that sensibility of principle, that chastity of honour, which felt a stain like a wound; which inspired courage, while it mitigated ferocity; which ennobled whatever it touched, and under which *vice lost half its evil by losing all its grossness.*"[20] Newman protests that Burke falls prey here to an aestheticist distortion of moral vice, since the grossness of which Burke speaks is an aesthetic category, not a moral category. This is why Newman insists that moral evil does not lose half of its evil, or any fraction of its evil, by losing all its grossness.

When then Newman acknowledges, as we heard, the "veracity, probity, equity, fairness, gentleness, benevolence, and amiableness" that grow in the mind of the liberally educated person, he is speaking of *moral qualities that are tainted by this aestheticism*. His praise of these virtues is spoken in an ironic tone of voice. He is speaking of an aestheticist substitute for real moral virtue, a substitute that comes natural to an intellectually cultivated person. Of course, liberally educated persons, no less than other persons, ought to possess these qualities as authentic moral virtues. But if they do, it will not be just because they are liberally educated, but because their conscience speaks with an imperative authority undiminished by aestheticism, and because, besides acquiring liberal education, they have also learned how to do battle with "those giants, the passion and the pride of man."

From this follows a consequence which leads us back to the misunderstanding that we warned against at the beginning. A university that prides itself on the liberal education that it offers must also offer more than liberal education. It must offer not only intellectual formation, but also moral and religious formation, this

---

17   *Idea*, 191.
18   *Idea*, 217.
19   *GA*, 110.
20   Quoted by Newman in *Idea*, 201.

latter being understood as an entirely distinct pedagogical project. And it must do so not only because moral and religious formation is supremely important, but also because this is the only way to protect liberal education against its own natural excesses.

Let us return to our point of departure: Newman's affirmation that intellectual culture does not by itself engender moral character. I said that for Newman intellectual culture no more engenders moral character than it produces things of practical utility. Let us conclude by hearing Newman unfold this thought:

> It is as real a mistake to burden it [liberal education] with virtue or religion as with the mechanical arts. Its direct business is not to steel the soul against temptation or to console it in affliction, any more than to set the loom in motion, or to direct the steam carriage . . . taken by and in itself, it as little mends our hearts as it improves our temporal circumstances. . . . Knowledge is one thing, virtue is another; good sense is not conscience, refinement is not humility, nor is largeness and justness of view faith. Philosophy, however enlightened, however profound, gives no command over the passions, no influential motives, no vivifying principles.

The passage ends with the sentence with which we began: "Quarry the granite rock with razors, or moor the vessel with a thread of silk; then may you hope with such keen and delicate instruments as human knowledge and human reason to contend against those giants, the passion and the pride of man."[21]

WISDOM AS THE UNITY OF INTELLECTUAL AND MORAL VIRTUE

But we are not finished. Once we have distinguished moral and intellectual virtue, we have to put them together. We want to see how they interpenetrate in the person who possesses both kinds of virtue. We want to understand why their interpenetration yields what Newman calls Wisdom.

---

21 Frank Turner articulates well the idea of Newman that liberal education aspires to intellectual but not moral formation. Problematic though some of his work on Newman is, he gets this idea of Newman right. He says: "Newman, unlike many persons in the late-twentieth century university, labored under no illusion that a liberal education can lead to either moral virtue or religious faith. Paradoxically, Newman's faith that human sinfulness requires supernatural redemption limited the moral aspirations of his university. In his view the liberal education addressed only the natural human being in a natural civic setting. The liberal education could not address the issues relating to human redemption. . . . For Newman, the liberal education led to 'intellectual excellence,' but that excellence was not to be confused with moral transformation. It was the Roman Catholic *Church* not the Roman Catholic *University* that opened the path to divine truth and human redemption." Frank M. Turner, "Newman's University and Ours," in his edition of *The Idea of a University* (New Haven: Yale University Press, 1996), 288–89.

In his great sermon, "Wisdom, as Contrasted with Faith and with Bigotry," Newman contrasts Wisdom and faith like this: they "are distinct, or even opposite gifts. Wisdom belongs to the perfect, and more especially to preachers of the Gospel; and Faith is the elementary grace which is required of all, especially of hearers."[22] "Wisdom is the last gift of the Spirit, and Faith the first."[23]

> Faith . . . acts promptly and boldly on the occasion, on slender evidence, as if guessing and reaching forward to the truth, amid darkness or confusion; but such is not the Wisdom of the perfect. Wisdom is the clear, calm, accurate vision, and comprehension of the whole course, the whole work of God . . . though there is none who has it in its fulness but He who "searcheth all things."[24]

We can discern in these words something of that vision of the whole that is cultivated by the person of intellectual virtue. Newman in fact says that "Christian Wisdom, as a habit or faculty of mind distinct from Faith, [is] the mature fruit of Reason, and nearly answering to what is meant by Philosophy."[25] Newman proceeds to give an account of Wisdom that almost coincides with his account of the comprehensiveness of mind proper to a liberally educated person.[26] The coinciding is such that Newman was able to incorporate a number of pages from this sermon into Discourse 6 of *The Idea of a University.*

Perhaps we can enlarge on Newman's understanding of Wisdom by saying that its specific opposite is heresy. In this sermon Newman says that the specific opposite is "bigotry," but I suggest that the concept of heresy brings greater precision to what Newman means. For a heresy is often said to be some truth that is pulled out of its place in the system of revealed truth and is given a primacy that it does not really have. It is a truth to which other truths are sacrificed. For instance, it is true that the conjugal act has a unitive meaning and also a procreative meaning. Affirming one or the other of these truths is not heresy; but when one gets affirmed at the expense of the other, whether the unitive at the expense of the procreative, or the procreative at the expense of the unitive, then it is that our affirmation of them becomes heretical. It takes a special comprehensiveness of mind and heart to know how to receive these truths without letting one or the other of them disrupt the delicate balance at the center of the Christian vision of human sexuality. It takes a certain anointing of Wisdom.[27]

---

22 *US*, 279.

23 *US*, 294.

24 *US*, 292–93.

25 *US*, 281. Note that the word Philosophy is capitalized in the quote. Newman is using the word in exactly that special sense explained above, that sense in which he will use it in *The Idea of a University* (this sermon is from 1841, and the Discourses of the *Idea* from 1852).

26 For mention of Aristotle's notion of practical wisdom and the Holy Spirit's gift of wisdom in Newman's thought, see ch. 16 of this volume by M. Dauphinais (editor's note).

27 I have long wondered why the Wisdom of which Newman speaks in this sermon

See what follows for our understanding of intellectual virtue in Newman's sense: this virtue is not only something worth having because it perfects our intellectual nature, it is also worth having because it provides the foundation for the high Christian grace of Wisdom. For without intellectual virtue there can be no Christian Wisdom. Wisdom is what results when a person of serious Christian faith cultivates the intellectual virtues and learns to "communicate the image of the whole to every separate portion" of knowledge.

Let us turn from the teaching of Newman on Wisdom to his own personal Wisdom. Some of his characterizations of Philosophy can serve as exact descriptions of his Wisdom, as when he says:

> But the intellect, which has been disciplined to the perfection of its powers, which knows, and thinks while it knows, which has learned to leaven the dense mass of facts and events with the elastic force of reason, such an intellect cannot be partial, cannot be exclusive, cannot be impetuous, cannot be at a loss, cannot but be patient, collected, and majestically calm, because it discerns the end in every beginning, the origin in every end, the law in every interruption, the limit in each delay; because it ever knows where it stands, and how its path lies from one point to another.[28]

In writing this Newman did not mean to speak about himself, but what he writes succeeds in capturing perfectly his own comprehensiveness of mind and his own Wisdom.

Here is a particular teaching of Newman that has the stamp of his Wisdom. In his *Essay on the Development of Christian Doctrine,* he says in one place, "But one aspect of revelation must not be allowed to exclude or obscure another; and Christianity is dogmatical, devotional, practical all at once; it is esoteric and exoteric; it is indulgent and strict; it is light and dark; it is love, and it is fear."[29] Minds deficient in intellectual virtue play off love against fear, and dogma against devotion, and indulgence against strictness; but Newman possesses the Wisdom that lets him find a place for all of these apparent opposites, and that lets him

---

is not taken up by him in *The Idea of a University.* He borrows so heavily from this sermon in writing Discourse 6: why not borrow also the theme of Wisdom? The reason, I have come to think, is that Wisdom, much as it builds upon Philosophy and intellectual virtue, goes beyond these and involves for Newman a certain anointing. It is a supernatural virtue and for this reason exceeds the scope of *The Idea of a University*, which limits itself to natural virtue.

28 *Idea*, 138. By the way, when we read these words of Newman about the "imperial intellect" that is formed by liberal education, it is difficult to understand why he says that liberal education aims at forming the gentleman (see *Idea*, end of discourse 8). For the imperial intellect seems to be something vastly more than the social polish that distinguishes the gentleman.

29 *Dev.*, 16.

show how they interpenetrate. Newman is a master of keeping disparate truths from getting in each other's way, of showing forth their *coincidentia oppositorum*. In his Wisdom, in his freedom from all heretical one-sidedness, we discern the comprehensiveness of his mind and the depth of his own intellectual virtue.

Suppose that Newman had been a simple priest of deep faith and of great moral integrity, but that he lacked the intellectual virtue that comes from liberal education. He might still be a saint, but of a very different cut from the Newman we know. He would be a saint like the Curé of Ars, but he would lack that which makes him a real doctor of the Church. What Newman had, and the Curé of Ars did not have, is great intellectual stature; he possessed to an eminent degree the intellectual virtue that he describes in *The Idea of a University*. Newman represents a pattern of holiness that builds on intellectual virtue. It follows that, though holiness is of course not to be reduced to the intellectual virtue wrought by liberal education, there is a kind of Christian Wisdom that cannot exist without this intellectual virtue.[30]

CONCLUSION

We could say, then, that Newman takes care not to claim too much for liberal education. He seeks from it only intellectual formation, not moral formation. And yet this "only" does not imply any disparagement of liberal education. He thinks that the intellectual virtue formed by liberal education, that is, the excellence of the imperial intellect, has a splendor all its own and is worth cultivating for its own sake. He thinks that intellectual virtue contributes something to the full flourishing of a person that is not contributed by moral virtue alone. In addition, he thinks, and shows by example, that intellectual virtue, if incorporated into a person's higher loves and commitments of faith, gives rise to a certain magisterial Wisdom. We saw at the beginning that Newman deplores the fact that individuals often have intellectual virtue at the expense of moral virtue, or moral virtue at the expense of intellectual; now we see at the end that he would restore this lost unity by cultivating Wisdom.

Suggested Reading

Newman, John Henry. *The Idea of a University* (1852), especially the nine discourses and the essay, "Discipline of Mind."

———. "Intellect, the Instrument of Religious Training." In *Sermons Preached on Various Occasions* (1857).

———. "Wisdom as Contrasted with Faith and with Bigotry." In *Oxford University Sermons* (1871).

---

30 Note that this Wisdom is not vulnerable to the aestheticism of which we spoke above. For Wisdom comprises not only intellectual virtue, but also moral and religious virtue, and this latter, as we saw, provides the antidote to aestheticism.

CHAPTER 15

THE POETRY OF JOHN HENRY NEWMAN: INTIMATIONS OF THE INVISIBLE WORLD

Barbara H. Wyman

S t. John Henry Newman was a man of letters.[1] His proficiency with the written word and his breadth of knowledge ranged across many areas, including that of poetry. Understanding Newman as poet illuminates all that he wrote; to put it another way, studying Newman's poetry brings a deeper appreciation of Newman's other work. Poetry mattered to Newman. That he consistently turned to poetry bears witness to the fact that he trusted poetry to say and do things that prose alone could not. This is an essential concept to grasp when studying any poetry but most especially religious poetry. After his conversion to Catholicism in 1845, Newman published poems written throughout his lifetime in a single volume called *Verses on Various Occasions*. The majority of the poems in the volume were written before his conversion, including the famous "The Pillar of the Cloud" written in 1833. Newman is most widely known by the general public as a poet because of this poem, commonly

---

1 For an overview of the breadth of Newman's expertise, see Mary Katherine Tillman, *John Henry Newman: Man of Letters,* Marquette Studies in Philosophy 86 (Milwaukee: Marquette University Press, 2015).

known by its first line, "Lead, Kindly Light," also sung as a hymn. It is not necessary to pass judgment on Newman's standing as a poet in order to realize that there is great merit in studying his poetry because it opens for us Newman's way of thinking.

There are many ways to approach Newman's verse. One can look to his verse to gain insight into the man Newman since there is a "thread of autobiography" running throughout his poetry which "reveals very specifically not only the changing moods and varying aspects of the author's mind but also its stable, cardinal principles."[2] He used poetry to share deep personal experience, turning to poetry at significant times of his life, especially during times of crisis.[3] Or one can study his poetry to learn his views of doctrine and theology, since along with the other Tractarians, he chose poetry for this purpose.[4] Newman's poetry presents his understanding of the Bible and biblical interpretation; many poems correspond to his sermons.[5] But there is an underlying intent and purpose in all of his poetry. He clearly stated this in 1839 when explaining the origins of the Oxford Movement: "Poetry then is our mysticism; and so far as any two characters of mind tend to penetrate below the surface of things, and to draw men away from the material *to the invisible world*, so far they may certainly be said to answer the same end; and that too a religious one."[6] Newman's profound awareness of the invisible world is formulated in what is known as the sacramental principle. This doctrine—that created things can be signs of God's presence and instruments of things unseen—is explained in his sermon, "The Invisible World,"[7] and later in the *Apologia Pro Vita Sua.*[8] Throughout his life, he repeatedly referred to God's harmonious ordering of both the seen and unseen world; poetry could "penetrate below the surface of thing" and "stimulate . . . a mode of thinking" leading others to God.[9] It was not the

---

2 Catherine A. Burns, "A Study of the Poetry of John Henry Newman" (PhD diss., University of Iowa, 1922), 1. Available at ir.uiowa.edu/etc/4283.

3 G. B. Tennyson, *Victorian Devotional Poetry: The Tractarian Mode* (Cambridge, Mass: Harvard University Press), 119.

4 Tennyson, *Victorian Devotional Poetry: The Tractarian Mode*, 49. I am indebted to Michael Pakaluk who has found that in Newman's *Philosophical Notebook* his poetry is important for his philosophy (see *PN* ii, 10). For example, at one point Newman puts forward the thesis that all of the perfections of a thing must, by the nature of the case, flow from a single point of unity within that thing. He suggests that one can argue that this is true of God, on the basis of an argument from analogy, which observes that the same is true in any creature which has perfections: the perfections are aspects of a unity in that creature. Newman wrote in the 1860s that he has been mulling over this thesis for many years and had expressed it in two poems, "The Watchman" and "The Course of Truth." *VO*, 80–82, 96–97.

5 Burns, "A Study in the Poetry of John Henry Newman," 28–44.

6 *EH* i, 291.

7 *PS* iv, no. 13: 200–13.

8 See *Apo.*, 49–50.

9 *EH* i, 291.

poet's will, but the will of God working through the poet.[10] Poetry, therefore, could give intimations of the invisible world by participating in the ongoing harmony of the divinely ordered universe.

THE MUSIC OF POETRY

The poetic impulse came naturally to Newman; he wrote verses as a young boy,[11] and he continued writing poetry throughout his life. He wrote and rewrote many of his poems, tinkering with the word choice and with the meter.[12] Newman also began studying violin as a youth.[13] He was a gifted musician, and he would eventually compose music.[14] Music, then, formed his ear from an early age; it was an integral part of Newman's sense of sound. Following the tradition of the ages,[15] he would have considered poetry like unto music, as did many in the Victorian period.[16] It was this musical quality of poetry that caused Newman, along with the other Tractarians, to realize that poetry was the best method for their cause of "recalling" and "recommending" important Christian doctrine.[17] Not surprisingly, the title given by the Tractarians to their collected poems, *Lyra Apostolica,* directly links the poems to the musical instrument of the poets of antiquity.[18] The relationship between poetry and religion for the Tractarians, beginning with Keble, was fundamental. "It is to the awakening of some moral or religious feeling, not by direct instruction (that is the office of morality or theology) but by way of association, that we would refer all poetical pleasure."[19] Poetry is pleasurable because it delights, but in so doing, it instructs, as Sir Philip Sidney in the sixteenth century famously wrote.[20] Devotional poetry instructs

---

10   For a study of Victorian poets' use of rhythm and form to explore agency and human will, see Matthew Campbell, *Rhythm and Will in Victorian Poetry* (Cambridge: Cambridge University Press, 1999), 15–63. See also Kirstie Blair, *Form and Faith in Victorian Poetry and Religion* (Oxford: Oxford University Press, 2012), 39.

11   Maisie Ward, *Young Mr. Newman* (New York: Sheed and Ward, 1948), 7.

12   Burns, "A Study in the Poetry of John Henry Newman," 45–87.

13   Ward, *Young Mr. Newman*, 5.

14   Edward Bellasis, *Cardinal Newman as a Musician* (London: Kegan Paul, Trench, Trübner, and Co., 1892). Online at www.gutenberg.org/files/26427/26427-h/26427-h.htm quoted by Susan Treacy, *Adoremus Bulletin* https://adoremus.org/author/Susan-Treacy/ November 2009.

15   Joseph Phelan, *The Music of Verse: Metrical Experimentation in Nineteenth-Century Poetry* (New York: Palgrave Macmillan, 2012). See also John Hollander, "The Music of Poetry," *The Journal of Aesthetics and Art Criticism* 15, no. 2 (Dec. 1956): 232–44.

16   John Keble taught that "music was the 'twin sister' to poetry because it 'draws out the secrets of the soul' through harmony and sequence." See Tennyson, *Victorian Devotional Poetry: The Tractarian Mode*, 64.

17   Tennyson, *Victorian Devotional Poetry: The Tractarian Mode*, 121.

18   Tennyson, *Victorian Devotional Poetry: The Tractarian Mode*, 122–23.

19   Tennyson, *Victorian Devotional Poetry: The Tractarian Mode*, 25.

20   Sir Philip Sidney, "An Apology for Poetry," in *Poets on Poetry*, ed. Charles Norman

by lifting the mind and heart to contemplation of divine truths, expressing a yearning for God, and leading others to do the same.[21] For Newman, poetry was more than just the craft of the poet; poetry, like music, could be "outpourings of *eternal harmony* in the medium of *created sound*."[22] That is, the audible aspect of earthly poetry, created sound, allowed it to participate in the inaudible harmony of the unseen world.

More than just words are necessary for poetry's aural effect; the words must be ordered in such a way that the rhythm, that is, the meter or beat within the line, accompanying word choice, accomplishes the effect. It is the ordered aspect of poetry which mimics the eternal harmony. This is the technical and practical side of composing poetry. Newman was an accomplished technical poet and made clever use of meter and rhyme. That he considered poetry and music as a path to the divine is evident in one of his discour*ses in The Idea of a University*:

> Education, is, it seems, not to impart any knowledge whatever, but to satisfy *anyhow desires after the Unseen* which will arise in our minds in spite of ourselves, to provide the mind with a means of self-command, to impress on it the beautiful ideas which saints and sages have struck out, *to embellish it with the bright hues of a celestial piety, to teach it the poetry of devotion, the music of well-ordered affections, and the luxury of doing* good.[23]

MUSIC OF WELL-ORDERED AFFECTIONS, A SYMBOL OF THE UNSEEN

This musical quality of poetry, the power of rhythm and meter (along with words) to move the listener "to do good,"[24] eliciting "desires after the unseen," is evident in Newman's verses from an early period onwards, including those which he contributed to the *Lyra Apostolica* (1836). The *Lyra* was a collection of 179 poems and hymns, previously printed in the *British Magazine*, to counter liberal forces arguing for the spiritual and ecclesial reform of the Anglican Church. Of

---

(New York: The Free Press, 1962), 28. Sidney based this axiom on Horace's statement in the *Ars Poetica*, "He who joins the instructive with the agreeable, carries off every vote, by delighting and at the same time admonishing the reader." *Ars Poetica* online https://www. poetryfoundation.org/articles/69381/ars-poetica. For a scientific examination of Sidney's axiom, see Ernst Pöppel and Frederick Turner, "The Neural Lyre: Poetic Meter, the Brain, and Time," *Poetry* 142, no. 5 (1983): 277–309.

21 See Michael D. Hurley, *Faith in Poetry: Verse Style as a Mode of Religious Belief* (New York: Bloomsbury Academic, 2018), 68–70.

22 *US*, no. 15: 347.

23 Discourse 2. "Theology a Branch of Knowledge," *Idea*, 19–42. Emphasis added.

24 For a short and concise history of this idea that poetry moves the listener to "do good" see: S. K Heninger, "Sidney and Boethian Music," *Studies in English Literature, 1500–1900* 23, no. 1 (1983): 43.

the poems, 109 were Newman's. His poetry written during the Oxford Movement is often complex, not only in language and meter, but also in the stanzaic form. This poetry was written for a different purpose than his later poetry; many of the *Lyra* poems are overtly polemical.[25] As an Oratorian years later, Newman would use his excellent technical skills for writing hymns. Before examining a few examples of Newman's metrical technique and the musicality of his verse, a short definition of the nature of meter is helpful. According to Paul Fussel in *Poetic Meter and Poetic Form*,

> Meter is what results when the natural rhythmical movements of colloquial speech are heightened, organized, and regulated so that pattern—which means repetition—emerges from the relative phoenetic haphazard of ordinary utterance. Because it inhabits the physical form of the words themselves, meter is the most fundamental technique of order available to the poet. The other poetic techniques of order—rhyme, line division, stanzaic form, and over-all structure—are all projections and magnifications of the kind of formalizing repetition which meter embodies. They are meter writ large. Everyone knows that poetic meter, even when unskillfully managed, tends to *produce a pleasant effect*, but metrical theorists disagree vigorously about the reason for the universal popularity of metered compositions.[26]

It is this "pleasant effect" of metered verse which unites it with music. In the *University Sermon* partially quoted above, Newman spoke of "Music a Symbol of the Unseen":

> Let us take another instance, of an outward and earthly form, or economy, under which great wonders unknown seem to be typified; I mean *musical sounds*, as they are exhibited most perfectly in instrumental *harmony* . . . [yet] is it possible that that inexhaustible evolution and disposition of notes, so rich yet so simple, so intricate yet so regulated, so various yet so majestic, should be a mere sound, which is gone and perishes? Can it be that those mysterious stirrings of heart, and keen emotions, and strange yearnings after we know not what, and awful impressions from we know not whence, should be wrought in us by what is unsubstantial, and comes and goes, and begins and ends in itself? It is not so; it cannot be. No; *they have escaped from some higher sphere; they are the outpourings of eternal harmony in the medium of created sound.* . . ."[27]

---

25   Juan R. Vélez, "Newman's Mediterranean 'Verses': Poetry at the Service of Doctrinal Teaching and Religious Renewal," *Newman Studies Journal* 3, no. 2 (2006): 80–81.

26   Paul Fussel, *Poetic Meter and Form* (New York: Random House, 1965), 5.

27   *US*, no. 15: 346–47. Emphasis added. See also Guy Nicholls, *Unearthly Beauty, The Aesthetic of St. John Henry Newman* (Leominster: Gracewing, 2019), 168–74.

The pleasant effect of the "musical sounds" brings "stirrings of heart" since these sounds are not only heard for a moment and then they perish; instead, since the musical sounds participate in the eternal, universal harmony, they are imperishable sounds echoing the divine music.

UNIVERSAL HARMONY

In this sermon, Newman is making reference to what is commonly known as "the music of the spheres" taken from the theory of Universal Harmony, a pervasive concept throughout philosophy and literature for two millennia. His claim that the power of sound and eternal harmony come from a "higher sphere" which illuminate "great wonders unknown" (the invisible world) flows from Newman's classical education. The *quadrivium* was used at both Cambridge and Oxford throughout the Renaissance, up to the nineteenth century. Boethius coined the term *quadrivium* of which "music" was a part.[28] This "music" was not in the form of instruments or song but that of number and proportions. The Pythagorean theory of Universal Harmony, Christianized by St. Augustine and Boethius, posited that the world was created in numerical harmony which was a reflection of the mind of the Creator. God was the generator of these numbers, and these numbers were manifested in the physical universe. Harmony in music reflected the harmony of the universe; understanding this numerical universe would lead a person to contemplate the divine ordering, inspiring the contemplation of God. The cosmos with its patterns of order at all levels of existence was also manifested in human nature—and proof of a creator. Music, then, according to Boethius and those who influenced him, could be understood by numbers. World music (music of the spheres) was related to music of instruments—and also *musica humana*; human nature itself was "part" of the cosmic harmony. When persons contemplate the order of the universe, they reach greater inner harmony. According to this ancient tradition of philosophy, the best way to hear the music of the spheres is to understand the harmony of one's own soul.[29] By this reasoning, instrumental or vocal music which imitates universal music raises and also heals the human soul whereas discordant music is harmful to the soul. Music, therefore, was considered a *universal* force (*musica universalis*). So there is a correspondence, according to Boethius, between the sounds given off by the strings of an instrument and the music of the spheres.[30] Music in the form of poetry had the power to heal, which explains Lady Philosophy's use of poetry

---

28   S. K. Heninger, Jr. *Touches of Sweet Harmony: Pythagorean Cosmology and Renaissance Poetics* (San Marino, Calif.: The Huntington Library, 1974), 53.

29   Throughout the Renaissance and forward, "That the universe reflects the number, weight, and measure of the divine scheme became the commonest of commonplaces." Heninger, "Sidney and Boethian Music," 43.

30   Heninger, *Touches of Sweet Harmony*, 91, 101–3.

to heal the prisoner in the *Consolation of Philosophy*.[31] The healing power of poetry was espoused by the Tractarian poets as well, and it was expressed as such in Keble's lectures: "Poetry, of whatever kind, is, in one way or another, closely associated with measure and a definite rhythm of sound . . . [which contributes to its] wonderful efficacy in soothing men's emotions and steadying the balance of their minds."[32]

This understanding of Universal Harmony was also accepted in the fields of science. Johannes Kepler, who devised the *Laws of Planetary Motion* (1609), believed this theory to be true. In his magnificent *Harmonices Mundi (Harmonies of the World)* he even composed musical scales for the planets, ascribing different tones to the different planets according to their orbits. Kepler (and Pythagoras many centuries earlier) believed human ears once could hear the music of the spheres, but humans have become so used to this sound that other earthly noises drown it out.[33] This concept of universal harmony fascinated Newman throughout his life, beginning as a schoolboy. At the age of sixteen, he wrote "On Music—A Fragment"[34]

> *Lo! by the word of power, the word supreme*
> *With heavenly lustre young creation beam*
> *Night flies appalled before the sov'reign voice,*
> *And new-formed orbs to run their course rejoice. . . .*
>
> *Did this alone the heav'nly chorus move*
> *To praise their great Creator and to love?*
> *O say, did nought arrest their ravished ears?*
> *Was there not heard the Music of the spheres?*
> *And angels joined the strain and heaven with Music rang.*
> *Thus good on good by Heav'n's high King bestowed. . . .*
>
> *God sent his sweetest gift, sent Music down.*
> *Soul of the world!—for thy harmonious force*
> *Retrains all nature in its proper course. . . .*

---

31 See Barbara H. Wyman, "Boethian Influence and Imagery in the Poetry of George Herbert," *Studies in Philology* 97, no. 1 (2000): 83.

32 Blair, *Form and Faith in Victorian Poetry and Religion*, 38. Keble also wrote: "the art naturally most fitted for this office (of healing and instructing) and therefore claiming it as her prerogative, is specially and peculiarly called Poetry; finally, that it is so fitted for this purpose, because it makes use of *rhythmical language.*" *Lectures on Poetry* i, 4:41.

33 Proust, Dominique. "The Harmony of the Spheres from Pythagoras to Voyager." *Proceedings of the International Astronomical Union* 5, no. S260 (2009): 362.

34 Diary entry for June 24, 1817, *LD* i, 23.

In this fragment the young Newman shows his familiarity with the notion from the *quadrivium* that God's gift was *music*, the harmonious order by which God set creation into being, placing the "orbs" or spheres into their courses; these orbs rejoice as they move in orderly pattern—literally the music of the spheres. Newman wonders, "Was [this music] not heard?" God sent the music with which he had ordered the heavens down to earth and this music by its harmonious force, "retrains all nature in its proper course."[35] That is, the divine rhythm and measure of this music has the ability to "retrain" creation, including humans, in effect "tuning" creation so as to bring all into this heavenly harmony. More than twenty years later Newman wrote, "One alone can be all things to us; One alone can supply our needs; One alone can train us up to our full perfection; One alone can give a meaning to our complex and intricate nature; *One alone can give us tune and harmony*."[36] And though the above fragment was not included in his *Verses on Various Occasions*, by the following year, the seventeen year-old Newman set the same thought down in the poem, "Solitude" (1818), which repeats many of the same elements found in the earlier fragment:

> *THERE is in stillness oft a magic power*
> *To calm the breast, when struggling passions lower;*
> *Touch'd by its influence, in the soul arise*
> *Diviner feelings, kindred with the skies. . . .*
>
> *No mortal measure swells that mystic sound,*
> *No mortal minstrel breathes such tones around,—*
> *The Angels' hymn,—the sovereign harmony*
> *That guides the rolling orbs along the sky,—*
> *And hence perchance the tales of saints who view'd*
> *And heard Angelic choirs in solitude.*
> *By most unheard,—because the earthly din*
> *Of toil or mirth has charms their ears to win.*
> *Alas for man! he knows not of the bliss,*
> *The heaven that brightens such a life as this.*

Newman refers explicitly to the "harmony" which guides the orbs (music of the spheres); and harkens back to Kepler—that this divine music could be heard by human ears if those ears weren't filled by "earthly din."[37] Poetry, like music,

---

35 For John Milton, "it is the Boethian *musica mundana*, the informing principle of the entire cosmos, keeping 'unsteady Nature to her law.'" Quoted by Rodney Stenning Edgecombe, "Melophrasis: Defining a Distinctive Genre of Literature/Music Dialogue," *Mosaic: A Journal for the Interdisciplinary Study of Literature* 26, no. 4 (1993): 4.

36 "The Thought of God, the Stay of the Soul," *PS* v, no. 22: 313–26.

37 John Keble believed that the religious poet had a role in retraining the listeners' ears by approximating the heavenly harmony in his poetry, helping "dull ears . . . scan

could influence a soul, bringing "diviner feelings" initiating desire for the unseen, "kindred with the skies"—by the rhythm of the measured and counted line. This rhythm is not arbitrary—"no mortal measure"—but rather, it is tied to divine ordering. When music moves us—often through a combination of the words and the rhythm—likewise for poetry. It is this ability of poetry or verse to instruct in a unique way, by means of pleasurable sound, which was cleverly put by George Herbert in the seventeenth century: "Hearken unto a Verser, who may chance/ Rhyme thee to good, and make a bait of pleasure:/ A verse may find him who a sermon flies/ And turn delight into a sacrifice."[38]

UNION OF MUSIC, POETRY,
AND INTERNAL AND EXTERNAL HARMONY

In another of his early poems, "Introduction: To an Album"[39] (1827), Newman particularly spells out the union of music and poetry, internal and external harmony. It exemplifies his understanding of God's ordering of the universe.

> I AM a harp of many chords, and each
> Strung by a separate hand;—most musical
> My notes, discoursing with the mental sense,
> Not the outward ear. Try them, they will reply
> With wisdom, fancy, graceful gaiety,
> Or ready wit, or happy sentiment.
> Come, add a string to my assort of sounds;
> Widen the compass of my harmony;
> And join thyself in fellowship of name
> With those, whose courteous labour and fair gifts
> Have given me voice, and made me what I am.

That Newman called himself "a harp of many chords" refers to God creating mankind with a musical numbering, that is, "my harmony," "discoursing" with inaudible sound, or the "mental sense," participating therefore in God's eternal, universal harmony. His use of harp or lyre is significant as well. The etymology of the word "lyric" shows the affinity of poetry and music, since the recitation of poetry from ancient times was often accompanied with the playing of the lyre, as noted earlier. However, by calling himself a harp or lyre, Newman implies that he is the instrument of God, who is the poet/musician. Therefore, Newman, the harp, is an instrument who will share his gifts (music) when his notes are "tried."

---

aright" and "outring Earth's drowsy chime." See Blair, *Form and Faith in Victorian Poetry and Religion*, 44.

38 George Herbert, "The Church Porch," in *The English Poems of George Herbert*, ed. C. A. Patrides (Totowa, N.J.: Rowman and Littlefield), 197.

39 *VO*, 20.

Equating the body with the lyre was a familiar image in poetry, most typically in love poetry.[40] Newman, as expected, Christianizes the symbol making God the musician. This, too, helps explain the choice of *Lyra Apostolica* for the title of the Tractarian poems.

By the advent of nineteenth century, enlightenment thought had stripped a lot of the "heavenly" meaning from poetry.[41] Nevertheless, the music of the spheres remained a familiar trope in poetry[42] and in hymns.[43] Newman and Keble[44] retained this earlier notion of the harmonious universe ordered by God, the visible world as a sign of the invisible, with music and poetry playing an integral role in the realm of created sound which elevated the soul to the divine.

In Discourse 4 of the *Idea of a University*, Newman expounds on this concept of universal harmony, specifying the cause and exemplar of such beauty, order and perfection:

> *Music*, I suppose . . . has an object of its own . . . *it is the expression of ideas greater and more profound than any in the visible world*, ideas, which center indeed in Him whom Catholicism manifests, who is the seat of all beauty, order, and perfection whatever, still ideas, after all, which are not those on which Revelation directly and principally fixes our gaze.[45]

And then in Discourse 6, he explicitly mentions "the music of the spheres" to explain the object of the intellect: the being and essence of things, and their heavenly source. In his own words:

> That perfection of the Intellect, which is the result of Education, and its beau ideal, to be imparted to individuals in their respective measures, is the clear, calm, accurate vision and *comprehension of all things*, as far as the finite mind can embrace them, each in its place, and with its own characteristics upon it . . . *it has almost the beauty and harmony of heavenly contemplation, so intimate is it with the eternal order of things and the music of the spheres.*[46]

---

40 For a treatment of poet as a stringed instrument, see John Hollander, *The Untuning of the Sky: Ideas of Music in English Poetry 1500-1700* (Princeton, N.J.: Princeton University Press 1961), 34–35, 43–45, and 269.

41 See Hollander, *The Untuning of the Sky*, 332–422.

42 Several nineteenth century poets repurposed the notion of the music of the spheres: see Edgecombe, "Melophrasis: Defining a Distinctive Genre of Literature/Music Dialogue," 9–19.

43 See "This is My Father's World" written by Maltbie Davenport Babcock in the nineteenth century and published in 1901, and "Eternal Ruler of the Ceaseless Round" by John W. Chadwick in 1864.

44 See Blair, *Form and Faith in Victorian Poetry and Religion*, 43–44.

45 Discourse 4. "Bearing of Other Branches of Knowledge on Theology," *Idea*, 80.

46 Discourse 6. "Knowledge Viewed in Relation to Learning," *Idea*, 139.

In these two passages Newman explains how comprehending the idea of the "eternal order of things" is the goal of true education, and how music expresses the eternal order inscribed into the music of the spheres in the visible world. Later, in 1877, when a new organ was being installed in the Birmingham Oratory, he reiterated the same idea, speaking to the fathers and brothers in the community on the efficacy of music. *The Tablet* (August 25, 1877) reported that Newman:

> preached a most beautiful discourse, upon the event of the day; and on music, first as a great natural gift, then as an instrument in the hands of the Church; its special prominence in the history of Saint Philip and the Oratory; the part played by music in the history of God's dealings with man from first to last, from the thunders of Mount Sinai to the trumpets of the Judgment; *the mysterious and intimate connection with the unseen world established by music*, as it were the unknown language of another state. Its quasi-sacramental efficacy, e.g., in driving away the evil spirit in Saul and in bringing upon Eliseus the spirit of prophecy; the grand pre- eminence of the organ in that it gave the nearest representation of the voice of God, while the sound of strings might be taken as more fitted to express the varying emotions of man's state here on earth.[47]

Besides recognizing this eternal order: "mysterious and intimate connection with the unseen world," Newman affirms its sacrament-like character, asserting that in it man can perceive "the voice of God."

And as would be expected, Newman's use of harmony extended to the Holy Family as well, this visible trinity a "shadow" of the Heavenly Trinity: "When, for our sakes, the Son came on earth and took our flesh, yet He would not live without the sympathy of others. For thirty years He lived with Mary and Joseph and thus formed a shadow of the Heavenly Trinity on earth. O the perfection of that sympathy which existed between the three! . . . It was like *three instruments absolutely in tune* which all vibrate when one vibrates, and vibrate either one and the same note, or in perfect *harmony*."[48]

UNTUNING THE MUSIC OF THE SPHERES

But just as the eternal harmony is laid out by God, so too can He break this harmony, if He so chooses, and for His own purposes. The opposite of this eternal harmony or tuning of the sky is their "untuning." In one of the *Discourses to Mixed Congregations*, "The Infinitude of the Divine Attributes," Newman echoes St. Paul's *Letter to the Romans* (chapter 1 and 8) writing of sceptics who deny Christ's miracles and the Creator's work:

---

47   Quoted in Bellasis, *Newman as Musician*, 24.
48   "Our Lord Refuses Sympathy," *MD*, 310.

They have denied the miracles of apostles and prophets, on the ground of their marring and spoiling what is so perfect and *harmonious*, as if the visible world were some work of human art . . . But He, the Eternal Maker of time and space . . . as if to pour contempt upon the . . . speculations of His ignorant creatures about His works and His will, in order to a fuller and richer harmony, and a higher and nobler order, *confuses the laws of this physical universe and untunes the music of the spheres*. Nay, He has done more . . . out of the infinitude of His greatness, He has defaced His own glory, and wounded and deformed His own beauty—not indeed as it is in itself, for He is ever the same, transcendently perfect and unchangeable, but in the contemplation of His creatures,—by the unutterable condescension of His incarnation.[49]

This tragic marring of creation must, however, be seen in light of the Incarnation and the promise of redemption in Christ, a new heaven and a new earth. For the classical educated Oxford scholar, poetry and music give man a glimpse of these mysteries.

Newman's understanding of music and harmony and ordering explains his use of numbered meter, not only in his early poetry for the *Lyra*, but also his later verses written as hymns for the oratory.

NEWMAN'S TECHNIQUE: MUSICAL PROSODY

The musicality of poetry comes from metrical adjustments within a set pattern of meter. Newman's poetry is typically composed in lines of varying length containing regular iambic feet, the iamb being two syllables, the first unstressed, the second stressed (^ /), as in the word re-**joice**. This gives his poetry a steady rhythm; it is this regulated pattern that makes metered verse pleasurable. The sort of musical technique employed by Newman (and others) is accomplished by substitution of metrical feet within a regular metrical line.[50] The regular metrical line creates the consistent beat, which is not necessarily apprehended by the reader or listener. This is like the beat in music. Once this regular metrical pattern is established, it becomes a sort of sound contract with the listener. When this musical agreement is mentally recognized, a substitution of metrical feet causes the effect of pausing the beat, thereby emphasizing the words or phrases which have been substituted. The poet often chooses the words used for the metrical substitution so that the consonance or affinity between the sound of

---

49 *Mix.*, no. 15: 315.

50 Blair notes, "through the drama of metrical adjustments . . . [Tractarian poets'] ideological work tends to go unnoticed by the reader, who reacts consciously and unconsciously to the steady underlying beat." Blair, *Form and Faith in Victorian Poetry and Religion*, 42.

word and the meaning of the word are echoed.[51] Thus, the regular meter establishes harmony and order, the recurring rhythm giving regulated expression to the words of the poem, and the metrical substitutions effectively though subliminally moves the reader.[52] In addition, Keble, who heavily influenced Newman who was some years his junior, believed that it was meter and form that help to contain emotion and religious fervor effectively. Keble states, "Let us therefore deem the glorious art of Poetry a kind of *medicine divinely bestowed* upon man: which gives healing relief to secret mental emotion, yet without detriment to modest reserve: and, while giving scope to enthusiasm, yet rules it with order and due control."[53] This reserve became an essential element in Newman's understanding of religious emotion in worship.

Newman's poem, "The Sign of the Cross" (1832) illustrates both his technique and belief in the unseen world. In a mere 76 words, Newman demonstrates the nature of poetry which can say and do so much in a few lines, influencing by both the word and the sound. The first stanza has regular iambic feet (^ /). However, in the third line, his substitution with a trochee (/ ^) and a spondee (/ /),[54] serve to emphasize the words being spoken, literally "stirring" the line, breaking the sound contract of the expected iambs. Newman's use of metrical adjustments is shown again, in the fifth line with another spondee (/ /) which "springs up" emphasizing these words. When stressed syllables are used with the iambic pattern set, they are like strong beats in a song. The poem begins thus:

> Whene'er across this sinful flesh of mine
> I draw the Holy Sign,
> **All** *good* **thoughts stir** *within me, and renew*
> *Their slumbering strength divine;*
> *Till there* **springs up** *a courage high and true*
> *To suffer and to do.*

Newman writes that after the "Holy Sign" is traced over the "sinful" body, this powerful sacramental causes the "slumbering" strength—that of the Holy Spirit's inspiration—to "*spring up*" within the soul, "*all* good *thoughts*," (emphasized

---

51 For an enlightening discussion on this theory see Richard Terry, "'The Sound Must Seem an Echo to the Sense': An Eighteenth-Century Controversy Revisited," *The Modern Language Review* 94, no. 4 (1999): 940–54.

52 Paul Fussel, *Poetic Meter and Form*, 37–73.

53 John Keble, *Lectures on Poetry*, 1:22 quoted in "Breaking Loose: Frederick Faber and the Failure of Reserve." See also Kirstie Blair, "Tractarian Poets," *Victorian Poetry* 44, no. 1 (Spring 2006), 29.

54 A trochee contains two syllables, the first stressed, the second unstressed as in NEWman; a spondee is two stressed syllables in a row.

by the meter) which gives courage to the person having signed himself "to suffer and to do." With this the poet returns to the expected iambic meter. The poem continues:

> *And who shall say, but hateful spirits around,*
> *For their brief hour unbound,*
> **Shud**der *to see, and wail their overthrow?*

Here again, the iambic meter is interrupted by metrical substitution. The initial trochee (/ ^) in place of the expected iamb literally makes the line "shudder" metrically and musically emphasizing Newman's lesson about how Satan and his demons fear the sign of the cross.

In the final three lines the poet reminds us of something remarkable, of the effects of prayer and poetry emphasized by the beat falling on the word "hails."

> *While on far heathen ground*
> *Some lonely Saint* **hails** *the fresh odor, though*
> *Its source he cannot know.*

In this verse lies the conviction which is at the heart of Christian prayer: that through the indwelling presence of God, when a person of faith is rightly disposed and praying, he or she is potentially in touch with the whole world, visible and invisible. And by making oneself available in the humble obedience of prayer, a channel is opened for God's grace to flow to any other in need, whether known or not. Prayers, which rise like incense to God, are in Revelation 5:8 called the odor of saints. And then there are the other spirits: the angels who minister to us, the counterparts of the demons. In his prose and verse, Newman refers to the "invisible" reality of God, grace, and the angelic world. Throughout, Newman's subtle use of metrical adjustment instructs by delighting.

Another short poem illustrating Newman's metrical technique is "The Isles of the Sirens" (1832),[55] composed on his Mediterranean voyage. The Sirens are mythical singing creatures whose irresistible song lured sailors to their deaths by crashing their ships into the shore while trying to reach them. Instead of the "siren choirs," Newman teaches that we should listen for heavenly music, which will purify not destroy us. Note the accented syllables that Newman uses to begin the first, third, and fifth lines. The initial accent emphasizes these first words, "ceasing" the meter before the pattern is set, in the otherwise iambic lines. An unaccented first syllable of the iamb would be expected; the trochaic substitution shows Newman's ability to vary meter to fit his message. In line 9, the bold spondee, two accented syllables in a row, is like a fist pounding on a desk. We take notice!

---

55 *VO*, 82.

Cease, *Stranger,* **cease** *those piercing notes,*
The craft of Siren choirs;
Hush *the seductive voice, that floats*
Upon the languid wires.
Music's ethereal fire was given
Not to dissolve our clay,
But draw Promethean beams from Heaven,
And purge the dross away.
Weak self! *with thee the mischief lies,*
Those throbs a tale disclose;
Nor age nor trial has made wise
The Man of many woes.

In the second stanza, Newman uses another classical reference—that of Prometheus, the Titan who stole fire from the gods for humans, whom he loved. Like the fire of Prometheus, the heavenly music will help mankind purge baser inclinations away. Newman chides weak humanity, urging us to remember these tales and to learn from antiquity, to choose rightly, not to give in to whatever siren song might be leading us astray. Therefore, the music from the invisible world will aid us in our path to heaven if we will only "listen;" these voices will keep us from crashing into the rocks attempting to reach the destructive siren song of earthly deceit.

NEWMAN'S TRANSLATIONS:
A SHIFT IN TECHNIQUE

Newman's output of verse slowed after the publication of the *Lyra*, but he never entirely gave it up. Between 1836–1838, just seven years before he entered the Roman Catholic Church, inspired by the ancient Latin hymns found in the Roman Breviary, he translated and rewrote many of these hymns. Although Newman's hymns are loosely based on the originals, he changed the words enough so that these can be considered his own poetry. Instead of employing metrical variation within regular lines as he did in the poems for the *Lyra* (which were not written with the intent that they be hymns), in translations and hymns composed for the Oratory Hymnbook, Newman expressly wrote for the purpose of hymnody. His technical ability and use of metrics is again exhibited. These hymn-poems are simpler in both language and stanzaic form and are easy to sing with their regular meter. Newman wrote his lyrics in set forms, most often in what is called Common Meter, followed by his use of Short Meter and Long Meter. Common Meter is listed in hymnals as 8.6.8.6. which indicate the number of syllables per line, repeated in each stanza. The first line has eight syllables, the second six syllables, and so on. Many well-known hymn tunes are written for Common Meter. Short Meter is 6.6.6.6. and Long Meter is 8.8.8.8.[56] The use of very regular metrical patterns allowed the meaning of the words to be released in a controlled form, and thus the singing of the hymn would be soothing like the recitation of form prayers.

One such composition by Newman, "Advent—Vespers,"[57] is based on the seventh century Latin hymn, "Conditor alme siderum" traditionally sung during the Advent season.[58] Newman's rewriting of this venerable chant has been beautifully and carefully rendered by him into Common Meter. There are many hymn tunes which have been composed for this hymn meter, making Newman's version highly accessible for congregational singing. This hymn matches the tune "Cheshire." The first two verses will illustrate:

> Creator of the starry pole, (8 syllables)
> Saviour of all who live, (6 syllables)
> And light of every faithful soul, (8 syllables)
> Jesu, these prayers receive (6 syllables)
> Who sooner than our foe malign (8)
> Should triumph, from above (6)
> Didst come, to be the medicine (8)
> Of a sick world, in love. . . . (6)

Newman's words and striking imagery powerfully remind us of the purpose for Christ's birth. For instance, in the second stanza, Newman has Christ coming to be the "medicine" of a "sick world," which Christ did for love. Newman continues the medicinal imagery in the remainder of the hymn (not included here), and he declares that Christ will "cleanse and cure" the "deep wounds" of the whole human race. The meter itself serves to emphasize the soothing words of this poem.

NEWMAN'S POETRY AND MUSIC:
THE ORATORY HYMN BOOK

The charism of St. Philip's Oratory inspired Newman to resume the writing of original poetry. To the Oratory Hymnbook Newman contributed not only the translations of Latin hymns but also original hymn lyrics as well as hymn tunes. These hymns again use Common Meter, Short Meter, and Long

---

56 The poems in John Keble's The Christian Year are largely written in these familiar meters which give them their soothing effect. See Tennyson, Victorian Devotional Poetry: The Tractarian Mode, 108.

57 VO, 262–63.

58 The hymn was first rewritten by Pope Urban VIII in 1632 and used in the Divine Office at Vespers. In 1852, the hymn was also translated into the well-known Advent hymn "Creator of the Stars of Night" by J. M. Neale.

Meter.[59] Newman crafted his hymn-poems in this manner so they could be easily sung to many familiar hymn tunes, as he did his translations. These hymn-poems are straightforward as were the translations since they were for communal worship.

An example is the ingenious poem, "Candlemas" (1849),[60] in which the Oratorian weaves together the entire liturgical year using the theme of light as the thread. In his day (and still in the traditional calendar), the Christmas season ended forty days after Christmas on February 2nd with the simultaneous feasts of the Purification of the Blessed Virgin Mary and the Presentation of Jesus in the Temple. These feasts are an extension of Christ's Nativity.

The regular rhythm and uniform lines of 4 iambic feet (8 syllables) alternating with lines of 3 iambic feet (6 syllables), make this lovely poem Common Meter. Though this beautiful hymn is not found in hymnals, nevertheless, it is sung in many oratories to the grand tune *Winchester Old* which is used for the familiar carol, "While Shepherds Watched Their Flocks by Night." The first and last verses will suffice:

> *The Angel-lights of Christmas morn,*
> *Which shot across the sky,*
> *Away they pass at Candlemas,*
> *They sparkle and they die. . . .*

> *And still, though Candlemas be spent*
> *And Alleluias o'er,*
> *Mary is music in our need,*
> *And Jesus light in store.*

In the last stanza, Newman brings this light from Christmas morning into all subsequent time by reminding us that Jesus is and ever shall be the light of the world, and His Mother, our mother, *music to us*, rest for the weary soul.

A final example of Newman's hymn-poems teaches the doctrine of purgatory, and it does indeed delight as it instructs. By the very name itself, "The Golden Prison" (1853),[61] Newman conveys his belief that purgatory is more like a "golden palace." As is the case with his other hymn-poems, it is composed in Common Meter and the meaning is plain. One hymn tune which matches this poem well is "Martyrdom" by Hugh Wilson. The first, fourth, and last verse will illustrate:

---

59 Other Newman hymns in CM: "The Month of Mary," "Guardian Angel," "A Martyr Convert," "The Two Worlds," "For the Dead."

60 *VO*, 279–80.

61 *VO*, 303–4.

Weep not for me, when I am gone,
Nor spend thy faithful breath
In grieving o'er the spot or hour
Of all-enshrouding death. . . .

To reach that golden palace bright,
Where souls elect abide,
Waiting their certain call to Heaven,
With Angels at their side. . . .

So pray, that, rescued from the storm
Of heaven's eternal ire,
I may lie down, then rise again,
Safe, and yet saved by fire.

In this poem, Newman reminds us that purgatory is to be a temporary place, where souls bear "willing agony" to be cleansed and purified before ascending to heaven. Purgatory involves a necessary purification; it is a "holy house of toll," but he compares it to "a golden palace bright." This poem is the perfect precursor for Newman's most celebrated poem, *The Dream of Gerontius* (1865),[62] made famous by Edward Elgar's musical composition (1900). The soul obtains forgiveness for the temporal punishment of faults already forgiven in the sacrament of confession but not fully expiated before death. For this reason, Newman requested in the first line that there be no mourning after his death, and "The Golden Prison" was read at his anniversary masses (before his beatification). The lines of this poem were as though St. John Henry Newman himself was leaving instructions on how he wished others to pray for him.

NEWMAN'S FULL POETIC POWER:
THE DREAM OF GERONTIUS

St. John Henry Newman's poetic masterpiece is *The Dream of Gerontius*. The poem, divided into seven parts, is about an old man (from the Greek "geron" for old man) and relates the emotions and prayers of this dying man, with corresponding angelic prayers and demonic taunts. The poem tells the story of a soul's journey through death and provides a meditation on the unseen world. "In effect, this poem is a sort of compendium of his [Newman's] insights into the teaching of the Catholic Faith on creation, grace, redemption and life after death. It is also the expression of his personal experience of illness and his perception of the death of many loved ones."[63] This poem too serves as a poetic

---

62 *VO*, 323–70.
63 Juan R. Vélez, "Newman's Theology in the 'Dream of Gerontius,'" *New Blackfriars* 82, no. 967 (2001): 388.

bridge between the two worlds: the dying man remains in the visible world, but soon he will be entering into the invisible world. Even as Gerontius clings to life, the angels sing to him from the invisible realm, gloriously teaching that this world and the next are an unbroken continuum.[64] This long poem is also a compendium of Newman's various verse techniques. He uses varying line length and varied meter representative of his early poems in the dying Gerontius's dialog, halting and unsure, whereas the well-known and frequently sung hymn from *The Dream*, "Praise to the Holiest in the Height," is composed in Newman's perfectly ordered Common Meter, measured and regular; it stands alone well since it is the song of angels, perfect and sure. Here is the first stanza:

> *Praise to the Holiest in the height,*
> *And in the depth be praise:*
> *In all His words most wonderful;*
> *Most sure in all His ways.*

The popularity of this hymn is shown by the fact that a specific tune was composed for it, aptly named "Gerontius" by the English musician and clergyman John Bacchus Dykes (1823–1876). Elgar's oratorio for voices and orchestra in two parts was first performed at the Birmingham Music Festival and became a success the following year in Düsseldorf.

CONCLUSION:
ST. JOHN HENRY NEWMAN'S POETIC
AND HARMONIOUS LIFE

St. John Henry Newman the poet used meter and rhythm to create sound, which he believed participated in the universal harmony of the divinely ordered universe. However, as he had written in an early essay, "Poetry, with Reference to Aristotle's Poetics" (1829),[65] he held that the idea that "poetic" could also refer to much more than just poetry. In this, he was agreeing with John Keble, who as noted earlier, influenced Newman greatly; Keble's idea of the poetic is fully defined in his Lectures.[66] To call something "poetic" was to refer to some quality, not at all limited to poetry; the poetic should make the world of sense, "from beginning to end, symbolic of the absent and unseen [world]."[67] Many things

---

64 Even within the text of the *Dream*, Newman refers to the harmonious ordering of the universe, when an Angel, speaking to the Soul, says, "By sun and moon, primeval ordinances— /By stars which rise and set harmoniously" (*VO*, 340). The moon, sun, and other stars are part of the universal harmony.

65 *EH* i, 1–27. This essay was originally published in the *London Review* in 1828.

66 See John Keble, *Lectures on Poetry*, 1832–1841, trans. E. K. Francis (Oxford: Clarendon Press, 1912), vol. 1, 2.

67 *Tract* 89 quoted in Gregory H. Goodwin, "Keble and Newman: Tractarian Aesthetics and the Romantic Tradition," *Victorian Studies* 30, no. 4 (1987): 483.

could be described as poetic, from a painting to a beautiful bridle-path to the Roman Catholic Church. Poetry in the form of rhythmic verse was his way of stirring religious feelings since it is the poet's duty to imitate God's music, in order that the listeners' hearts would be lifted from the visible world. Many years later, in the essay on "The Mission of St. Benedict" (1858),[68] Newman reflects on this idea: "Poetry does not address the reason, but the imagination and affections; it leads to admiration, enthusiasm, devotion, love."[69] The heart of John Henry Newman speaks to our hearts by means of his poetry. Things "poetic" lift the veil to the unseen world, giving a unity between things seen and unseen.

The literary outpouring from Newman's long and productive life fills entire shelves in libraries. The goal of his life and writing, simply put, was to draw others into a desire for the unseen, to give intimations of the invisible world. His verses are a consistent vehicle for this task, but furthermore, Newman's life and writing is one of harmony; his life itself is poetical. He is that "harp of many chords," giving us the poetry of devotion and the music of "well-ordered affections" in all his works. Newman's life leads us to "admiration, enthusiasm, devotion, love." More than Newman the Theologian, or Newman the Classicist, or Newman the Poet, or Newman the Priest, we have one Newman, St. John Henry Newman, whose visible harmonious life points the way for us to that invisible world, where he now participates in the perfect music of heaven.

Suggested Reading

Carpenter, Nan Cooke. *Music in the Medieval and Renaissance Universities.* Norman: University of Oklahoma Press, 1958.

Lewis, C. S. *The Discarded Image: An Introduction to Medieval and Renaissance Literature.* Cambridge: Cambridge University Press, 1964.

Hall, Jason David, ed. *Meter Matters: Verse Cultures of the Long Nineteenth Century.* Athens: Ohio University Press, 2011.

Hardison, O. B. *Prosody and Purpose in the English Renaissance.* Baltimore: Johns Hopkins University Press, 1989.

---

68   *HS* ii, 365–432. See ch. 3 of this volume by Stephen Morgan for an outline of Newman's thought on the imagination and its inseparable connection to the virtue of religion (editor's note).

69   *HS* ii, 387.

CHAPTER 16

NEWMAN,
A GREAT SPIRITUAL MASTER

Fr. Frédéric Libaud

At the end of this journey through various aspects of the personality, theology, and spirituality of St. Cardinal Newman, it is up to us to address the subject of holiness in Newman. It is entirely consistent that the chapter devoted to holiness is the last one of part 1 of this volume since holiness, that is, the intimate configuration of man to God, is the goal pursued by all believers. Jesus Christ taught: "Be ye therefore perfect, even as your Father who is in Heaven is perfect" (Mt 5:48). Holiness is the ultimate goal of Christian action and, at the same time, it is its origin. The chapter on holiness could well have appeared at the beginning of this work. Newman indeed places at the head of his eight volumes of *Parochial and Plain Sermons*, like a frontispiece, the sermon entitled: "Holiness necessary for future blessedness."[1] By the same token the preceding chapters lend cogency to Newman's sermons and teaching on the subject of holiness.

Although Newman remains very discreet about his personal spiritual life, all of his theological and spiritual teaching is steeped in his personal spiritual experience; it is the outward expression of his inner life with the Lord. "It is evident that his teaching is rooted in a deep experience of God's presence in the most intimate part of himself," as Fr. Keith Beaumont writes.[2] We must clarify,

---

1   *PS* i, no. 1.
2   John Henry Newman, *Sermons catholiques* (Paris: Éditions du Cerf), 2019, 13, Introduction by Keith Beaumont (my translation).

however, that he does not reveal his spiritual journey until after his entry into the Catholic Church as portrayed in *Loss and Gain* (1848), which is considered a sort of autobiography of his conversion; it is one of the rare texts written by Newman in which, under the guise of his character Charles Reding, he reveals his growing desire for God and his intellectual and spiritual development until his admission to the Catholic Church. All his teaching, transmitted in his sermons, his work, and even his correspondence, showcases the fruit of his own spiritual life and his intimate desire for holiness.

Therefore, since teaching is intimately linked to personal experience, dealing with holiness in John Henry Newman involves constantly addressing the question of holiness from both perspectives. First, it seems relevant to reflect on Newman's teaching on holiness. In order to do this, it is interesting to go through Newman's various writings, especially his theological discourses which, in various forms, all deal with the question of holiness. After this, the question of Newman's personal holiness—which he denied,[3] but which was already recognized by his contemporaries,[4] and later officially by the Church—proves relevant to study because his example is also a source of teaching for every believer today. From this examination, we can highlight six fundamental aspects of holiness according to John Henry Newman.

BAPTISM AS THE GATEWAY TO HOLINESS

The key to Newman's teaching on holiness is baptism. The evangelical movement played an important role in the spiritual development of the young student, but at Oxford he adopted an Anglican theology of "regeneration." This is the reason why, according to Newman, baptism allows the believer to enter a new state, the state of grace,[5] of salvation,[6] and holiness.[7]

---

3   "I have nothing of a Saint about me as everyone knows, and it is a severe (and salutary) mortification to be thought next door to one. . . . I have no tendency to be a saint—it is a sad thing to say. Saints are not literary men, they do not love the classics, they do not write Tales . . . It is enough for me to black the saints' shoes—if St Philip uses blacking, in heaven." *LD* xiii, 419.

4   Let us recall what the *London Times* said at the death of John Henry Newman: "Will Newman's memory survive in the estimation of his country? Will his books maintain it? That is a question which may be asked today, but which the future only can answer. Of one thing we may be sure, that the memory of his pure and noble life, untouched by worldliness, unsoured by any trace of fanaticism, will endure, and that whether Rome canonizes him or not he will be canonized in the thoughts of pious people of many creeds in England. The saint and the poet in him will survive." Quoted in *The Press on Cardinal Newman*, ed. Michael F. Glancey, found at www.newmanreader.org

5   See, for example, *PS* iv, no. 9; *PS* v, no. 15, *PS* v, no. 24; *Mix.*, no. 7; *Mix.*, no. 8.

6   See, for example, *PS* iv, no. 7; *PS* v, no. 13; *PS* v, no. 14; *PS* vi, no. 12.

7   *PS* v, no. 14.

Throughout their lives, Christians must watch over the full development of holiness. And it is in their daily lives that they will allow—or not—the germ of holiness to grow in them to become new icons of Christ. Christians are invited to welcome in the depths of themselves the love of God. Thanks to this sacrament, they are destined to become temples of the Holy Spirit and to live under the impulse of the Spirit of God. The Holy Spirit is "the inward light of God's presence."[8] Promised by Christ (Jn 15:26), he guides and supports the believers in their daily lives and helps them be ever more configured to Christ.[9] This is what St. Paul reminds us of in his Epistle to the Galatians: "If we live in the Spirit, let us also walk in the Spirit" (Gal 5:25).

Baptism is the gateway that allows every Christian to become a citizen of the invisible world, living in the presence of God and in the company of angels and saints. For Newman, by baptism, the Christian no longer lives only in the terrestrial world but is already living in the celestial world. As I have shown in my doctoral thesis,[10] it is the awareness of this reality that must lead every Christian to live and act in this world here below as a citizen of the invisible world. This is why Newman endorses the biblical quote: "Holiness, without which no man shall see the Lord" (Heb 12:14). Newman expresses this sea change as follows:

"He is brought into a new world, and, as being in that new world, is invested with powers and privileges which he absolutely had not in the way of nature. By nature, his will is enslaved to sin, his soul is full of darkness, his conscience is under the wroth of God; peace, hope, love, faith, purity, he has not; nothing of heaven is in him; nothing spiritual, nothing of light and life. But in Christ all these blessings are given: the will and the power; the heart and the knowledge; the light of faith, and the obedience of faith."[11]

In this sermon, Newman opposes the state of nature and the state of salvation, emphasizing that it is baptism itself and the grace flowing from it that bring the believers from the initial state of sin to the state of grace. This leads Newman to define the true Christian "as one who has a ruling sense of God's presence within him."[12] In another text, a lecture published as *Discourses to Mixed Congregations* (1849), the English convert offers a shorter definition of holiness: "Grace has vanquished nature; that is the whole history of the Saints."[13] Holiness

---

8   *PS* v, no. 22.

9   See ch. 18 of this volume for Keith Beaumont's presentation of Newman's doctrine on the transforming power of the Holy Spirit (editor's note).

10   See Frédéric Libaud, *Voir l'invisible* (Le Coudray-Macouard: Saint-Léger éditions), 2016.

11   *PS* v, no. 13: 178.

12   *PS* v, no. 16: 225.

13   *Mix.*, no. 3: 49.

is the victory of grace over nature, of this grace received at baptism which continues to grow day by day allowing the believer to be molded according to the divine will.

The reading of Newman's writings helps one to become aware of a reality: all the baptized are in some sense holy from the moment of their baptism. Holiness, as shown by Newman's pen, is therefore not something to be acquired, but something which is received in the baptismal water and needs to be preserved. "Men we remain, but not mere men, but gifted with a measure of all those perfections which Christ has in fulness, partaking each in his own degree of His Divine Nature so fully, that the only reason (so to speak) why His saints are not really like Him, is that it is impossible—that He is the Creator, and they His creatures."[14] The spiritual growth of human beings therefore consists in allowing the germ of holiness deposited in their heart when they are baptized to grow and develop according to the good will of God. They are holy, and they are called to become ever more so, to strive for the fullness of holiness in the image of God who is the three times holy God (Rev 4:8).

The consequence of this divine presence is that every baptized person is guided by the Spirit of God, both spiritually and morally. The individual cannot behave as if he were not a Temple of the Holy Spirit. All his being and all his actions must develop in coherence with the faith received at baptism. And it is according to the way the baptized allow themselves to be guided by this "indwelling Spirit"[15] that they grow in holiness. Holiness therefore consists in a person's welcoming the action of the Holy Spirit and in allowing him to take possession of his whole being; the more the baptized person is guided by the Spirit of God, molded by him and configured to God, the holier he will become. Indeed, every moment of his life is an opportunity for him to please God.

GNOTHI SEAUTON—"KNOW YOURSELF"

Thomas Aquinas taught: "*Gratia perficit naturam.*"[16] Grace does not destroy nature but presupposes it in order to perfect it. The starting point of any spiritual approach, according to Newman, is the recognition of one's human nature, torn between nature and grace. In his Catholic sermons, he constantly returns to this spiritual struggle between these two components of every human being. The faithful who wish to grow in holiness must accept themselves as they are and not as they imagine themselves to be. Of course, "it is very difficult to know ourselves even in part, and so far ignorance of ourselves is not a strange thing."[17] Self-knowledge is an invitation to become aware of one's true human nature,

---

14   *PS* viii, no. 17: 253.
15   *PS* ii, no. 19.
16   Thomas Aquinas, *Summa Theologiae*, I, q. 1, 8, ad 2.
17   *PS* i, no. 4: 41.

with its qualities and spiritual gifts but also with its finiteness, its strengths and weaknesses, its gifts and sins, aware that salvation is not acquired by one's own strength but obtained by Christ on the wood of the cross and offered freely to every believer. To recognize oneself as finite, limited, sinful is to accept the grace of redemption obtained and offered by God to heal and save created man. Thus, self-knowledge is not a goal in itself, but it opens a person to the knowledge of God and to welcome his indwelling.

This knowledge is possible only through a regular encounter with God, through prayer and meditation, and through reading with the help of a spiritual guide. For Newman, it is essential for the Christians to get to know themselves through the eyes of God and thus to discern God's plan for them. "God speaks to us primarily in our hearts. Self-knowledge is the key to the precepts and doctrines of Scripture. . . . And then, when we have experienced what it is to read ourselves, we shall profit by the doctrines of the Church and the Bible."[18] Let's not forget that Newman knew the King James Bible by heart! One of the riches of Newmanian spirituality is the knowledge and acceptance of the human condition, which is essential, and made possible through meditation on the Bible. By accepting their nature, human beings can accept divine grace. And conversely, it is by accepting divine grace that human beings can better accept their earthly condition. However, it is the divine light that enables them to become aware of their personal limitations and sins. Newman emphasizes this link between divine grace and human nature by saying:

"Only God's glories, His perfections, His holiness, His Majesty, His beauty, can teach us by the contrast how to think of sin; and since we do not see God here, till we see Him, we cannot form a just judgment what sin is; till we enter heaven, we must take what God tells us of sin, mainly on faith. Nay, even then, we shall be able to condemn sin, only so far as we are able to see and praise and glorify God."[19]

To sum up, holiness consists in turning one's gaze away from oneself in order to direct it and fix it on Christ Himself, the only model. Newman reminds us of the centrality of Christ in every step of the dynamic of sanctification. It is indeed from Jesus Himself that the believer will learn to grow in holiness, for only He can transmit this holiness. "The Son of God and we are of one; He has become "the firstborn of every creature;" He has taken our nature, and in and through it He sanctifies us. He is our brother by virtue of His Incarnation, and, as the text says, "He is not ashamed to call us brethren;" and, having sanctified our nature in Himself, He communicates it to us."[20]

---

18 *PS* i, no. 4: 43.
19 *Mix.*, no. 2: 33.
20 *PS* v, no. 7: 87.

In the preface of his celebrated *Apologia Pro Vita Sua* (1865), Newman states that he wants "to make him (the reader) understand, how I came to write a whole book about myself, and about my most private thoughts and feelings."[21] This shows that Newman was attentive to these aspects of himself throughout his life. This book is therefore the result of a practice of self-knowledge, of re-reading and analyzing his personal life and of a supernatural vision placing his whole life under the gaze of God. Newman never presents himself as a perfect man, above all the rest of humanity. On the contrary, he totally assumes his human condition, its defects and qualities, its doubts and certainties, because "our nature could not be perfect with a corruptible body; the body was treated now as a body of death."[22] This principle, clearly stated in the *Apologia*, is frequently expressed by his pen. His novels, his theological work, and his letters shed light on Newman as a man. He does not hide his frailties, his questionings or his certainties. Newman is a whole man for whom intelligence is not far removed from affectivity, the mind from the heart. This is perhaps the reason why Henri Brémond published in 1906 a book titled *Newman—Essai de biographie psychologique*[23] and, more recently, Cardinal Jean Honoré *Newman tel qu'en lui-même*,[24] to mention only two books with this perspective. Speaking of Newman's frailties, errors, sins, weaknesses, that is, his humanity, takes nothing away from his holiness. On the contrary, it makes him all the more contemporary and credible in his teaching and in the path of sanctification which he offers.

"Surely it is our duty ever to look off ourselves, and to look unto Jesus, that is, to shun the contemplation of our own feelings, emotions, frame and state of mind, as if that were the main business of religion, and to leave these mainly to be secured in their fruits."[25] For Newman, the spiritual life is not the search for personal and intimate well-being. It has nothing to do with a narcissistic self-study. For him, the spiritual life is the encounter with the risen Christ and the permanent configuration to the divine will. The spiritual life therefore supposes self-forgetfulness and self-denial in order to walk resolutely in the footsteps of Christ and grow in holiness. This is why in the *Apologia*, citing "An Autobiography in Miniature," he sums up his life as follows: "led on by God's hand blindly, not knowing whither He is taking me."[26] Unquestionably God was leading him to holiness.

---

21   *Apo.*, (1865), Preface, 483.

22   *LG*, 198.

23   Henri Brémond, Newman—*Essai de biographie psychologique* (Paris: Librairie Bloud & Cie), 1906.

24   Jean Honoré, *Newman tel qu'en lui-même* (Paris: Éditions du Cerf, 2012).

25   *PS* ii, no. 15:163.

26   *Apo.*, 215.

DOING AND ALLOWING GOD'S WILL

Newman reminds us that sanctification is not the fruit of the human will alone, but that it is above all the work of God, the fruit of divine grace at work in the heart of man. Holiness presupposes two seemingly paradoxical attitudes: the first consists in desiring, in wanting to grow holier, and the second in allowing oneself to be sanctified by God Himself. Thus, in every quest for holiness there are active and passive aspects.

The first act that one has to take is that of the will; Christians must want to become holy. And this desire is an aspiration of the whole being for holiness. After a Christian takes the decision to seek holiness, he must live in a coherent manner and make his entire life correspond in the smallest aspects to this ideal. Every moment of their lives is an opportunity for them "to please God."[27] Just as spouses must repeat the "yes" of their marriage vows daily, and as a priest must never stop repeating the "yes" of his ordination, so the baptized must reaffirm their "yes" to God day after day, their fervent desire to bow to the divine will, to become ever more holy. In this way the free will of the baptized person tends towards configuration to the divine will, in order to be able one day to say with the apostle: "I am crucified with Christ, nevertheless I live; yet not I, but Christ liveth in me" (Gal 2:20).

Holiness is not the fruit of personal effort alone. Just as Christ was resurrected on Easter morning, so too the believer is sanctified by God who operates His work of sanctification within each person. God does not sanctify against the free will of the individual; He waits until the person welcomes His divine action. Because Christians want to become saints, they desire to allow God to work within them. "We are reminded that we can do nothing, and that God does everything."[28] To grow in holiness implies letting oneself be fashioned more and more by God, to be molded and shaped according to His holy will. This supposes that those aspiring to holiness gradually give up their own will. The term "self-denial" is recurrent under Newman's pen.[29] To renounce one's will is not only to make the free choice to let oneself be molded by God, but also to dismiss and refuse all that could distance or divert from the goal of holiness. To be baptized is to discover and become aware, to discern and submit to the loving will of God. The Christian has the example of Newman who asks for kindly light "amid the encircling gloom" and prays to Jesus, "stay with me, and then I shall begin to shine as Thou shinest: so to shine as to be a light to others."[30]

---

27 *Mix.,* no. 1: 4.
28 *PS* v, no. 7: 97.
29 *PS* i, no. 5; *PS* i, no. 14; *PS* vi, no. 3; *PS* vii, no. 7; *VO*, 24; *Jfc.,* no. 11.
30 *MD*, 365.

IN PERMANENT CONVERSION

Newman, like other spiritual authors, describes Christian life in terms of a constant conversion.

> God deals with us very differently; conviction comes slowly to some men, quickly to others; in some it is the result of much thought and many reasonings, in others of a sudden illumination. . . . Some men are converted merely by entering a Catholic Church; others are converted by reading one book; others by one doctrine. They feel the weight of their sins, and they see that that religion must come from God which alone has the means of forgiving them. Or they are touched and overcome by the evident sanctity, beauty, and (as I may say) fragrance of the Catholic Religion. . . . God deals with them differently; but, if they are faithful to their light, at last, in their own time, though it may be a different time to each, He brings them to that one and the same state of mind, very definite and not to be mistaken, which we call conviction.[31]

Newman thus describes the conversion process as very personal and varying in time: sudden for some and slow for others. In his mind, conversion is conformity of the human will to the divine will; to convert is always to seek to obey God's will. It is clear for him, therefore, that conversion is a process which involves every moment in life and concerns every decision, leading to the point that a Christian can say with Christ: "Nevertheless not my will, but Thine, be done" (Lk 22:42).

In the case of Newman, conversion is not a single event but rather a long process, with ups and downs, which leads to an increasing personal configuration to the divine model. The factor of time was essential in the process of Newman's own conversion. The notion of conversion for Newman is a gradual exodus, tirelessly resumed over the course of life, "ex umbris et imaginibus, in veritatem"; it is an "ecstasy" brought about by the encounter with Christ and at the same time it is a purification of all that hinders the development of the life of grace in us."[32]

Two events in Newman's life receive the qualifier of "conversion." The first event is reported to us in his *Apologia* as follows:

> When I was fifteen, (in the autumn of 1816,) a great change of thought took place in me. I fell under the influences of a definite Creed, and received into my intellect impressions of dogma, which, through God's mercy, have never been effaced or obscured. . . . One of the first books I read was a work of Romaine's; I neither recollect the title nor

---

31 *Mix.*, no. 11: 234.
32 Grégory Solari, "Newman et le songe de Gérontius—Une poétique de la sainteté," in *Kephas* 37 (January–March 2011), 13 (my translation).

the contents, except one doctrine, which of course I do not include among those which I believe to have come from a divine source, viz. the doctrine of final perseverance. . . . I retained it till the age of twenty-one, when it gradually faded away; but I believe that it had some influence on my opinions, in the direction of those childish imaginations which I have already mentioned, viz. in isolating me from the objects which surrounded me, in confirming me in my mistrust of the reality of material phenomena, and making me rest in the thought of two and two only absolute and luminously self-evident beings, myself and my Creator;—for while I considered myself predestined to salvation, my mind did not dwell upon others, as fancying them simply passed over, not predestined to eternal death. I only thought of the mercy to myself."[33]

Ian Ker explains that Newman's conversion to a Calvinistic form of Evangelicalism "brought with it not only more definite Christian beliefs but also a sense of the importance of personal conversion to Christ which never left him."[34] The event thus reported is characteristic of the conversion process; it allows Newman to become aware of himself before God. God is not an abstract concept; instead He becomes a very real God, a Person with whom it is possible to establish and maintain a personal relationship. It's a person-to-person—*cor ad cor*—relationship that develops.[35] This event moves Newman from a belief in dogmas to a belief in an incarnate God. This personal encounter with God implies a radical change of life in the following of Christ. The way of seeing himself, others, and the whole of creation is fundamentally transformed. This conversion gives rise to the *sequella Christi*.

This first step in his conversion process opens the doors to a succession of insights, of "revelations" which, one after the other, lead him to a greater knowledge of God. In particular, this leads him to the discovery of the invisible world. This God, who is "higher than my highest and more inward than my innermost self"—to use the well-known formula of St. Augustine in his *Confessions*[36]—dwells in an invisible world surrounded by a heavenly court made up of the Blessed Virgin Mary, angels, and saints. Growing in the intellectual and personal knowledge of this God, he tastes His truth. And it is this search for truth that leads him, after many inner struggles, to the second great conversion.

---

33 *Apo.,* 4.

34 Ian Ker, "The Significance of Newman's Conversion," *Communio: International Catholic Review* 22 (Fall 1995): 444.

35 Newman used this expression for the motto of his cardinal's coat of arms. It originates in a letter by St. Francis de Sales to the Archbishop of Bourges. The original in French reads: "On a beau dire, mais le coeur parle au coeur, et la langue ne parle qu'aux oreilles." Francis de Sales, *Oeuvres de Saint François de Sales*, vol. 3, October 5, 1604 (1834).

36 The original text in Latin read: *"interior intimo meo et superior summo meo,"* Augustine of Hippo, *Confessions*, Bk III, 6, 11.

His second conversion was to the Roman Catholic Church. On October 9, 1845, Newman was received into full Catholic communion by Father Dominic Barberi. He states in his Memorandum: "In the Autumn of 1845 I was received at Littlemore into the Catholic Church by Fr. Dominic, a Passionist monk, whom I sent for by means of some friends."[37] But as he himself reports in his novel *Loss and Gain*, this conversion is the fruit of a long and slow intellectual and spiritual journey. Charles Reding's questions, doubts, and convictions are undoubtedly those of John Henry Newman. One need only read this novel to grasp the anguish and questioning that plagued Newman. But the power of truth, the desire to grow in intimacy with God, and the thirst for holiness forced Newman to renounce the Anglican Church and his academic status and privileges in order to take a real leap into the unknown and join a Church that he had previously considered the Antichrist. However, after joining the Roman Catholic Church, Newman did not lead a more pleasant or tranquil life. With complete honesty and humility, Newman writes in his diary: "O how forlorn and dreary has been my course since I have been a Catholic! Here has been the contrast—as a Protestant, I felt my religion dreary, but not my life—but, as a Catholic, my life dreary, not my religion."[38] His desire for holiness pushes him higher and higher, even if it forces him to wage a constant interior spiritual battle.

For all that, these two great events in Newman's life should not conceal all the other conversions, and there are plenty of them, which never ceased to mark his life: his election as fellow of Oriel, his illness in Sicily,[39] his choice to found the English Congregation of the Oratory in Maryvale and in London, the foundation of the new Catholic University of Ireland, and others. All these moments in Newman's life were opportunities for discernment and acceptance of God's plan, opportunities for conversion from his personal will to God's will. These conversions were less spectacular than the two commonly noted, but each of them allowed Newman to grow in divine obedience. This explains why Newman made his own Thomas Scott's famous maxim: "holiness rather than peace."[40] This formula alone sums up the whole life of Cardinal Newman who constantly sought holiness even at the expense of his personal tranquility. A saint never sits down and stops fighting the spiritual battle; a saint is always in conversion, moving towards God, growing in an intimate relationship with the Lord. Such was the life of John Henry Newman.

---

37 John Henry Newman, Memorandum for Mr. Henry J. Morgan, Quebec, Canada, October 26, 1863.

38 The Journal, 1859–79, *AW*, 254.

39 "I felt God was fighting agst me—& felt at last I knew *why*—it was for self will." "My Illness in Sicily," *AW*, 124.

40 *Apo.*, 5.

HOLINESS IN DAILY LIFE

The effectiveness of Newman's preaching lay even more in his own presence and bearing than in his masterful prose and capacity to enter into people's thoughts. Lord Coleridge, the chief justice who presided over the Achilli trial noted: "Oh! What a sweet musical, almost unearthly voice it was, so unlike any other we had heard."[41] But Newman's voice and manner were not affected or dramatic. They corresponded with his inner life which is the substance of holiness, and which was expressed in his relations with people, appearance, and gestures as well as his manner of speech.[42] For instance, the Oratorian priest John Bernard Dalgairns recounted his last meeting with Newman: "His eyes looked then just like a Saint's and he spoke and he acted like one, so disinterestedly, so gently."[43] James Bryce who visited him in 1875 described the reception Newman gave to him: "He received me . . . very kindly, with sort of grave sweet simplicity which coming from so old a man, has in it something inexpressibly touching."[44]

For many years Newman had preached and taught the lessons from Scripture, which are summed up in the theological and moral virtues lived out in the daily activities of work, study, and relations with people. The source of this daily Christian living was to be found in his prayer, especially of the breviary and in the celebration of the Holy Mass, as well as recitation of other prayers. He had practiced the advice which later in life he gave in a simple manner when explaining that "perfection" does not consist in "any extraordinary service, anything out of the way, or especially heroic," rather in doing what is complete, consistent, and sound.

In 1856, Newman summed this up in a reflection titled "A Short Road to Perfection":

> It is the saying of holy men that, if we wish to be perfect, we have nothing more to do than to perform the ordinary duties of the day well. A short road to perfection—short, not because easy, but because pertinent and intelligible. There are no short ways to perfection, but there are sure ones. . . . We must bear in mind what is meant by perfection. It does not mean any extraordinary service, anything out of the way, or especially heroic—not all have the opportunity of heroic acts, of sufferings—but it means what the word perfection ordinarily

---

41   Bernard Lord Coleridge, *This for Remembrance* (London: T. Fisher Unwin, 1925), 86, quoted in Guy Nicholls, *Unearthly Beauty: The Aesthetic of St. John Henry Newman* (Leominster: Gracewing, 2019), 7.

42   Guy Nicholls, *Unearthly Beauty*, 3–13.

43   *LD* xvii, 351.

44   *LD* xxvii, 238.

means. By perfect we mean that which has no flaw in it, that which is complete, that which is consistent, that which is sound—we mean the opposite to imperfect. As we know well what imperfection in religious service means, we know by the contrast what is meant by perfection. He, then, is perfect who does the work of the day perfectly, and we need not go beyond this to seek for perfection. You need not go out of the round of the day.[45]

These recommendations were like a description of his own life. Reflecting on Newman's life, Francis Joseph Bacchus, who after studying at the Oratory School became an Oratorian in 1881, wrote forty years after Newman's death that "he carried the art of being ordinary to perfection. He took his food, his recreation, went about his ordinary duties, conversed without any mannerisms whatsoever."[46]

Newman is, thus, rightly a spiritual master of holiness in everyday life, as Pope Francis pointed out during the holy mass of canonization on October 13, 2019: "Such is the holiness of daily life, which Saint John Henry Newman described in these words: 'The Christian has a deep, silent, hidden peace, which the world sees not. . . . The Christian is cheerful, easy, kind, gentle, courteous, candid, unassuming; he has no pretence . . . with so little that is unusual or striking in his bearing, that he may easily be taken at first sight for an ordinary man.'"[47] Holiness is not something flashy or exuberant. Holiness grows up in the concrete real life of each Christian, through a life of prayer, meditation on the Bible and Christian doctrine, and the exercise of faith, hope, and charity. The Christian is the one who lives, or who seeks to live, in a relationship with God within the most intimate part of himself. In Newman's words: "A true Christian, then, may almost be defined as one who has a ruling sense of God's presence within him. . . . A true Christian, or one who is in a state of acceptance with God, is he, who, in such sense, has faith in Him, as to live in the thought that He is present with him,—present not externally, not in nature merely, or in providence, but in his innermost heart, or in his conscience."[48]

Newman invites each and every one of his listeners or readers to inscribe their spiritual growth in time and to arm themselves with patience. Indeed, it takes time to allow the soul to grow in union with God, in a *cor ad cor* relationship with Him. Time allows one to move forward, to rise again in case of

---

45   *MD*, 285.

46   Father Martindale, "The Sibyl and the Sphinx: Newman and Manning in the 'Eighties," *The Eighteen-Eighties*, ed. Walter de la Mere (Cambridge, 1930), 70–71, quoted in Charles S. Dessain, *John Henry Newman* (Oxford, Oxford University Press, 1980), 166.

47   Francis, "Homily for the Canonization of St. John Henry Newman," October 13, 2019. Vatican documents available at http://www.vatican.va/. The pope quotes from *PS* v, no. 5: 71.

48   *PS* v, no. 16: 226.

a fall, and to deepen in intimacy with Him. The factor of time is an integral part of every spiritual journey. "If a man is in earnest in wishing to get at the depths of his own heart, to expel the evil, to purify the good, and to gain power over himself, so as to do as well as know the Truth, what is the difficulty?—a matter of time indeed, but not of uncertainty is the recovery of such a man."[49] As a "being in time" a Christian must be patient and prudent in building his relationship with God; as the Christian moves forward he inevitably has falls on his path of holiness, but he is convinced that each experience can bring him ever closer to God. Time also helps him to become aware of his own finiteness. Time, therefore, appears to be a necessary aspect of the process of sanctification of the Christian.

IN SEARCH OF THE TRUTH

As we have already pointed out, Newman's holiness is not something ethereal; on the contrary, it is embodied in reality, not only in the reality of his life but also in the reality of his thought and of his theological reflection. And what motivated and animated Newman throughout his life is the search for the truth, the search for God who reveals himself as the Truth: "I am the way, the truth, and the life: no man cometh unto the Father, but by me" (Jn 14:6). Indeed, for the Oxford convert, truth is not a concept but a person, Christ Jesus, whom he sought throughout his life, both in study and in prayer. And because he sought all his life to walk the path of truth, this conviction leads him as far as the Roman Catholic Church, to Birmingham, Dublin, and Rome where he receives the cardinalate. All this path is summarized in *Loss and Gain*, where Newman writes: "for our strength in this world is, to be the subjects of the reason, and our liberty, to be captives of the truth."[50] The only thing that motivated his whole life is the permanent search for the divine will, for the truth. Everything was an opportunity for him to unite himself to God, both his times of prayer and his intellectual reflection. Newman's search for truth undoubtedly involved a faithful and regular life of prayer. His life of prayer enabled him to nourish an intimate relationship with God, to know Him, to discern His will, to place his steps in His own. Prayer was inseparable from Newman's life. From the day he inherited the breviary of his friend Froude until his death, he never ceased to unite himself to the prayer of the Roman Catholic Church and to live heart to heart with his Lord. Indeed, for Newman,

> the inquirer into heavenly truths dwells in the cell and the oratory, pouring forth his heart in prayer, collecting his thoughts in meditation, dwelling on the idea of Jesus, or of Mary, or of grace, or of eternity, and

---

49 *PS* i, no. 3: 37.
50 *LG*, 18.

pondering the words of holy men who have gone before him, till before his mental sight arises the hidden wisdom of the perfect, "which God predestined before the world unto our glory," and which He "reveals unto them by His Spirit.[51]

Another primary source in the search for truth, according to Newman, is found in the intellectual life and study. He wrote many theological and philosophical texts, the common thread of which is always the quest for the truth. Reading the Fathers of the Church or the teachings of the Church enabled him to discern the face of God. Newman noted that the study of the Church Fathers and the doctrinal and historical development of the Church led him to conversion to the Roman Catholic Church. In *A Letter Addressed to the Rev. E. B. Pusey, D.D., on Occasion of His Eirenicon* he stated this explicitly: "The Fathers made me a Catholic, and I am not going to kick down the ladder by which I ascended into the Church."[52] Newman neither wrote nor studied primarily out of simple need for intellectual satisfaction; rather, through his reflection, it is the face of God himself that he sought and discovered. In this, Newman corresponds perfectly to the disposition of the theologian given by Pope Emeritus Benedict XVI, who during his visit to Heiligenkreuz Abbey said that "where theology is practised on bent knee . . . it will prove fruitful for the Church."[53] The place of study is never far from the place of prayer; Newman's desk in the Birmingham Oratory was in fact in the same room as his altar where he offered daily the sacrifice of the Holy Mass. The intellectual and spiritual lives were absolutely inseparable in John Henry Newman's life, for the Truth so much sought after through study is that same one found in silent prayer and contemplation.

In another lecture in *Discourses to Mixed Congregations* titled "Faith and Private Judgment," he speaks of the certainty of faith: "he who believes that God is true, and that this is His word, which He has committed to man, has no doubt at all. He is as certain that the doctrine taught is true, as that God is true; and he is certain, because God is true, because God has spoken, not because he sees its truth or can prove its truth."[54] Reading this extract, we understand that what animated Newman throughout his life was his personal meeting with the God of truth. This search for truth guides all his intellectual reflection and stimulated him to study the growth of doctrine throughout history and to write the *Essay on the Development of Christian Doctrine* (1845). On the other hand, the very meaning of his *Apologia pro vita sua* is the defense of the truth, and more than the personal truth about his religious belief—THE truth—which he sought his entire

---

51   *Mix.*, no. 17: 343.
52   In *Diff.* ii, §2.
53   Benedict XVI, "Address during His Visit to Heiligenkreuz Abbey," September 9, 2007. |
54   *Mix.*, no. 10: 195.

life and finally found in the Roman Catholic Church. The *Apologia* was precisely Newman's response to the criticism addressed to him by Charles Kingsley:

> Truth, for its own sake, had never been a virtue with the Roman clergy. Father Newman informs us that it need not, and on the whole ought not to be; that cunning is the weapon which heaven has given to the Saints wherewith to withstand the brute male force of the wicked world which marries and is given in marriage. Whether his notion be doctrinally correct or not, it is at least historically so.[55]

Newman does not shrink in the face of these attacks; instead he replies to them one by one, with courage and conviction, seeking to re-establish the truth about his own life, his own choices, and more broadly the truth about the Catholic priesthood and clergy. "In exculpating myself, it was plain I should be pursuing no mere personal quarrel;—I was offering my humble service to a sacred cause."[56] This episode in his life makes him experience the cross of Christ, because the search for truth inevitably leads to embracing the cross. The disciple must drink of the same cup from which the Master Himself has drunk. He experienced many trials in his long life, and each time found comfort in his faith in the risen Christ and in his love for the Roman Catholic Church.

Years earlier, after the life-threatening illness in Sicily (1833) he wrote in his diary:

> I had a strange feeling on my mind that God meets those who go on in *His* way, who remember Him in His way, in the paths of the Lord, that I must put myself in His path, His way, that I must do my part & that He met those who rejoiced & worked righteousness & remembered Him in His ways. . . .[57]

Newman never gave up the certainty of God's particular providence that guided him throughout his life.[58]

---

55 *Apo.*, Preface (1865), 484.

56 *Apo.*, Preface (1865), 486.

57 "My Illness in Sicily," *AW*, 127.

58 Dessain wrote about Newman: "All through he was buoyed up by his trust in Providence. Before he was sixteen he had come to the realisation that God was truly personal and present. The Presence and Providence of God was perhaps the lesson on which this champion of Revealed Religion insisted most." Dessain, *John Henry Newman*, 169.

CONCLUSION

As we have outlined throughout this paper, the spiritual theology of St. John Henry Newman addresses the human being in all his components, unlike spiritual masters who propose a disembodied holiness making the saint look like an angel. The starting point is the recognition and acceptance of the individual as he or she is, for it is this particular man or woman that God calls to grow in holiness. Fully accepting his or her humanity will allow God to sanctify the baptized. For Newman, the Incarnation is the way to sanctification. To deny one's own flesh and therefore one's own finitude is to deny the Incarnation of Christ and God's plan for each person. Nevertheless, he does not lock believers in their human condition but encourages them to rise in the truth and to let themselves be configured to God and by God. This path to holiness thus compels the believer to permanent conversion. This spiritual program is both demanding and very positive because it has as its sole objective the divinization of the human and Christian condition.

Christ and the Church, his spouse, accompany every man and woman from baptism to eternal life. The proposed path of sanctification is one of Truth, so dear to Newman: truth about oneself and Truth about and from God. By becoming aware of his human condition and of the perfection to which he is called, the baptized person is encouraged to abandon his certainties in order to advance with confidence and humility in the following of Christ, in a movement of permanent conversion. The holiness to which the Anglican convert calls everyone is, in fact, that of the Incarnation. It is in the reality of daily life that the baptized person is invited to live out his call to holiness. The Second Vatican Council will echo this aspect of holiness according to Newman when it affirms in regard to the apostolate of the laity: "They exercise the apostolate in fact by their activity directed to the evangelization and sanctification of men and to the penetrating and perfecting of the temporal order through the spirit of the Gospel."[59] Unquestionably, Newman is one of the greatest spiritual masters of the nineteenth century, not nostalgic for a past greatness of the Church but a promoter of a Church radiating the divine grace in the natural world. And, through his discourses, he makes each baptized responsible for his call to holiness and the building up of the Kingdom of God.

As noted above, Newman's life gave credence and ratified his teaching on holiness. This is what made him convincing in his lifetime, as testified by many of his contemporaries, and to men and women today. We can give the final word to Joseph Ratzinger, one who has studied and been inspired by Newman's thought. During the press conference on his flight to the United Kingdom on September 16, 2010, the Pope Benedict XVI said:

---

59   Vatican Council II, *Apostolicam Actuositatem* (November 18, 1965), 2.

He was a man whose whole life was a journey, a journey in which he allowed himself to be transformed by truth in a search marked by great sincerity and great openness, so as to know better and to find and accept the path that leads to true life. This interior modernity, in his being and in his life, demonstrates the modernity of his faith. It is not a faith of formulas of past ages; it is a very personal faith, a faith lived, suffered and found in a long path of renewal and conversion. He was a man of great culture, who on the other hand shared in our skeptical culture of today, in the question whether we can know something for certain regarding the truth of man and his being, and how we can come to convergent probabilities. He was a man with a great culture and knowledge of the Fathers of the Church. He studied and renewed the interior genesis of faith and recognized its inner form and construction. He was a man of great spirituality, of humanity, of prayer, with a profound relationship with God, a personal relationship, and hence a deep relationship with the people of his time and ours. So I would point to these three elements: modernity in his life with the same doubts and problems of our lives today; his great culture, his knowledge of the treasures of human culture, openness to permanent search, to permanent renewal and, spirituality, spiritual life, life with God; these elements give to this man an exceptional stature for our time. That is why he is like a Doctor of the Church for us and for all, and also a bridge between Anglicans and Catholics."[60]

Suggested Reading

Armogathe, Jean-Robert. *Newman: La sainteté de l'intelligence*. Paris: Parole et Silence, 2019.

Beaumont, Keith. *Comprendre John Henry Newman*. Le Coudray-Macouard: Saint-Léger Editions, 2015.

Libaud, Frédéric. *Voir l'invisible*. Le Coudray-Macouard: Saint-Léger Editions, 2016.

_____. *Remplir l'éternité: La sainteté à l'école de John Henry Newman*. Le Coudray-Macouard: Saint-Léger Editions, 2019.

Solari, Grégory. *John Henry Newman: L'argument de la sainteté*. Paris: Ad Solem Editions, 2019.

---

60 Benedict XVI, "Interview with Journalists during the Flight to the United Kingdom" September 16, 2010.

II. JOHN HENRY NEWMAN'S DOCTRINE

CHAPTER 17

"FAITH AND REASON" IN NEWMAN: LEARNING TO "SEE THINGS AS GOD SEES THEM"

Michael A. Dauphinais

David Hume (1711–1776) concludes his *Enquiry Concerning Human Understanding* with the following call to action:

> When we run over our libraries, persuaded of these principles, what havoc must we make? If we take in our hand any volume; of divinity or school metaphysics, for instance; let us ask, *Does it contain any abstract reasoning concerning quantity or number?* No. *Does it contain any experimental reasoning concerning matters of fact and existence?* No. Commit it then to the flames: for it can contain nothing but sophistry and illusion.

According to Hume's analysis, reasoning has but two valid modes: abstract reasoning about quantity, and experimental (or empirical) reasoning about material existence. In order to be justified, reasoning must be based upon

---

*   Quotation in chapter title from John Henry Newman, *Fifteen Sermons Preached before the University of Oxford between A. D. 1826 and 1843: Third Edition of 1872* (Notre Dame, Ind.: University of Notre Dame Press, 1997), 14: 311.

abstract laws and physical evidence. Abstract and empirical reasoning disclose a limited vision of reality by focusing only on what is replicable by theoretical or physical experimentation without respect for an individual person or a particular tradition. According to Hume, claims about God and religion are not only beyond reason but are meaningless and even harmful.

Such is the force of the British empiricism that John Henry Newman (1801–1890) and his contemporaries encountered a few generations later. How was Christianity to respond to such withering criticism that had seeped into the culture and society of the day? Some would follow David Hume's outright rejection of God's existence and Christianity. Others would follow William Paley's defense of Christianity according to the canons of British empiricism.[1] Still many others would supposedly safeguard religion by leaving the sphere of reason altogether and so view faith as exclusively the arena of emotion and sentiment.

Newman sought a different way forward, a way presenting faith as an intellectual act of accepting divine truth—an act moved by love and dependent upon grace and so higher than reason and, yet, an act compatible with reason. Newman presented an alternative to atheistic or theistic rationalism, on the one hand, and fideism, on the other hand, thus anticipating what the First Vatican Council would likewise do later in the nineteenth century.[2] Upon being created a cardinal toward the close of his life, Newman would aver that his lifelong opponent was liberalism, defining it thus: "Liberalism in religion is the doctrine that there is no positive truth in religion, but that one creed is as good as another . . . It is inconsistent with any recognition of any religion, as true."[3] Against the skepticism of empiricism, the deformity of liberalism, and the corruption of voluntarism or sentimentalism, Newman re-examines and re-presents faith and reason to his hearers and readers to show, firstly, that religious claims may be considered true and, ultimately, that the Catholic religion is true in fact.[4]

---

1   See John Locke (1632–1704) and his *An Essay Concerning Human Understanding* (1690) and *The Reasonableness of Christianity, As Delivered in the Scriptures* (1695). See William Paley (1743–1805) and his *Natural Theology or Evidences of the Existence and Attributes of the Deity* (1802).

2   See Vatican Council I, Dogmatic Constitution *Dei Filius* (April 24, 1870). Vatican documents available at www.vatican.va. On *Dei Filius* and its eschewal of rationalism and fideism, see Romanus Cessario, OP, "*Duplex Ordo Cognitionis*," in *Reason and the Reasons of Faith*, ed. Paul Griffiths and Reinhard Hütter (New York: T&T Clark, 2005), 327–38.

3   John Henry Newman, *Biglietto Speech*, May 12, 1879, published in *Addresses to Cardinal Newman with His Replies Etc. 1879–81*, ed. Rev. William P. Neville (New York: Longmans, 1905), accessed on www.newmanreader.org.

4   On the occasion of Newman's beatification, Pope Benedict drew attention to Newman's dedication to the truth: "In our day, when an intellectual and moral relativism threatens to sap the very foundations of our society, Newman reminds us that, as men and women made in the image and likeness of God, *we were created to know the truth, to find in that truth our ultimate freedom and the fulfilment of our deepest human aspirations*," (emphasis added) in "Prayer Vigil on the Eve of the Beatification of Cardinal John Henry Newman: Address Of His Holiness Benedict XVI," September 18, 2010.

Newman judged his nineteenth century British world as failing in many ways to receive and hand on the Christian faith despite the cultural trappings of Christianity present. In this way, Newman's writings speak more directly to our present age and its post-Christian trends than might at first appear. Newman dedicated his early Anglican years to the Oxford Movement, a movement designed to bring the Church of England back to a living continuity with the Church of the apostles and the Fathers, a Church free of government control, a Church with demands for moral conversion, for the sacramental life, and a rich doctrinal sense.[5] On becoming a Catholic and an Oratorian priest, he sacrificed his position at Oxford in the service of the truth, hoping to eventually see a second spring of Catholicism in England.[6] His vocation as a priest, scholar, and teacher was ever to help his hearers and readers to accept fully divine revelation and live their lives in accordance with it.

When Newman approaches the topic of faith and reason, he speaks and writes from his own experience of seeking truth in order to assist his readers in their movement toward embracing the truth. With abundant examples and an ever-deepening intellectual penetration, Newman seeks to move his audience away from erroneous conceptions of faith and reason and toward an understanding more adequate to the whole of reality.[7] The rhetorical character of his sermons and essays should not lead us to overlook that Newman displays an exceptionally keen philosophical mind and employs his philosophical reasoning in the service of defending the faith. Avery Dulles describes Newman "as one of the great apologists of his time" and praises Newman "for constructing his arguments in the light of [his] profound and realistic theory of religious knowledge."[8] Ultimately, Newman writes to assist his readers in coming to see the truth of the faith as moved by charity. When he became a cardinal late in his life, he

---

5   On Newman's central role in the Oxford Movement, see Ian Ker, *John Henry Newman: A Biography* (Oxford: Oxford University Press, 1988), 54–100. On the movement as a whole, see Marvin O'Connell, *The Oxford Conspirators: A History of the Oxford Movement, 1833–1845* (New York: Macmillan, 1969).

6   See his "The Ventures of Faith," *PS* iv, no. 20: 295–306. See also, "Second Spring," *OS*, no. 10: 163–82.

7   See, for example, his *Fifteen Sermons Preached before the University of Oxford between A. D. 1826 and 1843, Third Edition of 1872* (Notre Dame, Ind.: University of Notre Dame Press, 1997) with an extensive introduction by Mary Catherine Tillman (vii–lii). In an 1847 letter, Newman describes his high view of them, "After [re]reading these Sermons I must say I think they are, *as a whole*, the best things I have written, and I cannot believe that they are not Catholic, and will not be useful" in *LD* xii, 29–30 as cited by Mary Kathy Tillman in her introduction. Tillman describes Newman's iterative approach: "While Newman makes no pretense that his circle of views on the faith-reason relation is exhaustive or file, he presents a developing series of closely interrelated approaches to carefully selected aspects of the subject. By means of continuous, imaginative variation and shifts in perspective, by means of argument, especially from analogy, and by example and illustration, these distinct views work together even as a kind of *system* of integrated ideas" (xiii).

8   Avery Dulles, SJ, *John Henry Newman* (New York: Continuum, 2005), 58.

took as his motto "*Cor ad cor loquitur*" or "Heart speaks to heart." Not only does Newman speak to us, he wishes us to come to believe that God has spoken to us, *cor ad cor*, and that we may in turn speak to God. Throughout his analyses of faith and reason, Newman speaks ever as a Christian, a pastor, a theologian, and, now to us today, as a saint.[9]

Toward the end of his Anglican period, Newman addresses the relationship of faith and reason with penetrating and persuasive insight in the final six of his *Oxford University Sermons*.[10] He would return to the treatment of faith in his first published work as a Catholic priest in his *Discourses to Mixed Congregations*. Finally, he would treat faith and reason in a more systematic manner in his *Essay in the Aid of a Grammar of Assent*. For the purpose of this chapter, I will draw especially upon the earlier treatments since it is there that Newman first attempts to help his audience begin to see faith as a justified belief in the Christian revelation.[11] If this was necessary for his contemporary audience, burdened by empirical views of reason on one hand and by sentimental views of faith on the other, I suggest such an attempt in learning to see faith and reason anew is necessary for our times as well.

RETHINKING FAITH

Faith is never reducible to reason. Newman begins his considerations of faith and reason on the feast of the Epiphany by referring to the story of the three wise men who sought the Christ child. He writes, "To them Christ was manifest as He is to us, and in the same way; not to the eyes of their flesh, but to the illuminated mind, to their Faith."[12] Two things ought to be observed. First, Newman approaches these topics with the conviction that the assent of faith must be one across the world and across history. We are contemporaneous with the wise men in the presence of Christian revelation. Whatever faith was in their times, so it must be the same in its fundamental form today even with the greater complexity to be expected among historical living realities.[13] Second, the mind

---

9   See ch. 22 of this volume, for Keith Beaumont's explanation of Newman's unified vision of theology and spirituality (editor's note).

10   The last six sermons were preached between 1839 and 1843.

11   In the third edition of his *Oxford University Sermons* (1872), Newman includes a preface in which he notes that they "become more precise, as well as more accurate, in their doctrine" as they proceed. Further, he makes more explicit how they fit into the Catholic teaching on faith and reason and presents their teaching in "categorical form" with a list of fifteen propositions, or theses, on faith and reason. Thus, although discernment is required, it is safe to say that Newman never repudiated his earlier treatment of faith and reason in the *Oxford University Sermons* even in his later revisiting of the topic in his *Essay in Aid of a Grammar of Assent*, published in 1870.

12   *US*, no. 10: 176.

13   As Newman will subsequently show in *US* Sermon 15 and his *Essay on the Development of Doctrine*, such identity of form presupposes development in expression over time.

illumined by faith sees more than the eyes of the flesh or reason are able to see. Even the wise men who studied the stars and found a sign needed more than reason to see God's chosen king in the child Jesus.

Why does Newman think it so important to show that faith is distinct from reason? As we mentioned above, his world was dominated by powerful currents of rationalism, especially in the form of British empiricism. According to this view, what was truly trustworthy was that which we could see and touch and measure with our empirical senses. Empirical reason thus considered such tangible realities as evidences, observed the facts, reasoned about principles, and so came to conclusions filled with certitude. Newman thus freely admits that this kind of reason demands stronger evidence than does faith. Relatively speaking, faith requires less evidence. Such an admission would appear to damage Newman's defense of faith. Newman, however, distinguishes between the analytical and critical aspect of empirical reason and the receptive and creative role of faith.

Newman refers extensively to the idea of antecedent probability as key to understanding faith. Antecedent probability includes those starting points from which the rest of reasoning takes place. For instance, when we hear a report of a piece of news, the amount of credence we offer that report depends upon our trust in the messenger and our sense for the likelihood of the news. Such judgments come into play in faith in everyday communications as well as in our faith in reports of the miraculous events of the Gospel. Newman emphasizes that it is a regular part of life to trust in knowledge obtained from others since otherwise we would be extremely limited in what we could verify for ourselves. He uses the example that the ordinary Englishman is justified in having certainty that Great Britain is an island despite the fact that he has not circumnavigated its shores.[14] There are good reasons to believe in things not immediately available to our empirical reason. When reports of divine revelation are presented to us, we have to come to a judgment about their truthfulness to the best of our abilities. We do not have the luxury of dismissing them simply because they exceed empirical verification.

Due to his emphasis on antecedent probability, Newman's treatment of the so-called proofs of Christianity is more nuanced than it may at first seem. He famously criticizes Paley's *Evidences of Christianity* as insufficient for leading to faith. Rather than seeing faith as following upon rational proof, Newman relies upon the role of antecedent probability to maintain that much depends upon the disposition we bring to proofs such as Christ's miracles confirming his divinity or his fulfillment of Old Testament prophecies as confirmation of his revelation.[15] Newman does not, however, reject any role to such proofs; instead,

---

14 *GA*, 105.

15 For the roots of an alternative to an empirical approach within the Church of England, see Joseph Butler (1692–1752) and his *Analogy of Religion Natural and Revealed to the Constitution and Course of Nature* (1736). Offering an alternative to Paley's argument

he affirms their role in theology and their benefits to Christians. To religious persons struggling in the face of objections and difficulties, "the varied proofs of Christianity will be a stay, a refuge, an encouragement, a rallying point for Faith," and, to Christians strong in their faith, "they are a source of gratitude and reverent admiration, and a means of confirming faith and hope."[16] This positive, albeit non-sufficient, role of proofs allows Newman later to affirm the Catholic understanding of the motives of credibility that he explicitly encountered during his studies in Rome and that would be promulgated in the First Vatican Council.[17] Newman continued to hold that the proofs may prove revelation *credible* but may not prove *faith*. Faith, albeit supported by the natural knowledge of the moral and physical orders, remained a judgment of truth beyond what reason could prove and was necessarily inspired by divine grace.[18]

RETHINKING REASON

After Newman distinguishes faith from reason, he takes the next step by distinguishing between two types of reason: one of broader use and one of narrower scope. By this distinction, Newman challenges the common assumption that reason is only properly reason in its empirical and logical dimensions. Instead, these modes of reason are not the whole of reason but only subsets of the larger

---

that miracles are evidentiary proof of the truth of Christian revelation, Newman appeals explicitly to Butler, "Bishop Butler tells us that it is impossible to decide what evidence will be afforded of a Revelation, supposing it made; and certainly it might have been given without any supernatural display at all, being left (as it is in a manner even now) to be received or rejected by each man according as his heart sympathized in it, that is, on the influence of reasons, which, though practically persuasive, are weak when set forth as the argumentative grounds of conviction" (*US*, no. 13: 261–62). Newman likewise appeals to Butler in setting forth his account of development in *OUS*, no. 15: 318, in which he writes that the language of the Gospels with "its half sentences, its overflowings of language, admit of development [note 1]; . . . for they are representations of what is actual, and has a definite location and necessary bearings and a meaning in the great system of things, and a harmony in what it is, and a compatibility in what it involves" and therein cites "Butler's *Analogy*, part ii, ch. iii" (note 1).

16   *US*, no. 10: 199.

17   For an insightful discussion of Newman's integration of the Catholic theses on faith as articulated in mid-nineteenth century Rome, see Reinhard Hütter, *John Henry Newman on Truth and Its Counterfeits: A Guide for Our Times* (Washington, D.C.: The Catholic University of America Press, 2020), 96–98, 121–25.

18   Newman thus criticized evangelical tendencies to reduce faith to an act of the will or of feelings. In his *The Idea of a University*, he writes, "The old Catholic notion, which still lingers in the Established Church, was, that Faith was an intellectual act, its object truth, and its result knowledge. . . . But in proportion as the Lutheran leaven spread, it became fashionable to say that Faith was, not an acceptance of revealed doctrine, not an act of the intellect, but a feeling, an emotion, an affection, an appetency; and, as this view of Faith obtained, so was the connection of Faith with Truth and Knowledge more and more either forgotten or denied." *Idea*, 28.

field. Judgments stemming from antecedent probabilities remain acts of reason despite the fact that they may not be proved in a syllogistic or experimentally-re-peatable manner. Unlike modern philosophers such as Descartes and Hume, Newman refuses to treat the experience of the common person as immediately suspect. Instead, he thinks they navigate the world in a manner that engages their rationality even if they lack philosophical education.[19] He writes, "They may argue badly, but reason well; that is, their professed grounds are not suffi-cient measures of their real ones."[20] He illustrates his point with an example of a military general who assesses countless reports in real time, weighs the trust-worthiness of each report, and comes to a judgment about the next set of actions to take—all in the midst of a chaotically unfolding set of situations. The general may well judge rightly, yet without being able to defend his reasoning with rigor sufficient to satisfy a logician.

In our common and individual lives, Newman shows that we must rely on a reason broader than the constrictions afforded by empirical or logical ratio-nalism. Consider for a moment that no historical matter or remembrance may ever be experimentally repeated in order to meet the standard for empirical science. Yet, living in this world requires us constantly to assess the past in order to act in the present. In inspiring prose, Newman seeks to move his audience:

> We are so constituted, that if we insist upon being as sure as is conceiv-able, in every step of our course, we must be content to creep upon the ground, and can never soar. If we are intended for great ends, we are called to great hazards; and, whereas we are given absolute certainty in nothing, we must in all things choose between doubt and inactivity.[21]

In a *reductio ad absurdam*, Newman shows that if we held all human reasoning hostage to the same standards of logical certainty or empirical proof that are often alleged against faith, we would resign ourselves to live in a world without action.

Newman helps us to see that all reasoning, even empirical reasoning, requires certain assumptions. He reminds us that we must trust our memories, our senses, even our very process of reasoning in order to engage in any kind of argumentation. Newman is not so naïve as to believe that these faculties are always correct. Instead, he suggests that our ability to recognize mistakes in our memories and our senses is itself evidence of their overall trustworthiness.

---

19 Newman was not optimistic about a general ability to use reason well. In "The Tamworth Reading Room" he writes, "Now, without using exact theological language, we may surely take it for granted, from the experience of facts, that the human mind is at best in a very unformed or disordered state; passions and conscience, likings and reason, conflicting" in *DA*, 263. He is doubting here whether the restriction of reason to empirical reason was likely to generate greater wisdom.

20 *US*, no. 11: 212.

21 *US*, no. 11: 215.

He gives the example of walking at night, seeing a dark shadow ahead, and mistaking it at first for a man before discovering it to be a small tree. The reasonable response is not to give up in despair over one's fallible senses but to have confidence that we may well correct ourselves as long as we leave our senses, memories, and reasons open before reality. Even more than trusting our senses and our reason, we must trust others in countless areas that we could never verify for ourselves.[22]

As Newman slowly develops his argument, he draws the following conclusion: all rational inquiry presupposes certain assumptions. Newman writes, "there must ever be something assumed ultimately which is incapable of proof, and without which our conclusion will be as illogical as Faith is apt to seem to men of the world."[23] Newman does not make this point to make us doubt reason but simply to show that the reasoning in which we rightly place our trust begins with certain assumptions and principles. The historian Eamon Duffy summarizes Newman's project here in a way that highlights that Newman is not a skeptic but only skeptical of an excessive narrowing of reason:

> Newman was not here justifying irrationality, the triumph of heart over head: instead, he was proposing a different model of what human reason actually was. Instead of the simplistic Enlightenment image of rationality as a neutral weighing up of evidence until the balance tipped in favour of a conclusion, he pointed to the complex ways in which human beings actually arrive at their core convictions, in science and daily life as much as in religion.[24]

By enlarging reasoning beyond its critical mode, Newman shows that critical reasoning does not stand on its own but works upon an initial rationality that begins with trust.

With such a broader view of reason, Newman defends faith against the charge that it is absurd or against reason. Newman writes, "Faith is not the only exercise of Reason, which, when critically examined, would be called unreasonable, and *yet is not so*."[25] Faith, instead, belongs to a broader manner of reasoning essential to human living. Newman thus comes to describe faith as an act of reason beyond natural certainties: "Faith is the reasoning of a religious mind, or of what Scripture calls a right or renewed heart, which acts upon presumptions rather than evidence, which speculates and ventures on the future when it cannot

---

22 Newman treats the rationality of trust at length in "Religious Faith Rational" in which he summarizes his argument as follows: "The world could not go on without trust." *PS* i, no. 15: 196.

23 *US*, no. 11: 213.

24 Eamon Duffy, *John Henry Newman: A Very Brief History* (London: Society for Promoting Christian Knowledge, 2019), 42.

25 *US*, no. 11: 209; emphasis added.

make sure of it."[26] Reasoning is not less reasonable for relying on unavoidable presuppositions. Contemporary Newman scholar Frederick D. Aquino explains, "Newman rejects the claim that all the grounds of a belief accord with an explicit awareness of the features that make a belief reasonable or that these grounds need to be cognitively accessible to the believer."[27] The question is not whether we have presumptions but whether our presumptions are more or less accurate and our reasoning proper or not.

Newman does not eschew empirical or logical reasoning but rather reframes it as part of a larger whole of reasoning that is logical as well as presumptive, critical as well as trusting. When investigating physical facts, we learn to submit our antecedent probabilities to the experimental results. The success of the so-called scientific method may mislead us into thinking that we ought to apply the same critical method to matters of faith and reason. While Newman observes that Francis Bacon's restriction to empirical reasoning may well be appropriate for experimental science—since it is dealing with empirical realities—Newman argues that such a limitation would be absurd in matters of history, ethics, or religion in which the realities are not subject to physical examination.[28] For the areas of human life that are not materially present, we must have a broader scope of reasoning from antecedent judgments about how we look at the world and then subject those judgments to further questioning and judgments of a non-empirical sort.

Newman distinguishes between implicit and explicit reason to help his audience see reason more clearly and see how faith remains an act of the intelligence. Implicit reason is "the original process of reasoning," and explicit reason "the process of investigating our reasonings."[29] Newman helps the reader to grasp this distinction by observing that "all men have a reason, but not all men can give a reason."[30] In this way, Newman reshapes the debate with empiricism by refusing either to idolize or to demonize empirical and logical reason. He defends its place within the human community without requiring that all members practice this mode of investigating their reasonings in order to be justified in their beliefs. He also refuses to set up implicit reason against explicit reason as though one is good and the other bad or one is reliable and the other untrustworthy. Newman maintains that both form part of a larger whole:

---

26   *US*, no. 11: 203.

27   Frederick D. Aquino, "Epistemology," in *The Oxford Handbook of John Henry Newman*, ed. Frederick D. Aquino and Benjamin J. King (Oxford, United Kingdom: Oxford University Press, 2018), 379.

28   Newman claims a larger territory of reason than Bacon's circumscription of reasoning to experimental inquiry: "In subjects which belong to moral proof, such, I mean, as history, antiquities, political science, ethics, metaphysics, and theology, which are pre-eminently such, and especially in theology and ethics, antecedent probability may have a real weight and cogency which it cannot have in experimental science." *Dev.*, 112.

29   *US*, no. 13: 258.

30   *US*, no. 13: 259.

The process of reasoning, whether implicit or explicit, is the act of one and the same faculty, to which also belongs the power of analyzing that process, and of thereby passing from implicit to explicit. Reasoning, thus retrospectively employed in analyzing itself, results in a specific science or art, called logic, which is a sort of rhetoric, bringing out to advantage the implicit acts on which it has proceeded.[31]

By showing that explicit reasoning grows out of implicit reasoning, Newman sets up an asymmetrical relation between the two. Implicit reasoning maintains a primacy and an originality in the human encounter with the truth despite the fact that it also relies upon explicit reason to assess its claims, not as an outside neutral third-party, but as the reasoning mind reflecting upon itself. Newman notes that the beginning and ending of logical arguments exceed the ability of logic to determine. As Aidan Nichols, OP, helpfully summarizes:

A grasp of human beings' structure as knowing agents enables us, therefore, to say that not all assertions that transcend experience, but that the materials of experience prompt us to make, are abuses of reason. They will not be beyond reason simply because they go beyond the evidence.[32]

In Newman's evocative and rhetorical manner, speaking from one heart to another, he shows that it is ultimately an abuse of reason to reduce rationality to evidence.

JUDGMENTS OF FAITH

Just as Newman defends faith against the error of empiricism, so he also wants to avoid the error of sentimentalism or fideism as though they were only a feeling or without rational foundation. In his *Essay in Aid of a Grammar of Assent*, Newman develops the idea of implicit reason and represents it under the heading of the illative sense in order to show how faith remains an act of the intellect in arriving at truth. The illative sense describes how we come to judgments of truth not through logical reasoning alone but by means of a more informal, yet no less reliable, process.[33] In presenting the illative sense,

---

31   *US*, Preface to the 1871 edition, xii.

32   Aidan Nichols, OP, *A Grammar of Consent: The Existence of God in Christian Tradition* (Notre Dame, Ind.: University of Notre Dame Press, 1991), 13.

33   Eamon Duffy summarizes, "In the *Grammar* Newman refined, systematized and extended the ideas which had been set out in the *Oxford University Sermons* and the letters on the *Tamworth Reading Room*. The idea of 'Implicit Reasoning' was now given the name 'the Illative sense', an informal but generally reliable faculty of discernment that underlies all of our assents, which Newman likened to Aristotle's idea of *Phronesis*, wisdom or practical intelligence." *John Henry Newman*, 46–47.

Newman turns explicitly to Aristotle to explain it and to persuade his reader. For Aristotle, *phronesis*, or practical wisdom, describes the moral disposition of the man with practical wisdom, the *phronimos*, that allows him to act well in particular situations.[34] Newman takes this idea of practical wisdom in the judgment of moral action and brings it to the judgment of intellectual action. The illative sense thus describes the disposition of the man that allows him to think well. Just as Aristotle's prudential approach necessarily includes the perspective and character of the agent, so does Newman's approach. On this question, it is helpful to consider Aristotle's overall approach to ethics as neither universalistic nor relativistic.[35] Instead, Aristotle's approach may be best described as particularistic or agent-centered; the universal principles of human nature must be approached by particular individuals in particular situations. So also Newman's approach to reason is neither universalistic nor relativistic; Newman focuses on the particular person's ability to come to see higher truths. Such a person-centered approach to judgments of truth offers a substantive alternative to the reduction of reasoning to its abstract and empirical aspects, which seeks to be impersonal and repeatable. In addition to avoiding rationalism, Newman also eschews fideism in which the assent of faith has no rational basis. The agent may arrive at the assured judgments of the truth of faith on the basis of the illative sense, by taking in the whole of a matter and saying "yes, I believe this to be true."[36]

By arguing for a broader understanding of reason, Newman allows faith to be seen as harmonious with reason. No longer does faith appear to be against reason or without rational foundation. Instead, faith is the act of the intelligence by which one makes a judgment of truth. As such, faith may or may not include moments of explicit reasoning and analytical thought, but it always includes the role of implicit reasoning. Newman explains, "Faith, then, though in all cases a reasonable process, is not necessarily founded on an investigation, argument, or proof; these processes being but the explicit form which the reasoning takes

---

34 For an overview, see Michael Pakaluk, *Aristotle's Nicomachean Ethics: An Introduction* (New York: Cambridge University Press, 2005).

35 Stanley Jaki writes, "that illative sense that Newman defined as a judgment of prudence in which he saw a preeminently personal characteristic. Whenever he noted that the illative sense opened the door to subjectivism, he right away shut that door: 'Duties change, but truths never'" (citing *GA*, 278). Stanley Jaki, "Newman's Assent to Reality, Natural and Supernatural" in *Newman Today*, ed. Stanley Jaki (San Francisco, Calif.: Ignatius Press, 1988), 203.

36 Juan R. Vélez observes that the illative sense is not a leap of faith but growth of conviction: "A man reaches certitude through this illative sense. A skeptic might reply that this is tantamount to a leap of faith, but there is no such leap because the assent of faith has a cumulative and pain staking dimension; we grow into a conviction, rather than leap into it." "Newman's *Assent* of Faith" *First Things*, web exclusive, February 21, 2011, accessed www.firstthings.com. Aquino expresses the same judgment, "the illative sense is not an irrational leap in the dark, which abandons logic." "Epistemology," 383.

in the case of particular minds."[37] Newman summarizes three ways in which a proper understanding of faith is aided by the distinction between implicit and explicit reason: "that the reasonings and opinions which are involved in the act of Faith are latent and implicit; that the mind reflecting on itself is able to bring them out into some definite and methodical form; that Faith, however, is complete without this reflective faculty."[38] Just as was the case with reason, so also faith includes argumentation and logic without being reducible to either.

FAITH AND ITS DEVELOPMENT

Newman applies this distinction between implicit and explicit reason to what is believed in faith in his initial presentation of the development of doctrine in his fifteenth and final Oxford University Sermon.[39] He writes, "True Faith, then, admits, but does not require, the exercise of what is commonly understood by Reason [i.e., explicit reason]."[40] We make the assent of faith with implicit reason. Explicit reason then continues to investigate and argue over how the fullness of the initial act of faith is to be understood in greater depth and precision. As such, the Church's assent of faith is ever living and ever changing while remaining one and the same. Newman explains, "Theological dogmas are propositions expressive of the judgments which the mind forms, or the impression which it receives, of Revealed Truth."[41] Newman avoids the extremes of removing rational reflection from the sphere of faith and of necessitating rational reflection as necessary for faith.[42] Newman contends that faith naturally develops into a "body of dogmatic statements, till what was at first an impression on the Imagination has become a system or creed in the Reason."[43] In his *Essay on Development*, Newman writes, "the holy Apostles would *without words* know all the truths concerning the high doctrines of theology, which controversialists after them have piously and charitably reduced to formulae, and developed through argument."[44] Thus, we can see how Newman's foundational insight into the development of doctrine flows out of his understanding of faith as an act of reason in both its implicit and explicit forms. The initial faith of the apostles was an act of implicit reason that contains—and eventually would develop through explicit reason—the countless doctrines that would come over two millennia.

---

37 *US*, no. 13: 262.

38 *US*, no. 13: 277.

39 Newman delivered that final sermon in 1843 and soon afterwards began developing his initial insights into his justly famous work *An Essay on the Development of Christian Doctrine*, published in 1845.

40 *US*, no. 13: 255.

41 *US*, no. 15: 320.

42 *US*, no. 15: 319.

43 *US*, no. 15: 329.

44 *Dev.*, 191–92.

It is worth pausing here to respond to an interpretation of Newman's presentation of faith and reason as an early form of late nineteenth century Catholic modernism later condemned by Pius X in 1907. Gabriel Daly, for instance, argues that Newman shared the concerns of the modernists. Daly writes, "The phrase 'without words' in Newman's description of the apostles' knowledge of subsequent doctrines is worth noting together with the fact that he distinguishes between the truths and the doctrines which express them."[45] Daly's argument here is specious. In the very sentence referred to by Daly, Newman is not distinguishing between truths and doctrines but between the early assent of the apostles and the "truths concerning the high doctrines of theology" later developed. Truths and doctrines go hand in hand. Daly likewise shifts Newman's distinction between implicit and explicit reason to what Daly describes as "conscious and unconscious" reasoning: "First principles may lie deep in the unconscious and not be explicitly recognized for what they are."[46] In Daly's presentation, reliance upon unconscious reasoning would imply that the apostles would have been without rational judgment when they first assented to the report that "Christ has risen and appeared to Peter." Newman, however, does not present implicit reasoning as unconscious reasoning since "unconscious" implies a lack of judgment. Newman's point is the opposite of the one Daly presses. Implicit reason is a reasoning of the living and active mind making judgments and so has a natural continuity with further reflection upon such judgments. Rather than contrasting the truth of revelation from its later expressions, Newman is attempting to show that the truth of revelation remains the same both in its initial reception and later articulation. Reason is ever an act by which the person encounters truth.

It is worth considering further Daly's attempt to present Newman as one among the modernists since it helps to clarify what Newman does not mean by his appeal to antecedent probability and implicit reasoning. Daly writes,

> Perhaps the most significant contribution made to the theology of revelation by both Newman and the Modernists is their emphasis on experience, especially moral experience, and on the crucial role played by the imagination in the apprehension and interpretation of experience. . . . The appeal of both Newman and the Modernists to wordless and conceptless mental experience as the initial moment in the reception of revelation.[47]

---

45 Gabriel Daly, "Newman, Divine Revelation, and the Catholic Modernists," in *Newman and the Word*, ed. Terrence Merrigan and Ian T. Ker (Louvain: Peeters Press, 2000), 49–68, 58. For a history of the modernist crisis see Marvin O'Connell, *Critics on Trial: An Introduction to the Catholic Modernist Crisis* (Washington, D.C.: The Catholic University of America Press, 1995). See also, Pope Pius X, Encyclical Letter *Pascendi Dominici Gregis: On the Doctrines of the Modernists* (September 8, 1907).

46 Daly, "Newman, Divine Revelation, and the Catholic Modernists," 58.

47 Daly, "Newman, Divine Revelation, and the Catholic Modernists," 66.

This is a dubious claim about Newman's understanding of faith and revelation. Newman argues at length that it is the nature of Christian faith for believers to come to hear the word of God in the words of the apostles. When he says "without words," Newman is making the simple point that the Church over time developed many more words than those employed by the apostles in their original preaching and writing. Daly risks caricaturing Newman's reliance on implicit reason when he writes that Newman appealed to a "wordless and conceptless mental experience" as faith's encounter with revelation. Newman's writings point in the other direction. His chief aim is to show that faith remains a justified act of reason even when it does not fulfill the demands of logical and empirical reasoning. In coming to faith, the believer assents to Paul's verbal report that "Jesus is Lord" (1 Cor 12:3; Rom 10:9) or to its more developed creedal formulations. The content of faith develops from simpler words to more complex words, from the presumptive reasoning by which one first believes and then to the analytical reasoning employed over time to investigate the meanings and connections in the faith.[48] Newman's contention is that all of these remain conscious acts of human reasoning.

When reason is understood as including both its implicit and explicit forms, it becomes easier to see faith clearly as an act of the reasoning mind. Newman writes, "Faith . . . is an act of Reason, but of what the world would call weak, bad, or insufficient Reason; and that, because it rests on presumption more, and on evidence less."[49] Again, he writes, "Faith is an exercise of presumptive reasoning, or of Reason proceeding on antecedent grounds."[50] Rhetorically, this works to move his reader to see faith not as irrational or merely based upon sentiment. Newman will press the point further and show as long as one begins with the popular conception of reason as "the faculty of gaining knowledge upon grounds given," then one ought to conclude that "if this be Reason, [then] an act or process of Faith, simply considered, is certainly an exercise of reason."[51] In this way, both faith and reason gain knowledge based upon the testimony of others. Newman explains,

> Nothing, then, which Scripture says about Faith, however startling it may be at first sight, is inconsistent with the state in which we find ourselves by nature with reference to the acquisition of knowledge generally,—a state in which we must assume something to prove anything, and can gain nothing without a venture.[52]

---

48 Ian Ker comments, "the continuity of an idea is not conserved by remaining static; on the other hand, although it has to undergo change, this is not for the sake of change itself—if this were the case, then it would be the kind of change which Newman calls a corruption—but in order for the idea *to remain the same*" in his "Newman, Councils, and Vatican II," in *Newman and Faith*, ed. Ian Ker and Terrence Merrigan (Louvain: Peeters Press, 2004) 117–42, 134.

49 *US*, no. 11: 204.

50 *US*, no. 12: 231.

51 *US*, no. 11: 207.

52 *US*, no. 11: 214–15.

Life itself is so constituted that human beings must make judgments based upon trust and assumptions. This is true in acts of natural reasoning as well as graced reasoning. Questions about who we are, about the meaning of our lives, about the world and its source arise, and Newman wants to show that we are justified in holding judgments and embracing the risk and venture they entail. Not to make such judgments is already a judgment. Despite the criticisms of modern empirical reasoning, the Christian revelation remains a claim that calls for consideration by us. To assent to its claims as true and to live and be willing to die accordingly—to make "the ventures of faith"—is thus a proper use of human rationality.[53]

FAITH PERFECTED BY LOVE

Newman has thus far defended the necessity of relying on faith for our life within the world and the fact that we are not being irrational in doing so, and yet, how does one gain confidence about which testimonies to trust? After all, the realization that all rational inquiry is fiduciary might lead some to despair of finding truth. Newman faces the issue directly: "Antecedent probabilities may be equally available for what is true, and what pretends to be true, for a Revelation and its counterfeit."[54] How do we discern right faith from superstition or from believing in a counterfeit revelation? Newman does not think we may adjudicate among claims from a neutral perspective but must address this question from the perspective of the person encountering these truths.

Faith becomes rightly ordered to truth for Newman when it is directed by rightly-ordered love. Newman observes that we often see what we want to see when we look at the world. In particular, our own distorted ego inclines us not to see reality as it is in its fullness but rather as means for our own manipulation. Love of God and love of neighbor as oneself allow the person to begin to see things in a more realistic perspective. Newman describes this right faith as "faith working through love" or "*fides formata charitate*" and distinguishes it from "mere Faith."[55] Newman suffers no illusions that belief of any kind is virtuous. Mere faith, as he describes it, easily falls into superstition in attempts to change things to please the individual. Unlike mere faith, virtuous faith requires our fallen egos to submit to the wisdom and power of God. Newman writes,

---

53 In "The Ventures of Faith" Newman writes, "If then faith be the essence of a Christian life, and if it be what I have now described, it follows that our duty lies in risking upon Christ's word what we have, for what we have not; and doing so in a noble, generous way, not indeed rashly or lightly, still without knowing accurately what we are doing, not knowing either what we give up, nor again what we shall gain; uncertain about our reward, uncertain about our extent of sacrifice, in all respects leaning, waiting upon Him, trusting in Him to fulfil His promise, trusting in Him to enable us to fulfil our own vows, and so in all respects proceeding without carefulness or anxiety about the future." *PS* iv, no. 20: 299.

54 *US*, no. 12: 232.

55 *US*, no. 12: 234.

"Faith leads the mind to communion with the invisible God; its attempts at approaching and pleasing Him are acceptable or not, according as they are or are not self-willed; and they are self-willed when they are irrespective of God's revealed will."[56] True faith says yes to the revelation of God's will; love places God's goodness above our own and so desires God's will as the foundation of our will.

Newman's argument that right faith requires love may appear at first to be a retreat into sentimentality or away from faith as an act of reason. And, yes, there are certain truths in which it would be inappropriate to emphasize the moral disposition of the person. For instance, a mathematical truth once understood is simply seen to be true regardless of whether the person is good or bad. Even with mathematical truths, however, we know that many people fail to come to know them due to dispositions that prevent the person from dedicating the necessary time, study, and effort. Now what about truths concerning a person, especially a person with whom we are already in relation? If a young man holds significant resentments toward his parents, it is highly less likely that he will arrive at a reasonable assessment of their strengths and weaknesses than if he is deeply appreciative of their sacrifices on his behalf.[57] So also deep dispositions of resentment or ingratitude will impact how a person responds to the good news of our creation out of God's love, our entrance into sin and death as the result of free will turning from God, and our redemption and reconciliation with God through the death and resurrection of His incarnate Son, Jesus Christ.

Refusing to divorce moral dispositions from acts of reasoning, Newman writes, "Men do not choose light or darkness without Reason, but by an instinctive Reason, which is prior to argument and proof."[58] The full act of faith presupposes a willingness to trust God's revelation and so to trust in God's goodness; an act of unbelief presupposes an unwillingness to trust God's goodness. Newman distinguishes the mere act of faith from the proper act of faith that fully assents to divine truth:

> Right Faith is the faith or a right mind. Faith is an intellectual act; right Faith is an intellectual act, done in a certain moral disposition. Faith is an act of Reason, viz. a reasoning upon presumptions; right Faith is a reasoning upon holy, devout, and enlightened presumption.

---

56 *US*, no. 12: 242. See "Holiness Necessary for Future Blessedness" in *PS* i, no. 1: 1–14.

57 In an eloquent passage from *The Idea of a University*, Newman warns against the rationalistic tendency to discount the importance of the moral dimension of the human person: "Quarry the granite rock with razors, or moor the vessel with a thread of silk; then may you hope with such keen and delicate instruments as human knowledge and human reason to contend against those giants, the passion and the pride of man." *Idea*, 121.

58 *US*, no. 14: 280.

> Faith ventures and hazards; right Faith ventures and hazards deliber-
> ately, seriously, soberly, piously, and humbly, counting the costs and
> delighting in the sacrifice.[59]

Newman does not offer his audience a foolproof guarantee of absolute certainty
that the Christian revelation is true. Instead, he argues that we may be justified
in believing our faith to be true and in holding that judgment with certitude. As
we mentioned before, he thinks it reasonable that a man hold with certitude the
judgment that England is an island even though he may not be able to prove it
against all skeptical inquiries. So also, we are justified in holding our faith with
certitude. When one loves God and believes that He has spoken through His
incarnate Son, in fact, certitude is the only morally responsible response.[60]

Newman also shows how true love requires faith that is true. In other words,
the perfection of our moral relationship to one another and to God requires
knowledge of the truth about the world as revealed by God. In one of his *Parochial and Plain Sermons*, "Faith and Love," he addresses love's need for faith in
revealed truth:

> And thus it is that faith is to love as religion to holiness; for religion
> is the Divine Law as coming to us from without, as love is the acqui-
> escence in the same Law as written within. . . . Moreover it is plain,
> that, while love is the root out of which faith grows, faith by receiving
> the wonderful tidings of the Gospel, and presenting before the soul
> its sacred Objects, the mysteries of the faith, the Holy Trinity, and
> the Incarnate Saviour, expands our love, and raises it to a perfection
> which otherwise it could never reach. And thus our duty lies in faith
> working by love; love is the sacrifice we offer to God, and faith is the
> sacrificer. Yet they are not distinct from each other except in our way
> of viewing them. Priest and sacrifice are one; the loving faith and the
> believing love.[61]

Right love requires right faith. The necessity of right belief for loving properly
likely strikes us, and Newman's original audience, even more shockingly than
the reminder that love is necessary for the perfection of faith.[62] Love is not all

---

59 *US*, no. 12: 239.

60 Avery Dulles writes: "In exalting love as the way to heaven, Newman does not
make it a substitute for rational grounds. I take him to mean rather that where such love is
present, sincere inquirers will be able to find sufficient evidence for at least a rudimentary
faith in God. If they are privileged to encounter a religion accredited by divine signs, they
will be able to recognize and embrace it. But if their hearts are hardened, the evidences
will be wasted on them." *John Henry Newman*, 59.

61 *PS* iv, no. 21: 314–15.

62 Newman indicates that Butler's antecedent probabilities needed this added

we need. Love must believe, and faith must love. Newman addresses man in his existential unity as a being of both intellect and will who encounters the message of divine revelation.

FAITH AS REVEALED AND CATHOLIC

To what then or to whom does faith assent when it assents to divine revelation?[63] Newman pondered this question significantly from his earlier dedication of himself to God at the age of fifteen within the Church of England and then later in becoming a Catholic. He would describe his first conversion as a profound sense of grace and forgiveness for his sins and in particular as a faith that was definitely "creedal." The faith was capable of being expressed in true statements about the nature of God and his workings in the world: "I believe in God, the Father almighty, . . . and in Jesus Christ, His only Son Our Lord . . . who suffered under Pontius Pilate . . . who shall come again and judge the living and the dead." Newman's early experience of faith included the belief that Scripture was the true word of God, and yet, he described his faith as that he "fell under the influences of a definite Creed."[64] It was the voice of the Church expressing the realities of what God had done in Jesus Christ. Scripture spoke, yes, but with the Church and with the creeds, not alone. Newman's creedal faith would develop in his Anglican days in his defense of the Church of England as the inheritor of the truth of Christian revelation in the faith of the early Church through a retrieval of the Fathers, and the creedal, liturgical, moral, and spiritual practices of the early Church.

Newman would eventually argue that theological faith not only requires an assent to the truths revealed in Scripture and in the creeds and held by the Fathers of the Church, but specifically to the living teaching authority of the Catholic Church.[65] In arriving at the necessity of a faith both creedal and ecclesial,

---

moral dimension. See *Apo.*, 11: "Thus to Butler I trace those two principles of my teaching, which have led to a charge against me both of fancifulness and of scepticism." See also, *Apo.*, 19: "I considered that Mr. Keble met this difficulty by ascribing the firmness of assent which we give to religious doctrine, not to the probabilities which introduced it, but to the living power of faith and love which accepted it. In matters of religion, he seemed to say, it is not merely probability which makes us intellectually certain, but probability as it is put to account by faith and love. It is faith and love which give to probability a force which it has not in itself."

63 Ian Ker observes that Newman begins to use the language of "assent" in the 1850s and "certitude" in the 1860s, after the *Oxford University Sermons* (Ker, 621–22).

64 *Apo.*, 17–19, as cited by Ker, *John Henry Newman*, 4.

65 Avery Dulles, SJ, observes, "The organic and sacramental ecclesiology set forth in his Anglican sermons remained with him throughout his career. He never wavered in his conviction that the Church of Christ is a visible society, one, holy, catholic, and apostolic. From his boyhood, he firmly maintained that the revelation of Christ contained determinate truths to be proclaimed by the Church throughout all ages. When writing his treatise on

Newman distinguishes Christian faith from what he terms private judgment. Private judgment refers to the individual's determination by himself or herself of what he or she chooses to believe. Newman asks whether private judgement is compatible with true faith by putting before his audience the question of what Christian faith would have been in the time of the apostles. When the first generation of Christians encountered the preaching of Peter or Paul, they either believed their message or rejected it. There was no role for private judgment in determining what Christianity might mean or for private interpretation of Scripture. The apostles spoke with authority, as Jesus Himself had done. Newman thus describes faith as "assenting to a doctrine as true, which we do not see, which we cannot prove, because God says it is true, who cannot lie."[66] But we do not hear God speaking to us alone; instead, God speaks to us in and through his apostolic messengers.[67]

In the early Church, one believed "on the word of the Apostles, who were, as their powers showed, messengers from God."[68] Newman quotes Paul's praise of how the Thessalonians received his preaching, "not as the word of men, but (as it is indeed) the Word of God."[69] Newman articulates faith as the submission of "reason to a living authority." Faith had an unconditional aspect, "either the Apostles were from God, or they were not; if they were, everything that they preached was to be believed by their hearers; if they were not, there was nothing for their hearers to believe."[70] Newman's rather commonsensical argument is that if this is what faith was in the time of the apostles then it is what faith must ever be. Yes, the Scriptures are the true Word of God. Yes, the creeds summarize and present the true faith. Newman, however, says we need more than to submit to texts that we interpret for ourselves no matter how truthful or inspired those texts. He avers, "there is, I repeat, an essential difference between the act of submitting to a living oracle, and to his written words."[71]

---

the *Development of Doctrine* he became convinced that the 'additions' to the ancient faith in modern Roman Catholicism were legitimate developments, not corruptions or accretions." *John Henry Newman*, 95–96.

   66   *Mix.*, no. 10: 194.

   67   Sheridan Gilley shows how Newman's insistence on the need for the apostolic authority of the Church is a dominant theme of *The Grammar of Assent*: "The latter part of the *Grammar* is a passionate plea for the intrinsic reasonableness of Catholicism as the proper embodiment of a revelation given by God, not discovered by human reason, a revelation with divine authority. The whole of Newman's thought lies between the poles of two God-given popes, the private peremptory if fallible pope of conscience, the witness to the God within, creating that hunger for God which is satisfied and fulfilled by the public pope of the external revelation of God in Scripture and Tradition, as upheld in the witness of the infallible Church." Sheridan Gilley, *Newman and his Age* (London: Darton, Longman, and Todd, 2003), 372.

   68   *Mix.*, no. 10: 196.

   69   *Mix.*, no. 10: 198, quoting 1 Thes 2:13.

   70   *Mix.*, no. 10: 197.

   71   *Mix.*, no. 10: 200.

Thus, faith submits to the living authority of the Church as communicating the faithful interpretation of Scripture and the creeds.[72] Newman elegantly summarizes his argument,

> In the Apostles' days the peculiarity of faith was submission to a living authority; this is what made it so distinctive; this is what made it an act of submission at all; this is what destroyed private judgment in matters of religion. . . . Has faith changed its meaning, or is it less necessary now? Is it not still what it was in the Apostles' day, the very characteristic of Christianity, the special instrument of renovation, the first disposition of justification, one out of three theological virtues. . . . Since Apostolic faith was in the beginning reliance on man's word, as being God's word, since what faith was then such it is now, since faith is necessary for salvation, let them attempt to exercise it toward another, if they will not accept the Bride of the Lamb [the Catholic Church]. Let them, if they can, put faith in some of those religions which have lasted a whole two or three centuries in a corner of the earth.[73]

The counterfeit to true faith is private judgement. Private judgment leaves us in the world of our own inclinations, interpretations, and societies. By definition private judgment relies on our own judgments and so never crosses into faithful reception of divine revelation. As presented by Newman, the Church is not a third thing in between the believer and God, but, instead—as seen in his cardinal's motto, *cor ad cor loquitur*—the Church is the means through which God speaks to our hearts. Newman's ultimate understanding of faith was that the assent to God's speech requires the submission of the intellect and will to a judgment higher than our own as expressed in the Catholic Church.[74]

---

72 Newman summarizes the need for a living authority to assent to religious doctrine in his *Apo.*, 19: "Thus the argument from Probability, in the matter of religion, became an argument from Personality, which in fact is one form of the argument from Authority."

73 *Mix.*, no. 10: 207–11.

74 Frank M. Turner disagrees with this reading of Newman's Catholic faith as a deepening of his earlier faith and counters that Newman lost his earlier evangelical faith in becoming a Catholic. He writes, "[Newman's] reception into the Roman Catholic Church almost thirty years later [after his adolescent conversion] represented the final step in what had been a long process of separation from that adolescent faith. That the conclusion of the process, which commenced in his mid-twenties, was Roman Catholicism does not make it any less a loss of evangelical faith than if, like others of his and later generations, he had ended in Unitarianism, like his brother Francis, or in agnosticism," in *John Henry Newman: The Challenge to Evangelical Religion* (New Haven: Yale University Press, 2002), 11. Such an argument fails to account for the way in which Newman articulates his Catholic faith as in continuity with the faith of the early Christians in coming to believe in the good news of Jesus Christ not as a private discovery or the conclusion of a logical process but as preached authoritatively by the apostles and embraced by the believer.

CONCLUSION

For Newman, faith is an exercise of reason enlightened by grace and moved by charity that says yes to God's revelation through His Church and so comes to communion with God. By distinguishing between reasoning in its implicit and explicit modes, Newman challenges the presumptive hegemony of modern empirical and logical reason as expounded in figures such as David Hume. Reasoning is not merely abstract but is the way in which the living person encounters the world and makes implicit and explicit judgments about the truth of reality and the goodness of actions. As such, the dependence of faith upon antecedent probabilities of its truthfulness and upon the testimony of the apostles and Scripture does not mean that faith is irrational but only that faith is an act of the reasoning mind beyond the scope of empirical reason. Faith as an act of implicit reason may receive further consideration through the reflection of explicit reason so as to lead to the development of Christian teaching, but faith never loses its primacy as an assent of the living person to the Christian revelation.

Newman thus presents faith as a new way of seeing the whole of reality. With faith, the rational creature arrives at a new relationship to God and the rest of creation. Newman describes this process of coming to see the whole as the perfection of faith in Christian wisdom. At one point, he presents faith and wisdom as the first and last gifts of the Holy Spirit.[75] Newman suggests that he is undoubtedly saying what many others have thought but offers a rationale for his sustained engagement with faith and reason: "perhaps it is never without its use to bring together *in one view*, and *steadily contemplate truths*, which one by one may be familiar notwithstanding."[76] Newman here describes his own project as an attempt to present the complex realities of faith and reason "in one view" and look at them "steadily." In doing so, he offers his reader a new way of seeing things—not only the processes of faith and reason but, above all, their objects.

Newman's work thus serves its apologetic purpose in assisting his reader in at least three distinct steps to come to see ever-increasing dimensions of reality through renewed reason and faith. First, beyond the limited vision of empiricism that only sees what is measurable and quantifiable, Newman's defense of an expanded reason helps us to see the truth of the human person and the truth of God as the source of the universe. Second, beyond the limited vision of natural philosophical inquiry, Newman's defense of the revelation of Jesus Christ in the Catholic Church helps us to see God's plan of creation and redemption with certainty and hope. Third, beyond our limited, distorted, and ego-centric vision impacted by pride, Newman's recovery of faith working through charity helps us to see, at least in part, reality in its theo-centric dimension. Newman exhorts his audience to let God speak to us *cor ad cor* and so transform our hearts and minds by faith and love:

---

75 *US*, no. 14: 294.
76 *US*, no. 13: 277; emphasis added.

Let us ever make it our prayer and our endeavor, that we may know the whole counsel of God, and grow unto the measure of the stature of the fullness of Christ; that all prejudice, and self-confidence, and hollowness, and unreality, and positiveness, and partisanship, may be put away from us under the light of Wisdom, and the fire of Faith and Love; till *we see things as God sees them*, with the judgment of His Spirit, and according to the mind of Christ.[77]

Suggested Reading

Aquino, Frederick D. "Epistemology." In *The Oxford Handbook of John Henry Newman*, edited by Frederick D. Aquino and Benjamin J. King, 375–94. Oxford: Oxford University Press, 2018.

Barron, Robert. "John Henry Newman among the Postmoderns." In *Exploring Catholic Theology: Essays on God, Liturgy, and Evangelization*, 95–107. Grand Rapids, Mich.: Baker Academic, 2015.

Duffy, Eamon. "Faith and Doubt." In *John Henry Newman: A Very Brief History*, 41–50. London: Society for Promoting Christian Knowledge, 2019.

Gilley, Sheridan. "The Grammar." In *Newman and his Age*, 362–73. London: Darton, Longman, and Todd, 2003.

Hütter, Reinhard. "Faith and Its Counterfeit." In *John Henry Newman on Truth and its Counterfeits: A Guide for Our Times*, 90–129. Washington, D.C.: The Catholic University of America Press, 2020.

Newman, John Henry, *An Essay in Aid of a Grammar of Assent*.

_____. Sermons 4, 10–15. In *Oxford University Sermons*.

_____. "The Tamworth Reading Room." In *Discussions and Arguments*.

---

77 *US*, no. 14: 311; emphasis added. Newman also writes, "Wisdom is the clear, calm, accurate vision, and comprehension of the whole course, the whole work of God" (293).

CHAPTER 18

THE SPIRITUAL AND DOCTRINAL SIGNIFICANCE OF NEWMAN'S SERMONS

Fr. Keith Beaumont

I. INTRODUCTION: WAYS OF APPROACHING NEWMAN'S SERMONS

There are several ways of approaching the subject of Newman's preaching. One is to deal with his manner of preaching and its impact on contemporary audiences. Another is to engage in an essentially stylistic analysis of the sermons. A third approach is to look at the sermons as a record of Newman's changing ideas and of his personal dilemmas and dramas. All of these approaches have their interest and validity. However, the approach adopted in this chapter is different: it seeks to outline the principal themes of his sermons, emphasizing and illustrating in particular the nature and importance of the spiritual advice and teaching which they contain. It is all too often forgotten, in fact, that through his sermons and his spiritual direction—of which his voluminous correspondence also provides a record—Newman is one of the great spiritual teachers and guides of modern times.[1]

---

1   See, among others, Louis Bouyer, *Newman: Sa vie, sa spiritualité* (Paris: Éditions du Cerf, 1952). English translation: *Newman: His Life and Spirituality: An Intellectual and Spiritual Biography of John Henry Newman*, trans. J. Lewis May (San Francisco: Ignatius Press, 2011); and Louis Bouyer, *Newman's Vision of Faith: A Theology for Times of General*

THE PLACE OF NEWMAN'S SERMONS
IN HIS WORK AS A WHOLE

A word must first be said concerning the place occupied in Newman's published work by his sermons. The sheer quantity of his production in this domain is impressive. He published twelve volumes of sermons, ten as an Anglican[2] and two as a Catholic,[3] and these twelve volumes represent almost one third of the total number of volumes of his work which he himself published.[4] It is true that, since his death, a considerable number of other volumes have been published, made up in most cases of notes or drafts; no fewer than seven of these however are made up of sermons or sermon notes.[5] A further consideration worthy of note is the fact that Newman's sermons have remained continuously in print for close on two hundred years: of how many other authors of sermons can such a claim be made?

Yet his sermons are all too often neglected by scholars, as if the sermon were a minor genre not worthy of the same attention as his autobiographical, or theological, or philosophical, or historical works. Must we therefore conclude that questions of spirituality are unworthy of serious academic study? Or could it be that academics and intellectuals deem themselves incapable of dealing with such questions? Whatever the case, can one really justify such a neglect in a complete and balanced study of his work?

Apostasy (San Francisco: Ignatius Press, 1986.) See also Keith Beaumont, *Dieu intérieur: La théologie spirituelle de John Henry Newman* (Paris: Ad Solem, 2014).

2 These are the eight volumes of his *Parochial and Plain Sermons* (1834–1842, then 1868), his *Fifteen Sermons Preached Before the University of Oxford Between A.D. 1826 and 1843* (1843), and his *Sermons Bearing on Subjects of the Day* (1843).

3 *Discourses Addressed to Mixed Congregations* (1849) and *Sermons Preached on Various Occasions* (1857).

4 He wrote and preached far more than this, of course. It has been estimated that, as an Anglican, he rose into the pulpit to preach some 1270 times. He has left us 604 fully written out sermons from this period—many of them revised and preached more than once—of which he published roughly one-third, together with thirty-three published sermons and a handful of unpublished manuscripts dating from his Catholic period.

5 These are, for the Anglican period, the five volumes of unpublished sermons under the title of *Sermons 1824–1843*, edited by Placid Murray, Vincent Blehl, Francis McGrath, and others and published by the Clarendon Press, Oxford, 1991–2012. For the Catholic period they comprise a volume of nine sermons preached chiefly in 1848, first published by Sheed & Ward in 1956, in Britain as *Catholic Sermons of Cardinal Newman* and in the United States as (among other titles) *Faith and Prejudice and Other Sermons*, and a volume of *Sermon Notes of John Henry Cardinal Newman, 1849–1878* published in 1913 by Longmans, Green & Co. The general rule in regard to such works not published by the author himself is that, whatever their biographical or literary interest, they ought not to be accorded the same status in terms of expression of his thought as a work, and indeed the final edition of such a work, completed, revised, and published by the author himself.

NEWMAN'S CONCEPTION OF THE
NATURE AND PURPOSE OF A SERMON

A few words may be in order here concerning this subject. Newman himself has facilitated the task in an essay of 1855 entitled "University Preaching," published in the second part of *The Idea of a University*. It is true that he is speaking here of preaching to an educated congregation, and his words need to be supplemented by a few additional remarks; but the principles outlined here remain valid all the same for the whole of his preaching.

A sermon must never seek to say everything possible on a given subject but should aim at developing *one* particular theme or idea, exploring it in all its various dimensions. "Nothing is so fatal to the effect of a sermon," he remarks, "as the habit of preaching on three or four subjects at once."[6]

A sermon must not appeal simply to the emotions of the hearer (or reader) but to his or her *intellect* also; it must "convince" as well as "persuade." He quotes as an example of the wisdom of saints in this domain the words of St. Francis de Sales, "Necesse est ut *doceat* et moveat" (it is necessary both to *teach* and to move).[7]

In consequence, a sermon, without ever being a theological exposé, must "possess a reality,"[8] that is to say, it must have a solid *doctrinal* basis, for a sound grasp of Christian doctrine (or dogma) is essential to the correct orientation of our spiritual lives.

Preaching must be rooted in an intimate knowledge of and familiarity with the Bible. Newman himself quotes massively from both the Old and New Testaments, one of his Catholic sermons for example containing as many as fifty-one biblical quotations.[9]

Whilst a sermon must never be a pretext for self-indulgent talking about oneself, the preacher must *involve* himself personally, and totally, in the subject of his sermon. He must aim to "bring home to others, and to leave deep within them, what he has . . . brought home to himself."[10]

A preacher must address himself *directly* to his hearers and readers. It is necessary therefore that he must, as far as possible, have some knowledge of these; indeed, "we cannot determine how in detail we ought to preach, till we know whom we are to address."[11]

---

6   *Idea*, part II, 412.
7   *Idea*, 411. Newman's italics.
8   Letter of July 1836 to John Keble, *LD* v, 327.
9   See his sermon "Christ upon the Waters," *OS*, no. 9. This omnipresence of the Bible is such that it has even been suggested, with a touch of humour, that if by some unimaginable catastrophe all existing copies of the Bible were to disappear, it would be possible to reconstitute the text in large measure from Newman's Anglican sermons. W.F. Mandel, "Newman and his Audiences: 1825–1845," *Journal of Religious History* 24, no. 2 (June 2000): 143–58.
10   *Idea*, 412–13.
11   *Idea*, 415.

A key aim of all preaching must be to bring the hearer or reader to greater *self-knowledge*. Self-knowledge is in fact "at the root of all real religious knowledge" and is "the key to the precepts and doctrines of Scripture," for "God speaks to us primarily in our hearts." "The very utmost any outward notices of religion can do," he maintains, "is to startle us and make us turn inward and search our hearts; and then, when we have experienced what it is to read ourselves, we shall profit by the doctrines of the Church and the Bible."[12]

At the heart of all preaching must be the *person* of Christ, and not just a doctrine concerning Him. Newman invites us not just to serve Christ but to seek Him and to desire His presence within us.

Though Newman reveals himself in his sermons as a stern moralist, he never falls into the trap of mere moralising. Morality, like doctrine, is always placed at the service of a *spiritual* awakening. Though "talent, logic, learning, words, manner, voice, action" are all "required for the perfection of a preacher," the latter's ultimate aim must be to impart to those who hear and read him some "spiritual good," and indeed "some *definite* spiritual good."[13]

To sum up, preaching, for Newman, possesses a dual aim: it is that of making us "turn inward and search our hearts"[14] and that of "lighting up the image of the Incarnate Son in our hearts."[15]

SOME CONSEQUENCES OF THE
CIRCUMSTANCES OF NEWMAN'S SERMONS

As an Anglican, preaching for the most part from the pulpit of the University Church of St. Mary the Virgin, Newman addressed himself to a congregation all of whose members were, at least nominally, Anglican. His aim was therefore to bring them to a deeper understanding of themselves and to a Christianity which was "real" as opposed to purely nominal. This brings to his preaching a tone of "earnestness," a quality which he demands of his hearers and readers also.[16] But he was also deeply committed to a radical reform of his Church and was critical of the attitudes of certain of its members. He found himself in opposition to both of the two major currents of contemporary Anglicanism: the Evangelical movement, which he criticized for the narrowness of its theology—a theology he saw as concerned principally with the doctrine of "justification by faith"—and for its exacerbated emotionalism,[17] and the mainstream High Church, characterized

---

12   "Secret Faults," *PS* i, no. 4: 42–43.

13   *Idea*, 408, 410.

14   "Secret Faults," *PS* i, no. 4: 43.

15   "The Humiliation of the Eternal Son," *PS* iii, no. 12: 170.

16   See, among many others, the sermon "Self-Denial the Test of Religious Earnestness," *PS* i, no. 5.

17   For example, he refers scathingly, à propos of the Evangelicals, to their having placed "the life of a Christian" in "a sort of religious extasy, in a high-wrought sensibility on sacred subjects, in impassioned thoughts." "The Gift of the Spirit," *PS* iii, no. 18: 268.

all too often in his eyes by a purely formalistic worship and by a preaching that was dry and moralistic (he and his friends referred to its members scathingly as the "High and Dry").[18] As these examples reveal, one finds in Newman's sermons frequent expressions of irony and even at times a distinctly polemical strain (we sometimes forget that he is generally held to be one of the great polemical writers in the English language in a period—the Victorian age—renowned for its love of polemics). But the tone is far from being restricted to this. Some of the sermons in his last Anglican volume, *Sermons Preached on Subjects of the Day*, have an urgency and even pathos about them as he tries to cling to his Anglican faith and Church.

As a Catholic his situation was very different. He was now a member of a despised minority and of a Church that was hated and—paradoxically—at the same time feared. But it was a Church also which was gradually emerging from over three centuries of persecution and oppression. It is as a Catholic preacher, particularly in his first volume, *Discourses Addressed to Mixed Congregations* (the "mixed" congregations being made up of mainly Irish and poorly educated Catholics, Anglicans vaguely sympathetic or else hostile to Catholicism—whom he systematically now refers to as "Protestants"[19]—and those who rejected all religion), that the polemical strain is most in evidence. It is true also that, as Newman himself remarked, they are "more rhetorical than [his] former Sermons,"[20] and this has sometimes led modern readers to neglect unjustly the perspicacity and profundity of many of them. But the tone varies greatly, being alternately didactic, exhortatory, pleading, and combative; ironical interpellations alternate with impassioned appeals, while several sermons end with passages of tender devotion and even prayers of thanksgiving. His second volume of Catholic sermons, *Sermons Preached on Various Occasions*, is more heterogeneous, comprising the eight sermons preached in the newly opened church of the Catholic University of Ireland—in which he argues for the unity of the intellectual and the spiritual—four sermons celebrating various aspects of the "rebirth" of Catholicism in England, two personal homages and—curiously—a sermon preached (at his bishop's behest) on the temporal power of the pope. The tone in this volume is alternately exhortatory, meditative, lyrical, and celebratory.

---

18 He states for example that members of the High Church, by way of reaction against Evangelical emotionalism and a superficial spirituality, limit "the gift of the Holy Spirit" to making of us "decent and orderly members of society." *PS* iii, no. 18: 268.

19 This use of "Protestant" applied to Anglicans may surprise and even shock today's reader. But at the time, practically all Anglicans considered their Church to be a "Protestant" one and called themselves "Protestants." It was only in the second half of the nineteenth century—in large part owing to the influence of the Oxford Movement—that the term "Anglican" came progressively to be used.

20 To F. W. Faber, *LD* xiii, 335. Ian Ker remarks rather tartly that "the rhetoric is often more Italianate than Newmanian." Ian Ker, *John Henry Newman: A Biography* (Oxford University Press, 1988), 342–43. He tends, however, to be unfairly dismissive of these sermons.

It is important to note also the organisation or structure of the different volumes of his *Parochial and Plain Sermons*.[21] When readers complained of the "severity" of the first volume, Newman responded that he had intended it be so; he was in fact reacting against what he considered the too facile Christianity preached by many Evangelicals and members of the High Church. Later volumes, without losing this sternness, become progressively more "luminous," culminating in volumes V and VI, which contain some of his most inspiring Anglican sermons. Several volumes, also, are structured along liturgical lines, as Newman attempts to effect a rediscovery of the rich liturgical spirituality of earlier centuries: volume II commemorates chiefly saints' days, and volumes V and VI are organised according to the seasons and feasts of the liturgical calendar.[22] Each of these liturgical seasons or feasts imparts, to a certain degree, its own particular mood or tonality to the sermons concerned.

II. THE MAJOR THEMES OF NEWMAN'S SERMONS

Newman's twelve volumes of sermons cover a vast range of themes. For the sake of clarity, these are presented here in five broad groupings which form a kind of "constellation."[23]

1. FAITH

The subject of faith is at the heart of the last six of Newman's *Oxford University Sermons*; but it runs, in one form or another, through practically the whole of his preaching, both Anglican and Catholic.

However, his understanding of faith is, in part at least, at variance with the broader context of the evolution of Western thought over the past four centuries, which is marked by an *intellectualisation* of the concept of faith. Faith is identified generally with "believing" or with the holding of certain "beliefs." Newman shares of course this view: in the face of a corrosive relativism which reduces all religion to a mere matter of personal "opinion"—a phenomenon time and again

---

21   The series originally comprised only the first six volumes, published between 1834 and 1842, under the title *Parochial Sermons*. On the occasion of their republication in 1868 by an Anglican friend, William Copeland, with Newman's approval, two further volumes were added, as well as the words *"and Plain"* to the series title, because these last two volumes were made up of sermons drawn from a collective work, *Plain Sermons by Contributors to Tracts for the Times*, and possess a rather more heterogeneous character than the others.

22   Grouping sermons in this way may seem unsurprising to today's reader; but in Newman's day it represented something of a revolution in preaching practice.

23   The organisation proposed here reproduces that employed by the author of the present chapter in a thematic anthology of twenty-five sermons published in French translation. See *Être chrétien: Les plus beaux sermons*, ed. Keith Beaumont and Pierre Gauthier, with an introduction by Keith Beaumont (Paris: Éditions du Cerf, 2017).

denounced by him under the name of "private judgment"—he passionately defends what he calls "dogma."[24] As an Anglican he seeks to explore and to defend the theological basis of Anglicanism; as a Catholic, he embarks upon a defence and illustration of Catholic teaching.

At the same time, however, both as an Anglican and as a Catholic Newman seeks to broaden and to deepen our understanding of what constitutes faith. In the context of the contemporary debate between "faith" and "reason," he seeks to redefine and to enlarge the meaning of both terms. Faith is not simply believing but involves first and foremost an act of *confidence*. In this sense, it is not limited to religion but plays an important role in our everyday lives in which we are often required to make an "act of faith," acting or taking decisions without possessing an absolute certainty regarding the justification for our actions or decisions: faith is "a principle of action, and action does not allow time for minute and finished investigations. . . . This is the case with all Faith, and not merely religious."[25] He totally refuses however all forms of "fideism," the doctrine that faith has no need of intellectual justification: no "sober mind," he declares, can "run into the wild notion that actually no proof at all is implied in the maintenance, or may be exacted for the profession of Christianity."[26] He urges the need for faith to be "real" (in modern parlance one might say "existential"), denouncing in one of his most polemical Anglican sermons the use of what he calls "unreal words."[27] Against the corrosive rationalism inherited from the Enlightenment, he insists that belief is "reasonable," that is to say it is never without grounds or "reasons." But at the same time he recognizes that many persons may be unable to articulate those grounds, thus defending the reality of the faith of simple and uneducated persons: "Faith cannot exist without grounds or without an object; but it does not follow that all who have faith should recognize, and be able to state what they believe, and why."[28] As for the word "reason," he sees in it two basic meanings, neither of which is opposed to faith. One is that of "any process or act of the mind, by which, from knowing one thing, it advances on to know another"; in this case, he argues, "it includes of course Faith."[29] The other is that of an instrument of analysis, of investigation or of verification; in this sense there can be no conflict between reason and faith since they operate on two different

---

24 For a discussion of the meaning of this term, see my chapter on "The Connection between Theology, Spirituality, and Morality in Newman."

25 "Faith and Reason, Contrasted as Habits of Mind," *US*, no. 10, §27–28, 188.

26 "Faith and Reason, Contrasted as Habits of Mind," *US*, no. 10, §44, 199.

27 See the sermon "Unreal Words," *PS* v, no. 3.

28 "Implicit and Explicit Reason," *US*, no. 13, §4, 254.

29 "Love the Safeguard of Faith against Superstition," *US*, no. 12, §2, 223. See also the closing words of the *Grammar of Assent*: Christianity addresses itself "both through the intellect and through the imagination; creating a certitude of its truth by arguments too various for direct enumeration, too personal and deep for words, too powerful and concurrent for refutation. . . . It speaks to us one by one, and is received by us one by one, as the counterpart, so to say, of ourselves, and is real as we are real." *GA*, 491–92.

planes. Faith is in no way simply a "deduction" or "conclusion" resulting from the work of reason; but reason may legitimately examine and evaluate it: "Reason need not be the origin of Faith . . . , though it does test and verify it."[30]

These ideas are carried over into Newman's Catholic sermons. As a Catholic, he was ill at ease with the Church's essentially intellectualist conception of faith as adherence to a fixed and unchanging set of beliefs or propositions.[31] He distinguishes clearly between faith and theology, while recognising the necessity and interdependence of each. The notion of the "real" is developed in the *Grammar of Assent* in one of his key philosophical intuitions, namely the distinction between "real" and "notional" assent. "Real" assent is personal and relational, it involves things and more particularly *persons*; "notional" assent is that given to mere "propositions." The sense of "reality" which pervades his sermons is to be found in his philosophical works also.

From beginning to end, Newman possesses also an acute sense of the *complexity* of the human mind, and therefore of the phenomenon of faith: "No analysis," he argues, "is subtle and delicate enough to represent adequately the state of mind under which we believe, or the subjects of belief, as they are presented to our thoughts."[32] He possesses an equally acute sense of the *individuality* of each human being; and he is convinced that God too respects this individuality and seeks to lead each person along the path most suited to him (which does not mean, however, that all roads lead to God), declaring in a Catholic sermon that "God deals with us very differently; conviction comes slowly to some men, quickly to others; in some it is the result of much thought and many reasonings, in others of a sudden illumination. . . . Some men are converted merely by entering a Catholic Church; others are converted by reading one book; others by one doctrine. . . . Or they are touched and overcome by the evident sanctity, beauty, and (as I may say) fragrance of the Catholic Religion."[33]

He insists also on the need to distinguish between different forms of *knowledge*: however important knowing certain facts *about* or *concerning* God may be, it is not the same as an intimate, personal "knowledge" of Him, and only the "light" of divine grace can enable us to attain to the latter. In one of his finest Catholic sermons, "Illuminating Grace," he addresses himself to his congregation in these words:

---

30   "Faith and Reason, Contrasted as Habits of Mind," *US*, no. 10, §13, 183.

31   This intellectual or intellectualist conception of faith is well illustrated in the Dogmatic Constitution *Dei Filius* (1870) of the First Vatican Council. The "assent of faith" is here defined as a "movement of the intellect," and the object of faith is given as "all those things [which] must be believed which are contained in the written word of God and in tradition, and those which are proposed by the Church"; the Council adds that "we are bound by faith to give full obedience of intellect and will to God who reveals." "Faith," ch. 3.

32   "Implicit and Explicit Reason," *US*, no. 13, §22, 267.

33   "Faith and Doubt," *Mix.*, no. 11, 233–34.

> You ask, what it is you need, besides eyes, in order to see the truths of revelation: I will tell you at once; you need light. . . . Now, though your mind be the eye, the grace of God is the light; and you will as easily exercise your eyes in this sensible world without the sun, as you will be able to exercise your mind in the spiritual world without a parallel gift from without.

Without this divine Light, we "will not be able to do more than reason" about God, our thoughts "will not get beyond a mere reasoning" for "to infer a thing is not to see it in respect to the physical world, nor is it in the spiritual."[34]

Theology, however important, is therefore not faith—although it can lead to it—and faith is more than just believing, more than simply the work of our own minds. This active role of God in the birth and nourishment of faith is expressed by means of several terms frequent in Newman—"impression," "influence," and of course "grace." Yet if, as a Catholic, he defends the traditional Catholic conception of faith as a "gift of God," he insists also that we must *prepare* ourselves to *receive* this gift. Thus our moral selves are involved in the process of the reception and growth of faith. From beginning to end, in fact, Newman emphasizes the relationship between morality (or ethics) and our spiritual lives. In a scathing passage in the tenth of his *Oxford University Sermons* (in which many of us can no doubt recognize our own past, or perhaps even present, selves) he denounces the cavalier and superficial manner in which many approach the question of faith and emphasizes the need for a "preparation of heart":

> For is not this the error, the common and fatal error, of the world, to think itself a judge of Religious Truth without preparation of heart? . . . In the schools of the world the ways towards Truth are considered high roads open to all men, however disposed, at all times. Truth is to be approached without homage . . . the powers of the intellect, acuteness, sagacity, subtlety, and depth, are thought the guides into Truth. Men consider that they have as full a right to discuss religious subjects, as if they were themselves religious. They will enter upon the most sacred points of Faith at the moment, at their pleasure,—if it so happen, in a careless frame of mind, in their hours of recreation, over the wine cup.[35]

He insists on the importance of a disposition of humility and of what he calls "teachableness." He emphasizes the importance of openness of mind and even of intellectual curiosity: in his eyes, it is not belief but *un*belief which is often the result of a closed and incurious mind.[36] He distinguishes thus between

---

34 *Mix.,* no. 9, 172.
35 "Faith and Reason, Contrasted as Habits of Mind," *US,* no. 10, 198–99.
36 See the sermon "Dispositions for Faith," *OS,* no. 5, which Newman himself

the "religious" man and the "rationalist," the former displaying an openness of mind and the latter a closed mind.[37] He places particular emphasis, over and again, on the relationship between faith and what he calls "obedience"; by this he means not simply respect for the law or acting in a certain way but, once again, a certain *disposition* which underlies and determines these. Faith and obedience, far from standing in opposition to each other, are but two facets of one and the same disposition: "To believe is to look beyond this world to God, and to obey is to look beyond this world to God; to believe is of the heart, and to obey is of the heart."[38]

Newman frequently speaks also of the relationship between faith and "conscience." This word "conscience" signifies for him not just the moral conscience but the intimate sense, or "consciousness," of a Presence in the depths of our being; it is "like the echo of a voice," that of God. He perceives a double "movement," so to speak, within us: a "descent" into ourselves in search of the author of this "voice" and an experience of being "thrown out of ourselves":

> Every religious mind . . . will be in the habit of looking out of and beyond self, as regards all matters connected with its highest good. For a man of religious mind is he who attends to the rule of conscience, which is born with him, which he did not make for himself, and to which he feels bound in duty to submit. . . . Thus a man is at once thrown out of himself, by the very Voice which speaks within him; . . . that inward sense does not allow him to rest in itself, but sends him forth again from home to seek abroad for Him who has put His Word in him. . . . Such is faith as it exists in the multitude of those who believe, arising from their sense of the Presence of God, originally certified to them by the inward voice of conscience.[39]

---

described as a "re-writing" of an Anglican sermon preached twenty-two years earlier, "Faith without Sight" (*PS* ii, no. 2), a fact which underlines the continuity of his thought.

37   In an essay of 1836, published originally as *Tract* 73, he declares that whereas "the religious" man "[looks] out of [himself], trying to catch glimpses of God's workings, from any quarter,—throwing [himself] forward upon Him and waiting on Him," the "rationalist" "makes himself his own centre, not his Maker; he does not go to God, but he implies that God must come to him," he "sit[s] at home bringing everything to [himself], enthroning [himself] in [his] own views, and refusing to believe anything that does not force itself upon [him] as true." "On the Introduction of Rationalistic Principles into Revealed Religion," *EH* i, 33–34. The metaphors of "being thrown out of oneself" and "to sit at home" recur several times in Newman.

38   "Faith and Obedience," *PS* iii, no. 6: 80–81.

39   "Faith without Sight," *PS* ii, no. 2: 17–19. It is interesting to note that Joseph Ratzinger, the future Pope Benedict XVI, who has written extensively on the subject of conscience, was profoundly influenced by Newman when a seminarian, a fact which he recalls in a lecture given at a Newman symposium in 1990 entitled "Newman belongs to the great teachers of the Church." In this same lecture he declared that Newman's teaching on conscience and on doctrinal development constitutes "a decisive contribution

One further disposition is necessary, however, without which faith is fruit-less: it is the *love* of or the *desire* for God. "Let us understand," declares Newman, "as a first truth in religion, that *love* of God is the *only* way to heaven. . . . Let us understand that nothing but the love of God can make us believe in Him or obey Him."[40] And again: "Love is the condition of faith; and faith in turn is the cher-isher and maturer of love; it brings love out into works, and therefore is called the *works* of love."[41] The true object of faith then is not a doctrine but a person, with whom one can enter into a relationship of love and trust; and its foundation is an *interior disposition* of "openness" and a "capacity" to receive. Newman's thought echoes here that of the author of the Epistle to the Ephesians: "May Christ *dwell in your hearts* by faith."[42]

Newman's teaching on the subject of faith, therefore, in his sermons and elsewhere, goes far beyond a merely intellectual conception. Faith is above all confidence or trust in God: faith "does not crave or bargain to see the end of the journey . . . it is persuaded that it has quite enough light to walk by, more than sinful man has a right to expect, if it sees one step in advance."[43] Thus true faith leads us to place ourselves in God's hands, or to what Newman calls—using a traditional term employed by spiritual writers in English—"surrender" to God. Let it not be thought however that this involves some sort of passivity: on the contrary, spiritual "surrender" requires a powerful and unceasing act of the *will*, it can only be the fruit of a long and rigorous spiritual "training." An Anglican sermon describes in the following terms the relationship between faith and surrender:

> What is meant by faith? it is to feel in good earnest that we are crea-tures of God; it is a practical perception of the unseen world; it is to understand that this world is not enough for our happiness, to look beyond it on towards God, to realize His presence, to wait upon Him, to endeavour to learn and to do His will, and to seek our good from Him. . . . To have faith in God is to surrender one's-self to God, humbly to put one's interests, or to wish to be allowed to put them into His hands who is the Sovereign Giver of all good.[44]

---

to the renewal of theology." Joseph Ratzinger, "Newman gehört zu den grossen Lehrern der Kirche," in *John Henry Newman, Lover of Truth*, Academic Symposium and Celebration of the first Centenary of the Death of John Henry Newman (Rome: Pontificia Universitas Urbaniana, 1991), 144.

40 "Miracles No Remedy for Unbelief," *PS* viii, no. 6: 89–90. Newman's italics.

41 "Faith and Love," *PS* iv, no. 21: 315. Newman's italics.

42 Eph 3:17. My italics.

43 "Faith without Sight," *PS* ii, no. 2: 22. These words recall of course Newman's most famous prayer, "Lead, Kindly Light," written the previous year, on June 16, 1833.

44 "Faith and Obedience," *PS* iii, no. 6: 79–80. See also, on the subject of spiri-tual surrender, the sermons "Christian Repentance" (*PS* iii, no. 7) and "The Testimony of Conscience" (*PS* v, no. 17).

2. THE CHRISTIAN VOCATION TO HOLINESS

Every theology presupposes, and rests upon, an anthropology or conception of the human person. Newman's theology is intimately related to his conception of this, to his understanding of the meaning of life, and to his view of the Christian vocation.

The vision of man expressed by biblical authors such as St. John and St. Paul, followed by the Church Fathers, is essentially that of a "relational" being, capable of entering into a relationship with God in the depths of his or her own soul. This vision characterizes the Christian tradition from the time of the Fathers up until roughly the middle of the seventeenth century. Since then, however, we observe an increasing intellectualisation not only of our conception of faith but of our conception of the human person also. The latter is seen as a "thinking" being, then also, since the Romantic era, as a "feeling" being (and then today as one avid for new and exciting "sensations"). This evolution has gone hand in hand with a decline in interiority, with God being less and less seen as an interior "Presence" and more and more as an external "Judge" and "Ruler." Only in recent decades has a movement begun back to a more traditional vision; but it has yet to enter the consciousness of most Christians.

Newman, thanks to his familiarity with Scripture, to his intensive study of the Church Fathers, and no doubt also in part to his personal spiritual experience, offers us a vision of the human person whose first and most important characteristic is precisely this personal, interior relationship. Thus in an Anglican sermon of 1838 he declares:

> A true Christian, then, may almost be defined as one who has a ruling sense of God's presence within him. . . . A true Christian . . . is he, who, in such sense, has faith in Him, as to live in the thought that He is present with him,—present not externally, not in nature merely, or in providence, but in his innermost heart, or in his *conscience*.[45]

And in one of his last Anglican sermons, preached in February 1843, he proposes as a model for contemporary Christians the "Apostolical Christian" such as he is represented in Scripture. Such a person lives "in this world, but not for this world." He or she is "one who looks for Christ; not who looks for gain, or distinction, or power, or pleasure, or comfort, but who looks 'for the Saviour, the Lord Jesus Christ.'" Thus "watching is a special mark of the Scripture Christian"; prayer, too, "is another characteristic of Christians as described in Scripture." There was in fact "no barrier, no cloud, no earthly object, interposed between the soul of the primitive Christian and its Saviour and Redeemer. Christ was in his heart, and therefore all that came from his heart, his thoughts, words, and actions, savoured of Christ."[46]

---

45 "Sincerity and Hypocrisy," *PS* v, no. 16: 225–26. Newman's italics.
46 "The Apostolical Christian," *SD*, no. 19: 278–81.

The Christian then, for Newman, is one who does not simply "believe" or who does not simply strive to lead a morally upright life, but one who is called upon progressively to deepen an interior relationship, and thereby to undergo an inner transformation. He or she is called to holiness.

The theme of holiness occupies a privileged place in Newman's preaching. Following his first conversion of 1816, he had, he tells us, summed up the teaching of one of his early spiritual masters, Thomas Scott, in two formulae which "for years" he "used almost as proverbs": "Holiness rather than peace" and "Growth the only evidence of life."[47] He chose for the very first sermon in volume I of his *Parochial and Plain Sermons* one entitled "Holiness Necessary for Future Blessedness," and the position of this sermon in his work gave it a programmatic value. A Catholic sermon of 1849, "Saintliness the Standard of Christian Principle," takes up the same theme.[48]

How did Newman conceive of "holiness"? There are at times in his early sermons traces of a form of voluntarism typical of the whole of the nineteenth and early twentieth centuries: holiness is conceived of as a state of moral perfection, which we strive to attain by our own efforts. But gradually he came to realize that it is God who, little by little, makes us holy through the transforming power of his Holy Spirit working in us. As with conversion, the path to holiness is a process in which time and growth play a key role: "To obtain the gift of holiness is the work of a life."[49] It must be emphasized again however that this is no recipe for passivity: on the contrary, it involves what Newman would call a "work": we must strive to make ourselves receptive of the Spirit: "The more frequent are our prayers, the more humble, patient, and religious are our daily deeds, this communion with God, these holy works, will be the means of making our hearts holy, and of preparing ourselves for the future presence of God. Outward acts, done on principle, create inward habits."[50]

Nor does sin prevent us from becoming saints. In a Catholic sermon, Newman takes the example St. Augustine in order to show that not only can a sinner become a saint—on condition, obviously, that he repents—but that his former sinfulness can prove ultimately to be a positive force:

> And do you not think, my brethren, that he was better fitted than another to persuade his brethren as he had been persuaded, and to preach the holy doctrine which he had despised? Not that sin is better than obedience, or the sinner than the just; but that God in His mercy makes use of sin against itself, that He turns past sin into a present benefit, that, while He washes away its guilt and subdues its power, He

---

47 *Apo.*, 5.

48 *Mix.*, no. 5.

49 "Holiness Necessary for Future Blessedness," *PS* i, no. 1: 9, 12. Newman's italics.

50 "Holiness Necessary for Future Blessedness," *PS* i, no. 1: 9. Italics mine. The last sentence is a superb example of Newman's genius for pithy aphorisms. See Cardinal Jean Honoré, *Les Aphorismes de Newman* (Paris: Éditions du Cerf, 2007).

leaves it in the penitent in such sense as enables him, from his knowledge of its devices, to assault it more vigorously, and strike at it more truly, when it meets him in other men.[51]

A particularly interesting feature of Newman's thought on the subject of holiness is his association of the two categories of "holiness" and "beauty." Like many of the Church Fathers, he was attracted to the theme of the "Beauty" of God. And he seems to have been fascinated by a formula, found in the King James Bible and in the Anglican Book of Common Prayer, which he quotes roughly a dozen times in his sermons, "the beauty of holiness."[52] Through his participation in the very life of God, the Christian manifests "the beauty of holiness" which has its origin in the "beauty" of God Himself.

A further aspect of the Christian's vocation concerns his relationship to the "world." Newman takes up the distinction made in the Gospel of St. John between being in the world and being of the world. Many a passage in his sermons expresses a critical—and at times apparently negative—attitude towards the world. The word refers here however not to human society as a whole but to those attitudes and values, cherished by a majority of his (and our) contemporaries, that run counter to the Gospel message. But if the Christian is called upon to practice a critical discernment with regard to the values of the "world," Newman urges us to be on guard against the temptation to neglect our "duties" in this world on the pretext of concerning ourselves exclusively with "heaven." In a sermon, whose title "Doing Glory to God in Pursuits of the World" echoes the words of St. Paul who exhorts Christians to "do everything for the glory of God" (1 Cor 10:31), he declares that thankfulness to God and "the inward life of the Spirit itself" will cause the Christian to "labour diligently in his calling," in which case he will "see God in all things."[53] The Anglican Newman thus echoes the teaching of great spiritual masters such as St. Ignatius of Loyola and St. Francis de Sales (the second of whom was one of his favourite spiritual writers whose portrait hangs in his private chapel in the Birmingham Oratory).

Finally, for Newman, God alone can, in the end, meet all our desires and ensure our happiness. An Anglican sermon entitled "The Thought of God, the

---

51   "Men, not Angels, the Priests of the Gospel," *Mix.*, no. 3: 55–56. Newman's italics.

52   Here are just two examples out of a dozen or so:

"Let us pray God to give us *all* graces; and while, in the first place, we pray that He would make us holy, really holy, let us also pray Him to give us the *beauty* of holiness, which consists in tender and eager affection towards our Lord and Saviour: which is, in the case of the Christian, what beauty of person is to the outward man." "The Crucifixion," *PS* vii, no. 10: 134. Newman's italics.

"Christ and His Saints are alike destitute of form or comeliness in the eyes of the world, and it is only as we labour to change our nature, through God's help, and to serve Him truly, that we begin to discern the beauty of holiness." "Truth Hidden when not Sought After," *PS* viii, no. 13: 196–97.

53   "Doing Glory to God in Pursuits of the World," *PS* viii, no. 11: 164.

Stay of the Soul" echoes the celebrated words of St. Augustine: "You have made us for yourself, Lord, and our hearts will not find rest until they rest in you"[54]:

> The soul of man is made for the contemplation of its Maker; . . . nothing short of that high contemplation is its happiness; . . . whatever it may possess besides, it is unsatisfied until it is vouchsafed God's presence, and lives in the light of it. . . . He alone is sufficient for the heart who made it . . . the contemplation of Him, and nothing but it, is able fully to open and relieve the mind, to unlock, occupy, and fix our affections.[55]

It is in fact this deep *desire* for God, together with the conviction that God alone can fully satisfy this desire, which constitutes *the* chief motivating force of Newman's life and thought.[56] He was, in the fullest possible sense, "a man of God."

3. THE CHURCH, THE SACRAMENTS, AND PRAYER

While the mainstream Protestant tradition—present in the Anglican Evangelicalism that so deeply influenced the young Newman—tends to emphasize the personal relationship of each believer with God, often at the expense of the Church as an institution, Newman's Anglican sermons enable us to follow his progressive discovery—under the influence predominantly of the Church Fathers—of the Church as a visible, hierarchical and above all sacramental reality. There is something moving for the Catholic reader, and for the Anglican reader of today who has observed the immense changes which have taken place in his or her own Church, in following the stages of this progressive discovery by Newman and his fellow Tractarians.

It is important to grasp however that, amidst this discovery—or rediscovery—Newman never renounces his conception of the importance of the *personal* relationship of each individual Christian with God. An Anglican sermon of 1833 speaks—more than thirty years before the publication of the *Apologia* in which a celebrated passage evokes his discovery, at the time of his first conversion of 1816, of the existence of "two and two only absolute and luminously self-evident beings, myself and my Creator"[57]—of our perception, as we mature, that "there are but two beings in the whole universe, our soul, and the God who made it. . . . To every one of us there are but two beings in the whole world, himself and God."[58] It is no exaggeration to say that Newman, in becoming a Catholic, retained—a fact to which his Catholic sermons bear witness, and

---

54 Augustine of Hippo, *Confessions*, Bk. I, 1.
55 "The Thought of God, the Stay of the Soul," *PS* v, no. 22: 314–18.
56 In addition to his sermons, Newman's posthumously published *Meditations and Devotions* bears ample witness to this fact.
57 *Apo.*, 4.
58 "The Immortality of the Soul," *PS* i, no. 2: 20.

as he himself later acknowledged[59]—the best of what he had received from the Anglican and Protestant traditions.

Even more important is the discovery by Newman and his fellow-Tractarians—a century before the encyclical *Mystici Corporis* of Pope Pius XII (1943) and one hundred and thirty years before the Second Vatican Council—of the Pauline and patristic vision of the Church as the "*mystical* Body of Christ." Christ *lives* in his Church and in each of its members through the presence of His Holy Spirit. Thus, Newman declares, in a sermon of 1837 entitled "The Communion of Saints," that Christ

> formed His Apostles into a visible society; but when He came again in the Person of His Spirit, He made them all in a real sense one, not in name only . . . their separate persons were taken into a mysterious union with things unseen, were grafted upon and assimilated to the spiritual body of Christ, which is One, even by the Holy Ghost, in whom Christ has come again to us.[60]

Whereas the post-tridentine Catholic Church saw itself as first and foremost a visible, hierarchically structured body, Newman carried with him into that Church a vision of "the Christian Church" as "a *living* body, and *one*; not a mere framework artificially arranged to *look* like one. Its being alive is what makes it one," for "the Living *Spirit* of God came down upon it at Pentecost, and made it *one*, by giving it *life*."[61] Again as an Anglican, speaking in Pauline terms of Christians as members of the one body of Christ, he states that "the heart of every Christian ought to represent in miniature the Catholic Church, since one Spirit makes both the whole Church and every member of it to be His Temple," adding a few lines later that "these two operations of our Divine Comforter depend upon each other, and that while Christians do not seek after inward unity and peace in their own breasts, the Church itself will never be at unity and peace in the world around them."[62]

Newman sees clearly in the sacraments, and in particular in the Eucharist, a channel of divine grace. He and his fellow-Tractarians admit that they do not understand *how* Christ is present therein, and they accuse the Catholic doctrine of "transubstantiation" of destroying—through an undue attempt at conceptualisation—the "mystery" of this presence; but their conviction of this presence is unshakeable. It is particularly in volumes V and VI of the *Parochial*

---

59 See his autobiographical memoir of 1874 in *AW*, 79, and Newman's letter of February 24, 1887 to George Edwards, the secretary of the London Evangelization Society, *LD* xxxi, 189.

60 *PS* iv, no. 11: 169–70.

61 "The Communion of Saints," *PS* iv, no. 11: 171. Newman's italics.

62 "Connexion Between Personal and Public Improvement," *SD*, no. 10: 132.

and Plain Sermons that the understanding of the role of the sacraments reaches its fullest and finest expression. In an Easter sermon entitled "The Eucharistic Presence," speaking of the "Sacramental mystery" of Holy Communion, Newman states that

> Christ, who died and rose again for us, is in it spiritually present, in the fulness of His death and of His resurrection. . . . He who is present there can neither be seen nor heard . . . He is not present carnally, though He is really present. And how this is, of course is a mystery. All that we know or need to know is: He *is* given to us, and that in the Sacrament of Holy Communion.[63]

In the sermon immediately preceding, "The Spiritual Presence of Christ in the Church," he even goes so far as to declare that, although we have "lost the sensible and conscious perception" of Christ, we "enjoy the spiritual, immaterial, inward, mental, real sight and possession of Him, a possession more real and more present than that which the Apostles had in the days of His flesh, *because* it is spiritual, *because* it is invisible."[64]

Newman's sermons testify also to his and his fellow-Tractarians' rediscovery of the importance of the liturgy.[65] After the first volume of the *Parochial and Plain Sermons* that, in reaction against what he saw as a certain facile Christianity, stresses the austere and rigorous conditions of true Christian discipleship, several of the succeeding volumes, as already noted, are structured according to the Church's liturgical year. The intention here is no doubt to provide the faithful with a Christian "structuring" of time, or what Newman calls in one sermon the "redeeming of time."[66]

Newman is universally recognized as one of the great Christian preachers. Yet, paradoxically, he reverses the order of priority generally accorded at the time to preaching and to prayer. In an early unpublished sermon, he declares that, while most people come to church in order above all to listen to a sermon, in reality it is prayer which is most important:

> Now, if I were to ask what is the chief reason we come to Church, many persons, I conceive, would answer without hesitation, we come to hear the preaching of the word of God—but this is a very incorrect statement. . . .

---

63 "The Eucharistic Presence," *PS* vi, no. 11: 136–37. Newman's italics.

64 "The Spiritual Presence of Christ in the Church," *PS* vi, no. 10: 121. Newman's italics.

65 For a presentation of Newman's understanding of the liturgy see ch. 21 of this volume by Uwe Michael Lang and Juan R. Vélez (editor's note).

66 "Moral Effects of Communion with God," *PS* iv, no. 15: 233. The influence of Keble's *The Christian Year* upon all the Tractarians is of course paramount here.

Men in this day speak as if hearing so-called preaching was *the* great ordinance of the Christian religion, whereas the great ordinance, the difficult ordinance, and the most blessed and *joyful* ordinance of the Gospel is prayer and praise, and that not of one by one, but joint prayer and praise, of many together.[67]

Several Anglican sermons deal specifically with the subject of prayer (though the exhortation to pray runs through all his sermons, both Anglican and Catholic): for example, "Times of Private Prayer" (*PS* i, no. 19), "Forms of Private Prayer" (*PS* i, no. 20), "Moral Effects of Communion with God" (*PS* iv, no. 15), and "Watching" (*PS* iv, no. 22). His own attitude to prayer evolved. Though he always placed great emphasis on prayer of intercession, to which he himself devoted considerable time each day, he also saw prayer, and in particular continuous personal prayer, as an opening up of ourselves to the presence of the Holy Spirit:

But as our bodily life discovers itself by its activity, so is the presence of the Holy Spirit in us discovered by a spiritual activity; and this activity is the spirit of continual prayer. Prayer is to spiritual life what the beating of the pulse and the drawing of the breath are to the life of the body. . . . The state or habit of spiritual life exerts itself, consists, in the continual activity of prayer.[68]

He also criticizes existing forms of prayer. In the tradition of the Anglican High Church, the emphasis was placed on *set* prayers which were read, often somewhat mechanically. Among Evangelicals, on the other hand, the emphasis was on long, improvised, and often highly emotive prayer (Newman speaks ironically of "interminable invocations" addressed to God). He saw clearly that such constant improvisation demanded a creative tension which threw the person who prayed back upon him- or herself, thereby running the risk of falling into the trap of what he called "self-contemplation."[69] He found a perfect remedy to this in the Roman Breviary, which he discovered with delight in 1836 and which he himself thenceforth used regularly. He was struck by the brevity of the prayers and by the place accorded to the Psalms, the "objective" character of which avoided the danger of self-absorption. Later, as a Catholic, he would discover with even greater delight, on his journey to Rome in 1846 in order to "complete" his theological studies, the presence of Christ in the tabernacle of every church and chapel he visited on the way; henceforth the practice of prayer before the Blessed Sacrament became a regular feature of his own spiritual life

---

67 "On the Object and Effects of Preaching—(on the anniversary of my entering on my living)," *Serm.* i, 25 (first preached in 1831, then again in 1835). Newman's italics.

68 "Mental Prayer," *PS* vii, no. 15: 209. The biblical text on which the sermon is based is St. Paul's injunction to "pray without ceasing" (1 Thes 5:17).

69 See the sermon "Self-Contemplation," *PS* ii, no. 15.

(for example, during his long sojourn at the London Oratory at the time of the Achilli trial he spent many long hours praying before the Blessed Sacrament).[70]

Newman also saw in worship generally a "preparation" for communion with God:

> Appearing before God, and dwelling in His presence, is a very different thing from being merely subjected to a system of moral laws, and would seem to require another preparation, a special preparation of thought and affection, such as will enable us to endure His countenance, and to hold communion with Him as we ought. Nay, and, it may be, a preparation of the soul itself for His presence. . . . And in the worship and service of Almighty God, which Christ and His Apostles have left to us, we are vouchsafed means, both moral and mystical, of approaching God, and gradually learning to bear the sight of Him. This indeed is the most momentous reason for religious worship.[71]

Finally, he also saw in prayer a "duty" which the Christian was invited to take upon himself in order to acquire a "privilege," that of communion with God: "Prayer, praise, thanksgiving, contemplation, are the peculiar privilege and duty of a Christian, and that for their own sakes . . . , from a general sense of the blessedness of being under the shadow of God's throne."[72] He stresses, however, that "he who does not use a gift, loses it," and therefore "he who neglects to pray, not only suspends the enjoyment, but is in a way to lose the possession, of his divine citizenship."[73]

Thus prayer, liturgy, the sacraments and worship generally constitute for Newman a form of spiritual "training," which will be the subject of the next section.

4. CHRISTIAN LIFE AS A FORM OF SPIRITUAL "TRAINING"

In Newman's time, the same is largely true today, most Christians were content to live a morally good life in order to obtain the approbation of a God seen as purely external. Such was not the case, he argues, with the early Christians. These lived in the midst of a Greco-Roman civilisation dominated by two realities which are relevant here: the omnipresence of the Roman army, and the passion for the games or sports of the arena. They saw soldiers and athletes engaging in a rigorous "training" (designated by the Greek word *askésis*, which has given us in English "ascetic" and "asceticism") in order to be effective in combat or to win the victor's crown in one's chosen sport. Christians quickly saw in this training

---

70   See also "A Short Visit to the Blessed Sacrament before Meditation" in *Prayers, Verses and Devotions*, 335–36.

71   "Worship, a Preparation for Christ's Coming," *PS* v, no. 1: 6–7.

72   "Moral Effects of Communion with God," *PS* iv, no. 15: 227.

73   "Moral Effects of Communion with God," *PS* iv, no. 15: 228.

or *askésis* a source of inspiration for their own moral and spiritual efforts (the Epistles of Paul provide several examples of images borrowed from these two activities). The aim of the early Christians, or that of the more rigorous among them, was not just moral—a combat against sin—but also spiritual: it was to achieve a unity of thought and feeling, a greater attentiveness to God, a state of openness to and receptiveness of His presence in them.[74]

Newman's sermons show clearly the influence upon him of this concept of spiritual "training," of which we find numerous examples in his sermons. He refers specifically in an early Anglican sermon to the need to "train our hearts": "a Christian spirit is the growth of time," we "cannot force it upon our minds," however "if we strove to obey God's will in all things, we actually should be gradually training our hearts into the fulness of a Christian spirit."[75]

What are the key elements of this spiritual "training"? A first, already noted, is that of the acquisition of *self-knowledge*. Indeed, the absence of true self-knowledge leads us to use words "without attaching distinct meaning to them"; and it is only "in proportion as we search our hearts and understand our own nature" that we understand Christian doctrines. Self-knowledge must however exclude all morbid introspection, and above all any form of "self-contemplation."[76]

Newman also warns against the dangers of extreme *emotionalism*, as seen, according to him, amongst contemporary Evangelicals. Such emotionalism is usually superficial, incapable of effecting real change in a person. A "violent impulse," he declares, "is not the same as a firm *determination*," and "men may have their religious feelings roused, without being on that account at all the more likely to obey God in practice" (he adds ironically, "rather the less likely"). A little further on in the same sermon, he adds also: "As a general rule, the more religious men become, the calmer they become; . . . the highest Christian temper is free from all vehement and tumultuous feeling."[77] Elsewhere we find another ironical quip which conveys the same message: "by giving utterance to religious sentiments we do not become religious, rather the reverse."[78] Newman denounces in particular the conception of conversion held by certain Evangelical preachers and their flock. Such men "think that to be thus agitated is to be religious; they indulge themselves in these warm feelings . . . as if they were then engaged in a religious exercise"; and when their initial fervour begins to weaken, they "seek for potent stimulants to sustain their minds in that state of excitement which they have been taught to consider the essence of a religious life."[79]

---

74 See the sermon "The Apostolical Christian," *SD,* no. 19.

75 "Obedience the Remedy for Religious Perplexity," *PS* i, no. 18: 233.

76 See once again the sermon "Self-contemplation," *PS* ii, no. 15.

77 "Religious Emotion," *PS* i, no. 14: 177, 181, 185. Newman's italics.

78 "Obedience the Remedy for Religious Perplexity," *PS* i, no. 18: 232–33.

79 "The Religious Use of Excited Feelings," *PS* i, no. 9: 118–20. Though the context may be different, Newman's criticisms have lost none of their pertinence today.

The counterpart of this criticism of hyper-emotionalism is an emphasis on the importance of the *will* (we need to remember that the word designates not merely an order or a commandment but embraces also the category of "desire": God's "will" is also that which he *desires*). Our will—and our desire—are all too often weak; we must therefore allow *God* to strengthen them. Newman stresses over and again that if we fail to achieve the goals that we set ourselves, it is because we do not will, or desire, them strongly enough, and this is the reason why we cannot and do not "obey or make progress in holiness." He sees a subtle dialectic at work between our will and that of God: the Holy Spirit comes to our aid, *if* we allow Him to do so; divine grace strengthens our own will, *on condition* that we agree to make use of it. God has his work to do, and we have ours which consists of allowing Him to do His will in us:

> Is it that the *power* of God is not within us? Is it literally that we are *not able* to perform God's commandments? God forbid! We are able. We have that given us which makes us able. We are not in a state of nature. We have had the gift of grace implanted in us. We have a power within us to do what we are commanded to do. What is it we lack? The power? No; the will. What we lack is the real, simple, earnest, sincere inclination and aim to use what God has given us, and what we have in us.[80]

It is this which leads Newman to state in a Catholic sermon that "on the one hand, . . . our salvation depends on ourselves, and on the other, . . . it depends on God."[81]

One of the principal means available to us in order to "train" our will is that of *self-denial*. Christian self-denial does not involve a masochistic desire to inflict pain on ourselves but means *choosing*, from amongst several goals which may be good in themselves, the one which seems to us the best and putting aside all that hinders us from achieving this goal. In an early Anglican sermon Newman even makes of "rigorous self-denial" the "test whether we are Christ's disciples" or "whether we are living in a mere dream, which we mistake for Christian faith and obedience."[82] This self-denial does not consist, however, in performing some grand heroic gesture—Newman is the archenemy of all forms of spiritual "romanticism"—but must be practised in the ordinary actions of everyday life. By this daily practice of self-denial, we attain little by little to a mastery of self, to a non-dependence on things, and thus to a certain inner freedom. This has nothing to do with the Stoic search for "impassibility," nor with the desire to achieve a self-centred *power* over ourselves which becomes a source of pride. It is a question for the Christian of "unblocking" the "channel" of divine grace: "A smooth and easy life," Newman argues, "an uninterrupted enjoyment of the

---

80 "The Power of the Will," *PS* v, no. 24: 347–48. Newman's italics.
81 "Perseverance in Grace," *Mix.*, no. 7: 126.
82 "Self-denial the Test of Religious Earnestness," *PS* i, no. 5: 66.

goods of Providence, full meals, soft raiment, well-furnished homes, the plea-sures of sense, the feeling of security, the consciousness of wealth,—these, and the like, if we are not careful, choke up all the avenues of the soul, through which the light and breath of heaven might come to us. . . . We must, at least at seasons, defraud ourselves of nature, if we would not be defrauded of grace."[83]

This theme of self-denial is intimately related to that of *obedience*. As already indicated, this word signifies for Newman not merely compliance with a set of rules and injunctions but the creation of an inner *disposition* of attentiveness and openness to God. He fully recognizes the difficulty of attaining to such an inner disposition but prescribes a kind of dialectical therapy: our actions are the result of certain dispositions which we cannot easily change; but by exercising a constant vigilance in regard to our actions, and by endeavouring little by little to change *these*, we succeed in modifying, at least in part and with time, our character: "We have power over our deeds, under God's grace; we have no direct power over our habits. Let us but secure our actions, as God would have them, and our habits will follow."[84] Yet the role of divine grace remains all-important: we must labour, "under God's grace, to change [our] wills, to purify [our] hearts, and so prepare [ourselves] for the kingdom of God."[85] And then bit by bit, as we create in ourselves good habits, obedience will become progressively easier.

This does not however do away with the need for direct obedience to the "Law," in the form of the "commandments" of the Bible and of the Church. Contrary to what many believe, declares Newman, the Gospel has not done away with the Law, nor with the need for obedience: a host of biblical texts "show that the Gospel leaves us just where it found us, as regards the necessity of our obedi-ence to God; that Christ has not obeyed instead of us, but that obedience is quite as imperative as if Christ had never come." What has however changed—and this is of crucial importance—is the *means* enabling us to obey: Christ "gives us spiritual aids, which we have not except through Him, to enable us to keep" His commandments.[86] Our will to obey is weak, but divine grace comes to our aid; but we must *will* to make use of this grace.

Nevertheless, obedience for the Christian is not first and foremost to a Law but to a *person* and must go hand in hand with *love*. A purely legalistic obedience would have no value as regards our spiritual life, nor ultimately our salvation. For it is "possible to obey, not from love towards God and man, but from a sort of conscientiousness short of love; from some notion of acting up to a *law*; that is, more from the fear of God than from love of Him."[87] In the final resort, "to obey God is to be near Christ, and . . . to disobey is to be far from Him."[88]

---

83 "Love, the One Thing Needful," *PS* v, no. 23: 337–38.
84 "Saving Knowledge," *PS* ii, no. 14: 101.
85 "Obedience to God the Way to Faith in Christ," *PS* viii, no. 14: 203.
86 "Obedience to God the Way to Faith in Christ," *PS* viii, no. 14: 205.
87 "Love, the One Thing Needful," *PS* v, no. 23: 331. Newman's italics.
88 "Obedience to God, the Way to Faith in Christ," *PS* viii, no. 14: 214.

5. THE POWER OF DIVINE GRACE[89]

As the previous section makes clear, Newman is far from being a mere moralist: his lucid analysis of our weaknesses and failings is always placed in the service of our spiritual lives. Any study of his teaching which fails to take into account this fact passes over an essential element of that teaching and thereby distorts it.

It was stated earlier that Newman's sermons, though they are never theological discourses, always possess a solid theological foundation. Though he does not express himself in quite these terms, it is clear that for him our way of *thinking about* God determines our way of *praying* to Him and of *seeking* Him (as also, conversely, our inability, or indeed our refusal, to do so).

In this regard, two Christian dogmas, or doctrines, occupy a particular place in his sermons, that of the Incarnation and that of the Holy Trinity. Both speak of the *presence* of Christ among us, not only during His earthly life but also *here and now*, and of the "communication" of the divine Life, a communication which proceeds *from* the Father, *through* the Son and *in* (or *by*) the Holy Spirit. Both give rise to the doctrine of the "indwelling" of the Holy Spirit in our hearts or souls. The Holy Spirit dwells in us "as in a temple," he "pervades us (if it may be so said) as light pervades a building, or as a sweet perfume the folds of some honourable robe."[90] And, through the Holy Spirit (or Holy Ghost, as the Anglican Newman tends to say),

> we have communion with Father and Son. "In Christ we are builded together," says St. Paul, "for an habitation of God through the Spirit." "Ye are the temple of God, and the Spirit of God dwelleth in you." "Strengthened with might by His Spirit in the inner man, that Christ may dwell in your hearts by faith." The Holy Spirit causes, faith welcomes, the indwelling of Christ in the heart. Thus the Spirit does not take the place of Christ in the soul, but secures that place to Christ.[91]

Newman reflects also on the nature of salvation. Whilst recognizing that we have been saved by the death of Christ on the cross, he emphasizes the fact that Christ saves us also *here and now* by the transforming power of His presence

---

89   The title of this section is that given by me to the translation into French of Newman's first volume of Catholic sermons, *Discourses Addressed to Mixed Congregations* (1849). Quite apart from the fact that the titles given by Newman to several of his volumes of sermons were not particularly inspiring—his name alone was sufficient to cause a book to sell—this French title reflects one of the major themes of the volume. See John Henry Newman, *Sermons catholiques: La Puissance de la grâce* suivi de *Le Second printemps*, edited with an introduction by Keith Beaumont (Paris: Éditions du Cerf, 2019).

90   "The Indwelling Spirit," *PS* ii, no. 19: 222–23.

91   "The Spiritual Presence of Christ in the Church," *PS* vi, no. 10: 125–26. The biblical references, given by Newman, are Eph 2:22; 1 Cor 3:16; Eph 3, 17.

within us. One of his major theological works, his *Lectures on the Doctrine of Justification* (1838), deals with this and related themes; a sermon preached two years later returns to the same subject:

> Let us never lose sight of this great and simple view, which the whole of Scripture sets before us. What was actually done by Christ in the flesh eighteen hundred years ago, is in type and resemblance really wrought in us one by one even to the end of time. . . . Christ Himself vouchsafes to repeat in each of us in figure and mystery all that He did and suffered in the flesh. He is formed in us, born in us, suffers in us, rises again in us, lives in us; and this not by a succession of events, but all at once: for He comes to us as a Spirit, all dying, all rising again, all living. We are ever receiving our birth, our justification, our renewal, ever dying to sin, ever rising to righteousness.[92]

Such elevated terminology is rare in Newman's Catholic sermons, perhaps because the themes of Christ present within us and of the "indwelling" of the Holy Spirit fitted uneasily within the narrow confines of the neo-scholasticism which dominated Catholic theology at the time.[93] However, the word "grace," omnipresent in his Catholic sermons, fulfils much the same function. All too often the meaning of this word has been debased over recent centuries, signifying little more than the "favours" we ask of God, whereas its true meaning is that of the *gift* of God Himself, given freely, through Christ and in the Holy Spirit. It is divine grace which "purifies" us of sin, "transforms" us inwardly, and "sanctifies" us. Through grace, God Himself is at work within us.

Sin is also a recurrent theme throughout the whole of Newman's preaching. His emphasis on sin is in part a result of the depth and subtlety of his analysis of human psychology: true self-knowledge brings with it inevitably an awareness of our sinfulness. The life of the Christian is a constant "fight" against sin, indeed "fight is the very token of a Christian" who is a "soldier of Christ."[94] He emphasizes however that sin is *more* than simply a moral phenomenon: it concerns our relationship with God, and its foundation is the refusal, conscious or unconscious, of God's grace. He even goes so far as to define it as "a rebellion against God" and as "a traitor's act who aims at the overthrow and death of His sovereign."[95]

---

92 "Righteousness Not of Us, but in Us," *PS* v, no. 10: 138–39.

93 There are of course exceptions, for example the work of the German theologian Johann Adam Möhler about which Newman had knowledge. Although Newman knew no German, he may have read Möhler's *Symbolik*—translated into English in 1843—or a review of it. See Geoffrey Rowell, "Europe and the Oxford Movement" in *The Oxford Movement: Europe and the Wider World: 1830–1930*, ed. Stewart J. Brown and Peter Nockles (Cambridge: Cambridge University Press, 2012), 157. But the generalization remains true for the mainstream of Catholic theology.

94 "God's Will the End of Life," *Mix.*, no. 6: 120.

95 "Mental Sufferings of our Lord in His Passion," *Mix.*, no. 16: 335.

Our concern here however is the relationship between sin and grace. Several Catholic sermons focus on this theme. Whilst emphasizing our sinfulness, Newman affirms that the true nature of sin can only be understood by *contrast* with the reality of God: "We do not know what sin is, because we do not know what God is; we have no standard with which to compare it, till we know what God is. Only God's glories, His perfections, His holiness, His Majesty, His beauty, can teach us by the contrast how to think of sin."[96] He affirms also that the most inveterate sinner *can* become, through the work of divine grace, a saint; indeed, that the vast majority of saints began by being sinners: most often "those who have ended in being miracles of sanctity, and heroes in the Church, have passed a time in wilful disobedience, have thrown themselves out of the light of God's countenance, have been led captive by this or that sin."[97]

A closely related theme is that of the relationship between nature and grace. The "natural" man for Newman is he who believes he is self-sufficient, professing to have no need of any aid from outside of himself. In words which are even more relevant in our own increasingly secularized age than in Newman's time, he declares that "the world does not know of the existence of grace; nor is it wonderful, for it is ever contented with itself, and has never turned to account the supernatural aides bestowed upon it. Its highest idea of man lies in the order of nature; its pattern man is the natural man."[98] At times he appears to see an opposition between nature and grace. But this is in part, he admits, the result of a rhetorical strategy: if he has seemed at times to suggest an opposition, it is "for the sake of distinctness, that grace and nature might clearly be contrasted with each other."[99] In reality, however, grace is never absent from our human striving. God gives his grace to all human beings, and it is up to us whether we profit from it or not: "To all He gives grace sufficient for their salvation; to all He gives far more than they have any right to expect, and they can claim nothing."[100] And again: "No one has ever been deprived of the assistance of grace, both for illumination and conversion; even the heathen world as a whole had to a certain extent its darkness relieved by these fitful and recurrent gleams of light."[101]

Newman makes his own the traditional theological adage *gratia perfecit naturam*: grace does not destroy nature but builds upon it and, by transforming it from within, brings it to perfection. He sees a shining example of this, as an Oratorian, in his own patron saint, Philip Neri, founder of the first Oratory in Rome in 1575.[102] St. Philip exemplifies (as does also his faithful and

---

96 "Neglect of Divine Calls and Warnings," *Mix.*, no. 2: 33.

97 "Men, not Angels, the Priests of the Gospel," *Mix.*, no. 3: 51.

98 "Nature and Grace," *Mix.*, no. 8: 148.

99 "Illuminating Grace," *Mix.*, no. 9: 188.

100 "Neglect of Divine Calls and Warnings," *Mix.*, no. 2: 30–31.

101 "Nature and Grace," *Mix.*, no. 8: 159.

102 See, amongst other sources, his long two-part sermon of 1850 on "The Mission of St. Philip Neri" in *OS*, no. 12.

devoted disciple, St. John Henry Newman) what we may call Newman's "spiritual humanism": the ideal of a fully developed humanity, *transformed*—one might even say "spiritualized" and transfigured—by the inner workings of the Holy Spirit.

Despite the heavy emphasis on sin in many of Newman's sermons, Anglican and especially Catholic, many—and often the same—contain also a veritable hymn of praise to the power of divine grace which recalls the "how much more" of St. Paul.[103] Here are some examples of Newman in lyrical mode on the subject of grace. Grace is "that sovereign, energetic power, which forms and harmonises [man's] whole nature, and enables it to fulfil its own end, while it fills one higher than its own."[104] "There is no limit to be put to the bounty and power of God's grace. . . . It can undo the past, it can realise the hopeless. . . . Grace overcomes nature and grace only overcomes it."[105] "Grace is lodged in the heart; it purifies the thoughts and motives, it raises the soul to God, it sanctifies the body, it corrects and exalts human nature."[106] And finally: "That we are justified is of His grace; that we have the dispositions for justification is of His grace; that we are able to do good works when justified is of His grace; and that we persevere in those good works is of His grace."[107]

III. CONCLUSION:
THE RELEVANCE OF NEWMAN'S SERMONS TODAY

Why should we read Newman's sermons today? Some may read them for their literary qualities, Newman being one of the great masters of English prose. Others as a key to the evolution of his thought or to his personal dilemmas. Contemporaries were struck above all by the depth of psychological insight displayed and by his empathy even with those with whom he disagreed,[108] as

---

103 See Romans 5:15–17: "But the free gift is not like the trespass. For if many died through one man's trespass, how much more have the grace of God and the free gift in the grace of one man, Jesus Christ, abounded in many. . . . If, because of one man's trespass, death reigned through that one man, how much more will those who receive the abundance of grace and the free gift of righteousness reign in life through the one man, Jesus Christ" (RSV translation).

104 "Illuminating Grace," *Mix.*, no. 9: 169.

105 "Men, not Angels, the Priests of the Gospel," *Mix.*, no. 3: 56–57.

106 "Nature and Grace," *Mix.*, no. 8: 151.

107 "Perseverance in Grace," *Mix.*, no. 7: 124.

108 See this judgement of a particularly astute literary critic, James Mozley: "A sermon of Mr. Newman's enters into all our feelings, ideas, modes of viewing things. He wonderfully realises a state of mind, enters into a difficulty, a temptation, a disappointment, a grief . . . . Nay, he enters deeply into even what scepticism has to say for itself; he puts himself into the infidel's state of mind." Article published in *The Christian Remembrancer*, January 1846, 169, quoted by Richard W. Church, *The Oxford Movement. Twelve Years, 1833-1845* (London: Macmillan & Co., 1892) 139–41.

also by the powerful sense which emanated from his sermons on the presence of God.[109] All of these approaches and reactions remain valid. The most important question, however, and the one which this chapter seeks to answer, is: what can his sermons *teach* us today?

Newman was of course a man of his time, and some features of his sermons may today seem to certain readers outdated, or even at times "politically incorrect" (especially if we erect our notions of what is "politically correct" into absolutes and refuse to allow them to be called into question). But these are superficial reactions. Over and above these considerations, there is much in Newman's sermons which can speak to today's Christian, and indeed to all those who, whether Christian or not, retain an open mind in religious matters.

Above all, Newman challenges us to renew our understanding of what it *means* to be a Christian. Today Christianity is still too often seen principally in terms of "believing," and above all in moral terms, as acting in accordance with the law of God and of the Church. Whilst insisting on the importance of these two dimensions, Newman invites us to enlarge our conceptions of both. Correct *thinking* about God—doctrine or dogma—is essential to our *spiritual* lives since, as previously stated, our manner of thinking about God determines our manner of praying to Him and of seeking Him. Faith is not just a matter of "believing," however essential this may be, but of *confidence* in God and the *desire* to deepen a personal relationship with Him in the depths of our own being. Christian morality is not just a matter of choosing between right and wrong but a form of spiritual "training" designed to make us more open to God and more receptive of His presence in us. Men and women, for Newman, are "capable" of receiving God into their hearts and souls, and of allowing His Holy Spirit to "dwell" within them. And this "indwelling" of the Spirit in no way diminishes our human nature but, by transforming it from within—one might even say transfiguring it—brings it to "perfection"; this is the key intuition at the heart of what I have called Newman's "spiritual humanism." Finally, the aim of Christian life is holiness, conceived of not as an impossible form of moral perfection to which we would attain by our own efforts, but as the fruit of the transforming power of God's grace working within us.

Suggested Reading

Beaumont, Keith. *Dieu intérieur: La théologie spirituelle de John Henry Newman*. Paris: Ad Solem, 2014.

Bouyer, Louis. *Newman: Sa vie, sa spiritualité*. Paris: Éditions du Cerf, 1952 (English translation: *Newman: His Life and Spirituality*, 1958).

---

109 A former disciple, William Lockhart, declared that his sermons had the effect of "a new revelation. He had the wondrous, the supernatural power of raising the mind to God, and of rooting deeply in us a personal conviction of God, and a sense of His Presence." *Cardinal Newman* (London: Burns and Oates, 1891), 25–26.

_____. *Newman's Vision of Faith: A Theology for Times of General Apostasy.* San Francisco: Ignatius Press, 1986. (Written and first published in English).

Honoré, Jean. *Fais paraître ton jour: Newman, poète et prophète de l'au-delà.* Paris: Éditions du Cerf, 2000.

Newman, John Henry. *Être chrétien: Les plus beaux sermons.* Edited by Keith Beaumont and Pierre Gauthier, with an introduction by Keith Beaumont. Paris: Éditions du Cerf, 2017.

CHAPTER 19

VOICE OF GOD? CONSCIENCE, RELATIVISM, AND TRUTH IN ST. JOHN HENRY NEWMAN

Abp. Anthony Fisher, OP

CONSCIENCE TODAY

On October 13, 2019, the Church canonized a man whose life and work has been described by Pope Emeritus Benedict XVI as "one great commentary on the question of conscience,"[1] who was praised by St. John Paul II for his "deep intellectual honesty [and] fidelity to conscience and grace,"[2]

*   This chapter is a slightly revised version of an address delivered to the Conference on *Newman the Prophet: A Saint for Our Times* conducted by the Pontifical University of St. Thomas (Angelicum), Rome, October 12, 2019, on the eve of the canonisation. It was published in *Nova et Vetera* 18, no. 2 (Spring 2020): 337–53.

1   Joseph Ratzinger, "Conscience and Truth," in *Values in a Time of Upheaval* (New York: Crossroad, 2006), 75–100 at 84. Other texts of Ratzinger on conscience include: *On Conscience* (San Francisco: Ignatius, 2007); "Conscience in Its Age," in *Church, Ecumenism and Politics* (New York: Crossroads, 1987), 165–79; *The Nature and Mission of Theology* (San Francisco: Ignatius, 1995); *Without Roots: Europe, Relativism, Christianity, Islam* with Marcello Pera (New York: Basic, 2006), 51–80. See Vincent Twomey, *Pope Benedict XVI: The Conscience of Our Age* (San Francisco: Ignatius, 2007); Tracey Rowland, *Ratzinger's Faith: The Theology of Pope Benedict XVI* (Oxford: Oxford University Press, 2008), 39–40, 81–83.

2   John Paul II, *Letter for the Centenary of the Elevation of John Henry Newman to the Cardinalate* (May 21, 1979): "It is my hope that this centenary will be for all of

and who is celebrated by many as one worthy of the title of Doctor of the Church and specifically "doctor of conscience."[3]

That such a high authority on conscience is being celebrated in this way could not be more timely, for rights of conscience are regularly flouted today and the very idea of conscience much contested. Some treat it as mere sincerity or subjective intuition; others as personal rivalry with authority; others again dismiss it altogether as mythology. Oxford academic Julian Savalescu sounds like Newman's nineteenth century denigrators when he writes off appeals to conscience in health care practice and elsewhere as "idiosyncratic, bigoted, and discriminatory."[4] Behind disputes over whether religious or moral believers engaged in healthcare or other pursuits should have the space to pursue their conscientious beliefs—and even have conscience protections[5]—is the deeper question of the meaning, basis, and scope of conscience. There is no one better to explore this with than our new saint.

In the present chapter, I will review the sources and context of Newman's teaching on conscience and explore his particular take on the conscience idea. In particular, I will ask whether he thought conscience was a "voice" external to moral reasoning and discernment, whether he gave it primacy over religious faith, and how he thought conscience functions vis-à-vis intellect, will, and authority. I will then consider the influence of Newman's teaching on conscience both on the recent Magisterium of the Catholic Church and on the wider culture.

---

us an opportunity for studying more closely the inspiring thought of Newman's genius, which speaks to us of deep intellectual honesty, fidelity to conscience and grace, piety and priestly zeal, devotion to Christ's Church and love of her doctrine, unconditional trust in divine providence and absolute obedience to the will of God."

3   For instance, see Drew Morgan, "John Henry Newman—Doctor of Conscience: Doctor of the Church?" *Newman Studies Journal* 4, no. 1 (Spring 2007): 5–23; Philippe Lefebvre and Colin Mason, eds., *John Henry Newman: Doctor of the Church* (Oxford: Family Publications, 2007).

4   See Julian Savalescu, "Conscientious Objection in Medicine," *British Medical Journal* 332 (2006): 294–97; Udo Schuklenk, "Conscientious Objection in Medicine: Private Ideological Convictions Must Not Supersede Public Service Obligations," *Bioethics* 29, no. 5 (2015): ii–iii; Julian Savalescu and Udo Schuklenk, "Doctors Have No Right to Refuse Medical Assistance in Dying, Abortion or Contraception," *Bioethics* 31, no. 3 (2017): 162–70; Udo Schuklenk and Ricardo Smalling, "Why Medical Professionals Have No Moral Claim to Conscientious Objection Accommodation in Liberal Democracies," *Journal of Medical Ethics* 43 (2017): 234–40; Julian Savalescu and Udo Schuklenk, "Conscientious Objection and Compromising the Patient: Response to Hughes," *Bioethics* 32, no. 7 (2018): 473–76; Doug McConnell, "Conscientious Objection in Healthcare: How Much Discretionary Space Best Supports Good Medicine?" *Bioethics* 33, no. 1 (2019): 154–61.

5   See the special numbers of the *National Catholic Bioethics Quarterly* 4, no. 1 (Spring 2004), especially the contributions by Maureen Kramlich, Nikolas Nikas, Edward Furton, Mark Latkovic, and Peter Cataldo, and *The New Bioethics: A Multidisciplinary Journal of Biotechnology and the Body* 25, no. 3 (September 2019), especially the essays of David Oderberg, Mary Neal and Sara Fovargue, Toni Saad, Nathan Gamble and Michal Pruski.

CONSCIENCE IN NEWMAN'S DAY

Newman was heir to a long and rich tradition on conscience going back to Paul, Augustine, Aquinas, and Thomas More.[6] Joseph Butler mediated much of that tradition to Newman's generation. He described conscience as "moral Reason, moral Sense, or divine Reason . . . a Sentiment of the Understanding, or a Perception of the Heart" by which an agent reflects on action prospectively or retrospectively, applying moral principles available to all.[7] Butler reflected the turn away from metaphysical to more psychological explanations of ethics in that age. In Newman's own century new views of conscience were emerging: for Nonconformists, conscience was freedom of religion along with moral constraints on anything that made you smile; for the Kantians, it was stern-faced practical reason holding duty up before the agent for their acquittal or condemnation; for the liberals, it was about "doing it my way" constrained only by law and education; for the Darwinists, an evolved mechanism for managing conflict between competing natural impulses or species; for the Marxists and Nietzscheans, a social policeman, the construct of a controlling community. It was against such a background that Newman sought to teach his version of the tradition on conscience.

His most famous treatment was in his *Letter to the Duke of Norfolk*,[8] but we find thoughts on conscience in his sermons, treatises, hymns, and even novels. Conscience rates a mention 588 times in his letters and diaries alone. But, as with Thomas More, we see in Newman someone not just speculating about moral theory but often personally agonizing over what to do.[9]

---

6   See Eric D'Arcy, *Conscience and Its Right to Freedom* (New York: Sheed & Ward, 1961); Anthony Fisher, OP, "Conscience: The Crisis of Authority," in *Catholic Bioethics for a New Millennium* (Cambridge: Cambridge University Press, 2012), ch. 2; Douglas Langston, *Conscience and Other Virtues from Bonaventure to MacIntyre* (University Park, Pa.: Pennsylvania State University Press, 2001).

7   Joseph Butler, "Of the Nature of Virtue," in *The Analogy of Religion, Natural and Revealed, to the Constitution and Course of Nature*, 2nd ed. (London: Knapton, 1736), §1; *Fifteen Sermons Preached at Rolls Chapel*, rev. ed. (London: Knapton, 1729), Preface, III.6, XIII.7. On Butler on conscience see: Stephen Darwall, "Conscience as Self-Authorizing in Butler's Ethics," in *Joseph Butler's Moral and Religious Thought: Tercentenary Essays*, ed. Christopher Cunliffe (Oxford: Oxford University Press, 1992), 209–42; Aaron Garrett, "Reasoning about Morals from Butler to Hume," in *Philosophy and Religion in Enlightenment Britain*, ed. Ruth Savage (Oxford: Oxford University Press, 2012), 169–86; Amélie. Rorty, "Butler on Benevolence and Conscience," *Philosophy* 53, no. 204 (1978):171–84; Bob Tennant, *Conscience, Consciousness and Ethics in Joseph Butler's Philosophy and Ministry* (Suffolk: Boydell & Brewer, 2011); Aaron Garrett, "Joseph Butler's Moral Philosophy," *Stanford Encylopedia of Philosophy Online* (as revised February 18, 2018).

8   *Diff.* ii, 175–378.

9   Some of these quandaries are explored by his biographers and commentators: Frederick D. Aquino and Benjamin J. King, eds., *The Oxford Handbook of John Henry Newman* (Oxford University Press, 2018); Louis Bouyer, *Newman: His Life and Spirituality*

Newman gave his witness to Catholic conscience in an environment in which it was not always well-respected. Pope Emeritus Benedict attributes Newman's youthful conversion from rationalism to Christianity to the discovery of "the objective truth of a personal and living God, who speaks to the conscience and reveals to man his condition as a creature."[10] This first conversion—and the subsequent two, to High Churchman and then to Catholic—were not well received by all. Yet from the Calvinist Thomas Scott he learnt "his determination to adhere to the interior Master with his own conscience, confidently abandoning himself to the Father and living in faithfulness to the recognized truth."[11] Though "he was subjected to many trials, disappointments and misunderstandings . . . he never descended to false compromises. . . . He always remained honest in his search for the truth, faithful to the promptings of his conscience, and focused on the ideal of sanctity."[12]

After "popeing" in 1845, Newman's honesty was impeached by Rev. Charles Kingsley. This provoked his famous *Apologia Pro Vita Sua*, a spiritual autobiography that detailed his tussles of conscience and responds to the accusations of bad faith. A few years later (1852) Newman spoke out against a former Dominican friar, anti-Catholic demagogue, and serial rapist, Giacinto Achilli.[13] Newman was accused, tried, and convicted of criminal libel, despite overwhelming evidence from Achilli's victims of the truth of his claims.[14] He escaped imprisonment, and

(San Francisco: Ignatius Press, 2011); John Cornwell, *Newman's Unquiet Grave: The Reluctant Saint* (New York: Continuum, 2010); John Crosby, *The Personalism of John Henry Newman* (Washington, D.C.: The Catholic University of America Press, 2014); Eamon Duffy, *John Henry Newman: A Very Brief History* (London: Society for Promoting Christian Knowledge, 2019); Avery Dulles, *John Henry Newman* (New York: Continuum, 2009); Reinhard Hütter, *John Henry Newman on Truth and Its Counterfeits: A Guide for Our Times* (Washington, D.C.: The Catholic University of America Press, 2020); Ian Ker, *John Henry Newman: A Biography* (Oxford: Oxford University Press, 2010); Ian Ker and Alan Gill, eds., *Newman After a Hundred Years* (Oxford: Oxford University Press, 1990); Ian Ker and Terrence Merrigan, eds., *The Cambridge Companion to John Henry Newman* (Cambridge: Cambridge University Press, 2009); Gerard Skinner, *Newman the Priest—Father of Souls* (Leominster: Gracewing, 2010); Roderick Strange, *John Henry Newman: A Mind Alive* (London: Darton, Longman, and Todd, 2008) and *Newman 101: An Introduction to the Life and Philosophy of John Cardinal Newman* (Notre Dame, Ind.: Ave Maria Press, 2008); Joyce Sugg, *John Henry Newman: Snapdragon in the Wall* (Leominster: Gracewing, 2001); Frank M. Turner, *John Henry Newman: The Challenge to Evangelical Religion* (New Haven: Yale University Press, 2001); Juan R. Vélez, *Passion for Truth: The Life of John Henry Newman* (Charlotte, N.C.: TAN Books, 2012) and *Holiness in a Secular Age: The Witness of Cardinal Newman* (New York: Scepter Publishers, 2017).

10 Benedict XVI, *Message to Symposium of the Friends of Newman* (November 18, 2010), citing Newman's *Apologia Pro Vita Sua*, ch. 1.

11 Benedict XVI, *Message to the Friends of Newman.*

12 Benedict XVI, *Message to the Friends of Newman.*

13 See *Prepos.,* 207.

14 *The Times* recognized the verdict for the travesty it was, reporting: "We consider . . . that a great blow has been given to the administration of justice in this country, and Roman

his fine and court costs—the equivalent of more than £1.5 million in today's values—were paid by admirers. But first he received a humiliating tongue-lashing from the judge about his moral deterioration since becoming a Catholic. Another occasion on which Newman gave witness to conscience was in 1874 when former Prime Minister, William Gladstone, published a pamphlet declaring that following the Vatican Council the English Catholic was bound "to forfeit his moral and mental freedom, and to place his loyalty and civil duty at the mercy of another."[15] It fell to Newman to defend Catholics against these charges of disloyalty to the nation and subjection to papal tyranny in his *Letter to the Duke of Norfolk.*

NEWMAN ON THE VOICE OF CONSCIENCE

Writing on the occasion of the first centenary of Newman's death, John Paul II observed that Newman's "doctrine on conscience, like his teaching in general, is subtle and whole, and ought not to be oversimplified in its presentation."[16] Rather, Newman's complex account begins with an insistence that there is more to conscience than the English "sense of propriety, self-respect or good taste, formed by general culture, education and social custom. Rather is it the echo of God's voice within the heart of man, the pulse of the divine law beating within each person as a standard of right and wrong, with an unquestionable authority."[17] This "voice of God in the nature and heart of man, as distinct from the voice of Revelation"[18] is what tradition calls the natural law. Conscience applies that law in judgment that "bears immediately on conduct, on something to be done or not done."[19] Newman begins his account here.

But such obedience to natural conscience can be a preparation for obedience to divine revelation.[20] Thus, in his novel *Callista* the saint says:

Catholics will have henceforth only too good reason for asserting that there is no justice for them in matters tending to rouse the Protestant feelings of judges and juries." Wilfrid Ward, *Life of John Henry Cardinal Newman* (Charleston: BiblioLife, 2010), 292. On the trial see: M. C. Mirow, "Roman Catholicism on Trial in Victorian England: The Libel Case of John Henry Newman and Dr Achilli," *Catholic Lawyer* 36, no. 4 (1996): 401–53; Edward Short, "How the Achilli Trial Changed John Henry Newman," *Catholic World Report,* March 18, 2018.

    15 William Gladstone, *Vatican Decrees in Their Bearing on Civil Allegiance: A Political Expostulation* (1874).

    16 St. John Paul II, *Letter on the First Centenary of the Death of John Henry Newman* (July 16, 1990), 3. See Joseph Cardinal Ratzinger, "Address on the First Centenary of the Death of John Henry Newman," April 28, 1990.

    17 John Paul II, *Letter on the First Centenary of the Death of Newman,* 3.

    18 *Diff.* ii, 247.

    19 *Diff.* ii, 256.

    20 *PS* viii, no. 14: 202: "Obedience to conscience leads to obedience to the Gospel, which, instead of being something different altogether, is but the completion and perfection of that religion which natural conscience teaches."

I feel that God within my heart. I feel myself in His presence. He says to me, "Do this: don't do that." You may tell me that this dictate is a mere law of my nature, as it is to joy or to grieve. I cannot understand this. No, it is the echo of a person speaking to me. . . . It carries with it proof of its divine origin. My nature feels towards it as towards a person. When I obey it, I feel a satisfaction; when I disobey, a soreness—just like that which I feel in pleasing or offending some revered friend . . . An echo implies a voice; a voice a speaker. That speaker I love and I fear.[21]

In his *Letter to the Duke of Norfolk*, Newman explained whose voice that is:

Conscience is not a long-sighted selfishness, nor a desire to be consistent with oneself; but it is a messenger from Him, Who, both in nature and grace, speaks to us behind a veil, and teaches and rules us by His representatives. Conscience is the aboriginal Vicar of Christ, a prophet in its informations, a monarch in its peremptoriness, a priest in its blessings and anathemas, and, even though the eternal priesthood throughout the Church could cease to be, in it the sacerdotal principle would remain and would have a sway.[22]

Yet talk of inner lights and strange voices has a decidedly gnostic or even psychotic feel to it. If a person hears voices that no one else can hear, that person should probably see a doctor or an exorcist. And were conscience really a voice from *outside* our reasoning, it would play no part in moral philosophy and might suggest a double truth in moral theology: my merely-human practical reasoning tells me to do X, but my "divine voice" says to do Y, not X.[23]

So, does Newman think conscience is like an inbuilt sat-nav, or like the angel who appears on Fred Flintstone's right shoulder whispering into his right ear about his duty in contradiction to the bad angel whispering temptations into his left—which we must decide whether to obey? Several things might be said about this.

First, conscience is for Newman "a constituent element of the mind" like perception, reasoning, and aesthetic judgment, and its primary function is the rational judgment of the moral sense that interprets human nature.[24] It is the

---

21   *Cal.*, 314–15. See Ian Ker, *Newman on Vatican II* (Oxford: Oxford University Press, 2014), 134–38; Luc Terlinden, "Newman and Conscience," in Lefebvre and Mason, *John Henry Newman Doctor of the Church*, 201–19.

22   *Diff.* ii, 248.

23   See John Paul II, Encyclical Letter *Veritatis Splendor* (August 6, 1993), 56, where the pope noted a similar kind of "double truth" operative in attempts to legitimize supposedly "pastoral" solutions to moral dilemmas contrary to objective moral truth and also in seeking personal exceptions in conscience from universally binding norms.

24   *Diff.* ii, 248. See Gerard Magill, *Religious Morality in John Henry Newman: Hermeneutics of the Imagination* (Cham, Switzerland: Springer International Publishing, 2015), 199–201.

subjective experience of the objective moral law at play in the actor's life. Its reliable use requires moral education and practice. Here Newman is following the classical notion of *synderesis* and *conscientia* mediating a divine law even to unbelievers. The use of the metaphor of voice, then, is to emphasize that conscience does not invent its own principles but receives and recognizes them.

Secondly, it is this quality of conscience as "the rule of ethical truth, the standard of right and wrong, a sovereign, irreversible, absolute authority in the presence of men and angels"[25] that gives it its authority both with respect to the agent—who might otherwise choose the more convenient course—and the state, which should respect the individual not merely as a voter but as a voice of God. "We are accustomed to speak of conscience as a voice," Newman explains in the *Grammar of Assent*, "because it is so imperative and constraining, like no other dictate in the whole of our experience."[26] Conscience *must* be obeyed: "He who acts against his conscience loses his soul."[27] The voice metaphor, then, serves not only to highlight the givenness of conscience but also its "directing power," as he puts it in *The Development of Doctrine*.[28] Thus, as Pope Benedict has observed, conscience for Newman is both capacity for truth and obedience to that truth, both moral sense and moral judgment.[29]

Thirdly, natural conscience serves to plant "seeds" of faith and morals in the human soul, so that people are already ordered to receive the Gospel.

> It is by the universal sense of right and wrong, the consciousness of transgression, the pangs of guilt, and the dread of retribution, as first principles deeply lodged in the hearts of men, it is thus and only thus, that he has gained his footing in the world and achieved his success.[30]

Fourthly, once a person receives the gift of Christian faith, Newman implies this natural voice is transformed into the Christian sense of responsibility before God. In the *Apologia* Newman says believers would rather follow and, if necessary, be wrong with their religious conscience than follow and be right with their reason alone.[31] For the faithful, then, conscience is recognized as the voice of a God who is known and loved and whose instructions have even more imperative force than before.[32] "Left to itself and disregarded, it can become a counterfeit of the sacred power it is, and turn into a kind of self-confidence and deference to a

---

25 *Diff.* ii, 246.

26 *GA*, 107.

27 *Diff.* ii, 259.

28 *Dev.*, 361. In *The Letter to the Duke of Norfolk*, Newman describes conscience as "a messenger from Him, who, both in nature and in grace, speaks to us behind a veil." *Diff.* ii, 248.

29 See Benedict XVI, "Christmas Address to the Roman Curia," December 20, 2010.

30 *Diff.* ii, 253.

31 *Apo.*, 451.

32 John Paul II, *Veritatis Splendor*, 60.

person's own subjective judgment. Newman's words are unequivocal and perennially valid: 'Conscience has its rights because it has its duties'"[33]—duties to self, to one's fellows, above all to God. Thus, Reinhard Hütter argues that Newman's understanding of conscience is "essentially theonomic."[34]

Fifthly, in response to liberal tendencies of his day, Newman insisted that Christians must form their consciences in accord with the Scriptures, Tradition, and Magisterium.

> The sense of right and wrong is so delicate, so fitful, so easily puzzled, obscured, perverted, so subtle in its argumentative methods, so impressible by education, so biased by pride and passion, so unsteady in its course, that, in the struggle for existence amid the various exercises and triumphs of the human intellect, this sense is at once the highest of all teachers, yet the least luminous; and the Church, the Pope, the Hierarchy are, in the Divine purpose, the supply of an urgent demand.[35]

Ecclesiastical authority, on this account, is not so much an external force commanding us to act against our best judgments but rather a divinely ordained assistance for rooting out errors in our moral reasoning which the faithful willingly appropriate.[36] Famous for agreeing to toast the pope but only after toasting conscience first, Newman did not overstate the roles either of the Magisterium or of personal conscience but demonstrated their service to each other and the role of each in articulating God's purposes.[37] I explore what he meant by this in what follows.

Sixthly, if the light of reason and revelation is properly given to the intellect, conscience is then a property or function of the intellect. Yet in many places in Newman conscience seems to be a quality of the will as much as or more than of

---

33 John Paul II, *Letter on the First Centenary of the Death of Newman*, 4, quoting Newman, *Letter to the Duke of Norfolk* in *Diff.* ii, 250.

34 Reinhard Hütter, "Conscience 'Truly so called' and Its Counterfeit: John Henry Newman and Thomas Aquinas on What Conscience Is and Why It Matters," *Nova et Vetera* 12, no. 3 (2014): 701–67: "Conscience is not simply a human faculty, but is in its root constituted by the eternal law, the Divine Wisdom communicated to the human intellect. It is upon its theonomic nature and upon it alone that the prerogatives and the supreme authority of conscience are founded."

35 *Diff.* ii, 253.

36 Ryan Marr, "Newman Contra Liberalism: Conscience, Authority, and the Infidelity of the Future," *Public Discourse* 22 (July 2019).

37 On reading this highly contentious remark see: Benedict XVI, "Christmas Address to the Roman Curia"; December 20, 2010; Austin Cooper, OMI, "Newman and the Magisterium," in Lefebvre and Mason, *John Henry Newman: Doctor of the Church*, 173–87; Alan Donagan, *The Theory of Morality* (Chicago: University of Chicago Press, 1977), 418; John Finnis, "Conscience in the Letter to the Duke of Norfolk," in *Newman After a Hundred Years*, ed. Ian Ker and Alan Hill (Oxford: Clarendon Press, 1990), 401–18; Magill, *Religious Morality in John Henry Newman*, 199.

the intellect. This helps explain Newman's preference for the analogy of a voice rather than light for conscience. Reverence for and obedience to this "voice" make for sound conscience; self-sufficiency ("I loved to choose"), rebelliousness ("pride ruled my will"), and sensuality ("I loved the garish day"), on the other hand, distort judgment and behavior.[38]

The sound action of conscience thus requires a conversion or purification not just of intellect but also of will, a putting on of the mind and heart of Christ—to follow Paul's language—a trusting in the lead of the Kindly Light, not merely the consistent application of self-evident (or should-be-evident) principles. And without subjecting ourselves to the Church, which is the "undaunted and the only defender" of truth, conscience easily fades, as Newman puts it in *The Idea of a University*.[39]

NEWMAN ON CONSCIENCE
IN THE CONTEMPORARY MAGISTERIUM

It is here, at the intersection of the sovereignty of conscience and the fragility of conscience without guidance, that we find Newman's answer to the questions of relativism and truth that so often cloud discussion around his thinking. In his tussle with Gladstone, Newman insisted that the pope's authority rests precisely on the authority of conscience—for his magisterium is there to serve the consciences of the faithful by forming and informing them—and so can never contradict conscience without "cutting the ground from under his feet." Furthermore, he pointed out that the teaching of popes is mostly general and the judgments of conscience particular, and thus it would be very unlikely that they would come into conflict.[40]

The idea of making Newman a bishop had been abandoned long before the First Vatican Council, and he was unwilling to attend as a *peritus*.[41] He was very present at the Second Council, however, held long after his death. That Council readily adopted his language of the voice, echo, messenger or sanctuary of conscience. In *Gaudium et Spes* the Council fathers said:

> In the depths of his conscience, man detects a law which he does not impose upon himself, but which holds him to obedience. Always summoning him to love good and avoid evil, the voice of conscience

---

38 See "Lead, Kindly Light" in *VO*, 156–57.

39 *Idea*, 516. See Joseph Ratzinger, *Values in a Time of Upheaval* (San Francisco: Ignatius, 2006), 148.

40 *Diff.* ii, 221–22, 256–57. Quoted at 252.

41 B. C. Butler, OSB, "Newman and the Second Vatican Council," http://vatican-2voice.org/3butlerwrites/newman.htm; George Weigel, "Newman and Vatican II," *Catholic World Report*, April 15, 2015; Ian Ker, *Newman on Vatican II* (Oxford: Oxford University Press, 2014).

when necessary speaks to his heart: do this, shun that. For man has in his heart a law written by God; to obey it is his very dignity; according to it he will be judged. Conscience is the most secret core and sanctuary of a man: there he is alone with God, whose voice echoes in his depths.[42]

Conscience featured fifty-two times in the documents of the Second Vatican Council. The Council taught that:

- Human dignity consists in being creatures who by nature have the God-like ability to reason and choose. Thus all people are bound to seek, embrace and live the truth faithfully.[43]
- Every human agent has the capacity for and fundamental principles of conscience. Conscience is experienced as an inner "voice," "sanctuary," or "tribunal," yet one which mediates a universal moral law which is objectively given (by nature, reason, God) rather than personally invented.[44]
- Thus conscience summons us to inscribe the divine law in every aspect of life by seeking good and avoiding evil, loving God and neighbour, keeping the commandments and universal norms of morality.[45]
- To follow a well-formed conscience is not merely a right but a duty: persons are judged according to how they form and follow particular judgments of conscience.[46]
- Whether because of their own fault or not, agents may err in matters of conscience.[47] Catholics should therefore seek to form their consciences so that they are "dutifully conformed to the divine law itself and submissive toward the Church's teaching office, which authentically interprets that law in the light of the Gospel."[48]

---

42 Vatican Council II, *Gaudium et Spes* (December 7, 1965), 16. See John Paul II, *Veritatis Splendor*, 54; *Catechism of the Catholic Church* (hereafter *CCC*) 1778, 1795.

43 Vatican Council II, *Dignitatis Humanæ* (December 7, 1965), 1–2; *Gaudium et Spes*, 16, 41. See John Paul II, *Veritatis Splendor*, 31.

44 *Dignitatis Humanæ*, 3; *Gaudium et Spes*, 16. See John Paul II, *Veritatis Splendor*, 52–57; *Evangelium Vitae*, 29, 40; *CCC* 1778, 1795.

45 *Gaudium et Spes*, 16, 43, 74, 79; Vatican Council II, *Lumen Gentium* (November 21, 1964), 36; Vatican Council II, *Apostolicam Actuositatem* (November 18, 1965), 5; *Dignitatis Humanæ*, 3. See John Paul II, *Veritatis Splendor*, 57–59; *CCC* 1777, 1796.

46 *Gaudium et Spes*, 16; *Dignitatis Humanæ*, 1, 11. See *CCC* 1778. See John Paul II, *Veritatis Splendor*, 58–61; *CCC* 1778, 1798–1800.

47 *Gaudium et Spes*, 8, 16, 43, 47, 50. See John Paul II, *Veritatis Splendor*, 62–63; *CCC* 1799–1801.

48 *Dignitatis Humanæ*, 8, 14; Vatican Council II, *Gravissimum Educationis* (October 28, 1965), 1; *Apostolicam Actuositatem*, 20; Vatican Council II, *Inter Mirifica* (December 4, 1963), 9, 21; *Gaudium et Spes*, 31, 50, 87. See John Paul II, *Veritatis Splendor*, 64 etc.; *CCC* 1798.

- Claims of personal freedom or of obedience to civil laws or superiors do not excuse a failure to abide by the universal principles of conscience.[49]
- Freedom of thought, conscience and religion should be respected by civil authorities and people should not be coerced in matters of religion.[50]

Suffice it to say that this teaching is very much in the tradition of Paul, Augustine, Aquinas, More—and Newman. Paul VI attributed to Newman's wisdom much of the Council's thinking in this area.[51] Subsequent popes have regularly praised Newman's contribution on conscience and drawn upon it.[52] He is quoted directly in the *Catechism of the Catholic Church* and *Veritatis Splendor* in their treatments of conscience.[53]

NEWMAN ON CONSCIENCE
IN CONTEMPORARY SOCIETY

If Newman's influence on the Church's understanding of conscience is clear, has he also affected civil understandings? Several authors have recently explored how Newman's writings on conscience influenced the thinking and action of Sophie Scholl, leader of the White Rose resistance movement under Nazism.[54] In 1942 she gave two volumes of Newman's sermons as a parting gift to her boyfriend, Fritz Hartnagel, as he was sent to the eastern front. From the horrors of the battlefield, Fritz wrote to Scholl that Newman's writings were "like drops of precious wine."[55] Many others were also influenced by Newman's

---

49 *Dignitatis Humanæ*, 8; *Gaudium et Spes*, 79. See John Paul II, *Veritatis Splendor*, 32.

50 *Dignitatis Humanæ*, 3; *Gaudium et Spes*, 79; *Gravissimum Educationis*, 1, 6, 8.

51 Paul VI, "Address to Symposium on John Henry Newman," April 7, 1975. See Ker, *Newman on Vatican II*.

52 See Paul VI, "Address to Symposium on John Henry Newman," April 7, 1975, John Paul II, *Letter on the Centenary of the Elevation of Newman*; *Letter on the First Centenary of the Death of Newman*; "Address to Symposium on the Centenary of the Death of John Henry Newman," April 27, 1990; *Letter on the Second Centenary of the Birth of John Henry Newman*, January 22, 2001; Benedict XVI, "Address to Prayer Vigil on the Eve of the Beatification of John Henry Newman," September 18, 2010; "Homily for the Mass of Beatification of John Henry Newman," September 19, 2010; *Message to Symposium of the Friends of Newman*; "Christmas Address to the Roman Curia," 2010

53 John Paul II, *Veritatis Splendor*, 34; *CCC* 1778.

54 Dermot Fenlon, "From the White Star to the White Rose: Newman and the Conscience of the State," in *Realisation—Verwirklichung und Wirkungsgeschichte: Studien zur Grundlegung der Praktischen Theologie nach John Henry Newman*, ed. Günter Biemer and Bernd Trocholepczy (Frankfurt: Graf. Internationale Cardinal-Newman-Studien, 2010); Paul Shrimpton, *Conscience Before Conformity: Hans and Sophie Scholl and the White Rose Resistance in Nazi Germany* (Leominster: Gracewing, 2018); K. V. Turley, "How John Henry Newman's Writing Fought the Nazis," *National Catholic Register*, August 29, 2019, citing Fenlon, Shrimpton, and Marr.

55 Turley, "How John Henry Newman's Writing Fought the Nazis," quoting Ryan Marr.

teachings on conscience and took heroic stances for the truth at risk to their safety and comfort.

Yet conscience today is more often asserted in defense of following personal inclinations according to a subjectivist or relativist ethic. Servais Pinckaers noted that in Catholic circles "a certain allergic aversion to law [has] shifted the center of gravity in moral theology away from law and toward personal freedom, the individual subject and conscience."[56] "Follow your conscience" has come to be a code for pursuing personal preferences in sexuality, bioethics, remarriage, and Church practice.[57] The language of "the primacy of conscience," unknown for 1800 years of tradition from Paul to Newman, more often implies contest with Catholic teaching than with the spirit of the age or culture.[58] This is not the Christian conception of conscience at all. As Ratzinger observed, it is rather "a cloak thrown over human subjectivity, allowing man to elude the clutches of reality."[59]

Newman was alert to this tendency. "In this century," he said, conscience "has been superseded by a counterfeit, which the eighteen centuries prior to it never heard of, and could not have mistaken for it, if they had. It is the right of self-will . . . an Englishman's prerogative to be his own master in all things."[60]

> When men [today] advocate the rights of conscience, they in no sense mean the rights of the Creator, nor the duty to Him . . . but the right of thinking, speaking, writing, and acting, according to their judgment or their humour, without any thought of God at all. They do not even pretend to go by any moral rule, but they demand . . . for each to be his own master in all things, and to profess what he pleases, asking no one's leave, and accounting priest or preacher, speaker or writer, unutterably impertinent, who dares to say a word against his going to perdition, if he like it, in his own way . . . Conscience has rights because it has duties; but in this age, with a large portion of

---

56 Servais-Théodore Pinckaers, OP, *Morality: The Catholic View* (South Bend, Ind.: St. Augustine's Press, 2003), 56–57.

57 On these see: David Bohr, *In Christ a New Creation* (Our Sunday Visitor, 1993), 170; John Finnis, "Conscience, Infallibility and Contraception," *The Month* 239 (1978): 410–17; John Finnis, "IVF and the Catholic Tradition," *The Month* 246 (1984): 55–58; John Finnis, "'Faith and Morals': A Note," *The Month* 21, no. 2 (1988): 563–67; Germain Grisez, John Finnis, and William E. May, "Indissolubility, Divorce and Holy Communion," *New Blackfriars* 75 (June 1994): 321–30.

58 See, for example, Richard Gula, "Conscience," in *Christian Ethics*, ed. by Bernard Hoose (London: Cassall, 1998), 114; Linda Hogan, *Confronting the Truth: Conscience in the Catholic Tradition* (New York: Paulist, 2002); James Keenan, *Commandments of Compassion* (Franklin, WI: Sheed and Ward, 1999), 112, 134; Anne Patrick, *Liberating Conscience: Feminist Explorations in Catholic Theology* (New York: Continuum, 1996).

59 Ratzinger "Conscience and Truth," 79. See John Paul II, *Veritatis Splendor*, 32–33.

60 *Diff.* ii, 250.

the public, it is the very right and freedom of conscience to dispense with conscience, to ignore a Lawgiver and Judge, to be independent of unseen obligations.[61]

Thus, Newman already saw how revelation, tradition, community, even reason itself, could progressively be seen as adversaries of the free agent. Instead of being informed by right reason and Church teaching, appeals to conscience were more and more about personal preference.

He argued prophetically that conscience is only worthy of our respect because it is about hearing the truth and obeying God. But "left to itself, though it tells truly at first, it soon becomes wavering, ambiguous, and false; it needs good teachers and good examples to keep it up to the mark and the line of duty; and the misery is, that these external helps, teachers, and examples are in many instances wanting."[62] In critiquing misconceptions of conscience, Newman argued that just as the value of memory is in remembering accurately, so the value of conscience is in yielding right judgment and godly action. Truth always had primacy for him.

The Second Vatican Council followed Newman's lead in celebrating the dignity of conscience, but also habitually qualified the word with adjectives such as "right," "correct," "well-formed," "upright," or "Christian"—allowing that not a few consciences are confused, deformed, secularized, or otherwise misleading.[63] Conscience often goes astray, sometimes invincibly, that is, by no fault of the agent and so without losing its dignity; but at other times voluntarily, that is, because of negligence or vice, in which case conscience is degraded.[64] It is taught that

in the formation of their consciences, the Christian faithful ought carefully to attend to the sacred and certain doctrine of the Church. For the Church is, by the will of Christ, the teacher of the truth. It is her duty to give utterance to, and authoritatively to teach, that truth which is Christ Himself, and also to declare and confirm by her authority those principles of the moral order which have their origins in human nature itself. . . . The disciple is bound by a grave obligation toward Christ, his Master, ever more fully to understand the truth received from Him, faithfully to proclaim it, and vigorously to defend it, never—be it understood—having recourse to means that are incompatible with the spirit of the

---

61 *Diff.* ii, 250.

62 "Saintliness the standard of Christian principle," in *Mix.*, no. 5, 83.

63 See, for example, Vatican Council II, *Apostolicam Actuositatem*, 5, 20; *Inter Mirifica*, 9, 21; *Gravissimum Educationis*, 1; *Lumen Gentium*, 36; *Gaudium et Spes*, 16, 26, 43, 50, 52, 76, 87.

64 See John Paul II, *Veritatis Splendor*, 62–63.

Gospel. At the same time, the charity of Christ urges him to love and have prudence and patience in his dealings with those who are in error or in ignorance with regard to the faith.[65]

In response to the view that the Catholic conscience might come to conclusions at odds with the Magisterium, Newman said: "Natural Religion . . . needs, in order that it may speak to mankind with effect and subdue the world, to be sustained and completed by Revelation."[66] And "at first our conscience tells us, in a plain and straightforward way, what is right and what is wrong; but when we trifle with this warning, our reason becomes perverted and comes in aid of our wishes, and comes in aid of our wishes, and deceives us to our ruin."[67] It is Church teaching that keeps conscience to its proper course.[68]

Thus on the eve of Newman's beatification Pope Benedict noted that

at the end of his life, Newman would describe his life's work as a struggle against the growing tendency to view religion as a purely private and subjective matter, a question of personal opinion. Here is the first lesson we can learn from his life: in our day, when an intellectual and moral relativism threatens to sap the very foundations of our society, Newman reminds us that, as men and women made in the image and likeness of God, we were created to know the truth, to find in that truth our ultimate freedom and [deepest] fulfilment . . .[69]

CONCLUSION: DOCTOR OF CONSCIENCE

This short chapter has barely scratched the surface of Newman's teaching on conscience as the voice of God. Much is made of his insistence that conscience be respected and followed above all else. Yet on his account the authority of conscience lies in its pointing us to moral and religious truth and prompting us to follow the divine will. Far from being a cause or excuse for relativism, then, conscience is its ultimate rejection. But because conscience is also relativism's most vulnerable target, Newman insists on the Church's role as its defender and

---

65 *Dignitatis Humanæ*, 14.
66 *Diff.* ii, 254.
67 *PS* viii, no. 5: 67.
68 See *Diff.* ii, 132–33.
69 Benedict XVI, "Address on the Eve of the Beatification of John Henry Newman." See also his "Christmas Address to the Roman Curia." Likewise, John Paul II, *Letter on the First Centenary of the Death of Newman*, 4: "Few people championed the full rights of conscience as he did; few writers pleaded so persuasively on behalf of its authority and liberty, yet he never allowed any trace of subjectivism or relativism to taint his teaching."

formator. This brought a young *peritus* at the Second Vatican Council named Father Ratzinger to see that, without Church authority, conscience is the ready slave of personal passion and social fashion—what he would famously dub "the dictatorship of relativism."

On the centenary of the saint's death, the mature Cardinal Ratzinger paid tribute to Newman's "liberating and essential" truth that the "we" of the Church develops from and guarantees the "me" of personal conscience. For conscience, on Newman's account, is above all about discipleship: the implicit discipleship of those who hear and respond to God, even unknowingly, as they follow their best reason in their choices; and the more explicit discipleship of the faithful, who know that conscience, guided by the Gospel and the Church, is our surest guide.

Suggested Reading

Aquino, Frederick D., and Benjamin J. King, eds. *The Oxford Handbook of John Henry Newman*. Oxford: Oxford University Press, 2018.

Lefebvre, Philippe, and Colin Mason, eds., *John Henry Newman: Doctor of the Church*. Oxford: Family Publications, 2007.

Marr, Ryan. "Newman Contra Liberalism: Conscience, Authority, and the Infidelity of the Future." *Public Discourse* 22 (July 2019).

Newman, John Henry. "A Letter Addressed to His Grace the Duke of Norfolk on the Occasion of Mr Gladstone's Recent Expostulation" (1875). In *Diff.* ii.

Ratzinger, Joseph. "Conscience and Truth." In *Values in a Time of Upheaval*, 75–100. New York: Crossroad, 2006.

CHAPTER 20

JOHN HENRY NEWMAN ON THE DEVELOPMENT OF DOCTRINE: A *VIA MEDIA* BETWEEN INTELLECTUALISM AND HISTORICISM

Tracey Rowland

In an address delivered to mark the centenary of Cardinal Newman's death, Cardinal Ratzinger, as he was, remarked that an even deeper contribution to his appreciation of Newman than that of his *Doktor Vater*, Gottlieb Söhngen, was the contribution that Heinrich Fries published in connection with the Jubilee of Chalcedon.[1] This is the essay "Die Dogmengeschichte des fünften Jahrhunderts im theologischen Werdegang von John Henry Newman," published in volume III of the work *Das Konzil von Chalkedon: Geschichte und Gegenwart* (1954).[2] Here a young Fr. Ratzinger found access to Newman's teaching on the development of doctrine, which he regarded, along with Newman's doctrine

---

1   Joseph Ratzinger, "Presentation by His Eminence Card. Joseph Ratzinger on the Occasion of the First Centenary of the Death of Card. John Henry Newman," April 28, 1990. Available at www.vatican.va.

2   Heinrich Fries, "Die Dogmengeschichte des fünften Jahrhunderts im theologischen Werdegang von John Henry Newman," in *Das Konzil von Chalkedon: Geschichte und Gegenwart*, ed. Aloys Grillmeier, SJ, and Heinrich Bacht, SJ, vol. 3 (Echter-Verlag: 1954).

on conscience, as Newman's decisive contribution to the renewal of theology. As he wrote, Newman's work "placed the key in our hand to build historical thought into theology, or much more, [Newman] taught us to think historically in theology and so to recognize the identity of faith in all developments."[3]

Since the essay by Fries to celebrate the Jubilee of Chalcedon—in addition to his essay on Newman's contribution to fundamental theology, published in the journal *Newman Studien*—are not yet available in English translation, the first part of this chapter will seek to synthesize the main ideas in these two papers as they apply to Newman's idea of the development of doctrine. The second half of the chapter will then link the development of doctrine theme to Newman's idea of the *sensus fidelium*, specifically to contemporary elaborations on Newman's ideas on consulting the faithful in matters of doctrine. This is a live issue during the pontificate of Francis where encouragement has been given to processes eliciting lay opinion on a wide variety of subjects.

Ratzinger's reference to "thinking historically in theology" is a reference to what he regarded as the neuralgic point of modern Catholic theology—the theological significance of history. How does history relate to dogma, how does history relate to theological anthropology, how does history relate to scriptural hermeneutics, what is the relationship between salvation history and metaphysics, and what is the relationship between salvation history and eschatology? Is revelation something historical or something doctrinal, or both? Wherever one goes in the field of fundamental theology one runs into the land mine of history. In his *Principles of Catholic Theology* Ratzinger went so far as to identify a particular dimension of this neuralgic point—"understanding the mediation of history in the realm of ontology" as the most serious crisis faced by Catholic theology in the twentieth century.[4] In short hand terms, one might call this the Heideggerian "being in time" problem. This issue has had a significant impact upon the territory of moral theology, unsettling established teaching in many areas. The difficulty for anyone working in this field is that of explaining how history can be a relevant factor in Church teaching without landing in the ditch of cultural relativism. The fact that Newman was working in this dangerous quarry helps to explain the different appropriations of his thought. The image of Newman authors would like to project often depends on which dimension of his fundamental theology they decide to highlight. One can end up with very different images of Newman if, for example, one chooses to emphasize his theory of conscience while omitting any reference to his thoughts about the Petrine Office, or choosing to discuss his ideas about the doctrinal authority of the Magisterium, or what he calls the "*ecclesia docens*," while omitting to explain his understanding of the limits on the powers of the Petrine keys. For Newman the

---

3   Joseph Ratzinger, "On the Occasion of the First Centenary."

4   Joseph Ratzinger, *Principles of Catholic Theology* (San Francisco: Ignatius Press, 1986), 160.

papacy was no absolute monarchy, as he made clear in his famous *Letter to the Duke of Norfolk*.

The thesis advanced by Fries is that while Newman set out to defend the Church of England as the *Via Media* between Protestantism and Roman Catholicism, he ended up with a defense of Roman Catholicism as a *Via Media* between a pure intellectualism that acknowledged no role for history and a voluntarist-historicism with only the weakest of links to dogmatic theology. In other words, Newman came to have faith in Catholicism precisely because it was only in the Catholic resolution of the apparently discordant claims of history and dogma that Newman could find any way of effecting a reasonable relationship between the two. As Fries expressed the proposition: "Newman wants to raise the real content of dogmatism and historicism into a higher unity and thus to do justice to the whole of revelation, revelation as truth and revelation as reality and as history."[5]

Seen in this light Newman is very much a Church "Doctor"—someone whose special charism is the ability to resolve an intellectual crisis of enormous pastoral relevance. The fact that he was immensely popular in early twentieth century German Catholic circles is not surprising. In the world of German high culture the eighteenth century's era of Idealism with its exaltation of "pure reason" had been followed by the nineteenth century's era of Romanticism with its interest in history and tradition and ultimately in the early twentieth century with Heidegger's "being in time." For Fries, Newman offered a way forward that avoided the extremes of German Idealism or what he called "intellectualism" on the one side, and cultural relativism or "voluntarist-historicism," on the other.

To achieve the synthesis Newman operated with a number of building blocks. The first was his notion of revelation whose accent on the historical dimension anticipated the approach taken by the Second Vatican Council fathers in the document *Dei Verbum*. Fries observed:

> For Newman, revelation is not so much a summary of eternal truths that give our thinking and cognition a substantial increase and expansion beyond the natural possibilities, but first and foremost a reality of a historical nature and greatness, based on the Event that happened in Jesus Christ—an historical reality that did not freeze and die in the past but had and has a history, a history that pours into the space of history, spreads within it and with undiminished power extends into the present.[6]

Fries also explains that Newman did not simply declare revelation to be an historical event and then leave the subject at that point:

---

5 Heinrich Fries, "Newmans Bedeutung für die Theologie," in *Newman Studies Erste Folge* (Nürnberg: Glock und Lutz Verlag, 1948): 181–99 at 195.

6 Fries, "Newmans Bedeutung für die Theologie," 193.

Newman is not content to raise the character of revelation as an historical event, he also follows the laws and the structure of this history and historical development. If the revelation is delivered up to history, there is a double danger: that it is cursed in history and thereby loses its eternal content, or that it is changed in substance by history and historical development and thus corrupted.[7]

To avoid these two pitfalls Newman identified seven "Notes" or hallmarks of a real development as opposed to a corruption. In his own words:

> There is no corruption if it retains one and the same type, the same principles, the same organisation; if its beginnings anticipate its subsequent phases, and its later phenomena protect and subserve its earlier; if it has a power of assimilation and revival, and a vigorous action from first to last.[8]

SEVEN NOTES OF DEVELOPMENT

The reference to the "preservation of type" is an adoption of an organic metaphor earlier used by Vincent of Lérins in the famous *Commonitorium* composed in 434. This work became popular at the time of the Reformation, enjoying thirty-five new editions in one century, because it proposed an approach to the much-disputed notion of "tradition." This first Note is often summarised by the maxim: "young birds do not grow into fishes." In other words, a new idea will only be a legitimate development of a doctrine if it is an organic outgrowth of the original deposit of the faith. Baby birds do not grow up to be fish. An oak tree can grow from an acorn, but a pear tree cannot.

The second Note—that of the "continuity of principles"—means that the life of doctrines may be said to consist in the law or principle that they embody. For example, from the doctrine of the Incarnation, that God became incarnate in human form, certain other doctrines follow as a matter of logical consequence. We can reason, for example, that matter, including human nature, is capable of sanctification. Newman stated that for a development to be faithful, it "must retain both the doctrine and the principle with which it started."[9]

The third Note is the "power of assimilation." The harder it is to assimilate an idea the more likely it is to represent a corrupting influence rather than a legitimate development.

---

7   Fries, "Newmans Bedeutung für die Theologie," 194.

8   John Henry Newman, *An Essay on the Development of Christian Doctrine with an Introduction, Notes and Textual Appendices by James Tolhurst DD*, Newman Millennium Edition volume XII (London: Gracewing, 2018), 207.

9   *Dev.* (Gracewing), 219.

Newman described the fourth Note as the "logical sequence" principle. A doctrine is likely to be a true development, not a corruption, in proportion as it seems to be the *logical issue* of its original teaching. In this section of the *Essay on the Development of Doctrine* Newman wrote that "the holy Apostles would without words know all the truth concerning the high doctrines of theology, which controversialists after them have piously and charitably reduced to formulae, and developed through argument."[10] The significance of this statement is, as Michael Pakaluk has noted, that for Newman there is a single unchanging deposit of the faith.[11] It is set down at the beginning of Christian history in the apostolic era and subsequently develops in the sense that our passive reception and understanding of it grows. It is our understanding that grows and deepens, not the deposit of the faith itself.

The fifth Note is "anticipation of its future." Here Newman remarks:

> Since developments are in great measure only aspects of the idea from which they proceed, and all of them are natural consequences of it, it is often a matter of accident in what order they are carried out in individual minds; and it is no wise strange that here and there definite specimens of advanced teaching should very early occur, which in the historical course are not found till a late day. The fact, then, of such early or recurring intimations of tendencies which afterwards are fully realized, is a sort of evidence that those later and more systematic fulfil-ments are only in accordance with the original idea.[12]

In this context history can be a kind of midwife to the development of doctrine. For example, in the early twentieth century the rise of interest in personalist philosophy—fuelled in part by the demise of German Idealism which, metaphorically speaking, collapsed on the battlefields of World War I—fostered an interest in the theological significance of relationality. This is the way in which human identity is determined, at least in part, by relation-ships with other persons, including the Persons of the Holy Trinity. In his essay "Concerning the Notion of the Person in Theology," Joseph Ratzinger observed that the monks at the monastery of St. Victor (known as the Victorines) had been interested in this issue in the twelfth century but that, apart from them, in the medieval and late scholastic periods the notion of the Person was only considered by theologians in the context of the processions within the Holy Trinity.[13] Theologians did not extend the analysis from the Trinity to the human person. This only begins to happen in the twentieth century. The development is

---

10   *Dev.* (Gracewing), 231.
11   Michael Pakaluk, "An Introduction to John Henry Newman," Lecture Delivered to the Thomistic Institute, November 2019 at Columbia University.
12   *Dev.* (Gracewing), 236–37.
13   Joseph Ratzinger, "Concerning the Notion of the Person in Theology," *Communio: International Catholic Review* (Fall 1990): 439–54.

spurred on by the collapse of German Idealist philosophy, itself one of the many casualties of World War I, and the concomitant rise of personalism and existentialism.[14] Similarly, John Paul II's magisterial catechesis on human love significantly developed the theology of marriage as a response to the sexual revolution of the 1960s.[15] Without the development of the contraceptive pill there would have been no sexual revolution, and without the pill and the sexual revolution there would have been less impetus for the Church to develop her catechesis on human love as John Paul II did. Some questions simply do not arise until some historical development prompts their consideration. This does not mean however that history carries within it some new truths to be added to the original deposit of the faith, merely that history can be the midwife to a deepening of the Church's understanding of that original deposit.

The sixth Note is a "conservative action" upon its past. According to Newman, a true development "illustrates, not obscures, corroborates, not corrects, the body of thought from which it proceeds." Here Newman quotes St. Leo: "To be seeking for what has been disclosed, to reconsider what has been finished, to tear up what has been laid down, what is this but to be unthankful for what is gained?" Newman also refers to the principle of St. Vincent of Lérins that developments of doctrine must be *"profectus fidei non permutatio"*—a perfection of the faith not a permutation of the faith. In practice it is this Note that is often the most controversial and difficult to analyse. What for one scholar may look like a complete "doctrinal back-flip" for another is simply a "reading down" of the ambit of an earlier teaching. The *Declaratio circa Catholicam Doctrinam de Ecclesia: Contra Nonnullos Errores Hodiernos Tuendam* (1973) of the Congregation of the Doctrine of the Faith recognised that dogmatic truths bear the traces of a given epoch's conceptions of an issue and can be incomplete. This means that ecclesial doctrines share many similarities with legal doctrines as found in the British Common Law system insofar as the decisions of judges become doctrinal precedents that are subsequently clarified and both expanded and narrowed by later judicial decisions. The whole field of hermeneutics, of the interpretation of documents, can become relevant in this context of the development of doctrine. The International Theological Commission's document *The Interpretation of Dogma* (1989) can be read as a contemporary guide to issues thrown open by Note number six.

---

14   The link between World War I and the demise of German Idealism was summed up in the following statement of Paul Tillich: "All that horrible, long night I walked along the rows of dying men, and much of my German classical education philosophy broke down that night—the belief that man could master cognitively the essence of his being, the belief in the identity of essence and existence." See Paul Tillich, *Time* 73, March 11, 1959, 47. Quoted in Douglas John Hall, "The Great War and the Theologians" in *The Twentieth Century: A Theological Overview*, ed. Gregory Baum (New York: Orbis, 1999): 3–14 at 6.

15   For the best English translation of St. John Paul II's Catechesis on Human Love see: John Paul II, *Man and Woman He Created Them: A Theology of the Body*, ed. Michael Waldstein (New York: Pauline Books, 2006).

The seventh and final Note is described as the "chronic vigour" principle. Here a corruption is distinguished by its transitory character. Faddish ideas are like shooting stars. They glimmer for a moment but quickly fade.

Through his study of the history of early Christianity Newman reached the conclusion, in Fries's words, "that only in the revelation, as it is given in the Catholic Church and its historical development and representation up to the present reality, are these [above seven] characteristics and features of a real development present. The Catholic Church alone is the living bearer of divine revelation spanning centuries."[16]

Fries also observed that Newman formulated his concept of the development of doctrine at a time when the notion of development was at the centre of scientific and philosophical thinking. Darwin, Newman's contemporary, had applied the concept to the natural sciences and the theme was strong in German Idealist philosophy, especially in Hegel. Nonetheless, Fries also observes that Newman does not succumb "to a mechanical transfer of Darwinian thoughts to the realm of revelation" but "preserves their identity and constancy in the middle of all history."[17] Nor does Newman go down the path of Hegel with the idea of a purely logical dialectical development. He does not dissolve faith in knowledge as Fries suggests Anton Gunther, inspired by Hegel, did. He allows "revelation and mystery to persist in their captive transcendence."[18] Fries concluded that Newman adopted in his concept of development the attitude that he recognized as a characteristic feature of true Christianity and expressed as follows: "What man is in the midst of the unreasonable creatures, that is the Church in the middle of the schools of the world, as Adam gave the animals around him their names, the Church looked around the world from the first moment and took note of and visited the teachings it found."[19]

The above seven criteria could be described as the core of Newman's idea of "tradition," the second of his building blocks. Here too Newman's understanding was to anticipate and indeed even to feed into developments in twentieth century magisterial theology, especially the theology of *Dei Verbum*, where the idea of tradition is no longer so strongly reliant upon the *Commonitorium* of Vincent of Lérins. This document had been the standard Latin Catholic text for understanding the notion of tradition. The three basic principles offered by Lérins to distinguish the true tradition from heresy were that something had to have been held by everyone, everywhere in the Church from the earliest times. The principle is summarised by the Latin phrase *Quod ubique, quod semper, quod ab omnibus*. Newman's use of this principle is complex and changed over time. Initially Newman had been in favour of the *Quod ubique* maxim. Here Fries comments:

---

16   Fries, "Newmans Bedeutung für die Theologie," 194.
17   Fries, "Newmans Bedeutung für die Theologie," 195.
18   Fries, "Newmans Bedeutung für die Theologie," 195.
19   Fries, "Newmans Bedeutung für die Theologie," 195.

The Anglican Church and theology had adopted the well-known axiom from the *Commonitorium* of Vincent of Lérin (Lérins) as a rule of faith: Whatever has always, everywhere and by everyone, is credited as a revelation truth—"*quod semper, quod ubique, quod ab omnibus creditum est.*" Newman sees in this, with reason, "why we should make so much of the early centuries but not consider the later ones." He calls this rule majestic, understandable and in a very special way a rule that is related to the Anglican spirit, that "occupies a middle position by not rejecting the fathers but not recognizing the Pope. The principle establishes a simple rule by which to measure the value of every historical fact as it comes before us; thereby it establishes a stronghold against Rome, while at the same time opening an attack on Protestantism."[20]

However, Fries also observes that Newman "recognizes that there are considerable difficulties with this rule, namely in its application to the individual case. He thinks it is more of a rule in the sense of negative orientation than positive guidance." Newman himself wrote:

The rule is more useful in deciding what Christianity is not, than what it is. It is irresistible against Protestantism, and in one sense it is of course irresistible against Rome too, but in the same sense it is also against England. It strikes Rome through England. It can be interpreted in two ways: if it is narrowed down for the purpose of refuting the confession of Catholicism of Pope Pius, it also becomes an objection to the Athanasian confession; but if it is handled so laxly that it allows for the teachings retained in the English Church, then it no longer excludes certain teachings of Rome that England denies. It cannot condemn St. Thomas and St. Bernard and at the same time defend St. Athanasius and St. Gregory of Nazianzen.[21]

Fries concludes:

The [Anglican] Newman of the "Via media" already pointed out the extraordinary difficulties that the conditions "semper - ubique - ab omnibus" impose. Not only are they difficult to interpret in terms of their meaning and scope, but also they can hardly be met as conditions. They are in fact not given in the exclusive way in which the Anglican theologians understand them, not even in the first Christian period, for example in relation to the question of the Trinity. Indeed, Newman

---

20 Fries, "Die Dogmengeschichte des fünften Jahrhunderts im theologischen Werdegang von John Henry Newman," 439.
21 Fries, "Die Dogmengeschichte des fünften Jahrhunderts im theologischen Werdegang von John Henry Newman," 440.

declares categorically: With this canon of Vincent of Lérins alone, nothing would have been decided on what was dogmatically established in the first Christian centuries.[22]

It is not surprising therefore that criticism of Lérins abounded in twentieth century theological circles, preoccupied as they were with the relationship between history and dogma. In his essay "On the Transmission of Divine Revelation," a commentary on *Dei Verbum*, Ratzinger wrote that Vincent de Lérins's static *semper* no longer seems the right way of expressing the problem.[23] Vladimir Lossky was also critical of Lérins. He noted that the maxim "*quod semper, quod ubique, quod ab omnibus*" can be applied in full only to those apostolic traditions which were orally transmitted during two or three centuries. The New Testament Scriptures already escape from this rule, for they were neither "always," nor "everywhere," "received by all" before the definitive establishment of the scriptural canon. Cyril O'Regan also catalogued a number of Balthasar's criticisms of the position advocated by Lérins. His list included that Lérins does not acknowledge the variety of theological perspectives that is constitutive of the depth of the Catholic tradition and that he fails to appreciate "the *praxis* of the saints as forms of language that emerge unanticipated, yet answer specific communal and historical needs" and further, that "Lérins' definition is in danger of denying the symbolic nature of all language with respect to the divine and promoting the view that doctrine is adequate to the mystery to which it refers."[24] O'Regan summarized Balthasar's account of tradition with the statement: "truth is objective, yet refracted over time through Christian communities, and exemplary members of these communities."[25]

By the time he wrote the *Essay on the Development of Christian Doctrine* Newman had substantially revised his understanding of the concept of tradition and of the usefulness of Lérins's *Quod ubique, quod semper, quod ab omnibus* maxim. He declared: "It is indeed sometimes said that the stream is clearest near the Spring," but this "does not apply to the history of a philosophy or belief, which on the contrary is more equable and purer, and stronger, when its bed has become deep, and broad and full."[26]

Nonetheless, as noted above, Newman adopted Lérins's idea that development must be a *profectus* (advance) rather than a *permutation*—and used the principle as the foundation for his sixth Note. He also used Lérins's "preservation

---

22 Fries, "Die Dogmengeschichte des fünften Jahrhunderts im theologischen Werdegang von John Henry Newman," 440.

23 Joseph Ratzinger, "Transmission of Divine Revelation" in *Commentary on the Documents of Vatican II*, ed. Herbert Vorgrimler, vol. 3 (New York: Herder and Herder, 1969), 187.

24 Cyril O'Regan, "Balthasar between Tübingen and Postmodernity," *Modern Theology* 14, no. 3 (July 1998): 325–53 at 330.

25 O'Regan, "Balthasar between Tübingen and Postmodernity," 337.

26 *Dev.* (Gracewing), 60.

of type" principle for his First Note. Thus, one might conclude that he adopted some elements of Lérins's understanding of tradition within his own account of tradition, but that his own account differs significantly from Lérins in that it was a living and organic account, rather than a static account. In this way he was operating on parallel lines to those of the scholars of the Tübingen School, principally Adam Möhler. In *Unity in the Church, or The Principles of Catholicism: Presented in the Spirit of the Church Fathers of the First Three Centuries,* published in 1825, Möhler described the Church as the organic development of the work of the Holy Spirit through history. In the twentieth century Newman's organic understanding of tradition influenced the French philosopher Maurice Blondel, author of *History and Dogma* (1903). Blondel in turn influenced Henri de Lubac who influenced Hans Urs von Balthasar and both de Lubac and Balthasar influenced Ratzinger. By the time *Dei Verbum* was drafted in the early 1960s it was an organic rather than a static understanding of tradition that informed the document.

The historical account of Revelation and the organic account of tradition were not however Newman's only building blocks. A third very significant foundation stone was his understanding of the Petrine Office and more broadly the *ecclesia docens.* As Fries explained:

Another result of these dogma and church history studies was no less important. This, too, was particularly apparent to Newman when considering the Council of Chalcedon: it is the decisive and definitive role that the Pope played as the authoritative teaching authority . . . [Pope] Leo actually and energetically asserted his authority at the Council of Chalcedon, and it was recognized and confirmed by the council members, who mostly came from the East. Through Leo's strength and initiative, as documented above all in the *Epistula dogmatica ad Flavianum,* the theological and Christological questions about Chalcedon were decided as they were decided.[27]

Since the Anglican Church recognised the authority of the Council of Chalcedon, as a matter of logic, Newman concluded that the Anglican Church owed an important component of its intellectual patrimony to the exercise of the Petrine keys. As he wrote:

I saw that if the earlier times were my guide, the Pope had a completely different position in the Church than I had previously assumed. When this suspicion took hold of me and I looked at the facts of the story, the whole English system fell apart on all sides, the ground shook under my feet and in a short time I found myself in a completely different scene of things. What had passed could not be revoked.[28]

27 Fries, "Die Dogmengeschichte des fünften Jahrhunderts im theologischen Werdegang von John Henry Newman," 431.
28 *LD* x, 305.

As stated above, Newman did not regard the papacy as some kind of absolute monarchy with the Petrine keys holding magical power to change the laws of nature, to declare blue white and white blue, to announce that 4+4=7, to overturn the Scriptures and the very words of Christ himself. Newman was not Rex Mottram, the character in Evelyn Waugh's *Brideshead Revisited* who believed that if the pope said it was raining and the skies were perfectly clear and the sun shining then it must be "raining spiritually." Newman was not a fool. As a fifteenth century Viennese Dominican observed, "if the Supreme Pontiff, together with a Council, were to teach that Tobias's dog had no tail, he should not be believed."[29] Newman viewed the papacy as an office circumscribed by the deposit of the faith itself and manifested in the depths of the human conscience. As Ratzinger was later to write, the papacy is not an absolute monarchy.[30] It is more like a constitutional monarchy where the monarch holds certain "reserve powers" which must be exercised within the boundaries set by a constitution. In this analogy the Sacred Scriptures take the place of a constitution. Thus, Ratzinger's interpretation of Newman's statement that he would drink a toast to the pope but to conscience first was that Newman was making a point about the pope himself being bound by the voice of conscience. In his *God and the World* interview, Ratzinger declared:

> The Pope himself cannot even say, I am the Church, or I am tradition, but he is, on the contrary, under constraint; he incarnates this constraint laid upon the Church. . . . The Pope is thus not the instrument through which one could, so to speak, call a different Church into existence, but is a protective barrier against arbitrary action.[31]

Newman's understanding of conscience thus becomes a highly significant fourth building block. In this context Fries writes:

> According to Newman—especially considering its anthropological-psychological side—the belief in God is a separate, specific and original act of the human mind, not to be confused with or derived from knowing or striving or feeling, but stemming from a secret centre in a living relationship to everything standing in these components. This centre, in which faith is based on real approval, is the conscience, which is

---

29 This amusing comment was cited by Jared Wicks, "Six Texts by Prof. Joseph Ratzinger as *peritus* before and during Vatican Council II," *Gregorianum* 89, no. 2 (2008): 233–311 at 276.

30 Joseph Ratzinger, Preface to Alcuin Reid's *The Organic Development of the Liturgy* (Farnborough: St. Michael's Abbey Press, 2004).

31 Joseph Ratzinger, *God and the World: A Conversation with Peter Seewald* (San Francisco: Ignatius, 2002), 377.

more than knowing and striving and feeling, and yet combines all these powers and functions in one another . . . Newman knows the intellectualist and voluntarist-irrational solution to the problem of faith from a first-hand view. His answer is a truly creative "via media" between these two extremes, which in Newman's time were represented by a philosophical-theological liberalism, the fight against and surmounting of which he made his life's task.[32]

This is not, however, how the concept of the conscience is commonly understood in popular parlance. That Newman's understanding of conscience was distinctive is something the German Catholic scholars of the early twentieth century well understood. Gottlieb Söhngen wrote: "Conscience does not mean a purely ethical, but rather a religious fact of the human spirit. To speak with an expression of Kant: The categorical imperative or unconditional command is for a Newman, unlike a Kant, no longer purely ethical, but already in the peculiarly religious field."[33] Similarly, under the influence of Newman, Romano Guardini argued that conscience is "not a mirror or a camera, not a magnetic needle or any other kind of mechanical instrument," it is not a "law that hangs somewhere," "not a simple idea," "not a concept in the air," but rather "the living voice of God's holiness in us."[34] Fries noted that Newman understood that "unless human judgments are under the influence of the cognitive function of conscience, it could be that the god whom we gain from the study of nature is our own spirit, and our worship is the idolization of our own self."[35] Newman's idea of conscience is therefore much more sophisticated than a simple notion of doing whatever one feels comfortable doing. It includes an understanding that the work of the conscience can be either enhanced or impeded by the depths of the soul's holiness or depravity. This in turn means that a reliance upon this faculty of the soul in isolation from the other three of Newman's building blocks can be a recipe for moral error, as was later emphasised by Ratzinger in his short monograph on conscience.[36]

In summary, Newman's understanding of the development of doctrine rests on some four pillars: his notion of revelation, tradition, the powers of the magisterium, and the role of conscience. Each of these key concepts or intellectual building blocks need to be understood as Newman understood them in order to properly appreciate his synthesis.

---

32   Fries, "Newmans Bedeutung für die Theologie," 181–99 at 187.

33   Gottlieb Söhngen, *Kardinal Newman: Sein Gottesgedanke und seine Denkergestalt* (Bonn: Verlag Götz Schwippert, 1946), 20.

34   Romano Guardini, *La coscienza* (Brescia: Morcelliana, 2009), 18, 32–33.

35   Fries, "Newmans Bedeutung für die Theologie," 189.

36   Joseph Ratzinger, *On Conscience* (San Francisco: Ignatius, 2007).

THE *SENSUS FIDELIUM*

In the second decade of the twenty-first century yet another of Newman's key concepts presents itself as a live theological issue. This is his notion of the *sensus fidelium* derived from his essay "On Consulting the Faithful in Matters of Doctrine," first published in 1859. This essay can be seen to focus on one particular aspect of the development of doctrine—that of the role of the laity in this ecclesial work. This is not a fifth stand-alone building block but a concept that is intrinsically connected to each of the above four primary concepts. In this essay Newman made the following declaration of principle:

> I think I am right in saying that the tradition of the Apostles, committed to the whole Church in its various constituents and functions *per modum unius*, manifests itself variously at various times: sometimes by the mouth of the episcopacy, sometimes by the doctors, sometimes by the people, sometimes by liturgies, rites, ceremonies, and customs, by events, disputes, movements, and all those other phenomena which are comprised under the name of history. It follows that none of these channels of tradition may be treated with disrespect; granting at the same time fully, that the gift of discerning, discriminating, defining, promulgating, and enforcing any portion of that tradition resides solely in the *Ecclesia docens*.[37]

As lawyers would say, this statement of principle has two limbs. The first is that the tradition of the apostles—the deposit of the faith, as it were—manifests itself in many different ways, through many different agencies, including the beliefs of the lay faithful. The second is that "the gift of discerning, discriminating defining, promulgating and enforcing any portion of that tradition resides solely in the *Ecclesia docens*," that is, the magisterium, comprised of the pope and the college of bishops.

The logical conclusion to be drawn from Newman's "two limbs" theory is that the *ecclesia docens* and the *sensus fidelium* exist in an auxiliary relationship to one another. Each is a counterweight to the authority and weakness of the other. Another way to consider these issues is that of Balthasar's notion of there being different charisms in the life of the Church represented by different leaders in the early Church, especially St. John, St. James, St. Peter and St. Paul. St. Peter's charism is that of Church governance, St. Paul that of prophetic interventions, St. John that of prayer and contemplation, St. James that of defending the tradition. Each of the four operate to balance the other. The contemplative vocation of St. John is balanced by the active Petrine ministry; the prophetic charism of St. Paul is balanced by the more conservative care of the tradition of St. James.

---

37 *Cons.*, 63.

The charisms of James and John are mutually affirming since the contemplative life and the level of scholarship required to defend the tradition go well together, while the Pauline and Petrine charisms share an inner affinity in active apostolic works related to governance. It is therefore possible to analyse ecclesial crises by reference to weaknesses in one or other of the four charisms at work in the communion of the apostles and one or other of the four pillars for the development of doctrine identified by Newman.

In the nineteenth century, the Jesuit theologian Giovanni Perrone relied upon a notion of the *sensus fidelium* to defend what became the 1854 declaration of Pope Pius IX, in his papal bull *Ineffabilis Deus*, that Our Lady was conceived without original sin. A similar reliance undergirded the 1950 declaration of the assumption of Our Lady body and soul into heavenly glory by Pope Pius XII in the apostolic constitution *Munificentissimus Deus*. Newman knew Fr. Perrone and recent scholarship suggests that contrary to earlier scholarly judgments, the intellectual positions of Perrone and Newman on the subject of the *sensus fidelium* and the broader theme of the development of doctrine were very close.[38]

Of the above two papal applications of the *sensus fidelium* principle to Mariology Pope Benedict XVI said:

> Faith both in the Immaculate Conception and in the bodily Assumption of the Virgin was already present in the People of God, while theology had not yet found the key to interpreting it in the totality of the doctrine of the faith. The People of God therefore precede theologians and this is all thanks to that supernatural *sensus fidei*, namely, that capacity infused by the Holy Spirit that qualifies us to embrace the reality of the faith with humility of heart and mind. In this sense, the People of God is the 'teacher that goes first' and must then be more deeply examined and intellectually accepted by theology." In each case, the dogma was defined "not so much because of proofs in Scripture or ancient tradition, but due to a profound *sensus fidelium* and the Magisterium." Each of the two popes concerned consulted the bishops of the world about the faith of the Catholic community before proceeding to define the dogma.[39]

In a 2014 document of the International Theological Commission on the subject of the *sensus fidelium*, the ITC theologians described the *sensus fidelium* as "a sort of spiritual instinct that enables the believer to judge spontaneously whether a particular teaching or practice is or is not in conformity with the

---

38 See C. Michael Shea, "Father Giovanni Perrone and Doctrinal Development in Rome: An Overlooked Legacy of Newman's Essay on Development," *Journal for the History of Modern Theology/Zeitschrift für Neuere Theologiegeschichte* 20, no. 1 (2013): 85–116; Joseph Carola, "Newman and the Roman College," *Nova et Vetera* 18, no. 3 (Summer 2020): 741–57.

39 Benedict XVI, "General Audience," July 7, 2010.

Gospel and with apostolic faith."[40] The sense "is intrinsically linked to the virtue of faith itself; it flows from, and is a property of faith" and "it is compared to an instinct because it is not primarily the result of rational deliberation, but is rather a form of spontaneous and natural knowledge, a sort of perception (*aisthesis*)."[41]

The ITC theologians further spoke of "the connaturality that the virtue of faith establishes between the believing subject and the authentic object of faith, namely the truth of God revealed in Christ Jesus."[42] Generally speaking, the concept of connaturality refers to a situation in which entity A has such an intimate relationship with another entity B that A shares in the natural dispositions of B as if they were its own. In this context:

> Faith, as a theological virtue, enables the believer to participate in the knowledge that God has of himself and of all things. In the believer, it takes the form of a "second nature." By means of grace and the theological virtues, believers become "participants of the divine nature" (2 Pet 1:4), and are in a way con-naturalised to God. As a result, they react spontaneously on the basis of that participated divine nature, in the same way that living beings react instinctively to what does or does not suit their nature.[43]

Notwithstanding all the above, in paragraph 55 of the ITC document, it is acknowledged that in the actual mental universe of the believer, the correct intuitions of the *sensus fidei* can be mixed up with various purely human opinions, or even with errors linked to the narrow confines of a particular cultural context. Some people are simply not all that well catechised or formed in the faith. They have an understanding of bits of the tradition but there are also many gaps in their understanding. This means that "not all the ideas which circulate among the People of God are compatible with the faith."

This problem has been acknowledged by three recent popes—John Paul II, Benedict, and currently Francis. In the apostolic exhortation, *Familiaris Consortio* (1981), John Paul II considered the question as to how the "supernatural sense of faith" may be related to the "consensus of the faithful" and to majority opinion as determined by sociological and statistical research. The *sensus fidei*, he wrote:

> Does not consist solely or necessarily in the consensus of the faithful. Following Christ, the Church seeks the truth, which is not always the same as the majority opinion. She listens to conscience and not to

---

40 International Theological Commission, "*Sensus fidei* in the Life of the Church" (2014), 49.

41 ITC, "*Sensus fidei*," 49.

42 ITC, "*Sensus fidei*," 50–53.

43 ITC, "*Sensus fidei*," 53.

power, and in this way she defends the poor and the downtrodden. The Church values sociological and statistical research, when it proves helpful in understanding the historical context in which pastoral action has to be developed and when it leads to a better understanding of the truth. Such research alone, however, is not to be considered in itself an expression of the sense of faith.

Because it is the task of the apostolic ministry to ensure that the Church remains in the truth of Christ and to lead her ever more deeply into that truth, the Pastors must promote the sense of the faith in all the faithful, examine and authoritatively judge the genuineness of its expressions, and educate the faithful in an ever more mature evangelical discernment.[44]

In other words, St. John Paul II acknowledged that if the faithful have not first received the faith in all its wholeness, then their understanding will be limited and potentially flawed. Similarly, in an address to the International Theological Commission, Pope Benedict later stated that:

It is particularly important to clarify the criteria used to distinguish the authentic *sensus fidelium* from its counterfeits. In fact [the *sensus fidelium*] is not some kind of public opinion of the Church, and it is unthinkable to mention it in order to challenge the teachings of the Magisterium, this because the *sensus fidei* cannot grow authentically in the believer except to the extent in which he or she fully participates in the life of the Church, and this requires a responsible adherence to her Magisterium.[45]

In somewhat blunter language the papal theologian under the papacy of John Paul II, Cardinal Georges Cottier, wrote:

Obviously, the *sensus fidei* is not to be identified with the consensus of the majority, it is not defined on the basis of the statistics of polls. In the history of the Church it has happened that in certain contexts the *sensus fidei* has been manifested by isolated individuals, single saints, while general opinion hung on to doctrines not conforming to the apostolic faith.[46]

---

44 John Paul II, Apostolic Exhortation *Familaris Consortio* (November 22, 1981), 6.

45 Benedict XVI, "Address to the International Theological Commission," December 7, 2012.

46 Georges Cottier, "Reflections on the Mystery and Life of the Church," *30 Days*, 08/09/2010: www.30giorni.it/articoli_23083_13.htm

Addressing the ITC in December 2013, Pope Francis said:

> By the gift of the Holy Spirit, the members of the Church possess a 'sense of faith'. This is a kind of 'spiritual instinct' that makes us *sentire cum Ecclesia* and to discern that which is in conformity with the apostolic faith and is in the spirit of the Gospel. Of course, the *sensus fidelium* cannot be confused with the sociological reality of a majority opinion. It is, therefore, important—and one of your tasks— to develop criteria that allow the authentic expressions of the *sensus fidelium* to be discerned. . . . This attention is of greatest importance for theologians.[47]

In their response to Pope Francis's call to "develop criteria that allow the authentic expressions of the *sensus fidelium* to be discerned" the ITC theologians wrote that individual Catholics needed to possess at least the following six dispositions:

1. Participation in the Life of the Church

This means that people actually have to be practising Catholics in order to have any possibility of having a sense of the faith. Merely being baptised is not enough, one needs to be participating in the sacramental life of the Church. Yves Congar addressed this issue in his work *Lay People in the Church*. Congar noted that:

> We live in a world that is desacralized, individualistic, analytical and academic, a world in which ideas are investigated for their own sake and easily separated from their signs or their sensible embodiments. For us one of the faithful is a "believer," one who holds intellectually certain transcendent maxims, who has "religious convictions." But in the Christian tradition in which thought impregnated at least until the thirteenth century, a *fidelis* was someone sacramentally incorporated in the ecclesial reality. Not only was the faith he professed essentially the Trinitarian faith of the Symbol, it was the reality in him of baptism and his being part of the Church which, after having brought him to birth, formed him, nourished his life, governed all his actions, consecrated and united every moment of his existence to Christ.[48]

This is a good definition of a fully functional *fidelis*.

---

47   Francis, "Address to the International Theological Commission," December 6, 2013.
48   Yves Congar, *Lay People in the Church: A Study for a Theology of Laity* (London: Geoffrey Chapman, 1965), 36.

2. Listening to the Word of God

This means that Catholics need to be attentive to the Scriptures. It does not require them to be professors of biblical studies with a knowledge of biblical languages, but it does require them to be people who read the Scriptures and reflect upon them in prayer.

3. Openness to Reason

This disposition requires something like a rudimentary understanding of the Catholic couplet "faith and reason." It means an appreciation of the fact that Catholic intellectual life involves an interaction of the reasoning faculties with the theological virtue of faith in the service of truth.

4. Adherence to the Magisterium

This means that one must know and follow the magisterial teaching. This in turn requires a certain level of intellectual engagement with the life of the Church. One must know what the Church teaches and which teachings might reasonably be described as "magisterial" and what is mere speculative theology.

5. Holiness

Holiness is another way of saying that there is a high level of con-naturality between the person and God and for this high level of con-naturality to operate, then the person needs to have the three theological virtues of faith, hope, and love in abundance. Both the head and the heart need to be in good operational order since many spiritual pathologies arise when the heart operates without engaging the intellect, and when the intellect operates without engaging the heart. In paragraph 57 of the ITC document we find the statement that "the intensifying of faith within the believer particularly depends on the growth within him or her of charity, and the *sensus fidei fidelis* is therefore proportional to the holiness of one's life."

6. Seeking the Edification of the Church

This final disposition means that a person needs to be motivated by a desire for the good of the Church and by a respect for the deposit of the faith. An enthusiasm for some fashionable social theory or political ideology is not a disposition that seeks the edification of the Church. Faith is something received as a divine gift, not something humanly constructed. Again, in *Lay People in the Church* Congar wrote:

> The history of modern culture is dominated by various forms of immanentism, rationalism, the spirit of Faust; and eventually there is Marxism, the most consistent endeavour that has ever been made to give the world a purely immanent meaning, excluding all transcendence, an endeavour to overcome all contradictions and to attain integrity without any reference whatever to God. Even things that are in themselves good and true, authentic earthly values, are susceptible

of becoming idols and a "home-ground" for the Prince of this world. Think what can happen to country, production, progress, class, race, the body and sport, domestic comfort; and how many names can be given today to Egypt, Canaan or Babylon.[49]

These six attributes can be marshalled under the principle that there needs to be a right ordering of the heart and the intellect, as well as a certain deep level of holiness or sanctification. It is not surprising therefore that the theme of deification was strong in the theology of Newman, especially in his pre-Catholic *Lectures on Justification* and then in the *Essay on the Development of Doctrine*. In this *Essay* Newman wrote:

> The sanctification or rather the deification of man is one main subject of St. Athanasius's theology. Christ, in rising raises His Saints with Him to the right hand of power. They become instinct with His life, of one body with His flesh, divine sons, immortal kings, god. He is in them, because He is in human nature; and He communicates to them that nature, deified by becoming His, that them it may deify.[50]

Thus, for Newman, it is the saints who embody the *sensus fidei* to its highest power and especially the saints who stand out among the Church Doctors, foremost for Newman, St. Athanasius.

A work that addresses this topic of the significance of saintly scholars for the resolution of theological and pastoral crises is Matthew Levering's *The Feminine Genius of Catholic Theology*.[51] Levering outlines the contribution of various female scholar saints, some of whom are honoured as Church Doctors, to the development of Catholic theology. This is not a work of so-called feminist scholarship. It is simply an intellectual history that demonstrates that not only were women's voices being heard in the Church in earlier centuries, but, moreover, that some of these saintly women actually contributed to the development of the Church's theological tradition. Another highly valuable work is Andrew Meszaros's *The Prophetic Church: History and Doctrinal Development in John Henry Newman and Yves Congar*.[52] Meszaros includes a whole section on the significance of sanctifying grace and the gifts of the Holy Spirit for the effective operation of the *sensus fidelium*.

More recently, in 2018, the International Theological Commission published the document "Synodality in the Life and Mission of the Church." Synodality

---

49 Congar, *Lay People in the Church*, 100.

50 *Dev.* (Gracewing), 171.

51 Matthew Levering, *The Feminine Genius of Catholic Theology* (London: Bloomsbury, 2012).

52 Andrew Meszaros, *The Prophetic Church: History and Doctrinal Development in John Henry Newman and Yves Congar* (Oxford University Press, 2016).

and *sensus fidei* are related subjects because one would hope that those invited to take part in synods actually possess the *sensus fidei*. Merely being on the Church's payroll is no guarantee of this. As noted earlier the mere possession of a baptismal certificate is not sufficient evidence of the *sensus fidei*. Accordingly, the Synodality document affirms the dispositions listed in the 2014 International Theological Commission work on the *sensus fidei* and summarises them under the heading of a "spirituality in Communion." The "Eucharistic *synaxis*" is described as the "source and paradigm of the spirituality of communion" within which are "expressed the specific elements of Christian life that are called to mould the *affectus synodalis*." The International Theological Commission then lists five specific elements of Christian life relevant to the work of Synods: (a) the invocation of the Trinity, (b) reconciliation, (c) listening to the Word of God, (d) communion, and (e) mission.[53] Taken together these two documents from the International Theological Commission offer a spirituality of the *sensus fidei*.

CONCLUSION

Through an understanding of tradition and development in doctrine which changed and matured during his life, Newman was able to provide an account of the historical development of doctrine, acknowledging the limits of the *Quod ubique, quod semper, quod ab omnibus* maxim, and balancing the best insights of Vincent de Lérins with other "Notes of a Genuine Development." He thereby provided the Church with an organic account of tradition and an explanation of the work of the *sensus fidelium* in both building up and defending the tradition. In so doing he resolved one of the great theological crises of modern times with considerable pastoral consequences.

Newman's seminal work amplifies the importance of the relationship between spirituality and dogmatic theology and between holiness and conscience. The four pillars of his account of the development of doctrine— revelation, tradition, magisterial authority, and conscience—are all reliant on the spiritual capital of each generation. Holiness of life and intellectual formation are both essential for a proper and fruitful exercise of the *sensus fidelium* as noted in the two documents of the International Theological Commission. To cite O'Regan once more, summarising Balthasar: "Truth is objective, yet refracted over time through Christian communities, and exemplary members of these communities."

One of the practical conclusions of this study of Newman's *Essay on Development of Doctrine* and its "companion text" *On Consulting the Faithful in Matters of Doctrine* is that a heavy burden of responsibility falls on the shoulders of scholar-saints (both lay and clerical) and saintly pontiffs. In every generation

---

53 International Theological Commission, "Synodality in the Life and Mission of the Church" (2018), 109.

there needs to be people with extensive knowledge of the tradition, not just a knowledge of doctrinal propositions and dogmas but an understanding of the whole architectonic structure of the Christian mysteries so that pastoral problems that arise in relation to one particular area can be resolved without causing damage in ancillary areas. Newman was one of those exemplary members. Without such persons in the life of the Church there is always the risk, as Fries noted, of slipping over the edge of a dry and pastorally insensitive intellectualism on the one side, or a voluntarist-historicism—subservient to the *Zeitgeist*—on the other.

Suggested Reading

Congar, Yves. *Lay People in the Church: A Study for a Theology of Laity*. London: Geoffrey Chapman, 1965.

Fries, Heinrich. "Newmans Bedeutung für die Theologie." In *Newman Studies Erste Folge*, 181–99. Nürnberg: Glock und Lutz Verlag, 1948.

_____. "Die Dogmengeschichte des fünften Jahrhunderts im theologischen Werdegang von John Henry Newman." In *Das Konzil von Chalkedon: Geschichte und Gegenwart*, edited by Aloys Grillmeier, SJ, and Heinrich Bacht, SJ, vol 3. Echter-Verlag: 1954.

Newman, John Henry. *An Essay on the Development of Christian Doctrine with an Introduction, Notes and Textual Appendices by James Tolhurst DD*, Newman Millennium Edition volume XII. London: Gracewing, 2018.

Shea, C. Michael. "Father Giovanni Perrone and Doctrinal Development in Rome: An Overlooked Legacy of Newman's Essay on Development." *Journal for the History of Modern Theology/Zeitschrift für Neuere Theologiegeschichte* 20, no. 1 (2013): 85–116.

CHAPTER 21

FROM THE BOOK OF COMMON PRAYER TO THE SACRIFICE OF THE MASS AND THE ROMAN BREVIARY

Fr. Uwe Michael Lang and Fr. Juan R. Vélez

The liturgy is a part of Newman's life and thought that has received little scholarly attention. There are very few articles on this subject[1] and one monograph,[2] and yet Newman wrote many sermons and tracts as an Anglican on worship and the sacraments and arguably made a valuable contribution to liturgical renewal in the Church of England.[3] As Newman's

---

1   See Joseph Alencherry, "Newman, the Liturgist: An Introduction to the Liturgical Theology of John Henry Newman," *Newman Studies Journal* 13, no. 1 (2016): 6–21; Uwe Michael Lang, "'The Most Joyful and Blessed Ordinance of the Gospel': John Henry Newman on the Liturgy," Adoremus (November 8, 2019), https://adoremus.org/2019/11/08/the-most-joyful-and-blessed-ordinance-of-the-gospel-saint-john-henry-newman-on-the-liturgy/.

2   Donald A. Withey, *John Henry Newman: The Liturgy and the Breviary; Their Influence on his Life as an Anglican* (London: Sheed & Ward, 1992). Neither *The Cambridge Companion to John Henry Newman*, ed. Ian Ker and Terrence Merrigan (Cambridge: University Press, 2009), nor *The Oxford Handbook of John Henry Newman*, ed. Frederick D. Aquino and Benjamin J. King (Oxford: Oxford University Press, 2018) contains a chapter dedicated to liturgy or worship.

3   See the recently published collection of Newman's writings on the liturgy,

sacramental theology developed, so did his liturgical beliefs and practices. The result was his gradual restoring of elements in the Book of Common Prayer that had fallen into oblivion, and his discovery of Catholic principles which contributed in some measure to the Liturgical Movement of the twentieth century. His friend, Edward Bouverie Pusey (1800–1882), and the Tractarians of a second generation were responsible for recovering Catholic doctrine and rites in the liturgy of the Church of England. In this chapter, we first examine briefly the state of the Anglican liturgy in the early nineteenth century. Next, we look at the development of Newman's thought on the liturgy, followed by some of the principal ideas that he and his fellow Tractarians advanced. Lastly, we consider his personal discovery of Catholic doctrine and practice, and its expression in his life after his conversion in 1845.

ANGLICAN LITURGY
IN THE EARLY NINETEENTH CENTURY

The Protestant Reformation in England was implemented on the parish level through the Book of Common Prayer, published in two editions under Edward VI (1549 and 1552), and later revised under Elizabeth I (1559). The Anglican historian Diarmaid MacCulloch sums up the period from the death of Henry VIII in 1547 to the death of Elizabeth in 1603 as "the building of a Protestant Church which remained haunted by its Catholic past."[4] The Book of Common Prayer, first published in 1549—largely the work of Thomas Cranmer, Archbishop of Canterbury—became of obligatory use that same year under the Act of Uniformity. The Prayer Book provided for daily morning and evening prayer, the readings for Sundays and feast days, and the services for communion, baptism, matrimony, confirmation, visitation of the sick, and burial.[5] The rationale behind Cranmer's changes of the liturgy was his theology of justification and desire to remove the idea that there is any human merit contributing to man's salvation, and that the Mass is a sacrifice.

In his study *Eucharistic Sacrifice and the Reformation*, Francis Clark notes that the most striking difference between the 1549 Book of Common Prayer and the medieval liturgical books it substituted is "the omission of sacrificial language."[6] The Offertory rite was replaced, and the Canon of the Mass, while

---

Newman on Worship, Reverence and Ritual, ed. Peter Kwasniewski (Lulu.com, 2019), which numbers 524 pages.

4   Diarmaid MacCulloch, *The Later Reformation in England 1547–1603*, British History in Perspective (New York: St. Martin's Press, 1990), 6.

5   Gordon Jeanes, "Cranmer and Common Prayer," in *The Oxford Guide to the Book of Common Prayer*, ed. Charles Hefling and Cynthia Shattuck (Oxford: Oxford University Press, 2006), 21–38.

6   Francis Clark, *Eucharistic Sacrifice and the Reformation*, 2nd ed. (Oxford: Basil Blackwell, 1967), 183; for a detailed account, see also, 177–205 ("The Anglican Formularies in the Making").

retaining much of its structure, was rewritten in such a way as to remove any aspect of the eucharistic sacrifice as distinct from Christ's sacrifice on the cross.[7] The elevation of the consecrated host, with the congregation's adoration of the body of Christ now made present, which was considered the heart of the medieval Mass, was removed. While the 1549 Prayer Book thus broke with liturgical tradition in many ways, the Communion service still resembled the Mass and contained a number of ambiguities that appeared to allow for a Catholic interpretation. Cranmer's second edition of the Prayer Book in 1552 definitely embraced Reformed theology and removed any vestiges of Catholic eucharistic theology.[8] Significantly, the 1549 title "The Supper of the Lorde, and the holy Communion, commonly called the Masse" was replaced with "The ordre for the administracion of the Lordes Supper, or holy Communion."[9] The minister, no longer wearing traditional Mass vestments but only a surplice, presided by standing at the left side of a wooden table instead of an altar. These ritual changes were motivated by the intention to avoid any association with the Catholic Mass and its sacrificial character, a doctrine that was rejected in the authoritative "Articles of Religion" of 1562 (1571).[10] The dismantling of the liturgical tradition went even further than had been suggested by the Strasbourg Reformer Martin Bucer (1491–1551) in his critical *Censura* of the 1549 Prayer Book, which he wrote shortly before he died in English exile.[11]

The Elizabethan settlement was unable to establish a middle way between Catholicism and Puritanism, and seventeenth century England was marked by religious controversy. By the end of the eighteenth century, the Church of England was constituted by various parties with different doctrinal beliefs and liturgies, which have been labeled "Low Church" and "High Church."[12] The revival movements also led to the formation of Evangelical congregations within the Established Church.

C. G. Brown asserts that Evangelicals had an enthusiasm for the *Thirty-Nine Articles* that was matched by their reverence for the services of the Book of

---

7   Jeanes comments that "the eucharistic prayer removed all sense of offering the consecrated bread and wine to God, and replaced it with making a memorial of Christ's death and resurrection, together with the offering of praise and thanksgiving and the self-offering of the worshippers. Often the language evoked that of the medieval canon, but its theology was very different." Jeanes, "Cranmer and Common Prayer," 32.

8   Clark, *Eucharistic Sacrifice and the Reformation*, 194–201.

9   *The Book of Common Prayer: The Texts of 1549, 1559, and 1662*, ed. Brian Cummings (Oxford: Oxford University Press, 2011), 19 and 124.

10   The *Thirty-Nine Articles* are found conveniently in *Documents of the English Reformation 1526–1701*, ed. Gerald Bray, Corrected reprint (Cambridge: James Clarke & Co., 2004), 285–309.

11   Clark, *Eucharistic Sacrifice and the Reformation*, 197–201.

12   Peter B. Nockles's *The Oxford Movement in Context: Anglican High Churchmanship 1760–1857* (Cambridge: Cambridge University Press, 1994) presents the complexity of the liturgical debates between Cambridge Camdenites, pre-Tractarian High Churchmen, and others. See 184–227.

Common Prayer, yet he goes on to explain how John Newton (1725–1807), one of their best-known leaders, omitted clauses from it,[13] and others like William Grimshaw (1708–1763) and Samuel Walker (1714–1761) added extemporary prayers. Some Evangelicals conceived of "worship as utterance rather than action," and some went as far as to hold that liturgy had no life without preaching.[14] At the same time, Newton defended the need "for fixed forms of public worship on the grounds that few clergy are able to pray extemporaneously with ease and dignity, . . . and that the Bible provides examples of the use of set forms."[15] At some Evangelical parishes, Matins and Evensong were prayed on Sundays, and Holy Communion was a regular feature on Sundays and major feast days. According to Brown, some credit must be given to the Evangelicals for promoting more frequent communion in the Church of England.[16] During his early undergraduate years at Oxford, Newman was influenced by the piety and theology of the Evangelicals, but soon afterwards by High Church Anglicans such as John Keble (1792–1866) and Richard Hurrell Froude (1803–1836).

NEWMAN:
FROM EVANGELICAL TO ANGLO-CATHOLIC VIEWS

John Keble's *The Christian Year* (1827), with its poetical expression of the liturgical seasons and feast days of the Lord and the saints, made a strong impression on the young Newman. Through his friend Froude, Newman learned about the private lectures on liturgy by Charles Lloyd (1784–1829), Regius Professor of Divinity. Lloyd highlighted the pre-Reformation elements in the Book of Common Prayer and also introduced his hearers to the medieval liturgical tradition.

In 1831, Newman gave a sermon titled "Use of Saints' Days" in which he noted the importance of saints' festivals, since they mark the days and seasons of the Christian year. He lamented: "Our Church abridged the number of Holydays, thinking it right to have but a few; but we account any as too much. For, taking us as a nation, we are bent on gain; and grudge any time which is spent without reference to our worldly business."[17]

The same year, in another sermon, "Ceremonies of the Church," the Oxford don explained how Jesus had respected the Jewish ceremonies, and how Christians should respect the liturgical practices that the apostles or their immediate successors had instituted based on tradition and long usage. He argued that people need external forms and that when they do away with them, they end up

---

13   C. G. Brown, "Divided Loyalties? The Evangelicals, The Prayer-Book and The Articles," *Historical Magazine of the Protestant Episcopal Church* 44 (1975), 189–209 at 189.
   14   Brown, "Divided Loyalties?" 190.
   15   Brown, "Divided Loyalties?" 192.
   16   Brown, "Divided Loyalties?" 200.
   17   "The Use of Saints' Days," *PS* ii, no. 32: 395.

ceasing to pray. In the case of all forms "even the least binding in themselves, it continually happens that a speculative improvement is a practical folly, and the wise are taken in their own craftiness."[18]

The discovery of the Roman Breviary was another significant step in Newman's theological and spiritual development. Donald A. Withey's important work demonstrates what a profound impact the discovery of the breviary had on Newman's spiritual journey. In 1836, Newman inherited Froude's copy of the Roman Breviary after his friend's untimely death. He began to explore in depth the Divine Office, with the help of Bartolomeo Gavanti's *Thesaurus Sacrorum Rituum* (1628) and Francesco Zaccaria's *Bibliotheca Ritualis* (1776–1781). The result of this research was *Tract 75: On the Roman Breviary as embodying the substance of the Devotional Services of the Church Catholic*, dated June 24, 1836. The book-length publication consists of a historical overview of the breviary and a translation of selected offices. The praise Newman offers in his preface for "so much of excellence and beauty in the services of the Breviary" is still embedded in anti-Roman polemics, as he intends "to wrest a weapon out of our adversaries' hands." Stripped of its Roman additions, in particular the veneration of the Blessed Virgin Mary and the saints, the breviary, Newman claimed, is a witness to the prayer of primitive Christianity and "whatever is good and true in it" belongs to "the Church Catholic in opposition to the Roman Church."[19] Newman also wanted to show that the daily services of the Prayer Book derive from the Roman Breviary and can be better understood in the light of the latter. At the same time, Newman was deeply impressed by the breviary's daily round of prayer, with the psalms at its heart, and suggested Anglicans could use it for private devotions.

Newman's *Tract* 75 was widely received and inspired his friends Robert Williams (1811–1890) and Samuel Wood (1809–1843) to embark on an English translation of the entire *Breviarium Romanum*. The project was eventually abandoned, mainly because of Newman's concern about the hostility such a translation (even in an edited form) would meet at a time when antagonism towards the Tractarians was growing in the Anglican Establishment. In preparing *Tract* 75 and through his involvement in the breviary project, Newman produced English versions of Latin office hymns, which anticipated the better-known translations of the Anglican John Mason Neale (1818–1866) and of his fellow Oratorian Edward Caswall (1814–1878). Not all of Newman's forty-seven translations were printed during his lifetime, and Withey's study includes ten hymns that had not appeared in print before, taken from notebooks kept in the archives of the Birmingham Oratory.[20]

---

18 "Ceremonies of the Church," *PS* ii, no. 7: 78.
19 "On the Roman Breviary as Embodying the Substance of the Devotional Services of the Church Catholic," *Tract* 75: 1–2.
20 *Tract* 75: 115–23; see also Withey's annotated list of the hymns translated by Newman in *John Henry Newman: The Liturgy and the Breviary*, 124–36.

Earlier, writing in *Tract* 38 (1834), Newman decried the further protestantization of the Prayer Book from the time of King Edward to Queen Mary. In a fictitious dialogue between a clergyman and layperson he has the clergyman assert: "They took away the Liturgy altogether, and substituted a Directory."[21] He was careful not to cite Cranmer and wished to maintain a *Via Media* between the Reformers and Rome, but reading between the lines, his views of the Reformation were clear: "I am bound to the Articles by subscription; but I am bound, more solemnly even than by subscription, by my baptism and by my ordination, to believe and maintain the *whole* Gospel of CHRIST. The grace given at those seasons comes through the Apostles, not through Luther or Calvin, Bucer or Cartwright. You will presently agree with me in this statement. Let me ask, do you not hold the inspiration of Holy Scripture?"[22]

Newman thought it was possible to have "Calvinist Articles and a Popish liturgy."[23] It would seem that at this point he was still blinded to the fact that the liturgy of the Book of Common Prayer was anything other than popish. He would later realize that his *Via Media* was only a paper system. As noted earlier, the Reformers had changed the liturgy to fit with their beliefs. They did not believe in the sacrificial character of the Mass, transubstantiation, and the real presence, and thus changed the liturgy of the Mass accordingly.

In a sermon, "The Eucharistic Presence" (1838), we see Newman's eucharistic doctrine in transition from that of Protestant to Roman Catholic. He writes of the Holy Eucharist as a great mystery and gift: "That belief, which goes beyond ours, shows how great the gift is really. I allude to the doctrine of what is called Transubstantiation, which we do not admit; or that the bread and wine cease to be, and that Christ's sacred Body and Blood are directly seen, touched, and handled, under the appearances of Bread and Wine."[24] Newman asserts that the correct doctrine is more than what the Reformers held:

> It is what our Lord says it is, the gift of His own precious Body and Blood, really given, taken, and eaten as the manna might be (though in a way unknown), at a certain particular time, and a certain particular spot; namely, as I have already made it evident, at the time and spot when and where the Holy Communion is celebrated.[25]

At this point in his theological development, Newman noted that the Eucharist, as with Christ's other miracles, is intelligible but supernatural. Again, speaking of the mystery of the Eucharist, he reasoned: "If the marvellousness of the miracle of the loaves is no real objection to its truth, neither is the

---

21 *Tract* 38: 27.
22 *Tract* 38: 32.
23 *Tract* 38: 33.
24 "The Eucharistic Presence" (May 13, 1838), *PS* vi, no. 11: 141.
25 *PS* vi, no. 11: 144.

marvellousness of the Eucharistic presence any real difficulty in our believing that gift."[26] In effect, Newman believed that Christ's spiritual presence was more than that claimed by Bucer and other Reformers. Newman claimed:

> We call His presence in this Holy Sacrament a spiritual presence, not as if "spiritual" were but a name or mode of speech, and He were really absent, but by way of expressing that He who is present there can neither be seen nor heard; that He cannot be approached or ascertained by any of the senses; that He is not present in place, that He is not present carnally, though He is really present. And how this is, of course is a mystery. All that we know or need know is that He *is* given to us, and that in the Sacrament of Holy Communion.[27]

At about this point also we begin to see in his writings an understanding of the Mass as a sacrifice. For Newman, it became evident that altar (*thusiasterion*) for the early Christians implied a sacrifice (*prosphora*) and sacrifice implied priesthood.[28]

When Newman published parts of the diaries of his friend, *Remains of the Late Reverend Richard Hurrell Froude,* it was met with considerable indignation because of Froude's Roman Catholic beliefs. In response to Godfrey Faussett's criticism of Froude's use of the word "altar" as synonymous with the Lord's table, and that this use was attested only towards the end of the second century, Newman replied: "On the contrary I read it in as many as *four* out of the seven brief Epistles of St. Ignatius, at the end of the *first*."[29] And to the assertion that it was used merely in a figurative way and in accommodation to the Jewish and pagan customs, he asserted: "On the contrary, the word Altar is used after St. Ignatius by St. Irenaeus, Tertullian, St. Cyprian, Origen, Eusebius, St. Athanasius, St. Ambrose, St. Gregory Nazianzen, St. Optatus, St. Jerome, St. Chrysostom, and St. Austin."[30]

In "The Anglo-American Church" in *The British Critic* (1839), writing about the Anglican (now known as Episcopal) Church in the United States of America, Newman asserts: "She has got that truth in her; and with gratitude we add, that the most considerable of her bishops, living and dead, have developed it accurately no little way. They have gone forward from one truth to another; from the Apostolic Commission to the Succession, from the Succession to the Office,—in the office they have discerned the perpetual priesthood, in the priesthood the perpetual sacrifice, in the sacrifice the glory of the Christian Church,

---

28 "The Theology of St. Ignatius" in *Critic,* (January 1839), 222–24.
29 Newman, "Letter to the Margaret Professor of Divinity on Mr. R. H. Froude's Statements on the Holy Eucharist, 1838," *VM* ii, 222.
30 *VM* ii, 222.

26 *PS* vi, no. 11: 146.
27 *PS* vi, no. 11: 136–37.
28 "The Theology of St. Ignatius" in *Critic,* (January 1839), 222–24.
29 Newman, "Letter to the Margaret Professor of Divinity on Mr. R. H. Froude's Statements on the Holy Eucharist, 1838," *VM* ii, 222.
30 *VM* ii, 222.

its power as a fount of grace, and its blessedness as a gate of heaven."[31] Samuel Seabury (1729–1796) of Connecticut, the first Anglican bishop in America, who was consecrated by nonjuring Scottish bishops in 1784, preached on this uninterrupted apostolic succession and on the Holy Eucharist as "*a true and proper sacrifice*, commemorative of the original sacrifice and death of Christ."[32] Newman credits Seabury with "the restoration to the consecration prayer in the American Communion Service, of the oblatory words, and the invocation of the Holy Spirit."[33]

NEWMAN AND THE TRACTARIANS:
UNDERLYING PRINCIPLES

Among the original objectives of the Oxford Movement was the defence of the Anglican liturgy as received in the Book of Common Prayer.[34] Later, a second generation of Tractarians attempted to restore Catholic liturgical traditions, and this resulted in the Anglo-Catholic adaptations of the Daily Service (Office) and Communion, which gained momentum from the 1860s.[35] New monastic and religious communities began to pray the Daily Office and to create alternatives to the Book of Common Prayer.[36] Newman, Keble, Froude, and the other early Tractarians did not explicitly enunciate a series of principles concerning the liturgy, yet we can find some indication of them in Newman's writings.

In 1833, Newman published *Tract* 3: "On Alterations in the Liturgy," a short appeal to fellow clergymen to remain faithful to the rites of the Prayer Book. He argued that if each clergyman introduced changes to the liturgy at his own pleasure, the loss would be extensive, and what appeared to be nonessential alterations would lead to essential ones in doctrine. Newman warned against arbitrary innovations and invoked respect for episcopal authority over the liturgy. The problem, however, ran deeper because—as he acknowledged—agreement on doctrine and episcopal authority was lacking.

Some years later in an 1840 article for the *British Critic*, Newman wrote on Selina Hastings (1707–1791), Countess of Huntingdon, an influential figure in the religious revival of the eighteenth century and generous benefactor of the Methodist movement. He acknowledged the need for the preaching of conversion

---

31 "The Anglo-American Church," in *Critic* (1839), 336–37.

32 "The Anglo-American Church," 339.

33 "The Anglo-American Church," 339.

34 Lawrence F. Barmann, "The Liturgical Dimension of the Oxford Tracts, 1833–1841," *Journal of British Studies* 7, no. 2 (1968): 92–113.

35 George Herring, "Devotional and Liturgical Renewal: Ritualism and Protestant Reaction," in *The Oxford Handbook of the Oxford Movement*, ed. Stewart J. Brown, Peter Nockles, and James Pereiro (Oxford: Oxford University Press, 2017), 398–409.

36 John Gibaut, "The Daily Office," in *The Oxford Guide to the Book of Common Prayer*, 455–56.

but noted that various bishops opposed and censured practices of evangelical preachers while others softened towards the Methodists as they grew towards schism.[37] The Methodists "had a message to deliver, a position to defend, and that one and the same to all: [their antagonists] had none. Their opponents did not maintain any definite, or aggressive, or opposite doctrine, such as the sacramental power of the Church, or the catholic character of their own creed; they did not even agree together in opinion practically."[38]

From a theological point of view, one of the underlying principles for Newman's views on the liturgy was his notion of reverence and worship to the Creator with the necessary accompanying interior dispositions and external manifestations. Two of his Anglican sermons describe this Christian attitude that is the foundation of the liturgy: "Reverence in Worship" (1836), and "Reverence, A Belief in God's Presence" (1838). This notion of worship is a necessary consequence of the recognition of God as Maker, and Christ as Savior. In it there is an implicit theology of creation and redemption.

Another of the principles underlying the teaching of Newman and the Tractarians was that of restraint in religious emotions, whether perplexity or newfound joy, and the use of form in religious worship. He noted that often when persons have a religious turn, they seek greater strictness by attending a Dissenting Church, thinking that there they will have more of true religion. Instead, Newman advises such persons to take advantage of the Daily Service, praying the psalms and litanies of the Church.[39] Newman opposed the notion that preaching should eclipse ritual in worship as was the case with the Evangelicals.

Of particular note is a series of sermons preached between 1829 and 1831, which offer a rich liturgical and sacramental theology. In a sermon entitled "On Preaching," delivered first in 1831 and again in 1835, Newman affirms that "the most blessed and joyful ordinance of the Gospel is prayer and praise . . . , it is the peculiar office of public prayer to bring down Christ among us—it is as being many collected into one, that Christ recognizes us as His." Preaching is a means to an end, Newman says, which is "our praying better and living better." The public, sacramental prayer of the Church offers us access to God's grace, which makes us capable of living a Christian life and so offer the "acceptable sacrifice."[40]

Tractarians expressed devotion through the restrained use of emotion, with verses in regularly-ordered meter set by others to well-known hymn tunes. In his lectures on poetry, John Keble "expounded the commonly-held belief that poetry arises from heightened passion, but argued that its function is to tame this

37   "Selina, Countess of Huntingdon" in *Critic*, (October 1840), 409–10.

38   "Selina, Countess of Huntingdon," 410.

39   "Religious Worship a Remedy for Excitements," *PS* iii, no. 23: 336–39.

40   *Serm.* i, 25–26. On these sermons, see Alencherry, "Newman, the Liturgist," and Robert C. Christie, "Conversion through Liturgy: Newman's Liturgy Sermon Series of 1830," *Newman Studies Journal* 3, no. 2 (2006): 49–59.

passion rather than to give it stronger expression."[41] Frederick William Faber (1814–1863), a gifted poet, who became a follower of Newman and later the first Provost of the London Oratory, thought differently about reserve in the expression of emotions in his verses and hymns. Both Faber and Newman wrote hymns, but it was Faber's exuberant style that had a broader appeal in nineteenth century Catholicism. Still, during Newman's life, his emblematic poem "Lead, Kindly Light" was set to music and sung by many,[42] and after his death, his long poem *The Dream of Gerontius* inspired the hymn "Praise to the Holiest in the Height."[43]

An equally important principle for the Tractarians was the place of beauty in the liturgy and in church architecture. Beauty constitutes a reflection of the Eternal One, a fitting tribute, and an invitation to worship. In the sermon, "The Gospel Palaces" (1836), Newman said:

> Stability and permanence are, perhaps, the especial ideas which a Church brings before the mind. It represents, indeed, the beauty, the loftiness, the calmness, the mystery, and the sanctity of religion also, and that in many ways; still, I will say, more than all these, it represents to us its eternity. It is the witness of Him who is the beginning and the ending, the first and the last.[44]

The building of these temples was the fruit and pride of the community over generations:

> We, His members, who have but a portion of His fulness, execute but a part of His purpose. One lays the foundation, and another builds thereupon; one levels the mountain, and another "brings forth the headstone with shoutings." Thus were our Churches raised. One age would build a Chancel, and another a Nave, and a third would add a Chapel, and a fourth a Shrine, and a fifth a Spire. By little and little the work of grace went forward.[45]

Newman explained that this vast material work rests on spiritual foundations: "Their foundations are laid very deep, even in the preaching of Apostles, and the confession of Saints, and the first victories of the Gospel in our land. All that is so noble in their architecture, all that captivates the eye and makes its

---

41 Kirstie Blair, "Breaking Loose: Frederick Faber and the Failure of Reserve," *Victorian Poetry* 44, no. 1 (Spring 2006): 25–41.

42 The clergyman and hymnwriter John Bacchus Dykes (1823–1876), who was influenced by the Oxford Movement and choir director at Durham Cathedral, set "Lead, Kindly Light" to music. See https://hymnary.org/person/Dykes_John

43 Richard Runciman Terry (1865–1938), organist and choir director at Westminster Cathedral set "Praise to the Holiest" to music in 1912.

44 "The Gospel Palaces," *PS* vi, no. 19: 273.

45 *PS* vi, no. 19: 275.

way to the heart, is not a human imagination, but a divine gift, a moral result, a spiritual work."[46] These are the works of saints and the fruits of martyrdom: "Their simplicity, grandeur, solidity, elevation, grace, and exuberance of ornament, do but bring to remembrance the patience and purity, the courage, meekness, and great charity, the heavenly affections."[47]

Some of the Tractarians wished to embrace Catholic practices in the liturgy, but Newman, Keble, and Pusey did not go along with them.[48] Newman defended himself from the charge of popery in his writings, on the publication of Froude's *Remains*, the setting up of his monastic-like community at Littlemore, and his interpretation of the *Thirty-Nine Articles* in *Tract* 90. This need to defend his intentions, and his slow and deliberate movements, made him shun certain practices, including invocation of the saints or facing east in liturgical prayer. For the Communion service, it is reported that Newman, wearing surplice and hood, always stood at the "north end," that is, on the left side of the wooden table, unlike other Tractarians who strongly made a case for facing east in liturgical prayer to evoke the sacrificial character of the Eucharist.[49]

After Newman's reception into the Catholic Church, Pusey continued with his work in favor of Anglo-Catholicism, and his concern for parishes for the working poor, for instance, St. Savior's in Richmond Hill, Leeds, where he funded (anonymously) the building of the impressive Gothic revival church. Independent from him, some Anglican clergy, among them Charles Lowder (1820–1880), who had heard Newman preach at Oxford, began to bring back the use of eucharistic vestments, candlesticks for the altar, incense, and processions. This movement known as Ritualism spread to parishes and missions in the slums of the East and South side of London and other cities.[50] By the 1880s there were a dozen or more ritualist parishes in the poorer neighborhoods of London, Birmingham, Plymouth, Portsmouth, Leeds, and Leicester.[51] Its proponents counted clergymen such as Alexander Mackonochie, John Purchas, Arthur Stanton, and Charles Lowder. Some of them were prosecuted under The Public Worship Regulation Act (1874), introduced by Archibald Campbell Tait, Archbishop of Canterbury from 1868 until his death in 1882, to stem the growth of Anglo-Catholicism.[52] Before the Act, worship had been regulated by the Court of Arches (an ecclesiastical court with appeal to the Judicial Committee of the Privy

---

46 *PS* vi, no. 19: 278.

47 *PS* vi, no. 19: 278.

48 Aidan Nichols, *The Panther and the Hind: A Theological History of Anglicanism* (Edinburgh: T&T Clark, 1993), 126–27.

49 See Alf Härdelin, *The Tractarian Understanding of the Eucharist*, Acta Universitatis Upsaliensis 8 (Uppsala: Almqvist and Wiksell, 1965).

50 John Shelton Reed, "'Ritualism Rampant in East London': Anglo-Catholicism and the Urban Poor," *Victorian Studies* 31, no. 3 (Spring 1988): 375–76.

51 Reed, "Ritualism, Rampant in East London," 381.

52 See Nigel Yates, *Anglican Ritualism in Victorian Britain, 1810–1930* (Oxford: Oxford University Press, 1999).

Council). The act established a new court to regulate worship. The bishops did not look well on the ritualist movement or defend its adherents, but the zeal and generosity of priests and religious sisters in ritualist parishes and missions won a measure of tolerance and respect from outsiders.[53] It was precisely this government interference with doctrine and worship that Newman and the Tractarians had opposed half a century earlier.

NEWMAN AT LITTLEMORE,
AND REDISCOVERING CATHOLIC TRADITION

By the mid-1700s the practice of public prayer led by a minister was infrequent, although major urban centers had more weekday services.[54] Relatively soon after the beginning of the Oxford Movement, Newman began to enact various practices from the Edwardian Book of Common Prayer, which were inherited from Catholic tradition; the first one was the Daily Service of Matins and Evensong, followed two years later by the Sunday Communion service.

In the sermon on "The Daily Service" (1834) Newman told his congregation why he was reintroducing this ancient practice sanctioned by the Book of Common Prayer and attested in the Scriptures and in Christian Tradition.[55] He explained that private and public prayer in church should be considered a "privilege," much more than a duty. On June 30, 1834, one year after the start of the Oxford Movement, Newman began with the daily service of Matins in St. Mary the Virgin, and from 1836 he ensured that Evensong was celebrated every day in his newly-built church in Littlemore.

After some consideration, at Easter 1837, Newman instituted an early Sunday morning Communion service in the University church.[56] Although Sunday services were common in parish churches, reception of communion was infrequent.[57] Various reasons are adduced: fear of not being sufficiently prepared, the possibility of not being admitted by the parish minister, and associations of the Communion service with proper attire and with a higher social

---

53 Reed, "Ritualism, Rampant in East London," 402–3.

54 Jeremy Gregor, "The Prayer Book and the Parish Church: From Restoration to the Oxford Movement," in *The Oxford Guide to the Book of Common Prayer*, 97–98. In 1743, visitation returns for the diocese of York shows that out of 836 parishes only 24 had daily prayers. See also Stephen John Charles Taylor, "Church and State in England In the Mid-Eighteenth Century: The Newcastle Years 1742–1762" (PhD Diss., University of Cambridge, 1987), 31 at https://core.ac.uk/download/pdf/1333023.pdf

55 Newman told his parishioners: "I have now said enough to let you into the reasons why I have begun Daily Service in this Church. I felt that we were very unlike the early Christians, if we went on without it; and that it was my business to give you an opportunity of observing it, else I was keeping the privilege from you." "Daily Service," *PS* iii, no. 21: 310.

56 Withey, *John Henry Newman: The Liturgy and the Breviary*, 8–17.

57 Gregor, "The Prayer Book and the Parish Church," 98.

class.[58] Though these reasons were often given, in the sermon "Attendance on Holy Communion" (1842) Newman stated a deeper one: "The true reason why people will not come to this Holy Communion is this,—they do not wish to lead religious lives; they do not like to promise to lead religious lives; and they think that [the] blessed Sacrament does bind them to do so."[59]

On July 16, 1835, Newman wrote with great joy to Hurrell Froude, "My chapel, (Littlemore) was begun yesterday."[60] It was to be a church of Gothic style, intended to seat two hundred. Construction had required permission from the Provost and fellows of Oriel College who gave permission, a plot of land and £100 of the total £650 agreed upon with the architect. Newman's mother, Jemima, laid the first stone. It had an altar upon which Newman placed a stone cross and reredos. His sisters gave the church the gift of a beautiful altar cloth. The church of St. Mary the Virgin and St. Nicholas was dedicated by the Bishop of Oxford the following September. Newman's curate John Rouse Bloxam added five stained glass windows and a lectern.[61]

At Littlemore, Newman himself taught catechism to the children and instructed them in singing for the services. He also bought frocks for them. In 1840, the Oxford don, a gifted musician and violinist himself, taught Gregorian chants to the children,[62] although he later favoured polyphony for liturgical ceremonies.[63]

A few years later a group of young men in Cambridge founded the Cambridge Camden Society to promote the study of church architecture and ultimately the restoration of Gothic architecture in existing churches, and the construction of new churches in medieval form.[64] An important feature was the need for a chancel, elevated from the nave and a third of its length, with the altar at the most remote end and further elevated, emphasizing the altar and the role of the priest. Another innovation was adding stalls in the chancel facing one another for the use of lay people as a choir.[65] The church at Littlemore was soon hailed as a model for small churches, praised by the Society's journal, the *Ecclesiologist*, as a "temple of the MOST HIGH" rather than a "sermon house," and as "the first unqualified step of better things to come that England has long

---

58 Gregor, "The Prayer Book and the Parish Church," 98–99.

59 "Attendance on Holy Communion," *PS* vii, no. 11: 150.

60 *LD* v, 94.

61 Bernard Basset, *Newman at Littlemore* (Warley: Friends of Newman, 1983), 22–23.

62 Guido Milanese, "Newman and Gregorian Chant," *Antiphon* 20, no. 2 (2016): 123–50 at 132.

63 See ch. 11 of this volume for Daniel Seward's discussion of Newman's nuanced view of Gregorian chant and his preference for polyphonic music.

64 James F. White, "Prayer Book Architecture" in *The Oxford Guide to The Book of Common Prayer*, 111–12.

65 White, "Prayer Book Architecture," 112.

witnessed."[66] The church, with its simple Gothic style and solid materials, was soon imitated throughout England and in the wider Anglophone world.[67]

The Cambridge Camden Society, founded in 1839 and known from 1845 as the Ecclesiological Society, profoundly influenced Anglican church building in every detail for over a century,[68] and it managed to deflect its criticism as "popish" and "romanising" by forbidding theological debates in its bylaws and insisting on its architectural purpose. One author sees the immediate roots of the twentieth century Liturgical Movement in the revival of interest and study in patristic and medieval periods by Pusey, Newman, and other Tractarians in the 1830s and 1840s, and by John Mason Neale, Benjamin Webb, and other members of the Cambridge Movement.[69] Even though Newman liked Gothic architecture, he did not agree with all of the ideas behind the Camden Society, especially the aesthetic ideals of the leading English Catholic architect, Augustus Welby Pugin (1812–1852), which extolled the liturgy, art, and architecture of the Gothic period as normative.[70] As Sheridan Gilley comments, from the high medieval perspective Pugin had adopted, "anything later, from St Peter's in Rome to the smallest Baroque candlestick, was the product of the corruption of the church by Renaissance paganism."[71] To many of his contemporaries Pugin's principles seemed compelling, because they implied that there "is the most intimate connection between a religion and culture and its outward expression, and [that] the Gothic was the only architectural and artistic style which Christendom had created for itself."[72] Newman instead founded, with John R. Bloxam, Isaac Williams, and others, the Oxford Society for Promoting the Study of Gothic Architecture in 1839.

Newman did not remain for long in the Oxford Society but continued his interest in Gothic architecture, and as editor of the *British Critic* he included a number of articles by the Camden Society. James Patrick notes that as a convert Newman was still convinced by the beauty of Gothic architecture and its appropriateness for English church building.[73] In 1846, Newman visited St. Giles' Church built by Pugin for Lord Shrewsbury and commented in a letter

---

66   G. A. Bremner, "Littlemore Church," *Victorian Review* 39, no. 1 (2013): 18–22 at 19.

67   James Patrick, "Newman, Pugin, and Gothic," *Victorian Studies* 24, no. 2 (1981): 185–207 at 191.

68   White, "Prayer Book Architecture," 112.

69   John F. Baldovin, "The Liturgical Movement and Its Consequences" in *The Oxford Guide to The Book of Common Prayer*, 250.

70   Augustus W. N. Pugin, *The True Principles of Pointed or Christian Architecture* (London: John Neale, 1841).

71   Sheridan Gilley, "Newman, Pugin and the Architecture of the English Oratory," in *Modern Christianity and Cultural Aspirations*, ed. David Bebbington and Timothy Larsen (London: Sheffield Academic Press, 2003), 98–123 at 102. See also Patrick, "Newman, Pugin, and Gothic."

72   Gilley, "Newman, Pugin and the Architecture of the English Oratory," 103.

73   Patrick, "Newman, Pugin, and Gothic," 198.

to a friend that it was "the most splendid building I ever saw" adding "that the Chapel of the Blessed Sacrament is, on entering, a blaze of light—and I could not help saying to myself, 'Porta Coeli.'"[74] This letter clearly suggests the close relationship Newman saw between architecture and beauty. Yet Newman did not think the restoration of faith was tied to one architectural style. He told his friend Ambrose Phillipps, a wealthy convert to Catholicism, that Pugin was "notoriously engaged in a revival" while he had just written on *Development of Doctrine* and held "that the Church while one and the same in doctrine, is ever modifying, adapting and varying her discipline and ritual, according to the times. . . . It (Gothic) was once the perfect expression of the Church's ritual in those places in which it was in use; it is not the perfect expression now."[75]

In the early 1840s, Newman had begun to give more consideration to development in doctrine, sacramental practices, devotions, and ecclesial government.[76] Although in his *Essay on the Development of Christian Doctrine* (1845) there is only a short section referring to sacramental practice in reference to "assimilation," the third note of development, and another on devotion to the Mother of God as an application of "conservative action on the past," the sixth note,[77] he also applied the principles of development in continuity to the Catholic liturgy.

NEWMAN AS A CATHOLIC PRIEST

As an Anglican, Newman found contemporary Catholic liturgical and devotional life emotionally attractive but tended to avoid it because of his theological conviction that Rome had introduced many novelties and corruptions to the pure faith of the primitive Church. Ian Ker observes that Newman's embrace of Catholicism was to a large extent intellectual and preceded his actual experience of it.[78] Once the truth of the Catholic faith became a certainty to him, he threw himself fully into the Church's liturgical life. His prayers and devotions, which included litanies and two different sets of meditations for the Stations of the Cross, show a depth of devotion to Christ and the saints, based on a firm knowledge of Scripture and Tradition.

---

74 *LD* x, 210.

75 *LD* xii, 222, quoted in "Newman, Pugin, and Gothic," 200. Patrick describes well the unfortunate controversy that ensued between Newman and Pugin. See also Guy Nicholls, *Unearthly Beauty: The Aesthetic of St John Henry Newman* (Leominster: Gracewing, 2019), 245–60.

76 Nockles writes: "The liturgical revival of the 1840s was not the product of Tractarian endeavour alone." *The Oxford Movement in Context*, 219. He explains, for example, the influence of William Van Mildert, Bishop of Durham, of William Palmer in his *Origines Liturgicae* (1832), and of Bishop Charles Lloyd in this revival.

77 *Dev.*, 368–82, 425–36.

78 Ian Ker, "Newman's Post-Conversion Discovery of Catholicism," in *Newman and Conversion*, ed. Ian Ker (Notre Dame, Ind.: University of Notre Dame Press, 1997), 37–58 at 37.

Newman found strength and comfort especially in the eucharistic presence of Christ. The transporting beauty of adoration of the Blessed Sacrament
is portrayed in Newman's Catholic novel, *Loss and Gain*, where the protagonist Charles Reding, an Oxford don, steps into a Catholic church. "How
wonderful," said Charles to himself, "that people call this worship formal and
external; it seems to possess all classes, young and old, polished and vulgar,
men and women indiscriminately; it is the working of one Spirit in all, making
many one."[79] Newman valued the rites, sacred music, and religious architecture but considered them at the service of worship of God, coming before the
"Great Presence" in the tabernacle which makes a Catholic Church unique,
holy as no other place.

After his ordination to the priesthood on May 30, 1847, the daily celebration
of Holy Mass became the heart of his spiritual life. Newman's chosen vocation as
an Oratorian had a particular liturgical dimension. Since its foundation in 1575,
the Congregation of the Oratory had been known for its attention to solemn
liturgy and sacred music. The Oratorian houses in Birmingham and London
resumed this tradition from the moment of their foundation, despite their
limited initial resources and the occasional criticism they received for undue
attention to such matters.[80]

As rector of the Catholic University of Ireland, Newman set about to build a
church for the university. He worked on the design with his friend John Hunger-
ford Pollen, and the result was Our Lady, Seat of Wisdom, a beautiful church
with a surprising mix of Romanesque and Byzantine architecture, constructed in
1855–1856. The semi-circular apse was reminiscent of the church of St. Clement
in Rome, and the walls of the nave were decorated with three bands of marble of
different colors.[81] The Dublin University Church is a good example of Newman's
eclecticism that embraced various historical styles. While he admired Gothic art
and architecture, he refused to canonize it as the only Catholic style. Personally,
he liked the Greek, Roman, and Byzantine styles of building more, and understood the practical value of open spaces and a clear view of the altar, which could
be adapted to the development of rites.[82]

Newman's attitude was in keeping with the principles of development he
proposed in his famous *Essay* of 1845. He wished that the altar should be visible

---

79   *LG*, 427. See Milanese, "Newman and Gregorian Chant," 137–38.

80   In a letter to the editor of the Catholic weekly *The Tablet*, dated October 20,
1850, Newman writes in response to a disapproval of the Oratorians' regular celebration
of Vespers: *"we are bound by our rule* to the solemn Ritual services of the Church, *and
we keep it*. Both our own House here, and the Oratory in London, sings High Mass and
Vespers *every* Sunday, and other principal festivals. . . . The Congregations of the Oratory
have ever been remarkable for their exact attention to the rubrics of the Ritual." *LD* xiv, 106.

81   Nicholls, *Unearthly Beauty*, 236–43.

82   Nicholls, *Unearthly Beauty*, 200. The *Duomo* of Milan had a powerful effect on
him, as did St. Peter's Basilica in Rome, 258.

to the congregation so that the faithful could see the sacred action that takes place on the altar. According to Guy Nicholls this could be described as *participatio actuosa* in the liturgy, a term first mentioned in 1903 by Pius X.[83] Newman's thinking about such participation can be seen in a passage in *Callista* in which a congregation prays the Lord's prayer at Mass together, as opposed to it being prayed by the celebrant alone as in the historical form of the Roman Rite. In the novel, he was stating the belief that the laity were able to recite some of the prayers of the Mass, unlike in his own day. In 1855, the same year of the publication of *Callista*, Newman asked his bishop about the possibility of singing vernacular congregational hymns at Low Mass as an alternative to High Mass.[84] Although by means of this he wished to reduce the cost for suitable music, he also hoped to encourage a kind of congregational participation in the liturgy unknown in England.[85] Earlier he had experimented with a vernacular celebration of the office of Compline, with the same desire of encouraging the prayer of parts of the office by the congregation.

CATHOLIC SENSE OF THE LITURGY

The topics discussed in this chapter indicate Newman's deep grasp of the Catholic sense of the liturgy, which increased with time. Although in his study *The Organic Development of the Liturgy*, Alcuin Reid only dedicates two pages to Newman, it is noteworthy that he does incorporate him in a work of such a broad scope.[86] The only other person in the nineteenth century who receives more attention is Prosper Guéranger, the Benedictine who was a contemporary of Newman and the father of the Liturgical Movement.[87]

Romano Guardini (1885–1968) echoed a few notions held by Newman in his work *The Spirit of the Liturgy*, first published in German in 1918. He thought that the public and private nature of the liturgy called for the right balance of deep feeling and external restraint. For him, "In prayer we must find our entire life over again. On the other hand, it must be rich in ideas and powerful images, and speak a developed but restrained language; its construction must be clear and obvious to the simple man, stimulating and refreshing to the man of culture. It must be intimately blended with an erudition which is nowise intrusive, but which is rooted in breadth of spiritual outlook and inward restraint of thought,

---

83 Nicholls, *Unearthly Beauty*, 264.

84 *LD* xvi, 367–68.

85 Nicholls, *Unearthly Beauty*, 320–21.

86 Alcuin Reid, *The Organic Development of the Liturgy*, 2nd ed. (San Francisco: Ignatius Press, 2005), 67–69.

87 The contribution of Newman and the Oxford Movement is also briefly recognized, alongside theologians who followed in the path of Johann Adam Möhler, by William Barden, "Phases of the Liturgical Movement," *The Furrow* 5, no. 11 (1954): 667–75 at 672.

volition and emotion."[88] That is precisely the way in which liturgical prayer has been formed in the Church's tradition.

The splendour of the liturgy cannot be confused with aestheticism. Like Newman, Guardini understood the relationship of beauty with truth, which must be carefully sought so that the liturgy does not become an end in itself. Rather, in the liturgy "beauty is the triumphant splendor which breaks forth when the hidden truth is revealed, when the external phenomenon is at all points the perfect expression of the inner essence."[89] Newman would agree with Guardini's conclusion that "the liturgy must be regarded from the standpoint of salvation."[90]

After the rich theological development in the first half of the twentieth century of the concept of the paschal mystery and the role of the mystical body in the liturgy, an impoverishment of Catholic worship ensued from the late 1960s on. It was characterized by a banalization of the liturgy, loss of reverence, as well as precipitous changes and innovations in the rites. In response to these and other abuses, Pope John Paul II emphasized the sacrificial character of the Mass,[91] and Benedict XVI explained the connection between *lex credendi* and *lex orandi*, the meaning of "full participation," beauty in the liturgy, the value of liturgical norms, the bishop's responsibility for the liturgy, and other teachings on the Church's liturgical tradition.[92]

CONCLUSION

Newman's study of the Scriptures and of Church history, as well as his personal development, made him recognize the Catholic elements of the Book of Common Prayer of the Established Church and led him to restore the Daily Service to his parish in 1834 and the weekly Communion Service in 1837. This later prompted some Anglo-Catholic parish clergy to do likewise. Tractarians who remained Anglicans, especially Edward B. Pusey, contributed to a renewal of Anglican parish life and liturgy by reviving belief in the Real Presence,[93] and the founding of religious communities.[94]

---

88 Romano Guardini, *The Spirit of the Liturgy*, trans. Ada Lane (New York: The Crossroad Publishing Co., 1997), 35. For other possible influences of Newman on Guardini's *Spirit of the Liturgy*, see Francesco Zucchelli, "Da Newman a Guardini, Un percorso possible?" in *Rivista Liturgica, Quinta serie, anno CVIII, fascicolo 3, luglio-settembre* (2021), 211–25.

89 Guardini, *The Spirit of the Liturgy*, 77.

90 Guardini, *The Spirit of the Liturgy*, 83.

91 See John Paul II, Encyclical Letter *Ecclesia de Eucharistia* (April 17, 2003), 11–20.

92 Benedict XVI, Post-Synodal Exhortation *Sacramentum Caritatis* (February 22, 2007), 34–35, 38–40.

93 Other early Tractarians, Charles Marriot, Robert Wilberforce, and Isaac Williams, died relatively young in the 1850s.

94 Earl of Wicklow, "The Monastic Revival in the Anglican Communion," *Studies: An Irish Quarterly Review* 42, no. 168 (Winter 1953): 424–25. Marian Hughes, the first woman

For the Oxford scholar, the sacrificial character of the Eucharist was evident in the writings of the Church Fathers, especially on the priesthood, and in the liturgical tradition, for instance, the use of an altar and priestly vestments. Reflection on the Mass as a sacrifice helped him to accept elements of the Catholic liturgy while still an Anglican. Subsequently the axiom *ut legem credendi lex statuat supplicandi* ("let the law of prayer establish the law of belief") and its inverse *ut lex credendi legem statuat supplicandi* ("let the rule of belief establish the rule of prayer")[95] were verified in his gradual acceptance of the Roman Catholic liturgy and eucharistic doctrine.

Newman and the Tractarians contributed to a rediscovery of the sense of reverence and beauty by reconnecting the rites of the Book of Common Prayer with their Catholic heritage. The high regard of some of the Tractarians for Gothic architecture and its connection with the faith contributed to a new wave of church building in England, effected by the Cambridge Camden Society for the span of a century. Newman's appreciation of artistic beauty as an expression of God's beauty and the fitting praise of God was, however, not tied to one determined art form in music or architecture and much less associated to aestheticism.

There is no doubt that the sacred liturgy was at the heart of St. John Henry Newman's life and thought, even though it plays a minor role in his enormous written opus. He believed that private and public prayer—that "most blessed ordinance of the Gospel"—while respecting tradition, was enriched by development under episcopal authority. Once he became Catholic, he truly found peace and serenity in the liturgy, even in the midst of severe external trials, and his prayerful dedication to the Church's divine worship made his priestly life exemplary.

Suggested Reading

Alencherry, Joseph. "Newman, the Liturgist: An Introduction to the Liturgical Theology of John Henry Newman." *Newman Studies Journal* 13, no. 1 (2016): 6–21.

Barmann, Lawrence F. "The Liturgical Dimension of the Oxford Tracts, 1833–1841." *Journal of British Studies* 7, no. 3 (1968): 92–113.

Basset, Bernard. *Newman at Littlemore*. Warley: Friends of Newman, 1983; reprinted Leominster: Gracewing, 2019.

Bremner, G. A. "Littlemore Church." *Victorian Review* 39, no. 1 (2013): 18–22.

Christie, Robert C. "Conversion through Liturgy: Newman's Liturgy Sermon Series of 1830." *Newman Studies Journal* 3, no. 2 (2006): 49–59.

---

to take religious vows in this revival, did so at St. Mary the Virgin on Trinity Sunday, with Newman as the celebrant of Holy Communion. By 1950, there were forty-five communities of women, most of them with several houses (425–26).

95 The original axiom was coined by Prosper of Aquitaine in the early fifth century; see *Enchiridion symbolorum definitionum et declarationum de rebus fidei et morum*, ed. Heinrich Denzinger and Peter Hünermann, 43rd ed. (San Francisco: Ignatius Press, 2012), no. 246. For the inverse axiom, see Pius XII, Encyclical Letter *Mediator Dei* (November 20, 1947), 48.

Gilley, Sheridan. "Newman, Pugin and the Architecture of the English Oratory." In *Modern Christianity and Cultural Aspirations*, edited by David Bebbington and Timothy Larsen, 8–123. London: Sheffield Academic Press, 2003.

Härdelin, Alf. *The Tractarian Understanding of the Eucharist*. Acta Universitatis Upsaliensis 8. Uppsala: Almqvist and Wiksell, 1965.

Herring, George. "Devotional and Liturgical Renewal: Ritualism and Protestant Reaction." In *The Oxford Handbook of the Oxford Movement*, edited by Stewart J. Brown, Peter Nockles, and James Pereiro, 398–409. Oxford: Oxford University Press, 2017.

Kwasniekwski, Peter, ed. *Newman on Worship, Reverence and Ritual*. Lulu.com, 2019.

Lang, Uwe Michael. "'The Most Joyful and Blessed Ordinance of the Gospel': John Henry Newman on the Liturgy." Adoremus (November 8, 2019), https://adoremus. org/2019/11/08/the-most-joyful-and-blessed-ordinance-of-the-gospel-saint-john-henry-newman-on-the-liturgy/

Milanese, Guido. "Newman and Gregorian Chant." *Antiphon* 20, no. 2 (2016): 123–50.

Nicholls, Guy. *Unearthly Beauty: The Aesthetic of St John Henry Newman*. Leominster: Gracewing, 2019.

Patrick, James. "Newman, Pugin, and Gothic." *Victorian Studies* 24, no. 2 (1981): 185–207.

Withey, Donald A. *John Henry Newman: The Liturgy and the Breviary; Their Influence on his Life as an Anglican*. London: Sheed & Ward, 1992.

CHAPTER 22

THE CONNECTION BETWEEN THEOLOGY, SPIRITUALITY, AND MORALITY IN NEWMAN

Fr. Keith Beaumont

WAS NEWMAN A "THEOLOGIAN"?

This question may seem at first glance absurd, since he is after all universally recognized as one of the seminal Christian thinkers of the nineteenth century. Pope Pius IX offered him the position of "Consultor" at the First Vatican Council.[1] And numerous Popes since have stressed his importance as a theologian, most notably Paul VI,[2] John

---

* This chapter is a substantial revision of an earlier article: Keith Beaumont, "Was Newman a "Theologian"?" *Scripta Theologica* 51, no. 3 (2019): 679–710.

1   Letter of November 14, 1868 to E. B. Pusey, *LD* xiv, 171.

2   He declared in 1964 in a telegram addressed to the organizers of a Newman congress in Luxemburg that "the clarity of his insights and his teaching shed precious light on the problems of the Church today." *L'Osservatoro Romano* (English edition), June 4, 1970. In 1970, on the occasion of a further Newman congress in the same city, he described Newman as an "inspired precursor" who "had explored beforehand several of the paths to which our contemporaries are deeply committed." *L'Osservatoro Romano* (English edition), June 4, 1970. And in 1975, he spoke of the influence of Newman on the Second Vatican Council in the following terms: "Many of the problems which he treated with wisdom—although he himself was frequently misunderstood and misinterpreted in his own time—were the subjects of the discussion and study of the Fathers of the Second Vatican

Paul II,[3] and Benedict XVI.[4] He was capable of producing a series of powerful and original theological syntheses: his *Lectures on the Doctrine of Justification* (1838), his *Essay on the Development of Christian Doctrine* (1845), his *Essay in Aid of a Grammar of Assent* (1870), his *Letter to the Duke of Norfolk* (1875), and his long ecclesiological sketch that forms the Preface to volume I of the *Via Media* (1877) are outstanding examples of this.

Yet Newman himself resolutely and systematically refused the title of "theologian."[5] Some of these refusals can be explained by the context of the First Vatican Council and by Newman's reluctance to be drawn into acrimonious debates on the question of papal infallibility. Others can be seen as a tactic of self-defense in the face of Catholic attacks upon his orthodoxy, for example, in the response to the publication of his *Essay on Development* and in the context of the furore created by his article in *The Rambler* in July 1859, "On Consulting the Faithful in Matters of Doctrine." He was painfully aware also that at Oxford he had received little formal theological education and was largely self-taught in such matters; at Oxford—which was with Cambridge the place of formation of the vast majority

---

Council, as for example the question of ecumenism, the relationship between Christianity and the world, the emphasis on the role of the laity in the Church and the relationship of the Church to non-Christian religions. Not only this Council but also the present time can be considered in a special way as Newman's hour." *L'Osservatore Romano* (English edition), April 17, 1975.

   3   In an address of April 1990 at a symposium organized to commemorate the centenary of Newman's death, John Paul II referred to "the importance of this extraordinary figure, many of whose ideas enjoy a particular relevance in our own day" and to "the unity which he advocated between theology and science, between the world of faith and the world of reason." *John Henry Newman, Lover of Truth* (Rome: Pontificia Universitas Urbaniana, 1991), 7, 9. And in his encyclical *Fides et Ratio* he placed the name of Newman at the head of a long list of "great Christian theologians" of recent centuries "who also distinguished themselves as great philosophers." *Fides et Ratio* (September 14, 1998), 74.

   4   In a lecture given at the same Newman symposium in Rome in 1990, the then Cardinal Ratzinger declared that Newman's two teachings on conscience and doctrinal development constituted a "decisive contribution to the renewal of theology," adding that with his conception of doctrinal development he "placed the key in our hands to build historical thought into theology, or much more, he taught us to think historically in theology and so to recognize the identity of faith in all developments." "Newman gehört zu den grossen Lehrern der Kirche," *John Henry Newman: Lover of Truth*, 144.

   5   For example, writing in November 1867 to his former Tractarian colleague, Edward Pusey, after a series of comments on various philosophical points he declared: "Mind, I do not write as a theologian, which I am not" (*LD* xxiii, 369). He repeated this disclaimer exactly a year later in a letter to the same correspondent on the subject of his decision not to attend the Vatican Council: "I am not a theologian, and should only have been wasting my time in matters which I did not understand" (*LD* xv, 171). Two years later he stated in a letter to the Dominican Reginald Buckler: "I have no claim as a theologian" (letter of April 15, 1870, *LD* xxv, 100). And in 1871, in a letter to Henry James Coleridge, the Jesuit editor of *The Month*, on the subject of his *Grammar of Assent*, he confessed to his "ignorance of theology and philosophy." Letter of February 5, 1871, *LD* xxv, 278.

of Anglican clergy at the time—courses in theology, as opposed to biblical studies, were not compulsory for aspirants to Holy Orders (the first Anglican seminary was not created until 1854, at Cuddesdon just outside Oxford). By temperament, also, he was far removed from the mindset of the academic theologian, most of his works being, in the French phrase, *œuvres de circonstance*—written in response to an immediate need or challenge. And we too often forget that almost one-third of the books which he himself published were volumes of sermons, a reminder that, if Newman was in a sense a theologian despite his denials, he was also, and perhaps above all, a *pastor* and *spiritual guide*.

However, there was almost certainly a further reason for Newman's refusal of the term "theologian." Despite his best efforts, he remained ill at ease with the categories of thought of the neo-scholasticism which dominated Catholic philosophy and theology throughout the whole of the nineteenth century and the early years of the twentieth. Catholic theology at the time was essentially conceptual: it had lost contact with its biblical roots; it was devoid of a sense of history; and, most important of all, it had lost touch with the realm of spiritual experience.

A brief historical note may be useful here for it further underlines the gap between Newman's thought and that of his contemporaries. In the sixteenth century debate, initiated by the Lutheran theologian Philip Melanchthon, on the subject of *loci theologici* or authoritative sources of theology, the classical Catholic riposte was that formulated by the Spanish Dominican Melchior Cano in his *De locis theologicis* published in 1563. Cano distinguished seven such *loci*: Sacred Scripture; apostolic tradition; the teachings of the universal Church; the deliberations of Church councils; the pronouncements of popes and of the Magisterium; the Church Fathers; and the works of theologians and canonists. A striking absence from this list is that of individual spiritual experience (however one may define that term) as testified to by a host of Christian mystics and spiritual writers over the previous millennia and a half. The extent to which a gap exists been Cano's (and the Catholic Church's subsequent) fundamentally intellectualist conception, on the one hand, and the views of Newman on the other, is striking. It can be clearly seen in (amongst other examples) the following two statements in the *Apologia*, which Cano would doubtless have judged to be *a priori* invalid on account of their (supposedly) purely subjective character:

> The being of a God . . . is as certain to me as the certainty of my own existence, though when I try to put the grounds of that certainty into logical shape I find a difficulty in doing so in mood and figure to my satisfaction. . . . Were it not for this voice, speaking so clearly in my conscience and my heart, I should be an atheist, or a pantheist, or a polytheist when I looked into the world.[6]

---

6   *Apo.*, 241.

I am a Catholic by virtue of my believing in a God; and if I am asked why I believe in a God, I answer that it is because I believe in myself, for I feel it impossible to believe in my own existence (and of that fact I am quite sure) without believing also in the existence of Him, who lives as a Personal, All-seeing, All-judging Being in my conscience.[7]

The real question which needs to be asked, therefore, is not "*was* Newman a theologian?" but rather "what *kind* of theologian was he?" This chapter will attempt to answer that question by focusing firstly on the writings of the Church Fathers and on Christian tradition—for both of which a deep-seated *unity exists* between theology, spirituality, and morality—then on Newman's sermons which express that same unity of vision, on the reasons for his lifelong defense of "dogma" and opposition to "liberalism," and finally on the significance in this context of his distinction in the *Grammar of Assent* between "notional" and "real" assent.

THEOLOGY, SPIRITUALITY, AND MORALITY IN THE CHURCH FATHERS AND IN CHRISTIAN TRADITION

The influence of the Church Fathers is decisive here.[8] It was they, according to Newman, who were responsible for his embracing Catholicism.[9] But already as an Anglican he was profoundly influenced by them, and not just in propelling him in the direction of the Catholic Church; indeed, in a very real sense the Fathers were a major inspiration of the whole Oxford Movement.

What was the exact nature of this influence? In *The Arians of the Fourth Century*, based on the writings of early churchmen, Newman examines the relationship between doctrinal issues on the one hand and moral and spiritual questions on the other, his chief thesis being that Arianism—like the "liberalism" of his own day—by denying the divinity of the Son, and hence the reality of the Trinity, leads to a loss of Christian spirituality and the potential reduction of Christianity simply to its moral dimension. In the essays making up *The Church of the Fathers*,[10] however, he is concerned above all with portraits of men and of their struggles and trials rather than with questions of doctrine. In his sermons

---

7   *Apo.*, 198.

8   On Newman and the Fathers, see the chapter by Uwe Michael Lang.

9   In his 1850 lectures on *Difficulties Felt by Anglicans*, he declared that "the writings of the Fathers" constituted "simply and solely the one intellectual cause of his having renounced the religion in which he was born and submitted himself to [the Catholic Church]," and that "he joined the Catholic Church simply because be believed it, and it only, to be the Church of the Fathers" (*Diff.* i, 367). And in his *Letter to Pusey* (1866) he repeats this affirmation in the words: "The Fathers made me a Catholic, and I am not going to kick down the ladder by which I ascended into the Church." *Diff.* ii, 24.

10   Reproduced in *HS* ii, 1–216.

on the other hand (see my chapter on this subject), although he never quotes directly from the Fathers (in sharp contrast to the Bible which is massively present in his sermons) we find numerous themes that are almost certainly inspired by the Fathers—the Church as the mystical Body of Christ, the Trinity, the Incarnation, the Resurrection, the presence of the Risen Christ within the soul of the individual Christian, and the "indwelling" of the Holy Spirit. But I would argue that he found also in the Fathers, and largely made his own, a certain way of understanding the connection between theology, spirituality, and morality. For the Fathers refused to *separate* these three domains, as would occur many centuries later with disastrous consequences for Christian spirituality and indeed for our very conception of Christianity.

It is worth reflecting here on the changing meanings of certain terms. Today, "theology" refers to knowledge *concerning* or *about* God; it is the "science" of God, as geology for example (from the Greek *gé)* is the science of the earth or psychology (from the Greek *psuché*) is the science of the human mind. The word thus designates an essentially intellectual activity, as opposed to a form of direct or experiential "knowledge" such as that referred to by St. Paul when he speaks of "knowing Christ Jesus" and "the power of his resurrection" (Phil 3:8–10).[11] This modern meaning of the word, however, dates only from the mid-twelfth century onwards with Abelard. For the Church Fathers and for the medieval tradition of thought up until then, the "theologian" was first and foremost one who *sought* God through the meditative and prayerful reading of Scripture or simply in prayer. Thus Gregory of Nyssa, for example, in his fourth century *Life of Moses*, states that it is the "contemplation" of God which constitutes true "theology." (It is interesting that the Greek word employed here for "contemplation" is *theoria*, a further example of a word whose meaning has become "intellectualized.") Diadochus, the fifth century Bishop of Photice in northern Greece and a former monk, identified the "theological" and the "contemplative" minds, expressing the widely-held view that it is only *after* he has acquired an experience of God that the "theologian" can legitimately discourse upon Him.[12] And there is of course the celebrated formula of Evagrius Ponticus, one of the most intellectual of the desert Fathers: "If you are a theologian, you will truly pray, and if you truly pray you are a theologian."[13] In the patristic sense, therefore, "theology" was "not so much knowledge *about* God as knowledge *of* God through communion with him and union with him, knowing by 'being known.'"[14]

---

11 See also Gal 4:9: "now that you know God, or rather that you are known by him." It is unfortunate that the English language, so rich in many respects, possesses only one word for designating these two forms of "knowing," unlike other European languages such as French (with the two verbs savoir and *connaître*) or German (with *wissen* and *kennen*)

12 Quoted by Aimé Solignac, SJ, article "Théologie,," *Dictionnaire de spiritualité ascétique et mystique*, Paris: Beauchesne, vol. 15/1 (1990), col. 470.

13 *Traité de l'oraison*, quoted by Aimé Solignac, SJ, "Prière," *Dictionnaire de spiritualité* vol. 12/3 (1986), col. 2259.

14 Andrew Louth, "Denys the Areopagite," in *The Study of Spirituality*, ed. Cheslyn

"Theology" was thus intimately linked to, and the word even to an extent designated, what we would now call "spiritual" experience in the traditional Christian meaning of that (today) much abused term.[15] The word "spiritual" (the abstract noun "spirituality" is a more recent creation), employed in relation to human experience,[16] derives—via the Latin *spiritualis* (or *spiritalis*)—from the Greek *pneumatikos* as employed by St. Paul for whom the word designates the presence and the work of the *Pneuma*, the Spirit of God, or of Christ, or Holy Spirit dwelling within us.[17] To these two categories must be added that of morality or ethics, for the "knowledge" of God to which the "theologian" or "spiritual" man aspired was dependent upon a form of ethical "training"[18] designed to make us more open to and receptive of the presence of God. This association of ideas is found, according to one of the finest French historians of spirituality, the Jesuit Aimé Solignac, right up until the latter part of the thirteenth century; until then,

> *theologia* refers directly to the *knowledge* (*connaissance*) of God and this knowledge, to be authentic, always implies a spiritual attitude, at least in Christian writings . . . from the Fathers right up to the 13th century,

Jones, Geoffrey Wainwright, and Edward Yarnold, SJ, (London: Society for Promoting Christian Knowledge, 1986), 187. Italics mine.

15   Today the term "spirituality" is used in a multitude of senses that recall to mind the words of Humpty Dumpty in Lewis Carroll's *Through the Looking Glass:* "When I use a word, it means exactly what I choose it to mean, neither more nor less!" "Spiritual" and "spirituality" refer to everything from the "feel-good" factor in religion, via (real or imagined) communing with nature, to being a (preferred) substitute for the words "religious" and "religion." Thus many people claim to be "spiritual but not religious." The authors of the Charter of the European Union refused to speak of Europe's religious or Christian heritage but were quite happy to refer to its "spiritual" heritage. And a certain number of French philosophers (though in France, it is true, anyone who writes or speaks on a philosophical subject can claim to be a "philosopher") lay claim to a "secular" or even "atheistic" spirituality, basing their claim on a totally false etymology, the word "spiritual" being, so they argue, a translation of the Greek *psuchikos*.

16   There are of course other meanings in other contexts, for example the "spiritual" power of the Church as opposed to the exercise of "temporal" power, or "spiritual" goods as opposed to "worldly" goods, etc.

17   In 1 Cor 2:10–3:3, for example, one of the foundational texts of Christian spirituality. Paul distinguishes in the Christian three dimensions designated respectively by the terms *sarkikos* (generally translated as "carnal"), *psuchikos* (often translated by "natural," but in the RSV translated by "*un*spiritual"), and pneumatikos ("spiritual"), a clear reference to the Spirit of God or Holy Spirit.

18   This was the original meaning in Christian vocabulary of the Greek word *askésis*, which has given us in English "ascetic" and "asceticism." Its use was inspired by two massive realities of the Greco-Roman world: the omnipresence of the Roman army whose soldiers engaged in rigorous "training" in order to combat more effectively, and that of the games or sports of the arena for which athletes trained in order to win the victor's crown. St. Paul uses images drawn from both these realities. The Latin equivalent is to be found in the term "spiritual exercises," a generic term not by any means restricted to the work of St. Ignatius of Loyola.

theologia remains linked to the spiritual life (even, to a certain extent, in the case of Abelard). It always refers to a way of "knowing God" (*connaître Dieu*) and of "speaking of God." It therefore presupposes, and at the same time encourages, the humble submission of the human mind to the divine mystery, the opening up of the heart and the will to salvation and to the sanctification which the Old Testament promised and which the New Testament achieves.[19]

Numerous examples of this association of "theology," "spirituality," and ethics in the form of *askésis,* or spiritual "training," can be found in the writings of the Fathers. Thus, St. Athanasius of Alexandria declares that the man who "wishes to understand the thought of the 'theologians' must firstly purify his manner of living."[20] For Diadochus of Photice the "charisma of theology" requires a spiritual preparation involving the giving up of all one's goods for the sake of the Kingdom.[21] Athanasius, Augustine, and others—to be followed by Newman—employ the metaphor of the eyes that need to be cleansed of grit and dust if they are to "see" God. Many of the Fathers quote in this sense the sixth of the Beatitudes, "Blessed are the pure in heart, for they shall see God" (Mt 5:8) (the word "pure" being understood here in the sense of simple, undivided or unmixed, as in the modern expression "chemically pure"). Augustine employs the delightful image of the house which must be cleaned and tidied in order to prepare for the visit of God: "If I were to announce my visit, you would hasten to clean and to tidy up your house. And it is *God* who wishes to dwell in your heart and you do not hasten to prepare a place for Him!"[22]

From the fourteenth century onwards, however, Western Christianity generally is characterized by a gradual *loss* of this unified vision.[23] "Scholastic"

---

19 Aimé Solignac, "Théologie," *Dictionnaire de spiritualité,* vol. 15/1, col. 463–64, 481. Author's italics; my translation. An interesting case in point here is that of St. Thomas Aquinas. According to the Dominican Yves Congar, the term "theology" in the title of his *Summa theologiae* was not the work of Thomas but that of his pupils and disciples who wrote down, copied, and circulated his work after his death. Where we speak today of "theology," Thomas generally used the term *sacra doctrina*; to quote Congar: "*theologia* is found only three times in the authentic text . . . whereas the expression *sacra doctrina* is found close on eighty times: and moreover, *theologia* is not used in the modern sense of theology but in the etymological sense of reflection or discourse on God." Yves Congar, "Théologie," *Dictionnaire de Théologie catholique,* Paris: Letouzey et Ané, vol. 15 (1950), col. 346. My translation.

20 Quoted by Aimé Solignac, "Théologie," *Dictionnaire de spiritualité,* vol. 15/1, col. 467.

21 Aimé Solignac, "Théologie," *Dictionnaire de spiritualité,* vol. 15/1 col. 470.

22 Augustine of Hippo, *Sermon* 261.

23 This is in marked contrast to Eastern and Orthodox Christianity, which has always emphasized its direct descent from and dependence upon the (Greek) Fathers and has retained, in faithfulness to them, a *unified* vision of the relationship between theology, spirituality, and morality. The discovery of this in the first half of the twentieth century led to a radical rethinking of their subject by a number of Western theologians; it bore fruit

theology—that of the "schools" or universities—became increasingly conceptual and abstract, its practitioners tending to consider spiritual writers as intellectually inferior. This animosity was reciprocated by many spiritual writers: the author of that classic of late medieval spirituality, *The Imitation of Christ*, expresses in turn a marked contempt for "theologians." Theology increasingly lost contact with spirituality, whilst spirituality found itself increasingly lacking in a theological basis. At the same time, morality was seen less and less as a form of spiritual "training" intended to make a person more "capable"[24] of receiving God within his or her soul and more and more in terms of obedience to commandments and laws prescribed by a now largely "external" God. These are of course sweeping generalizations; but they remain globally true.[25]

Then, from the second half of the seventeenth century onwards, the patristic conception of the "spiritual" life, conceived of as the "indwelling" of Christ within the individual soul, gradually faded. This was part of a broader cultural evolution, as Western culture and its vision of humankind became progressively more intellectualised. The human person was more and more conceived of as a "*thinking* animal" (Descartes's celebrated formula "I think, therefore I am" can be seen as a symptom of this process). Correspondingly, the Christian was more and more defined in terms of the holding of certain "beliefs"; and Christianity itself became increasingly an affair of "dogma" and of moral "values," all too often finding itself reduced to a mere form of moralizing.[26] Only in the

---

in France in the major publishing venture, from 1942 onwards, of the collection *Sources chrétiennes* published by the Éditions du Cerf.

24 See the traditional formula "homo capax Dei," taken up and developed by Pierre de Bérulle, founder of the French Oratory, in his celebrated definition of man as "a nothingness surrounded by God, needful of God, capable of God, and filled with God, if he wishes it" (*un néant, environné de Dieu, indigent de Dieu, capable de Dieu, et rempli de Dieu, s'il le veut*), in *Oeuvres completes* vol. iv (Paris: Éditions du Cerf & Oratoire de France, 1996) 10. My translation.

25 There are of course honorable exceptions to this sweeping generalization. One of the most notable is that of the so-called "French school of spirituality" in the first half of the seventeenth century. Its chief inspirer, Bérulle, was both a brilliant theologian and a deeply spiritual man. Following St. Paul who declares in Gal 2:20: "It is no longer I who live, but Christ who lives in me," Bérulle defines the "spiritual life" as "the life of Jesus Christ" in us and declares that "the highest degree of a perfect spiritual life" consists in "allowing Jesus Christ to invade and dwell in our souls." *Œuvres complètes*, vol. 1 (1995), 184. And his disciple Jean-Jacques Olier, founder of the Company of Saint-Sulpice dedicated to the formation of the clergy, in the very first lesson of his *Catéchisme chrétien de la vie intérieure* defines the Christian (also quoting St. Paul) as "he who has within him the Spirit of Jesus Christ." *Catéchisme chrétien de la vie intérieure* (1656) (Paris: Le Rameau, 1954), 11. My translation in both cases. See St. Paul: "He who has not the Spirit of Christ does not belong to Him" (Rom 8:9).

26 There is an interesting example of the intellectualisation of Western thought and culture in the evolution, at least in the French language, of the word *spirituel*: in the literary and philosophical *salons* of the eighteenth century, the word came to designate a person of clever and witty conversation, Voltaire being seen by many of his contemporaries as a shining example of "the *spiritual* man."

twentieth century would Christians on the whole become conscious of the spiritual dimension of their religion—and then most often only in a partial and fragmentary way.

WHERE DOES NEWMAN STAND IN RELATION
TO THESE QUESTIONS?

It would be quite erroneous to assert that Newman uses the term "theology" in the sense of the Church Fathers. And there is no question, obviously, of an influence of contemporary Eastern Christianity upon his own thought. However, as Ian Ker and others have argued, many aspects of his theology appear to owe more to the influence of the Greek Fathers than to current Western theology.[27] And he shares implicitly their vision of the relationship between the three domains of theological reflection, spiritual life and experience, and morality. He declares in the *Essay on Development* that "Christianity is dogmatical, devotional [i.e., spiritual], practical [i.e., ethical] all at once."[28] He saw the need for a theology which places itself at the service of our spiritual lives; for a spirituality which possesses a sound theological foundation; and for an ethical system conceived of as a form of spiritual "training" or inner purification (in an Anglican sermon entitled "Obedience the Remedy for Religious Perplexity," he refers explicitly to the necessity of "training our hearts" into what he calls the "fulness of a Christian Spirit," that is openness to God).[29] If he appears to some as obsessed with tracking down "heresies," it is because he is keenly aware that our way of *thinking about* God influences and even determines our way of *seeking* Him and *praying to* Him—as also our inability, or our refusal, to do so.

One can see also in Newman's thought here an instance of a more general characteristic of his mind. In the Preface to *The Idea of a University*, he attributes to university education the aim of forming in the student "a connected view or grasp of things."[30] This idea is taken up again and developed in Discourse VI of the same work: a "truly great intellect," he declares, "is one which takes a connected view of old and new, past and present, far and near, and which has an insight into the influence of all these one on another. . . . It possesses a knowledge, not only of things, but also of their mutual and true relations."[31] Newman's own thought provides numerous illustrations of this characteristic of mind. We find it, for example, in the *Arians of the Fourth Century* where he is concerned to emphasize the consequences for the spiritual life of Christians of the Arian theology which denies the divinity of Christ. We find it also in his

---

27 See for example the chapter "Eastern Christianity," in Ian Ker, *Newman and the Fullness of Christianity* (Edinburgh: T. & T. Clark, 1993) 83–102.

28 *Dev.*, 36.

29 *PS* i, no. 18: 233.

30 *Idea*, xvii.

31 *Idea*, 134.

reflection on the relationship between change and continuity in his conception of "development,"[32] on the relationship between conscience and authority in the *Letter to the Duke of Norfolk*, and on the relationship between the theologian, the pastor, and the Magisterium in his 1877 Preface to volume I of the *Via Media*. In addition, of course, to his exploration of the relationship between theology, spirituality, and morality or ethics in his sermons, which is our concern in the section which follows.

EXAMPLES OF THE LINK BETWEEN THEOLOGY, SPIRITUALITY AND MORALITY IN NEWMAN'S SERMONS

The deep spirituality which pervades Newman's Anglican sermons has often been commented upon. However, this spirituality always has, in addition to a biblical basis, a solidly theological foundation. Conversely, it has been argued that the sermons of Newman and of several of his Tractarian colleagues, such as Edward Pusey and Isaac Williams, express the conviction that "theology is rooted in spirituality and worship,"[33] an example in point being their espousal of the patristic doctrine of the "indwelling" of the Holy Spirit that lies at the heart of the Tractarian movement. In either case, the two are inseparable.

Thus, we find a number of sermons exploring the spiritual implications of the doctrine of the Trinity, which, from a spiritual point of view, proposes a vision of God in terms of *communication* of the Divine Life, making us, in the words of 2 Pt 1:4 (several times quoted by Newman) "partakers of the divine nature." This communication proceeds *from* the Father (the source), *through* the Son, and *in* or *by* the Holy Spirit. God is not merely external to us but is—or rather can be— *within* us, as a living and transforming spiritual Presence. If Newman is consistently hostile to all forms of Christianity, such as Unitarianism, which deny the Trinity—and thus also the divinity of Christ—it is because they implicitly reduce Christianity to a simple moral code, devoid of any spiritual dimension.

The Incarnation constitutes also a recurrent theme, figuring in the title of several sermons both Anglican and Catholic. Newman emphasizes the *kenosis* or self-emptying of the Son of God in becoming man; but he sees also in the Incarnation the opening up of a "channel" of communication leading to a radical transformation of our whole being. As his beloved St. Athanasius put it in a formula subsequently embraced by the whole of Eastern and Orthodox Christianity, the Son of God "was made man that we might be made God."[34]

---

32 See for example the all too often misquoted passage in the *Essay on Development* where he speaks of the "idea" of Christianity which "changes" constantly, but *"in order to remain the same."* Dev., 43. My italics.

33 See Ralph Townsend, "The Catholic Revival in the Church of England," in *The Study of Spirituality*, ed. Cheslyn Jones (Oxford: Oxford University Press, 1986), 468.

34 Athanasius of Alexandria, *De Incarnatione*, quoted in *The Study of Spirituality*, 161–62.

As with the Trinity, his reflection on the Incarnation is also intimately linked to his view of our spiritual lives through the doctrine of the "indwelling" of the Holy Spirit. Numerous sermons contain an eloquent expression of this theme, for example:

> The Holy Ghost, I have said, dwells in body and soul, as in a temple. . . . He pervades us (if it may be so said) as light pervades a building, or as a sweet perfume the folds of some honourable robe; so that, in Scripture language, we are said to be in Him, and He in us. . . . In St. Peter's forcible language, he [the Christian] becomes "partaker of the Divine Nature," and has "power" or authority, as St. John says, "to become the son of God." Or, to use the words of St. Paul, "he is a new creation; old things are passed away, behold all things are become new."[35]

This indwelling of the Holy Spirit is also that of Christ Himself:

> Through the Holy Ghost we have communion with Father and Son. . . . The Holy Spirit causes, faith welcomes, the indwelling of Christ in the heart. Thus the Spirit does not take the place of Christ in the soul, but secures that place to Christ. . . . The Holy Spirit, then, vouchsafes to come to us, that by His coming Christ may come to us, not carnally or visibly, but may enter into us. And thus He is both present and absent; absent in that He has left the earth, present in that He has not left the faithful soul.[36]

This is no ethereal or otherworldly doctrine. Newman proposes a spirituality for people who live *in* the world and who seek "perfection" in the ordinary round of everyday activities. In this way the Christian will come to "see Christ revealed to his soul amid the ordinary actions of the day, as by a sort of sacrament."[37] The doctrine of the indwelling of the Holy Spirit thus leads *both* to an attitude of contemplation *and* to active service of God and our fellow humans, uniting the "contemplative" and "active" lives:

> In this, then, consists our whole duty, first in contemplating Almighty God, as in Heaven, so in our hearts and souls; and next, while we contemplate Him, in acting towards and for Him in the works of

---

35 "The Indwelling Spirit," *PS* ii, no. 19: 222–23. The biblical references given by Newman are 2 Pt 1:4; Jn 1:12; 2 Cor 5:17. Newman's language changes somewhat (though not totally) between his Anglican and Catholic sermons. In the latter he seldom refers to the doctrine of the "indwelling of the Holy Spirit"; however the word "grace" now expresses very much the same idea.

36 "The Spiritual Presence of Christ in the Church," *PS* vi, no. 10: 126–27.

37 "Doing Glory to God in Pursuits of the World," *PS* viii, no. 11: 165.

every day; in viewing by faith His glory without and within us, and in acknowledging it by our obedience. Thus we shall unite conceptions the most lofty concerning His majesty and bounty towards us, with the most lowly, minute, and unostentatious service to Him.[38]

Newman reflects also, at great length, on the crucial theological question of the nature of salvation, emphasizing in particular its spiritual implications. All are agreed today that it is Christ who saves us. But in what does "salvation" consist? And *how* exactly does Christ save us? Is it by a *past* action—his atoning death on the cross—or does he save us, here and now, by the *present* action of His Spirit? These and other questions regarding the nature of salvation have profound implications for our spiritual lives. For Newman, who in no way minimizes the sacrificial death of Christ on the cross, salvation is for each and every one of us essentially a *present* event, or rather *process*: it consists in our *receiving* into ourselves the Spirit of Christ and in *allowing* ourselves to be thereby transformed into what He was Himself. Salvation thus involves a communication, and a reception, of the very life of Christ. Thus he declares in 1838 in his *Lectures on Justification*:

> Christ, who is the Well-beloved, All-powerful Son of God, is possessed by every Christian as a Saviour in the full meaning of that title, or becomes to us righteousness; and in and after so becoming, really communicates a measure, and a continually increasing, measure, of what He is Himself. . . . He makes us gradually and eventually to be in our own persons, what He has been from eternity in Himself, what He is from our Baptism towards us, righteous.[39]

And in a sermon preached two years later, "Righteousness Not of Us, But in Us," he returns to this theme, emphasizing that we are not, and cannot be, the authors of our own salvation, but that salvation must nonetheless occur *within* each and every one of us:

> The Spirit came to finish in us, what Christ had finished in Himself, but left unfinished as regards us. . . . As then His mission proves on the one hand that salvation is not from ourselves, so does it on the other that it must be wrought in us. . . . As a light placed in a room pours out its rays on all sides, so the presence of the Holy Ghost imbues us with life, strength, holiness, love, acceptableness, righteousness.[40]

---

38 "The Gift of the Spirit," *PS* iii, no. 18: 269–70.
39 *Jfc.*, 104.
40 "Righteousness Not of Us, But in Us," *PS* v, no. 10: 138.

Newman's doctrine of conscience unites moral theology and spirituality. The word "conscience" designates for him not just a moral phenomenon—important though this is—but also, and inseparably, an awareness of God's mysterious presence within us, in the depths of our *consciousness*. Being attentive to the "law of conscience" involves therefore far more than simply distinguishing between right and wrong or good and evil: it involves cultivating an *inner disposition* of attentiveness to God, or of "receptivity." This conception of conscience is integral to his very definition of a Christian: "A true Christian, then, may almost be defined as one who has a ruling sense of God's presence within him . . . present not externally, not in nature merely, or in providence, but in his innermost heart, or in his *conscience*."[41]

Newman deals at length also, particularly in his Catholic sermons, with the relationship between "nature" and "grace." He makes his own the old scholastic adage *gratia perfecit naturam*: grace is not opposed to nature, it does not seek to destroy or to minimize it in order to take its place but transforms it from within and brings it to "perfection." Through the indwelling of the Holy Spirit we become by grace what Christ is by nature. Several of his Catholic sermons, in effect, are veritable hymns of praise to the transforming power of divine grace; they invite us not merely to reflect on the nature of grace but to *open up* our hearts or souls to it, thus deepening our spiritual lives.

He fiercely opposes the "rationalism" of the late seventeenth and eighteenth centuries that rejected the concept of "mystery" in religion.[42] This led to a rejection of the doctrines of the Trinity, of the Incarnation, and of the Resurrection in the name of "reason"; the result was either the rejection of Christianity or its reduction to a set of clear and explicable ideas and of moral principles. Newman defends the principle of "mystery" in religious matters,[43] arguing that, since God himself is "Mystery"—that is, beyond the ability to grasp or to comprehend of the human mind—Christianity necessarily contains mysteries which our intellect is unable to grasp fully. Conversely, a purely intellectualised Christianity can easily become a source of intellectual pride through the pretention to "know" and to "understand" everything.[44] All through the history of Christian spirituality this same recognition has gone hand in hand with an attitude of humility and of "receptiveness": to recognize God as "Mystery" is to open up the possibility of a relationship with Him in the innermost depths of our being. It

---

41 "Sincerity and Hypocrisy," *PS* v, no. 16: 225–26. Newman's italics.

42 One of the earliest and most virulent of these attacks was that of John Toland in his *Christianity Not Mysterious or, A Treatise Shewing That There is nothing in the Gospel Contrary to Reason, Nor Above it: And that no Christian Doctrine can be properly called a Mystery*, London, 1696.

43 Sermon "Mysteries in Religion," *PS* ii, no. 18: 206–16.

44 It is worth recalling that the verb "to comprehend" comes from the Latin *cumprehendere*, the literal meaning of which is "to seize," "to grasp," "to take hold of."

is this spiritual insight which underlies Newman's persistent opposition to the "intellectual" view of Christianity held by the theologian William Paley who, in his *Evidences of Christianity* (1794), sought to prove the truth of Christianity by an appeal to archaeology, to geology, and to the "realisation" of biblical prophecies, thus placing himself unwittingly, according to Newman, on the same intellectual ground as his opponents.

Finally, Newman's manifold reflections on the subject of faith seek to unite the intellectual, moral, and spiritual domains. Against those who see faith purely or chiefly in intellectual terms, as mere "believing," Newman conceives of it in the biblical sense: faith is above all looking to God, placing our trust wholly in him, and desiring to *receive* Him into our hearts. Quoting Ephesians 3:17, "Strengthened with might by His Spirit in the inner man, that Christ may dwell in your hearts by faith" (words which should be inscribed in letters of gold over the entrance of every Christian church and chapel), he comments: "The Holy Spirit causes, *faith welcomes*, the indwelling of Christ in the heart."[45] At the root of faith is a *desire*, and a *capacity*, to "receive."

He deals at length also with the relationship between faith and what he calls "obedience," in a reference to the debate initiated in the modern period by Martin Luther between "faith" and "works." He refuses to see an opposition between the two. "Faith" and "obedience" are simply "two states of mind" which are "altogether one and the same"; "to believe is to look beyond this world to God, and to obey is to look beyond this world to God; to believe is of the heart, and to obey is of the heart. . . . They are but one thing viewed differently."[46] Obedience, in fact, when it is based on humility, *leads to* belief; conversely, a man "may be obedient and yet proud of being so." In such a case, Newman argues,

> a man is proud, or (what is sometimes called) self-righteous, not when obedient, but in proportion to his disobedience. To be proud is to rest upon one's self . . . ; but a really obedient mind is necessarily dissatisfied with itself, and looks out of itself for help, from understanding the greatness of its task; in other words, in proportion as a man obeys, is he driven to faith, in order to learn the remedy of the imperfections of his obedience.[47]

Through "obedience," through embracing an attitude of humility and of what Newman calls "teachableness," we place ourselves "*in the way* to arrive at the knowledge of God."[48] Or as he declares in another sermon, "the supernatural

---

45   "The Spiritual Presence of Christ in the Church," *PS* vi, no. 10: 126. Italics mine.
46   "Faith and Obedience," *PS* iii, no. 6: 80–81.
47   "Faith and Obedience," *PS* iii, no. 6: 80–81.
48   "Inward Witness to the Truth of the Gospel," *PS* viii, no. 8: 113. Newman's italics.

works which [God] does towards us are in the heart, and impart grace; and if we disobey, we are not disobeying His command only, but *resisting His presence.*"[49]

He emphasizes also that if faith is a "gift of God," we must *prepare* ourselves to *receive* this gift. Finally, true faith leads us ultimately to place ourselves unreservedly in God's hands, or to what Newman calls an attitude of spiritual "surrender." To have faith is

> to feel in good earnest that we are creatures of God; it is a practical perception of the unseen world; it is to understand that this world is not enough for our happiness, to look beyond it on towards God, to realize His presence, to wait upon Him, to endeavour to learn and to do His will, and to seek our good from Him. . . . To have faith in God is to surrender one's-self to God, humbly to put one's interests, or to wish to be allowed to put them into His hands who is the Sovereign Giver of all good.[50]

If on the one hand, for Newman, our way of *thinking about* God determines our way of praying to Him and of seeking Him—whence the necessity of a sound and correct theology—it is the case also that our *moral dispositions* influence our *ideas* and hence both our ability to believe and our ability to seek and to find God.

NEWMAN'S DEFENSE OF "DOGMA" AND HIS OPPOSITION TO "LIBERALISM"

His whole life long, Newman championed the cause of "dogma." In the account given in the *Apologia* of his first "conversion" of 1816, the two key elements on which he insists are the discovery of dogma and his personal encounter with God: he "fell under the influences of a definite Creed, and received into [his] intellect impressions of dogma" and his mind came to "rest in the thought of two and two only absolute and luminously self-evident beings, myself and my Creator."[51] The juxtaposition suggests a link, even if the precise nature of this link is not here made explicit.

What exactly does Newman mean by "dogma"? Contrary to a widespread misapprehension today, the word does *not* designate a set of rigid ideas or an attitude of inflexibility. In the original Greek, *dogma* signifies "thought" or

---

49   "Miracles No Remedy for Unbelief," *PS* viii, no. 6: 87. Italics mine.

50   "Faith and Obedience," *PS* iii, no. 6: 79–80.

51   *Apo.*, 4. Newman is of course looking back here over a distance of nearly fifty years. But a similar expression can be found in a sermon written and delivered over thirty years earlier, in 1833: "we begin, by degrees, to perceive that there are *but two beings in the whole universe, our own soul, and the God who made it.* . . . To every one of us, there are *but two beings in the whole world, himself and God*." "The Immortality of the Soul," *PS* i, no. 2: 20. Italics mine.

"opinion." With the development of Christianity, however, the word took on a specific and technical meaning: the "dogmas" of the Church are the formulations, put forward and refined by theologians down the centuries and subsequently approved and promulgated by the Magisterium, of the great truths pertaining to the "Mystery" of God. A Christianity without dogmas is a Christianity without any intellectual substance, one which is purely personal and subjective, or a mere moral code or ideal. It is in this sense that we must understand the use of the word by Newman. From this fact, several important conclusions follow.

First of all, the existence of dogmas supposes and requires the existence of the *Church*, both as a teaching authority capable of defining and promulgating articles of faith, and as a "visible" body or institution with its rites and sacraments. Thus in the *Apologia*, Newman declares that if the first of the three principles on which the "Movement of 1833" was founded was that of dogma, the second, "based on this foundation of dogma," was the existence of "a visible Church, with sacraments and rites which are the channels of invisible grace."[52]

The second conclusion involves a paradox. Reflection on the subject of dogma leads to the conclusion of the inadequacy of all statements concerning God: dogma is both necessary yet falls short of its object. One can detect the influence here of the "apophatic" or "negative" theology of several of the Church Fathers, for whom God is "incomprehensible" and "unknowable" except through a certain form of "unknowing," in an experience which situates us beyond words and concepts. We can therefore only speak of Him in terms of analogy and metaphor, or through negative statements: "God is not this or that . . ." This is a tradition that runs through Christian spirituality from the Fathers to Meister Eckhart in the thirteenth century to the anonymous fourteenth century classic *The Cloud of Unknowing* and to St. John of the Cross, amongst others. As the fifteenth of his *Oxford University Sermons* suggests, Newman was clearly aware of this tradition, arguing for example that "the Catholic dogmas are, after all, but symbols of a Divine fact, which, far from being compassed by those very propositions, would not be exhausted, nor fathomed, by a thousand."[53]

But at the same time—and this is the third conclusion—dogma is absolutely indispensable. For its function is not just, as so many Christians have believed and believe, to ensure right thinking or believing as an end in itself, as if God were a kind of celestial schoolmaster judging us on our correct learning of the catechism; it is to guide us in our *spiritual* quest.

Newman reflects at length on this subject in the last of his *University Sermons*. He frequently employs the term "impression," in the sense of that which God has "impressed" directly upon our minds or hearts. In a long passage of this sermon, which Newman thought sufficiently important to quote parts of

---

52 *Apo.*, 48–49. The third principle, subsequently totally rejected by Newman, was a radical opposition to Roman Catholicism. See *Apo.*, 50–51.

53 *US* no. 15, § 23, 332.

it in his *Essay on Development*, he reflects on the relationship between theological affirmations and the "impression" which God gives us of Himself:

> As God is One, so the impression which He gives us of Himself is one; it is not a thing of parts; it is not a system; nor is it any thing imperfect, and needing a counterpart. It is the vision of an object. . . . Religious men, according to their measure, have an idea or vision of the Blessed Trinity in Unity, of the Son Incarnate and of His Presence, not as a number of qualities, attributes, and actions, not as the subject of a number of propositions, but as one, and individual, and independent of words, as an impression conveyed through the senses. . . . Creeds and dogmas live in the one idea which they are designed to express, and which alone is substantive; and are necessary only because the human mind cannot reflect upon that idea, except piecemeal, cannot use it in its oneness and entireness, nor without resolving it into a series of aspects and relations . . . ; and thus the Catholic dogmas are, after all, but symbols of a Divine fact, which, far from being compassed by those very propositions, would not be exhausted, nor fathomed, by a thousand.[54]

He even argues that dogmatic formulations may *proceed from* this spiritual experience:

> Further, I observe, that though the Christian mind reasons out a series of dogmatic statements, one from another, this it has ever done, and always must do, not from those statements taken in themselves, as logical propositions, but as being *itself enlightened and (as if) inhabited by that sacred impression* which is prior to them, which acts as a regulating principle, ever present, upon the reasoning, and without which no one has any warrant to reason at all.[55]

Similar reflections can be found in his *Parochial and Plain Sermons*. For example, in a sermon entitled "The Incarnation," speaking of the function of "Creeds," Newman declares that "the declarations made in them; the distinctions, cautions, and the like, supported and illuminated by Scripture, draw down, as it were, from heaven, *the image of Him who is on God's right hand*. . . ."[56] And in another sermon, also devoted to the theme of the Incarnation, he asks: "What do we gain from words, however correct and abundant, if they end with themselves, instead of lighting up *the image of the Incarnate Son in our hearts*?"[57]

---

54 *US* no. 15, §21–23, 330–32; *Dev.*, 53.
55 *US* no. 15, § 26, 334. Italics mine.
56 "The Incarnation," *PS* ii, no. 3: 29. Italics mine.
57 "The Humiliation of the Eternal Son," *PS* iii, no. 12: 169–70. Italics mine.

Once again, in this manner of conceiving the relationship between theological statements or dogma and spiritual experience, we can find a parallel with the traditions of Eastern Christianity. In a remarkable passage of a pioneering and now classic work first published in France in 1944 by the Russian Orthodox theologian Vladimir Lossky, *The Mystical Theology of the Eastern Church*, the author emphasizes the relationship seen by that tradition between "dogma" and "mystery," by which is meant here the realm of spiritual experience or the experiential "knowledge" of God as distinct from the mere knowledge *about* or *concerning* God which characterizes so much Western theology in recent centuries:

> The Eastern tradition has never made a sharp distinction between mysticism and theology; between personal experience of the divine mysteries and the dogma affirmed by the Church. The following words spoken a century ago by a great Orthodox theologian, the Metropolitan Philaret of Moscow, express this attitude perfectly: "none of the mysteries of the most secret wisdom of God ought to appear alien or altogether transcendent to us, but in all humility we must apply our spirit to the contemplation of divine things." To put it in another way, we must *live the dogma expressing a revealed truth, which appears to us as an unfathomable mystery, in such a fashion that instead of assimilating the mystery to our mode of understanding, we should, on the contrary, look for a profound change, an inner transformation of spirit*, enabling us to experience it mystically. Far from being mutually opposed, theology and mysticism support and complete each other. One is impossible without the other. . . . There is, therefore, no Christian mysticism without theology; but, above all, there is no theology without mysticism.[58]

Newman's defence of "dogma" is inseparable from his lifelong struggle against what he calls philosophical and theological "liberalism." This is a complex phenomenon of which he never gives one clear definition, but in which one can distinguish five separate but related strands of thought.

The first is obviously liberalism's refusal, on principle, of all "dogma"; thus in the *Apologia* Newman describes it as "the anti-dogmatic principle and its developments."[59]

In his *Biglietto Speech*, given on the occasion of receiving his cardinal's hat in 1879, he describes it as a form of relativism in religious matters: "Liberalism

---

58 Vladimir Lossky, *The Mystical Theology of the Eastern Church* (Crestwood, N.Y.: St Vladimir's Seminary Press, 1976), 8–9. Italics mine.

59 *Apo.*, 48. See also, in the appendix to the same work, Note A, (285–97), in which he undertakes to develop and clarify this formula.

in religion is the doctrine that there is no positive truth in religion, but that one creed is as good as another. . . . It is inconsistent with any recognition of any religion, as *true*."[60]

A third, closely related, element is the reduction of religion to a mere matter of personal and subjective "opinion." Liberalism "teaches that all are to be tolerated, for all are matters of opinion."[61] This criticism underlies Newman's repeated strictures and attacks upon the principle of "private judgment" that leads to the subjectivisation of religion.

A fourth element lies in what he considers to be an abusive use of "reason": thus he writes that "by liberalism I mean false liberty of thought, or the exercise of thought upon matters, in which, from the constitution of the human mind, thought cannot be brought to any successful issue, and is therefore out of place."[62] This is no call to obscurantism but a recognition that the "Mystery" of God will always be beyond the complete mastery of the human mind.

A fifth and final element of the liberalism attacked by Newman is more subtle but equally pernicious. Although this is never explicitly stated by him, one finds in his work an intuition concerning the evolution of Western thought since the seventeenth century, discussed earlier in this same chapter. Historians customarily speak of the "Age of Reason"; but it would be at least as appropriate to regard this period as an age of growing *intellectualism*. Thought is increasingly regarded as the highest human activity; and this in turn leads to a rejection of all forms of experience which are *not* reducible to a set of concepts or ideas— beginning with the experience of God, as testified to by a host of spiritual writers and mystics down the ages, and by Newman himself.

"NOTIONAL" AND "REAL" ASSENT

Finally, the idea of the interdependence of theology, spirituality, and morality is to be found also in the *Grammar of Assent* in Newman's crucial distinction— perhaps philosophically *the* most important aspect of his thought—between "notional" and "real" assent (the word "real" retaining here the sense of the Latin *res*, "object," or "thing," or eventually "person," a meaning which all of Newman's educated male contemporaries would have instantly recognized, a knowledge of Latin being then part of the intellectual accomplishments of a "gentleman").[63] "Notional" assent belongs to the domain of theology; "real" (or, as he sometimes calls it, "imaginative") assent to that of religion—which includes of course, for Newman, the domain of concrete relations and spiritual experience:

---

60 *Biglietto Speech*, in *Add*, 64. Newman's italics.
61 *Biglietto Speech*, 64.
62 *Apo.*, 289.
63 For a fuller discussion of the philosophical significance of Newman's distinction between the "real" and the "notional," see my article, "'Real' and 'Notional' in Newman's Thought," *American Catholic Philosophical Quarterly* 94, no. 1 (Winter 2020): 27–56.

A dogma is a proposition; it stands for a notion or for a thing; and to believe it is to give the assent of the mind to it, as it stands for the one or for the other. To give a real assent to it is an act of religion; to give a notional, is a theological act. It is discerned, rested in, and appropriated as a reality, by the religious imagination; it is held as a truth, by the theological intellect.[64]

"Religion," he argues, *needs* the intellectual foundation provided by theology, it "cannot maintain its ground at all without theology."[65] Indeed, theology must of necessity *precede* our spiritual quest:

[Propositions] are useful in their dogmatic aspect as ascertaining and making clear for us the truths on which the religious imagination has to rest. Knowledge must ever precede the exercise of the affections . . . we must know concerning God, before we can feel love, fear, hope, or trust towards Him.

Newman even admits that theology—as an intellectual exercise—can exist *without* "religion" (though adding the rider that it will necessarily, in this case, be lacking in "life"): "Theology may stand as a substantive science though it be without the life of religion."[66]

The fact remains, however, that for him it is the *spiritual* life which matters most, and it is therefore necessary to pass from the "notional" to the "real," from theology to religion, and to allow the presence of God to be "realized" in us.

But this "realization" is something that we all too often fail to accomplish, for reasons which are both moral and spiritual. Why is it, Newman asks à propos of our participation in the Church's liturgy, that we are so lacking in fervour for the great religious festivals, if not that "personally we often find ourselves so ill-fitted to take part in them, . . . that we are not good enough, that in our case the dogma is *far too much a theological notion, far too little an image living within us?*"[67]

In a highly intellectualized culture such as that of our age, to pass from the "notional" to the "real," from thinking *about* God to actually "realizing" His presence, represents a difficult and unending challenge. Yet it is one which all Christians are called upon to meet.

---

64 *GA*, 98.
65 *GA*, 120–21.
66 *GA*, 121.
67 *GA*, 139–40. Italics mine.

CONCLUSION

I have argued in this chapter that Newman, chiefly under the influence of the Church Fathers but in accordance with the whole of Christian tradition up until the beginning of the modern era, refuses to *separate* theology, spirituality, and morality. For him, theology (as we understand that term today) is absolutely necessary but cannot stand on its own. In a formula which is not Newman's but which I think admirably sums up his way of thinking, our manner of *thinking about* God determines, or at least profoundly influences, our manner of praying to Him and of seeking Him. And our moral selves influence both our way of thinking about God and our manner of relating to Him (as also our inability, or our refusal, to do so). The refusal of "dogma," properly understood, tends to the reduction of Christianity in most cases to mere moralism and to a religion devoid of any true spiritual dimension. Conversely, an exclusive insistence on "dogma" imprisons us in the domain of the "notional" as opposed to the "real," that is the domain of spiritual experience and of a personal, lived relationship with God.

These considerations determine Newman's very conception of Christianity. Christianity is, for him, of necessity a dogmatic religion, possessing a coherent and highly developed theology. But it is equally necessary that it should not be *simply* a dogmatic religion; nor that it be reduced *simply* to the level of moral "values," however noble and elevated these may be. Lastly, both the personal quest for theological truths concerning God, and the quest for an intimate "knowledge" of Him as a living Being, require a permanent form of *askésis* or ethical "training," designed to "purify" our hearts and minds in a way which will make us—at least in some small measure—"capable" of both.

Suggested Reading

Beaumont, Keith. *Dieu intérieur: la théologie spirituelle de John Henry Newman*. Paris: Ad Solem, 2014.

Bouyer, Louis. *Newman: Sa vie, sa spiritualité*. Paris: Éditions du Cerf, 1952 (English translation *Newman: His Life and Spirituality*, 1958).

———. *Newman's Vision of Faith: A Theology for Times of General Apostasy*. San Francisco: Ignatius Press, 1986 (Written and first published in English).

CHAPTER 23

NEWMAN ON JESUS AS SAVIOUR

Msgr. Roderick Strange

John Henry Newman is renowned for his understanding of doctrinal development, his awareness of the historical narrative that needs to be explored as Church teaching is examined and contemplated. At the same time, his own presentation of the Trinitarian and Christological mysteries of faith in particular remained remarkably consistent. There were some shifts in his thinking, of course, and especially there may appear to be shifts as he addressed what he had to say to different people, people whose intellectual frame of reference differed from his own. When he was in Rome preparing for ordination as a Catholic priest from 1846 to 1847, he presented four theses on patristic subjects in Latin in order to be better understood there, although the success of that attempt was limited[1] and in old age—still working on Athanasius—he has been thought to engage with the neo-Thomistic synthesis that was being promoted at that time.[2] Newman wrote and rewrote tirelessly in order to be understood. One major exception to this consistency, however, was his understanding of Jesus as saviour.[3] As the years passed, his approach to this key subject shifted, reflecting the course of his life and his own theological development. It is necessary, therefore, to begin at the beginning.

---

1   See *TT*, 7–91.
2   See Benjamin J. King, *Newman and the Alexandrian Fathers* (Oxford: Oxford University Press, 2009), 218–47.
3   An earlier version of this chapter was delivered as a talk to the Society of St. John Chrysostom in London on December 10, 2019.

In 1816, when he was only fifteen years of age, Newman remained at school throughout the long summer vacation because he was unwell and during that time underwent an experience of conversion. Although not a classically earnest evangelical conversion, it bore an evangelical stamp. In his *Apologia Pro Vita Sua*, nearly fifty years later, he described it as bringing him to "rest in the thought of two and two only absolute and luminously self-evident beings, myself and my Creator."[4] He was saying that, were he to believe nothing else, he knew that he existed and that he believed in God. The experience made its mark on him. As late as 1887 he was writing to his Evangelical correspondent, George Edwards, about his love for the Catholic Church and giving as his reason "that those great and burning truths, which I learned when a boy from evangelical teaching, I have found impressed upon my heart with fresh and ever increasing force by the Holy Roman Church."[5] And that evangelical teaching was evident in his earliest sermons, especially with their insistence on the atonement.

Newman was ordained as an Anglican deacon in 1824 and, already a fellow of Oriel College, he was appointed to St Clement's parish in Oxford, just over Magdalen bridge. In his first sermon he declared: "We must owe all to Christ—He died on the cross to redeem us from sin and misery."[6] Soon afterwards he told his congregation: "He is the Lord of Hosts, He is the King of glory,—Yea, it is the Son of the Highest who is offered up upon the cross for us, a mighty victim, an awful sacrifice, to atone for our sins."[7] And in another sermon a little later he made it plainer still: "This then is the grand and characteristic doctrine of our holy faith, an atonement for sin . . . Believe on the Lord Jesus and thou shalt be saved."[8] All these sermons were preached in 1824, when he was still just twenty-three years old. Their evangelical thrust is clear, although Newman was soon to reject in particular the appeal to the atonement as an instrument of conversion, a notion that was evident towards the end of this last sermon. This change will become clearer later. And in any case Newman himself was changing.

One reason for this change was his experience of parish visiting. His evangelicalism had led him to believe that more people were damned than were saved, but whatever his parishioners' failings may be, he noted in his journal, there were many who were not "altogether without grace."[9] He had come to see them differently, not necessarily damned after all. And, besides that pastoral experience, Newman was also becoming acclimatized to Oriel's Senior Common Room which at that time was regarded as the most prestigious in Oxford. It was said to "stink of logic."

---

4   *Apo.*, 4.
5   *LD* xxxi, 189.
6   *Serm.* v, 23.
7   *Serm.* v, 40.
8   *Serm.* i, 320–21.
9   *AW,* 206.

Reserved by nature, he was brought out of his shell notably by the colourful, rather eccentric Richard Whately, who was later to become the Archbishop of Dublin in the Church of Ireland. He was a great talker and Newman a great listener. If ever Newman could be said to have had a rationalist phase, this was it. There are two sermons he later noted as "Whateleyan," nos. 146 and 161, and another, no. 90, that he described as "a cross between Whateleyism and Evangelism."[10] Newman remarked later that he was being drawn towards what he called the liberalism of the day,[11] but that drift was stopped by his illness in November 1827, while invigilating examinations, and by the death of his sister, Mary, on January 5 the following year. Illness and bereavement forced him to take stock. What mattered to him? Was he to value intellectual excellence above everything else, or moral and spiritual excellence? He chose spiritual excellence. And a further influence, confirming that choice, was the friendships he was developing with Edward Pusey, John Keble, and Richard Hurrell Froude, friendships that led him moreover to turn to the Fathers of the Church. Their influence was to prove vital.

In 1860 Newman wrote a letter to Edgar Estcourt who was secretary to the Bishop of Birmingham, Bishop William Bernard Ullathorne. They had been discussing a scheme to build a Catholic Church in Oxford. Newman expressed his reservations, which Estcourt seemed largely to have shared. He argued that whatever weaknesses there might be in the Anglican Church more generally, he believed that the Church of England in Oxford had been till then "the seat of those traditions which constitute whatever there is of Catholic doctrine and principle in the Anglican Church. Nothing, therefore, should be done to undermine it. He also went on to state: Catholics did not make us Catholics; Oxford made us Catholics."[12] Six years later, in his controversy on Marian doctrine and devotion with his friend, Edward Pusey, he was to declare, "The Fathers made me a Catholic."[13] These statements, of course, do not clash. It was his study of the Fathers at Oxford, especially his enthusiasm for the Greek Fathers of the Church, St. John Chrysostom and the Cappadocians, the Alexandrian School, and especially St. Athanasius, that had had such an impact on him.[14] And those patristic studies can be discerned in his preaching on Jesus as saviour. In his book, *The Patristic Doctrine of Redemption*, H. E. W. Turner compared "'the forest track of patristic thinking' to 'the metalled road of Anselmic and post-Anselmic speculation.'"[15] It is time to explore that forest-track in Newman's writings.

---

10 *Serm.* v, 392; iii, 301; v, 252.
11 *Apo.*, 14.
12 *LD* xix, 352.
13 *Diff.* ii, 24.
14 See in ch. 8 of this volume Uwe Michael Lang's comments on Newman's study of St. John Chrysostom, St. Cyril, and St. Athanasius (editor's note).
15 H. E. W. Turner, *The Patristic Doctrine of Redemption* (London: Mowbray, 1952), 11.

Three major themes have been identified in patristic writing: Christ as illuminator, our pattern, model, or example; Christus Victor, Christ as victorious over Satan; and Christ as the atoning sacrifice. All three can be found in Newman's sermons.

CHRIST AS ILLUMINATOR

While still a deacon, in January 1825, Newman had asked, "Do we desire a pattern of holiness? In Christ again we possess that perfect example, and faultless specimen of every virtue."[16] Under Whately's influence at that time, it is probable that he was thinking of the pattern as something external, a view he was to correct ten years later, writing about the heresy of Apollinaris: "Much as it is to have a perfect pattern set before us, how is this pattern practically available, unless an inward grace is communicated from His Person to realise this pattern in us?"[17] Then, later still, on April 9, 1841 he preached a sermon on the cross as a pattern indeed to be followed, but as something interior, a reality to be contemplated.[18]

Newman began by speaking about people not reflecting on the state of the world in which they find themselves, but when they begin to reflect, they discover the world to be a maze and perplexity. How is it to be understood? There are different approaches, but in those early April days, the season of Passiontide, Newman urged those listening to him to consider the cross as the measure of the world. He asked about the worth of the world's kingdoms, drew attention to the strivings of the ambitious and the intrigues of the crafty in their search for political power, wondered about the great discoveries achieved by the intellect and science, the pride and confidence of reason, and referred as well to the evil that is found in the world, the misery, poverty, and destitution, the oppression and captivity, famine, homelessness, and disease. How is any of this to be rated? And his consistent answering refrain was, "Look at the Cross. Gaze upon the Cross." And so he concluded:

> The doctrine of the Cross does but teach, though infinitely more forcibly, still after all it does but teach the very same lesson which this world teaches to those who live long in it, who have much experience in it, who know it. The world is sweet to the lips, but bitter to the taste. It pleases at first, but not at last. It looks gay on the outside, but evil and misery lie concealed within. . . . Therefore the doctrine of the Cross of Christ does but anticipate for us our experience of the world.[19]

---

16 *Serm.* ii, 263.
17 *TT*, 319.
18 *PS* vi, no. 7: 83–93.
19 *PS* vi, no. 7: 87.

In other words, he was explaining how the world can deceive: it is sweet to the lips, but bitter to the taste, if that is all people have. Consider nowadays the colour supplements and magazines in the weekend newspapers. How many articles there are, advising people how to have more satisfying sex, or interviewing those who have become fabulously wealthy or have acquired great power or influence. Sex, money, and power: these are held up so often as the goals to admire, to which everyone should aspire. In themselves they may be good enough; but adored as idols, they can only deceive. Mammon deceives. As Newman explained, we have to "begin with the Cross of Christ, and in that Cross we shall at first find sorrow, but in a while peace and comfort will rise out of that sorrow . . . the Cross so wounds as to heal also."[20] He was to echo that thought in his poem, *The Dream of Gerontius*, when he referred to St. Francis of Assis receiving the stigmata: "Learn that the flame of the Everlasting Love / Doth burn ere it transform."[21]

CHRISTUS VICTOR

In his sermon, "Bodily Suffering," which he first preached in 1835, Newman had declared, "When lifted up upon the cursed tree, He [Christ] fought with all the hosts of evil, and conquered by suffering."[22] Here is the theme that focuses on the struggle between the Christ and Satan in which Christ's victory is acclaimed. And in a later sermon, "Christ Manifested in Remembrance" (1837), he stated the theme more fully.

An old difficulty for this theme, however, had been a concern that Satan had been defeated because he had been deceived. The true identity of his opponent, the Christ, had been hidden from him. Was the devil defeated by a trick? Could that be right? And various answers were proposed, for example, that all was well, because it would benefit Satan in the end. The end was justifying the means. But Newman's response was simpler and more satisfying. After exclaiming, "What wonderful providence indeed, which is so silent, yet so efficacious, so constant, so unerring!" he continued:

> This is what baffles the power of Satan. He cannot discern the Hand of God in what goes on; and though he would fain meet it and encounter it, in his mad and blasphemous rebellion against heaven, he cannot find it. Crafty and penetrating as he is, yet his thousand eyes and his many instruments avail him nothing against the majestic serene silence, the holy imperturbable calm which reigns through the providences of God. Crafty and experienced as he is, he appears like a child or a fool, like one made sport of, whose daily bread is but failure and mockery, before the deep and secret wisdom of the Divine Counsels.[23]

---

20 *PS* vi, no. 7: 91–92.
21 *VO*, 352.
22 *PS* iii, no. 11: 139.
23 *PS* iv, no. 17: 259–60.

The devil was not being deceived by God. His own evil blinded him. As Newman observed, "He accomplished the Atonement of the world, whose misery he was plotting. Wonderfully silent, yet resistless course of God's providence!"[24]

CHRIST THE ATONING SACRIFICE

So, Jesus who is the Christ is our pattern and victorious in the struggle for our redemption, but the forest-track does not end there. Indeed, to remain in particular focused on Christ as the pattern of human redemption would be inadequate. In another unpublished sermon, this one preached first in 1834, Newman warned: "Yet there is some danger, lest while we view His conduct in the light of a *pattern*, we should stop short of the full faith we should exercise towards Him as our Atoning Sacrifice . . . His sufferings must be adored as our atonement, not our pattern."[25] Besides being our pattern and example, and while his victory over Satan is cause for rejoicing, the Christ is also to be adored.

Newman taught about Christ's atoning work in a sermon preached two years later, in 1836. He called it, "The Incarnate Son, a Sufferer and Sacrifice." He explained:

> We believe, then, that when Christ suffered on the cross, our nature suffered in Him. Human nature, fallen and corrupt, was under the wrath of God, and it was impossible that it should be restored to His favour till it had expiated its sin by suffering. Why this was necessary, we know not; but we are told expressly, that we are "all by nature children of wrath," that "by the deeds of the law there shall no flesh be justified," and that "the wicked shall be turned into hell, and all the people that forget God." The Son of God then took our nature on Him, that in Him it might do and suffer what in itself was impossible to it. What it could not effect of itself, it could effect in Him. He carried it about Him through a life of penance. He carried it forward to agony and death. In Him our sinful nature died and rose again. When it died in Him on the cross, that death was its new creation. In Him it satisfied its old and heavy debt; for the presence of His Divinity gave it transcendent merit . . . And thus, when it had been offered up upon the Cross, and was made perfect by suffering, it became the first-fruits of a new man; it became a Divine leaven of holiness for the new birth and spiritual life of as many as should receive it.[26]

Christ atoned for humanity by assuming perfectly human nature. What had been disabled by sin was then restored by him sacrificing himself.

---

24 *PS* iv, no. 17: 260.
25 *Serm.* i, 255.
26 *PS* vi, no. 6: 79.

The key idea was again expressed movingly in *The Dream of Gerontius*, in words made familiar as the hymn, "Praise to the Holiest in the Height." One stanza reads:

> *O wisest love, that flesh and blood*
> *Which did in Adam fail,*
> *Should strive afresh against the foe,*
> *Should strive and should prevail.*[27]

The flesh and blood—ordinary, common humanity, that had failed at the beginning in Adam—had engaged in the struggle a second time, striving afresh and being victorious. How could that be possible? And the answer comes immediately: because it had been refined by "a higher gift than grace." There are scholars, however, who after reading Newman's words have asked, "What higher gift is there than grace?' And again the reply is immediate: "God's presence and His very Self, / And Essence all divine."[28] The gift is the Incarnation, the divine Son made man whose sacrifice is overwhelming.

It is important to recognize that this forest-track is not simply identifying three separate paths: pattern, victorious struggle, and sacrifice. There is moreover a dynamic process in play. Contemplating the cross as the measure of the world puts human experience into perspective. What really matters, Mammon or God?

Then, on the cross, Christ conquers, not by deceiving Satan, but because evil is blind to goodness. It cannot recognize how suffering, embraced with generosity, can be transformed. And if that idea seems improbable or blandly pious, an incident typical in tragedy may make it clearer.

On the night of May 31, 1944, an aircraft flew to mainland Europe over the Dutch coast to drop equipment for the forthcoming D-Day invasion. Poor weather conditions had delayed the flight for several days and, when the weather was not improving, the pilot asked the crew whether they would risk flying at a lower, more dangerous altitude than usual. They agreed. However, in the event they were attacked by German fighter planes and shot down. The pilot managed to keep the aircraft high enough for long enough for three crew members to parachute to land; they were captured and remained prisoners for the rest of the war. But the pilot himself and two others landed in the sea and were drowned. The pilot's mother, of course, was distraught when the news of her son's death reached her. She kept saying, "We'll never get over it, we'll never get over it." But her wise husband, a Shetland islander, said, "No, we'll never get over it. But we will get used to it." In other words, he was saying, "We'll learn to live with it."[29] To *live* with it. Suffering, embraced with generosity of heart, can be transformed.

---

27 *VO*, 363.

28 *VO*, 363–64.

29 This incident describes the death of my uncle, Graham Murray. He was the pilot, and those in his crew who were taken prisoner visited my grandfather after the war and told him what had happened.

That transformation is made real because the triumph of the cross is brought about by Christ assuming human nature, by becoming an ordinary human being. These three related paths along the forest-track then point to a further patristic pathway, known as divinization. It is the human nature Christ assumed that gains for humanity a share in the divine nature.

The Fathers of the Church spoke about God becoming man so that men could become gods. In his *De Incarnatione*, Athanasius, for example, wrote: "For He was made man that we might be made God."[30] This startling assertion needs to be explained. The parallel, of course, is not exact. God did not become human so that human beings might become further persons in the Godhead. The divine Son, the Word who became flesh, is God by nature, whereas men and women become gods by adoption, by grace. The vital element is the Son assuming common humanity. As Newman insisted, when explaining Athanasius's teaching, that "in truth, not Christ, but that human nature which He had assumed, was raised and glorified in Him . . . He is in [holy people], because He is in human nature; and he communicates to them that nature, deified by becoming His, that them It may deify."[31] And it was a teaching that he introduced into his own preaching.

In an Easter sermon in 1831 he explained: "Christ communicates life to us, one by one, by means of that holy and incorrupt nature which He assumed for our redemption; how, we know not; still, though by an unseen, surely by a real communication of Himself."[32] And in a later Christmas sermon, "Christian Sympathy," preached in 1839, Newman spoke of Christ who "took our nature, when He would redeem it; . . . so that, whereas He was God from everlasting, as the Only-begotten of the Father, He took on Him the thoughts, affections, and infirmities of man, thereby, through the fulness of His Divine Nature, to raise those thoughts and affections, and destroy those infirmities, that so, by God's becoming man, men, through brotherhood with Him, might in the end become as gods."[33] The humanity assumed by Christ was the vital instrument of human salvation. To grasp the kernel of this teaching, the unique character of the Incarnation may perhaps be compared analogously to someone accomplishing something unique.

Analogies are always limited, but it may help to consider records. When someone accomplishes something remarkable for the first time—Edmund Hillary climbing Everest, Roger Bannister running a mile in less than four minutes—we applaud their achievement, but there is a sense in which we are also applauding ourselves. No one perhaps has expressed it more exactly than Neil Armstrong. When he first stepped onto the surface of the moon on July 20,

---

30 Athanasius, *De Incarnatione* 54.3, in Archibald Robertson, ed., *The Nicene and Post-Nicene Fathers*, vol. 4 (Grand Rapids: Wm. B. Eerdmans Publishing Company, 1892), 65.

31 *Dev.*, 140.

32 *PS* ii, no. 13: 145.

33 *PS* v, no. 9: 117–18.

1969, it was not only, as he said, "one small step for a man," it was also truly "one giant leap for mankind." His small step made all men and women moon-walkers. At that moment he was the only person to have done it, but his step revealed that human beings were capable of walking on the moon. No human being will become a further person in the Godhead, but because Jesus—our brother, a human being, one of us—is also truly divine, truly a person in the Godhead, he reveals the height and the depth of human capacity for intimacy with God. Although by adoption, not by nature, we are all called to share in divine nature, and we are capable of realizing that vocation.

This range of patristic teaching was prominent in Newman's Anglican days and remained important for him after he had become a Catholic. He loved to return to the Fathers when he could and was again revising his work on *Select Treatises of St. Athanasius* in his eighties where he referred to Athanasius as "the great Saint in whose name and history years ago I began to write, and with whom I end."[34] All the same, he realized it was not as perfect a work as he had hoped it might be. And there were two further aspects of his understanding of Jesus as saviour that were characteristic of his Catholic days.

THE PRINCIPLE OF RESERVE

When young and still evangelical, Newman presented the atonement, as would then have been natural to him, as an argument to impress on his congregation a motive for conversion. In an early sermon he said: "The most convincing proof then of the malignity of sin is the fact of its having brought down the son of God from heaven to deliver us by His death from the punishment it justly merited . . . Believe on the Lord Jesus, and thou shalt be saved."[35] In his more mature Anglican years, however, he changed his mind. He rejected the view that saw the atonement as a manifestation, "a great argument addressed to the world, and in itself exciting faith, the one instrument of God's grace, convincing, satisfying the reason, and thereby the means of conversion."[36] He explained all this in a letter to George Edwards in 1883, where he also told him: "Now, with all that is good and spiritual in the Evangelical party, I think that they have forgotten that the Cross of Christ is a "mystery," and to be treated with deep reverence."[37] The Christ who is the saviour is to be adored.

That approach is the one he followed as an Anglican. Preaching in 1841, he observed that the doctrine of the atonement "is not one to be talked of, but to be lived upon; not to be put forth irreverently, but to be adored secretly; not to be used as a necessary instrument in the conversion of the ungodly, or for the satisfaction of reasoners of this world, but to be unfolded to the docile and

---

34 *Ath.* i, ix.
35 *Serm.* i, 320–21.
36 *LD* xxx, 204.
37 *LD* xxx, 204.

the obedient; to young children, whom the world has not corrupted; to the sorrowful, who need comfort; to the sincere and earnest, who need a rule of life; to the innocent, who need warning; and to the established, who have earned knowledge of it."[38] He was practising the principle of reserve. He did not want teaching about the atonement to be brandished about among people who were unfit to receive it. As he explained to an unknown correspondent in a letter two years after preaching this sermon,

> I do not object to bringing forward the Atonement explicitly and prominently *in itself*, but under circumstances, i.e. when people are *unfit* to receive it. I think it should be taught all baptized children—that it is the life of all true Christians—but that it is not the *means of conversion* (ordinarily speaking or in the divine appointment) of those who are not religious. I think it ought not to be preached to infidels, immoral men, backsliders, at first, and be *reserved* till they begin to feel the need of it. Consequently I object to the use of it so often in our pulpits as the *one* doctrine to be addressed to *all*. It is but one *out* of others, and *not* adapted to all.[39]

All the same, as a Catholic, Newman did not feel the need to employ the principle of reserve with regard to the atonement. He viewed it, as he said, as one doctrine, but there were others. He did not want it to be emphasized exclusively. As Robin Selby observed in his study of reserve in Newman's writings: "Newman started by wishing to lead people on by means of the principle of reserve, and . . . he ended by believing that the best and most manly course was to speak, whatever the consequences." And Selby concluded: "This change reflects the move from Tractarianism to Catholicism; he no longer had to induce people to accept Catholic doctrines, and so had no need to employ reserve."[40]

SCOTISM

Why did Christ come? Why was the Word made flesh? There is a common view that, while Thomas Aquinas taught that the Son of God only became man because of human sin, Duns Scotus believed that he would have become man in any case. The truth is rather more complex. To state the matter briefly, Aquinas was addressing what had in fact taken place, Adam's fall, while Scotus was considering something more speculative, what would have happened had Adam not fallen. But these contrasting emphases have led people to speak simplistically of two schools of thought on the question, Thomist and Scotist. And Newman

---

38 *PS* vi, no. 7: 90.
39 *LD* ix, 265.
40 R. C. Selby, *The Principle of Reserve in the Writings of John Henry Cardinal Newman*, (Oxford: Oxford University Press, 1975), 42.

favoured the Scotist approach. Frederick Faber, his fellow Oratorian, asked him about it in 1849 and Newman's reply was clear: "Certainly I wish to take the Scotist view on that point [the purpose of the Incarnation] . . . But as I understand the Scotist view it simply is, that He would have been incarnate, even had man not sinned—but when man sinned it was *for* our redemption; in *matter of fact* the end was to make satisfaction."[41] And he can be seen taking that view in his *Discourses to Mixed Congregations,* which had been published that same year.

In one of them he acknowledged the fact of what had happened: "He who ever does the best, saw in His infinite wisdom that it was fitting and expedient to take a ransom"[42:] Christ came to save humanity by dying on the cross. However, in another discourse his line follows the Scotist position: "He purposed even in man's first state of innocence a higher mercy, which in the fulness of time was was to be accomplished in his behalf."[43] And in yet another, he spoke still more plainly, imagining the thoughts of the incarnate Lord:

> I had had it in mind to come on earth among innocent creatures, more fair and lovely than them all, with a face more radiant than the Seraphim, and a form as royal as that of Archangels, to be their equal yet their God, to fill them with my grace, to receive their worship, to enjoy their company, and to prepare them for the heaven for which I destined them; but, before I carried my purpose into effect, they sinned, and lost their inheritance; and so I come indeed, but come, not in that brightness in which I went forth to create the morning stars and to fill the sons of God with melody, but in deformity and shame, in sighs and tears, with blood upon my cheek, and with My limbs laid bare and rent.[44]

CONCLUSION

Tracing the stages of Newman's understanding of Jesus as the saviour follows a path that leads from his early evangelicalism, through his brief flirtation with rationalism, and on to his exploration of the patristic understanding of atonement, and is rounded off by his distancing himself from the principle of reserve and his awareness of Scotism. It is a fascinating path.

As always with Newman, what was important was reality. In a sermon in 1837 he had declared: "The planting of Christ's Cross in the heart is sharp and trying; but the stately tree rears itself aloft, and has fair branches and rich fruit, and is good to look upon."[45] It is a statement that could be said to capture Newman's own lived experience. But that would be a story for another occasion.

---

41 *LD* xiii, 335.
42 *Mix.,* no. 15: 306.
43 *Mix.,* no. 14: 298.
44 *Mix.,* no. 15: 321–22.
45 *PS* iv, no. 17: 262.

Suggested Reading

King, Benjamin J. *Newman and the Alexandrian Fathers*. Oxford: Oxford University Press, 2009.

Morrone, Fortunato. *Cristo, il Figlio di Dio fatto Uomo: L'Incarnazione del Verbo nel pensiero cristologico di J. H. Newman*. Milan: Jaca Book, 1990.

Strange, Roderick. *Newman and the Gospel of Christ*. Oxford: Oxford University Press, 1981.

CHAPTER 24

NEWMAN'S MARIOLOGY: BIBLICAL AND PATRISTIC FOUNDATIONS OF HIS MARIAN DOCTRINE AND DEVOTION

Fr. Nicholas Gregoris

The life of John Henry Newman both as an Anglican and a Catholic was inexorably linked to the Blessed Virgin Mary. In his *Apologia Pro Vita Sua*, Newman recounts, "I had a true devotion to the Blessed Virgin, in whose College I lived, whose altar I served, and whose Immaculate Purity I had in one of my earliest printed sermons made much of."[1] Stephen Dessain, in discussing Mary's place in Newman's preaching, cites the aforementioned text from the *Apologia* and explains that "this was the sermon, 'The Reverence Due to the [Blessed] Virgin Mary,' first preached on 25 March 1832, more than a year before what is usually considered to be the beginning of the Oxford Movement."[2]

While at Oxford, Newman befriended the likes of Ambrose St John and Edward Pusey, who—as fellow "Tractarians"—spearheaded the Oxford Movement, which sought to re-catholicize Anglicanism by reviving patristic studies, the High Church liturgical traditions, Catholic theology, and Marian devotions

---

1   *Apo.*, 165.
2   Stephen C. Dessain, *Cardinal Newman's Teaching about the Blessed Virgin Mary* (Birmingham, England: The Friends of Cardinal Newman, 1979), 3.

of the "Caroline Divines." The more Newman studied the Fathers of the Church[3] and Church History, the more he overcame what he termed in his *Apologia Pro Vita Sua* the *crux* of Catholic Marian doctrine and devotion, and the more convinced he became that his herculean effort to establish Anglicanism as the *Via Media* between Catholicism and Protestantism was "absolutely pulverized."

From 1828 to 1843, Newman held the cherished post of Vicar at Oxford University's church, historically dedicated to St. Mary. He preached hundreds of sermons from St. Mary's pulpit, one of the most beautiful being entitled, "On Reverence Due to the Blessed Virgin Mary." His last sermon as an Anglican was preached on September 25, 1843 in his church at Littlemore (near Oxford) dedicated to the honor of St. Mary and St. Nicholas. He was received into full communion with the Catholic Church by a Passionist missionary to England, Blessed Dominic Barberi of the Mother of God, at Littlemore on October 9, 1845. On November 1, 1845, at Oscott, he was confirmed and chose "Mary" as his confirmation name.

When Newman returned from the Eternal City, where he had spent a year (1846–1847) studying at the College of the *Propaganda Fide*, he decided to introduce the first English Congregation of the Oratory—which he established at "Maryvale" on February 1, 1848, moving it a year later to Birmingham, where he spent the remainder of his life. As a Catholic, Newman's devotion to the Blessed Mother is evident in the Marian statues he insisted be placed in all the rooms of the Birmingham Oratory and in the decision to place the Oratory under Mary's patronage.

St. John Henry Newman was a most refined Mariologist, always thinking and feeling with the Church (*sentire cum ecclesia*) while, at the same time, undergoing a profound interior conversion that allowed him to ruminate and ponder in his heart, following the example of the Blessed Virgin Mary, those divine truths of the Catholic Faith that situate her at the heart of the mystery of redemption. Thus, Cardinal Newman understood how the cooperation of the humble handmaiden of Nazareth, Mother of God and Mother of the Church, was integral to the divine economy or plan of salvation.

Having undergone a personal conversion, Newman eventually advanced *ex umbris et imaginibus in veritatem*[4] in order to view Mary from the perspective of her most dignified and elevated place in the economy of salvation and the Church's mystical life of grace.

DOCTRINAL DEVELOPMENT AND NEWMAN'S MARIOLOGY

In his famous sermon, his last before the University of Oxford, entitled "The Theory of Developments in Religious Doctrine,"[5] Newman masterfully presents

---

3   Aidan Nichols, OP, *The Shape of Catholic Theology* (Collegeville, Minn.: The Liturgical Press, 1991), 225.

4   This is the epitaph on Newman's tomb at Rednal.

5   See Owen Chadwick, *From Bossuet to Newman: The Idea of Doctrinal Develop-*

Mary as the exemplar or type of *fides quærens intellectum* who, hearing and contemplating in the most profound way the Word of God ("she kept all these things, pondering them in her heart"), is able to understand its significance and its evolutionary process by making it an act of reasoned faith. For Mary, therefore, the knowledge of the truth is not "science" in an empirical and pragmatic sense but an authentic faith, hope, and charity that flow not so much from her notional comprehension of truthful propositions as much as from her capacity to integrate those real truths into the fabric of her life of faith.

The life of St. John Henry Newman[6] itself was in a certain way an epitome of *fides quærens intellectum*, a process of development and conversion by which faith working together with reason was able to shape and, at times, transform his religious thought, sensibilities, and personal relationships according to the logic of his motto as a cardinal, borrowed from St. Francis de Sales, namely, *cor ad cor loquitur*.

For Newman, in fact, Mary is the paradigm of the development of Christian doctrine. He traces and explains the development of Marian doctrine and devotion, seeking to ground them in what he calls the "rudimental" teaching of Sacred Scripture and Tradition, considering the image of Mary as the "Second Eve" to be the fundamental source for genuine development of Marian doctrine. Newman finds the process by which the dogmatic definition of the Immaculate Conception came about to be an enlightening and enlightened one. Cardinal Newman considered the development of the doctrine of the Immaculate Conception a logical consequence of the patristic theology concerning Mary as the New Eve[7] and also as a tremendous sign of the ongoing realization of Divine Providence[8] in the history of the Church.

This process was a turning point in the history of the Church since it was one of the few times when a pope, namely Pius IX in 1854, explicitly consulted not only the bishops but even through them the laity of the Catholic world before making this dogmatic definition.[9]

As an apologist, Cardinal Newman was also concerned with Protestant reaction to Marian doctrine and devotion. His critique of Protestant-Anglican difficulties is found primarily in his famous *Letter to Pusey*. Edward B. Pusey, Professor of Hebrew at Oxford, originally intended to construct a dialogue on

---

ment (Cambridge: Cambridge University Press, 1957); Aidan Nichols, OP, *From Newman to Congar: The Idea of Doctrinal Development from the Victorians to the Second Vatican Council* (Edinburgh: T&T Clark, 1990).

    6   Jean Stern, MS, *La Vierge Marie dans le Chemin de Foi Parcoura par John Henry Newman* (Rome: Marianum, 1991), 42–68.

    7   Thomas Joseph White, OP, *The Light of Christ: An Introduction to Catholicism* (Washington, D.C.: The Catholic University of America Press, 2017), 214–15.

    8   James Hitchcock, *History of the Catholic Church: From the Apostolic Church to the Third Millennium* (San Francisco: Ignatius Press, 2021), 15–16.

    9   Martin C. Albi, *Reason, Faith, and Tradition: Explorations in Catholic Theology*, rev. ed. (Winona, Minn.: Anselm Academic, 2015), 335–36.

disputed points of doctrine and devotion between Anglicans and Catholics. In his masterful response, Newman sought to provide answers to the questions, especially of a Mariological nature, posed by his lifelong friend.

In order to defend the Catholic position on Mary, Newman made numerous references to the Sacred Scriptures and Fathers of the Church. He believed Sacred Tradition to be the most efficacious and convenient argument to enable Catholics and Protestants to find agreement on Marian doctrine and devotion.

To take seriously some Protestant critiques, one might imagine that it is a question of pitting Christology against Mariology. On the contrary, according to Cardinal Newman as he explains in his discourse, "The Glories of Mary for the Sake of Her Son,"[10] the person and mission of Mary are by their very nature oriented toward the Person and mission of her Divine Son. In fact, Mary depends in everything upon her Son, cooperating in the economy of salvation, which the Fathers of the Church described as free, active, and responsible. At the same time, Mary cannot be opposed to Jesus or said to be in competition with Him as though she were His equal.

Cardinal Avery Dulles summarizes the import of Newman's Mariology in an interdisciplinary fashion:

> His own theology about Mary developed gradually from his early Anglican sermons, in which he shows a deep veneration toward her but refrains from clear dogmatic statements about her Immaculate Conception and Assumption. In his *Essay on Development* he frequently uses the Church's teaching on Mary as an example to be tested by his seven criteria of authentic development. In his *Discourses to Mixed Congregations*, representing his early enthusiasm with Roman Catholic thinking, he devotes the two final chapters to Mary. And finally, in his *Letter to Pusey*, he responds in a firm but friendly manner to the objections of his former associate in the Oxford Movement.[11]

THE LETTER TO PUSEY

In order to see how Newman's Anglican thought about the Virgin ties into his Catholic thought, one must turn to his response to Pusey's *Eirenicon*. Newman's response comprises the second part of his work, *Certain Difficulties Felt by Anglicans in Catholic Thinking*. Most scholars agree that this is the only so-called "systematic" treatise that Newman ever wrote on the subject of Marian doctrine and devotion—being both quite ecumenical in tone and yet uncompromising in its defense of the truth. Boyce affirms this latter point: "In an age when there was an inflation of popular and devotional writing on our Lady and when many

---

10 *Mix.*, no. 17.
11 Avery Dulles, SJ, *John Henry Newman* (New York: Continuum, 2002), 76.

Mariological treatises did not show a thoroughly theological knowledge of or respect for Patristic literature, Newman's *Letter to Pusey* appeared as a breath of fresh air. It dissipated many prejudices and was widely acclaimed."[12]

The *Letter to Pusey* gives us direct insight into Newman's use of the Fathers of the Church in support of his position on the Virgin. Bishop Philip Boyce elucidates the matter: "Even those Catholics who had a different outlook from Newman, such as Cardinal Manning and W.G. Ward and F.W. Faber, could not but acknowledge the theological depth and patristic knowledge displayed by the author."[13] It was a harbinger of much development in the field of Mariology, in ecumenism, and in many other areas of theological research. Friedel explains: "Newman, too, wished to give a new impulse to Catholic studies so as to enable the Catholic to meet the Protestant on the common footing of Antiquity. His small work, priceless for its profundity, solidity, and conformity to all the canons of historical criticism, was the forerunner of considerable subsequent research on similar lines and in other domains of theology."[14]

The *Letter to Pusey* is, in great part, an attempt to correct Pusey's misunderstandings concerning Catholic teaching on the intercession and invocation of the Blessed Virgin Mary. Pusey relied on Catholic sources such as Salazar, SS. Louis de Montfort (e.g., *Treatise on True Devotion to the Blessed Virgin Mary*), Bernardine of Siena, and Alphonsus Liguori, as well as on the writings of Suarez and Faber. His inability to distinguish between doctrinal and devotional statements in these writings led him to misinterpret and thus to reject some essential Marian teachings. Furthermore, Pusey's sources were limited, and he often latched onto more extreme, sentimental expressions of Catholic writers as so-called proofs of the falsehood of what was referred to by many Anglicans as "the Roman system of belief."

Newman accused Pusey of a superficial reading and misinterpretation, even misrepresentation, of the Catholic Church's teaching on Mary. Perhaps, here, Newman was guilty of overacting and misinterpreting Pusey's intent, insofar as Newman was initially convinced that the *Eirenicon* was partially intended as a direct attack on Catholicism, rather than a sincere attempt at ecumenical dialogue. In other words, Newman perceived at one point that Pusey's stated purpose of achieving greater understanding of Church teaching was, in effect, designed to create even further division.

Newman's letter was not meant to be a systematic treatment of Mariology; it was fundamentally a response of a friend and man of faith to a friend and man of faith. Newman's response, however, was not simply addressed to Pusey, for Newman had in mind a much larger audience, namely, all of Pusey's fellow

---

12   Philip Boyce, *Mary: The Virgin Mary in the Life and Writings of John Henry Newman* (Grand Rapids, Mich.: Eerdmans Publishing Co., 2001), 45.

13   Boyce, *Mary: The Virgin Mary in the Life and Writings of John Henry Newman*, 45–46.

14   Francis J. Friedel, *The Mariology of Cardinal Newman* (New York: Benziger Brothers, 1928), 140.

Anglicans with whom Newman could easily identify since he had had to over-come many of the same difficulties vis-à-vis Catholicism that they did. Likewise, Newman could easily sympathize with the desire to follow one's conscience in adhering to matters of faith and morals. Newman's *Letter to Pusey* is proof of his ultimate desire to establish further ground for unity between the Catholic and Anglican communions. It is a masterpiece of true ecumenism because Newman did not pursue this unity apart from truth and charity.

In doing so, Newman made clear to Pusey several important facts about himself, namely, that he had obviously taken stances on doctrinal and devotional matters that could not be considered of one accord with many of the official teachings of Anglicanism; that he had moved away from his positions in *Tract* 90, now admitting the full-blown consequences of his rediscovery of the Fathers of the Church and the authentic development of Christian doctrine represented by their teaching; that he believed that the combined witness of the Fathers of the Church (i.e., "Antiquity") was a confirmation of the truths of Sacred Scripture, Sacred Tradition, and the Magisterium of the Roman Catholic Church.

Newman's entire Marian apologetic in the "Letter to Pusey" can be summa-rized in his own emphatic words:

> The Fathers made me a Catholic, and I am not going to kick down the ladder which I ascended into the Church. It is a ladder quite as service-able for that purpose now, as it was twenty years ago. . . . And, in partic-ular as regards our teaching concerning the Blessed Virgin, with the Fathers I am content;—and to the subject of that teaching I mean to address myself at once. I do so, because you say, as I myself have said in former years, that "that vast system as to the Blessed Virgin . . . to all of us has been the special *crux* of the Roman system." Here, let me say, as on other points, the Fathers are enough for me, I do not wish to say more than they suggest to me, and will not say less.[15]

MARY IN THE BIBLE

Newman's evangelical Calvinistic and Anglican background provided him with a profound love of the Sacred Scriptures as is most clearly evident, for example, in his *Parochial and Plain Sermons*.[16] John R. Griffin writes:

---

15 *Diff.* ii, 24–25. It should also be noted that the only place in the Newmanian corpus where he mentions Mary as "Co-Redemptrix" (actually, he uses "Co-Redemptress") is in this work, doing so in a relatively neutral fashion (*Diff.* ii, 78). For a fuller discussion of this issue, see my *The Daughter of Eve Unfallen: Mary in the Theology and Spirituality of John Henry Newman* (Pine House, N.J.: Newman House Press, 2003), 413–41.

16 Philip Boyce, "John Henry Newman: The Birth and the Pursuit of an Ideal of Holiness," in *John Henry Newman: 1879–May 1979*, ed. M. K. Strolz (Rome: The International Centre of Newman Studies, 1979), 46.

In the *Plain and Parochial Sermons* [sic] we find abundant evidence of Newman's own devotion to Our Lady. Mary was always identified in Newman's mind as the person who was closest to Christ. In one of his sermons Newman went very close to an avowal of a belief in the doctrine of the Immaculate Conception, for it must be that the one who was chosen to bear the Son of God was unique in the history of mankind."[17]

Newman's hermeneutical and exegetical principles[18] stemmed from his appreciation of the literal and allegorical interpretation of Scripture in the ancient schools of Antioch and Alexandria to which the writings of the Fathers (e.g., St. John Chrysostom; St. Athanasius of Alexandria) bore for him a most noble witness. His reading of Sacred Writ is closely bound up with his belief in Divine Providence, the fundamental unity of Scripture (Old and New Testaments), the *nexus mysteriorum* in the *œconomia salutis*, and a theological and pastoral sense of the "hierarchy of truths." Furthermore, the Christocentricity of the Word of God necessarily calls into focus for Newman—and thus also for his congregation—the centrality of Mary's cooperation in the mysteries of her Son's salvific life and mission and in the whole of the *historia salutis*.[19]

Newman's first Marian sermon as an Anglican is entitled, "The Honor Due to the Blessed Virgin" (March 25, 1831). It is noteworthy among many things for its particular emphasis on the importance of venerating Mary both in accord with the veneration shown her in the Sacred Scriptures and as fulfillment of her own prophecy in her Canticle of Praise (*Magnificat*) that "all generations will call me blessed." Boyce highlights for us the genius of Newman's exegetical method in this sermon.

> It may seem strange that a young Anglican curate in Oxford should lament the lack of religious devotion and honour paid to our Lady by members of the Church of England. It shows how grounded in Scripture he was and how deeply he appreciated the full implications of the Incarnation—God the Son taking on our human nature and being born of a woman (cf. Gal 4:4). The fact that he had a human mother meant

---

17   John R. Griffin, "Newman and the Mother of God," *Faith and Reason* 15: *Essays in Honor of the Centenary of John Henry Cardinal Newman, 1801–1890,* no. 4 (Winter 1989): 93. See *PS* ii, no. 12: 145.

18   Among other texts see Adrian Boekraad, "Newman en die Heilege Schrift," *Schrift und Tradition* 7 (1954): 385–88; Norbert Schiffers, "Schrift und Tradition bei John Henry Newman," *Schrift und Tradition* (Essen, 1962): 250–66; J. Derek Holmes, "Newman's Attitude towards Historical Criticism and Biblical Inspiration," *Downside Review* 89 (January 1971): 20–37.

19   John Brit, "Newman's Use of Sacred Scripture in Texts on the Incarnation and Mary," *Marian Library Studies* 24 (1995): 215.

that he was truly one of us. As a result of Mary's association with her divine Son she shared in his honour and blessedness. Scripture itself urges us to venerate the Mother of Jesus.[20]

"The Reverence Due to the Blessed Virgin Mary"[21] (March 25, 1832), Newman's first Marian sermon to be published, is most striking for its treatment of Mary's extraordinary sanctity in the Scriptural data and insofar as the Anglican Newman postulates Mary's sinlessness, without, however, fully espousing the Catholic doctrine of the Immaculate Conception.

One of the first sermons that Newman preached after his Catholic conversion is entitled "Our Lady in the Gospel," which he preached after his return to England from Rome in December 1847 only a few months after his ordination in Rome to the Catholic priesthood. He preached this sermon in St. Chad's Cathedral of Birmingham on the Third Sunday of Lent, March 26, 1848, the previous day being the feast, known in England as "Lady Day," in honor of the Annunciation.

The sermon is primarily a reflection on the Lucan pericope concerning the praise of the anonymous woman in the crowd (Lk 11:27–28). It highlights Mary's two-fold blessedness, namely, her obedience of faith and divine maternity in accepting the message of the angel at the Annunciation.[22] In relying on the insights of SS. Augustine and John Chrysostom, Newman highlights[23] the belief that Mary was more blessed for having conceived the Word of God by means of a reasoned act of faith expressed in the *fiat* of the Annunciation than for having conceived Him in her womb through physical generation.

In one of his *Discourses to Mixed Congregations* (so called because Newman's audience consisted of both Catholics and Anglicans) entitled, "The Glories of Mary for the Sake of Her Son" (Spring–Summer of 1849), the Catholic Newman exhorts his listeners in the Oratory Church to contemplate the mystery of Mary's divine maternity and to invoke her maternal intercession as these two fundamental aspects of her cooperation are clearly expressed in the prophecies of the Old Testament and in the writings of the New Testament.

Newman, a convert of only three and a half years and a Catholic priest of two years, undertakes in this work to present a Catholic apologetic for Marian doctrine and devotion. Several years earlier in 1842, Charles Russell, an Irish priest and President of Maynooth College, sent Newman some of St. Alphonsus Liguori's sermons, including certain Marian writings. Much to his surprise, Newman found nothing in those works that disedified him. On the contrary, Newman believed them to be doctrinally sound works that engendered true

---

20 Boyce, *The Virgin Mary in the Writings of John Henry Newman*, 106, note 3.
21 *PS* ii, no. 12.
22 *Faith and Prejudice and Other Unpublished Sermons of Cardinal Newman*, ed. the Birmingham Oratory (New York: Sheed & Ward, 1956).
23 *Mix.*, no. 17.

devotion. Indeed, one can suppose that the title of St. Alphonsus's *Le Glorie di Maria* may have served as the basis for the title of Newman's discourse.

"On the Fitness of the Glories of Mary"[24] (circa August 15, 1849) is also one of Newman's *Discourses to Mixed Congregations*. Its particular literary and theological genius lies in the way Newman is able to show how the argument of convenience, evident in the natural and salvific economies, can be applied to the doctrine of Our Lady's bodily Assumption. Thus, Newman succeeds in demonstrating this doctrine's Scriptural roots and its full integration into the Sacred Tradition.

Furthermore, in "The Glories of Mary for the Sake of Her Son," Newman occupies himself with the question of the death of Our Lady. Did Mary actually experience a physical death? Newman seems to think that she did indeed experience a physical death, not as a consequence of sin, but as a participation in the Lord's Death and as it would be considered the end of the normal course of her human existence. Nevertheless, Newman argues that because Mary enjoyed the privilege of the Immaculate Conception and lived a life free from all sin, her holiness would, according to the divine economy of salvation, have been fittingly rewarded with a physical death without corruption.

Finally, we mention Newman's sermon "On the Purification of Mary"[25] (February 2, 1843), also entitled "The Theory of the Development in Religious Doctrine" which he delivered as the last of a series of sermons preached at Oxford. This sermon was a harbinger of Newman's *An Essay on the Development of Christian Doctrine* and served to underscore Mary's role of cooperation in the economy of salvation in terms of her having faithfully pondered the Word of God as its sacred and saving mysteries unfolded in her life.[26]

MARY AND THE FATHERS OF THE CHURCH

The influence of the Fathers of the Church on the theology and spirituality of John Henry Newman is undeniable.[27] Indeed, he has been referred to by some as a modern-day Father of the Church.[28] Giovanni Velocci writes: "The familiarity

---

24 *Mix.*, no. 18.

25 *US*, no. 15.

26 Dulles, *John Henry Newman*, 77.

27 H. John Chapman, "Newman and the Fathers," *Blackfriars* 14, no. 160 (1933): 578–90; Ernst Hammerschmidt, "John Henry Newman Patrischen Studien," *Internationale Kirchliche Zeitsschrift* 53 (1963): 105–15; Franz William, "Kardinal John Henry Newman und die Kirchlichen Lehrtradition," *Orientierung* 22 (1958): 61–66; Denys Gorce, *Newman et les Pères* (Bruges: Bayaert, 1947); *The Church of the Fathers*, with an Introduction and Notes by Francis McGrath, FMS (South Bend, Ind.: University of Notre Dame Press, 2002).

28 Jean Guitton, "Newman as a Modern Father of the Church," *Tablet* 218 (1964): 814; Giovanni Velocci, "John Henry Newman, l'Ultimo dei Padri" (*L'Osservatore Romano*, July 17, 1974); Walter Strolz, "Newman, Kirchvater der Neuzeit," *Wort und Wahrheit* 10 (1955): 396–99.

with those ancient teachers reveals itself in his Mariology, totally impregnated with his spirit and with his thought."[29] W. Ward remarked that once Newman had begun his preaching at St. Mary's Oxford, it seemed as though the spirit of an Ambrose or Augustine had been revived."[30] For Newman and many of his Anglican contemporaries, Catholic Marian doctrine and devotion were, however, at first tantamount to idolatry or what is sometimes termed "Mariolatry."

A notable exception was Richard Hurrell Froude, whom Newman met in 1826. Felicity O'Brien makes the point that "Froude, who was not, of course, a Roman Catholic, led Newman to develop an admiration for the Church of Rome, a belief in the Real Presence of Christ in the Eucharist, and the idea of devotion to the Blessed Virgin, whom Froude saw as the great pattern for virginity which he held in the highest esteem."[31] But, as Providence would have it, the more Newman systematically read the Fathers of the Church, the more he began to see how Mary's role in no way detracted from Christ's but was a direct consequence of her singular position in relation to Him.

The central doctrine of the Incarnation and its soteriological import formed the foundation of Newman's appropriation of the patristic patrimony. Newman's particular fondness for the thought of St. Athanasius of Alexandria, as most fully expounded in his controversy with the Arians, set the stage for Newman's love of Christology and was a sure inspiration for the development of his Mariology. Even though Athanasius himself does not concentrate on the figure of the Virgin *per se*, but vis-à-vis his defense of an orthodox Christology against the heresy of Arius, he implicitly establishes her link to the mystery of the Incarnation.[32]

Furthermore, Newman's reliance on St. Cyril of Alexandria and his writings in controversy with Nestorius, and the subsequent formulation of the Christological teaching at Ephesus, is most significant for Newman's development of a profound love for the doctrine of the *Theotokos*, officially ratified by that same Council in 431.

The "three-fold cord," as St. Newman terms it, of St. Justin Martyr, St. Irenæus of Lyons, and Tertullian of Carthage forms a powerful combined witness to the antiquity of the Church's doctrine of the New Eve as gleaned from these ancient Fathers' reflection on the antithetical parallelism of Christ and Adam in the Pauline corpus (Rom 5), the *Protoevangelium* of Genesis 3:15, and the apocalyptic vision of the woman in Revelation 12. Friedel comments: "This doctrine [the New Eve] is the central point of Newman's Mariology as exposed

---

29   Giovanni Velocci, *Newman: Il Coraggio della Verità* (Vatican City: Libreria del Vaticano, 2000), 160.
30   Wilfrid Ward, *Life of John Henry Cardinal Newman*, vol. 1 (London: Longmans, Green and Co., 1912), 42.
31   Felicity O'Brien, *Not Peace but a Sword* (Slough, England: St. Paul's Publication, 1990), 30.
32   See *Ath*, i and ii. Also, *The Arians of the Fourth Century*, with an Introduction by Rowan Williams (South Bend, Ind.: University of Notre Dame Press, 2002).

in his *Letter to Pusey*. From it he derives the doctrines of Mary's dignity, her sanctity, her Immaculate Conception, and Assumption."

Friedel lauds Newman's *Letter to Pusey* as a Mariological masterpiece precisely because he was able to harmonize his use of Sacred Scripture and the writings of the Fathers: "His treatment of Mary's position as Second Eve really merits the designation of "*magistrale*" as given it by Terrien. His method is not merely historical; the foundation for the belief is indirectly placed in Scripture. He explains it and then strengthens it by the testimony of the Fathers."[33]

The antithetical parallelism between Mary and Eve is a theme that pervades Newman's Mariological writing and is a direct consequence of his reliance on patristic sources. Michael Schmaus spells this out:

> The antithesis "Eve-Mary," stemming from the *Protoevangelium* and developed by Justin and still more by Irenæus, proved very fruitful. It was for a long time the keynote of Mariological thinking on the faith. The unbelief and disobedience of Eve brought ruin, the faith and obedience of Mary brought salvation. . . . A Mariology founded on the patristic data was introduced by J.H. Newman and M. J. Scheeben. The main questions centered on Mary's share in the redemption.[34]

The writings of St. Ambrose of Milan on Mary's cooperation in the economy of salvation indicate his predilection for certain Marian doctrines and dogmas. For example, Ambrose fought many a battle in defense of the dogma of Mary's perpetual virginity; he esteemed Mary as the example *par excellence* of Christian perfection and discipleship; he upheld Mary as the most exemplary model of virginal purity; and he praised Mary's spiritual maternity of the Church. Thus, for Ambrose, Mary is a *typus ecclesiae* and the model of Christian motherhood. Newman's Marian writings, both doctrinal and devotional, can be viewed as complementary to those of Ambrose since they underscore Mary's physical and spiritual fecundity as the Virgin-Mother of the Redeemer and the Redeemed. Hence, we note also Ambrose's reliance on the New Eve theology. Furthermore, both Ambrose and Newman emphasize the uniqueness of Mary's cooperation, for example, her obedience of faith, by way of reference to the antithetical parallelism of Mary-Zechariah in Luke's Gospel.

In the *Letter to Pusey*, Newman refers to St. Jerome and St. Ambrose as having deemed the Virgin Mary "the great pattern of Virgins."[35] Newman's own keen appreciation of the exemplarity of Mary's virginity and chastity is revealed in several passages from his *Meditations and Devotions*, where he dwells on the

---

33 Friedel, *The Mariology of Cardinal Newman*, 189.

34 Michael J. Schmaus, "Mariology," in *Encyclopedia of Theology: A Concise Sacramentum Mundi*, ed. Karl Rahner (New York: Seabury Press, 1975), 896–97.

35 *Diff.* ii, 52.

essence of *virginitas mentis, corporis et animæ* so emphasized in the theology of St. Ambrose.[36] Newman, in his *Essay on the Development of Christian Doctrine*, quotes St. Ambrose as saying: "Mary was alone and wrought the world's salvation," adding that Ambrose makes this point in connection to Mary's virginal conception of the Redeemer. Furthermore, as Newman points out, Mary is prefigured by the pillar of cloud which guided the Israelites, according to the same Father; and she had "thus great grace, as not only to have virginity herself, but to impart it to those to whom she came."[37]

Newman draws on St. Augustine's writings to defend the Church's dogma of the Immaculate Conception insofar as he clearly sees posited in them an implicit notion of the sinlessness of Mary based on what would later be termed by Duns Scotus as praevenient grace. For Augustine, *"propter honorem Domini"* ("for the honor of the Lord") was a good enough reason to exclude any mention of sin in relation to Mary.[38]

The themes of Mary's spiritual maternity of the Church and her two-fold blessedness (physical and spiritual) evident in Augustine's writings are likewise reflected on by Newman, especially in his Catholic sermon entitled "Our Lady in the Gospel,'" which is a reflection on Luke 11:27–28 whose key phrase is Augustine's: "More blessed was Mary in receiving the faith of Christ, than in receiving the flesh of Christ."[39]

Newman's critique of the anomalous and seemingly negative statements of SS. John Chrysostom, Basil of Caesarea, and Cyril of Alexandria concerning Mary's role in salvation history, as based on their interpretation of certain Marian passages of the Bible, is a noble attempt to temper the theological opinions of those respective Fathers of the Church in the light of the overall Tradition of the Church.[40]

Finally, St. Ephrem, nicknamed "the harp of the Spirit,"[41] provides us with several extraordinary examples of mystical and poetical interpretations of the Sacred Scriptures concerning the sublime mystery of the Incarnation. Several of Newman's sermons reveal his own mystical musings on the Sacred Text and his profound appreciation of Mary's role as Mother of the Incarnate Word, which have overtones of the great Syrian Doctor of the Church. Both SS. Ephrem and

---

36 Ambrose of Milan, *De Virginibus* 2, 7 (PL 16: 209): *"Virgo erat non solum corpore, sed etiam mente."*

37 *Dev.*, 146.

38 *Diff.* ii, 49–50.

39 *FP*, 86. See *Diff.* ii, 36.

40 *Diff.* ii, 141.

41 Owen Cummings, "The Mariology of St. Ephrem," *Lay Witness* (December 1998), 38; Patrick J. Hamell, *Handbook of Patrology* (New York: Alba House, 1968), 125; Sebastian Brock, *The Harp of the Spirit: Eighteen Poems of Saint Ephrem* (Fellowship of St. Alban and St. Sergius, 1983), 6.

Newman were enamored of the use of typology in reference to the Virgin Mary. This is most clearly evidenced in Ephrem's hymns on the Incarnation and in Newman's *Meditations* on the scripturally based Marian titles in the Litany of Loreto such as *Domus Aurea, Sedes Sapientiæ,* and *Janua Cæli.*

MARY'S COOPERATION
AS THEOTOKOS AND NEW EVE

The controlling factor in St. Newman's discussion of Mary's cooperation as *Theotokos* and New Eve is the *œconomia salutis.* For Newman, the economy of salvation embraces the entire mystery of God's relationship to man from the dawn of creation to original sin, from the work of Redemption to the distribution of the fruits of that redemptive work in and through the Church until its consummation in eternity.[42]

Cardinal Newman, being attuned to the Scriptures and historically conscious, surveyed Mary's place in the economy of salvation through the prism of the Marian titles, *Theotokos* and "Second Eve."[43] Mary dwells at the heart of the salvific economy.

St. Newman reminds us that the privilege of divine maternity is that from which all other Marian privileges and titles flow and from which they derive their essential meaning. St. John Damascene, the last Greek Father of the Church (eighth century) can be cited as having anticipated Newman's thought in this regard: "The name of the *Theotokos* contains the whole history of the divine economy in this world."[44] Newman leads Pusey in a reflection on the place of the *Theotokos* dogma in the *nexus mysteriorum.*[45]

Within the overall economy of salvation, the mystery of the Incarnation holds a central place for Newman as he follows a patristic line of thought exemplified by Fathers like Irenæus and Athanasius. Mary is both the "Mother of the Creator" and our spiritual mother through Baptism by which we became *filii in Filio* as members of Christ's Mystical Body, the Church.

Newman sees the title of *Theotokos* ratified at the Council of Ephesus as a succinct encapsulation of the fundamental Christological truths (indeed, it is primarily a Christological title, albeit with Mariological implications). This,

---

42   Gerard Magil observes how the principle of economy in the early Church fascinated Newman. He was attracted to the Alexandrian Church whose teachings were based upon the "various Economies or Dispensations of the Eternal" (*Apo.,* 26). See Gerard Magil, "Newman's Personal Reasoning: The Inspiration of the Early Church," *Irish Theological Quarterly* 58, no. 4 (1997): 307–8.

43   See among others Friedel, "Mother of God and Second Eve," *Catholic World* 141 (1935): 228–29; James E. McGuire, *Holy Virgin Mary: Mystery of Grace; A True Mystery of the Incarnation as Presented in the Writings of John Henry Cardinal Newman* (PhD Diss., *Pontificia Universitas Gregoriana,* 1975).

44   John Damascene, "On the Orthodox Faith," 3:12.

45   *Diff.* ii, 62–63.

in turn, becomes the *fons et culmen* ("source and summit") of all Mary's privileges as she safeguards the integral identity of her Divine Son, in no way ever
obscuring or compromising it.

Newman's theology, already from his Anglican period, reveals a particular
appreciation of Mary's cooperation as the New Eve and the sinless spouse of Christ
the beloved Bridegroom of our souls. This appreciation stems from his love of the
allegorical and mystical sense of the Scriptures, most especially with regard to the
Canticle of Canticles, and derives its inspiration, for example, from the writings of
Origen of Alexandria, St. Gregory of Nyssa, and St. Bernard of Clairvaux.[46]

Inasmuch as Newman is always concerned that genuine doctrinal development arises from the Scriptures and the Fathers (most notably, Justin, Irenæus,
and Tertullian), he resonates favorably to Mary's description as "the Second and
better Eve." This title helps Newman explain Mary's cooperation in the work
of redemption. Eve's involvement in the Fall was essential but subordinate to
Adam's. In like manner, Mary's participation in the reversal of the Fall was essential but subordinate to Christ's role as the New Adam.[47]

Newman keeps in the forefront such scriptural texts as the *Protoevangelium*
of Genesis 3:15 and the apocalyptic vision of Revelation 12 as he expounds on
the Fathers' development of the antitheses between Eve and Mary (disobedi-
ence/obedience; death/life) and their consequences. The title of Mary as "*Mater
omnium viventium*" ("Mother of all the living") indicates for Newman that
Mary's role as the New Eve encompasses her role as Mother of the Church and
therefore likewise her exercise of maternal mediation on behalf of our salvation.
In relying on the writings of such Fathers of the Church as Jerome, Ambrose, and
Peter Chrysologus, Newman emphasizes the active agency of both Eve and Mary
in their respective works, going so far as to speak of Mary's "real, meritorious"
share in the redemptive and salvific mission of Christ "in the economy of grace,"
so much so that she is worthy not only of our remembrance and imitation but
also of our filial invocation as part of our veneration of her timeless blessedness.

The cooperation of Mary in the work of our salvation begins with her
Immaculate Conception, whereby exempt from the contagion of original sin,
she became the antithesis of evil among creatures. Mary is justly called the New
Eve from the moment of her conception, that is, like the old or original Eve she
was created without sin (immaculate). However, it is at the Annunciation that
the title of New Eve takes on even greater significance as she consents to the
divine plan for our salvation.

St. Augustine says, "He who made you with you does not justify you without
you."[48] Therefore, Newman acknowledges that Mary's "real" and "meritorious"
cooperation "in bringing about our Redemption" extends from the moment of her

---

46 Michael J. Perrott, *Newman's Mariology* (Southampton, England: St. Austin
Press, 1997), 26–27.

47 *Diff.* ii, 36.

48 Augustine of Hippo, *Sermon* 169: *Qui fecit te sine te non te justificat sine te.*

salutary *fiat* at the Annunciation, through her extraordinary life of sanctity, virtue, and meritorious good deeds to its culmination and consummation on Calvary. At the foot of the cross, she exercises her *compassio*, which is more than a mere emotional or sympathetic feeling. Rather, it is a profound expression of her intimate union of mind and heart, body and soul with her Son as He accomplishes the work of redemption of which she is the primary and most perfect beneficiary.

In sum, Mary's cooperation "in the economy of Redemption," as the New Eve establishes her in the words of Newman as "a daughter of Eve unfallen,"[49] who took that first step in the salvation of mankind which Eve took in its ruin.[50] And, furthermore, in the words of one of Newman's favorite poets, William Wordsworth, whom he quotes in his *Letter to Pusey*, Mary is "our tainted nature's solitary boast."[51]

CO-SUFFERING AS AN INSTANCE
OF MARY'S COOPERATION

The biblical theology of co-suffering, already established in the Old Testament (e.g., the typological figures of Hagar and the Mother of the Maccabees) is foundational for Newman's theology of Christian co-suffering as a form of participation in the Paschal Mystery of Our Lord, based primarily on the Pauline theology of the cross. Newman considers the co-suffering of the Christian as a unique and privileged means of cooperation in the *œconomia salutis*, as exemplified in the life of the Blessed Virgin Mary and all the saints. Newman unequivocally asserts: "She had a meritorious share in bringing about our redemption."[52] Clearly, he understands Mary's cooperation in terms of her meritorious co-suffering as he reflects:

> And so, as regards the Blessed Virgin, it was God's will that she should undertake *willingly* and with *full understanding* to be the Mother of Our Lord, and not to be a mere passive instrument whose maternity would have no merit and no reward. The higher our gifts, the heavier our duties. It was no light lot to be so intimately near to the Redeemer of men, as she experienced afterwards when she suffered with Him.[53]

The *Compassio Mariae*, literally from the Latin, "Mary's suffering with" Jesus is highlighted by Newman in his *Meditations and Devotions*.[54] By this expression, he sought to understand the precise means according to which Mary participated

---

49 *Diff.* ii, 47.
50 *Diff.* ii, 36 and 45.
51 William Wordsworth, "The Virgin," quoted in *Diff.* ii, 85.
52 *Diff.* ii, 52.
53 *MD*, 37.
54 Vincent Ferrer Blehl, SJ, *The White Stone: The Spiritual Theology of John Henry Newman* (Petersham, Mass.: St. Bede's Publications, 1993), 119.

in the Passion of Christ. Therefore, he affirmed, "She suffered more keen and intimate anguish at Our Lord's passion and crucifixion . . . by reason of her being His mother." And Newman adds, "Not in the body, but in the soul, she suffered a fellow-passion; she was crucified with Him; the spear that pierced His breast pierced through her spirit." In his meditation on Mary as *Regina Martyrum*, Newman ruminates: "What an overwhelming horror to witness the Passion and Crucifixion of her Son! Her anguish was, as holy Simeon had announced to her, at the time of her Son's Presentation in the Temple, a sword piercing her soul."[55]

Newman underscores the important distinction between a physical type of co-suffering and a spiritual type of co-suffering. Furthermore, he clearly distinguishes between the unique salvific sufferings of Christ the God-Man, the sole Redeemer who dies the supreme martyr's death on the cross, and the singular participation of Mary in those same salvific sufferings by means of her co-suffering, which is more often than not characterized by Newman as a profound type of spiritual martyrdom.[56]

He traces Mary's singular cooperation, body and soul, from the moment of her Immaculate Conception to the moment of the Annunciation, culminating in her *fiat* on Calvary wherein she exercises her role as Mother of the Redeemer and the redeemed (see Jn 19:26–27). A careful analysis of Newman's *Meditations and Devotions*, as well as some of his other writings, demonstrates that Newman's spirituality was nourished by his understanding of the Marian dimension of the Paschal Mystery. Thus, St. Newman on numerous occasions employs the symbolism of the sword prophesied by Simeon as it reveals the depths of Our Lady's co-suffering. In sum, we can admire the tender and moving musings of Newman on Mary's maternal *compassion*—characteristic of her entire earthly sojourn from the crib of Bethlehem to the foot of the cross on Calvary.[57]

MARY'S SPIRITUAL MATERNITY AND
INTERCESSORY ROLE AS MEDIATRIX AND ADVOCATE

According to Newman, the *nexus mysteriorum* has as its central dogma the Incarnation, from which flow the doctrine of mediation, the sacramental principle, and the doctrines of the intercession of the saints, their merits, their invocation, and cult in the life of the Church.[58] For Newman,[59] Mary exercises her role of mediation

---

55 *MD*, 49.
56 *SN*, 91–92; *MD*, 60–61.
57 *SN*, 74–75.
58 *Dev.*, 93–94.
59 Newman's understanding of the communion of the saints was influenced by the writings of his Anglican friends, John Keble and Richard Hurrell Froude. See Roger Jupp, "'Awfully Gifted of the Children of Men': Some Aspects of Newman's Devotion to the Blessed Virgin Mary as an Anglican," in *Newman on Mary: Two Papers in Development* (Oxford: The Ecumenical Society of the Blessed Virgin Mary, 1996), 3–19.

as the preeminent member of the Mystical Body of Christ, which is made up of both visible and invisible members of which she is the first believer and the first redeemed. Mary, both in the practice of her faith and in the exercise of her privileges, especially that of mediation, is always treated within an ecclesial context.[60]

One of the principal activities by which the believer cooperates in the salvific work of Christ is prayer, and the chief work of the saints in heaven "in our behalf" (*pro nobis*) is that of intercession. Mary is the disciple of Christ *par excellence* and exemplifies the power of intercessory prayer to the highest degree as Mother of the Church and Queen of Heaven and Earth.[61] Newman makes an excellent synthesis for Pusey of his thoughts on the doctrines of intercessory prayer, Mary's singular intercessory power, and her privileged place in the communion of saints when he asserts:

> I consider it impossible then, for those who believe to be one vast body in heaven and on earth, in which every holy creature of God has its place, and of which prayer is the life, when once they recognize the sanctity and the dignity of the Blessed Virgin, not to perceive immediately that her office above is one of perpetual intercession for the faithful militant, and that our very relation to her must be that of clients to a patron, and that, in the eternal enmity which exists between the woman and the serpent, while the serpent's strength lies in being the tempter while the weapon of the Second Eve and the Mother of God is prayer.[62]

Mary's intercessory power is clearly a divine privilege which she exercises in subordination to the supreme mediation of Christ and by His sovereign will. The efficacy of Mary's prayer, like that of all believers, is dependent on that of Christ, Who makes continual intercession in our behalf at the right hand of the Father. In this way, Newman's theology of mediation anticipates the treatment of a creaturely participation in the one supreme mediation of Christ the God-Man and sole Redeemer as expounded on in *Lumen Gentium*.[63] Friedel comments:

> Newman is always careful to remind his audience that, though Mary is the Advocate of the Church, she did not effect the Atonement—she like all others were saved by her Son, through Whom she has been exalted to the office of Advocate of mankind. This position conferred on her is the result of God's merciful Providence, which permits us creatures to supplicate Him for the dispensation of His favors and graces.[64]

---

60 *Diff.* ii, 52.

61 *Diff.* ii, 76.

62 *Diff.* ii, 73.

63 Michael O'Carroll, "Our Lady in Newman and Vatican II," *Downside Review* 89, no. 294 (1971): 38–63.

64 Friedel, *The Mariology of Cardinal Newman*, 104.

Newman carefully distinguishes between *latria*, which is adoration that belongs by right to the Blessed Trinity alone, and *dulia*, which is the veneration rendered to the saints. Furthermore, Newman draws a clear line of demarcation between the mediation (intercessory prayer) of Our Lord as a Divine Person and that of Mary as a fellow creature with us, albeit the highest of all creatures.[65]

Moreover, Newman underscores the singularity of Our Lady's cult (*hyper-dulia*) within the broader cult of all the saints (*dulia*). Mary plays a pivotal role as Mother of both the Head and members of the Body of Christ. Mary's inter-cessory prayer is considered more powerful than that of all the angels and saints, precisely because Mary is their Queen. Indeed, Newman believes Mary's inter-cessory power to be all-powerful, insofar as it is the great exemplification of Christian intercessory prayer.[66] Furthermore, Mary's intercession in our behalf is a privileged means by which God communicates to us His saving grace. For Newman, however, Mary's intercession is fundamentally distinct from the mediation of Christ as the God-Man, the intercession of the Holy Spirit, and the mediation of the Church's sacraments.[67]

Newman argues that there is an essential difference between the interces-sion of the saints and our devotion to them by which we actively invoke their intercession. In other words, whether or not we directly invoke the saints, they nonetheless can and do intercede for us. This distinction Newman draws in part from the distinction of Suarez, who proposed that God communicated all saving grace through Mary's intercession but not necessarily through our direct invoca-tion of her and always in direct subordination to Christ, the only Redeemer and Supreme Mediator. In that context, Newman writes, "Our Lord died for those heathens who did not know Him; and His Mother intercedes for those Chris-tians who do not know her; and she intercedes according to His Will, and, when He wills to save a particular soul, she at once prays for it. I say, He wills indeed according to her prayer, but then she prays according to His will."[68]

One can safely infer from Cardinal Newman's writings his belief in Mary as the Mediatrix of All Grace. However, several important factors need to be taken into consideration in order to arrive at this conclusion. First and foremost, Newman's understanding of Mary's cooperation as *Theotokos* led him to regard Mary as the Mediatrix of all grace, insofar as she is the chosen instrument (not just physical) who cooperates with the Father's plan for the conception of the Author of Grace in Whose life she had a full participation from the moment of her own Immaculate Conception. Secondly, Newman believed that Mary's divine maternity included a spiritual maternity, whereby her cooperation in the *œconomia salutis* extended beyond her earthly life to encompass her active inter-cession on behalf of all the redeemed, especially the members of Christ's Mystical

---

65 *Diff.* ii, 85.
66 *MD*, 71.
67 *Diff.* ii, 84–85.
68 *Diff.* ii, 105.

Body, the Church. Consequently, Newman discerns continuity and fulfillment in her intercessory role which, beginning on earth, continues in the life of heaven and is there perfected.[69]

Newman's clear predilection for Our Lady's title of "Advocate"—as this title was applied to her, for example, in the writings of St. Irenæus of Lyons—stems from the patristic theology of the New Eve, which, in turn, is firmly based on the patristic interpretation of scriptural texts. In his meditation on Mary as "Refuge of Sinners," Newman ponders: "If the Creator comes on earth in the form of a servant and a creature, why may not His Mother on the other hand rise to be the Queen of Heaven, and be clothed with the sun, and have the moon under her feet?"[70]

Mary's mediation as "Our Advocate" is a most certain instance of her spiritual maternity (i.e., her motherhood of the Church) and therefore constitutes for Newman an indispensable and integral part of her cooperation in the economy of salvation. The early depictions of Mary in the catacombs in the *orans* position, which Newman considers to have been the fruit of the early Christians' profound reflection on the vision of the Mother and Child in Genesis 3:15 and Revelation 12, is concrete evidence in the Tradition of Mary's maternal mediation and of the Church's corresponding filial invocation of her.

Furthermore, due to Newman's acceptance of St. Alphonsus Liguori's belief that "God gives no grace except through Mary,"[71] one can safely infer from his writings that he accepted belief in Mary as "Mediatrix of All Grace," although he does not use the title *per se* and would likely modify this belief by saying that it is not so much a matter of our direct invocation of Mary as it is a matter of her all-powerful intercession in our behalf according to the will of Him Who "wills all men to be saved and come to the knowledge of the truth" (1 Tm 2:4).[72]

Newman affirms in his *Letter to Pusey* that devotion to the Blessed Virgin Mary is not a *sine qua non* of salvation. That having been said, Newman demonstrated a great personal devotion to Our Lady and encouraged such devotion among his flock. In his *Sermon Notes*, for example, he writes about the importance and efficacy of Mary's intercession at the moment of death such as is expressed in the last petition of the *Ave Maria* prayer. It should be noted that Newman as a Catholic developed a special devotion to the Holy Rosary, which he continued until his dying day.[73]

Of enormous influence on Newman's theological concept of Mary's mediation is the sagacious thought of the Greek Fathers, most noteworthy being the "panegyrical" language of St. Cyril of Alexandria at the Council of Ephesus; the "oratorical" language of St. Peter Chrysologus; and the theology of Mary's mediation of all salvific grace proffered by St. Basil of Seleucia. Bertrand de Margerie notes:

---

69 *Diff.* ii, 72, 84.

70 *MD*, 356.

71 *Diff.* ii, 105.

72 *Diff.* ii, 84.

73 Blehl, *The White Stone: The Spiritual Theology of John Henry Newman*, 119–20.

More than a century ago, J.H. Newman already took notice of the impressive thought of Basil of Seleucia.... For Basil, Mary's mediation is a result of divine Motherhood, a unique privilege that establishes her as Mediatrix between God and men. Basil justifies the viewpoint by a suggestive biblical reasoning: "If Peter was proclaimed 'blessed' for having confessed Christ, if Paul had been qualified by Him as 'chosen instrument' for having preached His name to the nations, what should we not think of Mary's great power, she who gave him a human body?"[74]

In fine, Newman differentiates the "Red Way," designating the redemptive sacrifice of Christ from the "White Way," which refers to the intercessory role of Mary and the saints, thereby stressing the latter's dependence on the former even as he shows their interrelatedness.

CONCLUSION

Although Newman also discussed the Blessed Mother in some of his more famous scholarly writings, including the *Apologia Pro Vita Sua* and *An Essay on the Development of Christian Doctrine*, his sole systematic Mariological treatise was his famed *Letter to Pusey*. Yet more than a treatise as such, it was a lengthy letter addressed to a dear friend and contemporary professor at Oxford, the Anglican Edward Bouverie Pusey. In his *Letter to Pusey*, Newman offers apologetical explanations of the Catholic Church's principal Marian doctrines and devotions, which Pusey and many of his fellow Anglicans called into question on grounds of their own ideas about biblical orthodoxy and historical credibility. Anyone attempting to grasp Newman's Mariology must commence with the *Letter to Pusey*.

Undoubtedly, Newman's Mariology hinges in large part on his rediscovery of the Fathers of the Church, who were the primary catalyst of his Catholic conversion. There are frequent references to the Fathers in the *Letter to Pusey*. Newman—being the consummate nineteenth century Victorian author and Oxford scholar, fluent in Latin and proficient in Greek—provides the original patristic texts as well as his own translations of numerous Fathers.

Another avenue by which to approach Newman's Mariology is one that passes not so much through the prism of his intellect as through that of his profound Marian devotion and piety. The pulsating heart of Newman's Marian spirituality is to be found in his *Meditations and Devotions*, particularly his meditations on select titles of the Litany of Loreto for the Marian month of May, which afford us special insight into the Marian heart of the saintly cardinal.

---

74   Bertrand de Margerie, SJ, "Mary, Co-Redemptrix in the Light of Patristics," in *Mary, Co-Redemptrix, Mediatrix, Advocate* (Santa Barbara, Calif.: Queenship Publishing, 1995), 20. The citation is from Basil's Homily 39 (PG 85: 448–49). In PG 77: 992, Basil of Seleusia uses the Greek word *mesiteuosa* "mediatrix" in reference to the Blessed Virgin Mary.

There one finds on full display the authentic Catholicity of Newman's devotion to Our Lady, whose beautiful titles receive from him a type of spiritual exegesis, at once theological and poetical, literal, and allegorical. We can venture to say that there exists in Newman's thought a "High Mariology" and a "Low Mariology," as well as an Alexandrian "High Christology" and an Antiochean "Low Christology," whose tensions are held together in perfect harmony in his devotional writings so as to shed light on and complement the more exuberant Mariological writings of such Doctors of the Church as St. Alphonsus Liguori, whom Newman discusses in his *Letter to Pusey*.

To know Newman—the quintessential Englishman, brilliant Oxford don, dutiful Oratorian, proud cardinal, and humble saint of the poor and working class of Birmingham—is to enter into the vicissitudes of his sufferings (e.g., an awful illness on a sea voyage off the coast of Sardinia, but which life-threatening sickness gave us his poem "The Pillar of the Cloud," more commonly known by its hymn-title, "Lead, Kindly Light"), his travails (e.g., the Achilli Trial), and his failures (e.g., the attempt to establish the Catholic University of Ireland). Therein, we catch a glimpse of his profound Christian humanism and personalism.

Thus, to familiarize oneself with Newman's biography is to glean many insights into his Mariology. In his dealings with friend and foe alike, with such illustrious men as Cardinal Nicholas Wiseman, Cardinal Edward Manning, Bishop William Ullathorne, Father Frederick Faber, the Duke of Norfolk, William Gladstone, Henry Wilberforce, and Charles Kingsley, Newman was both personalist to the core and a true imitator of the Marian virtues of humility, charity, and courageous forbearance amidst salvific suffering of body, mind, and spirit.

Beyond his correspondence with Pusey, Newman's exchanges with Hurrell Froude and John Keble, both Oxford luminaries who never converted to Catholicism, make clear his tender love for the Holy Mother of God. Even Newman's *Letters and Diaries* occasionally provide glimpses of his Mariology, while his *Sermon Notes* offer piecemeal reflections on the Blessed Virgin Mary in the context of the Sacred Liturgy.

Steeped in Sacred Scripture from his earliest childhood, Newman's predilection for God's Word was greatly enhanced by his coming into contact with the Holy Sacrifice of the Mass, which he celebrated daily and with great devotion until he was no longer physically able to do so. At last, poor eyesight greatly affected his ability to pray the Divine Office, but he continued to pray the Rosary until his fingers grew too numb to hold the beads. Thus, he continued until he relinquished Our Lady's "Corona" for the goal for which he had always longed, even as an Anglican, namely, to enter into God's eternal embrace in the company of the Virgin Mary and the whole Communion of Saints.

Newman's understanding of the Scriptures and Tradition, and the depth and clarity of his teaching gives weight to Pope Pius XII's prediction that one day Newman will be declared "Doctor of the Church."

Suggested Reading

Boyce, OCD, Philip. *Mary: The Virgin Mary in the Life and Writings of John Henry Newman.* Grand Rapids, Mich.: Eerdmans Publishing Co., 2001.

Friedel, Francis J. *The Mariology of Cardinal Newman.* New York: Benziger Books, 1928.

Govaert, Lutgart. *Kardinal Newmans Mariologie und Sein Persönlicher Wedergang.* Salzburg und München: Universitätsverlag Anton Puster, 1975.

Gregoris, Nicholas L. *The Daughter of Eve Unfallen: Mary in the Theology and Spirituality of John Henry Newman.* Pine Beach, N.J.: Newman House Press, 2003.

Perrott, Michael J. *Newman's Mariology.* Southampton, England: St. Austin Press, 1997.

CHAPTER 25

NEWMAN'S VIEWS
OF THE CHURCH:
A LEITMOTIV IN HIS WRITINGS

Fr. John T. Ford, CSC

"Church" was a recurring theme in the life and thought of John Henry Newman. Like the *leitmotiv* of a symphony, the church appears with many variations in Newman's writings: often like an *adagio* backgrounding his Anglican and Roman Catholic ministry; sometimes like an *andante*, expressing a compelling concern in his life; occasionally like an *allegro*, responding forcefully, even dramatically, to a "call" to challenge a contemporary thinker or to elaborate an ecclesiological position or to defend an ecclesial principle.[1]

Such "calls" for Newman to express his views regarding the church emerged in various but sometimes unanticipated ways: usually as part of his pastoral responsibility to explain different ecclesial teachings and liturgical practices to his congregation; frequently in the theological controversies that surfaced regularly at Oxford University; sometimes as part of the church-state debates that

---

*   This essay is an abridgement of "La Eclesiología de John Henry Newman," *Scripta Theologica* 51, no. 3 (December 2019): 741–73.

1   On Newman's need for a "call" to write, see *AW*, 272; on his love of music, see Bellasis, Edward, *Cardinal Newman as a Musician* (London: Kegan Paul, Trench, Trübner, and Co.), 1892 (available at: http://www.gutenberg.org/files/26427/26427-h/26427-h.htm).

were a staple of nineteenth-century British politics. In contrast to his *Grammar of Assent* (1870), which was a systematic analysis of the way the human mind knows, thinks, and believes, Newman did not write an academic treatise on ecclesiology. Rather his thinking about the church was expressed in a wide range of writings—sermons and tracts, essays and lectures, prefaces and occasional pieces, and so on. Sometimes he repeated the same ecclesiological point again and again—apparently to make sure his readers understood and hopefully accepted his views. Occasionally he proposed a hypothesis about the church as convincingly as possible—only later to abandon it—much to the confusion of his audience. Frequently, however, an ecclesiological position once taken became a lifelong conviction.

In terms of methodology, Newman customarily approached theological questions—not so much as theoretical positions to be analyzed—but as pressing pastoral questions to be answered. His approach was not *a priori* theoretical—beginning with a premise and then elaborating it in detail—but a personal question—analyzing a current pastoral concern and then proposing an appropriate solution. When one of his hypotheses unraveled—as sometimes happened—Newman abandoned them—sometimes rather casually, other times quite reluctantly. As a result, Newman's ecclesiology is a catena of answers to specific questions concerning various aspects of the church rather than a systematic theological treatise about the church.

Accordingly, those who want an ecclesiological tractate from Newman will likely be disappointed. Those willing to follow Newman in scrutinizing different facets of the church at various times in his life-journey should be fascinated, even delighted. Newman's ecclesiology is like a musical composition whose movements are keyed to different stages of his life with their concomitant challenges and concerns.

NEWMAN'S "FIRST CONVERSION": PERSONAL NOT ECCLESIAL (1801–1822)

In his *Apologia Pro Vita Sua* (1864), published almost two decades after his entrance into the Roman Catholic Church, Newman reminisced:

> I was brought up from a child to take great delight in reading the Bible; but I had no formed religious convictions till I was fifteen. Of course I had a perfect knowledge of my Catechism.[2]

In contrast to his detailed description of his teenage conversion, his autobiographical narrative did not detail his family members' religious practices at home nor their participation in the activities of their Anglican parish. One is

---

2   *Apo.*, 105.

then left speculating about what role the Church of England really played in his life prior to his entering Oxford University, where church attendance was a regular aspect of collegiate life.

If Newman's contacts with the church as a youngster are vague, it is clear from his *Apologia* that his religious convictions were basically formed in the course of a profound spiritual experience that occurred while he was completing his studies at Ealing and preparing to enter Trinity College, Oxford:

> I received it at once, and believed that the inward conversion of which I was conscious, (and of which I still am more certain than that I have hands and feet,) would last into the next life, and that I was elected to eternal glory.[3]

Newman's teenage experience, however, differed from typical "evangelical conversions"—which were usually instantaneous and associated with a specific time and place. Instead, his conversion occurred gradually over several months and in various locations. Yet his conversion resonated with the evangelical emphasis on the personal relationship of saved and Savior: his conversion made "me rest in the thought of two and two only absolute and luminously self-evident beings, myself and my Creator."[4]

Newman's encounter with the divine was then direct and personal, not mediated via a church-related experience. Thus, his conversion might be described as "churchless"—insofar as the essential focus was personal conversion: a "visible church" might be a helpful aid but not an absolute necessity. In theological terms, the "channels of grace" are direct and immediate, not necessarily mediated through an institutional church: whatever benefits and blessings the church may provide, the church is not absolutely essential. Accordingly, Newman might have become—like some of his contemporaries—a freelance Christian, seriously concerned about his personal salvation, yet only casually affiliated with a particular church. A decade later—after he had come to acknowledge the necessity of a visible church—he succinctly characterized the position of individualistic Christians:

> Had it so pleased God, each Christian might have been a Christian to himself alone—each Christian might have been required to look only to his own personal salvation, without concerning himself in the welfare of others.[5]

---

3   *Apo.*, 108.
4   *Apo.*, 108.
5   Sermon 157, "On the One Catholic and Apostolic Church" (November 19, 1826), in *Serm.* iv, 42–54 at 43; Newman numbered his Anglican sermons in the order in which he wrote them, not the order in which he delivered them; like many preachers, Newman sometimes revised and re-used previous sermons.

In tandem with his conversion, Newman read a variety of authors, whose spiritual influence continued during his Anglican years and even lifelong. For example, Newman appropriated Thomas Scott's emphasis on the "fundamental truth of religion" and "resolute opposition to Antinomianism."[6] Yet, unlike many evangelicals, Newman's "religious convictions" included belief in a definite creed; in particular, Joseph Milner's *History of the Church*[7] provided an introduction to "the religion of the primitive Christians." Simultaneously, from reading Thomas Newton's *Prophecies*,[8] Newman "became most firmly convinced that the pope was the Antichrist predicted by Daniel, St. Paul, and St. John."[9] Anti-papal prejudice was so deeply woven into the web and woof of nineteenth century English Protestantism that Newman had considerable difficulty in disentangling himself from its skeins.[10]

ORIEL COLLEGE (1822–1832):
"ONE HOLY CATHOLIC CHURCH"

On April 4, 1822, Newman was elected a fellow of Oriel College, then the most prestigious college in Oxford. As a fellow, Newman joined his colleagues in theological discussions about such topics as the nature of Christian revelation and the purpose of the church. Among the books that exerted an enduring influence on his ecclesiology was Bishop Butler's *The Analogy of Religion*:

> Its inculcation of a visible Church, the oracle of truth and a pattern of sanctity, of the duties of external religion, and of the historical character of Revelation, are characteristics of this great work which strike the reader at once.[11]

Newman also attended the lectures of the Regius Professor of Divinity, Charles Lloyd,[12] who characterized the Church of England as a direct descendant of the Apostolic Church and the sacraments as channels for communicating God's grace.

---

6 Thomas Scott (1747–1821), a founder of the Church Missionary Society, was described by Newman as the person "to whom (humanly speaking), I almost owe my soul" (*Apo*, 107). Antinomianism maintains that because believers live under divine grace, observance of the divine moral law is not necessary for their salvation; accordingly, Christians are not obliged to obey the commandments.

7 Joseph Milner (1744–1797) an Anglican evangelical, wrote a *History of the Church of Christ*.

8 The *Dissertations on the Prophecies* (1754) of Thomas Newton (1704–1782), Bishop of Bristol (1761–1782), portrayed the pope as anti-Christ.

9 *Apo.*, 110.

10 E. R. Norman, *Anti-Catholicism in Victorian England* (New York: Barnes and Noble, 1968).

11 *Apo.*, 113. Joseph Butler (1692–1752), Anglican Bishop of Bristol (1738–1750) and Durham (1750–1752), was the author of *Analogy of Religion, Natural and Revealed* (1736).

12 Charles Lloyd (1784–1829) was appointed Bishop of Oxford in 1827.

On June 13, 1824, Newman was ordained a deacon of the Church of England and began serving as curate at St. Clement's Church, a working-class parish at the edge of academic Oxford.[13] Newman's emerging "High Church"[14] views became evident in a sermon—"On the Use of the Visible Church"—preached at St. Clement's on December 4, 1825. He commented on the text—"The Church of the living God, the pillar and ground of the truth":

> By the expression, "church of God," is not only meant that general body of spiritual Christians who live by faith in their Saviour . . . —but also, that visible community which is regulated by certain laws, and directed by certain governors.[15]

Although only God can see the members of "the invisible or *unseen* church," in the case of "the visible church . . . we can actually discern its members—baptism is an ordinance we can see—the clergy, bishops and ministers are actually known by us to be such. . . ."[16] Newman emphasized that the visible church has "preserved our holy faith from being lost and given up" and that the apostles ordained their replacements whose succession has continued from generation to generation in order to "convey the saving truths of the Gospel to the next generation, and so on until the end of all that shall come."

At St. Clement's on November 19, 1826, Newman preached—"On the One Catholic and Apostolic Church."[17] Commenting on the "concluding words of St. Matthew's Gospel" (Mt 28:18–20), he emphasized that the "One Catholic and Apostolic Church" is an article of Christian faith, taught by both the Nicene and Apostles' Creed and asked rhetorically: what is this Church?

> By the *Church* in the Creeds is meant that visible Church in body and society instituted by Christ and His Apostles, professing the one faith of the Gospel, governed by certain officers and associated by certain laws, however the members of it may be divided by difference of country, language, manners or civilization.

---

13 At the time Newman served as deacon, St. Clement's Church was located on "The Plain" across Magdalen Bridge; that church was demolished in 1829, after a new church was built on Marston Road, about half a mile away.

14 The term "High Church" refers to Anglicans who interpret the *Thirty-Nine Articles* according to traditional catholic doctrines and celebrate the liturgy of *The Book of Common Prayer* with ceremonial formality.

15 Sermon 121: "On the Use of the Visible Church" (December 4, 1825) in *Serm.* iv, 28–34; the text is from 1 Tm 3:15.

16 Many evangelicals consider(ed) baptism an "ordinance" rather than a sacrament; during his early years as a fellow of Oriel College, Newman was persuaded by Pusey to accept baptism as a sacrament.

17 Sermon 157: "On the One Catholic and Apostolic Church" (November 19, 1826) in *Serm.* iv, 42–54; this sermon was one of Newman's first enunciations of High Church principles (*Serm.* iv, 42, no. 2).

Newman then enumerated four aspects of the Church's apostolic origins:

1. Christ instituted the Last Supper for the express purpose that His followers should meet *together* in remembrance of Him.
2. The one body of Christians that was formed by the apostles was governed by specific rulers appointed for the purpose—individuals whom St. Paul called *pillars*. These ministers—including Paul—were "formally ordained by the laying on of hands."
3. The visible body of the Church is regulated by laws and the apostles were invested with "power of spiritual censure."
4. Since apostolic times, there has existed a "systematic form of church government": (1) to preserve the Christian religion; (2) to preserve *purity of doctrine*; (3) to preserve Christian piety and holiness; and (4) to promote *order*.

Newman next discussed the Church's unity: the One Holy Apostolic Church, which was intended to continue as *one body* through the ages, has one branch in England, another in Scotland, still other branches in Ireland, France, Spain, Rome, Greece—"all members and descendants of that primitive church for which the Apostles laid down their lives." Lamenting the fact that many branches have fallen away from the faith and urging his congregation to pray for all branches of the church, he emphasized that the Church is a visible, public, outward church, a body of Christianity established by the apostles and continuing to the present, and he stressed that St. Paul condemned schism: God founded One Church, not many sects.

On January 28, 1827, Newman preached at St. Clement's "On the Mediatorial Kingdom of Christ." In contrast to the "divine Kingdom of Christ," which "is eternal, unbounded, absolute, independent of place or time," Christ's Mediatorial Kingdom is "a Kingdom over sinners whom He has redeemed and whom the Father has mercifully put into His hands for their final salvation;" Christ's Mediatorial Kingdom is "distinct from the general and Universal Kingdom of His Father."[18] Christ's Mediatorial Kingdom "is a Kingdom not over righteous men but over sinners."[19] Accordingly, "this Mediatorial Kingdom of Christ is not eternal, but for a time"—when "all people, nations and languages" recognize Christ, "then His Kingdom will close."[20] Newman concluded by urging the members of his congregation to partake of "the sacrament of the Lord's supper" as "subjects of His mediatorial Kingdom bound to Him by oaths of allegiance, grateful to Him for his mercy and suitor to Him for supplies of grace and comfort."[21]

---

18 Sermon 158: "On the Mediatorial Kingdom of Christ" (originally preached by Newman on December 25, 1826 at Brighton, where he was spending Christmas vacation, and repeated with a different ending at St. Clement's), *Serm.* i, 293–301 at 294–95.

19 *Serm.* i, 296.

20 *Serm.* i, 297–98.

21 Accordingly Newman bluntly admonished those of his congregation who left the service early and did not stay for communion (*Serm.* i, 299–301).

On April 15, 1827, Newman again preached "On the Mediatorial Kingdom of Christ"—this time in the Oriel College Chapel.[22] Newman pointed out that "On His resurrection from the dead He was no longer the man of sorrows and acquainted with grief, but the exalted Saviour of mankind, the one accepted and efficient Mediator between God and a sinful world"; just as Christ "was with His first disciples, so He is with us, and will be with His church, according to His promise . . . always, even unto the end of the world."[23] Newman then identified this Kingdom:

> The portion of mankind which he originally selected is called His church, the first fruits of His mediatorial Kingdom, the promise of His eventual triumph—over this He is already King, this He loves and justifies, for this He intercedes with the Father, this He governs, protects, disciplines, purifies by His Spirit, comforts, enlarges—till at length all nations shall flow into it, and the Kingdom of Satan shall be every where overthrown.[24]

Newman again emphasized that "the Mediatorial Kingdom of Christ is distinct from the absolute and eternal Kingdom of God the Creator"; this Kingdom is "*mediatorial and propitiatory*": "Christ *educates, purifies* those whom He takes out of the world for their future transference back again into the Kingdom of the Holy and Eternal God."[25] Accordingly, the "solemn judgment of mankind will be the last act of the Mediator."[26]

> Such then is the Kingdom of the Divine Mediator—a Kingdom over sinners for a gracious purpose to train and discipline them for the future enjoyment of heaven, a Kingdom in which He deigns to rejoice and glory, though nothing in reality can add to the *glory* or perfect *bliss* of that Infinite Being who is *over all* God *blessed* for ever.[27]

Recognizing that "the extension of Christ's Kingdom depends not wholly on His willingness, but partly on man," Newman was confident of "the slow but sure fulfillment of those prophecies which extend that Kingdom to the whole earth":[28]

---

22 Sermon 160: "On the Mediatorial Kingdom of Christ" (*Serm.* i, 329–43); Newman's statement that "the Son of God, as Mediator, *is inferior to the Father*" (*Serm.* i, 334) provoked stringent criticism from his Oriel colleagues, as indicated by the editorial additions to this sermon; Newman had made a similar statement in his previous sermon (158) on this topic (*Serm.* i, 297).

23 *Serm.* i, 330.

24 *Serm.* i, 331–32.

25 *Serm.* i, 333–34.

26 *Serm.* i, 338.

27 *Serm.* i, 338.

28 *Serm.* i, 338, 340.

And thus in spite of the manifold trials by which the church of God is visited, the attacks of open enemies, the teacher of false friends, the factions within, the defections of weak and misguided brethren, the errors of the good themselves, and the untimely loss of those who seem most adapted for its defense and extension, they learn practically to acquiesce in simple faith in the assurance of Christ, that all power *is* given to Him, that it is His *will* that His church should extend itself, and that He will be with His labourers in the good work always [sic] unto the end.[29]

Newman concluded this sermon by inviting his congregation to "the sacrament of the Lord's supper," where "we confess ourselves subjects of His Mediatorial Kingdom."[30]

THE CHURCH OF ENGLAND
AS *VIA MEDIA* (1833–1839)

During his first decade as a fellow of Oriel College, Newman described the visible church as one and apostolic. The church's apostolicity is evident in its celebration of the Eucharist and its hierarchical structure; the church's oneness is manifested by its branches in different places: not only England, Scotland, and Ireland— where there were churches of the Anglican Communion—but also Rome and Greece. This "branch theory," however, did not address the multiplicity of denominations nor the salvation of those outside the visible church. Newman needed to develop his idea of the Church both theologically and pastorally.

Following John Keble's Assize Sermon "National Apostasy" on July 14, 1833,[31] Newman, along with like-minded friends and colleagues, launched a campaign for religious renewal that came to be known as the *Oxford* or *Tractarian Movement*.[32] The Movement's main theological tenets were apostolic succession and ecclesial tradition, the renewal of church discipline and the universal call to Christian holiness, and the necessity of the sacraments and liturgical prayer. Along with his fellow "Oxford Conspirators," Newman employed a variety of means—sermons, lectures, conferences, essays, poetry, correspondence, and so on—to propagate this program of renewal.[33] One of his most notable endeavors was a series of *Tracts for the Times*.[34]

---

29 *Serm.* i, 340.
30 *Serm.* i, 340.
31 Keble's sermon, "National Apostasy," is available at: anglicanhistory.org/Keble/Keble1.html.
32 The term "Tractarian" was derived from the series of ninety *Tracts for the Times* (1833–1841), which were published, often anonymously, by participants in the Oxford Movement; the *Tracts* are available at: anglicanhistory.org/tracts/.
33 For a comprehensive view of the Oxford Movement, see Marvin O'Connell, *The Oxford Conspirators: A History of the Oxford Movement, 1833–45* (New York: Macmillan, 1969).
34 The *Tracts* attributed to Newman, who was the author of about one third of the

In *Tract* 2, "The Catholic Church" (September 9, 1833), after asking whether "the Clergy should abstain from politics," Newman pointed out "an unexceptionable sense in which a clergyman may, nay, must be political": "when the Nation interferes with the rights and possessions of the Church."[35] Such "an interference with things spiritual" is directly counter to Anglican belief in "The One Catholic and Apostolic Church":

> There is on earth an existing Society, Apostolic as founded by the Apostles, Catholic because it spreads its branches in every place; i.e. the Church Visible with its Bishops, Priests, and Deacons. And this surely *is* a most important doctrine; for what can be better news to the bulk of mankind than to be told that Christ when He ascended, did not leave us orphans, but appointed representatives of Himself to the end of time?[36]

In *Tract* 7, "The Episcopal Church Apostolical" (October 29, 1833), Newman criticized Presbyterian ministers because they "have presumed to exercise the power of ordination, and to perpetuate a succession of ministers, without having received a commission to do so":

> The Apostles appointed successors to their ministerial office and the latter in turn appointed others, and so on to the present day; and further that the Apostles and their Successors have in every age committed portions of their power and authority to others, who thus become their delegates, and in a measure their representatives, and are called Priests and Deacons.[37]

Newman then gave a three-point summary: (1) "the fact of the Apostolic Succession" is "too notorious to require proof"; (2) "the doctrine of a Succession" includes "a class of persons set apart from others for religious offices"; (3) "CHRIST promised He would be with His Apostles always, as ministers of His religion, even unto the end of the world."[38]

In *Tract* 11 (November 11, 1833), which took the form of two letters to a friend about "The Visible Church," Newman discussed his friend's claim that "The love of CHRIST is surely the one and only requisite for Christian communion here, and the joys of heaven hereafter."[39] In reply, Newman insisted that "the doctrine of 'the Church'" is "laid down *in Scripture*."[40] He emphasized that "the

---

Tracts, are available at: newmanreader.org/works/times/index.html; citations of Newman's *Tracts* are from this source.

   35   *Tract* 2, 1.
   36   *Tract* 2, 2–3.
   37   *Tract* 7, 1.
   38   *Tract* 7, 2–4.
   39   *Tract* 11, 1.
   40   *Tract* 11, 2.

Sacraments are evidently in the hands of the Church Visible," which "is not a voluntary association of the day, but a continuation of one which existed the age before us, . . . and so back till we come to the age of the Apostles."[41]

Acknowledging that God "might have left Christianity as a sort of sacred literature as contained in the Bible, which each person was to take and use by himself," Newman maintained that God "actually set up a Society, which exists even this day all over the world, and which (as a General rule) Christians are bound to join."[42] Comparing the Visible Church to a "Dispensary for medicine," he pointed out that "the Sacraments, which are the ordinary means of grace, are clearly in possession of the Church."[43]

In *Tract* 20, "The Visible Church" (December 24, 1833), Newman published a third letter to his anonymous friend. Apparently concerned that his friend might equate the Visible Church with "Papistical corruptions of the Gospel,"[44] Newman insisted that diminishing "the Divine Authority of our Apostolical Church" would be "plainly preparing the way for Popery in our land."[45] In contrast, God "has wonderfully preserved our [Anglican] Church as a true branch of the Church Universal, yet withal preserved it free from doctrinal error"; the Church of England "is Catholic and Apostolic, yet not Papistical;" accordingly, union with the Church of Rome is "IMPOSSIBLE. Their communion is infected with heterodoxy; we are bound to flee it, as a pestilence"; "Popery must be destroyed; it cannot be reformed." [46]

In a companion piece, *Tract* 19, "On Arguing Concerning the Apostolical Succession" (December 23, 1833), Newman discussed the scriptural basis for "the necessity of Episcopal Ordination, in order to constitute a Minister of Christ."[47] He contrasted his "argument for the Apostolical Succession" from "the ordination of St. Paul and St. Barnabas" (Acts 13:2–3) with the claim that "their ordination might have been an accidental rite, intended merely to commission them for their Missionary journey"; similarly, rejecting the claim that "St. Paul's direction to Timothy" to "lay hands suddenly on no man" might "refer to confirmation, not ordination," Newman insisted that "ordination has ever been thought necessary in the Church for the Ministerial Commission."[48]

Tract 47, Newman's fourth letter on "The Visible Church" (November 1, 1834), dealt with his friend's concern that Newman was implying that "Dissenters are without the pale of salvation."[49] Instead, while insisting that "Protestant sects

41 *Tract* 11, 3.
42 *Tract* 11, 4–5.
43 *Tract* 11, 5–6.
44 *Tract* 20, 1.
45 *Tract* 20, 4.
46 *Tract* 20, 3.
47 *Tract* 19, 1.
48 *Tract* 19, 2.
49 *Tract* 47, 2.

are not 'in CHRIST,' in the same fullness that we [Anglicans] are," he did not exclude Dissenters from the possibility of salvation.[50]

Earlier, in *Tract 31*, "The Reformed Church" (April 25, 1834), Newman compared the Church of England with "the state of the Jews after the captivity": just as those Jews were "at length through GOD'S mercy . . . brought back again from Babylon," similarly, "the Christian Church was, in the beginning, set up in unity; unity of doctrine, or *truth*, unity of discipline, or *Catholicism*, unity of heart, or *charity*."[51] Newman seemingly had little doubt that the prophecies of the past applied to the present; nonetheless, if it seemed "as if the Church were already dead, new forms of organization, multiplied varieties of life and action show themselves within her."[52]

Tract 38 (June 25, 1834), the first of two tracts on the *Via Media*, was a dialogue between *Laicus* and *Clericus*. *Laicus* began the conversation by observing that "the world accuses you of Popery."[53] *Clericus* was willing to concede a resemblance between his views of the Church and "the Popish system" on the grounds that "all corruptions of the truth must be like the truth which they corrupt," but asked rhetorically: "Are you quite sure we do not need A SECOND REFORMATION?"[54]

Laicus questioned the need for reform, since the Church of England has "Articles and a Liturgy, which keeps us from deviating from the standard of truth set up in the sixteenth century."[55] *Clericus* responded that many a "Churchman of this day has deviated from the opinions of our Reformers, and has become more opposed than they were to the system they protested against." *Clericus* then asserted: "The glory of the English Church is, that it has taken the VIA MEDIA, as it has been called. It lies between the (so called) Reformers and Romanists."[56] *Clericus* emphasized that the Reformers did not wish to reject "the doctrines which the Apostles spoke in Scripture and impressed upon the early Church."[57] While some of these doctrines were mentioned in the *Thirty-Nine Articles*, "there are many other doctrines unmentioned, only because they were not then disputed by either party."[58]

This discussion about the *Via Media* was resumed in *Tract 41* (August 24, 1834), where *Clericus* pointed out that "ignorance of our historical position as

---

50 *Tract* 47, 3. "Dissenters" included a broad range of Christians—Baptists, Presbyterians, Quakers, *et al.*—who refused to subscribe to the *Thirty-Nine Articles* of the Church of England and attended religious services in their own chapels or meeting houses.

51 *Tract* 31, 1.

52 *Tract* 31, 4.

53 *VM* ii, 21. Newman republished *Tracts* 38 and 41 in the second volume of his *Via Media*; this republication included Newman's comments and corrections.

54 *VM* ii, 21, 23.

55 *VM* ii, 23.

56 *VM* ii, 28.

57 *VM* ii, 31.

58 *VM* ii, 32–33.

Churchmen is one of the especial evils of the day."[59] *Laicus* pressed for further explanation about "the need of a *second Reformation*."[60] *Clericus* responded: "the Church . . . should not *change* the Articles, she should *add* to them; add protests against the erastianism and latitudiarianism which have encrusted them."[61] After *Clericus* listed various abuses in the Church of England, *Laicus* admitted that "as time goes on, fresh and fresh articles of faith are necessary to secure the Church's purity, according to the rise of successive heresies and errors."[62] *Laicus* also acknowledged that "the doctrines of the Church Catholic . . . are quite consistent with our Articles" but pressed for a description of "Protestantism"[63]—which *Clericus* described as:

> The religion of so-called freedom and independence, as hating superstition, suspicious of forms, jealous of priestcraft, advocating heart-worship; characteristics, which admit of a good or a bad interpretation, but which understood as they are instanced in the majority of persons who are zealous for what is called Protestant doctrine, are (I maintain) very inconsistent with the Liturgy of our Church.[64]

After pointing out that "the innovating spirit of this day" was resulting in "the comparative neglect of the details of duty," dropping "articles of faith and positive and ceremonial observance, as beneath the attention of a spiritual Christian, as monastic and superstitious, as forms, as minor points, as technical, lip-worship, narrow-minded, and bigoted," *Clericus* reiterated his conviction of the need for a Second Reformation.[65]

In addition to his tracts concerning the Church, Newman gave a series of lectures that were collectively published as *Lectures on the Prophetical Office of the Church viewed relatively to Romanism and popular Protestantism* (1837).[66] The "formal purpose" of these lectures was "the establishment of a doctrine of its own, the Anglican *Via Media*"; nonetheless these lectures were "'more or less' directed against points in [Roman] Catholic teaching."[67] While "Romanists have

---

59 *VM* ii, 35.

60 *VM* ii, 35.

61 *VM* ii, 38. Erastianism is the doctrine that the State has absolute authority over the Church; Latitudinarianism is the doctrine that Church teachings can be given a very broad interpretation.

62 *VM* ii, 40.

63 *VM* ii, 40.

64 *VM* ii, 41–42.

65 *VM* ii, 46.

66 For a detailed discussion of Newman's *Lectures on the Prophetical Office* (*VM* i), see Joseph Elamparayil, "John Henry Newman's 'Lectures on the Prophetical Office of the Church': A Contextual History and Ecclesiological Analysis" (unpublished PhD Diss., The Catholic University of America, 2012).

67 "Preface to the Third Edition," §1.1, *VM* i, xv.

ever insisted upon" the importance of the Church, "Protestants have neglected it" in spite of the fact that the Creed "binds them to faith 'in the Holy Catholic Church.'"[68] Accordingly, Newman not only tried to trace "the supposed evils which come of the doctrine of Infallibility" and other Roman Catholic doctrines such as purgatory, he also criticized "the abuse of Private Judgment," while candidly confessing "the shortcomings and reverses of the Anglican Establishment."[69]

THE CHURCH OF THE APOSTLES TODAY
(1840-1845)

Newman's *Lectures on the Prophetical Office* were an ambitious but flawed project; as he later acknowledged: "Protestantism and Popery are real religions . . . but the *Via Media* . . . has scarcely any existence, except on paper."[70] His effort to construct an Anglican ecclesiology midway between alleged Roman Catholic distortions and purported Protestant diminutions had two flaws: (1) theologically, he could not prove that the Anglican communion was an integral part of the One Church, on the ground of its teaching being Apostolic, without simultaneously acknowledging Roman Catholicism as part of the One Church; (2) personally, a series of events convinced him that instead of being a *Via Media* between Roman Catholicism and Protestantism, the Church of England was Protestant at its core. Prominent among these events was the popular reaction against his *Tract* 90, "Remarks on certain Passages of the Thirty-nine Articles" (1841), which attempted to show that the *Thirty-Nine Articles*—the official doctrinal statement of the Church of England—could be interpreted in a Catholic sense.

The outcry against *Tract* 90 was overwhelming: Anglican bishops condemned it in their official diocesan letters; Oxford clerics criticized it in their sermons and publications; the popular press published vociferous criticisms: Newman felt relentlessly pursued. It became abundantly clear to him that "there are but two alternatives, the way to Rome, and the way to Atheism: Anglicanism is the halfway house on the one side, and Liberalism is the halfway house on the other."[71]

Yet becoming a Roman Catholic was not an easy decision. For years, Newman had criticized Roman doctrines as unscriptural and described "papistical" devotions as superstitious; his anti-papalism was "almost a *consensus* of the divines of my Church."[72] In addition, he gradually came to the "deep,

---

68 §1.1, *VM* i, xxiv.
69 §1.2, *VM* i, xviii–xix.
70 §1.4, *VM* i, xxiv.
71 *Apo.*, 266.
72 "Retraction of Anti-Catholic Statements," *VM* ii, 427–33.

unvarying conviction that our Church is in schism, and that my salvation depends on my joining the Church of Rome."[73] While acknowledging that the "state of the Roman Catholics is at present so unsatisfactory," he felt that "nothing but a simple, direct call of duty is a warrant for any one leaving our Church"; his "simple question" was:

> Can *I* (it is personal, not whether another, but can *I*) be saved in the English Church? am *I* in safety, were I to die to-night? Is it a mortal sin in *me*, not joining another communion?[74]

Newman imaginatively asked: if Ambrose or Augustine came to Oxford, which church would they attend? He gradually came to the conclusion that Roman Catholicism is an authentic development of the Primitive Church.

CHURCH: HIERARCHY AND LAITY
(1846-1863)

After Newman entered the Roman Catholic Church, one might assume that his ecclesiological positions were determined for the rest of his life; as he stated in his *Apologia* (1864):

> From the time that I became a Catholic, of course I have no further history of my religious opinions to narrate. In saying this, I do not mean to say that my mind has been idle, or that I have given up thinking on theological subjects; but that I have had no variations to record, and have had no anxiety of heart whatever.[75]

In fact, this statement was stretching matters: just five years earlier, he had unexpectedly become embroiled in a controversy about the role of the laity in the Church.[76]

The immediate issue was government inspection of Catholic schools in view of receiving state subsidies. Some felt that Catholic schools should cooperate not only to receive government funding but also to benefit from educational expertise; moreover, Catholic cooperation would be a sign of good citizenship. Other Catholics—and eventually this became the position of the English hierarchy—felt that government supervision would effectively allow Protestant officials to supervise instruction in Catholic schools.

---

73 *Apo.*, 319.
74 *Apo.*, 322.
75 *Apo.*, 331.
76 *Cons.*, 1–49 (introduction by John Coulson).

One venue for this debate was *The Rambler,* a lay-owned and lay-edited journal, which occasionally was critical of ecclesiastical authority. Newman, a friend of the editors, wanted to see the journal continue, since it was a unique voice of the educated Catholic laity in England. When the bishops seemed on the verge of condemning the journal, Newman, at the urging of his bishop, reluctantly agreed to accept the editorship as a way of salvaging the situation. À propos of the controversy about state supervision of elementary education, Newman anonymously editorialized:

> Acknowledging, then, most fully the prerogatives of the episcopate, we do unfeignedly believe, both from the reasonableness of the matter, and especially from the prudence, gentleness, and considerateness which belong to them personally, that their Lordships [the English bishops] really desire to know the opinion of the laity on subjects in which the laity are especially concerned. If even in the preparation of a dogmatic definition the faithful are consulted, as lately in the instance of the Immaculate Conception, it is at least as natural to anticipate such an act of kind feeling and sympathy in great practical questions, out of the condescension which belongs to those who are *forma facti gregis ex animo* [made a pattern of the flock from the heart].[77]

In this passage, Newman maintained: (1) the bishops should consult the laity about the future of Catholic schools and (2) such consultation was ecclesiologically warranted, because Pope Pius IX—prior to the definition of the Immaculate Conception (December 8, 1854)—had mandated a world-wide investigation to ascertain whether the proposed dogma was really a belief of Catholics.

Nonetheless, Newman's editorial comment became so controversial that he felt constrained to reply with an essay "On Consulting the Faithful in Matters of Doctrine." After discussing the meaning of "consult," he focused on the central issue: "the body of the faithful is one of the witnesses to the fact of the tradition of revealed doctrine, and because their *consensus* through Christendom is the voice of the Infallible Church":

> The tradition of the Apostles, committed to the whole Church in its various constituents and functions *per modum unius* [as a unit], manifests itself variously at various times: sometimes by the mouth of the episocopcy [sic], sometimes by the doctors [teachers of the church], sometimes by the people, sometimes by liturgies, rites, ceremonies, and customs, by events, disputes, movements, and all those other phenomena which are comprised under the name of history.[78]

---

77 *Cons.,* 13; the Latin text is 1 Pt 5:3.
78 *Cons.,* 63.

As precedent, Newman pointed to Pius IX, who prior to the proclamation of the Immaculate Conception sought "the ascertainment of the feeling of the faithful both towards the doctrine and its definition." The rationale for such consultation had previously been well expressed by Bishop Bernard Ullathorne of Birmingham:

> And it is the devout who have the surest instinct in discerning the mysteries of which the Holy Spirit breathes the grace through the Church, and who, with as sure a fact, reject what is alien from her teaching.[79]

For Newman, the critical issue was that there is something in the "pastorum et fidelium *conspiratio*," which is not in the pastors alone."[80]

A dozen years later, Newman included a revised version of "On Consulting" in a new edition of *The Arians of the Fourth Century* and re-asserted his position:

> The episcopate . . . did not . . . play a good part in the troubles conse-quent upon the Council [of Nicaea]; and the laity did. The Catholic people, in the length and breadth of Christendom, were the obstinate champions of Catholic truth and the bishops were not.[81]

THE MAGISTERIUM OF THE CHURCH
(1864-1878)

Following the favorable reception of his *Apologia* (1865), Newman began repub-lishing many of his Anglican works. In 1877, the fortieth anniversary of its orig-inal appearance, he republished *On the Prophetical Office of the Church* with a new preface. In addition to apologizing for his anti-Roman statements in the original volume, he raised a neuralgic pastoral issue: why do some people—who "see the Catholic Religion a great substance and earnest of truth; a depth, strength, coherence, elasticity, and life, a nobleness and grandeur, a power of sympathy and resource in view of the various ailments of the soul, and a suitable-ness to all classes and circumstances of mankind"—not embrace Catholicism?[82]

In Newman's judgment, one major cause for this reluctance is the differ-ence between the Church's "formal teaching and its popular and political manifesta-tions."[83] The Church's "organization cannot be otherwise than complex, considering

---

79 *Cons.*, 73.

80 *Cons.*, 104: "pastorum et fidelium *conspiratio* literally means the '*breathing together* of pastors and faithful.'"

81 *Cons.*, 109.

82 *VM* i, xxxvi.

83 *VM* i, xxxvii. Newman addressed his other major concern—the contrast between "modern Catholicism" and "the religion of the Primitive Church"—in his *Essay on the Development of Christian Doctrine* (1845).

the many functions which she has to fulfil, the many aims to keep in view, the many interests to secure."[84] The Church's challenge is like the difficulty of finding "one and the same man to satisfy independent duties and incommensurable relations; to act at once as a parent and a judge, as a soldier and a minister of religion, as a philosopher and a statesman, as a courtier or a politician and a Catholic."[85] As a result, the Church's "rulers and authorities, as men, on certain occasions have come short of what was required of them, and have given occasion to criticism, just or unjust, on account of the special antagonisms or compromises by means of which her many-sided mission under their guidance has been carried out."[86]

In spite of such human shortcomings, Christ "left His representative behind Him. This was Holy Church, His mystical Body and Bride, a Divine Institution, and the shrine and organ of the Paraclete, who speaks through her till the end comes."[87] Accordingly, Christ entrusted His Church with His own offices of "Prophet, Priest, and King"—"three offices, which are indivisible, though diverse, viz. teaching, rule, and sacred ministry":

> Christianity, then, is at once a philosophy, a political power, and a religious rite: as a religion, it is Holy; as a philosophy, it is Apostolic; as a political power, it is imperial, that is, One and Catholic. As a religion, its special centre of action is pastor and flock; as a philosophy, the Schools; as a rule the Papacy and its Curia.[88]

For Newman, it is not only a challenge for the Church to discharge each of these three offices one by one, it is much more difficult to exercise these offices in harmony. Accordingly, God granted the Church "infallibility in her formal teaching," thereby protecting her "from serious error in worship and political action also."[89] Nonetheless, infallibility "does not secure her from all dangers"; "nothing but the gift of impeccability" would secure the Church's authorities from all mistakes, but "such a gift they have not received."[90] Accordingly, "there may indeed be holiness in the religious aspect of the Church, and soundness in her theological, but still there is in her the ambition, craft, and cruelty of a political power."[91]

Newman insisted that "Theology is the fundamental and regulating principle of the whole Church system":

---

84   *VM* i, xxxviii.
85   *VM* i, xxxviii–xxxix.
86   *VM* i, xxxix.
87   *VM* i, xl.
88   *VM* i, xl.
89   *VM* i, xli–xlii.
90   *VM* i, xliii.
91   *VM* i, xlvi.

It is commensurate with Revelation, and Revelation is the initial and essential idea of Christianity. It is the subject-matter, the formal cause, the expression, of the Prophetical Office, and, as being such, has created both the Regal Office and the Sacerdotal.[92]

Yet if theology is a restraining force, it has not always been able to curtail popes who "under secular inducements of the moment seem from time to time to have been wishing, though unsuccessfully, to venture beyond the lines of theology"; nor has theology been able to prevent "the faithful against putting trust in certain idle prophecies" or participating in questionable devotions.[93] In fact, it has been impossible to prevent "the theological and religious element of the Church being in antagonism with the political."[94]

Although "truth is the principle on which all intellectual, and therefore all theological inquiries proceed, and is the motive power which gives them effect," Newman recognized that "Novelty is often error to those who are unprepared for it."[95] Selecting a controversial case, Newman commented:

Galileo might be right in his conclusion that the earth moves; to consider him a heretic might have been wrong; but there was nothing wrong in censuring abrupt, startling, unsettling, unverified disclosures, if such they were, disclosures at once uncalled for and inopportune, at a time when the limits of revealed truth had not as yet been ascertained. A man ought to be very sure of what he is saying, before he risks the chance of contradicting the word of God.[96]

For Newman, "Veracity, like other virtues, lies in a mean"[97]: sometimes "it is the worst charity, and the most provoking, irritating rule of action, and the most unhappy policy, not to speak out, not to suffer to be spoken out, all that there is to say,"[98] especially when "concealment, accommodation, and evasion is to co-operate with the spirit of error."[99] However, "a proposition may be ever so true, yet at a particular time and place may be 'temerarious, offensive to pious ears, and scandalous,' though not 'heretical' nor 'erroneous.'"[100]

---

92   *VM* i, xlvii.
93   *VM* i, xlix.
94   *VM* i, li.
95   *VM* i, li–lii.
96   *VM* i, liv–lv.
97   *VM* i, lix; the Aristotelian principle—*virtus in medio stat*—was adopted by the Scholastics.
98   *VM* i, lvii.
99   *VM* i, lvi.
100   *VM* i, lvi; the phrase "temerarious, offensive to pious ears, and scandalous" was used in Vatican documents in the nineteenth century to categorize theological views that were considered erroneous, though not heretical.

Another case in point was the veneration of relics. Newman envisioned a situation in which a prelate might permit a popular devotion, even though "he is not sure it is true, and he does not guarantee its truth; he does but approve and praise the devotional enthusiasm of the people, which the legendary fact has awakened."[101] For Newman, it is difficult "to determine the point at which such religious manifestations become immoderate, and an allowance of them wrong; it would be well, if all suspicious facts could be got rid of altogether."[102] For Newman, there is a fundamental contrast between the teaching of the Church in matters of faith and its tolerance of popular devotions.

Turning to "the regal office of the Church," Newman pointed out that there are "instances in which the imperial and political expedience of religion stands out prominent, and both its theological and devotional duties are in the background."[103] After reviewing several "collisions and compromises" between the Regal and Prophetical offices of the Church," he asserted that "no act could be theologically an error, which was absolutely and undeniably necessary for the unity, sanctity, and peace of the Church."[104] It is "inconceivable" that Christ "intended that that the action of any one of her [the Church's] functions should be the destruction of another."[105]

Invoking the principle that "whatever is great refuses to be reduced to human rule, and to be made consistent in its many aspects with itself," Newman concluded his preface:

> We need not feel surprise then, if Holy Church too, the supernatural creation of God, is an instance of the same law, presenting to us an admirable consistency and unity in word and deed, as her general characteristic, but crossed and discredited now and then by apparent anomalies which need, and which claim, at our hands an exercise of faith.[106]

CONCLUSION

Just as concert audiences recognize the repeated *leitmotiv* of musical compositions, readers can recognize recurring ecclesiological themes in Newman's writings. As a teenager, he "fell under the influences of a definite Creed"[107] and began a lifelong pursuit of "Holiness." "Holiness," however, initially seems to have been more a personal spiritual journey than a commitment to the Church. Yet, once he began preaching as an Anglican cleric, "holiness" assumed an

---

101 *VM* i, lxv.
102 *VM* i, lvi.
103 *VM* i, lxxix.
104 *VM* i, lxxxiii.
105 *VM* i, lxxxvi.
106 *VM* i, xciv.
107 *Apo.*, 107.

ecclesial dimension: Christ calls people to holiness through the Church. Simultaneously, in his sermons, there was a growing emphasis on the apostolicity and sacramentality of the Church: Christ entrusted the sacramental means for achieving holiness to His apostles, who in turn entrusted these means of salvation to their successors in the Church. Through the sacraments of baptism and the Eucharist, Christians have access to the channels of holiness that are part of the Church's apostolic legacy.

Yet, if the Church's holiness and apostolicity became regular features of Newman's Anglican preaching, the Church's oneness and catholicity were problematic. He initially described different denominations as branches of the one Church; however, his "branch theory" faltered in the face of facts: most denominations claimed to be the only true church and refused to recognize their rivals as churches—not branches of the same vine. Newman then proposed an innovative hypothesis: the Church of England as the *Via Media* between Protestantism and Romanism. This hypothesis was torpedoed by a series of events that indicated that the Church of England was popularly Protestant. Yet Newman could not opt for Rome simply by default; a decisive question needed to be answered: what is the relationship of the Roman Catholic Church to the Apostolic Church? His eventual response was that the Roman Catholic Church is an authentic development of the Apostolic Church.[108]

Although Newman described entering the Roman Catholic Church "like coming into port after a rough sea,"[109] he felt "called" to address other important ecclesiological questions, particularly, the respective roles of laity and hierarchy. On the one hand, the laity are recipients of a *sensus fidei* at baptism—a divine gift enabling them to understand the Gospel and to reject its misrepresentations. On the other hand, the bishops as teachers of apostolic doctrine need to "consult" the *sensus fidelium* as part of their episcopal mission of teaching.

Envisioning the Church as exercising the three offices (*munera*) of Christ—Prophet, Priest, and King—Newman attempted to delineate both the prerogatives and the limitations of the ecclesial exercise of these offices. Although affording primacy to the prophetic office in teaching the doctrine of Christ, Newman candidly admitted that there have been occasions when the Church was reluctant, even unwilling, to acknowledge genuine doctrinal developments. Although the Church is responsible for exercising the offices of Christ the Mediator, the Church includes sinful human beings, who have frequently failed to exercise these offices in a Christ-like way.

---

108 At the time when Newman wrote his *Essay on the Development of Christian Doctrine* (1845), "doctrinal development" was an innovative theological idea; for a comprehensive discussion of Newman's *Essay on Development*, see Gerard McCarren, "'Tests' or 'Notes'? A Critical Evaluation of the Criteria for Genuine Doctrinal Development in John Henry Newman's Essay on the Development of Christian Doctrine" (PhD Diss., The Catholic University of America, 1998).

109 *Apo.*, 331.

In retrospect, Newman's ecclesiology began with an evangelical individualism that eventually metamorphosed into an ecclesial personalism, whose key elements were apostolic teaching, hierarchical government, and sacramental system. Nonetheless, various existential tensions prevail between these elements. Readers today should be both fascinated and encouraged by Newman's ecclesiological writings: fascinated by the way he conscientiously confronted the critical ecclesiological questions of his time and encouraged to follow his example by dealing with today's pressing ecclesiological problems.

Suggested Readings

Marr, Ryan. *To Be Perfect is to Have Changed Often*. Lanham, Md.: Fortress Academic, 2018.
Miller, Edward. *John Henry Newman on the Idea of the Church*. Shepherdstown, W. Va.: Patmos, 1987.
Misner, Paul. *Papacy and Development*. Leiden: E. J. Brill, 1976.
Nédoncelle, Maurice, ed. *L'Ecclésiologie au XIXe siècle*. Unam Sanctam 34. Paris: Cerf, 1960.
Norris, Thomas J. *Newman and His Theological Method*. Leiden: E. J. Brill, 1977.
Phan, Peter C., ed. *The Gift of the Church*. Collegeville, Minn.: Liturgical Press, 2000.

CHAPTER 26

NEWMAN'S FARSIGHTED UNDERSTANDING OF THE LAITY'S ROLE IN THE CHURCH

Fr. Juan R. Vélez

I n 1867 Msgr. George Talbot, papal chamberlain, wrote Cardinal Henry Manning a letter about Newman and his article *On Consulting the Faithful in Matters of Doctrine* (1859), which Bishop Brown of Newport had denounced to the Holy See. Talbot's letter serves to frame a study on Newman's view of the laity. The English prelate wrote: "It is perfectly true that a cloud has been hanging over Dr. Newman and that none of his writings since have removed the cloud." The laity "are beginning to show the cloven hoof. . . . They are only putting into practice the doctrine taught by Dr. Newman in his article in the *Rambler*." Talbot then asked his celebrated question: "What is the province of the laity? To hunt, to shoot, to entertain. These matters they understand, but to meddle with ecclesiastical matters they have no right at all, and this affair of Newman is a matter purely ecclesiastical. . . ."[1]

John Henry Newman's work corrects Talbot's mistaken vision, typical of nineteenth century ecclesiastics. By means of his teaching and interactions with laymen, Newman contributed to a better understanding of the vocation of the laity in the Church. This chapter briefly looks at some influences Newman received as an Anglican at Oxford and later as a Catholic living in Birmingham.

---

1   *Cons.*, 41.

After considering Newman's teaching on the laity, taken from his own writings, the chapter will then examine the development of doctrine on the laity by twentieth century writers Josemaría Escrivá and Yves M. Congar, and also the Magisterium, suggesting how some elements were already present in Newman's thinking.

Newman's vision of the Church, as noted by Ian Ker, was foremost that of a body of the baptized rather than that of a hierarchical body composed of clergy and laity.[2] In that body there are certainly clergy and laity, but Newman's emphasis is on the baptismal vocation of the believer and the believer's discipleship of Christ. In his writings Newman wrote more in terms of "Christians," the "faithful" and "witnesses."[3] By doing so he highlighted the common condition of the faithful Christian (*Christifideles*) that Vatican II would later teach in *Lumen Gentium*: "Everything that has been said above concerning the People of God is intended for the laity, religious and clergy alike."[4] While this is valid of Newman's way of looking at the Church as a whole, he saw much of his mission in life as the education of laymen; and so we must ask: What did Newman think was proper to the laity and what role does the laity exercise in the Church? His views on this subject can be gleaned from his sermons and letters, his work and writings on education, and his article "On Consulting the Faithful in Matters of Doctrine."[5]

Before exploring Newman's thought, it is helpful to look at the historical use of the term "laity." This word comes from the Greek *laikos* derived from *laos* (people) and was used to refer to members of the people of God, who are not clergy and have the characteristic of secularity.[6] The terminology was used by St. Clement of Rome in the first century and its usage extended into the second century. Until the third or fourth century, the dual distinction of laity and clergy was used; then beginning with the fifth we find the triad: laity, clergy, and monks. From this time on the term laity was used to refer to the secular work of laity.[7] Later on the clergy and monks are assimilated so that the distinction is again dual: clergy-monks and laity, men dedicated to worship and those dedicated to the world. The historical evolution of these concepts is problematic; and it is not until the twentieth century that these concepts have gradually been addressed from both theological and canonical perspectives. Misunderstandings of these roles presented several errors. One of the errors was the consideration that as a concession to human weakness the laity were inferior to those in a state of perfection; and another was the notion that the vocation to holiness was primarily for priests and members of religious orders.

---

2   Ian Ker, *Newman on Vatican II* (Oxford: Clarendon Press, 2014), 104–5.

3   For instance, see *PS* iii, no. 17: 242.

4   Vatican Council II, *Lumen Gentium* (November 21, 1964), 30.

5   Keith Beaumont, *Comprendre John Henry Newman: Vie et pensée d'un maître et témoin spirituel* (Le Coudray-Macouard: Saint-Léger Editions, 2015), 157–72.

6   Ignace de la Potterie, "L'origine et le sens primitif du mot 'laïc,'" *Nouvelle Revue Théologique* 80 (1958): 840–53.

7   Ramiro Pellitero, *La teología del laicado en la obra de Yves Congar* (Pamplona: Servicio de Publicaciones de la Universidad de Navarra, 1996), 55–56, 146.

As becomes evident upon examination, the role of the laity in the Church has varied significantly from the primitive Church, to Trent, and to Vatican II. St. Paul in his letter to the Romans taught that the Christians form the body of Christ in an organic unity (1 Cor 12:12–31) that has Christ as its head. Paul appointed elders through the laying on of hands to teach or hand on the tradition, administer the sacraments, and govern the communities of believers. At the end of the first and start of the second centuries we find in the letters of St. Ignatius of Antioch a clear mention of bishops (*episkopoi*) overseeing the Christian communities of Asia Minor and of the primacy of the bishop of Rome.[8]

The early Church had members pertaining to many different occupations and classes, and laymen were an active part of the Christian apostolate.[9] Among the martyrs we find many laymen and women. With the rise and growth of monastic orders, the number of priests and religious brothers grew as did their importance in the Church. Talented men such as Ambrose, Augustine, and Hilary of Poitiers were chosen from among the laity to be ordained priests and appointed as bishops. As the authority of bishops increased and the Church government filled the void left by the fall of the Roman Empire in the West, as well as the multiplication of religious communities, there began a clericalization of the Church. The natural talent and selection of intelligent laymen for the priesthood favored an increase in the authority granted to clergymen.

Moving into the Middle Ages, the term "lay" was identified with secular power, and the term "cleric" was identified with ecclesiastical work. In neither the early Church nor during the Middle Ages was there a theological reflection on the laity.[10] With the passage of time, the term laity became increasingly associated with a negative judgment because of the perceived incompatibility between holiness and living in the world, and the perception of a passive reception of the sacraments, which led to a failure of appreciation for the laymen's active responsibility in the Church's mission. From the sixteenth century forward, the Church was seen more in juridical terms,[11] and the institutional and hierarchical dimension of the Church was emphasized in response to the Protestant Reformation. The latter rejected the sacramental orders, but in doing so, revindicated the common priesthood of the faithful.

The *devotio moderna* in the Low Countries (beginning in the fourteenth century), guilds, third orders and movements in Italy, France, Spain, and the teaching of saints such as St. Philip Neri and St. Francis de Sales, contributed to the formation and spiritual life of the laity. This served as a counterbalance to the Protestant movement. But it was in the twentieth century that a significant

---

8 Johannes Quasten, *Patrology*, vol. 1 (Westminster, Md.: Christian Classics Inc., 1990), 66–70, and *TT* 125–26.

9 *Letter to Diognetus*, nn. 5–6, quoted in Quasten, *Patrology*, vol. 1, 250–51.

10 Pellitero, *La teología del laicado*, 57.

11 Pellitero, *La teología del laicado*, 57.

rediscovery of the position of the laity in the Church took place and a theology of the laity was elaborated.

Theologian Ramiro Pellitero indicates four motives for a reassessment in the twentieth century of the term and concept of laity: 1. The need to face a growing dechristianization of society led to a reflection on the laity; 2. The liturgical movement's understanding of the members of the Church; 3. A renewal of Christian spirituality underlying the possibility of holiness in the world and leading to the proclamation of the universal call to holiness by Vatican II; and 4. A response by the Church to liberalism, which sought to reduce religion to the sphere of the private.[12]

Newman's reading of history made him familiar with the historical framework outlined above and thus made him able to consider the laity in the Church in a different light. Furthermore, since he grew up as an Anglican and lived among educated laymen at Oxford, this gave him a firsthand understanding of the laity's contribution to the life and teaching of the Church.

OXFORD'S INFLUENCE

As a student at Trinity College and afterwards as tutor at Oriel, Newman met and interacted with educated laymen and clergymen. Although Oxford and Cambridge had many clergymen and prepared men to take orders in the Anglican Church, these centers of education were not seminaries. Newman was surrounded by laymen who later served in government, law, business, and other civil professions. He was thus in a community of educated persons who were or would later be leaders in society and in the Anglican Church.

Prior to this and during his first years at Oxford, Newman was inspired by devout Evangelicals, beginning with Walter Mayers, Classics master at the school at Ealing, and also Thomas Scott of Aston Sandford, author of *Force of Truth*. There was a host of others such as William Romaine, Joseph Milner, and John Bird Sumner, whose books taught the young Newman various religious truths. The influence of these men and many others on Newman has not been studied in any depth, and the information about their effect on Newman has relied on Newman's brief and selective autobiographical references to them.[13] The sincere and earnest love for God, the missionary zeal, and the social concern of these Evangelicals were an early example for him of devout Christian living. The Wilberforce family whom he befriended exemplified for him this Evangelical way of living. Newman thus drew a lasting influence from his Evangelical friends, but he would gradually part from the ecclesiology, fundamental theology, sacramental theology, and eschatology of his first teachers and friends.

---

12 Pellitero, *La teología de laicado*, 58.

13 Gareth Atkins, "Evangelicals," in *The Oxford Handbook of John Henry Newman,* ed. Frederick D. Aquino and Benjamin J. King (Oxford: Oxford University Press, 2018), 173–95.

Newman's circle of friends and acquaintances included members of the Oxford Missionary Society Association and the Bible Society. During his undergraduate years Newman wrote some articles for an encyclopedia and published a few letters in the *Record*, an Evangelical publication. While at Oriel College, his religious beliefs changed and he began to write some articles for The *British Critic*, a conservative and High Church review founded in 1792. In 1836 he began to provide writers for the *Critic* and became its editor from 1838 to 1841. During those years until 1843 the journal was dominated by the Tractarian views, and its scope became more narrowly theological. Newman and Thomas Mozley, his brother-in-law, edited the journal successively until it closed in 1843.

Newman's involvement in the *British Critic* indicates his acceptance and interest in priests and laity, writing and debating on theological and cultural matters, and the latitude he allowed his contributors.[14] Years later, however, he encouraged the editor of the *Rambler* to steer away from articles on theology since he considered journals an inadequate place for these discussions and wished to avoid any animosity with the hierarchy.[15] Both as an Anglican and later as a Catholic, Newman was opposed to lay people "doing" theology because he thought that they would only be amateur theologians, since there existed no place or means for them to obtain a sound theological formation. He explained to his friend J. M. Capes, who was proprietor of the *Rambler* and at various time editor, "I am opposed to laymen writing Theology, on the same principle that I am against amateur doctors and still more lawyers—not because they are laymen, but because they are αυτοδιδακτοι [self-taught]."[16] He suggested that rather than being taught theology *in extenso,* laymen should study its application to their secular affairs and its bearing on history and literature.[17]

AS A ROMAN CATHOLIC

Soon after becoming a Catholic, along with his convert friends, Newman chose to join the Oratory established by St. Philip Neri in the sixteenth century. The "apostle of Rome" had gathered laymen in Rome for prayer, discussions on the spiritual life, and works of charity. Newman admired various religious orders, such as the Benedictines and the Jesuits, and to a lesser extent the Dominicans. But he was personally attracted to the Oratorians by its founder, whose life exemplified a deep Christian joy and charity, and at the same time he was drawn to the way of life of the oratories which respected the individual gifts of its ordained

---

14   Meriol Trevor, *The Pillar of the Cloud: A Biography of John Henry Cardinal Newman* (New York: Doubleday & Co., 1962), 212.

15   Meriol Trevor, *Lion in Winter* (New York: Doubleday & Co., 1962), 192–203.

16   Letter to J. M. Capes, January 19, 1857, *LD* xvii, 504.

17   *Idea*, 376–77. In the same section, he mentions the names of some prominent laymen who had defended the Church by means of non-theological works (*Idea*, 379–80). Also *Campaign I*, Appendix VI, 276.

members, and that in its origins had a "Secular" Oratory or confraternity of laymen attached to each oratory.[18] Newman's respect and appreciation for the gifts of the faithful, in particular the laity, continued to grow and became even more evident in three events discussed below: the establishment of the Catholic University of Ireland, the founding of the Oratory School in Birmingham, and the *Rambler* Affair.

NEWMAN'S GROWING APPRECIATION OF GIFTS OF THE LAITY

Asked by the bishops of Ireland to establish a Catholic university in Ireland, Newman gladly accepted. He wished this to be a Catholic university for the English-speaking world.[19] He put all his energies into this educational project, selecting professors, raising funds, buying property, looking for students, and establishing faculties. In the first sermon delivered at the university church he expressed the ideal he sought for the students: that they be "oracles of philosophy and shrines of devotion"[20] by means of intellectual and moral discipline. He explained that: "Devotion is not a sort of finish given to the sciences; nor is science a sort of feather in the cap, if I may so express myself, an ornament and set-off to devotion. I want the intellectual layman to be religious, and the devout ecclesiastic to be intellectual."[21]

In addition to the inherent difficulties in such an educational project, Newman also experienced firsthand a vision of the Church in which the laity were expected to follow orders and have little say.[22] His first biographer, Wilfrid Ward, explained a strong opinion voiced by Newman in 1873 as to the necessity of giving the Catholic laity their full share of influence in any scheme for University education, if it were to have a chance of success: "His words on the subject were strong and weighty and deserve to be quoted: 'One of the chief evils which I deplored in the management of the affairs of the University 20 years ago when I was in Ireland was the absolute refusal, with which my urgent representations were met, that the Catholic laity should be allowed to co-operate with the Archbishops in the work.'"

The quote continues with Newman's account of his experience in Ireland: "So far as I can see, there are ecclesiastics all over Europe, whose policy it is to keep the laity at arms-length, and hence the laity have been disgusted and become infidel, and only two parties exist, both ultras in opposite directions. I came away from Ireland with the distressing fear, that in that Catholic country,

---

18   Ker, *Newman on Vatican II*, 102, 106.

19   Paul Shrimpton, *The 'Making of Men': The* Idea *and Reality of Newman's University in Oxford and Dublin* (Leominster: Gracewing, 2014), 107–12.

20   "Intellect, the Instrument of Religious Training," in *OS* no. 1, 13.

21   *OS* no. 1, 13.

22   Shrimpton, *Making of Men*, 291–97.

in like manner, there was to be an antagonism as time went on between the Hierarchy and the educated classes."[23]

In 1858, in the face of marked differences of opinion with Archbishop Cullen over the administration of the university, especially the role of laymen, Newman resigned from the rectorship and returned to England. Soon afterwards he became involved in another venture where he met with a similar resistance with regards to respect for the voice of the laity. This time it was with a Catholic periodical which had been begun by some of his friends. These men, fellow converts to Catholicism, owned *The Rambler*, which was originally a literary quarterly. Newman served as an informal theological consultant. He contributed some verses for the periodical, but avoided further involvement with it, hoping to eschew confrontation with the *Dublin Review*, the vehicle for Cardinal Wiseman's theological thought. Newman's involvement in the journal illustrates his view that it is important for educated laity to write on literature, history, architecture, as well as on religious matters of direct concern to them such as the education of children.

At this time in England there was debate about the requirement of government inspection of Catholic schools for the granting of financial subsidies. The bishops considered this to be government interference and a possible attack on religious freedom. In May 1859, the *Rambler* published an unsigned editorial by Newman that respectfully defended the rights of laity to voice their opinion and the need for the bishops to consult the faithful, made up in their majority by laity. He indicated that bishops should "desire to know the opinion of the laity on subjects in which the laity are especially concerned. If even in the preparation of a dogmatic definition the faithful are consulted, as lately in the instance of the Immaculate Conception, it is at least as natural to anticipate such an act of kind feeling and sympathy in great practical questions."[24] The editorial was contested by Dr. Gillow, the chair of theology at Ushaw, who objected that the infallibility of the Church rested exclusively with the *Ecclesia docens*. Shortly afterwards, in an interview with Ullathorne, the Bishop of Birmingham, Newman was asked to resign from the editorship which he promptly agreed to do in July.

Before giving up the editorship, however, Newman defended his position with an article titled "On Consulting the Faithful in Matters of Doctrine,"[25] a text which was considered almost heretical at that time.[26] It should be noted that Newman used the term "faithful" equivocally. Here he was referring to laity and their role in the education of their children, but at other times, as in an appendix

---

23 Wilfrid Ward, *Life of John Henry Cardinal Newman*, vol. 2 (London: Longmans, Green & Co., 1910), 397.

24 *Rambler* (May 1859), 122.

25 John T. Ford, "La eclesiología en John Henry Newman," *Scripta Theologica* 51, no. 3 (2019): 761–64.

26 For the history of this controversy see introduction by John Coulson to *Cons.*, 1–49, and Charles S. Dessain, *John Henry Newman* (Oxford: Oxford University Press, 1980), 111–20.

to an 1871 edition of the *Arians of the Fourth Century,* he had in mind both laity and clergy, including some bishops who in the fourth century remained faithful to the Church's Tradition. For Newman, the Church as a whole was infallible, rather than the hierarchy alone. He clearly and boldly asserted that the apostolic tradition was committed to the whole Church even though the role of discerning, discriminating, defining, and promulgating any part of the tradition resides solely in the *Ecclesia docens.* Although there is development in Newman's understanding of the laity's role in the prophetic tradition of the Church, he maintains that the body of the bishops have the ultimate teaching authority.[27]

In the *Rambler* article he explained the common meaning of the word "consult": "It includes the idea of inquiring into a matter of fact, as well as asking a judgment. Thus, we talk of "'consulting our barometer' about the weather . . . the matter of fact, viz. their belief, is sought for, as a testimony to that apostolical tradition."[28] Newman noted that consulting the faithful does not mean seeking their counsel or judgment but instead ascertaining if a belief they hold is a testimony to apostolical tradition. Their consensus is sought as an indication or instrument of the judgment of the infallible Church. Newman offered examples of the witness of the faithful during the Arian controversy, when the voice of tradition and Nicene dogma were maintained despite the divided voices of the Holy See, councils, and bishops. Despite the equivocal use of the word "faithful" in the article's title, he wrote: "Though the laity be but the reflection or echo of the clergy in matters of faith, yet there is something in the 'pastorum and fidelium *conspiratio,*' which is not in the pastors alone."[29] Newman took the expression "pastorum et fidelium conspiratio," the common spirit (or literally, breathing together) of the bishops and faithful, from a book on the Immaculate Conception (1847) by the Jesuit theologian Fr. Giovanni Perrone who helped him in his theological development as a Roman Catholic after Newman befriended him in Rome.[30]

The *Rambler* affair and Newman's article indicate his belief regarding the participation of the laity in the Church's prophetic mission. In the following century, the French theologian Yves Congar would refer to Newman on this very subject close to ten times in his *La Tradition et les traditions* (1960). In another work, Congar would specifically cite Newman's article in defense of this very proposition,[31] and Avery Dulles would point out that this was part of an "ecclesiology of checks and balances"[32] described by Newman.

---

27 Benjamin J. King, "Sensus Fidelium," in *The Oxford Handbook of John Henry Newman,* 264–83, for a detailed account of the context for Newman's idea of *sensus fidelium.*

28 *Cons.,* 54.

29 *Cons.,* 103–4. The italics are Newman's.

30 King, "Sensus Fidelium," 274, and C. Michael Shea, "Doctrinal Development" in *The Oxford Handbook of John Henry Newman,* 292–94.

31 Yves M. Congar, *Jalons por un théologie du laicat* (Paris: Éditions du Cerfs, 1953), 273.

32 Avery Dulles, SJ, *John Henry Newman* (London: Continuum, 2002), 111.

Along with these examples, The Oratory School, which Newman and a group of laymen opened in Birmingham in 1859, affords further evidence of the role which Newman realized that parents have in financing and directing the education of their children.[33] This role of the laity was not obvious then, nor is it now despite the intervening body of doctrine since Newman's time.[34]

NEWMAN ON THE LAITY AND ECCLESIOLOGY

Although Newman wrote sermons, tracts, and letters on specific questions such as apostolic succession and other notes of the Church, the relation of Church and state, and papal infallibility, he did not elaborate a treatise on ecclesiology.[35] However, his thinking contains some elements for an ecclesiology that goes beyond the ecclesiology of Trent and Vatican I, in particular in the exercise of three essential functions or powers in the Church, connected with the offices of Christ as priest, prophet, and king.[36] The successive changes in Newman's understanding of the Church, beginning in his youth as an evangelical Christian without a definite creed, to his membership in the visible Anglican Church, and finally in the Catholic Church, have been summarized by Newman scholar John T. Ford.[37]

For the nineteenth century English theologian, the Church is above all a visible and an invisible community of the baptized. He spoke of bishops, clergy, monks, and laity usually to address specific topics such as authority or the sacraments, celibacy or monastic life. But he always privileged the name and concept of "Christian" to denote the members of the Church.

In *Tracts for the Times,* 38 and 41 (1834), Newman asserted his belief that the Anglican Church held the teaching and traditions of the apostles, constituting a *Via Media* between the errors of Protestants and Romanists. And he called for a second reform of the Church to return it to the unity of doctrine and charity of the primitive Church. In these early tracts, Newman also identified two serious threats to the Anglican Church: the Erastian and Latitudinarian errors. The former is subordination of the Church to the State and the latter the increasing doctrinal and liturgical laxity.

---

33 Paul Shrimpton, *A Catholic Eton? Newman's Oratory School* (Leominster: Gracewing, 2005), 76–85, 178–87.

34 See Paul Shrimpton's chapter "Newman: An Educator 'from first to last,'" no. 12 in this volume.

35 In 1877 he wrote a long preface to the third edition of his *Lectures on the Prophetical Office of the Church viewed relatively to Romanism and Popular Protestantism* (1837) in which he offered some reflections for such a treatise. See Ford, "La eclesiología en John Henry Newman," 742–43, and the revised version of this article in ch. 24 of this volume.

36 See Dulles, *John Henry Newman,* 109–13.

37 Ford, "La eclesiología en John Henry Newman," 744–47, 761.

In his *Lectures on the Prophetical Office of the Church,* which later formed the first volume of his *The Via Media of the Anglican Church,* he decried the lack of teaching authority in his Church:

> In the English Church, however, we shall hardly find ten or twenty neighbouring clergymen who agree together; and that, not in the non-essentials of religion, but as to what are its elementary and necessary doctrines; or even as to the fact whether there are any necessary doctrines at all, any distinct and definite faith required for salvation. Much less do the laity receive that instruction in one and the same doctrine, which is a necessary characteristic, as may be fairly alleged, of their being "taught of the Lord."[38]

He also recognized the Protestant error of considering the true Church to be invisible. In the sermon "The Church Visible and Invisible," preached in 1835, Newman distinguished a Christian's admission to the Church and enjoyment of its privileges to dispel the objection that there are two Churches, a visible one made of sinners and an invisible one in heaven, the true Church. He explained that an adult who lacks faith will receive grace if baptized, but until he believes, will not enjoy the benefits of this baptismal grace. Of particular interest in this sermon is Newman's point about the laity in reference to the constitution of the Church. He notes that clergy represent the Church but the Church is one body: "we talk of clergy as the Church: here is a parallel instance, in which part of a body is viewed as the whole; still, who would say that the Laity are one Church by themselves, the Clergy by themselves another?"[39]

Newman did not see the pattern of the Church as two bodies: laity and clergy. Instead, he used the model of the body with various ranks and offices, enlivened by the Holy Spirit as described by St. Paul. In the Church the "sacraments are the instruments which the Holy Ghost uses."[40] Newman's concern at the time, and later as a Catholic, did not deal with the nature or extent of the laity's participation in the priestly office of Christ. His attention was focused on faith in God's action in the sacraments and the devout reception by the faithful of the sacraments.

For Newman, eschatology gave the proper perspective regarding man. He always conceived the Church on earth keeping in mind the eschatological reality of the Church in heaven. This is evident in another sermon, "The Visible Church, an Encouragement to Faith" (1834). We do not know them (the saints) but God knows them. The Christian "is one of a host, and all those blessed Saints he reads of are his brethren in the faith. He finds in the history of the past, a peculiar kind of consolation, counteracting the influence of the world that is seen . . . the

---

38 *VM* i, 333.

39 *PS* iii, no. 16: 223–24.

40 *PS* iii, no. 16: 226.

spirits of the just made perfect encourage him to follow them."[41] The Christian is a member of "the communion of the saints,"[42] an expression used by Newman.

In "The Visible Church," he mentioned bishops as the continuation of the apostles but does not speak of the clergy or laity. He noted that even though at various times some are unworthy, as are kings and princes as well, nevertheless the bishops—each bishop—is "the living monument of those who are dead," descendants of the apostles. He also referred to the unworthy lives of some bishops, yet the Church as a whole and in communion with the pope has the charism of infallibility in matters of faith. In the preface to the 1877 edition of his *Prophetical Office* he acknowledged that in the Church holiness and soundness of theology can coexist with ambition, scheming, and cruelty in its governance. Theology, far from being the cause of the latter, acts instead as a fundamental regulating principle for the entire ecclesiastical system.[43]

For the Anglican Newman, the focus of his attention was primarily on orthodoxy and growing religious indifference in the flock, but as a Catholic, it was more on relations with the Holy See. The controversy was polarized between ultramontane and liberal positions regarding the pope's temporal power. The formerly Catholic England in which Newman lived experienced a growing secularism and religious ignorance. He was, therefore, very interested in forming the faithful, in particularly children and university students, and spoke of enlarging their minds and creating in them a habit of thinking about God and the world.

Years later, in a public lecture delivered at the Birmingham Corn Exchange, he offered a summary of the formation he desired of the laity in matters of doctrine, religious practice, and history:

> I want a laity, not arrogant, not rash in speech, not disputatious, but men who know their religion, who enter into it, who know just where they stand, who know what they hold, and what they do not, who know their creed so well, that they can give an account of it, who know so much of history that they can defend it. I want an intelligent, well-instructed laity.[44]

The abundant spiritual direction that he provided, both in person and through correspondence, offered encouragement to laymen and women in the exercise of their gifts in the service of the Church, usually by means of their professional work, and also through the written media. Characteristic of this way of thinking is Newman's sermon, "Doing Glory to God in Pursuits of the World," in which he offered a short but insightful understanding of the value of human work done for the glory of God. Newman warned against the mistake

---

41 *PS* iii, no. 17: 244.
42 *PS* vi, no. 15: 17.
43 Preface, *VM*, i, no. 7.
44 *Prepos.*, 390.

made by some converts of seeking "a positive separation from active and social duties"[45] unless he has a clear calling to do so, "whereas what he ought to feel is this,—that *while* in it he is to glorify God, not *out* of it, but *in* it, and *by means* of it, according to the Apostle's direction 'not slothful in business, fervent in spirit, serving the Lord.'"[46] Newman's ideas and teaching would be shared and developed by various authors scarcely half a century after his death.

TWENTIETH CENTURY THEOLOGY

In the twentieth century, various spiritual writers and theologians such as Hans Urs von Balthasar, Karl Rahner, and Gérard Philips wrote theological articles and books on the laity. Here we will limit ourselves to mention Romano Guardini and take a look at the thought of St. Josemaría Escrivá, and theologians inspired by his work, as well as that of the Dominican Yves Congar because they developed ideas and intuitions held earlier by Newman.

Although as an Anglican, Newman showed some interest in the revival of religious life, both then and later as a Catholic, he thought that without making any vows the laity too could aspire to holiness in the exercise of their work. Romano Guardini (1885–1968), thirty years later, also dedicated himself to the intellectual, moral, and spiritual formation of many young laymen and women, first in the Catholic Youth movement "Quickborn" during the 1920s, and later in various German universities.[47] By means of this formation of the laity, Guardini, who greatly appreciated Newman[48] and tried to acquaint students with his works, sought the renewal of a Christian culture and society.

The most extensive treatment of the laity was offered by Yves Congar (1904–1995), who published his influential work, *Jalons pour une théologie du laïcat* (*Lay People in the Church*), in 1953. In this work and in shorter works preceding it he developed and formulated a theology of the laity as a part of a renewed ecclesiology. This was a comprehensive ecclesiology with its foundations in Christology.[49] In Congar's theology, some fundamental agreement is found with Newman's intuitions. Congar greatly admired the English theologian and quoted him in his works. In *Jalons* he cited Newman eight times, the first time in the

---

45 *PS* viii, no. 11: 154.

46 *PS* viii, no. 11: 158. The italics are Newman's.

47 Elizabeth Reinhardt, "Romano Guardini, amigo y maestro de la juventud," *Scripta Theologica* 50, no. 3 (2018): 591–610. Reinhart notes that Guardini was considered a real teacher, guide, and priest to many students, 609.

48 Guardini helped with one German translation of the *Apologia*, was familiar with Newman's sermons, and used the *Grammar of Assent* in teaching a university course on God. See Francesco Zucchelli, "Da Newman a Guardini, Un percorso possibile?" *Rivista Liturgica, Quinta serie, anno CVIII, fascicolo 3, luglio-settembre* (2021), 211–25 at 219–20.

49 Congar, *Jalons*, 15–17.

introduction, in which he quoted Newman: "In all times the laity have been the measure of Catholic spirit; they saved the Irish Church three centuries ago, and they betrayed the Church in England."[50]

Although *Jalons* is a theological work, it is set against the backdrop of laicism in the cultural milieu of France and Italy. In 1905, a French law on the separation of the Churches and State, based on the notion of *laïcité*, established a strict separation of the state and all religious bodies, which in practice was widely understood as the exclusion of the latter from public life. Faced with this cultural environment Catholic intellectuals debated whether to focus their thinking on the social action of the Church in the world, or on intellectual and spiritual formation of future leaders.

The social circumstance led theologians to think about a spirituality of action, which included a lay spirituality, as well as the meaning of being a Christian and of the baptismal vocation through a consideration of the first Christians.[51] Congar, Gustave Thils and others reflected on the relationship between the Church and the world. In *Jalons*, Congar postulated what he considered the correct relationship between the Church, the world, and the eschatological Kingdom of God within. It is here that he explains the role of the clergy and laity. Although in a very brief manner and in the form of a sermon titled "On the Mediatorial Kingdom of Christ" (1827), Newman had offered some ideas on the relationship between the Church, which he calls the Kingdom of Christ, and the future Kingdom of God. Newman concluded the sermon by inviting the congregation to participate in the sacrament of the Lord's Supper.

The French Dominican explained that the apostles and those who worked with them laid the foundations of the Church, which is like a house or temple. The Church receives its structure through them. But the Church is a living organism whose members are active; they are living stones. The members of the Church share in the kingly and priestly dignity of Christ; each one has a vocation determined by gifts and functions.[52] For Congar, only the lay people, who belong to the world and the Church in a way which is not true of clergy or monks, can open the way to the faith in every level of human structure. With regard to the Church's mission, he writes: "Lay people are the proper and irreplaceable subject of some of the activities through which this mission and this work are accomplished in their fullness."[53]

Congar described the relationship between the common and hierarchical priesthood (*Sacerdoce et laïcat dans l'Eglise, A Gospel Priesthood and Christians Active in the World*). Both the laity and ministerial priests participate in the one priesthood of Christ which gives rise to the original structure of the Church.

---

50 *Prepos.*, 390, cited in *Jalons*, xxxv.
51 Pellitero, *La teología del laicado*, 72.
52 Congar, *Jalons*, 429–31.
53 Congar, *Jalons*, 432.

For Aquinas, this participation takes place through the Christian's sacramental consecration in baptism and confirmation.[54] A contemporary theologian, José Luis Illanes, considers that other elements in the structuring of the Church are the charisms given by the Holy Spirit.[55]

Congar asked himself if the laity have a role in the government of the Church and answers that according to tradition they have some participation in its government and have the "right to be heard" because they form the *pleroma* of the mission of hierarchy.[56] There is a likely echo here of Newman's *On Consulting the Faithful*, who had to defend himself for his assertion that the faithful deserved a voice in such matters. Years later Congar openly asserted and developed the teaching on the laity's participation in the prophetic, priestly, and royal office of the Church. For him "the clergy bear witness to the amount of information, knowledge of conditions for apostolic work and even of doctrinal resources, they owe to listening to their lay fellows; their testimony bears out what such as Scheeben said from a theological point of view, Newman from a more concrete and pastoral angle."[57]

For the French theologian, the laity participates in apostolate in their specific circumstances, in their own place of work, and in the witness of their lives. Keeping in mind the organized work of Catholics generally known as "Catholic Action" at the turn of the century, the lay participation in apostolate has two aspects: one is the influence on institutions, and the other, depending on the hierarchy, is that of evangelization, understood as announcing the Gospel. Others, in addition to Congar, including contemporary theologian Pedro Rodríguez, have noted the negative definition of the laity found in canon 217 of the Code of Canon Law. A trace of this is found in the well-known passage of Vatican II's *Lumen Gentium*: "all the faithful except those in holy orders and those in the state of religious life."[58] Yet this same canon offers a positive definition of the laity that points out what is specific to them ("*proprium*"), distinguishing them from the baptismal condition common to all the faithful: "What specifically characterizes the laity is their secular nature."[59] Rodríguez highlights the secular nature of the lay faithful: the sanctification of earthly realities in the way that is proper to them (*indole saecularis*).[60] As noted above, Newman gave great importance to the personal witness of lay persons in their everyday life as well as their work in education, government, and other aspects of social life.

---

54 Thomas Aquinas, *Summa Theologiae*, III, q. 63, aa. 3 and 5.

55 José L. Illanes, *Laicado y Sacerdocio* (Pamplona: Eunsa, 2001), 104–7.

56 Congar, *Sacerdoce*, 22–23, 432; Pellitero, *La teología del laicado*, 90.

57 Congar, *Jalons*, 256.

58 Vatican Council II, *Lumen Gentium* (November 21, 1964), 31.

59 *Lumen Gentium*, 31.

60 Pedro Rodríguez, *Los Laicos en Eclesiología del Concilio Vaticano II*, ed. Ramiro Pellitero (Madrid: Rialp, S.A., 2006), 102–3, 113–15.

In line with Newman's and Congar's ideas, although independent of them, the Spanish priest, Josemaría Escrivá (1902–1975), founder of Opus Dei, taught and inspired others to understand the common priesthood of the faithful and personal apostolate. He pointed out that the characteristic mission of the laity in the world is the sanctification of human realities: family, work, culture.[61] Escrivá indicated that the reason for this is their participation in Christ's life and priesthood, and its corollary: the universal call to holiness. If the Christian is to sanctify the earthly realities he must strive for personal holiness through the sacramental life, prayer, and practice of the virtues in everyday life.[62]

Also like Newman, Escrivá encouraged the laity to carry out apostolate in their varied professional occupations, as well as in educational enterprises, urging them to exercise initiative and personal freedom. He found the basis for this in the Christian's baptismal consecration, which gives them a fundamental equality with the other faithful. Each Christian participates in the life of Christ through the grace of the Holy Spirit, becoming another Christ, and Christ himself.[63] This identification is most fully realized in and through the Eucharistic sacrifice. Congar, too, will later assert this, emphasizing that the Mass is the best expression of the unity of the Church in which different members fulfill diverse roles in the oneness of the whole.[64] This teaching and the universal call to holiness and apostolate were strongly reaffirmed by various Vatican II documents, especially *Lumen Gentium, Gaudium et Spes*, and *Apostolicam Actuositatem*.

Congar had the special merit of articulating a theological understanding of the Church in terms of both an institution and community of salvation in which some receive spiritual gifts he calls hierarchical, but all receive personal spiritual gifts that contribute to the constitution of the living body of the Church.[65] Since the twelfth century, however, the combination of the hierarchical and communal principle has suffered with the predominance given to the hierarchical in the west.[66]

The theological reflection and experience of Christians in the period between both councils led to a deeper understanding of the nature of the Church and to the fundamental equality and dignity of the laity and their place and mission in the Church, absent in Vatican I or the previous ecumenical councils. The Vatican II Constitution *Lumen Gentium* put forth the teaching of the Church

---

61 Alvaro del Portillo, *Fieles y Laicos en la Iglesia,* 2nd ed. (Pamplona: Eunsa, 1981), 199–200.

62 See Ernest Burkhart and Javier López, *Ordinary Life and Holiness in the Teaching of St. Josemaría: A Study in Spiritual Theology* (New York: Scepter, 2017), 146–58, 233–62. This theological and spiritual understanding is a central part of the teaching of Opus Dei, established by Escrivá in 1928.

63 Escrivá, *Christ Is Passing By,* 183.

64 Congar, *Jalons,* 435.

65 Congar, *Jalons,* 52–53.

66 Congar, *Jalons,* 434.

as a mystery rooted in the Trinity and structured by the sacraments (ch. 1), and as the people of God (ch. 2) made up by the baptized gathered by the Holy Spirit. This community of the faithful, structured by the hierarchy (ch. 3), constitutes the Church together with the laity (ch. 4) and the religious (ch. 6), who are all called to holiness of life (ch. 5). Ker has pointed out how this vision of the Church differs from the Tridentine model "as first and foremost hierarchical."[67] Some seeds for this new ecclesiology of communion are found in Newman's *On Consulting the Faithful in Matters of Doctrine* and in his sermons on the Church as a visible body animated and nourished by the Holy Spirit.[68]

After Vatican II some have wished to oppose a theology of communion (or Church as a "sacrament") to a theology of the people of God seen from a socio-political perspective. Rodríguez considers, instead, that the ecclesiology advanced by Vatican II attempted to understand the historic salvific reality in a trinitarian manner which affirms the mystery of the Church (the Church as a sacrament) and people of God. The essence of the notion "people of God" is communion of men with God and among themselves, and in its historical condition the "people of God" is, in and for the world, a sacrament of that mysterious communion.[69] Rodríguez explains how the Church is born and maintained in its organic structure through the anointing of the Holy Spirit in the sacraments of baptism and Holy Orders. Christ continues to rule, to teach, and to sanctify his Church through new donations of the Holy Spirit that are called charisms. It is through an understanding of the charisms that the theological identity of the laity is discovered.[70]

On a pastoral level, Escrivá deplored the clericalism or abuse of the spiritual power by the clergy for which Newman likewise expressed disdain along with the clericalization of the laity.[71] The laity should not be at the service of the clergy; rather, the clergy should be at the service of the laity. He employed an expression also used by Congar: the laity are not the *longa manus* of the clergy.[72] Escrivá and Congar were contemporaries who, independent of each other, thought alike and held the same view on this as Newman had before them. In sum, together, the clergy and laity form the body of Christ. Lay persons can contribute to the teaching and governing office of the Church but by their very number and their professional expertise their Christian vocation is lived out primarily in the exercise of family and professional obligations and projects. Newman did not write about this at any length, although his correspondence and advice bear witness to his similar way of thinking. In the letter cited above, he told his correspondent:

---

67 Ker, *Newman on Vatican II*, 104–5.

68 Ker, *Newman on Vatican II*, 103.

69 Pedro Rodríguez, "El Pueblo de Dios" in *Eclesiología 30 Años Después de "Lumen Gentium,"* ed. Pedro Rodríguez (Madrid: Rialp, S. A., 1994), 175–210.

70 Pedro Rodríguez, *Los Laicos en Eclesiología del Concilio Vaticano II*, 104–7.

71 Josemaría Escrivá, *Conversations with Monsignor Escrivá*, First Spanish edition, 1968 (New York: Scepter, 1993), 47.

72 Congar, *Jalons*, 419.

You will be doing the greatest possible benefit to the Catholic cause all over the world, if you succeed in making the University a middle station at which laity and clergy can meet, so as to learn to understand and yield to each other, and from which, as from a common ground, they may act in union upon an age which is running headlong into infidelity, and however evil in themselves may be the men and the measures which of late years have had so great a success against the Holy See, they will in the Providence of God be made the instruments of good, if they teach us priests that the "obsequium" which the laity owe religion is "rationabile."[73]

Newman grasped the notion of secularity without articulating it in a theological manner as was attempted during the subsequent century and put forth in *Lumen Gentium*, 31. Subsequently, in *Christifideles Laici*, 15, John Paul II explained further the secular character of the laity: "Certainly *all the members* of the Church are sharers in this secular dimension but *in different ways*. In particular, the sharing of the *lay faithful* has its own manner of realization and function, which, according to the Council, is 'properly and particularly' theirs. Such a manner is designated with the expression 'secular character.'" Again, we find similarities with Newman's thinking, illustrating just how well he understood the reality of the living Church.

The activities carried out by men here and now are not final realities but are open to and anticipate the fullness to be reached by eschatology. Escrivá taught that the greatness of ordinary life is to be found in the encounter with Christ and the building of a Christian fraternity that opens up to eternity.[74] The Christian faith does not call for separation from the world; the apostolic preaching, instead, urges the Christian to refer earthly realities to God.[75] Commenting on St. Paul's words "So whether you eat or drink or whatever you do, do it all for the glory of God" (1 Cor 10:31), Illanes writes: "The Church, in this sense, possesses a lay character by essence; a Church without laity would be an incomplete Church, lacking not only a material base without which in fact it could not subsist but rather one of the essential elements of the structure that Christ chose to grant it for the purpose of transmitting and communicating salvation to the world."[76]

These ideas seem self-evident today, but it took time for them to be developed and formulated as the Church necessarily moved into a postmodern secularist world. The underlying ecclesiology and theology of the laity highlight the contribution of ecclesial movements and institutions, popes, and other pastors

---

73   Ward, *The Life of John Henry Cardinal Newman*, 397–98.

74   Josemaría Escrivá, *Friends of God* (New York: Scepter, 1981), nn. 1–22.

75   José L. Illanes, "La Condición Laical en la Iglesia," in *Los Laicos en la Eclesiología del Concilio Vaticano II: Sanctificar el mundo desde dentro*, ed. Ramiro Pellitero (Madrid: Ediciones Rialp, 2006), 143–45.

76   José L. Illanes, "La Condición Laical en la Iglesia," 144.

that prompted the work of theologians. These developments were later reflected in the important addition of Book 2 to the 1983 revision of the Code of Canon Law. This revision enshrined the fundamental rights and duties of the laity in the Church.[77]

More than a century earlier Cardinal Newman had remarked to Bishop Ullathorne that "the Church would look foolish without them (the laity)."[78] This in itself shows how he grasped the importance of "the man in the pew," the everyday Christian who is immersed in the world. Without elaborating a doctrine on the laity, Newman's sermons and correspondence indicate a good understanding of the spiritual value of human work and the Christian's presence in the world, as well as his opposition to clericalism and narrow views on the Christian's role in the Church.

CONCLUSION:
NEWMAN'S FARSIGHTED UNDERSTANDING
OF THE ROLE OF THE LAITY IN THE CHURCH

Well ahead of his time, John Henry Newman defended the participation of the laity as members of the Church in Christ's prophetic and royal offices without undermining the role of the hierarchy in these or the clergy's exercise of Christ's priestly office. His sermons pointed toward what would be the ecclesiology of Vatican II in which the Church is the people of God constituted by the faithful: clergy, laity, and religious entrusted by the Holy Spirit with gifts and functions for the benefit of the Church and under the care of spiritual shepherds.

It seems, therefore, correct to consider Newman as precursor of some of the teaching of Vatican II[79] and the Post-Synodal Apostolic Exhortation *Christifideles Laici* (1988) on the laity, the universal call to holiness, and the laity's participation in the Church. Although he did not elaborate a treatise of ecclesiology, his life and works were known and respected by theologians who worked on the conciliar documents, in particular by Yves Congar whose theological work on this subject, and contribution to the council, were paramount. It is equally correct to hold that Josemaría Escrivá anticipated the teachings of the council on this subject and advanced our understanding of it, especially laying the foundations for a theology of work.[80]

For Newman, the identity of the lay person depends on the proper understanding of the Church, which requires an adequate eschatological point of view.

---

77 Del Portillo, *Fieles y Laicos en la Iglesia*, 175–231.

78 *BOA*, quoted in *Cons.*, 19. Reflecting on his mission on behalf of educated laity, Newman predicted correctly: "It may be God's will it should be done a hundred years later" (20).

79 Dessain, *John Henry Newman*, 116; and Ker, *Newman on Vatican II*, 2.

80 Javier Sesé, *Historia de la espiritualidad* (Pamplona: Eunsa, 2005), 289–94.

He always brought his listeners and readers to consider their lives in the light of God and last things, and to live by faith in obedience to Christ, both Savior and model for the Christian. He reminded them of the communion of the saints and of the charity that binds men here on earth and with the saints in heaven. At the same time, he taught Christians to take their calling in everyday life seriously, by building the kingdom of God which begins here on earth with their work in education, business, government life, and every other trade or profession. Newman recognized the importance of the laity's participation in teaching and running schools, and it is likely that he would equally recognize their contributions to theological research and teaching under other conditions such as those of the twentieth century.

The English Oratorian's works and example anticipated the teaching of Vatican II's decree *Apostolicam Actuositatem*, especially regarding the laity's participation in the Church's mission (no. 2), striving for holiness (no. 4), ordering the temporal realities (no. 7), and exercising personal influence among their peers (no. 13). Although this is now the teaching of the Magisterium and is widely accepted and developed by some theologians, it is one which in many ways remains a theory or ideal as evidenced by the degree of clericalism and clericalization of the faithful. Thus, Newman's life and teaching are both a refreshing vision and a challenging source of inspiration to Christians.

Lastly, Newman's consideration of the laity's role in the Church was a proper and necessary development, not a rupture, with tradition. There is tension regarding the prophetic role shared by the laity and the regal role of the pope and the bishops, but Newman does not ascribe "decision making power" to the laity in matters of faith and morals.[81] In his 1877 preface to the *Via Media* he noted that in the Church the three offices exert a sort of checks and balances on one another, yet he does not diminish the teaching authority of bishops.[82] Newman grasped the real value of the laity as Christ's body at work in the world, members of a visible Church under the teaching and ecclesial authority of the pope and the bishops, each person in his own life and occupation, living the gospel message, animated by the Holy Spirit, fortified by the sacraments.

---

81   While it can be acknowledged that there are tensions in Newman's writings on the subject along with his mixed reception in the twentieth century, it is incorrect to characterize his "rhetoric" on the subject, or find his development suspect, or suggest a "non-reception of doctrine" by the laity. See King, "Sensus Fidelium," 277–81.

82   Newman wrote thus of the three offices of teaching, rule, and sacred ministry in the Church: "Arduous as are the duties involved in these three offices, to discharge one by one, much more arduous are they to administer, when taken in combination. Each of the three has its separate scope and direction; each has its own interests to promote and further; each has to find room for the claims of the other two; and each will find its own line of action influenced and modified by the others, nay, sometimes in a particular case the necessity of the others converted into a rule of duty for itself." Preface, *VM*, xlii.

Suggested Reading

Illanes, José Luis. "La Condición Laical en la Iglesia." In *Los Laicos en la Eclesiología del Concilio Vaticano II: Sanctificar el mundo desde dentro*, edited by Ramiro Pellitero, 127–46. Madrid: Ediciones Rialp, 2006.

Ker, Ian. *Newman on Vatican II*. Oxford: Clarendon Press, 2014.

Newman, John Henry. *On Consulting the Faithful in Matters of Doctrine*. Edited with an Introduction by John Coulson. New York: Sheed & Ward, 1961.

Rodríguez, Pedro. "La identidad teológica del laico." In *Los Laicos en la Eclesiología del Concilio Vaticano II: Sanctificar el mundo desde dentro*, edited by Ramiro Pellitero, 91–126. Madrid: Ediciones Rialp, 2006.

Shrimpton, Paul. *The 'Making of Men': The Idea and Reality of Newman's University in Oxford and Dublin*. Leominster: Gracewing Publishing, 2014.

CHAPTER 27

LIBERALISM: PERSONAL AND SOCIAL ASPECTS IN NEWMAN'S THOUGHT

David P. Delio

S ince the publication of St. John Henry Newman's *Apologia Pro Vita Sua*,[1] there have been countless mentions of the term "liberalism" in biographical portraits,[2] systematic explorations,[3] and historiographic studies,[4] each contributing to why and how Newman used this particular word across the boundaries of his life and thought. In reviewing Newman's writings on liberalism and the commentaries and critiques that have followed, a kaleidoscopic scene

---

1   The title and contours of Newman's spiritual autobiography underwent several changes. Ian Ker, *John Henry Newman: A Biography* (Oxford: Oxford University Press, 1988), 545–50; hereafter, *Biography*.

2   Stephen Thomas, *Newman and Heresy: The Anglican Years* (Cambridge: Cambridge University Press, 2002); Frank M. Turner, *John Henry Newman: The Challenge to Evangelical Religion* (New Haven: Yale University Press, 2002); hereafter, *Challenge*.

3   Terrence Merrigan, "Newman and Theological Liberalism," *Theological Studies* 66 (2005): 605–21; Robert Carballo, "Newman and the Transition to Modern Liberalism," *Humanitas* 7, no. 2 (1994): 19–41.

4   Among the many that exist see, Robert Pattison, *The Great Dissent: John Henry Newman and the Liberal Heresy* (Oxford: Oxford University Press, 1991); Frank M. Turner, "Editor's Introduction: The Newman of the *Apologia* and the Newman of History," in *John Henry Newman: Apologia Pro Vita Sua and Six Sermons* (New Haven: Yale University Press, 2008), 54–85.

converges at points with colorful and varied arrays of meanings surrounding them. The accounts do not fully agree—as advocates and critics have reacted to Newman's thought in general, and on liberalism in particular, from their dispositions and assessments of the man, his character, and the Church in which he found his home.

Liberalism (the term and socio-political movement) had a genesis and growth during the nineteenth century in Continental, British, and American thought. In England, liberalism developed independent of and yet intersected with Newman's Oxford career and Catholic conversion. As the term gained currency from the 1820s onward, liberalism assumed traditional notions while also investing new meanings into older expressions.[5] Over the course of the nineteenth century, liberalism (the term and movement) increasingly acquired an elasticity and analogical breadth, while also coming into a visible form. Newman and his contemporaries' understanding of the word grew and they adapted it accordingly.

In his 1865 review of the *Apologia*, Fitzjames Stephen,[6] who perhaps inspired similar conclusions in later histories by Owen Chadwick, Stephen Thomas, and Frank Turner, accused Newman of using the word inconsistently or alienating it from common usage. However, other scholars[7] and the OED affirm that throughout the nineteenth century liberalism had a wide semantic range, and Newman's use was one among many possibilities. Newman shared in the general vicissitudes in British thought regarding this neologism. Yet, as is so characteristic of his mind, he saw the term from a religious perspective that was incisive but not unheralded: liberalism burnished a moral façade but in fact was the inverse of dogmatic religion. It denoted a personal habit of skepticism and eventually a social ethos that denied revealed truth and ecclesial authority. For Newman both senses of liberalism diminished dogmatic religious belief, ecclesial life, and therefore the socio-political fabric of a historically Christian people.

The Newman of Oxford described liberalism as a heresy, one with contemporary flora but ancient roots. He watched as it morphed into an emerging socio-religious fact: an idea always in transition contra Church and doctrine. Emerging from his Tractarian and early Catholic period, Newman refined the significance of liberalism in the *Apologia* to account for both the past and present. His final reflections on liberalism in his *Letter to the Duke of Norfolk* and especially in his *Biglietto Speech* outlined something akin to his understanding of an "idea" and its development.

In order to understand his insights into liberalism, a brief background of its cognates (e.g., liberal, liberals, and liberty) will be briefly traced as they

---

5   Patrick Deneen, *Why Liberalism Failed* (New Haven: Yale University Press, 2018), xiii; 24–27.

6   James Fitzjames Stephen, "Dr. Newman and Liberalism," *The Saturday Review* 504, no. 19 (June 1865): 768–70.

7   Nicholas Lash, "Tides and Twilight: Newman since Vatican II," in *Newman after a Hundred Years*, ed. Ian Ker and Alan G. Hill (Oxford: Clarendon Press, 1990), 460.

appear and change in Continental and British thought in the early to mid-nineteenth century. This will be set against select appearances of the word and corresponding meanings in Newman's public writings and letters prior to the *Apologia*. Although this study will draw upon scholars and the persons that shaped Newman's understanding of the term, it will not, for example, delve into his thick web of relationships and well-trod events such as the Hampden affair.[8] Approaching the genesis and development of the idea of liberalism in Newman's life and thought allows for an account of its historiography and integrity, while avoiding mistakes in predication of the term or undue suspicion of Newman's intentions.

DOGMATIC RESISTANCE

For many readers, the thematic power of the word liberalism in Newman's *Apologia* invokes a powerful impression of engagement and resistance. In his *Biglietto Speech* (1879),[9] occasioned by Pope Leo XIII elevating him to the Cardinalate, Newman expounded upon his lifelong resistance to "the spirit of Liberalism in religion." The source of this resistance was Newman's utter conviction that at fifteen years old he had had a direct and graced encounter with the Lord,[10] and as a result had an unwavering commitment to revealed truth or dogma.[11] This was not, as he recalled, a "violent" or an emotional epiphany but rather "a returning to, a renewing of, principles, under the power of the Holy Spirit, which I had already felt, and in a measure acted on, when young."[12]

Throughout his life, Newman continually bore witness to grace and doctrinal truth as he apprehended and awakened to it,[13] striving for holiness amid the tumult, digressions, broken and mended relationships, successes, and failures in his life.[14] Dogma presented a unique form of knowledge that he cultivated and shared with his students, from the pulpit, and in the pages of his

---

8   See for example Ker, *Biography*, 111–26.

9   Ian Ker, "Introduction to John Henry Cardinal Newman's *Biglietto Speech*," *Logos* 6, no. 4 (Fall 2003): 164–69.

10   This event, understood properly as an experience of God's grace, eludes critic Frank Turner (*Challenge*, 110–14), and so an explanation is sought in strictly human terms—his father's business failures, etc. In so doing, Turner belied his abilities as a historian, by wading into psychological musings (here and throughout) that actually require theological elucidations.

11   *Apo.*, 4, 49. See also, Louis Bouyer, *Newman: His Life and Spirituality*, trans. J. Lewis May (San Francisco: Ignatius Press, 2011), 10–25.

12   *AW*, 79–83.

13   For an insight into dogma in Newman's life see for example Keith Beaumont, "Newman as Theologian and Spiritual Guide," in *John Henry Newman: Doctor of the Church*, ed. Philippe Lefebrvre and Colin Mason (Oxford: Family Publications, 2007), 31–33.

14   See also Frédéric Libaud's chapter, no. 16 in this volume, for an account of Newman's teaching about holiness (editor's note).

written works. It was crucial for developing his arguments against liberalism. Amos Funkenstein has articulated how dogma *as knowledge* is, and always has been, both novel and controversial:

> An altogether new type of knowledge emerged with the advent and expansion of Christianity within the Roman Empire. Dogmatic knowledge, the truth claimed for dogmas, was unheard of within either the Greek-Hellenistic or the Jewish horizon. It is grounded in a new meaning of faith—a faith that is not a belief in someone or something, but a belief that some proposition is true; it is true even against all appearances to the contrary (without, however, being concealed or esoteric knowledge).[15]

What early Christians maintained about the propositional truth of dogma developed in Church tradition down to Newman's day. As a young man he accepted the doctrine of the Trinity from Thomas Scott's *The Force of Truth*, offered short disquisitions on the atonement,[16] wrote apologetic letters to his brother Charles,[17] and honed arguments in several university sermons, *The Arians of the Fourth Century*, and the *Tracts*. In his 1843 *Oxford University Sermon*, "The Theory of Developments in Religious Doctrine," Newman offered a concise statement of dogma that he had developed: "Theological dogmas are propositions expressive of the judgments which the mind forms, or the impressions which it receives, of Revealed Truth."[18] Although Newman's definition reflects Funkenstein's observation, he also found a depth to dogma; a believer's faith, which apprehends revealed truth, exceeds propositions. Dogma engaged persons to discover the profundities of God through Christ and the Christian mysteries. In 1835, Newman clarified dogma's two irreducible elements: manifestation in human propositions and mystery as divine presence:

> Revelation, as a Manifestation, is a doctrine variously received by various minds, but nothing more to each than that which each mind comprehends it to be. Considered as a Mystery, it is a doctrine enunciated by inspiration, in human language . . . a doctrine *lying hid* in language. . . . It is one and the same, independent and real, of depth unfathomable, and illimitable in its extent. . . . A Revelation is religious doctrine viewed on its illuminated side; a Mystery is the selfsame doctrine viewed on the side unilluminated. Thus Religious Truth is neither light nor darkness, but both together.[19]

---

15   Amos Funkenstein, "The Disenchantment of Knowledge: The Emergence of the Ideal of Open Knowledge in Ancient Israel and in Classical Greece," *Aleph* 3 (2003), 18.
16   Thomas, *Newman and Heresy*, 10–20.
17   *LD* i, 246.
18   *US*, no. 15: 320.
19   *EH* i, 41.

From the beginning of his priestly ministry and as a scholar, Newman understood that it would be an enduring struggle to uphold the dogmatic paradox of mystery and manifestation to nonbelievers and believers alike. His commitment to revealed truth led him in the *Apologia* to define liberalism as "the anti-dogmatic principle" or "the false liberty of thought . . . especially [in regards to] the truths of revelation."[20] Prior to the *Apologia*, he maintained this sense and so characterized the anti-dogmatic principle under many names in his sermons, tracts, poems, books, and letters: heresies, eclecticism, scepticism, the religion of the day, the world, latitudinarianism, rationalism, the infidel principle, and finally liberalism. These descriptions were analogues that Newman rhetorically used in different times and circumstances to express principles, ideas, persons, and movements that opposed Christian mysteries manifest in dogma.

Critics such as Frank Turner have misconstrued Newman's early writings and found his use of liberalism wanting in quantity and consistency. In his telling, Newman used the term occasionally, apart from conventional norms,[21] and associated it with groups that seemed so disparate—from Dissenters to High Churchmen to utilitarians and unbelievers alike. Turner believed ultimately that Newman conflated liberalism with evangelicalism, which expressed a more or less veiled attack on the latter.[22] Thus, his later use of liberalism in the *Apologia* was a false construct, and the Newman fabricated by Turner did not actually do "combat with a critical liberalism or [embark upon] a spiritual pilgrimage concluding in Roman Catholicism." Rather, Turner's Newman "more nearly resembled the typical pattern of Victorian loss of Protestant religious faith."[23]

Setting aside this bold yet discredited thesis,[24] it is as important to see that Newman did combat his understanding of liberalism under its many appearances and that in part issued in his conversion to the Catholic Church. In 1845, Newman actually made this direct connection in a handwritten note in

---

20 *Apo.*, 48; 288.

21 Stephen Thomas (*Newman and Heresy*, xiii) has also made such a claim. Thomas's work is helpful in seeing the analogical function of liberalism in Newman's early thought (43–48; 70–87), especially in terms of ancient heresy. However, his overall account is marred by thematic overreliance on heresy (like Turner with Evangelicalism), and thus weakens his argument.

22 Turner, "Editor's Introduction," 63.

23 Turner, *Challenge*, 11. Juan Alonso's description of Newman's lifelong process of conversion, in ch. 2 of this volume, indicates the complexity and gradualness of this process, which counters Turner's simplified anti-evangelical paradigm (editor's note).

24 See Eamon Duffy, "The Reception of Turner's Newman: A Reply to Simon Skinner," *Journal of Ecclesiastical History* 63, no. 3 (July 2012): 534–68; and Peter Nockles, "The Current State of Newman Scholarship," *British Catholic History* 35, no. 1 (2020): 120–25. Much of Turner's thesis falls apart when certain evidence is accounted for, e.g., see Newman's letter to Sir James Stephen in February 1835, *LD* v, 31.

the manuscript for the *Essay on the Development of Doctrine*, although without further elaboration: "This work must be looked at in connection to *Tract 85*— that delivered from Liberalism, this persuades to Rome."[25]

A GENESIS OF LIBERALISM

That Newman did not use the word liberalism exclusively in his early years has to do as much with the word's history as it does with Newman's mind and style of expression. He averts to this fact at the end of the *Apologia*, explaining:

> The Liberalism which gives a colour to society now, is very different from that character of thought which bore the name thirty or forty years ago. Now it is scarcely a party; it is the educated lay world. When I was young, I knew the word first as giving name to a periodical, set up by Lord Byron and others. Now, as then, I have no sympathy with the philosophy of Byron.[26]

This passage, in which Newman provides some reflection of the changes in the meaning of liberalism, contains an important historical fact overlooked by most commentators:[27] his first association of the word outside of customary usage was from Byron's ill-fated publication, *The Liberal*, in 1822–1823. In Byron's preface to the first edition, he declared that he and his compatriots "accept the title of enemies to religion, morals, and legitimacy" in contrast to the narrow, hypocritical religion of the day. Rather, as self-declared liberals, they desired to "see the mind of man exhibiting powers of its own, and at the same time helping to carry away on the best interests of human nature . . . there we recognize the demi-gods of liberal worship;—there we bow down and own our lords and masters."[28]

In part, Byron and his fellow travelers reflected the postrevolutionary mood of Continental Europe that was making its way into England in the early nineteenth century—the exaltation of humanity through secular knowledge and the reduction of religion to morality.[29] His attack was cultural—through literature,

---

25 Owen Chadwick, *From Bossuet to Newman* (Oxford: Oxford University Press, 1983), 129; 232.

26 *Apo.*, 261. Newman had also dealt briefly and curtly with Byron's poetry in his 1829 article "Poetry, with Reference to Aristotle's Poetics," republished in *EH* i, 1–27.

27 I too missed this in the *Apologia* and was alerted to the source in Brad Gregory, "The Prophetic Newman," *Newman Studies Journal* 11, no. 2 (Fall 2014): 47. See also, William H. Marshall, *Byron, Shelley, Hunt, and "The Liberal"* (Philadelphia: University of Pennsylvania Press, 1960), 50–89.

28 Lord Byron, preface to *The Liberal: Verse and Prose from the South* 1 (1822): vi, xii.

29 See Charles Taylor, *A Secular Age* (Cambridge, Mass.: Belknap Press, 2007), 225–26.

education, and religion—and only indirectly political. Moreover, Byron's "liberal" retained its Latinate roots in freedom and generosity reserved for the patricians and for an education in wisdom and virtue.

Beyond Byron, the term liberal had already been transformed under Christian influence, and especially seventeenth century England, through the King James Bible. The vernacular translation rendered "liberal" in a popular rather than exclusive sense of being generous and free, for example, "But the liberal deviseth liberal things; and by liberal things shall he stand" (Is 32:8); "Whiles by the experiment of this ministration they glorify God for your professed subjection unto the gospel of Christ, and for your liberal distribution unto them, and unto all men" (2 Cor 9:13). The biblical rendering of the term liberal gradually traversed into social and political thinking, although divested of its revelatory meaning.[30]

Finally, a conceptual tradition of political and religious freedom was ensconced in the cognate term, liberty. Pierre Manent has endeavored to explain that questions of liberty in the sixteenth century became answers as liberalism in the nineteenth century. This was the result of a sustained "theologico-political problem," specifically a war initiated by Machiavelli and Hobbes to displace the Roman and Anglican Church as the center of European political and religious life.[31] Locke sought to temper their bellicosity, offering an irenic solution (except for the Catholic Church) in tolerance. These two streams united in Rousseau: he imagined human nature as good, progressively able to improve, yielding in an almost Lockean toleration through social contract. Yet, for the Christian religion, Rousseau joined with Hobbes holding, "all the political misfortunes of European peoples come from Christianity, more precisely from the constitution of a Christian religious power distinct from and in rivalry with the political power."[32]

After the French Revolution, which had engendered a war of ideas into one of flesh and blood, liberty was given new life in the writings of Benjamin Constant and others. Manent argues that on the other side of the revolution, political thought moved away from considering distinct ends in human nature, that is, civic and religious, but rather toward humans as swept up into a progressive history and all-encompassing society.[33] Where once the Church had engendered a natural-supernatural distinction between the civic and religious orders, now there was an attempt at

---

30 Helena Rosenblatt, *The Lost History of Liberalism* (Princeton: Princeton University Press, 2018), 16–17.

31 Pierre Manent, *An Intellectual History of Liberalism*, trans. Rebecca Balinski (Princeton: Princeton University Press, 1995), 20–52. See also John Milbank's clarification and critique of Manent's thesis in "The Gift of Ruling: Secularization and Political Authority," *New Blackfriars* 85, no. 996 (March 2004): 213–19.

32 Manent, *Liberalism*, 68.

33 Manent, *Liberalism*, 78–81. Where Manent sees a discontinuity between Hobbes or Rousseau and the postrevolutionary "liberal society," Milbank sees continuity ("The Gift of Ruling," 222, n. 19). Milbank is more persuasive here than Manent.

a grand synthesis: the political and the ecclesial dissolved into an ascendant and dominant socio-historical reality.[34] In this dynamic shift modern liberalism was born, one that increasingly neutralized Catholic and Protestant claims to revealed truth while assimilating certain of Christianity's social and legal tenants into a seductive and comprehensive political, quasi-religious, and moral vision that developed over the course of the nineteenth century.

This is clear in liberalism's earliest popularizer, Benjamin Constant. In "The Liberty of the Ancients Compared with that of the Moderns," (1819) he declares "Individual liberty . . . is the true modern liberty. Political liberty is its guarantee." In this new social sphere where law, government, and vocation are on the side of the individual, "It is everyone's right to associate with other individuals, either to discuss their interests, or to profess the religion which they and their associates prefer, or even simply to occupy their days or hours in a way which is most compatible with their inclinations or whims."[35]

Helena Rosenblatt found that the term liberalism entered into the European lexicon in Spain somewhere around 1813, initially used as "a term of abuse" and related to Christian schisms such as Lutheranism, Jansenism, and so on.[36] In addition, "one of the earliest attacks on liberalism called it a 'religio-political heresy.'"[37] Rosenblatt recounts that while the new social understanding of liberalism often involved violent conflicts on the Continent, this word and meaning slowly imbedded itself into British language and thought—although not without opposition. Initially, the Tories resisted the implications of the new term, whereas "around 1817 the *Edinburgh Review*, informed its readers of the emergence of a French liberal party in a favorable way," while praising the work of Benjamin Constant.[38]

In the 1820s, "England became a favorite destination of many political refugees and another center of the European-wide liberal network." Tory backed papers and writers reacted:

> A writer in the *Morning Chronicle* had already in 1822 denounced the "influenza of liberalism" afflicting Europe, calling it a "moral plague." An *Essay on Liberalism* [1823] condemned what it called the "universal Liberalism" that was spreading confusion and chaos everywhere. France, it noted, was "the fountain head of liberalism." Its revolution had created the vile and dangerous ideas that were now spreading to the rest of Europe. Thanks to France, the word "liberal" no longer meant

---

34 Manent, *Liberalism*, 82.

35 Benjamin Constant, "The Liberty of Ancients Compared with that of the Moderns," https://oll.libertyfund.org/titles/constant-the-liberty-of-ancients-compared-with-that-of-moderns-1819, accessed September 19, 2020.

36 Rosenblatt, *History*, 63.

37 Rosenblatt, *History*, 5.

38 Rosenblatt, *History*, 71.

"a man of generous sentiments, of enlarged, expansive mind . . . [but]
a person [professing] political principles averse to most of the existing
governments of Europe."[39]

Although what seemed like an unwanted incursion of a Continental word
and philosophy, certain antecedent British traditions were fertile soil for liberalism: Locke's philosophy, Bentham's or Paley's utilitarianism, Deism, developments in Latitudinarian and Unitarian belief.[40] After some initial skirmishes,
liberalism as a word and social idea began to sprout and grow in the many
autochthonous habits of British practice and belief, including religion, education,
and politics. Within a relatively short interval, aspects of liberalism were accom-
modated to the plurality of British ecclesial traditions from High Churchmen
to Dissenters.[41] In education, questions of a national plan of "mixed" elementary education, secular universities, and repeals of tests and oaths increased and
intensified.[42] In politics, liberalism came to partial bloom in the Whig tradition
around 1835 and to full flower with Gladstone in 1859.[43]

LIBERAL(ISM)–PERSONAL AND
SOCIAL ASPECTS IN NEWMAN'S THOUGHT

From a young age Newman used the word liberal as most British did—in a
traditional-personal sense of noble, generous, free, and so on. Around 1829, he
expanded the scope of the term and its cognates (liberality, liberalistic, liberalism) to include two other senses: a skeptical-personal one and heretical-social
one. To develop these personal and social senses, Newman formed an analogy
that trades off of liberty. He consistently held that Christian liberty is freedom
in thought and conduct for Christ. However, skeptical-heretical liberal(ism) is
a false freedom moving away from dogmatic Christian faith. In one example of
many, Newman's 1837 Sermon "The Strictness of the Law of Christ," sets up this
contrast: "A number of persons . . . think their Christian liberty lies in being free
from all law, even from the law of God. . . . Religion . . . is a necessary service;
of course it is a privilege too. . . . The perfect Christian state is that in which
our duty and our pleasure are the same, when what is right and true is natural
to us, and in which God's 'service is perfect freedom.'"[44] For Newman, when a

---

39   Rosenblatt, *History*, 75–76.
40   Keith Beaumont, "Dogme et vie spirituelle," in *Dieu intérieur: La théologie spirituelle de John Henry Newman* (Paris: Éditions Ad Solem, 2014), 145–55.
41   Richard Brent, *Liberal Anglican Politics: Whiggery, Religion, and Reform: 1830–
1841* (Oxford: Clarendon Press, 1987), 144–84.
42   See David P. Delio, *"An Aristocracy of Exalted Spirits": The Idea of the Church in
Newman's Tamworth Reading Room* (Leominster: Gracewing, 2016), 11–12; 24–25; 31–34; 43–49.
43   See Eric J. Evans, *The Shaping of Modern Britain: Identity, Industry and Empire,
1780–1914* (Harlow: Pearson Educational, 2011), 215, 329–38.
44   *PS* iv, no. 1: 3–4.

Christian is liberal in the traditional sense she is free or open to revealed truth, Christ, and others. When liberal in the skeptical sense, she has begun a false step in freedom away from dogma, toward a personal liberalism. When this movement away from dogma is shared by many, liberalism yields a heretical system opposed to the Church.

Preceding the *Apologia*, Newman employed distinct senses of the term liberal and its cognates from 1818 through 1845. He used liberal(ism) in his private correspondences up to 1845 at least eighty-nine (89) times. In his published writings, he had at least thirty-five (35) separate instances. From 1845 until 1864 liberalism appeared at least fifteen (15) times in his correspondence, and eight (8) times publicly. His sense of liberal(ism) as skeptical or heretical was four to one (4:1) over the traditional sense.

There are multiple occasions before 1864 where Newman explains his meaning when referencing liberal(ism) as skeptical or heretical. For the most part his meaning is implied and revealed in context, functioning more as a label and marker in an observation or argument. Thus, Newman had analogically formed and frequently used the term well before writing the *Apologia*. Liberal(ism) appears seventy (70) times[45] in the *Apologia* (including "Note A"), and Newman denotes it in either a skeptical-personal or heretical-social sense. Indeed, there is only one instance in the *Apologia* where liberal(ity) appears in a traditional sense.[46]

Tracing the sheer quantity of Newman's contextual use of liberal(ism) in his writings would extend far beyond the scope of this chapter. Rather, it is enough to say that the personal and social patterns of the word emanate out of two very important periods early in his career and appear to correlate with the wider diffusion of liberalism in British society. In addition to use of the term liberal in the traditional sense, Newman tended toward use of the skeptical sense of the word in the late 1820s and later toward the understanding of liberalism as a religio-heretical social fact in the 1830s. These meanings, to which Newman continually returned, take shape in the *Apologia*, especially in regards to his involvement in the Oxford Movement, and later in The *Letter to the Duke of Norfolk* and his *Biglietto Speech*.

LIBERAL AS TRADITIONAL—
A POSITIVE, PERSONAL ASPECT

Although liberal(ism) as skeptical and heretical eventually prevailed in his thinking, Newman consistently used the traditional sense of "liberal" throughout his life,[47] especially in connection to education, for example, in The *Idea of a*

---

45   This counted past sources that include the word in quotes as well as in footnotes.

46   *Apo.*, 298.

47   See for example, letters to Maria Giberne in 1840 (*LD* vii, 381), to Edmund Ffoulkes in 1861 (*LD* xx, 72), and to John Cowley Fisher in 1877 (*LD* xxviii, 269).

University.[48] The first recorded mention of liberal in Newman's writings occurred in 1818, where he declared to his mother that his new friend Bowden "behaved in the most liberal manner possible."[49] Newman's correspondence until 1826 show liberal and liberality in a traditional sense approximately nine (9) times. He also used these words sparingly in his early published sermons.

This traditional sense provides a contrast to liberal(ism) in Newman's assessment of character and thought. A traditionally liberal person uses his or her liberty properly, is disposed toward others, inclined toward belief, while also having a mind that cultivates secular knowledge and is open to revealed truth in all its variety. It is an irony, and not an error, that Newman maintains this traditional sense for education over and against what he would see as liberalism in education: that which vaunts the majesty of secular knowledge over revealed truth while simultaneously pursing narrow specializations and utilitarian ends.[50]

LIBERAL(ISM) IN RELIGION—
THE SKEPTICAL, PERSONAL ASPECT

In his *Apologia*, Newman recollected that in his mid-twenties, "I was beginning to prefer intellectual excellence to moral; I was drifting in the direction of the liberalism of the day. I was rudely awakened from my dream at the end of 1827 by two great blows—illness and bereavement."[51] This recollection provides a clue to, but no confirmation of, the word liberalism in Newman's thought at this time. The word did not enter his writings until three years later, and this may correlate—in addition to his reading Byron—to its wider use in the press, his reading about the French Revolution, and his interest in French politics.[52] During the interval from 1826 to 1830, Newman had several distinct experiences that would transform how he eventually intended the word liberal(ism) and how he would incorporate liberalism, as a personal and social reality, into his lexicon.

Newman reflected in memoranda between 1821 and 1826,[53] letters,[54] and later reflections in his *Apologia* and *Autobiographical Writings*,[55] that he broke from Anglican evangelical teaching as a young man and had never fully committed to that tradition.[56] This break occurred through the ministrations of

---

48 See for example, Robert Barron, "'A Great Mischief': Newman on Liberalism in Religion," in Lefebrvre and Mason, *John Henry Newman: Doctor of the Church*, 99–111.

49 *LD* i, 57.

50 See this developed in Don Briel, *The University and the Church: Don J. Briel's Essays on Education*, ed. Jared Staudt (Providence, R.I.: Cluny Media, 2019), 83–108.

51 *Apo.*, 14.

52 *LD* ii, 114; 263; 280.

53 *AW*, 79–83.

54 *LD* ii, 185; v, 175–79.

55 *AW*, 211.

56 Gareth Atkins contests Newman's recollections but is unconvincing, for as with Turner he overlooks earlier evidence that corroborates Newman's later views. See

Richard Whately and Edward Hawkins, part of an influential, loosely affiliated group called the Noetics. Under their sway Newman began to exercise his reason in an independent way upon religious and philosophical subjects. Newman noted, however, that he could not agree to most of Whately's theological views. He revealed in 1852 to William Monsell, that "so powerful a mind [as Whately's] did, I doubt not, lead me in many thoughts and speculations which I had better never have had."[57] Newman intimated that although he learned to think independently, it was *upon* dogmatic truths, rather than *over* them. This became evident in a controversy he had in 1827 in which he took exception to Whately and others over a sermon he preached on Christ's sonship.[58] What Newman gradually concluded from this instance was that the Noetics[59] ran counter to his convictions, especially in theological speculations.[60] During this period Newman also clashed with his brothers Charles and Francis over the contours of Christian truth and composed a work on miracles that countered Hume's skepticism.[61] He engaged evangelical teachings, marveled at skepticism, drifted into noetic speculations, and decried the loss of faith of one brother. These experiences deeply impressed upon him a fundamental distinction between what he would later express as evangelicalism and liberalism. He saw the power and attraction of each but could accept neither—he believed the former depended on the heat of emotion, the latter, he recounted, was a "cold Arminian doctrine, the first stage of Liberalism, [and] the characteristic aspect for the high-and-dry Anglicans of that day and of the Oriel divines."[62]

For Newman the "first stage of Liberalism" constituted a dry, detached, and calculating rationality that usurped the power of dogmatic religious belief. Although he did not think the Noetics nor others who prized high culture and abstract rationality were outright skeptics, he found in them a tendency, depicted in his 1830 sermon, "The Self-Wise Inquirer":

Gareth Atkins, "Evangelicals," in *The Oxford Handbook of John Henry Newman*, ed. Frederick D. Aquino and Benjamin J. King (Oxford: Oxford University Press, 2018), 173–74. A more compelling and fair presentation of Evangelical traditions in Newman and the Oxford Movment is found in Grayson Carter, "The Evangelical Background," in *The Oxford Handbook of the Oxford Movement*, ed. Stewart J. Brown, Peter B. Nockles, and James Pereiro (Oxford: Oxford University Press, 2017): 45–49.

57   *LD* v, 177.

58   *LD* ii, 15. Newman later admitted that he had not prayerfully thought through the implications of the sermon, but seemed to take umbrage at their disapproval (*LD* ii, 185).

59   Brent notes that "the Noetics were possibly the last English representatives of a school of Christian apologetics which had its origins in Locke's *An Essay concerning Human Understanding* (1689)." See Brent, *Liberal Anglican Politics*, 150. It was his philosophy that Newman saw in their thought that lended itself to a personal skepticism, and he expanded on it as a Catholic in his *Essay in Aid of a Grammar of Assent (1870)*.

60   *Apo.*, 49.

61   *LD* i, 224; ii, 33; vii, 13–26. See Turner, "Editor's Introduction," 86–87; *Mir.*, 155–59.

62   *AW*, 80; 83.

But when that gift of reason is something especial,—clear, brilliant, or powerful,—then our danger is increased. The first sin of men of superior understanding is to *value* themselves upon it, and look down upon others. They make intellect the measure of praise and blame; and instead of considering a common *faith* to be the bond of union between Christian and Christian, they dream of some other fellowship of civilization, refinement, literature, science, or general mental illumination, to unite gifted minds one with another. Having thus cast down moral excellence from its true station, and set up the usurping empire of mere reason, next, they place a value upon all truths exactly in proportion to the possibility of proving them by means of that mere reason.[63]

This sense of liberal(ism) continued in his thought and it can be found in his public writings, for example, its analogous relationship to rationalism in *Tract* 73,[64] or latitudinarianism in *Tract* 85, in the *British Critic*, and down to his likening of personal liberalism to the myth of Phaeton in 1881.[65] In a revealing and generous reflection on Blanco White in 1845, Newman articulated in summary fashion how personal liberalism, although well intended, eventually sacrificed dogmatic truth for refined opinion:

[Blanco] "loved and sought truth," as liberals do, as Whately and Arnold, that is, as mathematicians love and seek *mathematical* truth I mean, *without fearing error*. Hence he was not afraid of theological mistakes—he never was sensitive (in appearance) of mistakes—and at length openly maintained that "opinions cannot be sinful," with Lord Brougham in his Glasgow speech.[66]

Finally, Newman believed he was not immune to the temptations of a skeptical liberalism, although he sought to resist his own inclinations. In the throes of his final year as an Anglican, he remarked to John Keble: "Indeed

---

63 *PS* i, no. 17: 223–24.

64 In *Tract* 73, he wrote: "Rationalism is a certain abuse of Reason. . . . To rationalize in matters of Revelation is to make our reason the standard and measure of the doctrines revealed. . . . It is Rationalism to accept the Revelation, and then to explain it away; to speak of it as the Word of God, and to treat it as the word of man; to refuse to let it speak for itself; to claim to be told the *why* and the *how* of God's dealings with us, as therein described, and to assign to Him a motive and a scope of our own; to stumble at the partial knowledge which He may give us of them; to put aside what is obscure, as if it had not been said at all; to accept one half of what has been told us, and not the other half; to assume that the contents of Revelation are also its proof; to frame some gratuitous hypothesis about them, and then to garble, gloss, and colour them, to trim, clip, pare away, and twist them, in order to bring them into conformity with the idea to which we have subjected them." *EH* i, 31–32.

65 *LD* xxx, 8.

66 *LD* x, 702.

I sometimes feel uncomfortable about myself—a sceptical, unrealizing temper is far from unnatural to me—and I may be suffered to relapse into it as a judgment."[67]

LIBERALISM IN RELIGION—
THE ADVERSARIAL, SOCIAL ASPECT

Although Newman ultimately did not follow Whately, among the several gifts his mentor bestowed upon him was "one momentous truth of Revelation . . . the idea of the Christian Church, as a divine appointment, and as a substantive visible body, independent of the State, and endowed with rights, prerogatives, and powers of its own."[68] Over time, this allowed Newman to think beyond the unity of Church and state that characterized Anglican religion and to also consider social alternatives and potential rivals. As he retreated from the liberal intellectual ethos of the Noetics, he was drawn into the orbit of Richard Hurrell Froude and John Keble. They impressed upon him the notion of authority and the power of assent and grace, almost reminding him of his first love of dogma.[69]

Their influence correlates to a distinct change in Newman's use of the word liberal in 1829—shifting away from the benevolent adjective. He began to designate liberal(ism), both adjective and noun, in a negative sense.[70] That same year Newman was involved in Catholic Emancipation row at Oxford, concerning Sir Robert Peel. It gave him a taste of ecclesial independence, of liberty in the Church. It also provided him a clear understanding of social opposition to the Church. Newman wrote to his mother in March,

> We live in a novel era—one in which there is an advance towards universal education. Men have hitherto depended on others, and especially on the Clergy, for religious truth; now each man attempts to judge for himself. Now, without meaning of course that Christianity is in itself opposed to free inquiry, still I think it in fact at the present time opposed to the particular form which that liberty of thought has now assumed. Christianity is of faith, modesty, lowliness, subordination; but the spirit at work against it is one of latitudinarianism, indifferentism, republicanism, and schism, a spirit which tends to overthrow doctrine, as if the fruit of bigotry.[71]

This passage reveals what Newman evinced as his understanding of the heresy of liberalism in a few years. For him, the term came to denote a false liberty (of thought) that tended to "overthrow doctrine." As the letter continues,

---

67 *LD* x, 262.
68 *AW*, 69; *Apo.*, 13.
69 *Apo.*, 17–24; 290.
70 *LD* ii, 115; 122; 119.
71 *LD* ii, 129–30.

Newman extended this argument to the many principles and parties (e.g., Woolers, Utilitarians, Schismatics) that he saw as against the Church. He also observed the vehicle which these groups employed to align together and grow—universal (e.g., utilitarian, secular) education. Toward the end of the letter Newman connected this to none other than Henry Brougham, who had heavily invested in secular education, was a writer for the *Edinburgh Review*, and by all accounts a prototypical liberal who would be central in developing the Whig liberalism of the 1830s.[72]

From the time of this letter forward Newman began to envision a systematic array of social opposition, which he would eventually call liberalism. Indeed, he sharpened his language a few months later, speaking of the "false liberality of the age" in which important ecclesial differences were suppressed purportedly for the sake of mutual benefit.[73]

In August of 1830, Newman wrote to Simeon Lloyd Pope about his resignation from the Bible Society and there defined and used liberalism for the first time: "The tendency of the age is towards liberalism—i.e. a thinking established notions worth nothing—in this system of opinions a disregard of religion is included."[74] Here Newman demonstrates liberalism in two senses—the first personal-skeptical by denying "established notions"—but carries it forward to talk about how these "system of opinions" can destroy not only one's sense of doctrine but the authority of the Church. Indeed, the preponderance of the letter reveals how Newman worried about the social implications of this liberalism and how "liberals" were seeking to break up the apostolic character of the Church.

Soon after Newman began actively using liberalism in both senses of the word, and his friends, many of whom became Tractarians, also evidenced remarkably similar uses.[75] Newman's first public mention of liberalism is found in his *Arians of the Fourth Century* (1833). In his discourse on the eclectic heresy of Ammonius, he created a striking parallel between the ancient Church and the modern (the dispute over dogma), while also displaying both senses of liberalism (personal and social) in the same passage,

> Who does not recognize in this old philosophy the chief features of that recent school of liberalism and false illumination, political and moral, which is now Satan's instrument in deluding the nations, but which is worse and more earthly than it, inasmuch as his former artifice, affecting a religious ceremonial, could not but leave so much of substantial truth

---

72 *LD* ii, 130–31. Turner mistakenly claimed that Newman shifted from a religious meaning of liberalism to a more secular "march-of-mind" liberalism much later ("Editor's Introduction," 64). However, by identifying Henry Brougham's utilitarian educational ideals with liberalism early on, Newman always understood its secular roots.

73 *LD* ii, 191.

74 *LD* ii, 265.

75 E.g., *LD* iii, 5; 29.

mixed in the system as to impress its disciples with somewhat of a lofty and serious character, utterly foreign to the cold, scoffing spirit of modern rationalism?[76]

In 1839, Newman reflected on liberalism in the *Arians of the Fourth Century*, writing to Pusey that he believed liberalism to be a modern heresy with ancient origins. He noted and said as much in the conclusion of the work.[77] Indeed, the final paragraph did not directly state the word liberalism but implied it from earlier uses. Newman's meaning was clear—that liberalism as a heresy, personally and socially, will challenge but never triumph over the Church.

Newman's insight into the personal and social dimensions of liberalism extended in many directions well before the *Apologia*. He did not confine liberalism to the ancient Church but (swayed by Hurrell Froude) also associated it with the Reformation. He had noted the excesses of the Reformation stretching back to his 1830 Oxford sermon, "The Usurpations of Reason," and in his 1834 *Tract* 45, "The Grounds of Our Faith."[78] That same year Newman wrote to John William Bowden that, "the flood of Puritanism is pouring over the Church, (as liberalism over the world)."[79] Perhaps his parenthetical remark referred to the Whig-liberal ascendancy that had become apparent in national politics.

The distinction and interrelation between Puritanism (evangelicanism) and liberalism and their social implications continued to develop in Newman's thought, for example, in his *Lectures on Justification*,[80] and especially in his *British Critic* article of 1839, "The State of Religious Parties."[81] In 1841, Newman provided a long essay on "Private Judgment" wherein he observed reason detached from tradition and a teaching authority can lead one astray.[82] Private judgment bereft of authority is a headwaters to a personal sense of liberalism, but also had socio-religious implications, for example in the Reformation. Around this time, Newman remarked to the Roman Catholic Ambrose Phillipps that "the spirit of lawlessness came in at the Reformation—and Liberalism is its offspring."[83]

---

76 *Ari.*, 106.

77 *LD* vii, 38; *Ari.*, 393–94. See Robert Pattison, *The Great Dissent: John Henry Newman and the Liberal Heresy* (Oxford: Oxford University Press, 1991), 128–29.

78 Turner, *Challenge*, 200.

79 *LD* iv, 321.

80 *Jfc.*, 330, 335. See Pattison, *The Great Dissent*, 212. See also Newman's "A Form of Infidelity of the Day," *Idea*, 381–404, which can be read as an extended commentary on liberalism in its two senses, including its historical developments.

81 He reprised these arguments in the *Apologia*. See *Apo.*, 102.

82 *EH* ii, 336–74.

83 *LD* viii, 270. See Sheridan Gilley, "Keble, Froude, Newman, and Pusey," in Aquino and King, *The Oxford Handbook of John Henry Newman*, 104. See also Brad Gregory, *The Unintended Reformation* (Cambridge: Belknap Press, 2012), 74–128. In many ways Gregory confirms Newman's trenchant assertion.

Beginning with Henry Brougham in 1829, Newman increasingly linked the power and spread of liberalism with the national push for utilitarian education shorn of religious truth. Nowhere was this more apparent than when Newman, under the pseudonym "Catholicus," tied Brougham and the political fortunes of Sir Robert Peel together in the *Tamworth Reading Room* letters.[84] Throughout, Newman defended the necessity of the Church and religious truth against what he called the "infidel principle," which was a creative analogy for liberalism.[85] Even with the quest for secular knowledge in education, Newman inveighed against the "anti-dogmatic principle," by showing the power of dogma beyond mundane knowledge,

> Many a man will live and die upon a dogma: no man will be a martyr for a conclusion. A conclusion is but an opinion; it is not a thing which *is*, but which *we are* "*certain about*;" and it has often been observed, that we never say we are certain without implying that we doubt. To say that a thing *must* be, is to admit that *it may not* be. No one, I say, will die for his own calculations; he dies for realities.[86]

Much of what Newman outlined in *Tamworth* was explained in his *Idea of a University*.[87] Indeed, during his tenure as rector of the Catholic University of Ireland, Newman returned to his critique of Brougham in the "Catholic University Gazette" and this time explicitly referred to him as "the very patriarch . . . of liberalism."[88] For Newman a liberal education engaged with religious truth was the converse of Brougham's desire to inculcate secular knowledge through the liberalistic infidel principle.

LIBERALISM AS AN "IDEA"

Examples of these two senses of liberalism appear throughout Newman's thought— indeed they seem ubiquitous.[89] Keeping this in mind, along with Newman's convictions about dogma and the authority of the Church, one can reread his *Apologia*,

---

84 Turner fails to see that the absence of liberalism, although its cognate liberal is present, does not mean an absence of its meaning ("Editor's Introduction," 57).

85 This was how he characterized Brougham's thoughts (which were very similar to Benjamin Constant's) about the relativity of religious belief. See Delio, *Aristocracy*, 99–101.

86 *DA*, 293.

87 For example, Newman's description of the "gentleman" in the *Idea* offers an indelible image of a liberal: a man with a cultivated mind and tastes but skeptical of true religious knowledge. *Idea*, 203–11.

88 *Campaign I*, 446.

89 To see a thematic development of how Newman understands liberalism, although without use of the term, see, *Newman Against the Liberals: 25 Classic Sermons by John Henry Newman*, ed. Michael Davies (Ridgefield, Conn.: Roman Catholic Books, 1978).

and even his tenets in "Note A," with fresh eyes. The term liberal(ism) and its meanings increasingly shaped Newman's understanding about his experiences of divine grace, intellectual growth, ecclesial commitments, human motivations, relationships, and events that culminated in his converting to the Roman Catholic Church in 1845. Soon after finishing his *Apologia*, and in response to the ponderous review by Fitzjames Stephen, Newman sensed he should "write a book" about liberalism but declared himself "so desperately lazy."[90]

In one sense Newman did provide a book length critique of British liberalism, albeit indirectly, in his *Letter to the Duke of Norfolk* (1875).[91] *The Letter* presents Newman's expository, immethodical refutation of William Gladstone's piercing question, "Can Catholics be trustworthy subjects of the State?"[92] As Manent had observed, liberalism desired to unite religion to the state and Gladstone, the British embodiment of liberalism, instinctively desired this union and demanded an answer. While scarcely using the term "liberalism," Newman's *Letter* denied ultimate primacy to the liberal order, especially in its chapter on conscience. Moreover, Newman wrily cited Puis IX's phrase from the "Syllabus of Errors" regarding "progress, liberalism, and the new civilization." He played with these terms, laced them with satire, yet acknowledged their power and omnipresence.[93] *The Letter* stands among other things as a riposte to Gladstonian liberalism, wherein Newman rejected it, not for an ultramontane fortress but for the mysterious and luminous sanctuaries of conscience and the Church in the world.

Newman mentioned liberalism in his letters and writings until the end of his days, and beyond *The Letter*, provided one clear, lasting statement on liberalism: the now posthumously named *Biglietto Speech*. Although fifteen years removed from the *Apologia* and fifty years from his first mention of the word, Newman sketched a portrait of liberalism that brought it into succinct yet comprehensive relief.

The speech presented a glimpse of an "idea," not only about "liberalism in religion" but liberalism *as* religion:[94] "A universal and a thoroughly secular education, calculated . . . to take the place of religion, . . . it provides—the broad fundamental ethical truths, of justice, benevolence, veracity, and the like."[95] Revealed religion embodied in the Church would be displaced by liberalism or what Robert Pattison termed an omnipotent, political "dark star."[96] The Church,

---

90 *LD* xxi, 502.

91 Special thanks to Austin Walker for pointing this out to me. See his "An Alexandrian Hermeneutic, or Theology in a Political Mode: A Study of John Henry Newman's Political Philosophy" (PhD diss., University of Chicago, 2022).

92 *Norfolk*, 179.

93 *Norfolk*, 268.

94 For an excellent presentation of this see, Lee Yearley, *The Ideas of Newman* (University Park, The University of Pennsylvania Press, 1978), 93–127.

95 *Add.*, 66–67.

96 Pattison, *The Great Dissent*, 212.

Newman feared, would orbit its outer rim or be discarded by many altogether.

Newman also delineated the "development" of liberalism as an idea, compressing its many variations over time and space in Britain and recasting much of what he had written from the 1830s. Newman respected liberalism's power yet alluded to the fact that Satan, the sovereign of the secular world, had co-opted it:

> There never was a device of the Enemy so cleverly framed and with such promise of success. And already it has answered to the expectations which have been formed of it. It is sweeping into its own ranks great numbers of able, earnest, virtuous men, elderly men of approved antecedents, young men with a career before them.[97]

Soon after this melancholic portrayal, he wrote that he nevertheless felt hope for the future of the Church: "The present spread of Liberalism may be, for what we know, another movement towards some great triumph which is to come."[98]

CONCLUSION

Newman's early commitment to dogma along with the development of his independent mind, allowed him to discern the core tenets of liberalism: skepticism of religious truth and the fusion of moral elements into the progressive modern state. His awareness of liberalism grew as he approached the most important decision of his life: conversion to the Catholic Church. What may have seemed to a few contemporaries and later commentators a strange account of liberalism, was rather Newman's original insight into its personal, political, and religious reality in history and in his own turbulent age. Newman saw clearly the ambiguities and aggression in the rise of religious and political liberalism and that the way to negotiate the liberal order was to seek true liberty in Christ and in Church.

Suggested Readings

Beaumont, Keith. "Dogme et vie spirituelle." In *Dieu intérieur: La théologie spirituelle de John Henry Newman*. Paris: Éditions Ad Solem, 2014.

Carballo, Robert. "Newman and the Transition to Modern Liberalism." *Humanitas* 7, no. 2 (1994): 19–41.

---

97 *Add.,* 68–69.

98 *LD* xxix, 143. Mahoney sees liberalism not as that end of "history" but rather as founded upon internal contradictions that are showing signs of stress if not collapse (*Why Liberalism Failed*, 3). Milbank, from a different angle, nevertheless arrives at a similar conclusion ("The Gift of Ruling," 215, 222–24). If their analyses are correct, Newman's hope for something other (and better) than liberalism will arise, something that truly reincorporates the Church.

Ker, Ian. "Introduction to John Henry Cardinal Newman's *Biglietto Speech*." *Logos* 6, no. 4 (Fall 2003): 164–69.

Manent, Pierre. *An Intellectual History of Liberalism*. Translated by Rebecca Balinski. Princeton: Princeton University Press, 1995.

Newman, John Henry. *Newman Against the Liberals: 25 Classic Sermons by John Henry Newman*. Edited by Michael Davies. Ridgefield, Conn.: Roman Catholic Books, 1978.

Yearley, Lee. *The Ideas of Newman*. University Park: The University of Pennsylvania Press, 1978.

CONTRIBUTORS

Juan Alonso is a priest and Associate Professor of Theology at the University of Navarra, Spain. He is Rector of the Bidasoa International Ecclesiastical College, Spain. Author of *La Conversión Cristiana: Estudios y Perspectivas*.

Keith Beaumont is a priest of the French Oratory and has taught theology and spirituality in several Catholic universities. Author of a dozen books on Newman, mostly in French, including *Dieu intérieur: La théologie spirituelle de John Henry Newman*, he is Hon. President of the French Newman Association.

Matthew C. Briel is Assistant Professor at Assumption University. He was awarded a Fulbright-Mach Scholarship and obtained his doctorate in Historical Theology from Fordham University. Author of *A Greek Thomist: Providence in Gennadios Scholarios*.

John F. Crosby is Professor Emeritus of Philosophy at Franciscan University of Steubenville, and co-founder of the Hildebrand Project where he serves as Senior Fellow. Author of many publications including *The Personalism of John Henry Newman*.

Michael Dauphinais is Professor and Chair of Theology at Ave Maria University, Florida. His main areas of publication are the study of Thomas Aquinas and theological exegesis. He is former co-editor with Matthew Levering of *Nova et Vetera: The English Edition of the International Theological Journal*.

David P. Delio is the President and Founder of the *Newman Idea*. He is Associate Professor of Theology, University of Holy Cross in New Orleans. Author of *"An Aristocracy of Exalted Spirits": The Idea of the Church in Newman's Tamworth Reading Room*.

Anthony Fisher, OP, is Archbishop of Sydney, Australia. He is *ex officio* Chancellor of the Catholic Institute of Sydney (having previously served as the deputy-chancellor) and Adjunct Professor of Bioethics at the University of Notre Dame Australia.

John T. Ford, **CSC**, was a Holy Cross priest and Professor of Theology and Religious Studies at the Catholic University of America, Washington D.C. He was former editor of *Newman Studies Journal.* Editor of *John Henry Newman: Spiritual Writings* (*Modern Spiritual Masters*).

Víctor García Ruiz is Professor of Spanish Philology and Literature at the University of Navarra, Spain. He has translated into Spanish close to a dozen volumes of Newman's works.

Scott Goins is Professor of Classics at McNeese State University, Louisiana, and Director of the Honors College. Co-editor and translator of the Ignatius Press Critical Edition of Boethius' *De Consolatione Philosophiae.*

Nicholas L. Gregoris is the Vice Provost of the Priestly Society of Saint John Henry Newman and author of *The Daughter of Eve Unfallen: Mary in the Theology and Spirituality of John Henry Newman.*

Carter Griffin is a priest of the Archdiocese of Washington, D.C., and Rector of the St. John Paul II Seminary. Author of *Why Celibacy? Reclaiming the Fatherhood of the Priesthood.*

Christopher J. Lane is Associate Professor of History, Christendom College, Virginia. Author of *Callings and Consequences: The Making of Catholic Vocational Culture in Early Modern France.*

Uwe Michael Lang is a priest of the Oratory of St. Philip Neri in London and teaches Church History and Patristics at Allen Hall Seminary and Mater Ecclesiae College. Editor of *Antiphon: A Journal for Liturgical Renewal.*

Frédéric Libaud is a priest of the Diocese of Strasbourg, France, and Director of the Diocesan Formation Programs and retreats. Author of *Remplir l'éternité—La sainteté à l'école de John Henry Newman.*

Stephen Morgan is a permanent deacon of the Diocese of Portsmouth, England, and Rector of the University of Saint Joseph, Macao, the only Catholic University in China, where he is also Associate Professor of Theology. Author of *John Henry Newman and the Development of Doctrine.*

Jeffrey L. Morrow is Professor of Theology at Seton Hall University, New Jersey, and Senior Fellow at the St. Paul Center for Biblical Theology. Author of various books, including *Alfred Loisy and Modern Biblical Studies.*

Michael Pakaluk is Professor of Ethics and Social Philosophy in the Busch School of Business at The Catholic University of America, Washington, D.C., and a member of the Pontifical Academy of St. Thomas Aquinas. Author of various books, his main area of research and publication has been Aristotle's ethics.

Tracey Rowland holds the St. John Paul II Chair of Theology at the University of Notre Dame (Australia). Author of various books, she is the editor of *Anglican Patrimony within Catholic Communion: The Gift of the Anglican Ordinariate.* She was a member of the Ninth International Theological Commission (2014–2019).

Daniel Seward is a priest of the Oratory of St. Philip Neri in York, England. He is the former Provost of the Oxford Oratory and lectures on early modern history at St. Mary's College, Oscott.

Paul Shrimpton teaches at Magdalen College School, Oxford, and is a historian of education. Author of *A Catholic Eton? Newman's Oratory School* and *The 'Making of Men': The Idea and Reality of Newman's University in Oxford and Dublin.*

Roderick Strange is a prelate of the Archdiocese of Westminster and Professor of Theology at St. Mary's University, Twickenham, London. Editor of *John Henry Newman: A Portrait in Letters.*

Juan R. Vélez is a priest of the Prelature of Opus Dei and an independent scholar living in Miami, Florida. Author of *Passion for Truth, the Life of John Henry Newman* and *Holiness in a Secular Age: The Witness of Cardinal Newman.*

Barbara H. Wyman is Assistant Professor of Classics at McNeese State University, Louisiana, and Associate Director of the Honors College. Co-editor and translator of the Ignatius Press Critical Edition of Boethius' *De Consolatione Philosophiae.*

INDEX

Abelard, Peter, 397, 399
Achilli, Giacinto, 340–41
Achilli, Giovanni, 98
Acts of the Apostles, 457
Adam, 358, 420, 439
Addington, Raleigh, 186
Adelphoe (Terence), 141
"Advent—Vespers" [hymn] (Newman),
   262
Aeneid (Virgil), 141n5
Aesop's Fables, 141
Aeterni Patris (Leo XIII), 137
After Virtue (MacIntyre), 216
Alonso, Juan, 5n7, 21–37, 24n13, 37,
   53n84, 493n23
Ambrose of Milan, 25, 123, 135,
   435–37, 439
Anabasis (Xenophon), 141, 150
Analogy of Religion, The (Butler), 451
Andria (Terence), 141, 148
Anglican Church: celibacy and, 57–58;
   Council of Chalcedon and, 361;
   Oxford Movement and, 4, 8, 14;
   Petrine keys and, 361; as *Via
   Media,* 455–60
"Anglo-American Church, The"
   (Newman), 379–80
Annals of the Christian Church
   (Baronius), 178–79, 186
Annunciation, 433, 439–40
Antichrist, 25, 276, 451
Apollonius of Tyana, 144
Apologia Pro Vita Sua (Newman):
   Ambrose St John and, 91–93;
   Birmingham Oratory in, 90;
   celibacy in, 28, 58–59, 61–62,
   74, 102n36; Classics in, 155;
   conscience in, 343, 396; dogma

in, 40, 54, 407–8, 410; ecclesiology
in, 451, 460, 502; Fathers of the
Church in, 74n2, 123–26, 131, 133,
158–59, 160n13, 163, 165, 438n42;
friendship in, 75–76, 82; history and,
171; holiness in, 321; imagination
in, 41, 47, 58; intellectualism in, 45,
395; Kingsley and, 82, 89–90, 171;
liberalism and, 489–91, 493–94,
498–99, 504n81, 505; Mary in,
426–27; Newman's conversion and,
22–25, 27, 29–36, 132, 274–76,
323n57, 415, 449–50, 461, 467;
Oxford Movement and, 5–7, 9–10,
17, 18, 29, 78–79, 127n20, 195;
philosophy in, 229; sacramental
principle in, 248; self-knowledge in,
272; Spark on, 63, 75; truth and,
280–81, 304n62, 306n72; Whately
and, 225–26; Woodgate and, 82
Apostles' Creed, 452
"Apostolical Christian, The" [sermon *SD*
   no. 19] (Newman), 320, 328n74
Apostolicam Actuositatem (Second
   Vatican Council), 483, 487
Aquinas, Thomas, 54, 270, 339, 347,
   399n19, 423
Aquino, Frederick D., 295
Arianism, 396
Arians, 115n72
Arians of the Fourth Century, The
   (Newman), 13n47, 31, 107–8,
   112n51, 123–27, 155, 158–60,
   160n13, 162–63; Alexandrian
   School and, 144; Christ in, 401;
   composition of, 45–46; as history,
   137; laity in, 463, 476; liberalism
   and, 503–4; Trinity in, 396

relics, 466
"Religious Emotion" [sermon *PS* i, no.
14] (Newman), 273n29, 328n77
"Religious Faith Rational" [sermon *PS*
i, no. 15] (Newman), 294n22
"Religious Joy" [sermon *PS* viii, no. 17]
(Newman), 270n14
"Religious Use of Excited Feelings, The"
[sermon *PS* i, no. 9] (Newman),
328n79
"Religious Worship a Remedy of
Excitements" [sermon *PS* iii, no. 23]
(Newman), 381n39
Reliquiae Sacrae, 8
*Remains of the late Rev. Richard Hurrell
Froude* (Froude), 78, 383
"Remarks on certain Passages of the
Thirty-nine Articles" [*Tract* 90]
(Newman), 17, 17n75, 18, 34, 85,
86, 132, 383, 431, 460
Renan, Ernest, 115
reserve, principle of, 422–23
Resurrection, 93, 302, 325, 375, 397, 405
Revelation, Book of, 270, 435, 439
revelation, Newman's understanding of,
109–12, 354–55
"Reverence, a Belief in God's Presence"
[sermon] (Newman), 381
"Reverence Due to the Blessed Virgin
Mary, The" [sermon *PS* ii, no. 12]
(Newman), 426, 427, 432n17, 433
"Reverence in Worship" [sermon]
(Newman), 381
"Review of Christ's sufferings and death"
[sermon no. 74] (Newman), 43
Rhetoric (Aristotle), 156
Rickards, Samuel, 58, 83
"Righteousness Not of Us, But in Us"
[sermon *PS* v, no. 10] (Newman),
332n92, 404
Rise and Progress of the Universities
(Newman), 142n16, 143n17, 144n27,
149n60, 151, 152n80, 156, 199n25,
200n27, 207n45, 207n47
"Rising with Christ" [sermon *PS* vi, no.
15] (Newman), 479n42
Rocha, Biff, 121n109

Rodríguez, Pedro, 482, 484
Roger, Francis, 147
Rogers, Frederic, 84–86, 92, 92n59
Romaine, William, 25, 472
Romans, Epistle to the, 257–58, 334n103,
435, 471
Rose, Hugh James, 12, 31, 125, 213
Rosenblatt, Helena, 496
Rosner, Mary, 143
Ross, W. D., 210
Rousseau, Jean-Jacques, 495
Routh, Martin, 8
Rowland, Tracey, 162n23, 337n1, 352–72
Ruiz, Victor Garcia, 22n5, 23n10, 24n12,
68n60, 73–93; 177n8
Rule of Faith, 13–14, 16, 18
Russell, Charles, 433
Ryder, Henry Ignatius Dudley, 90
Ryder, Sophia, 7, 19

Sacerdotalis Caelibatus (Paul VI), 70
sacramental principle, 32, 248, 441
Sacra Virginitas (Pius XII), 70
salus animarum suprema lex, 39, 39n1
salvation, 331–32, 404, 414–24, 438–39,
442, 453
"Salvation of the Hearer the Motive of
the Preacher, The" [sermon *Mix.*,
no. 1] (Newman), 273n27
"Saintliness the Standard of Christian
Principle" [sermon *Mix.*, no. 5]
(Newman), 321, 349n62
"Saving Knowledge" [sermon *PS* ii, no.
14] (Newman), 330n84
Schmaus, Michael, 436
Scholasticism, 399–400
Scotism, 423–24
Scott, Charles, 492
Scott, Thomas, 25, 276, 340, 451n6, 472,
492
Scott, Walter, 147n46
Scripture: Catholicism and, 112–20;
Christology and, 113; Church
Fathers and, 110–11, 129–30; faith
and, 113–14; historical criticism
and, 114–17; inspiration and, 112–13,
112n51, 114, 118–20; Judaism and,